FROMMER'S

COMPREHENSIVE TRAVEL GUIDE
NEW MEXICO '93-'94

by
Lisa Legarde and
John Gottberg

PRENTICE HALL TRAVEL

NEW YORK • LONDON • TORONTO • SYDNEY • TOKYO • SINGAPORE

FROMMER BOOKS

Published by Prentice Hall General Reference
A division of Simon & Schuster Inc
15 Columbus Circle
New York, NY 10023

ISBN: 0-671-84762-7
ISSN: 1053-2455

Design by Robert Bull Design
Maps by Geografix Inc.

FROMMER'S EDITORIAL STAFF
Vice President/Editorial Director: Marilyn Wood
Senior Editor/Editorial Manager: Alice Fellows
Senior Editor: Lisa Renaud
Editors: Charlotte Allstrom, Thomas F. Hirsch, Peter Katucki, Sara Hinsey Raveret, Theodore Stavrou
Assistant Editors: Margaret Bowen, Lee Gray, Chris Hollander, Ian Wilker
Editorial Assistant: Gretchen Henderson, Bethany Jewett
Managing Editor: Leanne Coupe

SPECIAL SALES
Bulk purchases of Frommer's Travel Guides are available at special discounts. The publishers are happy to custom-make publications for corporate clients who wish to use them as premiums or sales promotions. We can excerpt the contents, provide covers with corporate imprints, or create books to meet specific needs. For more information write to Special Sales, Prentice Hall Travel, Paramount Communications Building, 15 Columbus Circle, New York, NY 10023

CONTENTS

LIST OF MAPS

INVITATION TO THE READERS

In researching this book, I have come across many wonderful establishments, the best of which I have included here. I am sure that many of you will also come across appealing hotels, inns, restaurants, guesthouses, shops, and attractions. Please don't keep them to yourself. Share your experiences, especially if you want to comment on places that have been included in this edition that have changed for the worse. You can address your letters to:

Lisa Legarde
Frommer's New Mexico '93–'94
c/o Prentice Hall Travel
15 Columbus Circle
New York, NY 10023

A DISCLAIMER

Readers are advised that prices fluctuate in the course of time and travel information changes under the impact of the varied and volatile factors that affect the travel industry. Neither the author nor the publisher can be held responsible for the experiences of readers while traveling. Readers are invited to write to the publisher with ideas, comments, and suggestions for future editions.

SAFETY ADVISORY

Whenever you're traveling in an unfamiliar city or country, stay alert. Be aware of your immediate surroundings. Wear a moneybelt and keep a close eye on your possessions. Be particularly careful with cameras, purses, and wallets, all favorite targets of thieves and pickpockets.

CHAPTER 1

GETTING TO KNOW NEW MEXICO

Welcome to New Mexico. And prepare yourself for an assault on the senses.

The sights, sounds, smells, and tastes of this remarkable state have enraptured visitors for centuries. Probably no one who has ever trodden New Mexican soil can say they were unchanged.

What is it about the 47th state that is so special?

To some, it's the landscape. The state slopes gently upward from the Texas prairies and the Chihuahuan Desert to a wonderland of contorted canyons and high wilderness peaks, split by the life-sustaining river known as the Rio Grande. The mutable colors of the high plains, the sound of a coyote's howl, the smell of a storm-dampened creosote bush, the taste of a juicy prickly pear fruit—all these things are unforgettable.

Visitors also are entranced by New Mexico's unique blend of peoples and cultures. The most thoroughly tricultural of the contiguous 48 states, New Mexico is an overlay of Native Americans, Hispanics, and Anglos (non-Hispanic Caucasians). The groups live and work side by side, yet each preserves its distinct communities and cultural nuances.

Other visitors may point to its history for what makes New Mexico unique. Prehistoric culture reached its apex with the Anasazi (ca. A.D. 800–1300); when the Spanish first visited in the 16th century, they found a thriving post-Anasazi Pueblo culture. The newcomers built their capital at Santa Fe in 1610, spreading religion and politics across the region. In the 19th century, as the United States moved westward, New Mexico spawned legends like Billy the Kid and Geronimo, Kit Carson and the Cimarron Trail. Today, visitors can descend into the *kivas* of ancient Anasazi at Chaco Canyon and the Aztec Ruins; feel the damp earth at El Santuario de Chimayo, credited by pilgrims for two centuries of medical miracles; and relive the echoes of outlaws' gunfire in melodramatic re-creations at Fort Sumner and elsewhere.

There's something here for everyone. Hiking, skiing, and rafting for the outdoors lover; world-famous artists' and musicians' communities for the culture vulture; innovative and palate-pleasing cuisine for the gourmet; atomic and space museums for the amateur scientist. Excitement and relaxation for all.

A reminder: New Mexico *is* an integral part of the United States, and is not a foreign country. *New Mexico* magazine runs a regular monthly column entitled "One of Our Fifty Is Missing," with a plethora of instances in which the state has been placed south of the U.S. border. It is not: The dollar, not the peso, is the currency of preference, and no passport or visa is required for entry by American citizens.

1. GEOGRAPHY & HISTORY

GEOGRAPHY

It would be easy—and accurate—to call New Mexico's geography "high and dry" and leave it at that. The lowest point in the state, in the southeastern corner, is still over 2,800 feet in elevation, higher than the highest point in at least a dozen other states. The southern Rocky Mountains extend well into New Mexico, rising above 13,000 feet in the Sangre de Cristo range and sending a final afterthought above 10,000 feet, just east of Alamogordo. Most of New Mexico receives fewer than 20 inches of precipitation annually, the bulk of that coming either as summer afternoon thunderstorms or winter snowfall. In an area of 121,666 square miles—the fifth largest American state—there are only 221 square miles of water. Thus rivers and lakes occupy less than 0.2% of the landscape.

But look again: Statistics can lie, and there's a lot to meet the eye. New Mexico is bisected by the Rio Grande, the "Big River" of Hispanic lore. The Rio Grande nourishes hundreds of small farms from the Pueblo country of the north to the bone-dry Chihuahuan Desert of the far south. On either side of the river, sage-speckled plains are interrupted by mountains cloaked in forests of juniper and mesquite, and at higher elevations, denser stands of piñon, ponderosa, and aspen. Six of the earth's seven life zones are represented in New Mexico, from subtropical desert to alpine tundra.

New Mexico is nearly square in shape, about 350 miles north-south and 340 miles east-west, with a small panhandle tagged onto its southwestern corner. It is bordered on the west by Arizona, on the north by Colorado, on the east by Texas and a small piece of Oklahoma, and on the south by Texas and Mexico.

Picture New Mexico divided into vertical thirds. The eastern third of the state is an extension of the Great Plains of the Texas Panhandle. These flat plains, drained by the Pecos and Canadian rivers, and widely used for grazing, slope gently upward to meet the Rockies. Climaxing at 13,161-foot Wheeler Peak north of Taos, the range is incised by the Rio Grande: a stark canyon in the north, a wide, gentle stream in the south. New Mexico's western third is predominantly high plateau, including mesa land in the north and the rugged Gila Wilderness farther south.

Words can't do justice to the spectacular colors of the landscape: colors that have drawn contemporary artists from around the world for nearly a century, colors that have made Taos and Santa Fe synonymous with artists' communities. The blues of the sky, browns of the earth, greens of the plants, reds and oranges and yellows of the rock mesas and canyons, all in every imaginable variation and hue, make this land a living canvas. This is truly big sky country, where it seems you can see forever.

Visitors should be aware of New Mexico's high elevation for two reasons. The first is clothing: Don't come at any time of year, even in the middle of summer, without at least a warm sweater and rain gear. The second is health: Don't push yourself too hard during your first few days here. The air is thinner, the sun more direct. You should expect to sunburn more easily and stop to catch your breath more frequently.

DATELINE

- **3,000 B.C.** First evidence of stable farming settlements in region.
- **A.D. 700** Earliest evidence of Anasazi presence.
  (continues)

HISTORY

EARLY HISTORY Archaeologists say that humans first migrated to the Southwest, moving southward from the Bering Land Bridge, about 12,000 B.C. Sites such as Sandia Cave and Folsom—where weapon points were discovered that for the first time clearly established that our prehistoric ancestors hunted now-extinct mammals such as woolly mammoths—are internationally known. When these large animals died off during the late Ice Age (about 8,000 B.C.), people turned to hunting smaller game and gathering wild food.

Stable farming settlements, as evidenced by the remains of domestically grown maize, date from about 3,000 B.C. As the nomadic peoples became more sedentary, they built permanent residences—pit houses—and made pottery. Cultural differences began to emerge in their choice of architecture and decoration: The Mogollon people, in the southwestern part of modern New Mexico, created brown and red pottery and built large community lodges; the Anasazi, in the north, made gray pottery and smaller lodges for extended families.

The Mogollon, whose pottery dates from about 100 B.C., were the first of the sophisticated village cultures. They lived primarily in modern-day Catron and Grant counties. The most important Mogollon ruins extant today are in the Gila River Valley, including Gila Cliff Dwellings National Monument north of Silver City.

By about A.D. 700, and perhaps a couple of centuries earlier, the Anasazi of the northwest had absorbed village life and expanded through what is now known as the Four Corners Region (where New Mexico, Arizona, Utah, and Colorado come together). Around A.D. 1000, their culture eclipsed that of the Mogollon. Chaco Canyon National Historic Park, Aztec Ruins National Monument, and Salmon Ruins all exhibit an architectural excellence and skill, and a scientific sensitivity to nature, that marks this as one of America's classic pre-Columbian civilizations.

Condominium-style communities of stone and mud adobe bricks, three and four stories high, were focused around central plazas. The villages incorporated circular spiritual chambers called *kivas*. The Anasazi also developed means to irrigate their fields of corn, beans, and squash by controlling the flow of water from the San Juan River and its tributaries. From Chaco Canyon, they built a complex system of well-engineered roads leading in four directions to other towns or ceremonial centers. Artifacts found during excavation, such as seashells and macaw feathers, indicate they had a far-reaching trade network. The incorporation of solar alignments into some of their architecture has caused modern archaeoastronomers to speculate on the importance of the equinoxes to their religion.

The disappearance of the Anasazi culture, and the emergence of the Pueblo culture in its place, is something of a mystery today. Those who study such things are in disagreement as to why the Anasazi abandoned their villages around the 13th century. Some suggest drought or soil exhaustion; others, invasion, epidemic, or social unrest. But by the time the first Spanish arrived in the 1500s, the Anasazi were long gone and the Pueblo culture was well established throughout northern and western New Mexico, from Taos to Zuni, near Gallup. Most of the people lived on the east side of the Continental Divide, in the Rio Grande valley.

Certain elements of the Anasazi civilization had clearly been absorbed by the Pueblos, including the apartmentlike

DATELINE

- **1540** Francisco Vásquez de Coronado marches to Cíbola in search of a Native American "city of gold."
- **1542** Coronado returns to Spain, declaring his mission a failure.
- **1610** Immigration to New Mexico increases; Don Pedro de Peralta establishes Santa Fe as capital.
- **1680** Pueblo Indians revolt against Spanish.
- **1692** Spanish recapture Santa Fe.
- **1706** Albuquerque established.
- **1739** First French traders enter Santa Fe.
- **1779** Cuerno Verde, leader of rebellious Comanche tribes, falls to Spanish forces.
- **1786** Comanches and Utes sign treaty with Spanish.
- **1821** Mexico gains independence from Spain.
- **1828** Kit Carson, the legendary frontiersman, arrives in Taos.
- **1846** Mexican War breaks out; Gen. Stephen Kearny takes possession of New Mexico for United States.
- **1847** Revolt in Taos against U.S. control; newly appointed governor Charles Bent killed.

(continues)

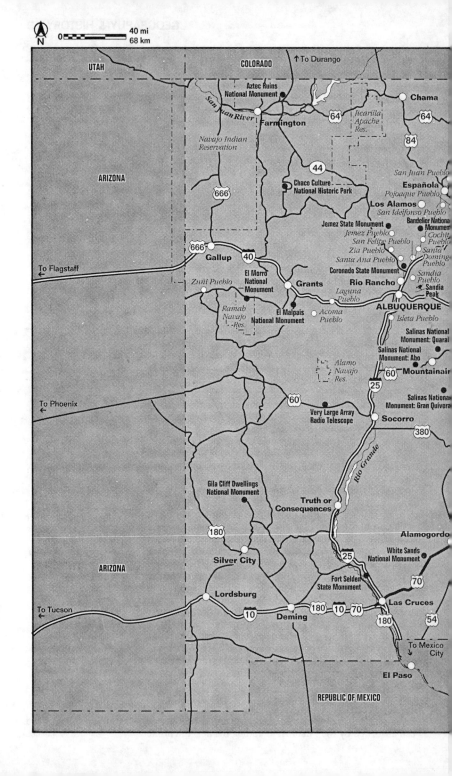

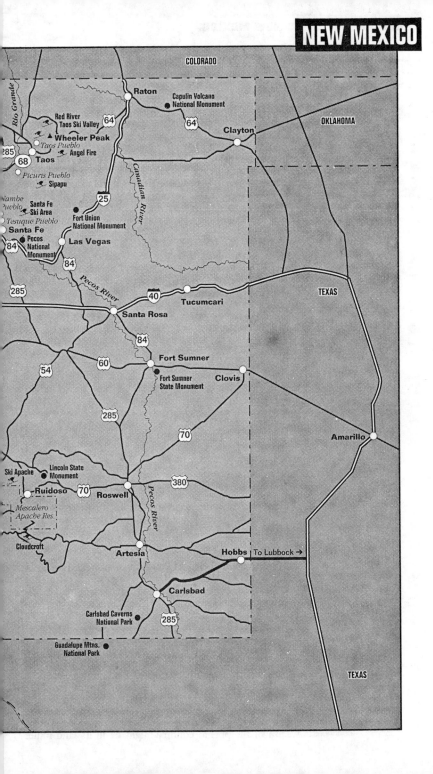

NEW MEXICO

adobe architecture, the creation of rather elaborate pottery, and the use of irrigation or flood farming in their fields. Agriculture, and especially corn, was the economic mainstay.

Each pueblo, as the scattered villages and surrounding farmlands were known, fiercely guarded its independence. When the Spanish arrived, there were no alliances between villages, even among those that shared a common language or dialect. No more than a few hundred people lived in any one pueblo, an indication that the natives had learned to keep their population (which totaled 40,000 to 50,000) down to preserve their soil and other natural resources. But not all was peaceful: They alternately fought and traded with each other, as well as with nomadic Apaches. Even before the Spanish arrived, a pattern had been established.

THE ARRIVAL OF THE SPANISH   The Spanish were the European rulers of New Mexico for 300 years, from the mid-16th to the mid-19th century. That's twice as long as the United States. The Hispanic legacy in language and culture is stronger today in New Mexico than anywhere else in the Southwest, no doubt a result of the prominence of the Rio Grande valley as the oldest and most populous fringe province of the viceroyalty of New Spain.

The spark that sent the first European explorers into what is now New Mexico was a fabulous medieval myth that seven Spanish bishops had fled the Moorish invasion of the 8th century, sailed westward to the legendary isle of Antilia, and built themselves seven cities of gold. Hernán Cortés's 1519 discovery and conquest of the Aztecs' treasure-laden capital of Tenochtitlán, now Mexico City, fueled belief in the myth. When a Franciscan friar 20 years later claimed to have sighted, from a distance, "a very beautiful city" in a region known as Cíbola while on a reconnaissance mission for the viceroyalty, the gates were open.

Francisco Vásquez de Coronado, the ambitious young governor of New Spain's western province of Nueva Galicia, was commissioned to lead an expedition to the "seven cities." Several hundred soldiers, accompanied by servants and missionaries, marched overland to Cíbola with him in 1540, along with a support fleet of three ships in the Gulf of California. What they discovered, after six hard months on the trail, was a bitter disappointment: Instead of a city of gold, they found a rock-and-mud pueblo at Hawikuh, the westernmost of the Zuni towns. The expedition wintered at Tiguex, on the Rio Grande near modern Santa Fe, before proceeding to the Great Plains seeking more treasure at Quivira, in what is now Kansas. The grass houses of the Wichita Indians were all they found.

Coronado returned to New Spain in 1542, admitting failure. Historically, though, his expedition was a great success, contributing the first widespread knowledge of the Southwest and Great Plains, and discovering en route the Grand Canyon.

By the 1580s, after important silver discoveries in the mountains of Mexico, the Spanish began to wonder if the wealth of the pueblo country might lie in its land rather than its cities. They were convinced that they had been divinely appointed to convert the natives of the New World to Christianity. And so a northward migration began, orchestrated and directed by the royal government. It was a mere trickle in the late 16th century. Juan de Onate established a capital in 1598 at San Gabriel, near San Juan Pueblo, but a variety of factors led to its failure. Then in 1610, under Don Pedro de Peralta, the migration began in earnest.

It was not dissimilar to America's schoolbook stereotype. Bands of armored conquistadors did troop through the desert, humble robed friars striding by their sides. But most of the pioneers came up the valley of the Rio Grande with ox carts and mule trains rather than armor, intent on transplanting their Hispanic traditions of government, religion, and material culture in this new world.

Peralta built his new capital at Santa Fe and named it La Villa Real de la Santa Fe de San Francisco de Asis, the Royal City of the Holy Faith of St. Francis of Assisi. His capitol building, the Palace of the Governors, has been continuously occupied as a public building ever since by Spanish, Mexicans, Americans, and for 12 years (1680–92) by the Pueblo Indians. Today it is a museum.

RELIGION & REVOLT Seventeenth-century New Mexico history was essentially a missionary era, as Franciscan priests attempted to turn the Indians into model Hispanic peasants. Their churches became the focal points of every pueblo, with Catholic schools a mandatory adjunct. By 1625 there were an estimated 50 churches in the Rio Grande valley. But the Indians weren't enthused about doing "God's work"—building new adobe missions, tilling fields for the Spanish, and weaving garments for export to Mexico—so soldiers backed the padres in extracting labor, a system known as *repartimiento*. Simultaneously, the *encomienda* system provided that a yearly tribute in corn and blankets be levied upon each Indian. The Pueblos were pleased to take part in Catholic religious ceremonies and proclaim themselves converts. To them, spiritual forces were actively involved in the material world. If establishing harmony with the cosmos meant absorbing Jesus Christ and various saints into their hierarchy of *kachinas* and other spiritual beings, so much the better. But the Spanish friars demanded they do away with their traditional singing and masked dancing, and with other "pagan practices." When the Pueblo religion was violently crushed and driven literally underground, resentment toward the Spanish grew and festered. Rebellions at Taos and Jemez in the 1630s left village priests dead, but they were savagely repressed.

A power struggle between church and state in Nuevo Mexico weakened the hand of the Spanish colonists, and a long drought in the 1660s and 1670s gave the warlike Apaches reason to scourge the Spanish and Pueblo settlements for food. The Pueblos blamed the friars, and their ban on traditional rain dances, for the drought. The hanging of four medicine men as "sorcerers," and the imprisonment of 43 others, was the last straw for the Rio Grande natives. In 1680, the Pueblo Revolt erupted.

Popé, a San Juan shaman, catalyzed the revolt. Assisted by other Pueblo leaders, he unified the far-flung Indians, who never before had confederated. They pillaged and burned the province's outlying settlements, then turned their attention upon Santa Fe, besieging the citizens who had fled to the Palace of the Governors. After nine days, having reconquered Spain's northernmost American province, they let the refugees retreat south to Mexico.

Popé ordered that the Pueblos should return to their life-style before the Spanish had arrived. All Hispanic items, from tools to livestock to fruit trees, were to be destroyed, and the blemish of baptism was to be washed away in the river. But the shaman misjudged the influence of the Spanish upon the Pueblo people. They were not the people they had been a century earlier, and they *liked* much of the material culture they had absorbed from the Europeans. What's more, they had no intention of remaining confederated; their independent streaks were too strong.

In 1692, led by newly appointed Gov. Don Diego de Vargas, the Spanish recaptured Santa Fe without bloodshed. Popé had died, and without a leader to reunify them, the Pueblos were no match for the Spanish. De Vargas pledged not to punish them, but to pardon and convert. Still, when he returned the following year with 70 families to recolonize the city, he had to use force. And for the next several years, bloody battles persisted throughout the Pueblo country.

By the turn of the 18th century, Nuevo Mexico was firmly in Spanish hands. This time, however, the colonists seemed to have learned from some of their past errors. They were more tolerant in their religion, less ruthless in their demands and punishments.

ARRIVAL OF THE ANGLOS By the 1700s, there were signals that new interlopers were about to arrive in New Mexico. The French had laid plans to begin colonizing the Mississippi River, and hostile Indian tribes were on the warpath. The viceroyalty fortified its position in Santa Fe as a defensive bastion, and established a new villa at Albuquerque in 1706.

In 1739, the first French trade mission entered Santa Fe, welcomed by the citizenry but not by the government. For 24 years, until 1763, a black-market trade thrived between Louisiana and New Mexico. It ended only when France lost its toehold on its North American claims during the French and Indian War against Great Britain.

The Natives were a more fearsome foe. Apache, Comanche, Ute, and Navajo launched repeated raids against each other and the Rio Grande settlements for most of the 18th century, which led to the Spanish and Pueblos pulling closer together for mutual protection. Pueblo and Hispanic militias fought side by side in campaigns against the invaders. But by the 1770s, the attacks had become so savage and destructive that the viceroy in Mexico City created a military jurisdiction in the province, and Gov. Juan Bautista de Anza led a force north to Colorado to defeat the most feared of the Comanche chiefs, Cuerno Verde ("Green Horn"), in 1779. Seven years later, the Comanches and Utes signed a lasting treaty with the Spanish, and thereafter helped keep the Apaches in check.

France sold the Louisiana Territory to the young United States in 1803, and the Spanish suddenly had a new intruder to fear. The Lewis and Clark expedition of 1803 went unchallenged, much as the Spanish would have liked to have challenged it; but in 1807, when Lt. Zebulon Pike built a stockade on a Rio Grande tributary in Colorado, he and his troops were taken prisoner by troops from Santa Fe. Pike was taken to the New Mexican capital, where he was interrogated extensively, and then to Chihuahua, Mexico. The report he wrote upon his return to the United States was Atlantic America's first inside look at Spain's frontier province.

At first, American merchants—excited by Pike's observations of New Mexico's economy—were summarily expelled from Santa Fe or jailed, their goods confiscated. But after Mexico gained independence from Spain in 1821, traders were welcomed. The wagon ruts of the Santa Fe Trail soon extended from Missouri to New Mexico, and from there to Chihuahua. (Later, it became the primary southern highway to California.)

As the merchants hied to Santa Fe, Anglo American and French Canadian fur trappers headed into the wilderness. Their commercial hub became Taos, a tiny village near a large pueblo a few days' ride north of Santa Fe. Many married into native or Hispanic families. Perhaps the best known was Kit Carson, a sometimes federal agent, sometimes Indian scout, whose legend is inextricably interwoven with that of early Taos. He spent 40 years in Taos, until his death in 1868.

Then in 1846, the Mexican War broke out, and New Mexico became a territory of the United States. There were several causes of the war—the U.S. annexation of Texas in 1845, disagreement over the international boundary, unpaid claims owed to American citizens by the Mexican government—but foremost was the prevailing U.S. sentiment of "manifest destiny," the belief that the union should extend "from sea to shining sea." Gen. Stephen Kearny marched south from Colorado and in the Las Vegas plaza announced that he had come to take possession of New Mexico for the United States. His arrival in Santa Fe on August 18, 1846, went un-opposed.

An 1847 revolt in Taos resulted in the slaying of the new governor of New Mexico, Charles Bent, but U.S. troops defeated the rebels and executed their leaders. That was the last threat to American sovereignty in the territory. In 1848, the Treaty of Guadalupe Hidalgo officially transferred title to New Mexico, along with Texas, Arizona, and California, to the United States.

Kearny promised New Mexicans that the United States would respect their religion and property rights, and would safeguard their homes and possessions from hostile Indians. His troops behaved with a rigid decorum. The United States upheld Spanish policy toward the Pueblos, assuring the survival of their ancestral lands, their traditional culture, and their old religion—which even three centuries of Hispanic Catholicism could not do away with.

THE CIVIL WAR As conflict between the North and South flared east of the Mississippi, New Mexico found itself caught in the debate over slavery. Southerners wanted to expand slavery to the western territories, but abolitionists fought a bitter campaign to prevent that from happening. New Mexicans themselves voted against slavery twice, while their delegate in Congress engineered the adoption of a slavery code. In 1861, the Confederacy, after its secession from the Union, laid plans to make New Mexico theirs as a first step toward capturing the West.

In fact, southern New Mexicans, including those in Tucson (Arizona was then a part of the New Mexico Territory), were disenchanted with the attention paid them by Santa Fe and already were threatening to form their own state. So when Confederate Lt. Col. John Baylor captured Fort Fillmore, near Mesilla, and on August 1, 1861, proclaimed all of New Mexico south of the 34th parallel to be the new territory of Arizona, there were few complaints.

The following year, Confederate Gen. Henry Sibley assembled three regiments of 2,600 Texans and moved up the Rio Grande. They defeated Union loyalists in a bloody battle at Valverde, near Socorro; easily took Albuquerque and Santa Fe, which were protected only by small garrisons; and proceeded toward the federal arsenal at Fort Union, 90 miles east of Santa Fe. Sibley planned to replenish his supplies there before continuing north to Colorado, then west to California.

On March 27-28, 1862, the Confederates were met head-on in Glorieta Pass, about 16 miles outside of Santa Fe, by regular troops from Fort Union supported by a regiment of Colorado Volunteers. By the second day, the rebels were in control—until a detachment of Coloradans circled behind the Confederate troops and destroyed their poorly defended supply train. Sibley was forced into a rapid retreat back down the Rio Grande. A few months later, Mesilla was reclaimed for the Union, and the Confederate presence in New Mexico was ended.

INDIANS & OUTLAWS The various tribes had not missed the fact that whites were fighting among themselves, and they took advantage of this weakness to step up their raids upon border settlements. In 1864, the Navajos, in what is known in tribal history as "The Long Walk," were relocated to the new Bosque Redondo Reservation on the Pecos River at Fort Sumner, in east central New Mexico. Militia Col. Kit Carson led New Mexico troops in this venture, a position to which he acceded as a moderating influence between the Indians and those who called for their unconditional surrender or extermination.

It was an ill-advised decision: The land could not support 9,000 Indians; the government failed to supply adequate provisions; and the Navajo were unable to live peacefully with the Mescalero. By late 1868, the tribes retraced their routes to their homelands, where the Navajos gave up their warlike past. The Mescalero's raids were squashed in the 1870s and they were confined to their own reservation in the Sacramento Mountains of southern New Mexico.

Corraling the rogue Apaches of southwestern New Mexico presented the territory with its biggest challenge. Led by chiefs Victorio, Nana, and Geronimo, these bands wreaked havoc upon the mining region around Silver City. Eventually, however, they succumbed, and the capture of Geronimo in 1886 was the final chapter in New Mexico's long history of Indian wars.

As the Indian threat decreased, more and more livestock and sheep ranchers established themselves on the vast plains east of the Rio Grande, in the San Juan basin of the northwest, and in other equally inviting parts of the territory. Cattle drives up the Pecos Valley, on the Goodnight-Loving Trail, are the stuff of legend; so, too, was Roswell cattle baron John Chisum, whose 80,000 head of beef probably represented the largest herd in America in the late 1870s.

Mining grew as well. Albuquerque blossomed in the wake of a series of major gold strikes in the Madrid Valley, close to ancient Indian turquoise mines; other gold and silver discoveries through the 1870s gave birth to boomtowns—now mostly ghost towns—like Hillsboro, Chloride, Mogollon, Pinos Altos, and White Oak. The copper mines of Santa Rita del Cobre, near Silver City, are still thriving.

In 1879, the Atchison, Topeka & Santa Fe Rail Road sent its main line through Las Vegas, Albuquerque, El Paso, and Deming, where it joined with the Southern Pacific line coming eastward from California. (The Santa Fe station was, and is, at Lamy, 17 miles southeast of the capital.) Now linked by rail to the great markets of America, New Mexico's economic boom period was assured.

But ranching invites cattle rustling and range wars, mining beckons feuds and land fraud, and the construction of railroads has often been tied to political corruption and swindles. New Mexico had all of them, especially during the latter part of the 19th century. Best known of a great many conflicts was the Lincoln County War (1878–81), which began as a feud between rival factions of ranchers and merchants. It led to such utter lawlessness that Pres. Rutherford B. Hayes ordered a federal investigation of the territorial government and the installation as governor of Gen. Lew Wallace—whose novel, *Ben Hur,* was published in 1880.

One of the central figures of the Lincoln County conflict was William "Billy the Kid" Bonney, a headstrong youth (b. 1858) who became probably the best-known outlaw of the American West. He blazed a trail of bloodshed from Silver City to Mesilla, Santa Fe to Lincoln, and Artesia to Fort Sumner, where he was finally killed by Sheriff Pat Garrett in July 1881.

By the turn of the century, most of the violence had been checked. The mineral lodes were drying up, and ranching was taking on increased importance. Economic and social stability were coming to New Mexico.

STATEHOOD, ART & ATOMS Early in the 20th century, its Hispanic citizens having proved their loyalty to the United States by serving gallantly with Theodore Roosevelt's Rough Riders during the Spanish-American War, New Mexico's long-awaited dream of becoming an integral part of the Union was finally recognized. On January 6, 1912, Pres. William Howard Taft signed a bill making New Mexico the 47th state.

Within a few years, Taos began gaining fame as an artists' community. Two painters from the East Coast, Ernest Blumenschein and Bert Phillips, settled in Taos in 1898, lured others to join them, and in 1914 formed the Taos Society of Artists, one of the most influential schools of art in America. Writers and other intellectuals soon followed, including Mabel Dodge Luhan, novelists D. H. Lawrence and Willa Cather, and poet-activist John Collier. Other artists settled in Santa Fe and elsewhere in northern New Mexico; the best known was Georgia O'Keeffe, who lived miles from anywhere in tiny Abiquiu. Today, Santa Fe and Taos are world renowned for their contributions to art and culture.

The construction in 1916 of the Elephant Butte Dam near Hot Springs (now Truth or Consequences) brought irrigated farming back to a drought-ravaged southern New Mexico. Potash mining boomed in the southeast in the 1930s. The Indians fared well, gaining full citizenship in 1924, two years after the All Pueblo Council was formed to fight passage in Congress of a bill that would have given white squatters right to Indian lands. And in 1934, with ex-Taos intellectual John Collier as commissioner of Indian Affairs, tribes were accorded partial self-government. The Hispanics, meanwhile, became the most powerful force in state politics, and remain so today.

But the most dramatic development in 20th-century New Mexico was induced by the Second World War. In 1943, the U.S. government sealed off a tract of land on the Pajarito Plateau, west of Santa Fe, that previously had been an exclusive boys' school. On the site, in utter secrecy, they built the Los Alamos National Laboratory, otherwise known as Project Y of the Manhattan Engineer District—the "Manhattan Project." Their goal: to split the atom and develop the world's first nuclear weapons.

Under the direction of J. Robert Oppenheimer, later succeeded by Norris E. Bradbury, a team of 30 to 100 scientists lived and worked in almost complete seclusion for two years. Their work resulted in the atomic bomb, tested for the first time at the Trinity Site, north of White Sands, on July 16, 1945. The bombings of Hiroshima and Nagasaki, Japan, three weeks later signaled to the world that the nuclear age had arrived.

Even before that time, New Mexico was climbing the ladder of stature in America's scientific community. Robert H. Goddard, considered the founder of modern rocketry, conducted many of his experiments near Roswell in the 1930s, during which time he became the first person to shoot a liquid-fuel rocket faster than the speed of sound. Clyde Tombaugh, the discoverer of the planet Pluto in 1930, helped establish the Department of Astronomy at New Mexico State University in Las Cruces; and former Sen. Harrison (Jack) Schmitt, an exogeologist and the first civilian to walk on the moon in 1972, is a native of the Silver City area.

Today the White Sands Missile Range is one of America's most important astrophysics sites, and the International Space Hall of Fame in nearby Alamogordo honors men and women from around the world who have devoted their lives to space exploration. Aerospace research and defense contracts are economic mainstays in Albuquerque, and Kirtland Air Force Base is the home of the Air Force Special Weapons Center. Los Alamos, of course, continues to be a national leader in nuclear technology.

Despite the rapid approach of the 21st century in many parts of the state, there are other areas still struggling to be a part of the 20th. The Natives, be they Pueblo, Navajo, or Apache, and the Hispanic farmers who till small plots in isolated rural regions both hearken to a time when life was slower paced. But life in New Mexico was never simple. For anyone.

2. ART, ARCHITECTURE & LITERATURE

ART   Since prehistoric times, New Mexico has been a cradle of artistic genius for its native peoples. Prehistoric Mogollon, Mimbres, and Anasazi pottery is unique in its design and color. Today's Pueblo Indians are noted not only for their pottery—each pueblo being distinctive in its touches from the next—but also for their textile crafts. Navajos are renowned for their silver jewelry, often with turquoise, and for their weaving and sand painting; Apaches are master basket makers.

Hispanic art was by nature either religious or rustic . . . or both. Cut off for centuries from most of the rest of the world, save through the rarely traveled colonial lifeline to Mexico, artisans handcrafted their own ornate furnishings. Paintings (*retablos*) and carved icons (*santos*) underscored the creators' devotion to their Roman Catholic faith. Traditional decorative tinwork and furniture are popular today, along with weaving and silversmithing.

New Mexico wasn't discovered by Anglo American artists until the end of the 19th century. Two East Coast painters, Ernest Blumenschein and Bert Phillips, happened upon Taos in 1898 and were hypnotized by the dramatic light. They returned to make the valley their home, and in 1914 founded the Taos Society of Artists. The society disbanded in 1927, a victim of its own success: It so widely marketed the works of the town's isolated masters that other artists thronged to Taos. Today, the art community is prolific, indeed: By some estimates, more than 10% of the permanent population of Taos are painters, sculptors, writers, musicians, or others who earn income from an artistic pursuit.

Santa Fe grew as an art community on the heels of Taos. By 1921, Los Cinco Pintores, a group of five avant-garde painters, were establishing names for themselves. The quintet included Jozef Bakos, Fremont Ellis, Walter Mruk, Willard Nash, and Will Shuster. The number of full-time professional artists in Santa Fe today exceeds 700, and that doesn't include writers or musicians. Thousands more dabble in the creative professions.

Santa Fe is home to the School of Indian Art, where many of today's leading native artists studied, including Apache sculptor Allan Houser. It's also the site of the Institute of American Indian Arts. The best-known Native American painter today is R. C. Gorman, an Arizona Navajo who has made his home in Taos since the 1960s. Now in his early 50s, Gorman is internationally acclaimed for his bright, somewhat surrealistic depictions of Navajo women.

ARCHITECTURE In a land as dry and treeless as most of New Mexico, it's not surprising that adobe has long been the principal construction material. Clay, mixed with grasses for strength, is placed in a mold and dried in the sun. The bricks are then stacked to create the building and reinforced with more wet clay. Almost every structure in New Mexico prior to 1879, when the railroad arrived, was built in this style by Pueblo Indians, Hispanics, and Anglos.

Architectural elements in adobe buildings usually include a network of *vigas,* long beams supporting the roof, their ends protruding through the facade; *latillas,* smaller stripped crossbeams layered between the *vigas;* corbels, carved wooden supports for the vertical posts and the *vigas;* a portal, usually shading a brick floor set into the ground; and a plastered adobe-brick *banco,* or fireplace, set into an outside wall.

The Territorial style of architecture became popular in the late 19th century, when railroads could carry in bricks, large logs, and other building materials. Today, adobe is again in vogue—for aesthetics, for price (it's cheap, and there's no shortage of mud!), and for its ability to retain heat for extended periods.

Modern architectural styles prevalent throughout the Western world are of course seen in New Mexico, especially in innovative downtown Albuquerque. But it's tradition that visitors find stunning. Santa Fe is the center of attention, as strict building codes have maintained the traditional architectural integrity of the city's core since the 1950s.

LITERATURE Many noted writers have made their homes in New Mexico in the 20th century. In the 1920s, the most noted were D. H. Lawrence and Willa Cather, both short-term Taos residents. Lawrence, the romantic and controversial English novelist, was here for parts of 1922–25, and reflected on that period in *Mornings in Mexico and Etruscan Places.* Though he died in Europe years later, a family shrine north of Taos is a popular place of pilgrimage for Lawrence devotees. Lawrence's Taos period is described in *Lorenzo in Taos,* written by his patron, Mabel Dodge Luhan. Cather, a Pulitzer Prize winner famous for her depictions of the pioneer spirit, penned *Death Comes for the Archbishop,* a fictionalization of the career of 19th-century Santa Fe Bishop Jean-Baptiste Lamy, as a result of her stay.

Many well-known contemporary authors live in and write about New Mexico. John Nichols of Taos, whose *The Milagro Beanfield War* was turned into a popular movie in 1987, writes with insight about the problems of poor Hispanic farming communities. Tony Hillerman of Albuquerque is renowned for two decades of weaving mysteries around Navajo tribal police in such books as *Listening Woman* and *Thief of Time*. Hispanic novelist Rudolfo Anaya's *Bless Me, Ultima,* and Pueblo writer Leslie Marmon Silko's *Ceremony,* capture the life-styles of their respective peoples. Of desert environment and politics, no one wrote better than the late Edward Abbey; *Fire on the Mountain,* set in New Mexico, was one of his most powerful works.

3. RELIGION & RITUAL

Religion has always been at the heart of Indian life. Throughout the Southwest, the cosmos is viewed as a single whole. Within that whole, all living creatures are seen as mutually dependent, and every relationship, whether with another person, an animal, or even a plant, carries spiritual meaning. A hunter will pray before killing a deer, for instance, to ask the creature to give itself to the tribe. The slain deer is then treated as a guest of honor before the hunter ritually sends its soul back to its comrades to be reborn. Even the harvesting of a plant requires prayer, thanks, and ritual.

Pueblo Indians believe their ancestors originally lived underground, the source of life (and the place from which plants spring). Encouraged by burrowing animals, they entered the world of humans—the "fifth" world—through a hole, a *sipapu,* by clinging to a web woven for them by Spider Woman.

The Pueblo peoples honor Mother Earth and Father Sun. In this dry land, the sun can mean life and death. The tribes watch the skies closely, tracking solstices and planetary movements, to determine the optimum timing for crop planting cycles.

Dances are ritual occasions. Usually held in conjunction with the feast days of Catholic saints (including Christmas Eve for Jesus Christ), the ceremonies demonstrate how the Pueblos absorbed certain aspects of Christianity from the Spanish without surrendering their traditional beliefs.

There are medicine dances, fertility rites, prayers for rain and for good harvests. The spring and summer corn or *tablita* dances are among the most impressive. Ceremonies begin with an early morning mass and procession to the plaza honoring an image of the saint. The rest of the day is devoted to song, dance, and feasting, with performers masked and clad as deer, buffalo, eagles, and other creatures.

The all-night Shalako festival at Zuni Pueblo in late November or early December is the most spectacular of Pueblo ceremonies. Colorfully costumed *kachinas,* or spirit dancers, act out the Zuni story of creation and evolution. Everyone awaits the arrival of the *shalakos,* 12-foot-tall *kachinas* who bless new and renovated homes in the village.

Visitors are normally welcome to attend Pueblo dances, but should respect the Indians' requests that they not be photographed or tape-recorded.

Navajos believe in a hierarchy of supernatural beings, the Holy Ones, who can travel on a sunbeam, a thunderbolt, or the wind. At their head is Changing Woman, the earth mother, who vigilantly assures humans' well-being by teaching them to live in harmony with nature. Her children, the Hero Twins, ward off our enemies—all but Old Age and Death. Religious symbolism, which pervades art and music, underscores the Navajo belief that their homeland was created by the Holy Ones for them to live in. Typical of Navajo dancing are the *yeibichai* rituals, curative ceremonies marked by circular social dances with long song cycles.

The Apaches have a similar creation belief. They were created by Father Sun and Mother Earth ("the White Painted Lady") to live in the Southwest region, and the Holy Ones' twin sons helped them ward off wicked creatures by teaching them how to ride horses and use a bow and arrow. The most important ceremony among the

Apaches today, including the Mescaleros, is the 4-day puberty ritual for young girls. The colorful masked *gahans,* or mountain spirits, perform to celebrate the subject's womanhood, when the White Painted Lady resides within her body.

Outside the pueblos and reservations, the most visible places of worship are those of the Roman Catholics. Santa Fe's Cathedral of St. Francis is the state's best-known church, but a close second is El Santuario de Chimayo, an hour north of the state capital. Constructed in 1816, it has long been a site of pilgrimage for Catholics who attribute miraculous powers of healing to the earth in the chapel's anteroom. Most Hispanic Catholics believe strongly in miracles.

4. SPORTS & RECREATION

Whether you're a spectator or a participant, there's year-round action in New Mexico.

There's professional baseball (the Albuquerque Dukes play in the AAA Pacific Coast League), major college football and basketball, and horse racing at Santa Fe (in summer) and near Las Cruces (in winter).

For outdoors lovers, New Mexico is famous for its fishing and hunting. There are German brown, rainbow, cutthroat, and lake trout in the streams and high lakes; bass, crappie, catfish, and pike are denizens of some of the larger bodies of water, like Elephant Butte and Navajo lakes. Fishing licenses, required of anyone 12 or older, cost $41. A 1-day license costs $8.50, and a 5-day license is $15. A Wildlife Habitat Improvement stamp ($5.25) must also be purchased for fishing in national forests or Bureau of Land Management–controlled waters. Fishing on an Indian reservation requires a permit from the reservation.

Hunters must also be licensed to hunt game birds—such as ducks, geese, quail, grouse, and wild turkey—and big-game animals, including mule deer, elk, pronghorn antelope, ibex, black bear, mountain lion, and javelina (peccary). For further information on hunting or fishing, contact the New Mexico Department of Game and Fish, Villagra Building, Galisteo Street, Santa Fe, NM 87503 (tel. 505/827-7911), or the New Mexico Council of Outfitters and Guides, 160 Washington Street SE, Suite 75, Albuquerque, NM 87108 (tel. 505/243-4461).

With so much national forest and wilderness, there are unlimited opportunities for backpackers and day hikers. There are 3,000 miles of trails in the 10 million acres of New Mexico national forests. Perhaps the most varied and interesting trails are in the Gila National Forest and Wilderness in southwestern New Mexico. For information, write the U.S. Forest Service, 517 Gold Ave. SW, Albuquerque, NM 87102 (tel. 505/842-3292); or specific forests: Carson National Forest, P.O. Box 558, Taos, NM 87571 (tel. 505/758-6201); Cíbola National Forest, 10308 Candelaria Blvd. NE, Albuquerque, NM 87112 (tel. 505/761-4650); Gila National Forest, 2610 N. Silver St., Silver City, NM 88061 (tel. 505/388-8201); Lincoln National Forest, 11th and New York streets, Alamogordo, NM 88310 (tel. 505/437-6030); or Santa Fe National Forest, 1220 St. Francis Dr., Santa Fe, NM 87504 (tel. 505/988-6940).

The Bureau of Land Management (BLM), P.O. Box 1449, Santa Fe, NM 87504 (tel. 505/438-7400), administrates 13 million acres around the state. Included is the upper Rio Grande, a popular destination for white-water rafting.

For winter visitors, Taos Ski Valley is considered one of the leading ski resorts in the United States. There are other ski resorts in the Taos area at Angel Fire, Red River, and Ski Rio; Santa Fe Ski Area; Sandia Peak at Albuquerque; at Ski Apache at Ruidoso. In addition, Cloudcroft, Los Alamos, Penasco, and Raton boast smaller hills. Cross-country skiing is popular on high-elevation trails in the national forests and on BLM land. You can get information from regional convention and visitors bureaus or chambers of commerce. Or contact Ski New Mexico Inc., P.O. Box 1104, Santa Fe, NM 87504 (tel. 505/982-5300). Check snow conditions by dialing New Mexico Snophone (tel. 505/984-0606) 24 hours daily.

Those who prefer less strenuous or time-consuming activities will find golf courses, tennis courts, and swimming pools in communities throughout the state.

And then there's ballooning: Albuquerque is the site of the world's largest hot-air balloon extravaganza every October, and trips operate in several cities throughout the year.

5. CUISINE

New Mexican cuisine isn't the same as Mexican cooking, or even those American concoctions sometimes called "Tex-Mex" or "Cal-Mex." It's a consequence of southwestern history, a unique blend of Hispanic and Pueblo Indian recipes. As the native population taught the Spanish conquerors about their corn—how to roast it, how to make corn pudding, stewed corn, cornbread, cornmeal, and posole (hominy)—the Spanish introduced their beloved chiles, adding spice to the cuisine.

Lovers of tacos, burritos, and enchiladas will find them here, although they may not be quite as you've had them before. Tacos, for instance, are more often served in soft rolled tortillas than in crispy shells. Tamales are made from cornmeal mush, wrapped in husks and steamed. Chile rellenos are stuffed with cheese, deep-fried, then covered with green chile.

Many dishes include unusual local ingredients, such as piñon nuts, jicama, and prickly pear cactus. Here's a sampling of some of the more regional dishes that might be hard to find outside the Southwest:

Blue corn Pueblo vegetable that produces a crumbly flour widely used in tortilla shells, especially for enchiladas

Carne adovada Tender pork marinated in red chile, herbs, and spiced, then baked

Chorizo burrito (also called a breakfast burrito) Mexican sausage, scrambled eggs, potatoes, and scallions wrapped in a flour tortilla with red or green chile and melted Jack cheese

Empanada A fried pie with nuts and currants

Fajitas Strips of beef or chicken sautéed with onions, green peppers, and other vegetables, and served on a sizzling platter

Green chile stew Locally grown chiles cooked in a stew with chunks of meat, beans, and potatoes

Huevos rancheros Fried eggs on corn tortillas, topped with cheese and red or green chile, served with pinto beans

Pan dulce Indian sweet bread

Posole A corn soup or stew (called hominy in other parts of the South), sometimes with pork and chiles

Sopaipillas A lightly fried puff pastry served with honey as a dessert, or stuffed with meat and vegetables as a side dish

6. RECOMMENDED BOOKS

General

Casey, Robert L. *Journey to the High Southwest: A Traveler's Guide* (Pacific Search Press, 1985).

Chilton, Lance and Katherine, et al. *New Mexico: A New Guide to the Colorful State* (University of New Mexico Press, 1984).

Horgan, Paul. *Great River: The Rio Grande in North American History* (Holt, Rinehart and Winston, 1960).

Jenkins, Myra Ellen, and Albert H. Schroeder. *A Brief History of New Mexico* (University of New Mexico Press, 1974).
Nichols, John, and William Davis. *If Mountains Die: A New Mexico Memoir* (Knopf, 1979).
Simmons, Marc. *New Mexico: An Interpretive History* (University of New Mexico Press, 1988).

Native & Hispanic Culture

Anaya, A. Rudolfo. *Bless Me, Ultima* (Quinto Sol, 1972).
Boyd, E. *Popular Arts of Spanish New Mexico* (Museum of New Mexico Press, 1974).
Dozier, Edward P. *The Pueblo Indians of North America* (Holt, Rinehart and Winston, 1970).
Silko, Leslie Marmon *Ceremony* (Viking, 1977).
Williamson, Ray A. *Living the Sky: The Cosmos of the American Indian* (University of Oklahoma Press, 1987).

Art, Architecture & Literature

Cather, Willa. *Death Comes for the Archbishop* (Random House, 1971).
Hillerman, Tony. *Thief of Time* (Harper & Row, 1988).
Lawrence, D. H. *Mornings in Mexico and Etruscan Places* (Penguin, 1967).
Luhan, Mabel Dodge. *Lorenzo in Taos* (Knopf, 1932).
Nichols, John. *The Milagro Beanfield War* (Ballantine, 1988).
O'Keeffe, Georgia. *O'Keeffe* (Viking, 1976).

CHAPTER 2

PLANNING A TRIP TO NEW MEXICO

As with any trip, a little preparation is essential before you start your journey to New Mexico. This chapter will provide you with a variety of planning tools, including information on when to go, how to get there, how to get around once you're there, and some suggested itineraries.

1. INFORMATION & CLIMATE

SOURCES OF INFORMATION   The best place to obtain detailed information is the **New Mexico Department of Tourism** in the Lamy Building, 491 Old Santa Fe Trail, Santa Fe, NM 87503 (tel. toll free 800/545-2040).

The various cities and regions of the state are represented by convention and visitors bureaus, and/or chambers of commerce. Their addresses and telephone numbers are listed in the appropriate chapters in this book.

CLIMATE   Summers are hot throughout most of the state, though distinctly cooler at higher elevations. Winters are relatively mild in the south, harsher in the north and in the mountains. Spring and fall are pleasant all over. Rainfall is sparse except in the higher mountains; summer afternoon thunderstorms and winter snows account for most precipitation.

Santa Fe and Taos, at 7,000 feet, have midsummer highs in the 80°s, overnight midwinter lows in the teens. Temperatures in Albuquerque, at 5,000 feet, often run about 10° warmer. Snowfall is common from November through March, and sometimes as late as May, though it seldom lasts long. Santa Fe averages 32 inches total annual snowfall. At the high-mountain ski resorts, as much as 300 inches (25 feet) may fall in a season—and stay. The plains and deserts of the southeast and south commonly have summer temperatures in excess of 100°.

NEW MEXICO TEMPERATURES & PRECIPITATION

	Jan High–Low	Apr High–Low	July High–Low	Oct High–Low	Annual Precip. (Inches)
Alamogordo	57–28	78–40	95–65	79–42	7.5
Albuquerque	47–28	70–41	91–66	72–45	8.9

Carlsbad	60–28	81–46	96–67	79–47	13.5
Chama	33–3	54–22	73–37	52–18	9.3
Cloudcroft	41–19	56–33	73–48	59–36	25.8
Farmington	44–16	70–36	92–58	70–37	7.5
Las Cruces	56–26	79–45	95–66	82–47	8.6
Roswell	56–24	78–42	91–65	75–45	12.7
Ruidoso	50–17	65–28	82–48	67–31	21.4
Santa Fe	40–18	59–35	80–57	62–38	14.0
Taos	40–10	62–30	87–50	64–32	12.1
Truth or Conseq	54–27	75–44	92–66	75–47	8.5

NEW MEXICO CALENDAR OF EVENTS

JANUARY

☐ **Three Kings' Day.** Most pueblos honor their new tribal officers with ceremonies. Traditional dancing is held at Cochiti, Jemez, Laguna, Nambe, Picuris, Sandia, San Felipe, San Ildefonso, San Juan, Santa Ana, Santa Clara, Santo Domingo, Taos, Tesuque, and Zia pueblos. January 6.

FEBRUARY

☐ **Mount Taylor Winter Quadrathlon.** Bicycling, running, cross-country skiing, and snowshoeing. Near Grants. Third weekend.

MARCH

☐ **Easter Celebrations.** At Cochiti, Nambe, Picuris, San Felipe, San Ildefonso, Santa Ana, Santo Domingo, and Zia pueblos, with masses, parades, and dances, including the corn dance. There's a street party in the historic district of Silver City, and a balloon rally at Truth or Consequences. Late March or early April.

APRIL

☐ **Albuquerque Founders' Day.** Parade, auction, and street entertainment in Old Town. Albuquerque. Third weekend.
☐ **Gathering of Nations Powwow.** Miss Indian World contest, dance competitions, arts and crafts exhibitions, fitness runs and walks. University of New Mexico arena. Albuquerque. Third weekend.

MAY

☐ **Cinco de Mayo Fiestas.** The restoration of the Mexican republic (from French occupation 1863–67) is celebrated at Hobbs, Las Cruces (Old Mesilla Plaza), Silver City, and Truth or Consequences. First weekend.
☐ **Taos Spring Arts Festival.** Three-week survey of visual, performing, and literary arts. Taos. Third week May to mid-June.
☐ **Spring Festival of the Arts.** Eleven-day celebration. Santa Fe. Ends Memorial Day weekend.
☐ **Great Rio Grande Raft Race.** Homemade boats launch from the Corrales and Central bridges. Albuquerque. Third Saturday.
☐ **Santa Fe Powwow.** Native dances, singing, games, crafts, and food. The Downs at Santa Fe. Memorial Day weekend.

JUNE

☐ **Rails and Trails Days.** Rodeo, train rides, fiddlers contest, quilt and art shows. Las Vegas. First weekend.
☐ **Old Fort Days.** Includes world's richest tombstone race. Fort Sumner. Second weekend.

JULY

☐ **Fourth of July Celebrations.** Parades, fireworks, and various other events at Albuquerque, Capitan, Carlsbad, Clayton, Farmington, Gallup, Grants, Las Vegas, Lordsburg, Moriarty, Red River, Roswell, and Socorro. July 4.
☐ **Apache Maidens' Puberty Rites.** Rodeo and ceremonial Dance of the Mountain Spirits, Mescalero. July 4.
☐ **Waterfall Ceremonial.** Several rarely seen traditional dances are presented at Nambe Falls, Nambe Pueblo. July 4.
☐ **Rodeo de Santa Fe.** Parade, dance, and four rodeo performances. Santa Fe. Weekend after July 4.
☐ **Taos Powwow.** Intertribal competitions in traditional and contemporary dances, Taos. Second weekend.
☐ **Billy the Kid–Pat Garrett Historical Days.** Lectures, tours, stew cook off, western music and dance, at Ruidoso. Second weekend.
☐ **Eight Northern Pueblos Artist and Craftsman Show.** More than 600 Indian artists exhibit their work. Traditional dances, food booths, at San Juan Pueblo. Third weekend.
☐ **Spanish Market.** Santa Fe Plaza. Last weekend.

AUGUST

☐ **Bat Flight Breakfast.** Carlsbad Caverns National Park. Early August.
☐ **Old Lincoln Days.** Billy the Kid pageant, Lincoln. First weekend.
☐ **Inter-Tribal Indian Ceremonial.** Fifty tribes from the United States and Mexico participate in rodeos, parades, dances, athletic competitions, and an arts and crafts show, at Red Rock State Park, east of Gallup. Second week.
☐ **Connie Mack World Series Baseball Tournament.** Teams of teenagers from throughout the United States and Puerto Rico compete in a 7-day, 17-game series. Ricketts Park, Farmington. Second week.
☐ **Annual Indian Market.** Juried Native art competition, musical entertainment, dances, food booths. Santa Fe Plaza. Third weekend.
☐ **Great American Duck Race.** Parade, ballooning, tortilla toss, dances—and, of course, the duck race. Deming. Fourth weekend.

SEPTEMBER

☐ **International Space Hall of Fame Induction.** Alamogordo.
☐ **Hatch Chile Festival.** Hatch. Labor Day weekend.
☐ **Hillsboro Apple Festival.** Crafts, flea market, food, dancing, at Hillsboro, west of Truth or Consequences. Labor Day weekend.
☐ **New Mexico State Fair.** Third-largest state fair in the United States. Seventeen days of Spanish and Indian villages, midway, livestock exhibits, arts and crafts, country-and-western entertainment. Albuquerque State Fairgrounds. Begins Friday after Labor Day.
☐ **Fat Tire Fiesta,** Socorro. Last weekend in September.
☐ **Fiesta de Santa Fe.** Santa Fe Plaza. Second weekend.
☐ **Stone Lake Fiesta.** Apache festival with rodeo, ceremonial dances, and footrace. Jicarilla Reservation. Dulce. September 14 to 15.
☐ **Mexican Independence Day.** Parade and dances in Carlsbad (San Jose Plaza) and Las Cruces (Old Mesilla Plaza), with a rodeo in Carlsbad. September 16.

☐ **Old Taos Trade Fair.** Reenactment of Spanish colonial living in the 1820s, with craft demonstrations, food, and entertainment. Martinez Hacienda, Taos. Third weekend.

☐ **Taos Fall Arts Festival.** Gallery openings, concerts, crafts fair. Taos. Third weekend to first weekend October.

☐ **Shiprock Navajo Fair.** Rodeo, traditional dancing and singing, parade, arts and crafts exhibits. Shiprock. Last weekend.

OCTOBER

☐ **Fall Festival of the Arts.** Eleven-day event focusing on New Mexican painters, sculptors, and craftspeople. Santa Fe. Ends Columbus Day.

☐ **Albuquerque International Balloon Fiesta.** World's largest balloon rally, with races, contests, and special events, including weekend mass ascensions. Albuquerque. First to second weekend.

NOVEMBER

☐ **Bosque Fall Fest.** Bosque del Apache Wildlife Refuge, San Antonio, Socorro County.

☐ **Festival of the Cranes.** Socorro. Late November.

☐ **Indian National Finals Rodeo.** Indian rodeo riders from throughout the United States and Canada compete. Powwow, ceremonial dancing, Miss Indian Rodeo pageant, arts and crafts. Albuquerque State Fairgrounds. Third weekend.

DECEMBER

☐ **Shalako Ceremony.** Night-long chanting and dances, Zuni Pueblo. First or second weekend.

☐ **Yuletide in Taos.** *Farolito* tours, candlelight dinners, dance performances, art events, ski-area activities. Taos. First to third weekends.

☐ **Our Lady of Guadalupe Fiesta.** Pilgrimage to Tortugas Mountain and torchlight descent, followed by mass and traditional Hispanic dances. Tortugas, near Las Cruces. December 10 to 12.

☐ **Christmas in Cloudcroft.** Snow Queen contest, skating party, lighting contests, caroling, snowmobile races. Cloudcroft. Weekend before Christmas.

☐ **Sundown Torchlight Procession of the Virgin.** Vespers and Matachines dance at San Ildefonso, Santa Clara, Taos, and Tesuque pueblos. December 24.

2. HEALTH & INSURANCE

HEALTH PREPARATIONS One thing that sets New Mexico aside from most other states is its altitude. Most of the state is above 4,000 feet in elevation, and many heavily touristed areas—including Santa Fe—are at 7,000 feet or above. Getting plenty of rest, avoiding large meals, and drinking lots of nonalcoholic fluids (especially water) can help make the adjustment easier for flatlanders.

The reduced oxygen and humidity can bring on some unique problems, not the least of which is acute mountain sickness. Characterized in its early stages by headaches, shortness of breath, appetite loss and/or nausea, tingling in the fingers or toes, and lethargy and insomnia, it ordinarily can be treated with aspirin and a slower pace. If it persists or worsens, you must descend to a lower altitude.

Sunburn and hypothermia are other dangers of higher elevations, and should not be lightly regarded.

INSURANCE Before setting out on your trip, check your medical insurance policy to be sure it covers you away from home. If it doesn't, it's wise to purchase a traveler's policy, widely available at banks, travel agencies, and automobile clubs. Coverage offered by numerous companies is relatively inexpensive. In addition to medical assistance, including hospitalization and surgery, it should include the cost of an accident, death, or repatriation; loss or theft of baggage; costs of trip cancellation; and guaranteed bail in the event of a suit or other legal difficulties.

3. WHAT TO PACK

The traveler's first rule of packing for a trip is to *travel as light as possible*.

Except perhaps for underwear and socks, carry no more than three changes of clothing. Ideally you shouldn't have more than one suitcase and a small bag of essentials that fits neatly under an airplane seat or in the upper rack of a train or bus.

Don't fail to pack a sweater or rainproof jacket. Even in summer, it can get cold at night. You'll want shorts and a swimsuit (for hotel pools) in the summer, and several layers of warm clothing, including gloves and hat, in winter. Unless you plan to dine in one of the handful of very elegant restaurants in the state, you probably won't need a coat and tie or an evening dress. No matter what your plans, a good pair of walking shoes (not just tennis shoes) is essential.

A few other easily forgotten items that could prove priceless during your stay: (1) a travel alarm clock, so as not to be at the mercy of your hotel for wake-up calls; (2) a Swiss army knife, which has a multitude of uses, from bottle opener to screwdriver; (3) a magnifying glass to read the small print on maps; and (4) a small first-aid kit (containing an antibiotic ointment, bandages, aspirin, soap, a thermometer, motion-sickness pills, and required medications) to avoid dependence on others in minor emergencies.

4. GETTING THERE

BY PLANE Albuquerque is the hub for travel to most parts of New Mexico. A secondary hub for southern New Mexico is El Paso, Texas. Both airports are served by **American** (tel. toll free 800/433-7300), **America West** (tel. toll free 800/247-5692), **Continental** (tel. toll free 800/525-0280), **Delta** (tel. toll free 800/221-1212), **Southwest** (tel. 505/831-1211), and **United** (tel. toll free 800/241-6522). In addition, Albuquerque is served by **TWA** (tel. toll free 800/221-2000), **USAir** tel. toll free 800/428-4322), and the regional carrier, **Mesa** (tel. toll free 800/637-2247).

BY TRAIN **AMTRAK** has two routes through the state. The *Southwest Chief,* which runs between Chicago and Los Angeles, passes through New Mexico once daily in each direction, with stops in Gallup, Grants, Albuquerque, Lamy (for Santa Fe), Las Vegas, and Raton. A second train, the *Sunset Unlimited,* skims through the southwest corner of the state three times weekly in each direction—between Los Angeles and New Orleans—with stops in Lordsburg, Deming, and El Paso, Texas.

You can get a copy of AMTRAK's National Timetable from any AMTRAK station, from travel agents, or by contacting AMTRAK, 400 N. Capitol St. NW, Washington, DC 20001 (tel. toll free 800/USA-RAIL).

BY BUS **Greyhound Lines, Inc.** and **TNM&O Coaches** (Texas, New Mexico & Oklahoma) have extensive networks that penetrate every corner of the state, with daily connections virtually everywhere. Call 505/243-4435 for information on schedules and rates.

BY CAR Three interstate highways cross New Mexico. The north-south I-25 bisects the state, passing through Albuquerque and Las Cruces. The east-west I-40 follows the path of the old Route 66 through Gallup, Albuquerque, and Tucumcari in the north; while I-10 from San Diego crosses southwestern New Mexico until intersecting I-25 at Las Cruces.

Here are the approximate mileages to Albuquerque from various cities around the United States:

City	Mileage	City	Mileage
Atlanta	1,424	Minneapolis	1,257
Boston	2,248	New Orleans	1,188
Chicago	1,351	New York	2,029
Cleveland	1,616	Oklahoma City	540
Dallas	670	Phoenix	537
Denver	449	St. Louis	1,051
Detroit	1,572	Salt Lake City	617
Houston	907	San Francisco	1,091
Los Angeles	802	Seattle	1,460
Miami	2,018	Washington, D.C.	1,883

PACKAGE TOURS Tours within the state of New Mexico are offered by the following inbound operators:

Jack Allen Tours, P.O. Box 11940, Albuquerque, NM 87192 (tel. 505/266-9688).

Discover New Mexico, 6303 Indian School Rd. NE, Albuquerque, NM 87110 (tel. 505/888-2444).

Mary's Dream Tours, 8300 San Pedro Blvd. NE, Albuquerque, NM 87113 (tel. 505/831-4184 or toll free 800/344-0626).

Photo Adventure Tours, 2035 Park St., Atlantic Beach, NY 11509-1236 (tel. 516/371-0067).

Rojo Tours & Services, 228 Old Santa Fe Trail, Santa Fe, NM 87501 (tel. 505/983-8333).

Rocky Mountain Tours, 142 Lincoln Ave., Suite 203, Santa Fe, NM 87501 (tel. 505/984-1684).

Sun Tours, Ltd., 4300 San Mateo Blvd. NE, Suite B-155, Albuquerque, NM 87110 (tel. 505/881-5346).

Southwest Gray Line Tours, P.O. Box 25381, Albuquerque, NM 87125 (tel. 505/764-9464 or toll free 800/452-2665).

Tours of Enchantment, 5801 Jones Place NW, Albuquerque, NM 87120 (tel. 505/831-4285).

Wild West Shows & Tours, 2430 Juan Tabo Blvd. NE, Suite 142, Albuquerque, NM 87112 (tel. 505/293-3326).

5. GETTING AROUND

BY PLANE **Mesa Airlines** (tel. toll free 800/637-2247) flies from Albuq
to Alamogordo, Carlsbad, Clovis, Farmington, Gallup, Hobbs, Las Cruces, Rosw
Santa Fe, Silver City, and Taos. **Ross Aviation** (Albuquerque tel. 505/242-2811)
provides commuter service between Albuquerque and Los Alamos.

BY TRAIN **AMTRAK**'s northern New Mexico line, the *Southwest Chief,* runs
west-east and east-west once daily, with stops in Gallup, Grants, Albuquerque, Lamy
(for Santa Fe), Las Vegas, and Raton. The *Sunset Unlimited* connects Lordsburg and
Deming with El Paso, Texas, three times weekly each direction. Greyhound/Trailways
bus lines provide through-ticketing for AMTRAK between Albuquerque and El Paso.
Call for information (Albuquerque tel. 505/842-9650 or toll free 800/USA-RAIL).

BY BUS Service links every sizable city in the state: Alamogordo, Albuquerque,
Artesia, Belen, Carlsbad, Clayton, Clovis, Costilla, Cuba, Deming, Espanola, Farming-
ton, Gallup, Grants, Hatch, Hobbs, Jal, Las Cruces, Las Vegas, Lordsburg, Portales,
Raton, Roswell, Ruidoso, Santa Fe, Santa Rosa, Shiprock, Silver City, Socorro,
Springer, Taos, Truth or Consequences, Tucumcari, and other communities en route.
   Service is provided by **Greyhound Lines, Inc.** (Albuquerque tel. 505/243-4435)
and **TNM&O** (Texas, New Mexico & Oklahoma; tel. 505/243-4435 in Albuquer-
que). Many of the two coach companies' routes are now combined.

BY CAR Visitors who plan to drive their own car to and around New Mexico
should give their vehicle a thorough road check before starting out. There are lots of
wide-open desert and wilderness spaces in New Mexico, and it is not fun to be
stranded in the heat or cold with a vehicle that doesn't run. Check your lights,
windshield wipers, horn, tires, battery, drive belts, fluid levels, alignment, and other
possible trouble spots.
   Make sure your driver's license, vehicle registration, safety-inspection sticker, and
auto-club membership (if you have one) are valid. Check with your auto insurance
company to make sure you're covered when out of state, and/or when driving a rental
car.
   Unless otherwise posted, the speed level on open roads is 65 m.p.h. (105 kmph).
Minimum age for drivers is 16. Safety belts are required for drivers and all passengers
age 5 and over; children under 5 must use approved child seats.
   Indian reservations are considered sovereign nations, and they enforce their own
laws. For instance, on the Navajo reservation (New Mexico's largest), it is prohibited
to transport alcoholic beverages, to leave established roadways, or to travel without a
seat belt. Motorcyclists must wear helmets.
   Gas is readily available at service stations throughout the state. Prices are cheapest
in Albuquerque (about $1.25 a gallon in the fall of 1992), and 10% to 15% more
expensive in more isolated communities. All prices are subject to the same fluctuations
as elsewhere in the United States.
   An excellent state highway map can be obtained from the New Mexico
Department of Tourism, Lamy Building, 491 Old Santa Fe Trail, Santa Fe, NM 87503
(tel. toll free 800/545-2040). More specific county and city maps are available from
the State Highway and Transportation Department, 1120 Cerrillos Rd., Santa Fe, NM
87501 (tel. 505/827-5250).
   The State Highway and Transportation Department has a toll-free hot line (tel.
800/432-4269) providing up-to-the-hour information on road closures and conditions.
   In case of an accident or road emergency, contact the New Mexico State Police.
District offices are in Alamogordo (tel. 437-1313), Albuquerque (tel. 841-9256), Clovis
(tel. 763-3426), Espanola (tel. 753-2277), Farmington (tel. 325-7547), Gallup (tel.
287-4141), Hobbs (tel. 392-5588), Las Cruces (tel. 524-6111), Las Vegas (tel.

1), Roswell (tel. 622-7200), Santa Fe (tel. 827-9300), aos (tel. 758-8878).

Automobile Association can get free emergency road hours, by calling AAA's emergency number (tel. toll free

in every sizable town and city in the state, always at the lso downtown. **Rich Ford Payless** (tel. 505/247-9255) ely represented agencies include: **Alamo** (tel. toll free . toll free 800/331-1212), **Budget** (tel. toll free 800/527- ree 800/421-6878), **General** (tel. toll free 800/327-7607), 0/654-3131), **National** (tel. toll free 800/227-7368), and 00/367-2277).

Woras ., : U.S. 666 between Gallup and Shiprock has been labeled America's "most dangerous highway" by *USA Today*. New Mexico has the highest per capita rate of traffic deaths of any American state. Drive carefully!

SUGGESTED ITINERARIES

IF YOU HAVE 1 WEEK

Days 1–2 Spend your first 2 nights in Albuquerque. Wander around Old Town, visit the Albuquerque Museum and Indian Pueblo Cultural Center, take the tramway up Sandia Peak. Then drive to Santa Fe, not much more than an hour north.

Days 3–5 Stay 3 nights in Santa Fe, and be sure to include a day trip to Los Alamos and Bandelier National Monument.

Days 6–7 Drive to Taos in the morning, taking the "High Road" through Chimayo. Stay overnight in Taos to see the pueblo, the art galleries, and the historic properties.

Day 7 In the afternoon, return to Albuquerque for the flight home.

IF YOU HAVE 2 WEEKS

Spend days 1 to 6 as described above.

Day 7 In the afternoon drive west from Taos on U.S 64 to Chama to spend the night.

Day 8 Spend the day in Chama on the famous Cumbres & Toltec narrow-gauge steam railroad. After the train trip, continue west on U.S. 64 to Farmington to spend 2 nights.

Day 9 Take an easy day trip from Farmington to Aztec Ruins National Monument, the Salmon Ruins, or Shiprock, on the Navajo Reservation.

Day 10 Start out early to spend most of the day at fascinating Chaco Culture National Historic Park. Then drive to Gallup for 2 nights.

Day 11 Explore the pawn shops of Gallup, and visit Zuni Pueblo, perhaps the most culturally unique in New Mexico.

Day 12 Drive to Grants for lunch, passing El Morro National Monument on the way. In the afternoon visit historic Acoma Pueblo as you head back to Albuquerque.

Day 13 Do a loop tour of the pueblos north of the city, or to drive to the three divisions of Salinas National Monument southeast of Albuquerque.

Day 14 Day 14 is your departure date from Albuquerque airport.

IF YOU HAVE 3 WEEKS

Spend the first 2 weeks as described above.

Day 15 Drive south from Albuquerque on I-25, stopping en route to explore Socorro and the Bosque del Apache National Wildlife Refuge. Stay the night in Truth or Consequences.

Day 16 Get an early start and visit Gila Cliff Dwellings National Monument. Spend the night in Silver City.

Day 17 Drive to Las Cruces, southern New Mexico's largest city, and its historic suburb of La Mesilla via City of Rocks State Park and Deming.

Day 18 Drive over the Organ Mountains to Alamogordo, being sure not to miss White Sands National Monument or the International Space Hall of Fame.

Day 19 If you get an early start, you can lunch in Carlsbad, check into your hotel, then spend the entire afternoon at Carlsbad Caverns.

Day 20 Take a trip to Ruidoso, a picturesque mountain resort town, via Roswell and the Old West village of Lincoln.

Day 21 Head back to Albuquerque for your departure.

FAST FACTS: NEW MEXICO

American Express Atlas American Express, 5301 Central Ave. NE, Albuquerque (tel. 505/262-2255). To report a lost card, call toll free 800/528-4800. To report lost traveler's checks, call toll free 800/221-7282.

Banks Major statewide banks are the Bank of New Mexico, First Interstate Bank, First National Bank in Albuquerque, SunWest Bank, United New Mexico Bank, and Western Bank. They're typically open Monday to Thursday 10am to 3pm and Friday 10am to 6pm. Drive-up windows may be open later. Some may also open Saturday morning. Most branches have cash machines available 24 hours.

Business Hours In general, Monday to Friday 9am to 5pm, with many stores also open Friday night and Saturday. Some cities may have different hours; in Las Cruces, for instance, many merchants close their doors on Monday but are open all day Saturday.

Camera & Film Film of all kinds is widely available at camera stores throughout the state, and simple repairs can be handled in the major cities.

Drugstores 24-hour prescription services are available at selected Walgreens Drug Stores around the state. Prices at Thrifty and Wal-Mart outlets might be somewhat less. If you're having trouble getting a prescription filled, call the nearest hospital pharmacy.

Electricity As throughout the U.S., 110 to 115 volts, 60 cycles.

Embassies & Consulates There are two in New Mexico, both in Albuquerque: the Mexican Consulate, 505 Marquette Ave. NW (tel. 247-2139), and the German Consulate, 5700 Harper Dr. NE, Suite 430 (tel. 822-8826).

Emergencies For emergency medical help or information call the New Mexico Medical Crisis Center toll free at 800/432-6866. The center is open 24 hours a day. In most cities, for police, sheriff, fire department, or ambulance, dial 911 at any time; otherwise, dial 0, and ask the operator to connect you.

Hitchhiking Hitching a ride is legal in New Mexico, and in summer you may find backpack-laden vagabonds at interstate highway entrances, at road junctions, in the Navajo Indian Reservation, and on secondary roads.

Language English is the lingua franca, but Spanish is almost as frequently spoken. You'll also hear Indian languages—Navajo (the most widely spoken surviving North American Indian dialect), Apache, Zuni, Tanoan, and Keresan.

Liquor Laws Drinking age is 21. Bars close at 2am; on Sunday they are open noon to midnight. Wine, beer, and spirits are sold at licensed supermarkets and liquor stores. A special allowance must be granted for liquor to be dispensed in proximity to any church. It is illegal to transport liquor through most Indian reservations.

Mail   It takes two to three days for mail from major New Mexico cities to reach other major American cities. Figure an extra day from and/or to smaller communities. Domestic postage for letters is 29¢ for the first ounce, 23¢ per additional ounce, and 19¢ for a postcard. Postage to most foreign countries is 50¢ per half-ounce. (It's 40¢ per ounce to Canada, 35¢ per ounce to Mexico.) Buy stamps and send parcels from post offices in any city, town, or village. Major city post offices are open Monday to Friday 8am to 4pm, Sat 9am to noon; smaller communities often have limited hours.

You can have mail sent to you in any city in New Mexico. Have it addressed to you, c/o General Delivery, Main Post Office, Name of City. The post office will hold it for one month. You must pick it up in person and show proof of identification. A passport will suffice.

Maps   The official state highway map is published by the State Tourism and Travel Division; county and city maps can be obtained from the State Highway and Transportation Department. Many local visitors bureaus or chambers of commerce publish their own city or regional maps. The American Automobile Association (AAA) supplies detailed state and city maps free to members. The best regional maps are the Highroad maps for each quadrant of the state. Priced at $1.95 each, they are published by Highroad Publications, 7701 Spring Ave. NE, Albuquerque, NM 87110, and are available at bookstores.

Newspapers & Magazines   Larger cities and regional hubs have daily newspapers, and many smaller towns publish weeklies. The *Albuquerque Tribune,* published mornings, and the *Albuquerque Journal,* published evenings, are widely available around the state. The *El Paso Times* is favored in southern New Mexico. National newspapers like *USA Today* and the *Wall Street Journal* can be purchased in cities and major hotels. The state's favorite magazine is *New Mexico,* a high-quality monthly published by the State Tourism and Travel Division since 1923.

Pets   Dogs, cats, and other small pets are accepted at motels in most parts of the state, though not as universally in Albuquerque and Santa Fe as elsewhere. Some properties require owners to pay a damage deposit in advance. If you bring your pet, keep it well dusted with flea powder: Plague bacilli, a disease borne by fleas, is endemic to New Mexico.

Police   In the event of any emergency, contact the New Mexico State Police. Call 911 or 0 for an operator. Regional telephone numbers are listed in "Getting Around," above.

Radio & TV   There are 125 AM and FM radio stations in New Mexico, so if you have a car radio or other receiver, you'll never be far from the rest of the world. Albuquerque has five television stations, including ABC, CBS, NBC, and PBS affiliates. Santa Fe has one station. Southern New Mexico gets reception from El Paso, Texas.

Safety   Whenever you're traveling in an unfamiliar city or region, stay alert. Be aware of your immediate surroundings. Wear a money belt and keep a close eye on your possessions. Be particularly careful with cameras, purses, and wallets, all favorite targets of thieves and pickpockets.

Taxes   The 6% state tax on gross receipts includes hotel bills. Local governments tack their own lodging tax on top of that, which ranges from 2.75% to 5.25% depending upon the city.

Telephone & Fax   The area code for the entire state of New Mexico is 505. Local calls are normally 25¢. Facsimiles can be transmitted by most major hotels at a nominal cost to guests.

Time   New Mexico is on mountain standard time, one hour ahead of the West Coast and two hours behind the East Coast. Daylight saving time is in effect from April to October.

Tipping   A tip of 50¢ per bag is appropriate for hotel valets and airport porters. If you're staying longer than a night or two in a hotel or motel, tip about $1 per night for chamber service. Restaurant servers should get 15% to 20% of your bill for service.
Water   You can drink the water everywhere.

CHAPTER 3

FOR FOREIGN VISITORS

1. PREPARING FOR YOUR TRIP

2. GETTING TO & AROUND THE U.S.

- **FAST FACTS: FOR THE FOREIGN TRAVELER**

As New Mexico is a part of the United States, all foreign visitors must satisfy the entrance requirements for a visit to the USA before continuing their trip to the Southwest. This chapter is designed to explain the intricacies.

1. PREPARING FOR YOUR TRIP

NECESSARY DOCUMENTS   Most foreigners entering the United States must carry two documents: (1) a valid **passport,** expiring not fewer than six months prior to the scheduled end of their visit to the United States; and (2) a **tourist visa,** which can be obtained without charge at any American consulate.

Exceptions are Canadian nationals, who must merely carry proof of residence, and British and Japanese nationals, who require a passport but no visa.

To obtain a visa you merely complete a form and submit a passport photo. At most consulates, it's an overnight process, though it can take longer during the busy summer period of June, July, and August. Those who apply by mail should enclose a large, self-addressed, stamped envelope, and expect a response in about two weeks. Visa application forms, available at consulates, can also be obtained from airline offices and leading travel agencies.

In theory, a tourist visa (Visa B) is valid for single or multiple entries for a period of one year. In practice, the consulate that issues the visa uses its discretion in granting length of stay. Applicants of good appearance, who can supply the address of a relative, friend, or business acquaintance in the United States, are most likely to be granted longer stays. (American resident contacts are also useful in passing through Customs quickly and for numerous other details.)

MEDICAL REQUIREMENTS   New arrivals in the United States do not need any inoculations unless they are coming from, or have stopped over in, an area known to be suffering from an epidemic, particularly cholera or yellow fever.

Anyone applying for an immigrant's visa must undergo a screening test for the AIDS-associated HIV virus, under a law passed in 1987. This test does not apply to tourists.

Any visitor with a medical condition that requires treatment with narcotics or other drugs, or with paraphernalia such as syringes, must carry a valid, signed prescription from a physician. This will show Customs officials and others that you are carrying drugs for a legitimate purpose.

TRAVEL INSURANCE   All such insurance is optional in the United States. Medical care is very costly in the United States, however, and every traveler is strongly advised to secure full insurance coverage before starting a trip.

For a relatively low premium, numerous specialized insurance companies will cover (1) loss or theft of baggage, (2) costs of trip cancellation, (3) guaranteed bail in the event of a suit or other legal difficulties, (4) the cost of medical assistance—including surgery and hospitalization—in the event of sickness or injury, and (5) the cost of an accident, death, or repatriation. Travel agencies, automobile clubs, and banks are among those selling travel insurance packages at attractive rates.

2. GETTING TO & AROUND THE U.S.

Nearly all major airlines, including those of the United States, Europe, Asia, Australia, and New Zealand, offer **APEX (advance purchase excursion) fares** that significantly reduce the cost of transoceanic air travel. This enables travelers to pick their dates and ports, but requires that they prepurchase their ticket, and meet minimum- and maximum-stay requirements—often 15 to 90 days. Season of travel and individual airline discounts also affect fares, but this is the most widely acknowledged means of cheap, flexible travel.

Some large airlines, including Delta, Eastern, Northwest, TWA, and United, have in the past offered foreign travelers special add-on discount fares under the name **Visit USA.** Though not currently available, they may be repeated in the future, and are worth asking a travel agent about. These tickets (which could be purchased overseas only) allowed unlimited travel between U.S. destinations at minimum rates for specified time periods, such as 21, 30, or 60 days. Short of bus or train travel, which can be inconvenient and time-consuming, this was the best way of traveling around the country at low cost.

AMTRAK, the American rail system, offers a **USA Railpass** to non-U.S. citizens. Available only overseas, it allows unlimited stopovers during a 45-day period of validity. Fares vary according to the size of the region being traveled.

Foreign students can obtain the **International Ameripass** for unlimited bus travel on Greyhound/Trailways throughout the United States and Canada. Available for 7 to 30 days, it can be purchased with a student ID and a passport in New York, Orlando, Miami, San Francisco, and Los Angeles.

Foreign visitors who plan to rent a car can visit an American Automobile Association (AAA) office to obtain a "touring permit," which validates a foreign driver's licenses.

For detailed information on travel by car, train, and bus, see "Getting Around," Chapter 2.

 FOR THE FOREIGN TRAVELER

Business Hours   Banks open weekdays from 9am to 3pm, although there's 24-hour access to the automatic tellers (ATMs) at most banks and other outlets. Generally, offices open weekdays from 9am to 5pm. Stores are open six days a week with may open on Sundays, too; most department stores usually stay open until 9pm one day a week.

Climate   See "Information & Climate," Chapter 2.

Currency & Exchange   In the American monetary system, 100¢ equal one dollar ($1).

Foreign visitors used to paper money of varied colors should look carefully at the U.S. "greenbacks"—all bills are green, and all are the same size regardless of value. Aside from the numbers, Americans often differentiate them by the portrait they bear: The $1 bill ("a buck") depicts George Washington; the seldom-seen $2, Thomas Jefferson; the $5, Abraham Lincoln; the $10, Alexander Hamilton; the $20, Andrew

Jackson. Larger bills, including the $50 (Ulysses S. Grant) and the $100 (William McKinley), are not welcome in payment for small purchases.

There are six coins, four of them widely used: 1¢ ("penny") is brown copper; 5¢ ("nickel"); 10¢ ("dime"); and 25¢ ("quarter"). The 50¢ piece ("half-dollar") is less widely circulated and $1 coins—including the older, large silver dollar and the newer, small Susan B. Anthony coin—are rare.

Traveler's checks in *U.S. dollars* are easily cashed in payment for goods or services at most hotels, motels, restaurants, and large stores. The best rates, however, are given at banks; a major bank is also the only place where you can confidently cash traveler's checks in any currency *but* U.S. dollars. In fact, don't plan on changing any foreign currency here; the foreign-exchange bureaus common in other countries are largely absent from U.S. cities.

Credit cards are the most widely used method of payment by travelers in the United States. In New Mexico, VISA (BarclayCard in Britain, Chargex in Canada) and MasterCard (EuroCard in Europe, Access in Britain, Diamond in Japan) are accepted almost everywhere; American Express, by most establishments; Diners Club and Carte Blanche, by a large number; Discover, by an increasing number. EnRoute and JCB, the Japanese Credit Bank card, are beginning to come into favor as well.

Use of this "plastic money" reduces the necessity to carry large sums of cash or traveler's checks. It is accepted almost everywhere, except in food stores selling groceries and liquor. Credit cards can be recorded as a deposit for car rental, as proof of identity (often preferred to a passport) when cashing a check, or as a "cash card" for withdrawing money from banks that accept them.

Customs & Immigration U.S. Customs allow each adult visitor to import the following, duty free: (1) one liter of wine or hard liquor; (2) 1,000 cigarettes or 100 cigars (*not* from Cuba) or three pounds of smoking tobacco; and (3) $400 worth of gifts. The only restrictions are that the visitor must spend at least 72 hours in the United States, and must not have claimed them within the preceding six months. Food and plants are forbidden from import.

Foreign tourists may import or export up to $5,000 in U.S. or foreign currency, with no formalities. Larger amounts of money must be declared to Customs.

Visitors arriving by air, no matter what the port of entry, are well advised to be exceedingly patient and to resign themselves to a wait in the Customs and immigration line. At busy times, especially when several overseas flights arrive within a few minutes of each other, it can take two or three hours just to get a passport stamped for arrival. Allot *plenty* of time for connections between international and domestic flights!

Border formalities by road or rail from Canada are relatively quick and easy.

Electric Current The United States uses 110 to 120 volts, 60 cycles, compared to 220 to 240 volts, 50 cycles, as in most of Europe. Besides a 100-volt converter, small appliances of non-American manufacture, such as hair dryers or shavers, will require a plug adapter with two flat, parallel pins.

Embassies & Consulates All embassies are located in the national capital, Washington D.C.; some consulates are located in major cities, and most nations have a mission to the United Nations in New York City.

Listed here are the embassies and East and West Coast consulates of the major English-speaking countries. Travelers from other countries can get telephone numbers for their embassies and consulates by calling "Information" in Washington D.C. (202/555-1212).

The **Australian embassy** is at 1601 Massachusetts Ave. NW, Washington, DC 20036 (tel. 202/797-3000). The **consulate** in New York is located at the International Building, 630 Fifth Ave., Suite 420, New York, NY 10111 (tel. 212/245-4000). The consulate in Los Angeles is located at 611 N. Larchmont, Los Angeles, CA 90004 (tel. 213/469-4300).

The **Canadian embassy** is at 501 Pennsylvania Ave. NW, Washington, DC 20001 (tel. 202/682-1740). The **consulate** in New York is located at 1251 Avenue of the Americas, New York, NY 10020 (tel. 212/768-2400). The consulate in Los Angeles is located at 300 Santa Grand Ave., Suite 1000, Los Angeles, CA 90071 (tel. 213/687-7432).

The **Irish embassy** is at 2234 Massachusetts Ave. NW, Washington, DC 20008 (tel. 202/462-3939). The **consulate** in New York is located at 515 Madison Ave., New York, NY 10022 (tel. 212/319-2555). The consulate in San Francisco is located at 655 Montgomery St., Suite 930, San Francisco, CA 94111 (tel. 415/392-4214).

The **New Zealand embassy** is at 37 Observatory Circle NW Washington, DC 20008 (tel. 202/328-4800). The **consulate** in Los Angeles is located at 10960 Wiltshire Blvd., Los Angeles, CA 90024 (tel. 213/477-8241). There is no consulate in New York.

The **British embassy** is at 3100 Massachusetts Ave., NW Washington, DC 20008 (tel. 202/462-1340). The **consulate** in New York is located at 845 Third Ave., New York, NY 10022 (tel. 212/745-0200). The consulate in Los Angeles is located at 1766 Wilshire Blvd., Suite 400, Los Angeles, CA 90025 (tel. 310/477-3322).

Emergencies   A single emergency telephone number, **911,** will put you in touch with police, ambulance, or fire department in Albuquerque, Santa Fe, and other major New Mexico cities. In Taos and smaller towns without a 911 line, dial **0** (zero) for the operator.

Holidays   On the following national and legal holidays, banks, government offices, post offices, and many stores, restaurants, and museums are closed: January 1 (New Year's Day), third Monday in January (Martin Luther King Day), third Monday in February (President's Day), last Monday in May (Memorial Day), July 4 (Independence Day) first Monday in September (Labor Day), second Monday in October (Columbus Day), November 11 (Veteran's Day/Armistice Day), last Thursday in November (Thanksgiving Day), and December 25 (Christmas).

The Tuesday following the first Monday in November, Election Day, is a legal holiday in presidential-election years.

Information   See Chapter 2, Section 1.

Legal Aid   Those accused of serious offenses are advised to say and do nothing before consulting a lawyer. Under U.S. law, an arrested person is allowed one telephone call to a party of his or her choice: Call your embassy. If you are pulled up for a minor infraction, such as a traffic offense, never attempt to pay the fine directly to a police officer. You may wind up arrested on the much more serious charge of attempted bribery. Pay fines by mail, or directly into the hands of the clerk of a court.

Mail   If you aren't sure of your address while visiting New Mexico, your mail can be sent to you, in your name, **c/o General Delivery** at the main post office in the city of your destination. The addressee must pick it up in person, and must produce proof of identity (driver's license, credit card, passport, and so on).

Mailboxes are blue with a red-and-white logo, and carry the inscription "U.S. MAIL." A first-class stamp costs 29¢.

Newspapers & Magazines   Foreign publications, other than Spanish-language periodicals from Mexico, may be hard to find in New Mexico. There are newsstands in Santa Fe and Albuquerque that carry a few magazines from overseas, but no newspapers. Your best bet for staying abreast of foreign news is to pick up a copy of the *New York Times* or an American weekly newsmagazine.

Post Office   See "Mail" above or in the individual city and region chapters.

Radio & Television   There are dozens of radio stations (both AM and FM), each broadcasting talk shows, continuous news, or a particular kind of music—classical, country, jazz, pop, gospel—punctuated by frequent commercials. Television, with three coast-to-coast networks—ABC, CBS, and NBC—joined in recent years by the Public Broadcasting System (PBS) and a growing network of cable channels, plays a major part in American life.

Safety   Whenever you're traveling in an unfamiliar city or country, stay alert. Be aware of your immediate surroundings. Wear a money belt and don't flash expensive jewelry and cameras in public. This will minimize the possibility of your becoming a crime victim. Be alert even in heavily touristed areas.

Taxes   In the United States, there is no VAT (Value-Added Tax) or other indirect tax at a national level. New Mexico levies a 6% state tax on gross receipts, including hotel checks and shop purchases. Food is exempt. In addition, each city or county levies an additional lodging tax to support the local tax base.

Telephone, Telegraph, Telex & Fax **Pay phones** can be found on street corners, as well as in bars, restaurants, public buildings, stores, and service stations. Local calls cost 25¢.

For **long-distance** or **international calls,** stock up with a supply of quarters; the pay phone will instruct you when you should put them into the slot. For long-distance calls in the United States, dial 1 followed by the area code and number you want. For direct overseas calls, first dial 011, followed by the country code (Australia, 61; Republic of Ireland, 253; New Zealand, 64; United Kingdom, 44; and so on) and then by the city code (for example, 71 or 81 for London, 21 for Birmingham) and the number of the person you wish to call.

Before calling from a hotel room, always ask the hotel phone operator if there are any telephone surcharges. These are best avoided by using a public phone, calling collect, or using a telephone charge card.

For **reversed-charge** or **collect calls,** and for person-to-person calls, dial 0 (zero, not the letter "O") followed by the area code and number you want; an operator will then come on the line and you should specify that you are calling collect, or **person-to-person,** or both. If your operator-assisted call is international, ask for the overseas operator.

For local **directory assistance** ("Information"), dial 555-1212; for **long-distance information** dial 1, then the appropriate area code and 555-1212.

Like the telephone system, **telegraph** and **telex** services are provided by private corporations like ITT, MCI, and above all, Western Union. You can bring your telegram to the nearest Western Union office (there are hundreds across the country), or dictate it over the phone (a toll-free call, 800/325-6000). You can also telegraph money, or have it telegraphed to you, very quickly over the Western Union system.

Most hotels have fax machines available to their customers (ask if there is a charge to use it). You will also see signs for public faxes in the windows of small shops.

Time The United States is divided into six **time zones.** From east to west, they are: eastern standard time (EST), central standard time (CST), mountain standard time (MST), Pacific standard time (PST), Alaska standard time (AST), and Hawaii standard time (HST). Keep time zones in mind when traveling or telephoning long distances in the United States. For example, noon in New York City (EST) is 11am in Chicago (CST), 10am in Salt Lake City (MST), 9am in San Francisco (PST), 8am in Anchorage (AST), and 7am in Honolulu (HST). **Daylight saving time** is in effect from the last Sunday in April through the last Saturday in October; this alters the clock so that sunrise and sunset are an hour later.

Toilets Some foreign visitors complain that public "johns" are hard to find in the States. There are none on the streets, but most hotels, restaurants, bars, department stores, gasoline stations, museums, and other tourist attractions have them available. In a restaurant or bar, it's usually appropriate to order a cup of coffee or soft drink to qualify you as a customer.

Yellow Pages There are two kinds of telephone directories available. The general directory is called "white pages," and includes individuals and businesses alphabetically by name. The second directory, called "yellow pages," lists all local services, businesses, and industries alphabetically by category, with an index in the back. Listings include not only the obvious, such as automobile repairs and drugstores (pharmacies), but also restaurants by cuisine and location, places of worship by religious denomination, and other information that a tourist might not otherwise readily find. The yellow pages also include city plans or detailed area maps and often show postal ZIP codes and public transportation routes.

CHAPTER 4

ALBUQUERQUE

With a population of about half a million, Albuquerque is New Mexico's largest city. But it holds onto the bustling spirit of western towns of half a century ago when "progress" was a fashionable word and growing bigger was unquestionably synonymous with getting better.

The historic center of Albuquerque is Old Town, where it was founded in 1706. The city jumped away from its origins when the railroad came through in 1880 and caused a new Albuquerque to be planted around the passenger and freight depots. This *Saturday Evening Post*-style center, so reminiscent of hundreds of small plains cities of the thirties and forties, still exists along Central Avenue between second and sixth streets. But a new downtown, with an impressive new convention center, luxury hotels, financial district of glass skyscrapers, and underground shopping mall, is emerging just a few steps north. And vast commercial and shopping complexes are part of the urban expanse east of downtown, within quick reach by car via the long, wide, straight, flat streets and avenues of the sprawling grid that reach nearly to the foot of the Sandia Mountains 20 miles east of the old center.

In spite of the leveling, gentrifying effect of the spread of chain restaurants, interchangeable condos, and placeless superhighways, Albuquerque retains strong elements of its original western spirit. It feels somehow closer to the plains to the east, the directness of the Texan, than to the thin, chic optimism and faddishness of California. It is a young city: The people are young in years and in energy. The University of New Mexico plays a central role in life here, both by its geography just east of downtown and for the part it takes in the life of its city through its outstanding museums and cultural programs.

The city does have its unsightly commercial strips along the main east-west highway. The notorious old Route 66, where mid-20th-century pioneers heading west used to "get their kicks," still goes straight through town though most of its traffic has been diverted to I-40. But it was not all that long ago that Albuquerque had for a main drag a movie set—like row of false-front hotels, bars, and stores lined in front with hitching posts and wooden sidewalks along a muddy, rutted roadway crowded with wagons and buggies and figures on horseback.

That shot-in-the-arm railroad connection a little over a century ago gave Albuquerque the impetus to grow, to build, to move out in every direction without a thought for the future—without any plan at all. The city grew so big and so much, before there was any thought of saving any of its land for public use, that it wasn't until 1975 that any serious attempt at growth control took place. That action has provided citizens (and visitors) with some green spaces, and there are more to come. First-time visitors, viewing the city from a car speeding in over the interstate, which makes a huge cross in the middle of town with its east-west and north-south trajectories meeting and corkscrewing in and around one another, might suppose themselves lost in a Los Angeles–style wasteland of urban sprawl. But parts of Albuquerque are very special indeed—you just have to make sure to find them.

One of these is the Plaza of Old Town, which rivals the plazas of Santa Fe and Taos for historical interest, architectural beauty, and lively shopping and restaurant-going scenes. Another is the innovative complex of glass-and-steel bank buildings clustered around a tiled open space, containing a pool and a fountain, terraces and tables with parasols, the whole of which conceals First Plaza—a brightly lighted futuristic warren of underground shops, bars, and eating places that could make you imagine you'd come to Montreal on the Rio Grande. That good old western-style downtown is just outside in case you feel a dire need for a touch of reality.

The city was long a supply center for the region. Today it has added to its original mercantile base by developing supply depots for military bases and building experimental scientific laboratories in a wide variety of specialized fields. Its warm, sunny climate and healthful altitude—varying from 4,200 to 6,000 feet—also bring in many vacationers and retirement residents.

The fairgrounds is the site for the annual State Fair and for a colorful and locally renowned annual arts-and-crafts show. Indian pueblos in the area welcome tourists, and along with other pueblos throughout New Mexico have worked together to create the Pueblo Cultural Center, a showplace of Indian crafts of both past and present. The country's longest aerial tramway takes visitors to the top of Sandia Peak, which protects the city's eastern flank.

1. ORIENTATION

ARRIVING

BY PLANE **Albuquerque International Airport** is in the south central part of the city, between I-25 on the west and Kirtland Air Force Base on the east, just south of Gibson Boulevard. A major renovation and expansion, completed in early 1990, gave the city a sleek and efficient air terminal.

The airport is served by eight national airlines—**America West** (tel. 247-0737), **American** (tel. toll free 800/433-7300), **Continental** (tel. 842-8220), **Delta** (tel. 243-2794), **Southwest** (tel. 831-1221), **TWA** (tel. 842-4010), **USAir** (tel. toll free 800/428-4322), and **United** (tel. toll free 800/241-6522)—plus one regional carrier, **Mesa** (tel. 842-4218), and a commuter line, **Ross Aviation** (tel. 842-4161).

Most hotels have courtesy vans to take new arrivals to their accommodations. **Shuttlejack** (tel. 243-3244) also runs a service to city hotels and on to Santa Fe. **Sun Tran** (tel. 843-9200), Albuquerque's public bus system, also makes airport stops. There's efficient taxi service to and from the airport, and numerous car-rental agencies.

BY TRAIN Amtrak's *Southwest Chief* arrives and departs daily from and to Los Angeles and Chicago. The station is at 314 First St. SW, two blocks south of Central Avenue (tel. 842-9650).

BY BUS **Greyhound Lines, Inc.** (tel. 243-4435) and **TNM&O Coaches** (tel. 243-4435) arrive and depart from the Albuquerque Bus Transportation Center, adjacent to the train station at 300 Second St. SW.

BY CAR If you're driving yourself, you'll probably arrive in the city either via the east-west Interstate 40 or the north-south Interstate 25. Exits are well-marked. For information and advice on driving in New Mexico, see the "Getting Around" section in Chapter 2.

TOURIST INFORMATION

The head office of the **Albuquerque Convention and Visitors Bureau** is at 121 Tijeras Ave. NE, First floor (P.O. Box 26866) (tel. 505/243-3696 or toll free 800/284-2282). It's open Monday to Friday from 8am to 5pm. In addition, the bureau operates information centers at the airport, bottom of the escalator in the lower level, open from 9:30am to 8pm daily; and in Old Town next to Aceve's Basket Shop on Romero Street, open Monday to Saturday 10am to 5pm and Sunday 11am to

5pm. The bureau publishes a wide variety of visitor information, including the city's official annual visitors guide, brochures about local and regional attractions and accommodations, and quarterly calendars of events.

Tape-recorded information on current local events is available from the bureau Monday to Friday after 5pm and all day Saturday and Sunday. Call 243-3696 or toll free 800/284-2282.

CITY LAYOUT

Lay a map of Albuquerque before you and notice how the crossroads of I-40 and I-25 divide the city into four neat quadrants. The southwest quadrant is the location of downtown and Old Town. Central Avenue (the old "Route 66") and Lomas Boulevard flank downtown on the south and north, respectively; they come together 2 miles west of downtown near the Old Town Plaza. The Rio Grande greenbelt lies about a half mile southwest of Old Town.

Lomas and Central continue east across I-25, staying about a half mile apart as they pass by first the University of New Mexico, then the New Mexico State Fairgrounds. The airport is due south of the UNM campus, about 3 miles via Yale Boulevard. Kirtland Air Force Base—site of Sandia National Laboratories and the National Atomic Museum—is an equal distance south of the fairgrounds on Louisiana Boulevard.

Roughly paralleling I-40 to the north is Menaul Boulevard, focus of the Midtown and Uptown shopping and hotel districts. (Think of Midtown as extending from I-25 to San Mateo Boulevard, about 2½ miles, and Uptown from there to Eubank Boulevard, another 3 miles.) As Albuquerque expands northward, the Journal Center business park area, about 4½ miles north of the freeway interchange, is getting more attention. Broad San Mateo links Journal Center with Midtown and Uptown. East of Eubank are the Sandia Foothills, where the alluvial plain slants a bit more steeply toward the mountain.

For address purposes, Central Avenue divides the city into north and south, and the railroad tracks—which run just east of First Street, downtown—split it into east and west. Street names are followed by a directional: NE, NW, SE, or SW.

The most comprehensive Albuquerque street map is the one published by Sun West Bank and distributed by the Convention and Visitors Bureau.

2. GETTING AROUND

BY BUS   **Sun Tran of Albuquerque** (tel. 843-9200) cloaks the arterials with its city bus network. Call for information on routes and fares.

BY TAXI   **Albuquerque Cab** (tel. 883-4888), **Checker Cab** and **Yellow Cab** (tel. 247-8888 or 243-7777, for either) serve the city and surrounding area 24 hours a day.

BY CAR   The yellow pages list more than 30 **car-rental** agencies in Albuquerque. **Rich Ford Payless** (tel. 247-9255) offers some of the best rates around. It's located one-eighth of a mile from the airport. Among the well-known national firms are **Alamo,** at the airport (tel. 842-4057), **Avis,** airport (tel. 842-4080), **Budget,** airport (tel. 884-2666), **Dollar,** airport (tel. 842-4224), **Hertz,** airport (tel. 842-4235), **Rent-a-Wreck,** 500 Yale Blvd. SE (tel. 256-9693), and **Thrifty,** 2039 Yale Blvd. SE (tel. 842-8733). Those not in the airport itself are nearby, and provide rapid airport pick up and delivery service.

When you return your vehicle to the rental agency, fill the tank before you get directly back to the airport. Service stations near the airport often jack their prices for gasoline up 33% higher than stations a mile or two away.

Parking is generally not difficult in Albuquerque—nor, for that matter, is rush hour a serious problem (yet). Meters operate from 8am to 6pm weekdays and are not monitored at other times. Most hotels do not charge for parking, with the exception of the large downtown properties.

BY BICYCLE The wide streets and gentle slopes make Albuquerque an ideal city for cycling. There is a large network of designated bike lanes, as well as a citywide system of bike trails. However, be careful to obey all traffic laws when not in an area with designated bike lanes.

Numerous bicycle shops sell bikes and accessories, handle repairs, and supply parts. Among them is centrally located **Two Wheel Drive,** 1706 Central Ave. SE, near University Boulevard (tel. 243-8443) and **Gardenswartz Sportz,** 2720 San Mateo Blvd. NE (tel. 884-6787).

FAST ALBUQUERQUE

American Express A travel service representative is the **Atlas Travel American Express Travel Agency,** 3412 Central Ave. NE (tel. 255-5558). To report lost cards, call toll free 800/528-4800. To report lost traveler's checks, call toll free 800/221-7282.

Area Code 505.

Babysitters Most hotels can arrange on request. Otherwise, try **Albuquerque Nursery and Kindergarten,** 1423 Wyoming Blvd. NE (tel. 298-7547); or **The Children's Center,** 4001 Montgomery Blvd. NE (tel. 881-9565). Both offer sitting services from early morning to late night.

Business Hours In general, Monday to Friday 9am to 5pm, with many stores also open Saturday.

Doctor **Presbyterian Hospital** (tel. 841-1234) makes referrals for visitors.

Drugstores **Walgreens** offers 24-hour prescription service at 2950 Central Ave. SE (tel. 262-1745).

Embassies & Consulates See "Fast Facts: For the Foreign Traveler" in Chapter 3.

Emergencies For police, fire, or ambulance, dial 911.

Eyeglasses Downtown, **Wohl Optical,** 216 Gold Ave. SW (tel. 242-4262), offers lunch-hour service. Uptown, look for **LensCrafters,** 133 Winrock Center NE (tel. 889-3464), open daily.

Hairdressers & Barbers Many of the better hotels have in-house salons or can recommend nearby parlors. For budget watchers, **SuperCuts** has nine locations in Albuquerque, most of them in the northeastern part of the city. Consult your yellow pages.

Hospitals The major facilities are **Presbyterian Hospital,** 1100 Central Ave. SE (tel. 841-1234, emergency 841-1111); and **University of New Mexico Hospital,** 2211 Lomas Blvd. NE (emergency tel. 843-2411). **Lovelace Medical Center,** 5400 Gibson Blvd. SE (tel. 262-7000, emergency 262-7222) has seven other urgent care facilities around the city, open daily 8am to 8pm year-round.

Information See "Information," Chapter 2. The **Albuquerque Convention and Visitors Bureau** head office is at 121 Tijeras Ave. NE, Suite 1000 (P.O. Box 26866), Albuquerque, NM 87102 (tel. 505/243-3696 or toll free 800/284-2282). Branch centers are at Albuquerque International Airport, at the lower level in front of the escalator, open 9:30am to 8pm daily; and in Old Town on Romero Street NW, next to Aceve's Basket Shop, open Monday to Saturday 10am to 5pm, Sunday 11am to 5pm.

Laundry & Dry Cleaning Virtually all hotels provide either valet and laundry service or guest laundry facilities. A 24-hour self-service laundry is **Harold's Laundries,** 1512 Girard Blvd. NE (tel. 268-9834).

Libraries The main branch of the **Albuquerque/Bernalillo County Public Library** is downtown at 501 Copper Ave. NW (tel. 768-5140). There are 11 other

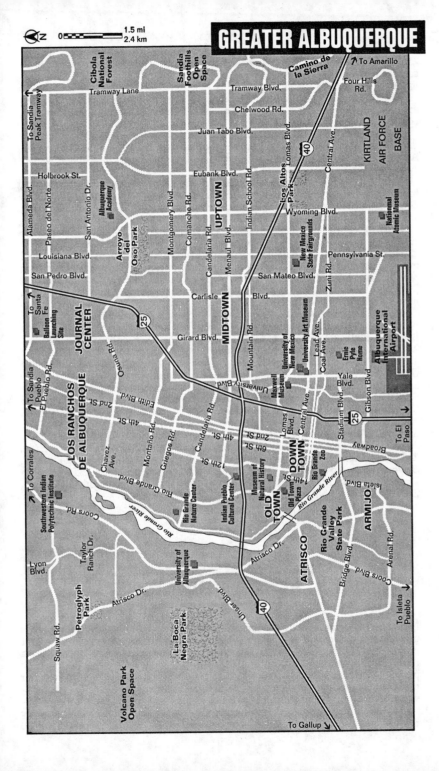

branches, including the notable **Ernie Pyle Branch** at 900 Girard Ave. SE (tel. 256-2065). The **University of New Mexico Libraries** are headquartered on campus near Central Avenue and University Boulevard (tel. 277-5761).

Lost Property   Contact city police (tel. 768-2020).

Mail   The main post office, 1135 Broadway NE (tel. 848-3872), is open 8am to 4pm daily. There are 14 branch post offices, and another 13 in surrounding communities.

Newspapers & Magazines   The two daily newspapers are the *Albuquerque Journal,* published mornings, and the *Albuquerque Tribune,* published evenings. *Albuquerque Monthly* magazine covers many aspects of city life and is widely available.

Photographic Needs   Kurt's Camera Corral, with three locations, handles sales, repairs, rentals, and processing. Find them at 3417 Central Ave. NE (tel. 266-7766); 6909 Menaul Blvd. NE, beside the Ramada Hotel Classic (tel. 883-5373); and 1713 Juan Tabo Blvd. NE (tel. 296-4888).

Police   For emergencies, call 911. For other business, contact Albuquerque City Police (tel. 768-2020) or the New Mexico State Police (tel. 841-9256).

Radio & TV   Albuquerque has some 30 local radio stations catering to all musical tastes. Albuquerque television stations include KOB Channel 4 (NBC affiliate), KOAT Channel 7 (ABC affiliate), KGGM Channel 13 (CBS affiliate), KNME Channel 5 (PBS affiliate), and KGSW Channel 14 (Fox and independent). There are, of course, numerous local cable channels as well.

Religious Services   Anglican, Church of St. Peter, Eubank and Paseo del Norte (tel. 822-1192). **Assemblies of God,** First Family Church, 4701 Wyoming Blvd. (tel. 299-7202). **Baptist,** First Baptist Church, 101 Broadway Blvd. NE (tel. 247-3611). **Church of Christ,** Albuquerque Church of Christ, 1908 Sunshine Terrace SE (tel. 764-9277). **Episcopal,** Episcopal Diocese of the Rio Grande, 4304 Carlisle Blvd. NE (tel. 881-0636). **Jewish,** Congregation B'nai Israel, 4401 Indian School Rd. NE (tel. 266-0155). **Lutheran,** St. Paul Lutheran Church, 1100 Indian School Rd. NE (tel. 242-5942). **Methodist,** Central United Methodist Church, 1615 Copper Ave. NE (tel. 243-7834). **Mormon,** 1100 Montano Rd. NW (tel. 345-7642). **Nazarene,** Sandia Church of the Nazarene, 2801 Louisiana Blvd. NE (tel. 881-0267). **Presbyterian,** La Mesa Presbyterian Church, 7401 Copper Ave. NE (tel. 255-8095). **Roman Catholic,** San Felipe Church, 2005 Plaza NW, Old Town (tel. 243-4628); Immaculate Conception Church, 619 Copper Ave. NW (tel. 247-4271). **Seventh-day Adventist,** Central Seventh Day Adventist Church, 2201 Estancia Dr. NW (tel. 836-1845). **United Church of Christ,** First Congregational Church, 2801 Lomas Blvd. NE (tel. 265-5749).

3. ACCOMMODATIONS

New Mexico's largest city has some 9,000 hotel rooms. Although Albuquerque is growing as a convention destination, a high percentage of the rooms remain vacant during much of the year. That means visitors can frequently request, and obtain, a room rate lower than the one posted. The exceptions would be during peak periods—the New Mexico Arts & Crafts Fair in late June, the New Mexico State Fair in September, and the Albuquerque International Balloon Fiesta in early October—when hoteliers may raise their rates as much as 50% and still fill every room.

In the listings below, the following categories define price ranges: **very expensive,** over $120 per night double; **expensive,** $90 to $120; **moderate,** $60

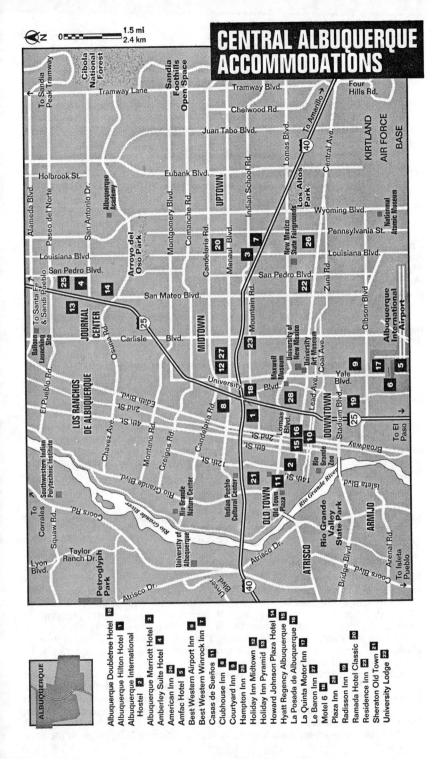

CENTRAL ALBUQUERQUE ACCOMMODATIONS

1.5 mi
2.4 km

Cibola National Forest

Sandia Foothills Open Space

Tramway Lane

Tramway Blvd.

Four Hills Rd.

To Sandia Peak Tramway

Chelwood Rd.

Juan Tabo Blvd.

To Amarillo

KIRTLAND AIR FORCE BASE

Central Ave.

Holbrook St.

Eubank Blvd.

UPTOWN

Alameda Blvd

Paseo del Norte

San Antonio Dr.

Albuquerque Academy

Indian School Rd.

Lomas Blvd.

Los Altos Park

Wyoming Blvd.

National Atomic Museum

Arroyo del Oso Park

Montgomery Blvd.

Comanche Rd.

Candelaria Rd.

Menaul Blvd.

New Mexico State Fairgrounds

Pennsylvania St.

Louisiana Blvd

San Pedro Blvd.

Louisiana Blvd.

To Santa Fe & Sandi Pueblo

San Pedro Blvd.

Zuni Rd.

Gibson Blvd

Albuquerque International Airport

Balloon Launching Site

JOURNAL CENTER

El Pueblo Rd.

Osuna Rd.

Carlisle

Blvd.

San Mateo Blvd.

Mountain Rd.

LOS RANCHOS DE ALBUQUERQUE

University

Blvd.

Maxwell Museum

University of New Mexico

University Art Museum

Yale Blvd.

To El Paso

Edith Blvd.

2nd St.

4th St.

Candelaria Rd.

Lomas Blvd.

Coal Ave.

Lead Ave.

Stadium Blvd.

DOWNTOWN

Chavez Ave.

Montano Rd.

Greigos Rd.

12th St.

6th St.

2nd St.

14th St.

Broadway

MIDTOWN

Rio Grande Nature Center

Indian Pueblo Cultural Center

OLD TOWN

Old Town Plaza

Rio Grande Zoo

Isleta Blvd.

Southwestern Indian Polytechnic Institute

To Corrales

Squaw Rd.

Coors Rd.

University of Albuquerque

Rio Grande Blvd.

Rio Grande River

Rio Grande Valley State Park

ARMIJO

To Isleta Pueblo

Arenal Rd.

Coors Blvd.

Bridge Blvd.

Taylor Ranch Dr.

Lyon Blvd.

Petroglyph Park

Atrisco Dr.

Atrisco Dr.

Unser Blvd.

Linser Blvd.

ATRISCO

ALBUQUERQUE

Albuquerque Doubletree Hotel 10
Albuquerque Hilton Hotel 1
Albuquerque International Hostel 2
Albuquerque Marriott Hotel 3
Amberley Suite Hotel 4
American Inn 26
Amfac Hotel 5
Best Western Airport Inn 6
Best Western Winrock Inn 7
Casas de Sueños 11
Clubhouse Inn 9
Courtyard Inn 8
Hampton Inn 25
Holiday Inn Midtown 12
Holiday Inn Pyramid 27
Howard Johnson Plaza Hotel 14
Hyatt Regency Albuquerque 15
La Posada de Albuquerque 16
La Quinta Motor Inn 17
Le Baron Inn 22
Motel 6 18
Plaza Inn 28
Radisson Inn 19
Ramada Hotel Classic 20
Residence Inn 23
Sheraton Old Town 21
University Lodge 22

to $90; **inexpensive,** $30 to $60; **budget,** less than $30 per night double. An additional 11% tax (6% state tax, 5% city lodging tax) is imposed on every hotel bill.

DOWNTOWN/OLD TOWN

This area is the best location to stay if you want to be close to many of the major sights and attractions. All of the following accommodations are between I-25 and the Rio Grande, and between I-40 and Route 66 (Central Avenue).

VERY EXPENSIVE

HYATT REGENCY ALBUQUERQUE, 330 Tijeras Ave. NW, Albuquerque, NM 87102. Tel. 505/842-1234 or toll free 800/233-1234. Fax 505/842-1184. 395 rms, 14 suites. A/C TV TEL

$ Rates: $110–$120 single, $130–$145 double, $310–$725 suite. Weekends $79 single or double. AE, CB, DC, DISC, MC, V. **Parking:** $2 daily per entry for guests; $5 valet with in-out privileges.

This 20-story, $60-million property became a city landmark the day it opened in August 1990. The boldly appointed Hyatt makes a statement unlike any other in New Mexico. Marble pillars, Irish carpets, and an extensive use of mahogany contribute to the feeling of opulence. A pyramid skylight nourishes palms surrounding a fountain in the lobby. The hotel boasts a $500,000 collection of public art in contemporary and western genres, including an original sculpture by Frederic Remington.

Spacious rooms, decorated in mauves and forest greens, feature such touches as remote-control television, clock radios, full-length mirrors, mahogany desks, even data-port jacks for business travelers. In southwestern fashion, each boasts a potted cactus.

Dining/Entertainment: McGrath's, open daily from 6:30am–2:30pm and 5–10pm, offers a gourmet grill menu in a rich atmosphere of black cherry and mahogany. A casual lounge adjoins the restaurant. A lobby bar has whimsical oil paintings on its walls, depicting saloons where the deer and the antelope play.

Services: Room service from 6am–midnight, concierge, valet laundry, courtesy van.

Facilities: Rooms for nonsmokers and the disabled, heated outdoor swimming pool, health club with massage service and large weight and exercise room, gift shop, several upscale art galleries, Delta airlines desk, Budget auto rental desk, hair salon, florist, optician, travel agency.

EXPENSIVE

CASAS DE SUEÑOS, 310 Rio Grande Blvd. SW, Albuquerque, NM 87102. Tel. 505/247-4560. 12 rms. TV

$ Rates: $85–$200 single or double. AE, MC, V.

You'll know Casas de Sueños by the bright sign and the snail-shaped front of the main building (you'll know exactly what I mean when you see it, and you can't miss it). The buildings that comprise Casas de Sueños were once private homes—apparently somewhat of an artists' colony. Most of them face a courtyard that was cooperatively maintained for many years by the residents. In the spring and summer, the gardens, filled with roses, are maintained by today's owners of Casas de Sueños, making the place somewhat of an oasis right in the middle of Albuquerque.

Each of the rooms follows an individual theme; for instance, Cupid is done in black, white, and pink and has a claw-foot bathtub—a nice romantic getaway. La Cascada, so named because of the fountain outside its door, has a Monet theme with its pastel colors, Monet posters, and Monet print comforter. The Kachina room has many little *kachinas* (the storytellers) scattered about. Some of the rooms have kitchens, and La Miradora has two bedrooms (one with two twin beds), a living room with a fireplace, a full bath, and a back porch with a swing. All the rooms have private entrances, and most have telephones.

Mari Penhurst-Gerste, the manager, serves a delicious full breakfast in the main building every morning. Works by local artists are displayed in the breakfast room. Guests have executive sports club privileges, and there is a massage therapist on premises. No smoking is permitted. Pets are not accepted, but children 12 and older are welcome.

DOUBLETREE HOTEL, 201 Marquette St. NW, Albuquerque, NM 87102.
  Tel. 505/247-3344 or toll free 800/528-0444. Fax 505/247-7025. 280 rms, 14 suites. A/C TV TEL
  $ Rates (including breakfast): $118 single or double, $180–$350 suite. Weekends $61 single or double. AE, CB, DC, DISC, ER, MC, V. **Parking:** Free.
A pillared lobby with a marble floor greets arrivals to this elegant property. But perhaps the most remarkable feature of the Doubletree, which adjoins the Albuquerque Convention Center, is the two-story waterfall that cascades against a marble backdrop from the lobby to the restaurant and lounge below. An underground passageway links the hotel to the convention center and a shopping mall.
All rooms in this 15-story hotel are decorated in pastel shades and southwestern designs, including custom-made furnishings. Each has a cable TV (with in-house movies) hidden in an armoire, clock radio, full mirror on the bathroom door, and good-sized desk for business travelers.
  Dining/Entertainment: La Cascada Restaurant is an airy coffee shop, with trees and mirrors to make it appear larger than it is, open from 6am–11pm daily. A variety of food is served, from sandwiches and pastas to New Mexican specialties and meat, fish and chicken main courses; dinners run from $9.95–$17.95. Drinks are served in the Bistro Bar, adjacent to the waterfall, and the Lobby Lounge, with its marble-top bar, has live music daily during happy hour (4:30–6:30pm).
  Services: Room service from 6am–midnight, valet laundry, airport courtesy van.
  Facilities: Rooms for nonsmokers and the disabled, swimming pool, weight room, gift/sundry shop, American Airlines ticket counter.

LA POSADA DE ALBUQUERQUE, 125 2nd St. NW (at Copper St.),
  Albuquerque, NM 87102. Tel. 505/242-9090 or toll free 800/777-5732. Fax 505/242-8664. 114 rms, 5 suites. A/C TV TEL
  $ Rates: $75–$95 single, $85–$105 double, $180–$235 suite. AE, CB, DC, DISC, MC, V. **Parking:** Complimentary valet.
Built in 1939 by Conrad Hilton as the famed hotelier's first inn in his home state of New Mexico, this hotel is listed on the National Register of Historic Places. The atmosphere is of a 19th-century hacienda courtyard in Old Mexico. In the center of a tile floor is an elaborate Moorish brass-and-mosaic tile fountain, and beyond it, a piano bar surrounded by plush leather-upholstered seating. Tin chandeliers hang from the two-story high ceiling.
The guest rooms are somewhat outdated but equally charming. As in the lobby, all furniture is handcrafted, but here it's covered with cushions of stereotypically southwestern design. There are limited-edition lithographs by R. C. Gorman and Amado Pena on the white walls, and an ample desk opposite the wood-shuttered windows. The heating and ventilation system is the original.
  Dining/Entertainment: Eulalia's, serving continental cuisine with a contemporary flair, is one of Albuquerque's exclusive dinner clubs (see "Dining," below). Hours are 7am–2pm Mon–Sat for breakfast and lunch, 6–10pm nightly for dinner. The Plaza Coffee Shop is open Mon–Fri from 6am–3pm and Sat from 7–11am for breakfast and lunch. All-you-can-eat lobby buffets are served for $5.95–$7.95 during weekday noon hours, and a bar menu is offered in the lobby until 11pm.
  Services: Room service, valet laundry, 24-hour courtesy van.
  Facilities: Rooms for nonsmokers and the disabled, gift shop.

SHERATON OLD TOWN, 800 Rio Grande Blvd. NW, Albuquerque, NM
  87104. Tel. 505/843-6300 or toll free 800/237-2133 or 800/325-3535. Fax 505/842-9863. 190 rms, 20 suites. A/C MINIBAR TV TEL

$ Rates: $85–$98 single, $95–$108 double, $120 suite. Children free with adult. AE, CB, DC, MC, V. **Parking:** Free.

Within five minutes' walk of the Old Town Plaza and overlooking two of Albuquerque's major museums, the Sheraton is an ideal spot for visitors without their own vehicles who don't want to be at the mercy of taxis or rental cars. Mezzanine-level windows light the adobe-toned lobby, which is separated from the Fireside Lounge by a double-sided fireplace.

Each guest room is characterized by a Pueblo Indian craft on the wall over the beds. Southwest colors are the preferred shades of decoration. All furniture, including dressers, desks, and chairs, is handmade. Southside rooms, facing Old Town, have private balconies.

Dining/Entertainment: The Customs House Restaurant, designed with a southwestern flair, is the main dining room. It specializes in seafood and regional cuisine, with dinner main courses priced in the $10–$17 range. Open for lunch weekdays from 11:30am–2pm; dinner daily from 5:30–10:30pm; Sun champagne brunch from 11:30am–2pm. Café del Sol is the Sheraton's coffeehouse; open daily from 6am–9pm, its dinner main courses are priced from $6–$12. Taverna Don Alberto, serving drinks off the main lobby, features dance bands Fri and Sat nights.

Services: Room service, concierge, valet laundry, 24-hour courtesy van, secretarial, babysitting.

Facilities: Rooms for nonsmokers and the disabled, outdoor swimming pool and Jacuzzi, exercise room. Sheraton owns and operates Old Town Place, a shopping center to which it is directly connected. Shops include art dealers, bookstore, beauty salon, and manicurist.

MODERATE

THE W. E. MAUGER ESTATE, 701 Roma Ave. NW, Albuquerque, NM 87102. Tel. 505/242-8755. 8 rms, 1 suite.
$ Rates (including full breakfast): $49–$79 single, $59–$99 double. AE, DC, MC, V.

A restored Queen Anne–style residence constructed in 1897, this former residence of wool baron William Mauger is listed on the National Register of Historic Places. Today it is a wonderfully atmospheric bed-and-breakfast, with high ceilings and rich brass appointments. It's located close to downtown, just five blocks from the convention center. All rooms feature period furnishings, private baths and showers. Some also have a fireplace or balcony. A full breakfast is served each morning that includes tea or coffee, juice, freshly baked pastries, a hot egg dish, and a breakfast meat.

BUDGET

ALBUQUERQUE INTERNATIONAL HOSTEL, 1012 Central Ave. SW, Albuquerque, NM 87106. Tel. 505/243-6101. 15 private rms, 34 dorm beds.
$ Rates: $10–$12 nightly for dorm beds, $27 private rooms. No credit cards.

This pleasant hostel is located two blocks west of Robinson Park, halfway between downtown and Old Town. As with all hostels, toilets, showers, kitchen, TV room, telephone, laundry, and other facilities are shared. The hostel is open for registration daily from 7:30am to noon and 4:30 to 11pm.

MIDTOWN/UPTOWN

This area, which extends from I-25 to Eubank Boulevard, and between Central Avenue and Montgomery Boulevard, is a popular resting place for business travelers, shoppers, and other visitors seeking a central location. It includes Freeway Loop, which surrounds the interchange of I-25 and I-40; several major hotels are on Menaul or University boulevards nearby.

VERY EXPENSIVE

ALBUQUERQUE MARRIOTT HOTEL, 2101 Louisiana Blvd. NE, at I-40, Albuquerque, NM 87110. Tel. 505/881-8600 or toll-free 800/228-9290. Fax 505/881-1780. 410 rms, 6 suites. A/C TV TEL

$ Rates: $119–$135 single, $134–$155 double, $225–$250 suite; weekends $64 double ($69 including breakfast). AE, CB, DC, DISC, JCB, MC, V. **Parking:** Free.

One of Albuquerque's most elegant hotels looms over I-40 as it enters the city from the east. A classically beautiful lobby, with plush red seating surrounding a player piano, beneath the ceiling of a two-story atrium, greets the visitor.

Most rooms are decorated in pastel shades of green, peach, or lilac, with a palm or similar plant against the window. Many have an unusual Oriental motif, which extends from cane-and-rattan furniture to prints of Japanese cranes on the walls. Half-size refrigerators are provided on request; big closets have full-size mirrors on the doors. The two-floor Concierge Level caters to business travelers with a private lounge, complimentary continental breakfast, evening hors d'oeuvres, and a well-stocked honor bar.

Dining/Entertainment: Nicole's is widely considered one of Albuquerque's finest restaurants (see "Dining," below). The Herbs & Roses coffee shop serves three meals daily in a southwestern-style decor. Nicole's Lounge is a quiet spot for a chat; there's a bar menu, and light jazz and classical music are piped.

Services: Room service, telephone concierge, valet laundry, 24-hour courtesy van.

Facilities: Rooms for nonsmokers and the disabled, indoor and outdoor swimming pools, saunas, Jacuzzi, health club with weight/exercise room, guest Laundromat, games room, gift shop.

EXPENSIVE

ALBUQUERQUE HILTON HOTEL, 1901 University Blvd. NE, Albuquerque, NM 87102. Tel. 505/884-2500 or toll free 800/27-HOTEL. Fax 505/889-9118. 250 rms, 2 suites. A/C TV TEL

$ Rates: $91–$105 single, $95–$105 double, $375–$400 suite. AE, CB, DC, DISC, MC, V. **Parking:** Free.

White stuccoed corridors with petroglyph-style paintings are a trademark of this hotel. Many of the rooms are in a high-rise tower which underwent a multimillion-dollar renovation in 1988. Two floors of rooms comprise a VIP level for business travelers; cabana rooms with 15-foot cathedral ceilings surround the outdoor pool.

Standard rooms, if there is such a thing, typically have maroon carpeting and peach walls with limited-edition prints by Susan Brooke. Furnishings include a queen-size bed, sofa bed, desk, dresser, satellite TV, full-wall mirror, radio/alarm clock, and two telephones—desk and bedside.

Restaurant/Entertainment: The Ranchers Club (see "Dining," below) is considered by many to be Albuquerque's number-one restaurant. A less formal mealtime option is Casa Chaco, open daily from 6am–10pm for coffee shop–style breakfasts and lunches, and highly regarded contemporary southwestern dinners. The Cantina, with its fajitas grill and piano bar, serves as the hotel lounge.

Services: Room service during restaurant hours, valet laundry, courtesy van. No pets.

Facilities: Rooms for nonsmokers and the disabled, indoor and outdoor swimming pools, whirlpool, saunas, tennis courts. Gift shop.

RAMADA HOTEL CLASSIC, 6815 Menaul Blvd. NE at Louisiana Blvd., Albuquerque, NM 87110. Tel. 505/881-0000 or toll free 800/2-RAMADA. Fax 505/881-3736. 296 rms, 23 suites. A/C FRIDGE TV TEL

$ Rates: $74–$94 single, $84–$104 double, $125–$250 suite. AE, CB, DC, DISC, MC, V. **Parking:** Free.

White Spanish pillars and tile floors lend a hacienda feeling to the lobby of the

Ramada. Known as the "classic" in honor of owner Phil Maloof's collection of vintage automobiles, it once exhibited a classic beauty outside the hotel's main doors until vandals convinced management that wasn't wise.

The spacious rooms are decorated with southwestern abstracts and light-wood decor. All have twin sinks, refrigerators, and good-sized working desks. Rooms earmarked for women travelers have hairdryers. Corporate accounts get a complimentary continental breakfast and a free copy of *USA Today* delivered to their rooms.

Dining/Entertainment: Chardonnay offers fine continental dining in an atmosphere of turn-of-the-century elegance, with china and crystal service amid mahogany room dividers. Open for lunches weekdays, for dinners daily, its main-course prices range from $11.95–$39.50. Café Fennel, a garden-style coffee shop, serves three meals from 6am–11pm daily. The Quest Lounge has live music Mon through Thurs and a disc jockey weekends. The Lobby Lounge features a piano bar and happy-hour buffet.

Services: Room service during restaurant hours, valet laundry, 24-hour courtesy van.

Facilities: Rooms for nonsmokers and the disabled, indoor swimming pool, Jacuzzi, saunas, fitness center with weight and exercise room, hair salon, gift shop, American Airlines desk. Spa affiliation.

RESIDENCE INN, 3300 Prospect Ave. NE, Albuquerque, NM 87107. Tel. 505/881-2661 or toll free 800/331-3131. Fax 505/884-5551. 112 rms, all suites. A/C FRIDGE TV TEL

$ Rates (including continental breakfast): Weekdays $109 studio suite, $135 penthouse suite; weekends, $89 studio suite. $114 penthouse suite. Weekly and monthly rates on request. AE, CB, DC, DISC, MC, V. **Parking:** Free.

Located just off I-40 at its Carlisle Boulevard exit, this Marriott property caters to those planning extended stays. The average guest, in fact, makes the inn home for 10 nights. It's constructed like a condominium complex, with 8 units in each of 14 different buildings.

The suites are entirely residential, with full kitchens (refrigerator, stove, microwave, dishwasher, coffee maker, toaster, and the like) and all utensils provided. Every living room has a wood-burning fireplace; each unit has its own hot-water heater and air conditioner. Decor has a southwestern theme. Bedrooms contain either two queen-size beds or a king-size bed and a full working desk. Penthouse units feature a bedroom in a loft above the living area.

Dining/Entertainment: Continental breakfast is served in Gatehouse room off lobby. Social hour weekdays from 5:30–7pm, also in Gatehouse, includes complimentary buffet. No alcohol is served.

Services: Valet laundry, courtesy van, complimentary grocery-shopping service, free daily newspaper.

Facilities: Rooms for nonsmokers and the disabled, outdoor swimming pool, Jacuzzi, weight/exercise room, sports court, guest Laundromat.

MODERATE

BEST WESTERN WINROCK INN, 18 Winrock Center NE, Albuquerque, NM 87110. Tel. 505/883-5252 or toll free 800/866-5252. Fax 505/889-3206. 174 rms, 4 suites. A/C TV TEL

$ Rates (including breakfast buffet): $50–$68 single, $56–$74 double, $95 suite. AE, CB, DC, DISC, MC, V. **Parking:** Free.

Located just off I-40 at the Louisiana Boulevard interchange, the Winrock is attached to Albuquerque's second-largest shopping center: Winrock Center. A hotel with prime appeal to international visitors, its two separate buildings are wrapped around a private lagoon and garden featuring Mandarin ducks, giant *koi* (carp), and an impressive waterfall.

The comfortable rooms, many of which have private patios overlooking the lagoon, feature a pastel southwestern-motif decor. There are rooms for nonsmokers and the disabled. The Club Room offers a breakfast buffet each morning and

complimentary happy-hour drinks each evening. Upstairs, but under separate ownership, is the Japanese Kitchen, a hibachi-style steak house (see "Restaurants," below).
The hotel offers valet laundry, 24-hour courtesy van, a heated outdoor swimming
pool, and guest Laundromat.

**CLUBHOUSE INN, 1315 Menaul Blvd. NE at I-25, Albuquerque, NM
87107. Tel. 505/345-0010** or toll free 800/258-2466. Fax 505/344-3931.
137 rms, 17 suites. A/C TV TEL
$ Rates (including breakfast): $59 single, $69 double, $80–$85 suite. Children
under 10 free with parent. AE, CB, DC, DISC, MC, V. **Parking:** Free.

The ClubHouse lobby sets the tone for the rest of the inn by looking just like a
living room, complete with fireplace, sofas, and lush plants. Furnishings in each
of the brightly appointed, oversized rooms include a free-standing desk with
phone (free local calls), cable TV, and sofa or easy chair with ottoman. The suites
include kitchenettes and numerous other special touches. Complimentary buffet
breakfast served from 6:30 to 9am; complimentary cocktails, from 5 to 7pm daily.
The hotel provides valet laundry service, rooms for nonsmokers and the disabled, a
swimming pool, Jacuzzi, guest laundry, and barbecues.

**HOLIDAY INN MIDTOWN, 2020 Menaul Blvd. NE, Albuquerque, NM
87107. Tel. 505/884-2511** or toll free 800/545-0599 or 800/HOLIDAY. Fax
505/884-5720. 360 rms. A/C TV TEL
$ Rates: $74–$80 single, $84–$90 double. AE, CB, DC, DISC, JCB, MC, V.
Parking: Free.
As headquarters lodge for Albuquerque's annual International Balloon Fiesta in
October, the Midtown keeps a "high" profile. Miniature balloons dangle high above a
spacious, two-story atrium, and the rest of the hotel has a similar airy appeal.
Nicely appointed rooms have all standard furnishings, including satellite television
and radio/alarm clocks. The Sandia Springs Restaurant, famous for its frequent
all-you-can-eat buffets, is open daily from 6:30am to 2pm and 4 to 10pm. Lunches
run $6.09 to $10.98; dinners, $6.95 to $13.95. It's adjoined by the popular Sandia
Springs Lounge, featuring live country-and-western music nightly except Sunday. The
Springwater Deli (open from 6am to 11pm daily) serves sandwiches and snacks under
the atrium roof, and the adjacent Conversations Lounge offers drinks. The hotel has
room service during restaurant hours, valet laundry, courtesy van, and rooms for
nonsmokers; pets are permitted. Facilities include an indoor swimming pool,
weight/exercise room, sauna, whirlpool, games room, guest Laundromat, gift shop.

INEXPENSIVE

**AMERICAN INN, 4501 Central Ave. NE, Albuquerque, NM 87108. Tel.
505/262-1681** or toll free 800/343-2597. Fax 505/255-0309. 130 rms, 24
suites. A/C TV TEL
$ Rates (including full breakfast): $28–$43 single, $36–$56 double, $180 suite. AE,
CB, DC, DISC, MC, V.

One of the nicer properties in the Nob Hill area of Route 66, between the
University of New Mexico and the State Fairgrounds, the friendly American
Inn underwent a complete renovation in 1989. Rooms are clean and sufficiently
spacious, with Southwestern decor, one king-size or two double beds, and standard
motel furnishings. All suites have kitchenettes, including a refrigerator with freezer
and a microwave oven. Full breakfasts, served at the 24-hour American Café, are
included in the room price. There is complimentary shuttle service to airport, bus and
train stations. Pets are permitted with payment of a damage deposit. The hotel has an
outdoor swimming pool and hot tub.

**LE BARON INN, 2126 Menaul Blvd. NE, Albuquerque, NM 87107. Tel.
505/884-0250** or toll free 800/444-7378. Fax 505/883-0594. 189 rms, 24
suites. A/C TV TEL
$ Rates: $45–$49 single, $57 double, $65–$85 suite. AE, CB, DC, DISC, MC, V.
Of special note at this large motel are two dozen two-room suites, all of which have

microwaves and refrigerators. A rich navy blue or maroon color scheme dominates the other rooms, which have standard furnishings including satellite TV and two phones, one in the bath (free local calls). Free coffee and doughnuts are served in the lobby each morning. The Village Inn, a 24-hour restaurant, is on adjoining property. The hotel offers valet laundry and 24-hour courtesy van service; 50% of rooms are designated for nonsmokers. No pets are permitted. Facilities include a swimming pool and a guest Laundromat.

PLAZA INN, 900 Medical Arts Ave. NE (at Lomas Blvd. and I-25), Albuquerque, NM 87102. Tel. 505/243-5693 or toll free 800/237-1307. Fax 505/843-6229. 120 rms. A/C TV TEL

$ Rates: $50–$55 single, $60–$80 double. AE, CB, DC, DISC, MC, V.

Centrally located just east of downtown and west of the University of New Mexico campus, the Plaza offers amenities of larger, pricier hotels with the rates and convenience of a motel. Services include round-the-clock airport shuttle and lobby coffee service, secretarial assistance, meeting space for up to 60 people, and valet laundry. The inn has a heated outdoor swimming pool, a coin-op guest Laundromat, and pay in-house movies. Rooms are average size, with pastel decor and standard furnishings, including a working desk. Parking is free, and pets are accepted. JB's Restaurant and Lounge is adjacent.

BUDGET

MOTEL 6, 1701 University Blvd. NE at I-40, Albuquerque, NM 87102. Tel. 505/843-9228 or 505/891-6161. 118 rms. A/C TV TEL

$ Rates: May–Oct $27.95 single, $39.95 double; Nov–Apr $23.95 single, $29.95 double. AE, DC, DISC, MC, V.

Typical of the 16 other members of this chain scattered around New Mexico, the midtown Motel 6 is a no-frills accommodation with the essentials for a comfortable stay. It's just big enough, it's clean, it has a phone and television, and there's even a swimming pool for summer afternoon dips.

Other Motel 6s in Albuquerque are at 13141 Central Ave. NE, I-40 at Tramway Boulevard Exit 67 (tel. 505/294-4600), and 6015 Iliff Rd. NW, I-40 at Coors Road Exit 155 (tel. 505/831-3400).

UNIVERSITY LODGE, 3711 Central Ave. NE, Albuquerque, NM 87108. Tel. 505/266-7663. 53 rms. A/C TV TEL

$ Rates: $19.95 single, $24.95 double. AE, CB, DC, DISC, ER, MC, V.

This Nob Hill property, a former TraveLodge six blocks east of UNM, is average in every way. Its pastel-decor rooms are adequate in size, clean and comfortable, with standard motel furnishings. Complimentary morning coffee is available in the lobby, and there's an outdoor swimming pool, open seasonally. Rooms for nonsmokers and the disabled are available. Pets are discouraged.

AIRPORT

This district lies south of Central Avenue (Route 66) and primarily east of I-25, and includes Kirtland Air Force Base and Albuquerque International Airport. Most accommodations here are along Yale or Gibson boulevards near the airport entrance.

MODERATE

AMFAC HOTEL, 2910 Yale Blvd. SE, Albuquerque, NM 87106. Tel. 505/843-7000 or toll free 800/227-1117. Fax 505/843-6307. 266 rms, 13 suites. A/C TV TEL

$ Rates: $74 single, $94 double, $124–$320 suite. AE, CB, DC, DISC, MC, V. **Parking:** Free.

No accommodation is closer to the airport than the Amfac (soon to be a Best

Western), which is literally a stone's throw north of the main terminal. It caters to air travelers with a 24-hour desk and shuttle service, overnight valet laundry, and free admission to the Club, a full-service athletic facility a block away.

Rooms are appointed in pastel decor with a southwestern flavor and are furnished with king-size or double beds, four-drawer dressers, leather easy chairs with ottomans, cable TV/radios, and phones (local calls are 50¢).

Lil's is an exclusive Victorian restaurant serving continental cuisine beneath crystal chandeliers. The Harvey House Restaurant offers breakfast, lunch, and dinner for more reasonable prices. Room service, courtesy van, valet laundry, complimentary shoeshine, and rooms for nonsmokers and the disabled are available. Pets are not permitted. Facilities include an outdoor swimming pool, coed sauna, two all-weather tennis courts, free athletic-club admission, gift shop.

COURTYARD BY MARRIOTT, 1920 Yale Blvd. SE, Albuquerque, NM 87106. Tel. 505/843-6600 or toll free 800/321-2211. Fax 505/843-8740. 136 rms, 14 suites. A/C FRIDGE TV TEL

$ Rates: $70 single, $80 double, $84–$103 suite. Weekend packages available. AE, CB, DC, DISC, MC, V. **Parking:** Free.

Opened in 1990, this four-story member of the Marriott family is built around an attractively landscaped courtyard with a shake-roofed bandstand reminiscent of a village green. The lobby's white marble floor is also surrounded by greenery. Families appreciate the security system: Access is by key card only between 11pm and 6am.

The rooms feature walnut furniture and decor in pastel tones. Among the nicer touches are coffee and tea service from a 190-degree faucet, full-length mirrors, full-size writing desks, 100-foot telephone cords, clock radios, and massage shower heads. Refrigerators are available by request at no charge in any room.

The coffee shop, separated by planter boxes from the main lobby, is open from 7am to 2pm and 5 to 10pm daily. It features breakfast and lunch buffets, and a variety of all-American dinners priced from $6.95 to $12.50. An adjacent lounge opens from 4 to 11pm daily. The hotel provides valet laundry, courtesy van, and rooms for nonsmokers. Guest facilities include an indoor swimming pool, whirlpool, exercise room, and Laundromat.

RADISSON INN, 1901 University Blvd. SE, Albuquerque, NM 87106. Tel. 505/247-0512 or toll free 800/333-3333. Fax 505/843-7148. 148 rms. A/C MINIBAR TV TEL

$ Rates: $75–$85 single, $85–$95 double. AE, CB, DC, DISC, MC, V. **Parking:** Free.

The Spanish colonial–style Radisson is a mile from the airport. It's nice to be away from the hubbub, especially lounging on the spacious deck of the swimming pool in the center of the landscaped grounds. The rooms are decorated in emerald green, navy blue, or dusty rose, and are furnished with king- or queen-size beds, two-drawer credenzas, tables and chairs, cable TV/radios, and telephones.

Diamondback's Restaurant, open daily from 6am to 2pm and 5 to 10pm, specializes in steaks and regional dishes like pollo a la parrilla and trout Rio de Pecos. Breakfasts run from $2.25 to $7.50; lunches, $4.75 to $7.95; dinners, $7.95 to $15.95. The restaurant features live classical guitar Thursday through Saturday evenings. Coyote's Cantina is a popular watering hole.

The hotel offers room service from 6am to 10pm, valet laundry, and a 24-hour courtesy van. Rooms for nonsmokers are available; small pets are accepted. Guests enjoy a year-round outdoor swimming pool, whirlpool, lobby art gallery, and free use of a nearby health club.

INEXPENSIVE

BEST WESTERN AIRPORT INN, 2400 Yale Blvd. SE, Albuquerque, NM 87106. Tel. 505/242-7022 or toll free 800/528-1234. Fax 505/243-0620. 120 rms. A/C TV TEL

$ Rates (including breakfast): $52–$57 single, $62–$67 double. AE, CB, DC, DISC, MC, V.

A landscaped garden courtyard behind the hotel is a lovely place to relax on cloudless days. The rooms, with dark-brown carpets and beige-checkered bedspreads, contain standard furnishings plus cable TV and free local phone calls. Deluxe units have refrigerators and other special touches. Breakfast is served free in rooms, or guests can get a coupon good for $3 off their morning meal at the adjacent Village Inn. The hotel has a courtesy van on call from 6am to midnight, valet laundry, and non smoking and handicapped rooms. No pets are accepted. Guests may use the outdoor swimming pool and Jacuzzi, or a nearby health club.

LA QUINTA MOTOR INN, 2116 Yale Blvd. SE, Albuquerque, NM 87106. Tel. 505/243-5500 or toll free 800/531-5900. Fax 505/247-8288. 105 rms. A/C TV TEL

$ Rates: $58 single, $66 double. AE, CB, DC, DISC, ER, JCB, MC, V.

A *quinta* (pronounced "*keen*-ta") is a villa in the Spanish language, and like vacation homes, La Quinta motels—a 240-strong Texas-based chain—are friendly and gracious toward visitors.

Rooms are appointed in pleasant modern tones. Each has one king-size or two extra-long double beds, a credenza, a table and chairs, a satellite TV/radio with pay in-house movies, a direct-dial phone (free local calls), and individually controlled heating and air conditioning. Rooms for nonsmokers and the disabled are available, and small pets are permitted. La Quinta has an outdoor swimming pool. Coffee is on 24 hours in the lobby, and Goody's restaurant is adjacent to the motel.

Other La Quinta Motor Inns in Albuquerque are located at 5241 San Antonio Dr. NE, off I-25 at Journal Center (tel. 505/821-9000, fax 505/821-2399; 130 rooms); and at I-40 and San Mateo Boulevard (tel. 505/884-3591; 106 rooms). All have the same rates and facilities, including adjacent restaurants.

JOURNAL CENTER/NORTH CITY

North of Montgomery Boulevard, the focal point is the I-25 interchange with Osuna Road and San Mateo Boulevard. On the west side of the freeway, the Journal Center business park is dominated by the giant pyramid of the Holiday Inn. East of the freeway, at San Mateo and Academy boulevards, numerous hotels, restaurants, and shopping complexes dominate.

EXPENSIVE

HOLIDAY INN PYRAMID, 5151 San Francisco Rd., Albuquerque, NM 87109. Tel. 505/821-3333 or toll free 800/544-0623 or 800/HOLIDAY. Fax 505/828-0230. 312 rms, 60 suites. A/C TV TEL

$ Rates: $92–$105 single, $105–$115 double. $110–$270 suite. AE, CB, DC, DISC, JCB, MC, V. **Parking:** Free.

Driving north from Albuquerque toward Santa Fe, you can't help being startled by the spectacular stepped Aztec pyramid that seems to rise from nowhere on the west side of the I-25 freeway. It's not there by accident: this is a major hotel and convention complex. Reached via the Paseo del Norte Exit 232 from I-25, it's a monument to what modern-day hotel architecture can be like.

The 10 guest floors focus around a "hollow" skylit core. Vines drape from planter boxes on the balconies, and a fountain falls five stories to a pool between the two glass elevators. The Aztec theme pervades in the sand-and-cream color tones and the figures etched into the glass facing the fountain, opposite the entrance. The color scheme carries to the spacious rooms, furnished with king- or queen-size beds, two easy chairs, a desk, four-drawer dresser, fully lit dressing table, cable TV with in-room movies, radio/alarm clock, and direct-dial phone (local calls are 50¢). Kitchenettes are available.

Dining/Entertainment: The Pyramid has two restaurants and two lounges. The Gallery is open for fine dining from 5:30 to 10pm nightly except Sunday. Main courses, priced from $12.50–$24.25, include oysters Tasso in cream, boneless duck breast Chambord, and fresh salmon in raspberry and green-peppercorn sauce. The Terrace, an atrium café surrounded by planter boxes, is open from 6am to 2pm and 5 to 10pm daily; dinner prices top out at $23, and even vegetarians are catered to with a tofu stir-fry. The Palm Court, next to the Terrace, has a baby grand piano bar open until 10pm every day. The Pyramid Club attracts the younger set with a disc jockey providing video music for dancing until 2am Monday through Saturday nights.

Services: Room service, full-service concierge, 24-hour courtesy car, valet laundry.

Facilities: Rooms for nonsmokers and the disabled, indoor/outdoor swimming pool, sauna, two whirlpools, health club with weights and exercise room. Jogging trails wind through 313-acre Journal Center business park.

MODERATE

AMBERLEY SUITE HOTEL, 7620 Pan American Fwy. NE, Albuquerque, NM 87109. Tel. 505/823-1300 or toll free 800/333-9806. Fax 505/823-1300, ext. 775. 170 rms, all suites. A/C FRIDGE TV TEL

$ Rates: $83 single, $93 double. $17 higher during balloon fiesta. Discounts for longer stays, weekend arrivals, or corporate or government travelers. AE, CB, DC, DISC, MC, V. **Parking:** Free.

Every room here is a one- or two-room suite. They're fully carpeted units, most with a living room/kitchenette and separate bedroom; the deluxe king is an efficiency studio with a kitchen area. Kitchen facilities include a refrigerator (with complimentary beverages), microwave oven, coffee maker, pots, pans, and utensils. Each living room has a swivel rocker with ottoman and a cable television. Every bathroom is provided with a built-in hair dryer. Watson's Café and Deli, open from 6am to 10pm daily, serves an all-you-can-eat breakfast buffet ($4.95) until 10am and a summer patio barbecue Tuesday through Thursday from 5 to 9pm. The hotel manager hosts a happy-hour reception Wednesday at 5:30pm with cocktails, hors d'oeuvres, live music, and trivia games. The hotel also provides 24-hour courtesy car (within 2-mile radius), free airport shuttle, valet laundry, rooms for nonsmokers and the disabled. Guest facilities include an outdoor swimming pool, sauna, hot tub, weight/exercise room, and Laundromat.

HOWARD JOHNSON PLAZA HOTEL, 6000 Pan American Fwy. NE at San Mateo Blvd., Albuquerque, NM 87109. Tel. 505/821-9451 or toll free 800/654-2000. Fax 505/821-9451, ext. 157. 150 rms, 12 suites. A/C TV TEL

$ Rates: $48–$110 single, $58–$145 double. $75–$145 suite. $20 extra during the balloon fest. Various discount packages available. AE, CB, DC, DISC, MC, V. **Parking:** Free.

Howard Johnson's doesn't try to be as grand as the Pyramid. But it does have a five-story lobby atrium with fountains of its own. A three-story-high tapestry reminds viewers of Albuquerque's obsession with hot-air ballooning, and there are old-fashioned flower-topped lampposts on the mezzanine deck.

Private balconies are an outstanding feature of every room. They've got all standard furnishings, including remote-control cable TV and phones. Earl's Café, open from 6am to 2pm and 5 to 9pm daily, offers southwestern fare ($5 to $14). The Atrium Lounge has a big-screen TV for watching sports events, and a Top-40 DJ for dancing. The hotel offers room service during restaurant hours, 24-hour courtesy van, valet laundry; and rooms for nonsmokers and the disabled. Pets are permitted with manager's prior approval. Facilities include an indoor/outdoor swimming pool, sauna, Jacuzzi, weight/exercise room, guest laundry, and gift shop.

INEXPENSIVE

HAMPTON INN, 7433 Pan American Fwy. NE, Albuquerque, NM 87109. Tel. 505/344-1555 or toll free 800/HAMPTON. Fax 505/345-2216. 125 rms. A/C TV TEL

$ Rates (including continental breakfast): $50.50 single, $55.50 double. AE, CB, DC, DISC, MC, V. **Parking:** Free.

These sound-insulated rooms for cost-conscious travelers have all standard furnishings, plus remote-control cable TV and free local phone calls. The inn has an outdoor swimming pool, but no courtesy car or other exercise facilities. It's okay to bring your pet. The coffee pot is on in the lobby 24 hours.

CAMPING

ALBUQUERQUE CENTRAL KOA, 12400 Skyline Rd. NE, Albuquerque, NM 87123. Tel. 505/296-2729.
  200 sites, bathhouse, guest laundry, outdoor swimming pool (open summers only), convenience store. Cabins available.

ALBUQUERQUE NORTH KOA, 1021 Hill Rd., Bernalillo, NM 87004. Tel. 505/867-5227.
  108 sites, bathhouse, guest laundry, outdoor swimming pool (open summer only), playground, convenience store; café open May to October, shows outdoor movies. Free breakfast off-season.

AMERICAN RV PARK OF ALBUQUERQUE, I-40 west at Exit 149, Albuquerque, NM 87121. Tel. 505/831-3545.
  186 sites, picnic area, bathhouse, guest laundry, heated swimming pool, playground, outdoor games area, movies convenience store.

PALISADES RV PARK, 9201 Central Ave. NW, Albuquerque, NM 87121. Tel. 505/831-5000
  110 sites, bathhouse, guest laundry, recreation room, small convenience store, propane available. Near Old Town.

4. DINING

In these listings, the following categories define price ranges: very expensive—most dinner main courses over $20; expensive—most dinner main courses $15 to $20; moderate—most dinner main courses $10 to $15; inexpensive—most dinner main courses $6 to $10; budget—most dinner main courses under $6.

DOWNTOWN/OLD TOWN

EXPENSIVE

EULALIA'S, in La Posada de Albuquerque, 125 Second St. NW. Tel. 242-9090.
  Cuisine: SPANISH/CONTINENTAL. **Reservations:** Recommended, especially at dinner.
$ **Prices:** Appetizers $5.95–$7.95; lunch $5.95–$10.95; dinner $13.50–$17.95. AE, CB, DC, DISC, MC, V.
  Open: Daily 7am–2pm and 6–10pm.

Eulalia's offers diners the best of two worlds. The atmosphere is old-world Spanish colonial, an extension of La Posada's hotel lobby. Diners can lock themselves into intimate conversations in candlelit, semicircular booths, upholstered in pastel patterns.

  The cuisine can best be described as continental with a Spanish contemporary flair, serving everything from filet mignon to swordfish fajitas. The house pâté is invariably

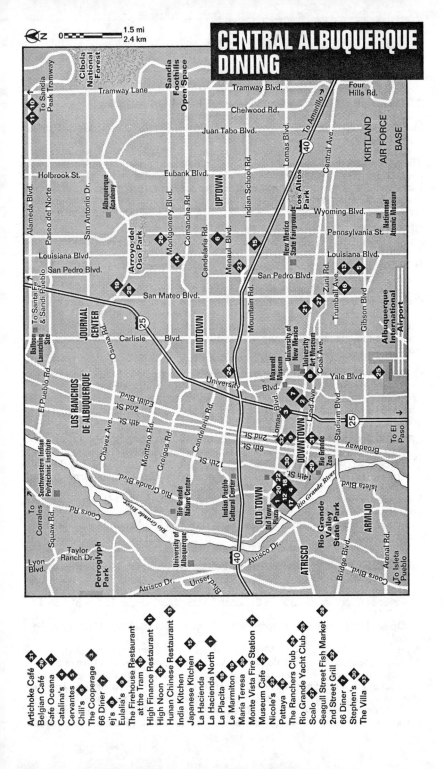

CENTRAL ALBUQUERQUE DINING

Artichoke Café
Belgian Café
Cafe Oceana
Catalina's
Cervantes
Chili's
The Cooperage
66 Diner
ej's
Eulalia's
The Firehouse Restaurant at the Tram
High Finance Restaurant
High Noon
Hunan Chinese Restaurant
India Kitchen
Japanese Kitchen
La Hacienda
La Hacienda North
La Placita
Le Marmiton
Maria Teresa
Monte Vista Fire Station
Museum Cafe
Nicole's
Pattaya
The Ranchers Club
Rio Grande Yacht Club
Scalo
Seagull Street Fish Market
2nd Street Grill
66 Diner
Stephen's
The Villa

excellent as a starter. Many diners savor the tableside service of Caesar salad preparation and flambé desserts.

MODERATE

ARTICHOKE CAFE, 424 Central Ave. SE. Tel. 243-0200.

Cuisine: CONTINENTAL. **Reservations:** Recommended.
$ Prices: Appetizers $4.50–$5.95; lunch $6.95–$11.95; dinner $8.95–$16.95. AE, MC, V.
Open: Lunch Mon–Fri 11am–2:30pm, dinner Mon–Sat 5:30–10pm.

The no-frills decor is clean and tasteful, with modern-art prints on azure walls, white linens on tables shaded by standing plants, and classical music playing in the background. Start your meal with an artichoke appetizer, then go on to a main dish like veal scallopine with Duxelle mushrooms. Crêpes, pastas, salads and sandwiches are popular at lunch. The café has an excellent list of California and French wines.

HIGH NOON, 425 San Felipe St. NW. Tel. 765-1455.

Cuisine: STEAKS, SEAFOOD & NEW MEXICAN. **Reservations:** Recommended.
$ Prices: Appetizers $3–$7.95; lunch $4.95–$7.95; dinner $6.95–$16.95. AE, CB, DC, DISC, MC, V.
Open: Mon–Sat 11am–3pm and 5–10pm, Sun noon–9pm.

One of Albuquerque's oldest existing buildings, this restaurant boasts a 19th-century saloon atmosphere with stuccoed walls, high and low ceiling beams, and historical photos on the walls. One photo depicts the original 1785 structure, which now comprises the building's foyer and *santo* room. Additional rooms were added in the late 1960s.

The dinner menu offers a choice of beef dishes, like the house-specialty pepper steak sautéed with brandy; fish dishes, including red trout with avocado margarita salsa; and regional favorites, among them burritos and enchiladas. Sandwiches dominate the lunch menu, along with fine salads and pastas. A flamenco guitarist performs in the rustic bar Thursday, Friday, and Saturday evenings beginning at 6:30pm.

LA HACIENDA, 1306 Rio Grande Blvd. NW. Tel. 243-3709.

Cuisine: ITALIAN & NEW MEXICAN. **Reservations:** Recommended.
$ Prices: Appetizers $2.50–$5.95, main courses $3.25–$9.95. AE, DC, MC, V.
Open: Brunch Sat–Sun 11:30am–3pm. Lunch Mon–Fri 11:30am–2:30pm; dinner Mon–Thurs 6–10pm, Fri–Sat 6–10:30pm.

La Hacienda got its start in the 1950s as a journalists' bar. The bar is still there, but now it's upstaged by a Spanish colonial–style restaurant and bistro. Rich wood furnishings are complemented by chile ristras on a *kiva* fireplace and southwestern art on the walls.

The menu includes a variety of beef, veal, chicken, and seafood dishes.

LA HACIENDA NORTH, 302 San Felipe St. NW, at North Plaza. Tel. 242-4866.

Cuisine: NEW MEXICAN & AMERICAN. **Reservations:** For large parties.
$ Prices: Appetizers $3.50–$6.25; lunch $4.95–$7.50; dinner $6.50–$13.95. DC, MC, V.
Open: Daily, lunch 11am–4pm, dinner 4–9pm; breakfast 8:30–11am June–Sept only.

A mural on La Hacienda North's outer wall tells of the establishment of the city of Albuquerque and the construction of this Villa de Albuquerque at the turn of the 18th century. The cozy restaurant within is approached through a large and interesting gift shop; adorned by hanging plants and chile *ristras,* the room has an intimate, laid-back atmosphere. There's outside seating facing the San Felipe de Neri church.

The menu is predominantly regional, with house specialties including beef or chicken fajitas, carne adovada, tostadas compuestas, and tortilla-chile soup. Steaks, shrimp, and other American meals also are offered. Guitarists play daily beginning at noon. La Hacienda North has a full-service bar.

MARIA TERESA, 618 Rio Grande Blvd. NW. Tel. 242-3900.

Cuisine: CONTEMPORARY AMERICAN. **Reservations:** Recommended.
$ Prices: Appetizers $3.95–$7.25; lunch $4.45–$15.25; dinner $8.95–$29. AE, MC, V.
Open: Mon–Sat 11:30am–2pm and 5–9pm, Sun 11am–9pm.

The city's most beautiful and classically elegant restaurant, Maria Teresa is located in the 1840s Salvador Armijo House, a national historic property furnished with Victorian antiques and paintings. Built with 32-inch adobe bricks, the house exemplifies 19th-century New Mexico architecture, when building materials were few and defense a prime consideration. The house had 12 rooms, 7 of which (along with a large patio) are now reserved for diners. Another room is home to the 1840 Bar and Lounge.

The menu features salads, pastas, and sandwiches for lunch; and a wide choice of gourmet dinners, from raspberry chicken to fresh swordfish with tequila lime butter, and from baby back ribs to regional dishes like carne y pollo asada burrito. It runs $16.25, including cover charge and a full dinner.

STEPHEN'S, 1311 Tijeras Ave. NW (at 14th and Central). Tel. 842-1773.

Cuisine: CONTEMPORARY AMERICAN. **Reservations:** Recommended.
$ Prices: Appetizers $5.50–$6.95; lunch $5.50–$9.95; dinner $10.95–$21.95. AE, MC, V.
Open: Lunch Mon–Fri 11am–2pm; dinner Sun–Thurs 5:30–9:30pm, Fri–Sat 5:30–10:30pm.

Big bay windows face on Central Avenue, and foliage shades an enclosed patio. This modern, open and airy restaurant was inspired by Mexico City's Hacienda Angel and features interior decor by the noted designer Richard Worthen, whose gallery adjoins the restaurant.

The eclectic menu is described as "fresh American and southwestern ingredients prepared with continental inspiration." Dishes include everything from scallops Provençale to braised lamb shank, veal schnitzel to stuffed tortellini, poached trout with piñon nuts to New York strip steak. Homemade pastas, salads, and Mexican foods are served at lunch. Stephen's also has a full bar.

INEXPENSIVE

CATALINA'S, 400 San Felipe St. NW. Tel. 842-6907.

Cuisine: MEXICAN.
$ Prices: $3.50–$8.25. MC, V.
Open: Breakfast Mon–Sat 8–11am; lunch daily 11am–2pm; dinner daily (summer only) 4–8pm Sun 8am–4pm. **Closed:** Usually mid-Jan to Mar.

Right in the heart of Old Town, set back in the rear of the Patio San Felipe del Norte courtyard, is this oft-overlooked gem in an old adobe home. The white stuccoed interior, covered with Mexican handcrafts, still has its original log beams. All meals are homemade by Catalina Walsh; the chile rellenos are superb, as are the tacos, tostadas, enchiladas, and so forth.

LA PLACITA, 208 San Felipe St. NW at South Plaza. Tel. 247-2204.

Cuisine: NEW MEXICAN & AMERICAN. **Reservations:** For large parties.
$ Prices: Lunch $3.40–$5.20; dinner $5.25–$13.25. AE, CB, DC, ER, MC, V.
Open: Daily 11am–9pm. (Hours vary according to business.)

Native American artisans spread their wares on the sidewalk outside the old Casa de Armijo, built by a wealthy Hispanic family in the early 18th century. The adobe hacienda, which faces the Old Town Plaza, features hand-carved wooden doorways, deep-sunk windows, and an ancient patio. Fine regional art and furnishings decorate the five dining rooms and an upstairs gallery.

The house favorite is a full Mexican dinner ($9.35) that includes an enchilada Colorado de queso, chile relleno, taco de carne, frijoles con queso, arroz español, ensalada, and two sopaipillas. There are also a variety of beef, chicken, and fish main courses, including a 14-ounce New York cut ($13.25) and sandwiches. Children's plates are available. The restaurant is licensed to serve beer and wine only.

THE VILLA, 722 Central Ave. SW, at 8th Street. Tel. 242-2006.
Cuisine: ITALIAN. **Reservations:** Recommended at dinner.
$ **Prices:** Appetizers $2.50–$6.25; lunch $3.75–$6.75; dinner $6.25–$10.25. AE, MC, V.
Open: Mon–Thurs 11am–9pm, Fri 11am–10pm, Sat 5–10pm.

Roman-style porticoes overlook an elegant decor of polished-wood tables and hanging chandeliers. There's even a Roman fountain in a lovely garden, but you must book ahead to sit there. The lunch menu features sandwiches, salads, and pastas; dinners include pasta marinara with stuffed mushrooms, and lasagne's a customer favorite anytime. The Villa is fully licensed.

BUDGET

MUSEUM CAFE, at New Mexico Museum of Natural History, 1801 Mountain Rd. NW. Tel. 764-0058.
Cuisine: NOUVELLE AMERICAN.
$ **Prices:** $2.95–$8.95. MC, V.
Open: Daily 9am–5pm.

Beneath the shadow of a pterodactyl suspended high above, this "find" on the museum mezzanine is the stronghold of chef Beauregard Detterman, well known in Albuquerque for his catering business. The menu ranges from gazpacho soup and Brie cheese with crackers to barbecued chicken breast and gourmet club sandwiches. The desserts are sinful but delicious, particularly the pies.

MIDTOWN/UPTOWN

VERY EXPENSIVE

NICOLE'S, in the Albuquerque Marriott Hotel, 2101 Louisiana Blvd. NE. Tel. 881-6800.
Cuisine: CONTINENTAL. **Reservations:** Essential.
$ **Prices:** Appetizers $5–$13; lunch $6–$15; dinner $18–$22. AE, CB, DC, DISC, JCB, MC, V.
Open: Lunch Mon–Fri 11:30am–2pm; dinner nightly 6–10pm.

A classically intimate restaurant, Nicole's ranks among the handful of Albuquerque's finest. Hand-carved chairs with rich green upholstery sit at candlelit tables amid an atmosphere of plants and reproductions of 19th-century oils hanging on the walls.

Creative continental cuisine, with seafood specialties, is the kitchen's forte. Diners can start with black lobster ravioli in a marinara sauce, or wilted spinach salad prepared tableside. Main courses include salmon relleno with green chile, shrimp sautéed with a hazelnut liqueur, and chateaubriand with béarnaise sauce. Chocolate macadamia-nut pie is a featured dessert. Lunch main courses include scallops sautéed in a Szechuan sauce or New York sirloin with cognac-mustard sauce. Nicole's also has an extensive wine list.

EXPENSIVE

JAPANESE KITCHEN, 10 Winrock Center NE at I-40 and Louisiana Blvd. Tel. 884-8937.
Cuisine: JAPANESE. **Reservations:** Recommended.

$ Prices: Lunch $5–$8, dinner $10–$25. AE, CB, DC, DISC, MC, V.
Open: Lunch Mon–Sat 11:30am–2:30pm; dinner Sun–Thurs 5–9:30pm, Fri–Sat 5–10:30pm.

The Japanese Kitchen comes in two sections: a hibachi-style steak house with fourteen eight-seat hibachi grills on which master chefs slice and cook steaks, seafood, and chicken before your eyes; and a separate full sushi bar. Teppanyaki dinners include chicken, steak, lobster, and prawns. Don't miss the museum-quality samurai uniform just outside the entrance. A cocktail lounge is attached: Ever try a banzai?

THE RANCHERS CLUB, in the Albuquerque Hilton Hotel, 1901 University Blvd. NE. Tel. 884-2500.
  Cuisine: CONTINENTAL. **Reservations:** Recommended, especially at dinner.
$ Prices: Appetizers $5.95–$9.95; lunch $5.95–$10.95; dinner $13.50–$25.95. AE, CB, DC, DISC, MC, V.
  Open: Lunch Mon–Fri 11:30am–2pm; Sun brunch buffet 10am–2pm. Dinner Mon–Thurs 5:30–10pm, Fri–Sat 5:30–11pm.

⭐ Like a British hunting lodge transplanted to the high plains, the Ranchers Club creates a mood of western elegance with its polished oak decor, flagstone fireplace, and remarkable longhorn chandelier. Established in 1986 to offer Albuquerque "something unique and different," the Club consistently ranks number one in the list of the city's favorite restaurants.

But the food outdoes the atmosphere, thanks in part to its unique preparation over aromatic woods. Cucumber dill complements swordfish, for instance, and garlic butter is great with lobster or steak. Then there's the "small" (14-ounce) New York sirloin, grilled over sassafras with wild mushroom sauce, and the Norwegian salmon, grilled over mesquite with curried apple chutney. All main courses are served with a choice of vegetables.

MODERATE

CAFE OCEANA, 1414 Central Ave. SE. Tel. 247-2233.
  Cuisine: SEAFOOD. **Reservations:** Recommended.
$ Prices: Lunch $5.95–$10.95; dinner $6.95–$17.95. AE, MC, V.
  Open: Lunch Mon–Fri 11am–3pm; dinner Mon–Thurs 5–11pm, Fri–Sat 5–11:30pm.

Café Oceana is and has been Albuquerque's favorite oyster bar and fresh seafood café for years. In a New Orleans–style atmosphere in a dining room with high ceilings and hardwood floors, you can enjoy fresh oysters, fresh fish daily, scallops, crab rellenos (for the New Mexican touch), and the house special, shrimp Oceana. If you're really in the mood for New Orleans cuisine, you can also get some red beans and rice here.

COOPERAGE RESTAURANT & LOUNGE, 7220 Lomas Blvd. NE. Tel. 255-1657.
  Cuisine: STEAKS & SEAFOOD. **Reservations:** Recommended.
$ Prices: Lunch $4–$8; dinner $9–$22. AE, CB, DC, DISC, MC, V.
  Open: Lunch Mon–Fri 11am–2:30pm, Sat noon–2:30pm; dinner Mon–Thurs 5–10pm, Fri–Sat 5–11pm, Sun noon–9pm.

The Cooperage is shaped to make you feel as if you're in a gigantic beer barrel. Circular and wood paneled, its walls are decorated with reproductions of 19th-century paintings and depictions of coopers at work making barrels.

The dinner menu features a variety of seafood and beef dishes, including trout parmesan and prime rib. The restaurant also has a great 30-item salad bar, and is fully licensed. There's live music for dancing Wednesday through Saturday nights.

Cooperage West is at 10200 Corrales Rd. NW, in Corrales (tel. 898-5555).

MONTE VISTA FIRE STATION, 3201 Central Ave. NE, Nob Hill. Tel. 255-2424.

Cuisine: CONTEMPORARY AMERICAN. **Reservations:** Recommended.
$ **Prices:** Appetizers $3.95–$7.95; lunch $5.95–$9.50; dinner $8.95–$17.50. AE, MC, V.
Open: Mon–Fri 11am–2pm; Sun–Thurs 5–10pm; Fri–Sat 5–11pm. Bar open to 1:30am Mon–Sat, to midnight Sun.

The Fire Station has been a city landmark since it was built in pure Pueblo Revival style in 1936. Its occupants no longer make fire calls, however, concentrating instead on serving a unique menu within an art deco interior. Both the lunch and dinner menus focus on creative cookery. Luncheon diners can start with crab cakes and goat cheese, then go on to sliced sirloin with green peppercorn and cognac cream. Popular dinner appetizers are wild mushroom ravioli, tossed with scallops and spinach ricotta, in a champagne sauce; and grilled duck and pepper sausage with zinfandel sauce. Main courses include leg of lamb, stuffed with sun-dried tomatoes and chile, with a roasted garlic sauce; and quail with wild mushrooms in a tawny port sauce.

There's a popular singles bar on the fourth-story landing.

SCALO, 3500 Central Ave. SE, Nob Hill. Tel. 255-8782.
Cuisine: NORTHERN ITALIAN. **Reservations:** Recommended.
$ **Prices:** Appetizers $2.50–$6.50; lunch $4.75–$9.50; dinner $6.95–$17.95. AE, MC, V.
Open: Lunch Mon–Fri 11:30am–2:30pm; dinner Mon–Sat 5–11pm. Bar open Mon–Sat 11am–1am.

Scalo has a simple bistro-style elegance, with white-linen indoor seating and umbrella-shaded outdoor tables. The kitchen, which makes its own pasta and breads, specializes in contemporary adaptations of classical northern Italian cuisine. Featured appetizers are calamaretti fritti (fried baby squid with garlic aioli) and caprini con pumante (goat cheese with toast, sun-dried tomatoes, capers, and roasted garlic). There's a fine selection of pastas for both lunch and dinner, and a choice of meat, chicken, and fish dishes—among them pollo affumicato (apple-smoked chicken with red potatoes and onions in a Madeira gravy) and filetto con salsa balsamica (grilled filet of beef with fresh garlic, green peppercorns, and balsamic sauce). The wine list focuses on Italian imports and California wines.

INEXPENSIVE

BELGIAN CAFE, 7400 Montgomery Blvd. NE. Tel. 881-3323.
Cuisine: BELGIAN.
$ **Prices:** Lunch $6–$8. AE, MC, V.
Open: Tues–Sun 8am–4pm.
This is a rare eating experience: Belgian decor, Belgian cuisine, Belgian chef. Soups are a specialty, including carrot soup with puréed vegetables, and beer stew with beef and onions. The cocorico salad—diced breast of chicken, mandarin orange slices, and sliced almond in homemade brandy mayonnaise—is wonderful. Belgian waffles are of course a big draw, served plain or with fruit and whipped cream.

CHILI'S, 6909 Menaul Blvd. NE. Tel. 883-4321.
Cuisine: TEX-MEX.
$ **Prices:** Appetizers $2.25–$5.25; main courses $2.95–$9.95. AE, CB, DC, DISC, MC, V.
Open: Mon–Thurs 11am–10:30pm; Fri–Sat 11am–11:30pm; Sun 11:30am–10pm.
A casual bar and grill adjacent to the Ramada Classic Hotel, Chili's is like a small greenhouse. There are plants in baskets and pots, standing and hanging, dispersed among the antique bric-a-brac suspended from the ceilings or on shelves high above the red tile floors. The menu focuses on hamburgers (like the verde burger, with guacamole) and southwestern grill—fajitas, chicken, ribs, steaks, and the like. There

are also salads, sandwiches, and chili. The bar, which has a happy hour from 3 to 6pm weekdays, is noted for its margaritas.

INDIA KITCHEN, 6910 Montgomery Blvd. NE. Tel. 884-2333.
   Cuisine: INDIAN. **Reservations:** Suggested at dinner.
$ Prices: Lunch $3.95–$6.95; dinner $6.95–$9.95. AE, CB, DISC, MC, V.
   Open: Lunch Tues–Fri 11:30am–2pm; dinner Tues–Sun 5–9pm.

In a shopping strip near Louisiana Boulevard is this little restaurant. It is the pride and joy of Ajay Gupta, a 20-year U.S. resident who left his job as a Chicago engineer to start cooking. He does it well! Main courses, all served with *pullao* (rice), *puri* (wheat bread), and *bhujia* (mixed vegetables), include the likes of *korma* (beef with almonds, pecans, and sour cream) and shrimp curry in coconut-cream sauce. There are also vegetarian dishes like jackfruit *vindaloo* or chickpea curry. Wash your meal down with a yogurt *lassi*. Raga music from sitars plays continuously in the background as you dine, and there are Mogul-style paintings and batiks on the walls.

BUDGET

ej's, 2201 Silver Ave. SE. Tel. 268-2233.
   Cuisine: VEGETARIAN/NATURAL FOOD.
$ Prices: Breakfast $2.50–$5.95; lunch $3.95–$7.50; dinner $5.25–$8.75. MC, V.
   Open: Mon–Thurs 7am–11pm; Fri 7am–midnight; Sat 8am–midnight; Sun 8am–9:30pm.

A popular coffeehouse just a couple of blocks from the UNM campus, ej's roasts its own specialty coffees—and also caters to natural-foods lovers. Breakfasts include granola and croissants from ej's own bakery. Lunch features homemade vegetarian soups, tempeh burgers, organic turkey sandwiches, and cheese enchiladas. The gourmet dinner menu lists shrimp linguine, spinach fettucine Alfredo, Monterey chicken, and a vegetarian stir-fry.

66 DINER, 1405 Central Ave. NE. Tel. 247-1421.
   Cuisine: AMERICAN.
$ Prices: $3–$5.95. AE, MC, V.
   Open: Mon–Thurs 9am–11pm; Fri 9am–midnight; Sat 8am–midnight; Sun 8am–10pm.

Like a trip back in time to the days when Martin Milner and George Maharis got "their kicks on Route 66," this thoroughly 1950s-style diner comes complete with Seeburg jukebox and full-service soda fountain. The white caps make great hamburgers, along with meat-loaf sandwiches, grilled liver and onions, and chicken-fried steaks. Ham-and-egg and pancake breakfasts are served every morning.

AIRPORT
MODERATE

RIO GRANDE YACHT CLUB, 2500 Yale Blvd. SE. Tel. 243-6111.
   Cuisine: SEAFOOD. **Reservations:** Suggested at dinner.
$ Prices: Appetizers $1.95–$8.95; lunch $3.50–$7.95; dinner $8.95–$14.50. AE, CB, DC, MC, V.
   Open: Lunch Mon–Fri 11am–2pm; dinner Mon–Thurs 5:30–10:30pm, Fri–Sat 5:30–11:30pm, Sun 5–10:30pm.

Red-white-and-blue sails are draped beneath the skylight of a large room dominated by a tropical garden. The walls are of wood strips like those of a ship's deck, and yachting prints and photos hang on the walls. The intercom pipes the music of Jimmy

Buffett and other soft-rock performers. Buffett, the contemporary sailor's chanteur, couldn't have created a better milieu for the Caribbean yachtsman-wannabe.

Fresh fish, of course, is the order of the day. Catfish, whitefish, bluefish, salmon, grouper, sole, mahimahi, and other denizens of the deep are prepared in a variety of ways—broiled, poached, blackened, teriyaki, Veracruz, au gratin, Mornay, amandine, and more. Diners can also opt for shrimp, steaks, ribs, chicken, and seafood-and-steak or prime rib combinations. Sandwiches and salads are served at lunch. Desserts include the Aspen snowball and frozen mud pie. The cozy lounge has a full bar with an outdoor courtyard.

INEXPENSIVE

CERVANTES, 5801 Gibson Blvd. at San Pedro Blvd. Tel. 262-2253.
  Cuisine: NEW MEXICAN. **Reservations:** Suggested at dinner.
$ Prices: Lunch $3.50–$6.25; dinner $5.75–$12.50. AE, CB, DC, MC, V.
  Open: Mon–Sat 11am–10pm.
An impressive classical Spanish decor hides behind a rather unimpressive exterior near Kirtland Air Force Base. Miguel Cervantes, author of the classic *Don Quixote,* has a portrait in a place of honor, though he only shares a name with the owners. New Mexican dinners with all the trimmings are extremely reasonably priced: A combination plate of a taco, tamale, enchilada, and carne adovada, for instance, is just $5.75, including beans, rice, chile, and sopaipillas.

There's another Cervantes—this one with a piano bar—at 10030 Central Ave. NE, near Manzano Mesa (tel. 275-3266).

HUNAN CHINESE RESTAURANT, 1218 San Pedro Blvd. SE. Tel. 266-3300.
  Cuisine: CHINESE (HUNAN & PEKING).
$ Prices: Individual dishes $4.25–$22.95; lunch buffet $5.50; dinner buffet $6.95. AE, MC, V.
  Open: Daily 11am–9:30pm.
The atmosphere here, a garish overload of red-and-gold decor, reflects the spiciness of the cuisine in what may be Albuquerque's most authentic Chinese restaurant. You can start with hot-and-sour soup, then try sizzling beef (sautéed with peanuts, water chestnuts, and green onions) or whole fish with hot bean sauce. The lunch and dinner buffets offer a variety of spicy and not-so-spicy options.

PATTAYA, 843 San Mateo Blvd. SE, near Trumbull Ave. Tel. 255-5930.
  Cuisine: THAI.
$ Prices: Most dishes $3.25–$8.25. MC, V.
  Open: Daily lunch 11am–2pm, dinner 5–9pm.
Thai food is the rage on the East and West coasts, but it hasn't penetrated far into America's hinterlands. The Pattaya is a pleasant exception. A wide selection of spicy dishes, characterized by coconut milk, lemongrass, peanut sauce, and/or chiles, are on the menu—from *tom yum goong,* Thai cuisine's trademark hot-and-sour shrimp soup, to *pahd thai,* spicy stir-fried noodles, and an exquisite chicken curry.

JOURNAL CENTER/NORTH CITY

EXPENSIVE

HIGH FINANCE RESTAURANT, 40 Tramway Rd., atop Sandia Peak. Tel. 243-9742.
  Cuisine: CONTINENTAL. **Reservations:** Requested.
$ Prices: Appetizers $3–$7; lunch $3–$7; dinner $11–$29. Tramway $8 with dinner reservations ($10.50 without). DC, DISC, MC, V.

Open: Lunch daily 11am–2:30pm; dinner Sun–Thurs 5–8:30pm, Fri–Sat 5–9:30pm.

Perched atop Sandia Peak, two miles above Albuquerque and the Rio Grande valley, diners at High Finance have a breathtaking panorama of New Mexico's largest city. The atmosphere inside is elegant yet casual. The menu focuses on prime rib, steaks (including a wonderful steak Diane), and fresh seafood, from fresh fish to crab and lobster. Diners can also choose pasta or Mexican main courses. Many tram riders just drop in for the view and a drink at the casual full-service bar.

LE MARMITON, 5415 Academy Blvd. NE. Tel. 821-6279.
   Cuisine: FRENCH. **Reservations:** Highly recommended.
$ **Prices:** Appetizers $3–$5.95; lunch $5.75–$7.95; dinner $13.95–$19.95. AE, DC, MC, V.
   Open: Lunch Tues–Fri 11:30am–2pm; dinner daily 5:30–9:30pm.

The name means "the apprentice," but there's nothing novice about the food or presentation. The 12 tables seat 30 people in a romantic French provincial atmosphere, with lace curtains and antique plates on shelves.

Recommended main courses include *fantaisie aux fruits de mer,* a mixture of shrimp, scallops, and crab in a mushroom-cream sauce on pastry, and *cailles,* two whole quail finished with a shallot sherry-cream sauce. There's a long wine list and great cinnamon-apple crêpes for dessert.

MODERATE

THE FIREHOUSE RESTAURANT AT THE TRAM, 38 Tramway Rd. Tel. 292-3473.
   Cuisine: STEAKS & SEAFOOD. **Reservations:** Highly recommended.
$ **Prices:** Main courses $12–$18. AE, MC, V.
   Open: Dinner daily 5–10pm. Bar open daily from noon.

Located at the bottom of the Sandia Peak Tramway, the Firehouse has an old steam-powered fire engine serving as its bar and windows on all sides: The views of the city and the Rio Grande valley are great. Seafood, steaks, chicken, and baby pork ribs get special treatment on the mesquite grill. There's nightly entertainment; guests with reservations get a discount on tram tickets.

SEAGULL STREET FISH MARKET, 5410 Academy Blvd. NE. Tel. 821-0020.
   Cuisine: SEAFOOD. **Reservations:** Recommended at dinner.
$ **Prices:** Lunch $3.95–$7.95; dinner $11.95–$21.95. AE, DC, MC, V.
   Open: Lunch Mon–Fri 11am–2:30pm; brunch Sun 10am–2:30pm; dinner Sun–Thurs 5–10pm, Fri–Sat 5–11pm.

An average of 15 different selections of fresh mesquite-grilled fish are available here on any given day. If the weather is fine, seafood lovers can dine in true maritime fashion on an outdoor dock beside a freshwater lagoon on Bear Canyon Arroyo. Steaks are also on the menu, and there's full bar service.

OUT OF TOWN

Some of Albuquerque's finest restaurants are outside the city. Prairie Star is about 20 miles north, via I-25 and N.M. 44, near Bernalillo; the Luna Mansion is about 24 miles south, also via I-25.

EXPENSIVE

PRAIRIE STAR, 1000 Jemez Canyon Dam Rd., Bernalillo. Tel. 867-3327.

Cuisine: CONTEMPORARY REGIONAL. **Reservations:** Essential.
$ **Prices:** Appetizers $3.50–$8; main courses $12–$23. AE, MC, V.
Open: Mon–Thurs 5–10pm, Fri–Sat 5–11pm.

A sprawling adobe home, with a marvelous view across an adjacent golf course and the high plains to Sandia Peak, is host to this intimate dining experience. The 6,000-square-foot house, on a rural site leased from Santa Ana Pueblo, was built in the 1940s in Mission architectural style. Exposed *vigas* and full *latilla* ceilings, hand-carved fireplaces and *bancos,* complement the thick adobe walls in the dining room. All art displayed on the walls is for sale.

Diners can start with smoked quail or green chile strips. Main courses include shrimp margarita, veal sweetbreads, stuffed lamb loin, and panfried Truchas trout with piñon nuts. There are daily specials and a lounge at the top of a circular stairway. Private parties often reserve the patio and tiled swimming pool.

MODERATE

THE LUNA MANSION, Hwys. 6 and 85, Los Lunas. Tel. 865-7333.
Cuisine: STEAK & SEAFOOD. **Reservations:** Essential.
$ **Prices:** Appetizers $3–$8.50; main courses $8.95–$17.95. AE, DC, MC, V.
Open: Brunch Sun 11am–2pm; dinner Mon–Thurs 5–10pm; Fri–Sat 5–10:30pm; Sun 4:30–9:30pm.

A mile and a half east of I-25 is this national historic landmark, built in 1881 by the Santa Fe Railroad as compensation to the Don Antonio Jose Luna family when the railroad built a track through their existing hacienda. While the two-story mansion is Southern Colonial in style, its basic construction material is adobe. A solarium, front portico, and impressive ironwork were added in the 1920s.

The menu offers such gourmet dishes as blackened prime rib, Sonoma stuffed chicken breasts (with sun-dried tomatoes, goat cheese, and fresh parsley), and the Mansion steak (a 9-ounce filet topped with king crab and béarnaise). There are fresh seafood specials daily and a full bar.

SPECIALTY DINING

Local favorites, all of them specializing in New Mexican cuisine, include **La Hacienda** (*p. 52*), **La Hacienda North** (*p. 52*), and **La Placita** (*p. 53*).

The best hotel dining is found at **the Ranchers Club** in the Albuquerque Hilton (*p. 55*), **Nicole's** in the Albuquerque Marriott (*p. 54*), and **Eulalia's** in La Posada de Albuquerque (*p. 50*).

For dining with a view, head for the Sandia Peak Tramway, where you can choose between the **Firehouse Restaurant** (*p. 59*) at the base or **High Finance** (*p. 58*) at the summit.

Light, casual, and fast food is readily found throughout the city. Personal favorites include **ej's** (*p. 57*), the **Kachina Kitchen,** the **66 Diner** (*p. 57*).

Good spots for breakfast include the **Belgian Café** (*p. 56*), **ej's** (*p. 57*), **Catalina's** (*p. 53*), and **La Hacienda (North)** (*p. 52*) in summer.

Looking for afternoon tea? The **Museum Café** (*p. 54*), in the New Mexico Museum of Natural History, is a good option.

Late-night dining (after 10pm) is available at **Café Oceana** (*p. 55*), **Chili's** (*p. 56*), **ej's** (*p. 57*), the **Rio Grande Yacht Club** (*p. 57*), and **Scalo** (*p. 56*), among others.

For 24-hour dining, your best bet may be **Village Inn,** 2437 Central Ave. NW (tel. 247-2579), where most main courses are $3 to $10. It's not flashy, but it serves good American food at reasonable prices. Seven other locations around the city include: 5505 Central Ave. NE (tel. 265-2811); 2039 Fourth St. NW (tel. 242-3440); 840 Juan Tabo Blvd. NE (tel. 298-3444); 2118 Menaul Blvd. NE (tel. 884-0316); 6300

San Mateo Blvd. NE (tel. 821-5900); 2282 Wyoming Blvd. NE (tel. 294-6191); and 2340 Yale Blvd. SE (tel. 243-5476).

5. ATTRACTIONS

Albuquerque's original town site, today known as Old Town, is the central point of interest for visitors to the city today. Here, centered around the Plaza, are the venerable Church of San Felipe de Neri and numerous restaurants, art galleries, and crafts shops. Several important museums stand nearby.

But don't get stuck in Old Town. Elsewhere in the city are the Sandia Peak Tramway, Kirtland Air Force Base and the National Atomic Museum, the University of New Mexico with its museums, and a number of natural attractions. Within day-trip range are several Indian pueblos and a trio of national monuments.

SUGGESTED ITINERARIES

IF YOU HAVE 1 DAY Focus your attention on Old Town. Take in the ambience of the Plaza, the old church, and the numerous shops and galleries. Don't miss the nearby Albuquerque Museum, and if time permits (or you have the kids along), the New Mexico Museum of Natural History. Late in the day, head for Sandia Peak and its justly famed tramway. Watch the sun set while dining or sipping an apéritif at High Finance.

IF YOU HAVE 2 DAYS Spend the morning at the Indian Pueblo Cultural Center. After lunch there, spend the rest of the day in the anthropological past (Indian Petroglyphs State Park, the Maxwell Museum at the University of New Mexico), in the nuclear future (National Atomic Museum at Kirtland Air Force Base), or in the environmental present (Rio Grande Nature Center State Park, Rio Grande Zoological Park).

IF YOU HAVE 3 DAYS Get out of town, ideally to the Acoma Pueblo, a little over an hour's drive west via I-40. Here you'll get a true taste of the pueblo life that you merely sampled at the Cultural Center. There are numerous other pueblos in the Albuquerque area. If history intrigues you, Coronado State Monument, near Bernalillo, and the three divisions of Salinas National Monument, near Mountainair, are all within 90 minutes drive.

IF YOU HAVE 5 DAYS OR MORE Spend at least one of them in Santa Fe, traveling either there or back via N.M. Highway 14, the "Turquoise Trail" of all-but-abandoned mining metropolises. The more time you have, the more of New Mexico you can uncover—the mountain mecca of Taos, the gripping ruins of Chaco Canyon, hypnotizing White Sands, awesome Carlsbad Caverns, and so on.

THE TOP ATTRACTIONS

OLD TOWN, northeast of Central Ave. and Rio Grande Blvd. NW.

A maze of cobbled courtyard walkways lead to hidden patios and gardens where many of Old Town's 150 galleries and shops are located. Adobe buildings, many refurbished in Pueblo Revival style in the 1950s, focus around the tree shaded Old Town Plaza, created in 1780. Pueblo and Navajo Indian artisans often display their pottery, blankets, and silver jewelry on the sidewalks lining the plaza.

The buildings of Old Town once served as mercantile shops, grocery stores, and government offices; but the importance of Old Town as Albuquerque's commercial center declined after 1880, when the railroad came through 1.2 miles east of the plaza and businesses relocated nearer the tracks. Old Town clung to its historical and sentimental roots, but the quarter was disintegrating until it was rediscovered in the 1930s and 1940s by artisans and other shop owners and tourism took off.

The first structure built when colonists established Albuquerque in 1706 was the **Church of San Felipe de Neri,** facing the Plaza on its north side. The house of worship has been in almost continuous use for 285 years. When the original building collapsed about 1790, it was reconstructed and subsequently expanded several times, all the while remaining the spiritual heart of the city. The windows are some 20 feet from the ground and its walls are four feet thick—structural details needed to make the church also serviceable as a fortress against Indian attack. A spiral stairway leading to the choir loft is built around the trunk of an ancient spruce. Confessionals, altars, and images are hand carved; Gothic spires, added in the late 19th century, give the church a European air from the outside. The annual parish fiesta, held the first weekend in June, brings food and traditional dancing to the Plaza.

Next door to the church is the **Rectory,** built about 1793. Also on the North Plaza is **Loyola Hall,** the Sister Blandina Convent, built originally of adobe in 1881 as a residence for Sisters of Charity teachers who worked in the region. When the Jesuit fathers built **Our Lady of the Angels School,** 320 Romero St., in 1877, it was the only public school in Albuquerque.

The **Antonio Vigil House,** 413 Romero St., is an adobe-style residence with traditional *viga* ends sticking out over the entrance door. The **Florencio Zamora Store,** 301 Romero St., was built in the 1890s of "pugmill" adobe for a butcher and grocer. The **Jesus Romero House,** 205 Romero St., was constructed by another grocer in 1915 in "Prairie and Mediterranean" style. Just down the street, the **Jesus Romero Store,** built in 1893, has Territorial and Queen Anne structural features. On the South Plaza, the **Manuel Springer House** had a hipped roof and bay windows, still visible under its commercial facade today. The adjacent **Cristobal Armijo House,** a banker's two-story adobe, was completed in 1886 in combined Italianate and Queen Anne architectural styles.

Casa Armijo, in the 200 block of San Felipe Street, dates from before 1840; it was a headquarters for both Union and Confederate troops during the Civil War days. The nearby **Ambrosio Armijo House and Store,** also in San Felipe, an 1882 adobe structure, once had the high false front of wooden boards so typical of Old West towns in movies. The **Herman Blueher House,** at 302 San Felipe St., built by a businessman in 1898, is a three-story Italianate mansion with fancy porches on two levels, now obscured by storefronts.

The Albuquerque Museum conducts guided **walking tours** of Old Town's historic buildings during the summer at 11am Tuesday through Friday and 1pm Saturday and Sunday. The $2-per-person price includes museum admission. For visitors who don't find those times convenient, the museum publishes a brochure for a self-guided walking tour of Old Town.

For suggestions on shops and galleries to visit in Old Town, obtain a shopping guide from the **Old Town Association,** P.O. Box 7483, Albuquerque, NM 87194 (tel. 505/842-9100).

The Old Town Easter Parade, held annually on the Saturday preceding Easter, brings the Easter Bunny to the streets of the quarter, along with a variety of floats and marching bands. On Christmas Eve, thousands of *luminarias* or *farolitos*—brown paper bags filled with sand and lighted candles—line the narrow streets and flat-roofed buildings surrounding the Plaza.

SANDIA PEAK TRAMWAY, 10 Tramway Loop NE. Tel. 298-8518 or 296-9585.

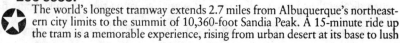

The world's longest tramway extends 2.7 miles from Albuquerque's northeastern city limits to the summit of 10,360-foot Sandia Peak. A 15-minute ride up the tram is a memorable experience, rising from urban desert at its base to lush

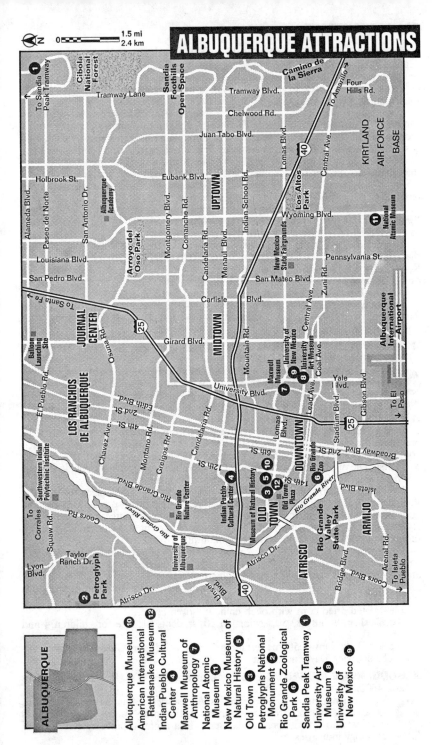

ALBUQUERQUE ATTRACTIONS

0 —— 1.5 mi
—— 2.4 km

N

Cibola National Forest

To Sandia Peak Tramway

Tramway Lane

Sandia Foothills Open Space

Camino de la Sierra

Tramway Blvd.

Chelwood Rd.

Juan Tabo Blvd.

Lomas Blvd.

To Amarillo

Four Hills Rd.

KIRTLAND AIR FORCE BASE

Central Ave.

Holbrook St.

Alameda Blvd.

Paseo del Norte

San Antonio Dr.

Albuquerque Academy

Eubank Blvd.

Montgomery Blvd.

Comanche Rd.

UPTOWN

Indian School Rd.

Los Altos Park

Wyoming Blvd.

National Atomic Museum

Louisiana Blvd.

San Pedro Blvd.

Arroyo del Oso Park

Candelaria Rd.

Menaul Blvd.

New Mexico State Fairgrounds

Pennsylvania St.

Carlisle Blvd.

San Mateo Blvd.

Zuni Rd.

Albuquerque International Airport

To Santa Fe

Balloon Launching Site

JOURNAL CENTER

Osuna Rd.

Girard Blvd.

MIDTOWN

Mountain Rd.

Maxwell Museum

University of New Mexico

University Art Museum

Coal Ave.

Yale Blvd.

Gibson Blvd.

To El Paso

El Pueblo Rd.

LOS RANCHOS DE ALBUQUERQUE

Edith Blvd.

2nd St.

University Blvd.

Lomas Blvd.

Central Ave.

Lead Ave.

Stadium Blvd.

Broadway Blvd.

Southwestern Indian Polytechnic Institute

Chavez Ave.

4th St.

Montano Rd.

Greigos Rd.

Candelaria Rd.

12th St.

Rio Grande Nature Center

Indian Pueblo Cultural Center

Museum of Natural History

OLD TOWN

8th St.

6th St.

Old Town Plaza

14th St.

2nd St.

Rio Grande Blvd.

DOWNTOWN

Zoo

Rio Grande River

To Corrales

Coors Rd.

Squaw Rd.

University of Albuquerque

Taylor Ranch Dr.

Lyon Blvd.

Petroglyph Park

Atrisco Dr.

Unser Blvd.

ATRISCO

Rio Grande Valley State Park

Bridge Blvd.

ARMIJO

Isleta Blvd.

Arenal Rd.

Coors Blvd.

To Isleta Pueblo

ALBUQUERQUE

Albuquerque Museum ⑩
American International Rattlesnake Museum ⑫
Indian Pueblo Cultural Center ④
Maxwell Museum of Anthropology ⑦
National Atomic Museum ⑪
New Mexico Museum of Natural History ⑤
Old Town ③
Petroglyphs National Monument ②
Rio Grande Zoological Park ⑥
Sandia Peak Tramway ①
University Art Museum ⑧
University of New Mexico ⑨

mountain foliage in the Cíbola National Forest at its peak . . . and dropping about 20 degrees in temperature in the process. Animals viewed on the wild slopes from the tram occasionally include bears, bighorn sheep, deer, eagles, hawks, and a rare mountain lion. The view from the observation deck encompasses more than 11,000 square miles, well beyond Santa Fe and Los Alamos to the north.

Winter skiers often take the tram to the **Sandia Peak Ski Area,** where visitors can couple their trip with a ride on the resort's 7,500-foot double-chair lift through the spruce and ponderosa pine forests on the mountain's eastern slope. (A single ride costs $4; the chair operates from 10am to 3pm in summer, 9am to 4pm in winter.)

The Sandia Peak tram is a "jigback"; in other words, as one car approaches the top, the other nears the bottom. The two pass halfway through the trip, in the midst of a 1.5-mile "clear span" of unsupported cable between the second tower and the upper terminal.

There is a popular and high-priced restaurant at the tramway's summit, **High Finance** (tel. 243-9742); at the base is the **Firehouse** (tel. 292-3473) another upscale eatery. Special tram rates apply with dinner reservations.

To reach the base of the tram, take I-25 north to the Tramway Road/Alameda exit, then proceed east about five miles on Tramway Road (N.M. 556); or take Tramway Road (N.M. 541) north of I-40 approximately 8.5 miles. Turn east the last half-mile on Sandia Heights Road to Tramway Loop.

Admission: Adults $11, seniors and children 5–12 $8.50.

Open: Memorial Day–Labor Day daily 9am–10pm; spring and fall Thurs–Tues 9am–9pm, Wed 5–9pm; ski season Mon–Tues and Thurs–Fri 9am–9pm, Wed noon–9pm, Sat–Sun 8am–9pm.

INDIAN PUEBLO CULTURAL CENTER, 2401 12th St. NW. Tel. 843-7270 or toll free 800/288-0721.

Owned and operated as a nonprofit organization by the 19 pueblos of northern New Mexico, this is a fine place to begin an exploration of native culture. Located about a mile northeast of Old Town, this museum—modeled after Pueblo Bonito, a spectacular 9th-century ruin in Chaco Culture National Historic Park—consists of several parts.

In the basement, a permanent exhibit depicts the evolution from prehistory to present of the various pueblos, including displays of the distinctive handcrafts of each community. Note, especially, how pottery differs in concept and design from pueblo to pueblo. The displays include a series of remarkable photographs of Pueblo Indians taken between 1880 and 1910, a gift of the Smithsonian Institution.

Upstairs is an enormous (7,000-square-foot) gift shop—a fine place to price the Pueblo peoples' colorful creations of art before bartering with private artisans. The code of ethics of the Indian Arts and Crafts Association guarantees work here to be stylistically authentic. A gallery displays a variety of ancient and modern works from different pueblos, with exhibits changing monthly.

Every weekend throughout the year, native dancers perform and artisans demonstrate their crafts expertise in an outdoor arena surrounded by original murals. An annual craft fair is held on the July 4 holiday weekend.

A restaurant, open from 7:30am to 3:30pm, emphasizes the cornmeal-based foods of the Pueblo people. Daily specials are priced at $4, although an ample meal is posole, treated dried corn with beef, chili, and oven bread.

Admission: Adults $2.50, seniors $1.50, students $1; free for children 4 and under.

Open: Daily 9am–5:50pm; restaurant 7:30am–3:30pm. **Closed:** New Year's Day, Thanksgiving Day, and Christmas.

ALBUQUERQUE MUSEUM, 2000 Mountain Rd. NW. Tel. 243-7255 or 242-4600.

A permanent exhibit, "Four Centuries: A History of Albuquerque," chronicles the city's evolution from the earliest 16th-century forays of Coronado's *conquistadores* to its present-day status as a center of military research and high-technology industries.

Among objects held in the museum's collection are arms and armor used during the Hispanic conquest, medieval religious artifacts and weavings, maps from the 16th to 18th centuries, and coins and domestic goods traded during that same period. Of special note is a 17th-century *repostero,* or tapestry, once belonging to the Spanish House of Albuquerque. It was given to the city in 1956 by the 18th duke of Albuquerque to commemorate the 200th anniversary of the founding of the Spanish settlement here. Made of silk with gold and silver thread, it is 12 feet square and displays a dragon.

A multimedia audiovisual presentation, *Albuquerque: The Crossroads,* depicts the development of the city since 1875. The photography around the turn of the 20th century shows a rip-roaring Main Street scene aswarm with buggies, wagons, horses, draymen, cowboys, and cattle drivers, with the typical false-front stores, saloons, and hotels in the background. A first-rate unsentimental narration and apposite music help the sharp overall impression that you are getting something of a taste of the real life that was lived in this place.

There's also a gallery of early and modern New Mexico art, with permanent and changing exhibits; and a major photo archive. Lectures and workshops are offered in an auditorium and classroom. A gift shop offers souvenirs and other wares.

Admission: Free; donation appreciated.
Open: Tues–Sun 9am–5pm. **Closed:** Holidays.

MORE ATTRACTIONS

UNIVERSITY OF NEW MEXICO, Yale Blvd. NE north of Central Ave. Tel. 277-0111.
The state's largest institution of higher learning stretches across an attractive 700-acre campus about two miles east of downtown Albuquerque, north of Central Avenue and east of University Boulevard. The six campus museums, none of which charge admission, are constructed (like other UNM buildings) in a modified pueblo style. Popejoy Hall, in the south-central part of campus opposite Yale Park, hosts many performing arts presentations, including those of the New Mexico Symphony Orchestra; other public events are held in nearby Keller Hall and Woodward Hall.

The **Maxwell Museum of Anthropology** (tel. 277-4405) is an internationally acclaimed repository of southwestern anthropological finds, situated on the west side of campus on Redondo Drive at Ash Street NE. Permanent galleries include "Ancestors," describing 4 million years of human evolution, and "Peoples of the Southwest," a 10,000-year summary. Mimbres and Pueblo pottery, Hopi *kachina* dolls, Navajo weavings, and a variety of regional jewelry, basketry, and textiles are on display. The collections support education and research in anthropology, archaeology, and ethnology. Native arts and books about the state's cultural heritage are on sale in the museum's gift shop. It's open Monday through Friday from 9am to 4pm, Saturday from 10am to 4pm, and Sunday from noon to 4pm closed holidays.

The **University Art Museum** (tel. 277-4001), in the Fine Arts Center adjoining Popejoy Hall on Cornell Street, just north of Central Avenue, is a multilevel museum focusing on 19th- and 20th-century American and European artists. The prides of its permanent collection are an exhibit of early modernist work, and exhibitions covering the history of photography and prints. It's open from September through May, Tuesday from 9am to 4pm and 5 to 9pm, Wednesday through Friday from 9am to 4pm, and Sunday from 1 to 4pm; closed holidays. A gift shop offers many art books and periodicals, as well as some prints of the works displayed.

The small **Jonson Gallery** (tel. 277-4967), at 1909 Las Lomas Blvd. NE on the north side of the central campus, features more than 2,000 works by the late Raymond Jonson, a leading modernist painter in early 20th-century New Mexico. Open Tuesday 9am to 4pm and 5 to 9pm, Wednesday to Friday 9am to 4pm.

Located in Northrop Hall (tel. 277-4204), about halfway between the Maxwell Museum and Popejoy Hall in the southern part of campus, the adjacent **Geology Museum** and **Meteoritic Museum** (tel. 277-1644) cover the gamut of recorded time from dinosaur bones to meteorites. The 3,000 meteorite specimens held here comprise the sixth-largest collection in the United States. The Geology Museum is open Monday through Friday from 8am to 5pm; the Meteoritic Museum, Monday through Friday from 9am to noon and 1 to 4pm.

Finally, the **Museum of Southwestern Biology** (tel. 277-3411) in the basement of Castetter Hall (the biology building next to Northup Hall) has few displays, but has extensive research holdings of global flora and fauna. The holdings especially represent southwestern North America, Central America, South America, eastern Asia, and parts of Europe. Visitors must call ahead for an appointment.

NATIONAL ATOMIC MUSEUM, Wyoming Blvd. and K St., Kirtland Air Force Base. Tel. 845-6670.

This museum is the next best introduction to the nuclear age after the Bradbury Science Museum in Los Alamos. It traces the history of nuclear-weapons development beginning with the top-secret Manhattan Project of the 1940s, including a copy of the letter Albert Einstein wrote to Pres. Franklin D. Roosevelt suggesting the possible development of an atomic bomb. A 50-minute film, *Ten Seconds That Shook the World,* is shown four times daily, at 10:30 and 11:30am, and 2 and 3:30pm. There are full-scale models of the "Fat Man" and "Little Boy" bombs, displays and films on peaceful applications of nuclear technology and other alternative energy sources. Fusion is explained in a manner that a layperson can begin to understand; other exhibits deal with the problem of nuclear waste. Outdoor exhibits include missiles and bombers. The museum is directly across the street from the International Nuclear Weapons School, adjacent to Sandia National Laboratory.

Admission: Free. Visitors must obtain passes at the Wyoming or Gibson gate of the base. Children under 12 not admitted without parent or adult guardian.

Open: Daily 9am–5pm. **Closed:** New Year's Day, Easter Day, Thanksgiving Day, and Christmas.

RIO GRANDE NATURE CENTER STATE PARK, 2901 Candelaria Rd. NW. Tel. 344-7240.

Located on the Rio Grande Flyway, an important migratory route for many birds, this wildlife refuge extends for nearly a mile along the east bank of the Rio Grande. Numerous nature trails wind through the cottonwood *bosque,* where a great variety of native and migratory species can be seen at any time of year. The center publishes a checklist to help visitors identify them, as well as several self-guiding trail brochures.

Housed in a unique building constructed half aboveground and half below, the visitor's center contains classrooms, laboratory space, a library, and exhibits describing the history, geology, and ecology of the Rio Grande valley. Films and interpreted hikes are scheduled every weekend.

Admission: $1 adults, 50¢ children 6 and older.

Open: Daily 10am–5pm. **Closed:** New Year's Day, Thanksgiving Day, and Christmas.

PETROGLYPH NATIONAL MONUMENT, 6900 Unser Blvd. NW, west of Coors Rd. Tel. 839-4429.

Albuquerque's western city limits are marked by five extinct volcanoes. The ancient lava flows here were a hunting ground for prehistoric Indians, who camped among the rocks and left a cryptic chronicle of their life-style etched and chipped in the dark basalt. Some 10,500 of these petroglyphs have been found in several concentrated groups at this archaeological preserve. Plaques interpret the rock drawings—animal, human, and ceremonial forms—to visitors, who may take four hiking trails, ranging from easy to moderately difficult, winding through the lava. The 45-minute Mesa Point trail is the most strenuous but also the most rewarding.

Camping is not permitted in the park; it is strictly for day use, with picnic areas, drinking water, and rest rooms.

Admission: $1 per vehicle.

Open: Summer daily 9am–6pm; winter 8am–5pm. **Closed:** State holidays.

SPANISH HISTORY MUSEUM, 2221 Lead St. SE. Tel. 268-9981.

This exclusive gallery features "From Kingdom to Statehood," an exhibit outlining

Hispanics' role in New Mexico's pursuit of statehood from 1848 to 1912. There's also documentation of Spain's assistance to the 13 original colonies during the American Revolution, information about New Mexico's founding Hispanic families and their heraldic coats-of-arms, and family history booklets. The Columbus display is an in-depth study of the great navigator's life.

Admission: $1 donation requested.

Open: Summer 10am–5pm; rest of year 1–5pm. **Closed:** Major holidays.

ERNIE PYLE MEMORIAL LIBRARY, 900 Girard Blvd. NE. Tel. 256-2065.

The 1939 home of America's favorite war correspondent is now a library. Memorabilia and poignant exhibits recalling the Pulitzer Prize–winning journalist, killed in action during World War II, stand in display shelves between the book racks.

Admission: Free.

Open: Tues and Thurs 12:30–8pm; Wed and Fri–Sat 9am–5:30pm.

COOL FOR KIDS

If you're traveling with children, you'll be happy to know that there are a number of Albuquerque attractions that are guaranteed to keep the kids interested. One of the city's best child-oriented activities takes place on Sundays year round on Romero Street in the Old Town, where costumed actors re-create **Wild West shoot-outs.** On weekends, there are also regular puppet plays at the **Old Town Puppet Theatre** (tel. 243-0208).

NEW MEXICO MUSEUM OF NATURAL HISTORY, 1801 Mountain Rd. NW. Tel. 841-8837.

Two life-size bronze dinosaurs stand outside the entrance to this modern museum, opposite the Albuquerque Museum. The pentaceratops and albertosaur are only the first of the museum's displays that kids will love.

When the museum opened in 1986 on money drawn mostly from taxes on oil, gas, and coal produced in the state, it began nearly from scratch, without any major collections of artifacts or other materials. Today it contains permanent and changing exhibits on regional zoology, botany, geology, and paleontology.

Innovative video displays, polarizing lenses, and black lighting enable visitors to stroll through geologic time. You can walk a rocky path through the Hall of Giants, as dinosaurs fight and winged reptiles swoop overhead; step into a seemingly live volcano, complete with simulated magma flow; or share an Ice Age cave, festooned with stalagmites, with saber-toothed tigers and woolly mammoths. Hands-on exhibits in the Naturalist Center permit use of a video microscope, viewing of an active beehive, and participation in a variety of other activities. An atrium in the lobby features a 22-foot relief map of the earth showing the surfaces of continents and seabeds; a network of 2,500 fiber-optic elements monitors the pulse of the planet, flashing wherever earthquakes or eruptions occur—about every three seconds.

There's a gift shop on the ground floor, and the highly regarded Museum Café (see "Dining," above) on the mezzanine.

Admission: Adults $4, seniors $3, children 3–11 $2. Children under 12 must be accompanied by an adult.

Open: Daily 9am–5pm, to 6pm May–Sept. **Closed:** Christmas.

AMERICAN INTERNATIONAL RATTLESNAKE MUSEUM, 202 San Felipe St. NW. Tel. 242-6569.

This unique museum has living specimens in naturally landscaped habitats of common, not so common, and rare rattlesnakes of North, Central, and South America. Over 20 species can be seen, including such oddities as albinos and patternless rattlesnakes. Especially popular with the kids are the baby rattlesnakes. A 7-minute film explains the rattlesnake's contribution to the ecological balance of our hemisphere. Throughout the museum are rattlesnake artifacts from early American history, Indian culture, medicine, the arts, and advertising. A gift shop sells Indian jewelry, T-shirts, and other mementos of the Southwest—with an emphasis on rattlesnakes of course.

Admission: $1.
Open: Daily 10am–9pm.

RIO GRANDE ZOOLOGICAL PARK, 903 10th St. SW. Tel. 843-7413.

Open-motif exhibits, including an African savanna and Amazon rain forest, are the highlights of this fine zoo, located a short distance south of downtown. More than 1,200 animals of 300 species live on 60 acres of riverside *bosque* among ancient cottonwoods. The zoo has an especially fine collection of endangered African hoofed animals, including bongo, gerenuk, and sable, as well as the requisite apes, big cats, elephants, giraffes, and native southwestern species. A children's petting zoo is open during the summer. There are numerous snack bars on the zoo grounds, and La Ventana Gift Shop carries film and souvenirs.

Admission: Adults $4.25, children and seniors $2.25. Children under 12 must be accompanied by an adult.

Open: Daily 9am–5pm, with extended hours in summer. **Closed:** New Year's Day, Thanksgiving Day, and Christmas.

CLIFF'S AMUSEMENT PARK, 4800 Osuna Rd. NE. Tel. 883-9063.

This is New Mexico's largest amusement park. Children of all ages love the 23 rides, video arcades, recording studio, picnic ground, and live entertainment.

Admission: $7.25.

Open: May Fri 7–11pm, Sat 1–11pm, Sun 1–7pm; Memorial Day–Labor Day Fri 2–11pm, Sat 1–11pm, Sun 1–9pm, Mon–Thurs 6–10pm (1–7pm Mon holidays); Sept Sat 1–10pm, Sun 1–6pm.

TOURS

Albuquerque is very spread out and doesn't lend itself to **walking tours**—except in Old Town. The Albuquerque Museum, 2000 Mountain Rd. NW (tel. 243-7255 or 242-4600), publishes a brochure for self-guided walking tours of Old Town and conducts guided tours during the summer Tuesday through Friday at 11am and Saturday and Sunday at 1pm. Many of the buildings included on that tour are discussed above, in this chapter's treatment of Old Town.

Consult any of the following **tour operators** for city and regional tours: **Jack Allen Tours,** P.O. Box 11940, Albuquerque, NM 87192 (tel. 505/266-9688); **Discover Travel,** 6303 Indian School Rd. NE, Albuquerque, NM 87110 (tel. 505/888-2444); **Sun Tours,** 4300 San Mateo Blvd. NE, Suite B-155, Albuquerque, NM 87110 (tel. 505/881-5346).

6. SPORTS & RECREATION

SPECTATOR SPORTS

BASEBALL   The Albuquerque Dukes, 1990 champions of the Class AAA Pacific Coast League, are the number-one farm team of the Los Angeles Dodgers. They play 72 home games from mid-April to early September in the city-owned 30,000-seat Albuquerque Sports Stadium, 1601 Stadium Blvd. SE at University Boulevard (tel. 243-1791). Among the former Dukes now playing major-league baseball are John Franco, Sid Fernandez, Pedro Guerrero, Orel Hershiser, Candy Maldonado, and Dave Stewart.

BASKETBALL   The University of New Mexico team, nicknamed the Lobos, plays an average of 16 home games from late November to early March. Capacity crowds cheer the team at the 17,121-seat University Arena (fondly called "the Pit") at University and Stadium boulevards. The arena was the site in 1983 of the annual National Collegiate Athletic Association championship tournament.

BOXING   Albuquerque has several professional boxing gyms. Local bouts, whose sites have varied, have featured top contenders in various weight divisions. Several nationally ranked boxers live and train in the Albuquerque area.

FOOTBALL   The UNM Lobos football team plays a September-to-November season, usually including five home games, at the 30,000-seat University of New Mexico Stadium, opposite both Albuquerque Sports Stadium and University Arena at University and Stadium boulevards.

HORSE RACING   The Downs at Albuquerque, 201 California St. (tel. 265-1188 for post times), is in the State Fairgrounds near Lomas and Louisiana boulevards NE. Racing and betting—on thoroughbreds and quarter horses—take place Wednesdays, Fridays, and Saturdays from late January to June and during the state fair in September. The Downs has a glass-enclosed grandstand, exclusive club seating, valet parking, complimentary racing programs and tip sheets.

RODEO   The All-American Pro Rodeo, a key event on the national professional rodeo circuit, takes place the second through third weekends of September each year as a part of the New Mexico State Fair. Tickets—at $5 general, $9 reserved—must be ordered from fair officials (tel. toll free 800/235-FAIR).

RECREATION

✪ **BALLOONING**   Visitors not content to watch the colorful craft rise into the clear blue skies have a choice of several hot-air balloon operators from whom to get a ride, at rates starting about $35 per person. They include: **Braden's Balloons Aloft,** 9935-B Trumbull Ave. SE (tel. 281-2714 or toll free 800/367-6625); **Cameron Balloons,** 2950 San Joaquin Ave. SE (tel. 265-4007); **Rainbow Ryders, Inc.** 430 Montclaire Dr. SE (tel. 268-3401 or toll free 800/725-7477); **Southwest Aviation Management,** 2730 San Pedro Blvd. NE (tel. 889-6318); **World Balloon Corporation,** 4800 Eubank Blvd. NE (tel. 293-6800).

BICYCLING   Albuquerque is a major bicycling hub in the summer, both for road racers and mountain bikers. Full information on competitive events and touring, as well as rentals, can be obtained from **Gardenswartz Sportz,** 2720 San Mateo Blvd. NE (tel. 884-6787), or **R.E.I.,** 1905 Mountain Rd. NW (tel. 247-1191).

BOWLING   There are 10 bowling alleys in Albuquerque. They include the 40-lane **Fiesta Lanes,** 6001 Menaul Blvd. NE, at San Pedro Boulevard (tel. 881-4040), open daily from 8am to midnight, with a pro shop, private locker rooms, child care, and a restaurant; and the 32-lane **Leisure Bowl,** 7400 Lomas Blvd. NE, near Louisiana Boulevard (tel. 268-4371), open daily from 9am to 1am, with a 15-minute break from 5:45 to 6pm, with a pro shop, sports bar, and "bumper bowling" for children.

FISHING   Although most avid anglers head for high-mountain lakes or outlying streams, the Rio Grande, even as it flows through Albuquerque, remains an attraction to some fishermen. Youngsters may catch their first trout or crappie at **Shady Lakes,** 11033 Fourth St. NW (tel. 898-2568). Licenses, equipment, and bait can be purchased from numerous sporting goods outlets, including **Charlie's Sporting Goods,** 7401-H Menaul Blvd. NE (tel. 884-4545), and **Quality Baits,** 4257 Isleta Blvd. SW (tel. 877-0780). Fly fishermen patronize **Backwoods,** 6307 Menaul Blvd. NE (tel. 881-5223).

GOLF   There are 11 public and private courses in Albuquerque, all of them open year-round, sunrise to sunset. Clubhouses will make arrangements for partners on request. Public courses include: **Arroyo del Oso Golf Course** (18 holes), 7001 Osuna Blvd. NE (tel. 884-7505); **Los Altos Golf Course** (18 holes), 9717 Copper St. NE (tel. 298-1897); **Puerto del Sol Golf Course** (9 holes), 1600 Girard Blvd. SE (tel. 265-5636); **Ladera Golf Course** (18 holes), 3401 Ladera Dr. NW (tel. 836-4449); **University of New Mexico South Course** (18 holes), 3601 University Blvd. SE (tel. 277-4546); **University of New Mexico North Course** (9 holes), Yale Boulevard at Tucker Road (tel. 277-4146). Private courses offering reciprocity include: **Albuquerque Country Club** (18 holes), 601 Laguna Blvd. SW (tel.

247-4111); **Four Hills Country Club** (18 holes), 911 Four Hills Rd. SE (tel. 299-9555); **Paradise Hills Country Club** (18 holes), 10035 Country Club Lane NW (tel. 898-0960); **Rio Rancho Country Club** (18 holes), 500 Country Club Dr. SE, Rio Rancho (tel. 892-5813); **Tanoan Country Club** (18 holes), 10801 Academy Blvd. NE (tel. 822-0433). There's miniature golf at **Highland Swing,** 312 Adams St. SE off Zuni Avenue (tel. 255-9992). Near Highland High School, it's a tree-shaded course.

HIKING & BACKPACKING The 1.6-million-acre **Cíbola National Forest** offers ample opportunities. In the Sandia Mountain section alone are 18 recreation sites, though only one—Cedro Peak, four miles southeast of Tijeras—allows overnight camping. For details, contact Sandia Ranger Station, NM-337, south toward Tijeras (tel. 381-3304).

    Elena Gallegos/Albert G. Simms Park, near the base of the Sandia Peak Tramway at 1700 Tramway Blvd. NE (tel. 291-6224 or 768-3550), is a 640-acre mountain picnic area with hiking trail access to the Sandia Mountain Wilderness. Nature programs and hikes are guided during the summer.

    Llama pack trips, guided backpacking trips, and gourmet day hikes are offered by **Southwest Wilderness Trails,** Star Route Box 303, Placitas, NM 87043 (tel. 505/867-3442). Trips into Bandelier National Monument and the Pecos Wilderness are regularly scheduled and cost as little as $35 per person per day.

    Sporting goods stores specializing in this type of outdoor equipment include **R.E.I.,** 1905 Mountain Rd. NW (tel. 247-1191); **Sandia Mountain Outfitters,** 1560 Juan Tabo Blvd. NE (tel. 293-9725); and the **Wilderness Centre,** 4900 Lomas Blvd. NE (tel. 268-6767).

HORSEBACK RIDING Many urban riders make use of the 20-mile path along the irrigation ditches flanking the Rio Grande from Bernalillo through Albuquerque to Belen. Others head up the slopes of Sandia Mountain. Local stables rent horses, offer instruction, and provide outfitters as required. Try **Los Amigos Stables,** 10601 Fourth St. NW, Alameda (tel. 898-8173), with more than 300 acres of trails on the Sandia Indian Reservation; or **Turkey Track Stables,** 1306 U.S. Hwy. 66 East, Tijeras (tel. 281-1772).

HUNTING In the Albuquerque area, **Cíbola National Forest** is popular among hunters for game birds and some big-game animals, including mule deer, bear, and mountain lion. Licenses and information can be obtained from **Charlie's,** 7401-H Menaul Blvd. NE (tel. 884-4545), or **Los Ranchos Gun & Tackle Shop,** 6542 Fourth St. NW (tel. 345-4276). Guided hunting expeditions can be arranged by the **New Mexico Council of Outfitters and Guides,** 160 Washington St. SE, Suite 75, Albuquerque, NM 87108 (tel. 505/243-4461).

    Bow hunters can practice their craft indoors at the **Albuquerque Archery** shooting range, 5000-B Menaul Blvd. NE (tel. 881-0808), open daily until 9pm.

RIVER RAFTING This mainly takes place farther north, in the Santa Fe and especially Taos areas. Check with **Wolf Whitewater Rafting Co.,** P.O. Box 666, Sandia Park, NM 87047 (tel. 281-5042 or toll free 800/552-0070), or **Rio Grande Rapid Transit,** Box A Pilar, NM 87571 (tel. 758-9700 or toll free 800/222-RAFT).

    In mid-May each year, the **Great Race** takes place on a 14-mile stretch of the Rio Grande through Albuquerque. Eleven categories of craft, including rafts, kayaks, and canoes, race down the river. Call 768-3490 for details.

RUNNING Albuquerque Parks & Recreation (tel. 768-3550) maintains numerous recreational trails. Bicyclists and walkers enjoy them, too, but they're ideal for runners. They include **Paseo del Nordeste,** a 6.1-mile asphalt trail beginning at Tucker Avenue, north of the UNM campus, and ending at Sandia High School on Pennsylvania Boulevard NE; **Paseo del Bosque,** a 5-mile trail running parallel to the irrigation ditch on the east side of the Rio Grande, with access from Candelaria

Road NW, Campbell Road NW, Mountain Road NW, Central Avenue SW, and other streets; **Paseo de las Montanas,** following Embudo Arroyo 4.2 miles from Pennsylvania Boulevard NE, east of Winrock Center, to Lynnwood Park near Tramway Boulevard NE; **Tramway,** 4 miles, along the east side of Tramway Boulevard from Montgomery Boulevard to I-40; **La Mariposa,** 1.5 miles, between Montano Road NW and Dellyne Avenue NW, west of Taylor Ranch Road NW; and **Jefferson-Osuna,** 0.4 mile, following the Bear Arroyo between Jefferson Street NE and Osuna Boulevard NE.

SKATING The **Outpost Ice Arena,** 9530 Tramway Blvd. NE (tel. 298-6855), has a year-round rink, with instructors and a hockey league. There's also a fitness center and a restaurant. Skaters who prefer a maple floor can try the **Rainbow Garden Roller Drome,** 204 San Mateo Blvd. SE (tel. 255-2480), an enormous air-conditioned facility with a pro shop.

SKIING The **Sandia Peak Ski Area** has twin base-to-summit chair lifts to its upper slopes at 10,360 feet and a 1,700-foot vertical drop. There are 25 trails, 14 of them geared to intermediates, and several beginners' runs above the day lodge and ski-rental shop. Three chairs and two pomas accommodate 3,400 skiers an hour. All-day lift tickets are $25 for adults, $18 for children; rental packages are $11 for adults, $9 for kids. The season usually runs from the Christmas holidays through March. Contact the ski area's offices at 10 Tramway Loop NE (tel. 296-9585) for more information, or call the hot line for ski conditions (tel. 242-9052).

Cross-country skiers can enjoy the trails of the **Sandia Wilderness** from the ski area or can go an hour north to the remote **Jemez Wilderness** and its hot springs.

Among the many shops in Albuquerque renting full ski equipment are **R.E.I.,** 1905 Mountain Rd. NW (tel. 247-1191), and **Sports Venture Ski Systems,** 1605 Juan Tabo Blvd. NE, Suite A (tel. 296-9111).

SWIMMING There are five indoor and nine outdoor swimming pools in Albuquerque, allowing year-round swimming in all parts of the city. Open 12 months a year are the following pools: **Highland,** 400 Jackson St. SE (tel. 256-2096), **Los Altos,** 10300 Lomas Blvd. NE (tel. 291-6290), **Sandia,** 7801 Candelaria Blvd. NE (tel. 291-6279), and **Valley,** 1505 Candelaria Blvd. NW (tel. 761-4086). Among those open summers only are **Sierra Vista West,** 5001 Montano Rd. NW (tel. 897-4517), **South Valley,** 3912 Isleta Blvd. SW (tel. 877-3959), and **West Mesa,** 6705 Fortuna Rd. NW (tel. 836-0686). For more information, call **Albuquerque Culture and Recreational Services** (tel. 768-3520).

Slightly more off-beat water entertainment is available at the **Beach,** I-25 and Montano Road (tel. 344-6111). This 15-acre water park, including a wave pool, five water slides, and two restaurants, is open daily in summer from 11am to 8pm.

TENNIS There are some 140 public tennis courts at 29 parks in and near Albuquerque. Many of them can be reserved in advance. There are tennis complexes at **UNM South Campus,** 1903 Stadium Blvd. SE (tel. 848-1389), and **Jerry Cline Park,** Louisiana Boulevard NE and Constitution Avenue NE, at I-40 (tel. 256-2032).

7. SAVVY SHOPPING

Nowhere in the state could one get a better shopping "fix" than in Albuquerque. The city has the two largest shopping malls in the state within two blocks of one another, both on Louisiana Boulevard just north of I-40—Coronado Center and Winrock Center.

Visitors interested in regional specialties will find many artists and galleries, although not so concentrated as in Santa Fe and Taos. The galleries and regional fashion designers around the plaza in Old Town make a sort of shopping center of their own for tourists, with more than 40 merchants represented. The Sandia Pueblo

Indians run their own crafts market on their reservation land off I-25 at Tramway Road, just beyond Albuquerque's northern city limits.

Business hours vary from store to store and from shopping center to shopping center. In general, it's safe to say that shops will be open Monday through Saturday from 10am to 6pm, but many have extended hours; some have reduced hours; and a few, especially in shopping malls or during the high tourist season, are open Sunday.

BEST BUYS

Look for southwestern regional items in Albuquerque. That includes arts and crafts of all kinds, from traditional Indian and Hispanic to contemporary works. In native art, look for silver and turquoise jewelry, pottery, weavings, baskets, sand paintings, and Hopi *kachina* dolls. Hispanic folk art, including handcrafted furniture, tinwork and *retablos,* religious paintings, are worth seeking out. Contemporary art focuses primarily on paintings, sculpture, jewelry, ceramics, and fiber art, including weaving.

By far the greatest concentration of galleries is in Old Town; others are spread around the city, with smaller groupings in the university district and the northeast heights. Consult the brochure published by the Albuquerque Gallery Association, *A Select Guide to Albuquerque Galleries,* or Wingspread Communications' annual *The Collector's Guide to Albuquerque,* widely distributed at shops. Once a month, usually the third Friday from 5:30 to 8:30pm, the Albuquerque Art Business Association (tel. 292-7537) sponsors an ArtsCrawl to dozens of galleries and studios. If you're in town, it's a great way to get to know the artists.

Other things to keep your eyes open for are fashions in southwestern print designs; gourmet items, including blue-corn flour and chile *ristras;* and souvenirs unique to the region, especially Indian and Hispanic creations.

SHOPPING A TO Z
ANTIQUES

ANDREW NAGEN OLD NAVAJO RUGS, 14 Corrales Rd., Corrales. Tel. 898-5058.

Very much a specialty dealer, Nagen buys, sells, and appraises historic Navajo, Pueblo, and Hispanic weavings. He opens by appointment only.

BRANDYWINE GALLERIES, 120 Morningside Dr. SE. Tel. 255-0266.

In an elegant setting of period furniture, porcelain, and silver are displayed some of the outstanding representational works of art of 19th- and 20th-century New Mexico, including pieces by the original Taos and Santa Fe schools. The gallery specializes in art and antique appraisals and restorations.

CLASSIC CENTURY SQUARE, 4616 Central Ave. SE. Tel. 265-3161.

More than 100 individual dealers in antiques, collectibles, and arts and crafts exhibit here, between the University of New Mexico and the State Fairgrounds. Jewelry, china, crystal, silver, books, dolls, home accessories, and other items are available.

A second location, **Classic Century Square II,** is at 3100 Juan Tabo Blvd. NE (tel. 294-9904), in the eastern foothills. Both centers are open Monday through Saturday from 10am to 6pm and Sunday from noon to 5pm.

RICHARD WORTHEN GALLERIES, 1331 Tijeras Ave., NW. Tel. 764-9595.

Worthen made his name nationally as an interior designer. Now most of his energy goes into his extensive collection of Spanish colonial art and antiques.

ART

ADOBE GALLERY, 413 Romero St. NW, Old Town. Tel. 243-8485.

Art of southwestern Native Americans is featured here. The gallery also carries numerous contemporary and antique Indian items, including pottery, weavings, and *kachina* dolls. Open Monday through Saturday from 10am to 6pm, Sunday from 1 to 4pm.

R. C. GORMAN'S NAVAJO GALLERY, 323 Romero St. NW, Old Town. Tel. 843-7666.
The painting and sculpture of famed Navajo artist Gorman, a resident of Taos, are shown here daily from 11am to 5pm. Most works are available in limited-edition lithographs.

WEYRICH GALLERY (Rare Vision Art Galerie), 2935-D Louisiana Blvd. at Candelaria Rd. Tel. 883-7410.
Contemporary paintings, sculpture, textiles, jewelry, and ceramics by regional and nonregional artists are exhibited at this spacious midtown gallery. Open Monday through Saturday from 10am to 5:30pm.

BOOKS

In addition to the independent bookstores in Albuquerque, the nationwide chain stores B. Dalton and Waldenbooks are represented. Among the most interesting bookstores are:

BOOKWORKS, 4022 Rio Grande Blvd. NW. Tel. 344-8139.
This store has one of the most complete southwestern nonfiction and fiction sections, with both new and used books. Recently enlarged, the store carries major offerings in children's books and gift books.

CORNER BOOKSTORE, 3500 Central Ave. SE. Tel. 266-2044.
Albuquerque's newest bookstore is located in the nostalgic Nob Hill section. They have an especially fine collection of nonfiction, as well as fine arts books. A superb source for a wide collection of travel books.

CANTWELL'S BOOKS & FINE PAPERS, 8236 Menaul Blvd. NE. Tel. 294-4454.
Cantwell's is noteworthy as the center for codependency books and serious modern fiction, as well as a large selection of children's books. Their gift and paper sidelines are worth checking out.

PAGE ONE, 11200 Montgomery Blvd. NE, at Juan Tabo Blvd. Tel. 294-2026 or toll free 800/521-4122.
New Mexico's largest bookstore has more than 135,000 titles in stock, close to 5,000 foreign and domestic magazines, and more than 150 out-of-state and foreign newspapers. It also carries road maps, computer books and software, and compact discs. Open daily from 8am to 10pm.

TOM DAVIES BOOKSHOP, 414 Central Ave. SE. Tel. 247-2072.
A specialist in rare and out-of-print books, maps, and documents since 1956, they carry a fine collection of hard-to-find southwestern regional literature. Open Monday through Saturday from 12:30 to 5pm, or by appointment.
Other specialty bookstores include **Birdsong Books,** 139 Harvard Ave. SE, near the University of New Mexico (tel. 268-7204), for used books and records; **Blue Eagle Book & Metaphysical Center,** 4807 Central Ave. NE (tel. 268-3682), for New Age materials; **Holman's,** 401 Wyoming Blvd. NE (tel. 265-7981), for professional and technical texts; **Hosanna,** 2421 Aztec Blvd. NE, at Girard Boulevard (tel. 881-3321), for Christian literature; **Murder Unlimited,** 2510 San Mateo Blvd. NE (tel. 884-5491), for mystery titles; and **Trespassers William,** 5003 Lomas Blvd. NE (tel. 268-4601), for children's books.

CRAFTS

AMERICAN INDIAN GALLERY AT THE COVERED WAGON, 2034 S. Plaza NW, Old Town. Tel. 242-4481.
Prehistoric, historic, and contemporary Indian arts of North America, including

pottery, weaving, and costumes, are featured. Open Monday through Saturday from 9am to 10pm and Sunday from 10am to 7pm.

ANDREWS PUEBLO POTTERY & ART GALLERY, 400 San Felipe St. NW, Suite 8, Old Town. Tel. 243-0414.
Probably nowhere in New Mexico has a wider selection of contemporary and Pre-Columbian Pueblo pottery. The gallery also carries baskets, serigraphs, fetishes, and *kachina* dolls. Open daily from 10am to 6pm, until 8pm in summer.

BIEN MUR INDIAN MARKET CENTER, I-25 at Tramway Rd. NE. Tel. 821-5400.
★ The Sandia Pueblo Indians' crafts market is on their reservation, just beyond Albuquerque's northern city limits. The market sells turquoise and silver jewelry, pottery, baskets, *kachina* dolls, handwoven rugs, sand paintings, and other arts and crafts. Open Monday through Saturday from 9am to 5:30pm and Sunday from 11am to 5pm.

HOUSE OF THE SHALAKO, First Plaza Galeria no. 65. Tel. 242-4579.
Traditional and contemporary Southwest Indian art—including Pueblo pottery, Navajo rugs, fetishes, jewelry, sand paintings, baskets, *kachinas,* and miniatures—can be found here. Open Monday through Friday from 10am to 5:30pm and Saturday from 10am to 5pm.

MARIPOSA GALLERY, 113 Romero St. NW, Old Town. Tel. 842-9097.
Five rooms of contemporary crafts display everything from small-scale regional works to major national acquisitions. The collection includes fine jewelry, porcelain, furniture, rugs and tapestries, mixed-media works, photography, and an otherwise eclectic variety of pieces.

NIZHONI MOSES LTD., 326 San Felipe St. NW, Old Town. Tel. 842-1808.
Fine Indian art is featured here, including Pueblo pottery, Navajo weavings and mud toys, and a variety of contemporary and antique jewelry. Open daily from 10am to 7pm, later in spring and summer.

TANNER CHANEY GALLERY, 410 Romero St. NW, Old Town. Tel. 247-2242 or toll free 800/444-2242.
Contemporary and traditional Indian art, jewelry, weavings, sculpture, pottery, and baskets are displayed in this gallery, one of New Mexico's oldest. Lodged in a Civil War era adobe hacienda, it also has notable historic collections. Open Monday through Saturday from 10am to 6pm and Sunday from noon to 6pm.

WRIGHT'S COLLECTION, Park Square, 6600 Indian School Rd. NE. Tel. 883-6122.
★ This free private museum, first opened in 1907, carries fine handmade Indian arts and crafts, both contemporary and traditional. Open Monday through Friday from 10am to 6pm, Saturday 10am to 5pm.

FASHIONS

FASHION SQUARE, San Mateo and Lomas Blvds. NE.
Upscale boutique lovers congregate at this award-winning midtown shopping area. The various shops retail fashions, jewelry, gift items, home furnishings, and luggage. There's also a florist, a beauty salon, and restaurants. Most shops are open Monday through Saturday from 10am to 6pm; some remain open Monday and Friday until 8pm and Sunday from noon to 5pm. Extended holiday hours are in effect Thanksgiving through Christmas.
Shops include **Kistler Collister,** with retail men's and women's fashions, shoes,

accessories, furs, lingerie, cosmetics, and fragrances; **Ashlynn Fine Lines,** contemporary fashions and accessories; and **Santa Fe Pendleton,** with men's and women's clothing, Indian trade blankets, sweaters, and accessories.

WESTERN WAREHOUSE, 6210 San Mateo Blvd. NE. Tel. 883-7161.
Family western wear, including an enormous collection of boots, is retailed here. Open Monday through Friday from 9:30am to 8pm, Saturday from 9:30am to 6pm, and Sunday from 11am to 5pm.

FOOD

THE CANDY LADY, 524 Romero St. NW, Old Town. Tel. 243-6239.
What a fun place to visit, even if you're not a chocoholic! Chocolate candies and cakes of all kinds are made on the premises, and there's a side room "for over 18 only" with more ribald chocolate delights. Open Monday through Saturday from 10am to 6pm and Sunday from 10am to 5pm. Opposite the intersection of Mountain Road and Rio Grande Boulevard NW.

CHILI PEPPER EMPORIUM, 328 San Felipe St. NW, Old Town. Tel. 242-7538.
Old Town's "Hot Spot" carries every imaginable chile product—from ground powder and dried pods to jam and jelly beans, red or green, hot or mild. They'll ship it home for you, too. And they're glad to share recipes.

MY SANTA FE CONNECTION, 517½ Central Ave. NW. Tel. 842-9564.
This mail-order company specializes in native New Mexican food and gift items, including decorated chile *ristras,* and ships them anywhere. Open Monday through Friday from 8:30am to 5pm.

FURNITURE

ERNEST THOMPSON SOUTHWESTERN FURNITURE, 2618 Coors Blvd. SW. Tel. 873-4652.
Original design, handmade southwestern furniture is exhibited in the factory showroom. Thompson is a fifth-generation furniture maker who still uses traditional production techniques. Open Monday through Friday from 8am to 5pm and Saturday from 10am to 4pm.

SCHELU INTERIORS GALLERY, 306 San Felipe St. NW, Old Town. Tel. 765-5869.
Featured are the American Southwest Home Collection—weavings, rugs, handcrafted pottery, stoneware, and designer sculpture for contemporary homes. Open Monday through Saturday from 10am to 6pm and Sunday from 11am to 6pm.

STRICTLY SOUTHWESTERN, 1321 Eubank Blvd. NE. Tel. 292-7337.
Solid oak southwestern-style furniture is manufactured and sold directly to the buyer. Lighting, art, pottery, and other interior items are available. Open Monday through Saturday from 9am to 5pm.

GIFTS/SOUVENIRS

CASA DE AVILA, 324 San Felipe St. NW, Old Town. Tel. 242-3753.
Southwest contemporary gifts, jewelry, and interior decor are retailed here. Open in summer weekdays from 9am to 9pm, weekends from 9am to 8pm; in winter weekdays from 10am to 7pm, weekends from 10am to 6pm.

ELAINE'S CANDLES & GIFTS, 1919 Old Town Rd. NW, Old Town. Tel. 242-2608.

Indian pottery, sand paintings, chimes, bells, southwestern prints, T-shirts, and other popular souvenirs are sold. Open Monday through Saturday from 10am to 5pm and Sunday from 11am to 5pm.

LA PIÑATA, 2 Patio Market NW, Old Town. Tel. 242-2400.
Pinatas and paper flowers are the specialty here; they can be custom ordered and shipped. Open in winter daily from 10am to 5pm; in summer daily from 9:30am to 8:30pm.

TREASURE HOUSE, 2012 S. Plaza NW, Old Town. Tel. 242-7204.
Decorative tiles, ironwood carvings, Navajo sand paintings, Indian and gemstone jewelry, and other interesting items are available. The shop has been open since the 1940s. Open daily.

JEWELRY

ESTEVAN'S CUSTOM JEWELRY, 2 Patio Market NW, Old Town. Tel. 247-4615.
Master goldsmith Estevan B. Garcia designs and handcrafts his own contemporary southwestern pieces. Open daily from 10am to 5pm (longer in summer).

FELIPE'S INDIAN JEWELRY, 2038 S. Plaza NW, Old Town. Tel. 242-4784.
Turquoise-and-silver jewelry isn't the only thing Felipe sells; he's also got a fine selection of gold and diamond jewelry. Open Monday through Saturday from 9am to 8pm and Sunday from 9am to 6:30pm.

GUS'S TRADING COMPANY, 2026 Central Ave. SW, Old Town. Tel. 843-6381.
Gus sells and repairs Hopi, Navajo, Zuni, and Santo Domingo Indian jewelry. He also carries *kachina* dolls, pottery, and original paintings by Indian artists. Open Monday through Saturday from 9am to 5:30pm and Sunday from 10am to 5pm.

JEWELER'S REPAIR SHOP, 6910 Central Ave. SE. Tel. 266-9057.
Besides repairs, this excellent shop opposite the State Fairgrounds sells diamonds, gold and silver jewelry, pottery, and *kachinas*. Open Monday through Friday from 9am to 5:30pm and Saturday from 9am to 3pm.

ORTEGA'S INDIAN ARTS AND CRAFTS, 726 Coronado Center NE. Tel. 881-1231.
An institution in Gallup, adjacent to the Navajo Indian Reservation, Ortega's now has this Albuquerque store. They emphasize sales, repairs, engravings, and appraisals of silver and turquoise jewelry. Open Monday through Friday from 10am to 9pm, Saturday from 10am to 6pm, and Sunday noon to 6pm.

THE SILVER BIRD, 3821 Menaul Blvd. NE, at Carlisle Blvd. Tel. 881-2780.
Visitors can make appointments to view the factory workshop, where Indians make jewelry and concho belts. Pottery, ceramics, paintings, mandalas, storytellers, sand paintings, and other crafts are also sold here. Open Monday through Friday from 8:30am to 6pm and Saturday from 9am to 5pm. A second location is at 2436 Menaul Blvd. NE.

SKIP MAISEL'S WHOLESALE INDIAN JEWELRY & CRAFTS, 510 Central Ave. SW, at 5th St. Tel. 242-6526.
The largest selection of native jewelry, along with other arts and crafts, can be found at this downtown outlet. Zuni, Hopi, Navajo, and Santo Domingo Pueblo jewelry is featured. Open Monday through Friday from 9am to 5:30pm and Saturday from 9am to 5pm.

MARKETS

FLEA MARKET, New Mexico State Fairgrounds.
Every Saturday and Sunday, year-round, the fairgrounds hosts this market from 8am to 5pm. There's no admission; just come and look around.

WINES

ANDERSON VALLEY VINEYARDS, 4920 Rio Grande Blvd. NW. Tel. 344-7266.

Patty Anderson, widow of world-famous balloonist Maxie Anderson, owns and operates this small winery, which has been producing award-winning vintages since 1976. There are complimentary tours. They also offer wine tastings, picnic facilities, and a gift shop. Open Tuesday through Saturday from noon to 5:30pm.

SANDIA SHADOWS VINEYARD AND WINERY, 11704 Coronado Ave. Tel. 298-8826.

A small winery at the western foot of Sandia Peak, not far from the tramway terminal, it offers a tasting room, gift shop, and picnic facilities beneath a grape arbor. A wine festival is included as part of the international balloon fiesta in October. Open Wednesday through Friday from noon to 5pm and Saturday from 10am to 5pm; closed national holidays. Reached via San Rafael Avenue, 0.6 mile west of Tramway Boulevard.

8. EVENING ENTERTAINMENT

Albuquerque has an active performing arts and nightlife scene, as befits a city of half a million people. The performing arts are naturally multicultural, with Hispanic and (to a lesser extent) Indian productions sharing time with Anglo works—they include theater, opera, symphony, and dance. In addition, many national touring companies appear in the city. Country music predominates in nightclubs, though aficionados of rock, jazz, and other forms of music can find them here as well.

Full information on all major cultural events can be obtained from the Albuquerque Convention and Visitors Bureau (tel. 243-3696, with a tape recording of local events after business hours). Current listings can be found in the two daily newspapers; detailed weekend arts calendars can be found in the Thursday evening *Tribune* and the Friday morning *Journal.* The weekly *Albuquerque Voice,* launched in September 1990, and the monthly *On the Scene* also carry entertainment listings.

Tickets for nearly all major entertainment and sporting events can be obtained from **TicketMaster,** 4004 Carlisle Blvd. NE (tel. 884-0999 for information, or 842-5387 to place credit-card orders on American Express, MasterCard, or VISA). This computerized ticket service is located in Smith's Food & Drug Stores, with 10 outlets in the greater Albuquerque area, and at box offices of the New Mexico Symphony Orchestra, the Albuquerque Civic Light Opera Association, and Popejoy Hall on the University of New Mexico campus.

Discount tickets are often available for midweek and matinee performances. Check with specific theaters or concert halls.

Don't miss the free entertainment May to August on Civic Plaza, at Third and Marquette streets NW. Musicians serenade outdoor diners during the Friday noon hour, while ethnic performers take to the plaza every Saturday evening, from 5 to 10pm, as part of Summerfest.

THE PERFORMING ARTS

MAJOR PERFORMING ARTS COMPANIES

Classical Music & Opera

NEW MEXICO SYMPHONY ORCHESTRA, 220 Gold Ave. SW (P.O. 769), Albuquerque, NM 87103. Tel. 843-7657 for information, 842-8565 or 800/251-6676 for tickets.

★ NMSO musicians may be the busiest performing artists in New Mexico. As the orchestra enters its 61st season in 1992–93, and its 16th as the official state symphony orchestra, it continues a hectic agenda with approximately 60 performances of classics, pops, and chamber concerts scheduled in a September to May season.

Nine pairs of classics and six pops concerts are presented at Popejoy Hall. A chamber series is heard on six Sunday afternoons at the Sunshine Music Hall, 120 Central Ave. SW. The NMSO emphasizes touring; another 10 dates are set in cities throughout the state.

Prices: Popejoy Hall concerts, adults $15–$25.50, students $12–$21, $5 Hot Tix (available 15 minutes prior to Popejoy Hall concerts). Symphony in the Sunshine, adults $10, students and seniors $6.

CHAMBER ORCHESTRA OF ALBUQUERQUE, 2730 San Pedro Dr. NE, Suite H-23. Tel. 881-0844.

The 31-member professional orchestra, conducted by music director David Oberg, performs an October to June season primarily at St. John's United Methodist Church, 2626 Arizona St. NE. The concerts include a subscription series of six classical concerts (in October, November, January, March, May, and June); an all-baroque concert in February; concerts for children in February and April; a joint concert with the University of New Mexico Chorus; and outreach programs for seniors in December. The orchestra regularly features guest artists of national and international renown.

Prices: $8–$20 depending on seating and performance.

ALBUQUERQUE CIVIC LIGHT OPERA ASSOCIATION, 4201 Ellison Rd. NE. Tel. 345-6577.

Five major Broadway musicals are presented each year at Popejoy Hall during a March to December season. Each production is staged for three consecutive weekends, including two Sunday matinees.

In 1992, its 25th season, ACLOA presented *Into the Woods, Grease, Once Upon a Mattress, Peter Pan,* and *The King and I.*

Prices: Adults $9–$17, students and seniors $7–$15.

OPERA SOUTHWEST IN ALBUQUERQUE, 809 Morningside Dr. NE. Tel. 243-0591.

Most years, this regional company, established in 1972, presents three European operas (with English lyrics) between October and May. Performances are at the KiMo Theatre on Saturday, Tuesday, and Friday evenings, followed by a Sunday matinee.

Prices: Adults $8–$25, student rush (day of performance) $3.

Theater Companies

NEW MEXICO REPERTORY THEATRE, 419 Central Ave. NW (P.O. Box 789, Albuquerque, NM 87103). Tel. 243-4577 for information, Box office, 228 Gold Ave. SW (tel. 243-4500).

★ The state's only resident professional theater company, the Rep is developing a solid reputation for its innovative productions of classical works and contemporary American and European plays. It splits its production schedule equally between Santa Fe and Albuquerque, where it performs at the KiMo Theatre. Six productions are staged each year in a mid-October to early May season.

The Rep does few premieres—although a few years ago it presented the world premiere of *Children of a Lesser God,* subsequently an Oscar-nominated Hollywood movie. A recent season included Shakespeare's *Othello* and Shaw's *Man and Superman,* acclaimed contemporary plays *Other People's Money* and *The Heidi Chronicles,* and two lesser known 20th-century plays. Each opens its run with two weeks in Santa Fe, and closes with two weeks in Albuquerque at the KiMo Theatre.

Prices: In Albuquerque, adults $8.50–$22, depending upon performance and seatings; students and seniors $5–$21.50. Military and group discounts also apply. See Santa Fe chapter for prices of performances there.

LA COMPAÑIA DE TEATRO DE ALBUQUERQUE, 518 1st St. NW. Tel. 242-7929.

One of only 10 major professional Hispanic companies in the United States and Puerto Rico presents four productions at the KiMo Theatre in October, December, April, and June. The company also does barrio tours and takes its productions to local community centers and churches. The semiprofessional company's mix of contemporary and classic comedies, dramas, and musicals includes one Spanish play a year; others in English or bilingual.

Prices: Thurs and Sun, adults $7, students and seniors $6; Fri–Sat, adults $8, students and seniors $7.

Dance Companies

THE NEW MEXICO BALLET COMPANY, 3620 Wyoming Blvd. NE Suite 105D. (P.O. Box 21518), Albuquerque, NM 87154. Tel. 299-7798.

Founded 1972, the state's oldest ballet company performs an October-to-April season at Popejoy Hall. It typically includes a fall production like *Legend of Sleepy Hollow,* a December performance of *The Nutcracker* or *A Christmas Carol,* and a contemporary spring production. Professional guest artists fill the leading roles in some productions, but most of the cast of 60 to 150 is local and amateur. The New Mexico Symphony Orchestra sometimes provides the music.

Prices: Adults $10–$20, students $5–$10.

MAJOR CONCERT HALLS & ALL-PURPOSE AUDITORIUMS

KELLER HALL, Cornell St. at Redondo Dr. S, University of New Mexico. Tel. 277-4402.

The fine arts department's main auditorium, with seating for 336, hosts numerous musical concerts throughout the year, including student recitals and concerts. It's best known for its two annual distinguished faculty and guest artist series, with seven chamber music and solo concerts each from August to December and from January to June.

Tickets: General admission $6; students $3, faculty, staff, and seniors $2.50.

KIMO THEATRE, 419 Central Ave. NW at 5th St. Tel. 848-1370 for information, 764-1700 for tickets (Mon–Fri 11am–5pm).

Albuquerque's historic showcase of the performing arts is a tribute to the region's Native American cultures. Opened in 1927, the KiMo's architecture is a colorful adaptation of the adobe pueblo and its interior decor emphasizes Native American motifs. Handmade tiles adorn the lobby; wall paintings simulate Navajo sand paintings; murals of the legendary "Seven Cities of Cíbola" stand outside the balcony seating area; even the design of the box office is based on a *kiva.* And then there's the remarkable lighting: White plaster buffalo heads with lights in their eye sockets adorn the mezzanine columns and outline the ceiling of the theater itself.

The 750-seat theater, owned by the city of Albuquerque, is the home of the New Mexico Repertory Theatre, Opera Southwest, and La Compañia de Teatro de Albuquerque. In addition, it hosts numerous dance, music, and theater groups. The KiMo and the city also sponsor a series of touring shows of national and international importance.

Prices: $5–$25 depending on seating and performance. Series tickets are available at a discount, and there are discounts for children.

POPEJOY HALL, Cornell St. at Redondo Dr. S, University of New Mexico. Tel. 277-3121.

A multipurpose performing arts facility, Popejoy Hall is Albuquerque's leading venue for major musical entertainment. Seating 2,094, it is the home of the New Mexico Symphony Orchestra, the Albuquerque Civic Light Opera Association, the New Mexico Ballet Company, and UNM's highly popular September to April

"Broadway" series, featuring major New York productions. For information on each of the local companies, see the descriptions above and below.

Adjacent Woodward Hall is the site of Albuquerque's **June Music Festival** (tel. 888-1842), a series of five concerts, featuring nationally and internationally known string quartets with guests artists from leading symphony orchestras, during the first two weeks following Memorial Day. The festival celebrated its 50th anniversary year in 1991. Season subscription tickets are $65 to $80; single tickets, $16 to $20 for adults, $10 for students.

Tickets: Broadway series, $20–$38 general admission (depending upon production), with discounts for students, faculty, staff, and seniors. For prices of other events, see descriptions of specific companies.

SOUTH BROADWAY CULTURAL CENTER, 1025 Broadway Blvd. SE. Tel. 848-1320.

Funded, like the KiMo Theatre, by the Cultural Affairs Division of the city of Albuquerque, SBCC presents a diversity of multicultural programming in the performing arts—from blues singers to avant-garde comedy, Mexican dance theater to medieval troubador melodies. The center, which seats 214, doubles as an art gallery (with exhibits changing monthly), a book and film-rental library, and a workshop center. Open Monday through Saturday from 8:30am to 5pm (with performances normally at 8pm), it's located west of I-25 and just east of the railroad tracks, near Bridge Boulevard.

Tickets: Adults $8, children 12 and under $5, for touring shows.

THEATERS

ALBUQUERQUE LITTLE THEATRE, 224 San Pasquale Ave. SW. Tel. 242-4750.

The 63-year-old amateur theater presents six plays annually during a September-to-May season. Each year, productions cover the gamut from classic to contemporary, comedy to mystery, drama to musical. The 1992–93 calendar included *On Golden Pond, Arsenic and Old Lace, Annie, Children of a Lesser God, The Importance of Being Earnest,* and *Rumors.*

The 570-seat Little Theatre Building, a masterpiece of Territorial architecture, was designed by noted regional architect John Gaw Meem and built in the 1930s with WPA funds. It's located just south of Old Town.

Prices: Adults $9–$11, seniors and students $7–$9.

RODEY THEATRE AND EXPERIMENTAL THEATRE, Fine Arts Center, University of New Mexico. Tel. 277-4332.

Major student dramatic productions and dance recitals, from classical ballet to modern jazz dance, hold forth at the 440-seat Rodey Theatre. The adjacent Experimental Theatre, which seats 75 to 150 (depending upon configuration), hosts a variety of unique productions, from one-acts to dance recitals.

Prices: General admission $8, faculty $6, students $4.50.

THE VORTEX THEATRE, 2204½ Central Ave. SE. Tel. 247-8600.

A 15-year-old community theater known for its innovative productions, the Vortex is Albuquerque's "Off Broadway," presenting plays ranging from classic to original scripts. The company mounts 10 to 12 shows a year, including (in 1992) works by Shakespeare and the classic *Trip to Bountiful.* The black-box theater seats 90.

Prices: Adults $7, students and seniors $6, children 13 and under $5. All tickets $5 Sun.

ALBUQUERQUE CHILDREN'S THEATRE, 4139 Prospect Ave. NE. Tel. 888-3644.

Playwright Bill Hayden established this troupe at his ballet school in the late

1950s, and it has grown to become one of the country's most unique children's theaters. Hayden's philosophy was to produce shows for children, by children, and to give those kids a nonstressful introduction to theater: just 90 minutes of rehearsal each week. When he died in 1989, after three decades of instruction, he left a legacy of original plays and adaptations of such classics as *Cinderella, Snow White,* and *Puss in Boots.* There are three companies: seniors (ages 12 to 16) do January and July shows at Popejoy Hall or Rodey Theatre at UNM. Juniors (ages 8 to 11) and play actors (ages 4 to 7) also do two shows a year, but theirs are at the Hayden School of Ballet.

Prices: $4 for public (senior) shows.

LOCAL CULTURAL ENTERTAINMENTS

Attracted in large part by its Hispanic heritage, there are several local **flamenco** troupes, and others of national renown often visit Albuquerque. Eva Encinias's **Ritmo Flamenco Dance Company** is among the outstanding local troupes.

The Rodey Theatre (see above) at the University of New Mexico hosts an annual **Flamenco Festival** in late June, with four performances in one long weekend. Tickets run $13 to $15 per show. Call 277-6122 for information.

THE CLUB & MUSIC SCENE

COMEDY CLUBS

LAFFS COMEDY CAFFE, 3100 Juan Tabo Blvd. at Candelaria Rd. NE. Tel. 296-JOKE.

Top acts from each coast, including comedians who have appeared on the Tonight Show, David Letterman, and HBO, also appear at Albuquerque's top comedy club. Show times are Tuesday through Thursday and Sunday at 8pm, with second shows Friday and Saturday at 10:30pm.

Tuesday is "Best of Albuquerque night." Wednesday is men's night; Thursday is ladies' night; and Sunday is Laff's T-shirt night. The Caffé serves dinner nightly from 6pm. Happy hour is from 6:30 to 7:30pm daily.

Admission: $7.

COUNTRY MUSIC

CARAVAN EAST, 7605 Central Ave. NE. Tel. 265-7877.

"Always a dance partner," boasts this large country-and-western club east of the State Fairgrounds. Two bands share stage time Monday through Saturday from 5pm to 2am and Sunday from 4:30pm to midnight; there are occasional national acts. Tuesday is ladies' night. Happy hour is from 4:30 to 7pm, and there's a free dinner buffet from 5 to 7pm.

Admission: Fri–Sat women $2, men $3; free other nights.

MIDNIGHT RODEO, 4901 McLeod Rd. NE, near San Mateo Blvd. Tel. 888-0100.

The Southwest's largest nightclub of any kind, Midnight Rodeo not only has bars in all corners of its enormous domicile; it even has its own shopping arcade, including a boutique and gift shop. A DJ spins records daily until closing; the hardwood dance floor is so big (5,000 square feet) it resembles an indoor horse track. Free dance lessons are offered Sunday from 5:30 to 7pm and Tuesday from 7 to 8pm. A busy kitchen serves simple but hearty meals to dancers who work up appetites, and there's a free buffet Monday to Friday from 5 to 7pm.

Admission: Fri–Sat women $2, men $3; free other nights.

SUNDANCE SALOON & DANCE HALL, 12000 Candelaria Rd. NE, near Tramway Blvd. Tel. 296-6761.

An atmospheric club with the feel of a 19th-century Wild West saloon, the Sundance features top country bands Monday through Saturday from 4pm to 2am and Sunday from 4pm to midnight. Happy hour starts at 4pm nightly, with cheap drinks and free pool. It's followed by free dance lessons (Monday to Thursday 7 to 8:30pm) on the 1,000-square-foot dance floor. The Sundance Sports Connection (Sports Bar) is adjacent to the saloon.
Admission: Fri–Sat women $2, men $3; free other nights.

ROCK

CONFETTI, 9800 Montgomery Blvd. NE. Tel. 298-2113.
Ensconced in a small shopping strip, this big hard-rock club features a sunken dance floor and pool tables for a young (20s) crowd. It's open Monday through Saturday from 6pm to 2am, with live music nightly.
Admission: $5.

SEÑOR BUCKETS, 4100 San Mateo Blvd. NE. Tel. 881-3110.
A very casual hangout for students and others in their early 20s, Señor Buckets features Top-40 and hard-rock bands—like local favorites Problem Child and Whiplash Bash—starting at 9:30pm nightly except Sunday. Bands also play for happy hour, Tuesday through Friday from 5 to 9pm. Sunday night is jam night (8pm to midnight). The club opens at 2pm during the week, 6pm weekend.
Admission: Free.

JAZZ, BLUES & FOLK

THE COOPERAGE, 7220 Lomas Blvd. NE. Tel. 255-1657.
Jazz, rhythm-and-blues, rock, and other sounds keep dancers hopping Friday and Saturday nights inside this gigantic wooden barrel. (See "Dining," above.)
Admission: $2.

DANCE CLUBS & DISCOS

AMERICAN ROCK CAFE, 5850 Eubank Blvd. NE. Tel. 296-5772.
This is a fun place to hang out: Not only does the DJ play dance music from the fifties through the nineties; weeknights are livened up by creative contests like scooter races (around the dance floor) and the waterski bunny bash (don't ask). There's a free buffet Saturday and Monday through Thursday 5 to 8pm, Friday 5 to 7pm, and a special late-night bar menu. Thursday is ladies' night. Open Monday through Saturday from 4pm to 2am.
Admission: $2 after 8pm.

BEYOND ORDINARY, 211 Gold Ave. SW. Tel. 764-8858.
Albuquerque's alternative rock hangout has live music, including reggae, and a DJ spinning progressive disks Friday and Saturday from 7pm to 1:30am and Sunday from 7pm to midnight. An art gallery exhibits equally alternative paintings. Happy hour is Wednesday through Friday from 4 to 8pm.
Admission: $4.

THE BAR SCENE

DOC & EDDY'S, 6040 Brentwood Lane NE, near Osuna and San Mateo Blvds. Tel. 884-2271.
Nineteen solid-oak billiard tables attract the biggest pool-playing clientele in the city. There are eight TV's operated by two satellite dishes so you can watch your favorite sporting events. The restaurant serves knockout burgers and salads.

LA POSADA DE ALBUQUERQUE, 125 2nd St. NW Tel. 242-9090.

There's music nightly in this popular piano bar in the hotel's atmospheric hacienda-style courtyard.

RICO'S SPORTS PAGE, 4214 Central Ave. SE. Tel. 255-5932.
Rico's 10-foot TV and satellite feed attract sports fans from all over the city.

MORE ENTERTAINMENT

Albuquerque's best nighttime attraction is the **Sandia Peak Tramway** (see "Attractions," above) and its two restaurants, **High Finance** at the summit and the **Firehouse** at the base (see "Dining," above). Both offer a view nonpareil of the Rio Grande valley and the city lights.

The best place to catch foreign films, art films, and limited-release productions is the **Guild Cinema** 3405 Central Ave. NE (tel. 255-1848). For film classics, check out the **UNM SUB Theater,** on the UNM campus, with double features Wednesday through Saturday, changing nightly.

Major Albuquerque first-run theaters include **Coronado Six Theater,** 6401 Uptown Blvd. NE (tel. 881-5266); **Del Norte Cinema Four,** 7120 Wyoming Blvd. NE (tel. 823-6666); **Four Hills 12 UA Cinema,** 13160 Central Ave. SE, at Tramway Blvd. (tel. 275-2114); **Ladera Six Cinema,** 3301 Coors Blvd. NW (tel. 836-5606); **Montgomery Plaza-5,** San Mateo Boulevard at 165 Montgomery Plaza NE (tel. 881-1080); **San Mateo Cinema 8,** 6311 San Mateo Blvd. NE (tel. 889-3051); **United Artists 8 at High Ridge,** Tramway Boulevard at Indian School Road (tel. 275-0038); and **Winrock 6 UA Cinema,** 201 Winrock Center NE (tel. 883-6022). The **Albuquerque 6 Drive-In Theatre,** Montgomery Boulevard NE and I-25 (tel. 345-8641), has six theaters, all showing double features beginning at 8pm.

The **Isleta Bingo Palace,** 11000 Broadway Blvd. SE (tel. 869-2614), is a luxurious, air-conditioned bingo parlor with a full-service restaurant, nonsmoking section, and free bus transportation on request. **Sandia Indian Bingo,** on the Sandia Reservation at Bernalillo (tel. 897-2173), also provides transportation.

The **Albuquerque International Folkdance Association** teaches dances every Saturday from 7 to 10:30pm at Carlisle Gym, UNM. Beginners are welcome; admission is $1.

9. EASY EXCURSIONS

PUEBLOS

Ten Indian pueblos are located within an hour's drive of central Albuquerque. Two of them, Acoma and Laguna, are discussed in Chapter 8, "Northwestern New Mexico." The others, from south to north, are discussed here along with Coronado and Jemez state monuments, which preserve ancient pueblo ruins.

In visiting pueblos, remember to respect them as people's homes. Don't peek into doors and windows, and don't climb on top of buildings. Stay out of cemeteries and ceremonial rooms, such as *kivas,* as these are sacred grounds. Do not speak during dances or ceremonies, nor applaud after its conclusion; silence is mandatory. Most pueblos require a permit to carry a camera or to sketch or paint on location. Many pueblos prohibit picture taking at any time.

ISLETA PUEBLO, P.O. Box 1270, Isleta, NM 87022. Tel. 869-3111.
Just 14 miles south of Albuquerque, off I-25 or U.S. 85, is the largest of the Tiwa-speaking pueblos, comprising several settlements on the west side of the Rio Grande. The largest village, Shiaw-iba, contains the Mission of San Agustin de Isleta, one of the few mission churches not destroyed in the 17th-century Pueblo rebellion.

Grasslands and wooded *bosque* along the river are gradually becoming part of Albuquerque's growing urban sprawl; already, some governmental agencies and commercial interests are leasing property from the Isleta. Most of the pueblo's 3,000 residents work in Albuquerque; others are employed in farming and ranching or private business.

Isleta women potters make red wares distinctive for their red-and-black designs on white backgrounds. The tribe operates a modern bingo hall at 11000 Broadway Blvd. SE (tel. 869-2614), and fishing and camping areas at Isleta Lakes. Permits ($2 to $7 daily) can be purchased at the recreation area.

The Isleta hold an evergreen dance in late February, and stage a Spanish fiesta with a carnival, food stands, and religious events on August 28. The big day of the year is the feast day honoring St. Augustine, September 4, when a midmorning mass and procession are followed by an afternoon harvest dance.

Admission: Free. Photography limited to church only.
Open: Daylight hours, seven days a week.

SANDIA PUEBLO, P.O. Box 6008, Bernalillo, NM 87004. Tel. 867-3317.

Established about 1300, this was one of the few pueblos visited by Coronado's contingent in 1540. Remains of that village, known as Nafiat, or "sandy," are still visible near the present church. The Sandia people temporarily fled to Hopi country after the Pueblo rebellion of 1680, but returned to the Rio Grande in 1742. Many of today's 300 Tiwa (Tanoan) speaking inhabitants work in Albuquerque or at Pueblo Enterprises. They also run the bingo hall (sessions Monday to Thursday 12:30 and 6:30pm) and the Bien Mur Indian Market Center on Tramway Road (tel. 821-5400). Both are about 14 miles north of Albuquerque off I-25.

The pueblo celebrates its St. Anthony feast day on June 13 with a midmorning mass, procession, and afternoon corn dance. Another dance honors newly elected governors in January.

Admission: Free. No photography, recording, or sketching allowed.
Open: Daylight hours.

CORONADO STATE MONUMENT, N.M. 44 (P.O. Box 95), Bernalillo, NM 87004. Tel. 867-5351.

When the Spanish explorer Coronado traveled through this region in 1540-41 while searching for the Seven Cities of Cíbola, he wintered at a village on the west bank of the Rio Grande—probably one located on the ruins of the ancient Anasazi pueblo known as Kuaua. Those excavated ruins have been preserved in this state monument. Hundreds of rooms can be seen, and a *kiva* has been restored so that visitors may descend a ladder into the enclosed space, once the site of sacred rites. Unique multicolored murals, depicting human and animal forms, were found on successive layers of wall plaster in this and other *kivas* here; some examples are displayed in the monument's small archaeological museum.

An adjacent state park has sheltered campsites, hot showers and RV hookups. The site is 20 miles north of Albuquerque, via I-25 to Bernalillo and N.M. 44 west.

Admission: Adults $2.10. Children 15 and under free.
Open: May 1–Sept 15 9am–6pm; Sept 16–Apr 30 8am–5pm; closed major holidays.

SANTA ANA PUEBLO, Star Route, Box 37, Bernalillo, NM 87004. Tel. 867-3301.

Though partially abandoned and closed to visitors except for ceremonial events, this pueblo on the lower Jemez River claims a population of about 550. Many "residents" who maintain family homes at the pueblo actually live nearer the stream's confluence with the Rio Grande, in a settlement known as Ranchos de Santa Ana near Bernalillo, where farming is more productive.

Pottery, wood carvings, ceremonial bands, red cloth belts, and unique wooden crosses with straw inlay are produced in the old village by a handful of craftspeople. Marketing is handled by the Ta-Ma-Myia Co-operative Association.

Guests are normally welcomed only on ceremonial days. Pueblo members perform the turtle and corn dances on New Year's Day; the eagle, elk, buffalo, and deer dances on January 6, Three Kings Day; the spring corn basket dance at Easter; various dances for St. Anthony's Day on June 29 and St. Anne's Day on July 26; and several days of dances at Christmastime.

The pueblo is about 30 miles north of Albuquerque, reached via I-25 to Bernalillo, then 8 miles northwest on N.M. 44.

Admission: Free. No photography is permitted.

Open: Daylight hours, certain ceremonial days only.

ZIA PUEBLO, San Ysidro, NM 87053. Tel. 867-3304.

This pueblo of 720 inhabitants blends in so perfectly with the soft tans of the stone and sand of the desertlike land around it, that it's very hard to see, like a chameleon on a tree trunk. The pueblo is best known for its famous sun symbol—now the official symbol of the state of New Mexico—adapted from a pottery design showing three rays going in each of the four directions from a sun, or circle. It is hailed in the pledge to the state flag as "a symbol of perfect friendship among united cultures."

Zia has a reputation for excellence in pottery making. The Zia pottery is identified by it's unglazed terra-cotta coloring and traditional geometric designs and plant and animal motifs painted on a white slip. Paintings, weaving, and sculptures are also prized products of the artists of the Zia community, and their work can be viewed and purchased at the Zia Cultural Center located at the pueblo. Our Lady of the Assumption, the patron saint, is given a celebratory corn dance on her day, August 15.

The pueblo is about eight miles northwest of the Santa Ana Pueblo, just off N.M. 44.

Admission: Free. No photography is permitted.

Open: Daylight hours.

JEMEZ PUEBLO, P.O. Box 78, Jemez, NM 87024. Tel. 834-7359.

The 2,400 Jemez natives—including descendants of families from the Pecos Pueblo, east of Santa Fe, abandoned in 1838—are the only remaining people to speak the Towa dialect of the Tanoan group. Famous for their excellent dancing, Jemez feast days attract Indians from other pueblos, turning the celebrations into Indian fairs. Two rectangular *kivas* are central points for groups of dancers. Try to attend the Feast of Our Lady of Angels on August 12; the Feast of San Diego on November 12, when the Pecos bull dance is performed; or the Feast of Our Lady of Guadalupe on December 12, featuring the Matachines dance, based on a Spanish morality play.

Woven belts, plaited yucca-fiber baskets, and cloth for garments are the primary crafts. A famous native potter who lives at Jemez Pueblo is Estella Loretto (tel. 834-7444), who has studied ceramics from Italy to Japan, the South Pacific to the Himalayas.

There is fishing and picnicking along the Jemez River on government forest lands, and camping at the Dragonfly Recreation Area. Pueblo stores sell fishing permits at $2 to $5 daily, and permits for game hunting may be bought from the pueblo governor's office.

The pueblo is 42 miles northwest of Albuquerque via I-25 to Bernalillo, N.M. 44 to San Ysidro, and N.M. 43 final miles.

Admission: Free. No photography is permitted.

Open: Daylight hours daily. (May be closed certain ceremonial days.)

JEMEZ STATE MONUMENT, N.M. 4, (P.O. Box 143) Jemez Springs, NM 87025. Tel. 829-3530.

All that's left of the Mission of San Jose de los Jemez, founded by Franciscan missionaries in 1621, is preserved at this site. Visitors find massive walls standing alone, its sparse, small door and window openings underscoring the need for security and permanence in those times. The mission was excavated between 1921 and 1937, along with portions of a prehistoric Jemez pueblo. The pueblo, near the Jemez Hot Springs, was called Giusewa—"place of the boiling waters."

A small museum at the site exhibits artifacts found during the excavation, describes traditional crafts and foods, and weaves a thread of history from Anasazi to the 21st century in a series of displays. An interpretive trail winds through the ruins. The monument is located about 18 miles north on N.M. 4 from N.M. 44.

Admission: $2.10 per person 16 and over, 15 and under free.

Open: May 1–Sept 15 9:30am–5:30pm, Sept 16–Apr 30 8:30am–4:30pm; closed major holidays.

SAN FELIPE PUEBLO, P.O. Box A, San Felipe, NM 87001. Tel. 867-3381.

A conservative pueblo of 2,400 people located on a mesa on the west bank of the Rio Grande, San Felipe is known for its beautiful ritual ceremonies. The plaza has been worn into the shape of a bowl by the feet of the dancers over the centuries.

In the biggest of these dances, hundreds of men, women, and children move through their rhythmic steps all day long in the spring corn dance on May 1, performed in honor of the pueblo's patron, St. Philip (San Felipe). The dancing is done to a great chorus of male singers intoning music that reaches back into prehistory and evokes strong emotions in participants and in visitors, too. Other ceremonial events here are a January 6 corn dance, a February 2 buffalo dance for Candelaria Day, and many dances over several days around Christmastime.

San Felipe is 30 miles northeast of Albuquerque via I-25 and an access road.

Admission: Free. Photography is not permitted.

Open: Daylight hours.

SANTO DOMINGO PUEBLO, P.O. Box 99, Santo Domingo, NM 87052. Tel. 465-2214.

One of New Mexico's largest pueblos with 3,450 residents, this farming community on the east bank of the Rio Grande is also one of the state's most traditional. Craftspeople make beautiful silver jewelry; unique necklaces of *heishi,* or shell fragments; innovative pottery; and fine weaving. They are renowned as astute traders and often will swap with visitors for the value of their crafts rather than selling them for cash.

The dramatic Santo Domingo Pueblo feast day, August 4, sees the corn dance performed as it is done nowhere else. It is a lavish production involving clowns, scores of singers and drummers, and 500 tireless and skilled dancers in imaginative traditional costumes. Other festive occasions during the year include Three Kings Day, January 6, with elk, eagle, buffalo, and deer dances; Candelaria Day, February 2, with the buffalo dance; the Easter spring corn dance and basket dance; the San Pedro's Day corn dance, June 29; and many traditional dances in the Christmas season.

Santo Domingo is 50 miles northeast of Albuquerque via I-25 north to N.M. 22.

Admission: Free. No photography or sketching is permitted.

Open: Daylight hours.

COCHITI PUEBLO, P.O. Box 70, Cochiti Pueblo, NM 87041. Tel. 465-2244.

Occupied continuously since the 14th century, the northernmost of the Keresan-speaking pueblos (pop. 920) stretches along the Rio Grande. Its Church of San Buenaventura, though rebuilt and remodeled since, still contains sections of its original 1628 structure.

Cochiti is well known for its pottery, especially the famous "storyteller" figures created by Helen Cordero. Beadwork and soft leather moccasins are other specialties. The pueblo's double-headed dance drums, made from hollowed-out cottonwood logs and covered with leather, are used in ceremonies throughout the Rio Grande area.

San Buenaventura Feast Day is July 14, when the corn dance and rain dance are performed. Other events include a New Year's Day turtle dance and corn dance; eagle, elk, buffalo, and deer dances on January 6, Three Kings Day; the spring corn dance and basket dance for Easter; more such dances on May 3, Santa Cruz Day; and ceremonies for several days around Christmas.

Fishing and bird hunting on pueblo grounds requires purchase of a permit from the pueblo governor for $2 to $7. Cochiti Lake is popular for water sports among Albuquerque citizens.

The pueblo is about 40 miles north of Albuquerque, via U.S. 85, then north on N.M. 22 and N.M. 16.
Admission: Free. No photography or sketching is permitted.
Open: Daylight hours daily.

THE TURQUOISE TRAIL

New Mexico Highway 14 begins 16 miles east of downtown Albuquerque, at I-40's Cedar Crest exit, and winds 46 miles to Santa Fe along the east side of the Sandia Mountains. Best known as the Turquoise Trail, this state-designated scenic and historic route traverses the revived "ghost towns" of Golden, Madrid, and Cerrillos, where gold, silver, coal, and turquoise were once mined in great quantities. Modern-day settlers, mostly artists and craftspeople, have brought a renewed frontier spirit to the old mining towns.

Before reaching the first of these towns, however, travelers can make a turn at **Sandia Park,** 6 miles north of the I-40 junction, to begin climbing 10,678-foot **Sandia Crest** on N.M. 536. The road is paved and well maintained and wide enough to accommodate tour buses, with no severe hairpin turns; and there is parking at the summit overlook. Sandia Crest is the high point of the Sandia Mountains and, like Sandia Peak, offers a spectacular panoramic view in all directions. Many miles of Cíbola National Forest trails, including the popular north-south Sandia Crest Trail, run through here; box lunches can be provided for day hikers by the **Sandia Crest House Restaurant & Gift Shop** (tel. 243-0605). The restaurant is open daily May to October from 10am to 9pm, 10am to one hour after sunset the rest of the year.

En route to the summit, on N.M. 536 in Sandia Park, is the **Tinkertown Museum** (tel. 281-5233), a miniature wood-carved western village with more than 10,000 objects on display, including 500 animations—among them a turn-of-the-century circus. There are also antique dolls and old-time music machines. It's April 1 to October 31 daily from 9am to 6pm. Admission is $2 for adults, 50¢ for children under 16.

If you turn north off N.M. 536 onto the unpaved N.M. 165, and proceed about 5 tortuous miles on the rough, narrow byway, you'll come to **Sandia Cave,** a short walk from the road. Artifacts identified as those of "Sandia Man," dating back to 23,000 B.C., were found in this cave. They are some of the oldest evidence of humankind ever discovered in the United States.

Golden is 10 miles north of the Sandia Park junction on N.M. 14. Its sagging houses with their missing boards, and the wind whistling through the broken eaves, make it a purist's ghost town. There is a general store open, though, as well as a bottle seller's "glass garden." Nearby are ruins of an Indian pueblo called Paako, abandoned around 1670. Such communities of mud huts were all the Spaniards ever found on their avid quests for the gold of Cíbola.

Madrid is 12 miles north of Golden. Madrid and neighboring Cerrillos were in a fabled turquoise-mining area dating back into prehistory. This semiprecious stone, known in the Old World since 4000 B.C., got its name from the French for "Turkish." In Mexico it was sacred to the Aztec royal house and was forbidden to commoners; it was believed to have an affinity to its owner, to grow pale in prophecy of a coming misfortune, or to glow richly with its wearer's good health. A visitor might still find a bit of raw turquoise in the tailings of an ancient pit mine. The Spanish worked these mines, using local Indian slave labor, until 1680, when a rockfall killed 30 of the miners. Their lack of concern was one of the final sparks contributing to the Pueblo revolt of that year.

Gold and silver mines followed, and when they faltered, there was still coal. The Turquoise Trail towns supplied fuel to locomotives of the Santa Fe Railroad until the 1950s, when the railroad converted to diesel fuel. Madrid (pronounced with the accent on the first syllable) used to produce 100,000 tons of coal a year.

In 1919, an idealistic mine owner named Huber transformed a gloomy scene into a showcase village with a new recreation center, hotel, hospital, school, church, post office, department store, drugstore, auto showroom, beauty shop, fire station, dental office, tennis and basketball courts, golf course, shooting range, a brass band, and a Christmas light show; early transcontinental planes used to detour over the town for a look. But the town emptied when the mine closed in 1956.

Twenty years later, the owner's son sold everything at auction: tipple, breaker, tavern, church, store, houses, roads—the lot. A handful of diehards, many of them artists and craftspeople, bought property and stayed on. Today the village seems stuck in the 1960s: Its funky, ramshackle houses have many counterculture residents, the "hippies" of yore, who operate several crafts stores and import shops.

The **Old Coal Mine Museum** (tel. 473-0743) is an on-site museum that features mining and railroad relics, including antique cars, tools, workshops, and a fully restored 1900 Baldwin Steam Locomotive—you can even climb aboard and ring the bell! The museum is open daily, weather permitting, and the admission price is $2.50 for adults.

Next door, the **Mine Shaft Tavern** continues its lively career with buffalo steaks on the menu and live music daily, attracting folks from Santa Fe and Albuquerque. It's adjoined by the **Madrid Opera House,** claimed to be the only such establishment on earth with a built-in steam locomotive on its stage. (The structure was an engine repair shed; the balcony is made of railroad track.)

Cerrillos, 3 miles north of Madrid, is a village of dirt roads that sprawls along Galisteo Creek. It appears to have changed very little since it was founded during a lead strike in 1879; the old hotel, the saloon, even the sheriff's office have a flavor very much like an Old West movie set.

Cerrillos once had eight daily newspapers, several hotels, and two dozen saloons, serving miners from 30 mines. Today only the Palace Hotel stands, in ruins, used as a stable for llamas that go on backcountry pack trips. The general store sells flea-market items, antiques, and some old turquoise. The Cerrillos Bar—part of the original Tiffany Saloon, founded by the New York jewelry family—has billiard tables in an ornate Victorian setting. And an old adobe house called Casa Grande shelters an unusual trading post.

I-25 at Santa Fe is 15 miles on.

SALINAS PUEBLO MISSIONS NATIONAL MONUMENT, P.O. Box 496, Mountainair, NM 87036. Tel. 847-2585.

The Spanish conquistador's Salinas Jurisdiction, on the east side of the Manzano Mountains (southeast of Albuquerque), was an important 17th-century trade center because of the salt extracted by the Indians from the salt lakes. Franciscan priests, utilizing Indian labor, constructed missions of adobe, sandstone, and limestone for the native converts. The ruins of some of the most durable—along with evidence of preexisting Anasazi and Mogollon cultures—are highlights of a visit to Salinas Pueblo Missions National Monument. The monument consists of three separate units: the ruins of Abo, Quarai, and Gran Quivira. They are centered around the quiet town of Mountainair, 75 miles southeast of Albuquerque at the junction of U.S. 60 and N.M. 55.

Abo (tel. 847-2400) boasts the 40-foot-high ruins of the Mission San Gregorio de Abo, a rare example of medieval architecture in the United States. Quarai (tel. 847-2290) preserves the largely intact remains of the Mission La Purisima Concepción de Cuarac (1630). Its vast size, 100 feet long and 40 feet high, contrasts with the modest size of the pueblo mounds. A small museum in the visitor center has a scale model of the original church, with a selection of artifacts found at the site. Gran Quivira (tel. 847-2770) once had a population of 1,500. Las Humanes has 300 rooms and 7 kivas. Rooms dating to 1300 can be seen. There are indications that an older village, dating to A.D. 800, may have previously stood here. Ruins of two churches (one almost 140 feet long) and a convent have been preserved. A museum with many artifacts from the site, a 40-minute movie showing the excavation of some 200 rooms, plus a short history video of Las Humanes are in the visitor center.

All three pueblos and the churches that rose above them are believed to have been abandoned in the 1670s. Self-guided tour pamphlets can be obtained at the units' respective visitor centers and at the Salinas Pueblo Missions National Monument Visitor Center in Mountainair, one block west of the intersection of U.S. 60 and N.M. 55 on U.S. 60. The visitor center offers an audiovisual presentation on the region's history, a bookstore, and an art exhibit.

Admission: Free.

Open: Sites, daily 9am–5pm. Visitor center in Mountainair, daily 8am–5pm. **Closed:** Christmas and New Year's Day. **Directions:** Abo is 9 miles west of Mountainair on U.S. 60. Quarai is 9 miles north of Mountainair on N.M. 55. Gran Quivira is 25 miles south of Mountainair on N.M. 55. All roads are paved.

SANTA FE

The New Mexico state capital is caught in a time warp between the 17th and 21st centuries, between traditional Indian and Hispanic cultures and the modern onslaught of tourism. The longest continuously occupied capital city in the United States, it has been under the rule of five governments: Spain (1610–80 and 1692–1821), the Pueblo Indians (1680–92), Mexico (1821–46), the United States (since 1846), and the Confederacy (for a short time in 1862).

Nestled at 7,000 feet in the pastel foothills of the Sangre de Cristo Mountains is this community of 60,000 people. Residents call it "The City Different."

A carefully considered plan to preserve and perpetuate pre-20th-century architecture has made downtown Santa Fe look like an adobe enclave. Much of the rest of the city has followed suit. For miles in all directions, flat-topped, earth-colored homes, many of them valued in the millions of dollars, speckle the hills amid sparse piñon and mesquite forests. Most of the construction is actually stuccoed concrete. A standing joke in Santa Fe art circles is that the city sanctions the use of 42 shades of brown.

But therein lies much of its charm. Santa Fe is nothing if not aesthetically pleasing and artistically involved. It has a famous art colony, larger (though not as historically rich, perhaps) than that of Taos; the world-renowned Santa Fe Opera and other acclaimed performing-arts companies; a highbrow literary segment; an active festival life; and more than its fair share of energetic, creative citizens in all pursuits.

Santa Fe has always been close to the earth. For its first two centuries and longer, it was a town of one- and two-story adobes. When the United States took over the territory from Mexico in 1846 and trade began flowing from the eastern states, new tools and materials began to change the face of the city. The old adobe took on brick facades and roof decoration in what became known as the Territorial style. But the flat roofs were retained so that the city never lost its unique, low profile, giving a serenity to be found in no other American city, and only in a few of the smaller towns of the Southwest, such as Taos.

Bishop Jean-Baptiste Lamy, the inspiration for the character of Bishop Latour in Willa Cather's *Death Comes for the Archbishop,* built the French Romanesque St. Francis Cathedral shortly after he was appointed to head the diocese in 1851. Other structures still standing include what is claimed to be the oldest house in the United States, built of adobe by Indians an alleged 800 years ago. The San Miguel Mission is the oldest mission church in the country, while the state capital, built in the circular form of a ceremonial Indian *kiva,* is among the newest in the United States.

The city was originally named La Villa Real de la Santa Fe de San Francisco de Asis (The Royal City of the Holy Faith of St. Francis of Assisi) by Spanish governor Don Pedro de Peralta, who founded it. Peralta built the Palace of the Governors as his capitol on the north side of the central Plaza, where it stands today as an excellent museum of the city's four centuries of history. It is one of the major attractions in the Southwest, and under its portico, Pueblo Indians sit cross-legged, hawking their crafts to eager tourists, as they have done for decades.

The Plaza is the focus of Santa Fe's mid-September fiesta, celebrated annually since 1770 to commemorate the reconquest of the city by Spanish governor Don Diego de Vargas in 1692, following the years of the Pueblo revolt. It was also the terminus of the Santa Fe Trail from Missouri, and of the earlier Camino Real (the Royal Road) up from Mexico, when the city thrived on the wool and fur of the Chihuahua trade.

1. ORIENTATION

Part of the charm of Santa Fe is that it's so easy to get around in. Like most cities of Hispanic origin, it was built around a parklike central plaza, with its centuries-old adobe buildings and churches lining the narrow streets. Many of them now house shops, restaurants, art galleries, and museums.

Santa Fe sits high and dry at the foot of the Sangre de Cristo range. Santa Fe Baldy rises to more than 12,600 feet a mere 12 miles northeast of the Plaza. The city's downtown straddles the Santa Fe River, a tiny tributary of the Rio Grande that is little more than a trickle for much of the year. North is the Espanola valley (a beautiful view of which is afforded from the Santa Fe Opera grounds) and beyond that, the village of Taos, 66 miles distant. South are ancient Indian turquoise mines in the Cerrillos Hills; southwest is metropolitan Albuquerque, 58 miles away. To the west, across the Caja del Rio Plateau, is the Rio Grande, and beyond that, the 11,000-foot Jemez Mountains and Valle Grande, an ancient and massive volcanic caldera. Indian pueblos dot the entire Rio Grande valley an hour's drive in any direction.

ARRIVING

BY PLANE The **Santa Fe County Municipal Airport** (tel. 473-7243), just outside the southwest city limits on Airport Road off Cerrillos Road, is primarily used by private planes. Commercial service is offered by **Mesa Airlines** (tel. 473-4118 or toll free 800/MESA AIR), which shuttles up to seven times a day between Albuquerque and Santa Fe and has direct flights to Taos and Denver. The nine-passenger Cessna Caravans have a 25-minute flying time to Albuquerque International Airport, with interline connections with all major carriers. Charter services include **Capital Aviation** (tel. 471-2525) and **Santa Fe Aviation** (tel. 471-6533).

Typically, air travelers to Santa Fe arrive in Albuquerque and either rent a car there or take the **Shuttlejack** bus (tel. 982-4311 in Santa Fe, 243-3244 in Albuquerque, or toll free 800/452-2665 outside New Mexico). This express service travels direct from the Albuquerque airport to central Santa Fe hotels and back. The fare is $20, payable to the driver, and there's service every 2½ hours or so between 5am and 10:15pm. **Greyhound Lines, Inc.** (tel. 471-0008) also runs two round-trips daily between the Albuquerque airport and the Santa Fe bus station at 858 St. Michael's Dr. **Faust's Transportation** (tel. 758-3410) shuttles between Albuquerque and Taos with a stop in Santa Fe each direction.

BY TRAIN **Amtrak** (tel. 842-9650 or toll free 800/872-7245) runs the *Southwest Chief* between Los Angeles and Chicago, making a stop at the frontier village of Lamy, 14 miles southeast of Santa Fe. (Lamy ticket office phone: 988-4511). There is one arrival and one departure in each direction daily, each arriving about 2:45pm. A shuttle van leaves for Santa Fe at 3:30pm, for a charge of $10.

BY BUS **Greyhound Lines, Inc.** and **TNM&O Coaches** (tel. 471-0008 or toll free 800/528-0447) offer regular daily service between Santa Fe and Albuquerque, Taos, Denver, Phoenix, Dallas, and points around the state and the country. The

Santa Fe bus station is at 858 St. Michael's Dr.; fare to or from Albuquerque runs around $12. Because the bus station is several miles south of the city center, travelers often need a taxi to get to their hotels. It may be more convenient to pay a few extra dollars for an airport-to-hotel shuttle.

BY CAR I-25 skims past Santa Fe's southern city limits, connecting it north and south with points from Billings, Montana, to El Paso, Texas. I-40, the state's major east-west thoroughfare that bisects Albuquerque, affords coast-to-coast access to "The City Different." (From the west, motorists leave I-40 in Albuquerque and take I-25 north; from the east, travelers exit I-40 at Clines Corners, an hour's drive east of Albuquerque, and continue 52 miles to Santa Fe via U.S. 285.) For travelers coming from the northwest, the most direct route is via Durango, Colorado, entering Santa Fe on U.S. 84.

TOURIST INFORMATION

The **Santa Fe Convention and Visitors Bureau** is located at 201 W. Marcy St., in Sweeney Center at the corner of Grant Street downtown (P.O. Box 909), Santa Fe, NM 87504 (tel. 505/984-6760 or toll free 800/777-CITY). The **New Mexico Department of Tourism** is in the Lamy Building, 491 Old Santa Fe Trail (tel. toll free 800/545-2040). The **Santa Fe Chamber of Commerce** is at 333 Montezuma St. (tel. 505/983-7317).

CITY LAYOUT

The limits of downtown Santa Fe are demarcated on three sides by the horseshoe-shaped **Paseo de Peralta,** and on the west by **St. Francis Drive,** otherwise known as U.S. 84/285. **Alameda Street** follows the north shore of the Santa Fe River through downtown, with the State Capitol and other federal buildings on the south side of the stream, and most buildings of historic and tourist interest on the north, east of Guadalupe Street.

The **Plaza** is Santa Fe's universally accepted point of orientation. Its four diagonal walkways meet at a central fountain, around which a strange and wonderful assortment of people, of all ages, nationalities, and life-styles, can be found at nearly any hour of the day or night.

If you stand in the center of the Plaza looking north, you're gazing directly at the Palace of the Governors. In front of you is Palace Avenue; behind you, San Francisco Street. To your left is Lincoln Avenue and to your right **Washington Avenue,** which divides downtown avenues into "East" and "West." St. Francis Cathedral is the massive Romanesque structure a block east, down San Francisco Street. Alameda Street is two blocks behind you.

Streaking diagonally to the southwest from the downtown area, beginning opposite the state office buildings on Galisteo Avenue, is **Cerrillos Road.** Once the main north-south highway connecting New Mexico's state capital with its largest city, it is now a 6-mile-long motel and fast-food "strip." St. Francis Drive, which crosses Cerrillos Road three blocks south of Guadalupe Street, is a far less pretentious byway, linking Santa Fe with I-25 four miles southeast of downtown. The **Old Pecos Trail,** on the east side of the city, also joins downtown and the freeway. **St. Michael's Drive** interconnects the three arterials.

Free city and state maps are easily obtained at tourist information offices. Members of the **American Automobile Association,** 1511 Fifth St. (tel. 982-4633), can get maps at no cost from the AAA office.

2. GETTING AROUND

BY TAXI It's best to telephone for a cab, for they are difficult to flag from the street. Taxis have no meters; fares are set for given distances. Expect to pay an average of about $2.50 per mile—unless you get coupons at the public library downtown for a 50% discount. **Capital City Cab** (tel. 982-9990) is the main company in Santa Fe.

BY CAR   Cars may be rented from any of the following firms in Santa Fe: **Adopt-a-Car,** 3570 Cerrillos Rd. (tel. 473-3189); **Agency,** 3157 Cerrillos Rd. (tel. 473-2983); **Avis,** Garrett's Desert Inn, 311 Old Santa Fe Trail (tel. 982-4361); **Budget,** 1946 Cerrillos Rd. (tel. 984-8028); **Capitol Ford,** 4490 Cerrillos Rd. (tel. 473-3673); **Enterprise,** 1911 Fifth St. (tel. 473-3600); **Hertz,** 100 Sandoval St. (tel. 471-7189); **Snappy,** 3012 Cielo Court (tel. 473-2277); and **Thrifty,** 1718 Cerrillos Rd. (tel. 984-1961).

If you're having car trouble, many garages, including import specialists, are listed in the telephone directory. For **AAA Towing Service,** call 471-6620.

Street parking is difficult to find during the summer months. There is a parking lot near the Federal Courthouse, two blocks north of the Plaza; another one behind Santa Fe Village, a block south of the Plaza; and a third at Water and Sandoval streets.

BY BICYCLE   A bicycle is a perfect way to get around town. Check with **First Powder** (tel. 982-0495) or **Schwinn** (tel. 983-4473) about rentals.

FAST FACTS: SANTA FE

American Express   There is no representative in Santa Fe. To report lost cards, call toll free 800/528-4800. To report lost traveler's checks, dial toll free 800/221-7282.

Area Code   505.

Babysitters   Most hotels can arrange on request. Alternatively, call the **Santa Fe Kid Connection,** 1015 Valerie Circle (tel. 471-3100).

Business Hours   In general, Monday to Friday 9am to 5pm, with many stores also open Saturday and Sunday in the summer season. Most banks are open Monday to Thursday 9am to 3pm and Friday 9am to 6pm.

Currency Exchange   Four banks in Santa Fe will exchange foreign currency. **SunWest Bank,** 1234 St. Michael's Dr. (tel. 471-1234) offers same-day sales of 20 different currencies. **First Interstate Bank,** 150 Washington Ave. (tel. 982-3671), **First National Bank of Santa Fe,** Plaza (tel. 984-7500), and the **Bank of Santa Fe,** 241 Washington Ave. (tel. 984-0509), as well as SunWest, will buy currencies—but this usually takes two to three days.

Dentist   Most work in the medical office area several miles south of downtown. Among those near downtown, **Dr. Leslie E. La Kind,** 623 Don Gaspar Ave. (tel. 988-3500), offers 24-hour emergency service.

Doctor   The **Lovelace Alameda** clinic, 901 W. Alameda St. (tel. 986-3666 for urgent care, 986-3600 for family care) is in the Solano Center near St. Francis Drive. It's open every day of the year 8am to 8pm for urgent care, with no appointments required.

Drugstores   Three-quarters of a block north of the Plaza is the **Santa Fe Drug Co.,** 125 Lincoln Ave, Suite 115 (tel. 984-8202), open Monday to Friday 8am to 6pm and Saturday 9am to 5pm. Emergency and delivery service can be arranged with the **Medical Center Pharmacy** (tel. 983-4359), adjacent to St. Vincent Hospital at 465 St. Michael's Dr.

Emergencies   For police, fire or ambulance emergency, dial 911. For fast advice on any kind of difficulty, call the **Crisis Intervention Center** at 982-2255.

Eyeglasses   Quintana Optical Dispensary, 109 E. Marcy St. (tel. 988-4234), offers 1-hour prescription service Monday to Friday 9am to 5pm and Saturday 9am to noon.

Hairdressers & Barbers   You can get your hair cut in the Inn at Loretto, the La Fonda Hotel, or numerous other locations throughout the city. Santa Fe's **Supercuts** franchise is at 1936 Cerrillos Rd. (tel. 988-7559).

Hospitals   The **St. Vincent Hospital,** 455 St. Michael's Dr. (tel. 983-3361), is a 268-bed regional health center. Patient services include urgent and emergency-room care, ambulatory surgery, diagnostic radiology, cancer diagnosis and treatment, behavioral sciences, and a family recovery center for adolescent substance abuse.

Hot lines   Crisis Intervention, 982-2255. **Battered Families,** 473-5200. **Poison Control,** toll free 800/432-6866. **Psychiatric Emergencies,** 983-3361. **Sexual Assault,** 473-7818. **Teen Suicide,** 989-5242. **Emergency Lodging,** 988-4252 after 4pm daily.

Information   The **Santa Fe Council on International Relations,** P.O. Box 1223, Santa Fe, NM 87504 (tel. 982-4931), assists foreign visitors by providing home hospitality, professional and academic introductions, and a language bank. An office in Room 145 of La Fonda Hotel on the Plaza is open Monday to Friday 9am to noon.

Laundry & Dry Cleaning   Just outside the downtown perimeter is **Shockey's Coin-op Laundry,** 755 Cerrillos Rd. (tel. 983-9881), open daily 6am to 10pm. You can drop off laundry ($5 a load) at **Adobe Econ-O-Wash,** 411 W. Water St. (tel. 982-9063). **One Hour Martinizing,** in five locations including 200 E. Water St. (tel. 982-8606), handles dry cleaning Monday to Saturday 7am to 6pm.

Libraries   The **Santa Fe Public Library** is a block from the Plaza at 145 Washington Ave. (tel. 984-6780). There are branch libraries at Villa Linda Mall and at 1713 Llano St., just off St. Michael's Drive.

Lost Property   Contact city police at 473-5000.

Newspapers & Magazines   The *New Mexican,* a Gannett property, is Santa Fe's daily newspaper. Offices are at 202 E. Marcy St. (tel. 983-3303). The weekly *Santa Fe Reporter,* published on Wednesdays, is often more willing to be controversial; its entertainment listings are excellent. Regional magazines published locally are *New Mexico Magazine* (monthly, statewide interest), the *Santa Fean Magazine* (monthly, local interest), *Santa Fe Lifestyle* (quarterly, local interest), and *Southwest Profile* (eight times a year, regional art).

Photographic Needs   Everything from film purchases to camera repairs to 1-hour processing can be handled by the **Camera Shop,** 109 E. San Francisco St. (tel. 983-6591). **Camera & Darkroom,** 216 Galisteo St. (tel. 983-2948) also processes film.

Police   In case of emergency, dial 911. All other inquiries should be directed to the main **Santa Fe Police Station,** 2515 Camino Entrada (tel. 473-5000 or 473-5080 after 5pm and weekends). The **Santa Fe County Sheriff's Office** is in the county courthouse, Grant Avenue and Johnson Street (tel. 984-5060). The **New Mexico State Police** search-and-rescue line is 827-9300.

Postal Services   The Main Post Office (988-6351) is at 120 South Federal Place, two blocks north and a block west of the Plaza. The branch Coronado Station is at 541 W. Cordova Rd. (tel. 438-8452). Most of the major hotels have stamp machines and mailboxes with twice-daily pickup. The **ZIP code** for central Santa Fe is 87501.

Radio   Santa Fe's radio stations include KMIK-AM 810 (all-news CBS affiliate), KTRC-AM 1400 (nostalgia music and early radio dramas), KSFR-FM 90.7 (classical), KNYN-FM 95.5 (country), KBAC-FM 98.1 (adult contemporary), KLSK-FM 104.1 (adult alternative), and KBOM-FM (Spanish). Albuquerque stations are easily heard from Santa Fe.

Religious Services   Roman Catholics are the highest-profile group in Santa Fe, with eight churches and the venerable **St. Francis Cathedral.** Visitors may attend services at the Franciscan cathedral, 131 Cathedral Place, one block east of the Plaza (tel. 982-5619).

Other denominations active in Santa Fe include Anglican, Assembly of God, Baptist, Charismatic, Christian and Missionary Alliance, Christian Science, Church of Christ, Church of God, Disciples of Christ, Episcopal, Foursquare Gospel, Friends, Jehovah's Witnesses, Lutheran, Methodist, Mormon, Nazarene, Seventh-day Adventist, and United Church of Christ. There is also a Jewish synagogue. The **Galisteo News & Ticket Center,** 201 Galisteo St. (tel. 984-1316), is a good clearing house of information on metaphysical pursuits.

Shoe Repairs   Most convenient to downtown Santa Fe is the **Jacobs Shoe Repair Shop,** 646 Old Santa Fe Trail (tel. 982-9774).

Taxes   A city lodging tax of 3.875% is added onto all lodging bills, over and above the state gross receipts tax of 6%.

Telegrams, Telex & Fax   Telegrams can be sent through **Western Union,** 519 Airport Rd. (tel. 438-3141). Numerous agencies, including most hotels, will send and receive faxes, among them **Kinko's Copies,** 333 Montezuma Ave. (tel. 982-6311).

Television   Two local independent television stations are KKTO-TV (Channel 2) and KCHF-TV (Channel 11), the latter offering Christian programming. The three Albuquerque network affiliates—KOB-TV (Channel 4, NBC), KOAT-TV (Channel 7, ABC) and KGGM-TV (Channel 13, CBS)—all have offices at the state Capitol.

Useful Telephone Numbers   Information on road conditions in the Santa Fe area can be obtained from the state police (tel. 827-9300). For time and temperature, call 473-2211.

Weather   For weather forecasts, call 988-5151.

3. ACCOMMODATIONS

Although Santa Fe has over 50 hotels, motels, bed-and-breakfast establishments, and other accommodations, rooms can still be hard to come by at the peak of the tourist season. You can get year-round assistance from **Santa Fe Central Reservations,** 1210 Luisa St, Suite 10 (tel. 505/983-8200 or toll free 800/982-7669). The service will also book transportation and activities. **Emergency Lodging Assistance**—especially helpful around Fiesta time in September—is available free after 4pm daily at 988-4252.

Accommodations are often booked solid through the summer months, and most establishments raise their prices accordingly. Rates are usually increased further for Indian Market, the third weekend of August. But there's little agreement on the dates marking the beginning and end of the tourist season; whereas one hotel may not raise its rates until July 1 and may drop them again in mid-September, another may have higher rates from May to November. Some hotels recognize a shoulder season or increase rates again over the Christmas holidays. It pays to shop around during these "in-between" seasons of May-June and September-October.

In any season, senior, group, corporate, and other special rates are often available. If you have any questions about your eligibility for these rates, be sure to ask.

In these listings, the following categories define midsummer price ranges: **very expensive,** most rooms over $150 per night double; **expensive,** $110 to $150; **moderate,** $75 to $110; **inexpensive,** $45 to $75; **budget,** less than $45 per night double. Remember that an additional 9.875% tax is imposed on every hotel bill.

DOWNTOWN

Everything within the horseshoe-shaped Paseo de Peralta, and east a few blocks on either side of the Santa Fe River, is considered downtown Santa Fe. None of these accommodations is beyond walking distance from the Plaza.

VERY EXPENSIVE

ELDORADO HOTEL, 309 W. San Francisco St., Santa Fe, NM 87501. Tel. 505/988-4455 or toll free 800/955-4455. Fax 505/982-0713. 200 rms, 18 suites. A/C MINIBAR TV TEL

$ Rates: July–Aug and major holidays $195 single, $215 double, $265–$675 suite; Mar–June and Sept–Oct $165 single, $185 double, $215–$500 suite; Nov–Feb excluding holidays $115 single, $135 double, $195–$500 suite. AE, DC, DISC, MC, V. **Parking:** Free for guests.

In 16th- and 17th-century Spanish folklore, Eldorado was a fabled city of gold. This hotel carries on the image of luxury. With five-story pueblo architecture built around a lovely courtyard two blocks west of the Plaza, the Eldorado boasts a southwestern interior with an art collection appraised at more than $500,000, including antique furniture, Native American pottery, carved animals, and other works mainly by Santa Fe artists.

The guest rooms continue the regional theme. Many of them have traditional *kiva* fireplaces, handmade furniture, and decks or terraces. The upper rooms in particular afford outstanding views of the surrounding mountains. Each room—tastefully appointed in shades of lilac and red—has one king-size bed or two double beds, easy chairs, a double closet, a remote-control TV in an armoire, and a minirefrigerator with an honor bar.

Dining/Entertainment: The innovative and elegant Old House restaurant was built on the preserved foundation of a Santa Fe house that was originally built in the early 1800's. It's *vigas* and *latilla* ceiling, polished wood floor, pottery and kachinas in niches give it a distinct regional touch that carries over to its preparation of creative continental cuisine. Open for dinner from 6pm Tuesday through Sunday, its main courses are in the $14 to $21 price range. The Old House Tavern is open from 6 to 11pm Tuesday through Sunday. More casual meals are served in the spacious Eldorado court, open for breakfast 7am to 11am and lunch 11:30am to 2pm. Dinner is served from 5:30pm to 9:30pm Monday through Saturday, and Sunday brunch is offered from 11:30am to 2pm. Dinner prices range from $6 to $16 for anything from cheese enchiladas to seared filet of salmon. The lobby lounge has low-key entertainment Monday through Saturday evenings.

Services: Room service, concierge, valet, laundry, twice-daily maid service, and safe-deposit boxes.

Facilities: Rooms for nonsmokers and the handicapped, pets are welcome, heated rooftop swimming pool and Jacuzzi, his-and-hers saunas, professional masseuse; free membership in Santa Fe Spa; shopping arcade with Southwest artifacts, jewelry, gifts, news, and a real estate showcase.

HILTON OF SANTA FE, 100 Sandoval St. (P.O. Box 25104), Santa Fe, NM 87504-2387. Tel. 505/988-2811 or toll free 800/336-3676 or 800/ HILTONS. Fax 505/988-1730. 155 rms, 5 suites. A/C MINIBAR TV TEL
$ Rates: (based on single or double occupancy) Jan 1–May 6 $90–$160. May 7–June 24 and Sept 8–Oct 25, $110–$205. June 25–Sept 7 $165–$260. Oct 25–Dec 31 $90–$235. Extra person $20. AE, CB, DC, DISC, MC, V. **Parking:** Free for guests.

With its city-landmark bell tower, the Hilton covers a full city block two blocks west of the Plaza, between Sandoval, San Francisco, Guadalupe, and Alameda streets. It's built around a central pool and patio area. There's cozy lobby seating around a traditional fireplace, flanked on one side by a cactus, on the other by a folk-art sculpture of a howling coyote.

The units are clean and spacious, furnished with king-size, queen-size, or double beds. Each room—with forest-green carpets and drapes, pastel-patterned bedspreads, and potted plants—has a deck or balcony, couch or two easy chairs and a table, four-drawer credenza, in-room movies, modern-art prints, and a mirror on the walls. There are two sinks, one inside the bathroom, one outside at a dressing table; and every room has a coffee pot.

Dining/Entertainment: Two restaurants occupy the premises of the early 18th-century Casa de Ortiz, which has been incorporated into the hotel. In the Piñon Grill, with its intimate candlelight service from 5 to 11pm daily, you can't miss the

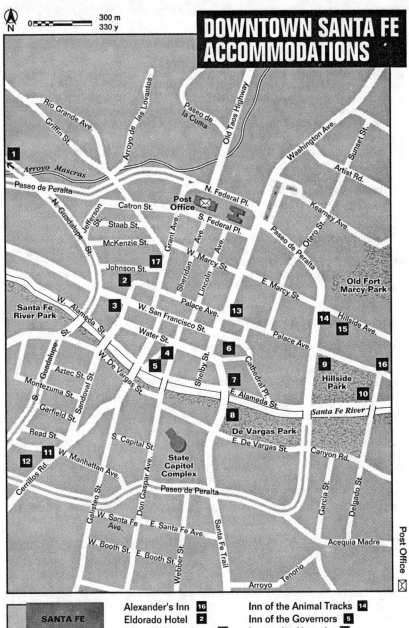

DOWNTOWN SANTA FE ACCOMMODATIONS

N

0   300 m
     330 y

Post Office ⊠

SANTA FE

Downtown

Alexander's Inn	**16**	
Eldorado Hotel	**2**	
Garrett's Desert Inn	**8**	
Grant Corner Inn	**17**	
Hilton of Santa Fe	**3**	
Hotel Santa Fe	**12**	
Hotel St. Francis	**4**	
The Inn at Loretto	**7**	
Inn of the Anasazi	**13**	

Inn of the Animal Tracks	**14**	
Inn of the Governors	**5**	
Inn on the Alameda	**10**	
La Fonda	**6**	
La Posada de Santa Fe	**9**	
Picacho Plaza Hotel	**1**	
Preston House	**15**	
Santa Fe Motel	**11**	

ancient beams and pillars of the main house construction. All main courses are prepared on the piñon-and-mesquite grill, including quail (with roasted peppers), chile-marinated lamb, and Rocky Mountain trout; dinner prices range from $14.95 to $19.95. The Chamisa Courtyard serves breakfast and lunch daily from 6:30am to 2pm; featuring casual garden-style tables amid lush greenery under a large skylight, it is built on the home's enclosed patio.

Services: Room service, concierge, courtesy car, valet laundry.
Facilities: Outdoor swimming pool, Jacuzzi, gift shop, car-rental agency. Rooms for nonsmokers and the disabled.

INN OF THE ANASAZI, 113 Washington Ave., Santa Fe, NM 87501. Tel. 505/988-3030 or toll free 800/688-8100. Fax 505/988-3277. 59 rms, all with bath. A/C MINIBAR TV TEL
$ Rates: Jan–Feb $150–$200 single, $170–$225 double, $275–$305 suite; Mar–Apr and Nov–Dec excluding Thanksgiving Day and Christmas $185–$230 single, $195–$250 double, $325–$360 suite. AE, DC, MC, V. **Parking:** $7 per night.

The Inn of the Anasazi, located near the Palace of the Governors, can definitely be described as a luxury hostelry. It is named in a celebration of the "enduring and creative spirit" of the Native American Indians known as the Anasazi. It opened in July of 1991, and is one of the projects of Robert Zimmer, who is well-known for his exciting concepts in hotels like the Inn of the Anasazi, which is "committed to ecological and environmental awareness, the interconnectedness and diversity of all people, land, heritage and sentient beings, and makes every effort to operate in a sound and conscious manner." Basically, the inn seeks to teach by example. Every piece of paper used in the inn is recycled; the fireplaces are gas, rather than wood burning; the linens, soaps, and shampoos are all natural, and the food in the restaurant is chemical free and organic.

None of this is to say that the hotel skimps on amenities—there are TVs, VCRs, and stereos in all the rooms, as well as minibars, private safes, coffee makers, telephones in the bathrooms, and walk-in closets. The artwork is original, and there is a living room with a fireplace, as well as a library where you can sit and relax before dinner.

Dining/Entertainment: The Inn of the Anasazi restaurant serves breakfast, lunch, and dinner every day, and it features Native American and northern New Mexican food (see "Santa Fe Dining," below).
Services: Room service, twice-daily maid service, complimentary newspaper, tours of galleries and museums, concierge, massage and aroma-therapy treatments, stationary bicycles available for use in guest rooms.

INN ON THE ALAMEDA, 303 E. Alameda St., Santa Fe, NM 87501. Tel. 505/984-2121 or toll free 800/289-2122. Fax 505/986-8325. 50 rms, (11 suites). A/C TV TEL
$ Rates (including breakfast): Nov–Mar $120–$160 single; $130–$170 double; $185–$290 suite. Apr–Oct $150–$190 single; $165–$200 double; $240–$315 suite. Holiday and special events rates may be higher. AE, CB, DC, MC, V. **Parking:** Free.

⭐ This might be just the ticket for visitors who prefer more intimacy than large hotels can offer. Four blocks from the Plaza and a block from gallery-intense Canyon Road, opposite the Santa Fe River at the corner of Paseo de Peralta, the inn preserves the spirit of old Santa Fe behind an exterior of adobe and adzed-wood pillars. You'll catch the flavor as soon as you walk into the lobby, with its traditional *viga-latilla* ceiling construction. Just past the unobtrusive reception desk is a sitting room/library with handcrafted furnishings, soft pillows, and a rocking chair placed around a big fireplace.

The mood continues to the guest rooms, characterized by the pastel shades of contemporary southwestern decor. Each room features a king-size bed or two queen-size beds, a desk with three-drawer credenza, an additional table and chairs, and cable TV with built-in AM/FM radio. There are prints on the walls and wood-slat blinds on the windows and heating and air conditioning is individually controlled. Some rooms have outdoor patios or private balconies.

Eight new individually designed suites have recently been added to this inn, and they include such luxuries as enclosed courtyards and portals, traditional *kiva* fireplaces and TVs in both the living room and bedroom, and minirefrigerators. Their furnishings are much the same as the rest of the hotel, but they are set away from the main building and have their own parking areas.

Dining/Entertainment: An elaborate continental breakfast is served each morning in the sitting room. Refreshments are available at a full-service bar nightly.

Services: Room service 7 to 11am, concierge, valet laundry, complimentary morning newspaper. Child care can be arranged. Small pets are accepted.

Facilities: Hot tub/spa by reservation. Rooms for nonsmokers and the disabled.

EXPENSIVE

HOTEL SANTA FE, 1501 Paseo de Peralta at Cerrillos Rd., Santa Fe, NM 87501. Tel. 505/982-1200 or toll free 800/825-9876. Fax 505/984-2211. 131 rms, 91 suites. A/C MINIBAR TV TEL

$ Rates: Late June–early Nov, Thanksgiving Day and Christmas, $100 single, $120 double, $135–$155 junior suite, $175–$200 deluxe suite; rest of year $75 single; $95 double; $110–$125 junior suite; $145–$165 deluxe suite. Extra person $20. Children 17 and under stay free with parents. AE, CB, DC, DISC, MC, V. **Parking:** Free.

⑤ Open since March 1991, this is the first-ever partnership in New Mexico between a Native American tribe—in this case, Picuris Pueblo—and private business located off reservation trust land. The three-story, pueblo-style building, cruciform in shape and featuring Picuris tribal motifs throughout, is about a half mile south of the Plaza.

The hotel has 40 superior rooms (30 with king-size beds), 51 junior suites (all with kings), and 40 deluxe suites (30 with kings). All rooms boast Taos-style furnishings, remote-control television, and fully stocked minibars. Each of the suites has a microwave oven. Each suite has a separate living room and bedroom, with a TV and phone in each room.

Dining/Entertainment: The hotel offers an extensive continental breakfast and a deli on the lobby level. The Lobby Lounge serves complimentary hors d'oeuvres from 5pm to 7pm daily.

Services: Valet laundry, courtesy shuttle to Plaza and Canyon Rd., 24-hour security, safe-deposit boxes.

Facilities: Rooms for nonsmokers and the disabled, massage room, guest Laundromat, Picuris Pueblo gift shop, outdoor pool and hot tub.

THE INN AT LORETTO, 211 Old Santa Fe Trail (P.O. Box 1417), Santa Fe, NM 87501. Tel. 505/988-5531 or toll free 800/528-1234. Fax 505/984-7988. 136 rms, 3 suites. A/C FRIDGE TV TEL

$ Rates: $95–$160 single; $110–$180 double; $275–$550 suite. Extra person $15. Children 12 and under free with parent. AE, CB, DC, DISC, MC, V. **Parking:** Free.

★ This handsome, Pueblo revival–style building was originally the Loretto Academy, a Catholic girls' school built in the late 19th century under the direction of Bishop Lamy. Although the building—which reopened as a hotel in 1975—has been fully renovated and expanded, bits and pieces of the original academy remain, including the famous chapel of Our Lady of Light with its mysterious spiral staircase (see "Attractions," below). Another unique element of the Inn at Loretto is the use of hand-painted Mimbres designs. There are about 1,000 of these colorful motifs, all different, on lobby, corridor, guest room, meeting room, and restaurant walls throughout the building. Staff artist Ross Martinez re-created work found on pottery of the 11th- and 12th-century Mimbres people of southwestern New Mexico.

The hotel, a little over one block from the southeast corner of the Plaza, is horseshoe-shaped, with room balconies or patios surrounding a landscaped outdoor courtyard with a fountain and pool. Half of the guest rooms have a single king-size bed, the remainder, a pair of double beds. Southwest decor dominates with etched-tin shades on intricate pottery-style lamps, Mexican tiles inset in writing and bedside tables, dried flower arrangements, and blue-toned regional motifs on bedspreads and drapes. All rooms have either a sofa or an easy chair with ottoman.

Dining/Entertainment: Los Rincones, noted for its intricate etched-tin chandeliers, is open daily from 6:30am to 10pm. On warm summer days, service is extended to the courtyard. Breakfasts run $5.95–$8.50; lunches, $6.95–$11.50. Dinners, including pastas, regional specialties, and continental cuisine, range from $9.25–$17.95. The warm, mezzanine-ringed hotel lounge has live entertainment nightly; hot spiced shrimp are cooked up during happy hour every Friday afternoon.

Services: Room service, concierge, valet laundry.

Facilities: Outdoor swimming pool. Shopping arcade with three art galleries, four boutiques, a jeweler, a bookstore, a liquor store, a gift shop, a sundries shop, and a hair salon. Rooms for nonsmokers and the disabled are available.

LA FONDA, 100 E. San Francisco St. (P.O. Box 1209), Santa Fe, NM 87501. Tel. 505/982-5511 or toll free 800/523-5002. Fax 505/982-6367. 160 rms, 15 suites. A/C TV TEL

$ Rates: $120–$135 single or double; $150–$165 deluxe or minisuite; $225–$345 suite. Extra person $15. Children under 8 free with parent. AE, CB, DC, MC, V.

Parking: $2 a day in three-story garage.

"The Inn at the End of the Trail" occupies a full block between the southeast corner of the Plaza, where a marker denotes the terminus of the Santa Fe Trail, and Bishop Lamy's St. Francis Cathedral. When the first Americans to pioneer the trail arrived in Santa Fe in 1821, they found an inn—a *fonda*—on this site. As trappers, traders, and merchants began flocking to Santa Fe, a saloon and casino were added. Among the inn's 19th-century patrons were Pres. Rutherford B. Hayes, Gen. Ulysses S. Grant, and Gen. William Tecumseh Sherman. It is said that even Billy the Kid worked at La Fonda for a time washing dishes. The original inn was dying of old age in 1920 when it was razed and replaced by what is today La Fonda. Its architecture is Pueblo revival, imitation adobe with wooden balconies and beam ends protruding over the tops of windows.

Every room is a bit different from the next. Each piece of hand-carved Spanish-style furniture is painted in a Hispanic folk motif color coordinated to other pieces in the room (but to nothing outside the room). Beds are king-size, doubles, or high, old-fashioned twins. Suites and deluxe rooms have minirefrigerators, tiled baths, and sophisticated artwork, including etched tin and stonework. Full suites, two of them with kitchen facilities, have fireplaces, private balconies, antique furniture, Oriental carpets, and a large amount of closet and shelf space.

Dining/Entertainment: La Plazuela Restaurant, a tiled skylit garden patio, is open for three meals daily from 7am–10pm. Furniture is solid-wood Spanish colonial, and the waiters and waitresses are garbed accordingly. Cuisine is regional with contemporary flair, ranging at dinner from blue-corn enchiladas to shrimp scampi cilantro. The adjacent La Fiesta Lounge, open Mon–Sat from 11am–2am and Sun noon–midnight, has nightly swing or mariachi entertainment. La Terraza, an enclosed outdoor patio on the third floor, offers lunches daily in summer. The Bell Tower Bar, at the southwest corner of the hotel, is the highest point in downtown Santa Fe, a great place for a view of the city.

Services: Room service, concierge, tour desk, valet laundry.

Facilities: Rooms for nonsmokers and the disabled, outdoor swimming pool, two indoor Jacuzzis, cold plunge, massage room. Shopping arcade with four arts-and-crafts galleries, leather shop, boutique, French pastry shop, and newsstand with sundries.

LA POSADA DE SANTA FE, 350 E. Palace Ave., Santa Fe, NM 87501. Tel. 505/986-0000 or toll free 800/727-5276. Fax 505/982-6850. 116 rms, 20 suites. TV TEL

$ Rates: May–Oct, Thanksgiving and Christmas seasons, $123–$283 single or double, $203–$393 suite. Nov–Apr except holidays $80–$225 single or double, $135–$293 suite. Various packages available. AE, CB, DC, MC, V. **Parking:** Free.

This lovely hotel has 19 adobe-style buildings spread across six acres of thoughtfully landscaped grounds. It is built around the Staab House, a historic mansion built four blocks east of the Plaza in 1882 by Abraham Staab, a German immigrant, for his bride, Julia. Santa Fe's first brick building was equally well known for its richly carved walnut interior woodwork and the decorative scrolls and fluting on its doors and windows. Today, several rooms of the house have been fully restored in classical fashion as a Victorian lounge, with period furnishings and museum-quality 19th-century art. Julia Staab, who died in 1896 at the age of 52, continues to haunt a half-dozen upstairs sleeping rooms. Mischievous but good-natured, she is Santa Fe's best-known and most frequently witnessed ghost.

Each of the hotel's charming rooms is a little different from the next, with variations in size, shape, layout, and detail. Many objets d'art are one of a kind—a factor which inspires repeat visitors to request "their" room year after year. But the *casitas,* "little houses," share many common traits: outside entrances with wood-carved portals, handcrafted furniture and wrought-iron garden chairs, wood floors with throw rugs, painted tiles built into walls. Eighty-six rooms have fireplaces or wood stoves; piñon firewood is provided daily. Some larger units have wet bars or refrigerators, walk-in closets, and dressing tables. Suites have full kitchenettes. But finding your way around the hotel grounds may be confusing: Get a map from the desk. The room numbers are in no particular order. No. 143, for instance, is between nos. 195 and 196 and across from 116.

Dining/Entertainment: The Staab House Restaurant, open for three meals daily from 7am–2pm and 5–10pm, has been fully restored with ceiling *vigas* and pueblo weavings and tinwork on the walls. From spring to early fall, food is also served outside on a big patio. New Mexico cuisine is a house specialty, with breakfasts like eggs Robles (with chorizo sausage and cactus chile), lunch including fresh fish in corn husks and a jicama chicken salad, dinner featuring scallops Encinada, pork Mezcal, and prime rib. The lounge has frequent happy-hour entertainment.

Services: Room service, valet laundry.

Facilities: Rooms for nonsmokers and the disabled. Outdoor swimming pool, guest use of local health club; boutique, beauty salon.

MODERATE

GARRETT'S DESERT INN, 311 Old Santa Fe Trail, Santa Fe, NM 87501. Tel. 505/982-1851 or toll free 800/888-2145. Fax 505/984-8959. 83 rms, 6 suites. A/C TV TEL

$ Rates: May–Oct, Nov–Feb, and major holidays $80 single, $90 double or suite. (Rates increase 33% for Indian Market.) Mar–Apr $70 single, $80 double or suite. AE, MC, V. **Parking:** Free.

The nearest motel to the Plaza, just three blocks south on the Santa Fe River, the Desert Inn is clean and comfortable, if a step down in elegance from the midcity hotels. Rooms have standard furnishings and unobtrusive southwestern decor. There's an outdoor swimming pool, valet laundry service, and car-rental and travel agencies attached. China Gate, a Chinese restaurant is also attached. Geno's Lounge, off the cozy motel lobby, has live entertainment Tuesday through Friday evenings.

INEXPENSIVE

SANTA FE MOTEL, 510 Cerrillos Rd., Santa Fe, NM 87501. Tel. 505/ 982-1039 or toll free 800/999-1039. 22 rms. A/C TV TEL

$ Rates: May–Oct $65–$75 single, $70–$80 double, $145 Thomas House; Nov–Apr $55–$65 single, $60–$70 double, $150 Thomas House. AE, MC, V.

S One of the bonuses of staying at this adobe-style motel is that most rooms have kitchenettes, complete with two-burner stoves and minirefrigerators, fully stocked with pans, dishes, and utensils. Southwestern motifs predominate in the comfortable rooms, spread across four turn-of-the-century buildings. Fresh-brewed coffee is served each morning in the office, where a bulletin board posts listings of Santa Fe activities. The nearby Thomas House, on West Manhattan Drive, is a fully equipped rental home with living and dining rooms and off-street parking.

NORTHSIDE

This area, within easy reach of the Plaza, includes accommodations that lie beyond the loop of the Paseo de Peralta on the north.

VERY EXPENSIVE

THE BISHOP'S LODGE, Bishop's Lodge Rd. (P.O. Box 2367), Santa Fe, NM 87504. Tel. 505/983-6377. Fax 505/989-8739. 74 rms and suites. A/C TV TEL

$ Rates: European Plan (meals not included): Apr 1–June 30 and early Sept–Jan 2, $95–$125 standard (for two); $140–$195 deluxe; $150–$200 super deluxe; $175–$215 deluxe suite. Modified American Plan (includes breakfast and lunch or dinner daily) July 1–Labor Day $190–$215 standard; $245–$285 deluxe; $280–$315 super deluxe; $305–$365 deluxe suite. A 15% service fee added to all charges. No credit cards, but out-of-state personal checks accepted. **Parking:** Free. **Closed:** Jan–Mar.

★ More than a century ago, when Bishop Jean-Baptiste Lamy was the spiritual leader of northern New Mexico's Roman Catholic population, he often escaped clerical politics by hiking 3½ miles north over a ridge into the Little Tesuque Valley. There he built a retreat he named Villa Pintoresca (Picturesque Villa) for its lovely vistas and a humble chapel (now on the National Register of Historic Places) with high-vaulted ceilings and a hand-built altar. Today Lamy's 1,000-acre getaway has become the Bishop's Lodge. Purchased in 1918 from the Pulitzer family (of publishing fame) by Denver mining executive James R. Thorpe, it has remained in that one family's hands for more than seven decades. That gives it continuity in theme and direction not often found in the visitor industry. It's been rewarded with a Mobil four-star rating.

The guest rooms are spread through seven buildings. All feature handcrafted cottonwood furniture, regional artwork, and etched-tin trim. Guests receive a complimentary fruit basket upon arrival. Standard rooms have balconies and king-size or two twin beds. Deluxe rooms have traditional *kiva* fireplaces, private decks or patios, and walk-in closets; some older units have flagstone floors and *viga* ceilings. Super deluxe rooms have a combination bedroom/sitting room. Deluxe suites are extremely spacious; they have living rooms, separate bedrooms, private patios and decks, and artwork of near-museum quality throughout. All units classified as "deluxe" have fireplaces and refrigerators.

Dining/Entertainment: Three large adjoining rooms with wrought-iron chandeliers and wall-size Indian-theme oil paintings comprise the Bishop's Lodge dining room. Santa Feans flock here for its buffets—breakfast $15 (7:30–9:30am), lunch $18 (noon–1:30pm), Sun brunch $25 (11:30am–2pm)—and its dinners (main courses $16–$32), creative regional cuisine with continental flair, served from 6:30–8:30pm daily. Attire is casual at breakfast and lunch but more formal at dinner, when men are asked to wear a sport coat and women a dress or pants suit. There's a full vintage wine list, and El Charro Bar serves pre- and postdinner drinks.

Services: Room service, valet laundry.

Facilities: Daily guided horseback rides, introductory riding lessons, children's pony ring; four surfaced tennis courts, pro shop and instruction; exercise room;

supervised skeet and trap shooting; outdoor pool with lifeguard, saunas, and whirlpool; stocked trout pond for children; shuffleboard, croquet, Ping-Pong; summer daytime program with counselors for children 4–12.

EXPENSIVE

PICACHO PLAZA HOTEL, 750 N. St. Francis Dr., Santa Fe, NM 87501.
   Tel. 505/982-5591 or toll free 800/441-5591 or 800/542-5523. Fax 505/988-2821. 211 rms, 33 suites and 34 condominium units. A/C TV TEL
$ Rates: Jan 1–June 15 and Nov 1–Dec 16, $78–$108 single, $88–$118 double, $138–$294 suite. Rest of year $98–$138 single, $113–$153 double, $178–$374 suite. Children 12 and under free with parent. AE, DC, MC, V. **Parking:** Free.

If you're in town for the Santa Fe Opera, you'll have a hard time finding an accommodation closer than this one. The amphitheater is only three miles north up U.S. 84/285; the Picacho Plaza provides free drop off and pick up. In fact, there's complimentary shuttle service anywhere within the city limits—including the Santa Fe Plaza, 1¼ miles southeast—from 6am to 10pm daily. Once you're in this landscaped garden-style hotel, though, you may find it hard to leave. You can watch an in-house artist convert a blank canvas into a stirring portrait or regional landscape. You can have free run of facilities at the adjacent Santa Fe Spa, the city's top health club. Standard rooms, with soft southwestern decor, have king-size or two double beds and other typical hotel furnishings. Minisuites are more spacious, with Santa Fe–style furnishings—including an armoire containing the TV—and private balconies. In addition to all the above, each parlor suite has a Murphy bed and traditional *kiva* fireplace in the living room, a big dining area, a hot-plate kitchenette with a wet bar and refrigerator, and a jetted bathtub. Cielo Grande condo units have fully equipped kitchens, fireplaces, and private decks.

   Dining/Entertainment: The Petroglyph Bar and Restaurant serves three meals a day from 6:30am–10pm amid antique local crafts and reproductions of rock drawings. Dinner main courses ($11.75–$18.50) are international cuisine with a bit of southwestern flair, like grilled chicken jalapeño marinated in olive oil and fresh herbs, grilled and basted with orange jalepeño marmalade; or shrimp spaghetti with mussels, crushed red peppers, and "lots of garlic." A jazz combo plays Thursday through Saturday in the Petroglyph Bar, and the nightclub features the Spanish quicksteps of New Mexico's best-known flamenco dancer and her Estampa Flamenco troupe.

   Services: Room service, complimentary shuttle, valet laundry, complimentary *USA Today* to each room. Child care can be arranged.

   Facilities: Rooms for nonsmokers and the disabled, outdoor swimming pool, hot tub, Santa Fe Spa (indoor pool, racquetball courts, weights, massage, steamrooms, aerobics, dance, yoga, and karate classes), coin-op guest Laundromat, gift and sundries shop.

SOUTHSIDE

Santa Fe's major commercial strip, Cerrillos Road, is U.S. 85, the main route to and from Albuquerque and the I-25 freeway. It's about 5¼ miles from the Plaza to the Villa Linda Mall, which marks the southern extent of the city limits. Most motels are on this strip, although one—the Residence Inn—is a couple of miles east, closer to St. Francis Drive (U.S. 84).

MODERATE

BEST WESTERN HIGH MESA INN, 3347 Cerrillos Rd., Santa Fe, NM
   87501. Tel. 505/473-2800 or toll free 800/777-3347. Fax 505/473-5128. 211 rms, 33 suites. A/C FRIDGE TV TEL
$ Rates: High-season $96–$125 single or double; low-season $64–$72 single or

double; suites $85–$120 most of year. Guests over 55 get 10% discount; children under 17 stay free with parent. AE, CB, DC, DISC, MC, V. **Parking:** Free.

The High Mesa wins kudos as one of the city's better properties. In the user-friendly lobby is a message board with information on current local events. The rooms feature Southwest regional decor, with a king-size or two queen-size beds, plush carpeting, wet bar and refrigerator, desk/dresser, and satellite TV with in-room movies. Suites have a separate sitting room with a couch and TV. Five luxury suites have full kitchens and huge desks. Alfredo's restaurant is open for three meals daily (6:30am–2pm and 5–10pm, in summer; 7am–2pm and 5:30–10pm in winter). You can expect gourmet coffee shop fare here, with dinner main courses priced from $8 to $15. Kids' menus are available. Room service, courtesy car, valet and coin-op guest laundry, child care, rooms for nonsmokers and the disabled are all available. Facilities include a skylit indoor pool, two Jacuzzis, a weight/exercise room, and a gift shop.

EL REY INN, 1862 Cerrillos Rd. (P.O. Box 130), Santa Fe, NM 87504. Tel. 505/982-1931 or 800/521-1349. 56 rms, 8 suites. A/C TV TEL
$ Rates (including continental breakfast): July–Aug $54–$92, depending upon size and type of room required; $85–$130 suite. Rest of year $47–$83; $75–$110 suite. AE, CB, DC, MC, V.

"The King" is notable for its carefully tended, shaded grounds and thoughtfully maintained units. The white-stucco buildings are adorned with bright trim around the doors and hand-painted Mexican tiles in the walls. No two rooms are alike. Most have *viga* ceilings and Santa Fe–style wood furnishings, a walk-in closet and a handsome blue-and-white tiled bathroom. Some have kitchenettes, others refrigerators and/or fireplaces. Eight stylish poolside terrace units feature private outdoor patio areas. Facilities include a Territorial-style sitting room with library and game tables, a swimming pool, hot tub, picnic area, children's play area, and coin-op laundry.

BUDGET

SANTA FE INTERNATIONAL HOSTEL, 1412 Cerrillos Rd., Santa Fe, NM 87501. Tel. 505/988-1153 or 983-9896. 40 dorm beds, 9 private rms. A/C
$ Rates: Dorm beds $9 American Youth Hostel members, $12 nonmembers; private rooms $23–$30 single or double.

Located 1½ miles south of the Plaza, this is a liberal hostel: There's no curfew and the office is open continually from 7am to 11pm. But there's also no smoking, and everyone must do a daily chore to help keep maintenance costs down. Bathrooms, kitchen ($1 a day includes basic foods), laundry ($1 includes soap), and common room with a piano, book rack, and pay phones are shared. Hostel owner Preston Ellsworth runs the Rio Bravo River Tours service from an office at the rear of the hostel.

WARREN INN, 3357 Cerrillos Rd., Santa Fe, NM 87501. Tel. 505/471-2033. 166 rms. A/C TV TEL
$ Rates: $36–$39 single; $46–$49 double. Children under 12 free with parents. AE, CB, DC, DISC, MC, V.

What a bargain! All rooms have kitchenettes, complete with sink, a microwave in the smaller rooms and full stores in the larger rooms, and refrigerator. You provide the food, pans, and utensils. The rooms are sufficient in other ways, too, with large dressers and closets, and standard features like cable television. Guest facilities include a swimming pool, coin-op laundry, and barbecue grills in the garden.

BED & BREAKFASTS

ALEXANDER'S INN, 529 E. Palace Ave., Santa Fe, NM 87501. Tel. 505/986-1431. 5 rms (3 with bath). A/C
$ Rates: $80–$120 double. MC, V.

Located not too far from the center of downtown Santa Fe in a quiet residential area, Alexander's Inn is unlike most of the places in Santa Fe because it isn't done in Southwest decor. Instead, the 5-year old inn is done in a Victorian/New England style with stenciling on the walls, pastel dhurrie rugs, muted colors like apricot and lilac, and white-iron or four-poster queen-size beds. You might begin to think you're in a country inn in Vermont. One of the rooms has a private deck, and all guests can enjoy privileges at the Santa Fe Country Club. Mountain bikes are available for guest use. A continental breakfast of homemade baked goods is served every morning.

GRANT CORNER INN, 122 Grant Ave., Santa Fe, NM 87501. Tel. 983-6678 for reservations or 984-9001 for guest rooms. 11 rms. A/C TV TEL

$ Rates (including breakfast): June–Oct and major holidays $55–$65 single, $55–$130 standard double, $90–$130 deluxe double. Nov–May except holidays $50 single, $65–$85 standard double, $100–$120 deluxe double. No children 6 or under. MC, V.

This early 20th-century manor at the corner of Johnson Street is just three blocks west of the Plaza. Each room is furnished with antiques, from brass or four-poster beds to armoires and quilts. Each has a portable cable TV, private phone and clock radio, limited-edition lithographs on the walls, and mono-grammed terry-cloth robes. Most rooms also have ceiling fans and small refrigerators, and five have private baths. But each room also has its own character. No. 3, for instance, has a hand-painted German wardrobe closet dating from 1772 and a wash basin with brass fittings in the shape of a fish. No. 8 has an exclusive outdoor deck which catches the morning sun. No. 11 has an antique collection of dolls and stuffed animals. The inn's office doubles as a library and gift shop and has hot coffee and tea at all hours.

Breakfast is served each morning in front of the living-room fireplace, or on the front veranda during the warm months of summer. The meals are so good, an enthusiastic public pays $10.50 a head ($7 for young children) to brunch here Saturday from 8 to 11am and Sunday from 8am to 1pm. (It's included in the room price for Grant Corner Inn guests, of course.) The menu changes daily, but always includes a fruit frappé, a choice of two gourmet main courses, homemade pastries, and coffee and tea.

INN OF THE ANIMAL TRACKS, 707 Paseo de Peralta, Santa Fe, NM 87501. Tel. 505/988-1546. 5 rms (all with bath).

$ Rates: $95–$110 single or double. AE, MC, V.

Inn of the Animal Tracks is a great little inn. All of the rooms, including the common spaces, are named under the sign of different animals. There are five in all, the sign of the rabbit, the soaring eagle, the gentle deer, the playful otter, and the loyal wolf. They are patron spirits of the different rooms. All of the rooms have platform beds and private baths, and all reflect the presence of the patron animal. The Sign of the Rabbit room, for instance, is just overflowing with rabbits—stuffed rabbits, rabbit paintings, and rabbit books. There are handmade furnishings, and the rooms are all pleasant and bright. The Sign of the Soaring Eagle room is the only one with a fireplace.

The Sign of the Bear room is a wonderful living room with a fireplace and a big overstuffed sofa. There's a small library from which you can borrow a book. Breakfast is served in the Sign of the Buffalo room, and it includes fresh bread, juice, fruit, and a different egg recipe daily. In the afternoon tea is served. The Inn is nonsmoking.

THE PRESTON HOUSE, 106 Faithway St., Santa Fe, NM 87501. Tel. 505/982-3465. 15 rms. A/C

$ Rates: High-season $58–$68 double with shared bath, $88–$115 private bath, $128 cottage or adobe home; low-season $48–$58 double with shared bath, $78–$98 private bath, $115 cottage or adobe home. Extra person $7. Children over 10 only. MC, V.

S This is a different sort of building for the City Different—a century-old Queen Anne home. That style of architecture is rarely seen in New Mexico, especially painted sky blue with white trim. The house's owner, noted silk-screen artist and muralist Signe Bergman, adores its original stained glass.

Located three blocks east of the Plaza, off Palace Avenue near La Posada hotel, the Preston House has several types of rooms. Six in the main house have period antiques and exquisitely feminine decor, with floral wallpaper and lace drapes. Many have brass beds covered with quilts; some have decks, several have fireplaces, and only two must share a bath. TV and phone are in the living room. Seven more rooms with private baths and TVs are in an adobe building catercorner from the house. Two private cottages in the rear of the Preston House, and an adobe home across the street, have more deluxe facilities. All rooms are stocked with sherry and terry-cloth robes. A continental buffet breakfast is served daily from 8 to 10am, and full tea and dessert are served every afternoon.

4. DINING

There are literally hundreds of restaurants in Santa Fe, from luxury establishments with strict dress codes right down to corner hamburger stands. This is a sophisticated city, and there is a great variety of cuisines here. Some chefs create new recipes incorporating traditional southwestern foods with nonindigenous ingredients; their restaurants are referred to in this listing as "creative Southwestern."

The categories below define a very expensive restaurant as one in which most dinner main courses are priced above $25; expensive, most main courses $18 to $25; moderate, $12 to $18; inexpensive, $7 to $12; budget, most main courses cost less than $7.

DOWNTOWN

VERY EXPENSIVE

THE COMPOUND, 653 Canyon Rd. Tel. 982-4353.
  Cuisine: CONTINENTAL. **Reservations:** Essential.
$ Prices: Prix-fixe menu $45. AE and all personal checks.
  Open: Tues–Sat 6pm–closing.
Many consider the Compound to be at the head of its class in Santa Fe dining. A past winner of several national awards, this restaurant—designed by noted architect Alexander Girard—is set on beautifully landscaped grounds amid tall firs and pines on the south bank of the Santa Fe River. It's reached by a long driveway off Canyon Road, at the rear of an exclusive housing compound. The interior decor is simple but refined, yielding to the natural setting. Service is attentive and elegant: a coat and tie is *de rigueur* for gentlemen, and young children are not admitted. Meals are prix fixe, including a salad, appetizer, main course, vegetables, rice or potatoes, dinner roll, dessert, and coffee. There's typically a wide choice of seafood (scallops, salmon, Dover sole), chicken, and meat dishes, including pepper steak, tournedos, lamb, and veal. Seafood and vegetables are delivered daily; bread and pastries are baked on the premises. There is, of course, an extensive wine list.

EXPENSIVE

COYOTE CAFE, 132 W. Water St. Tel. 983-1615.
  Cuisine: CREATIVE SOUTHWESTERN. **Reservations:** Required.

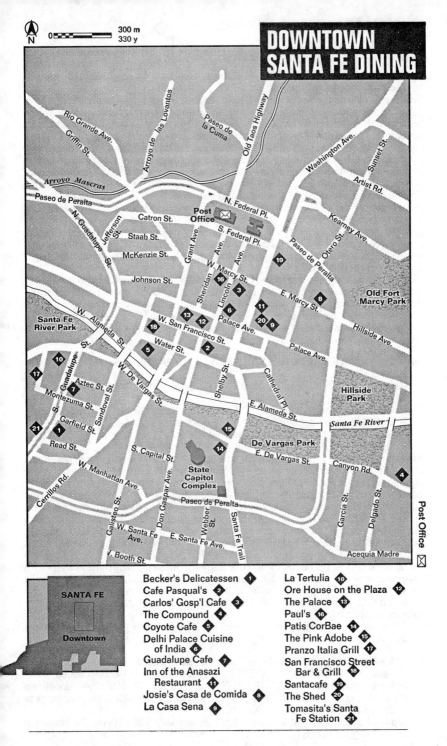

DOWNTOWN SANTA FE DINING

N

0 ___ 300 m
   ___ 330 y

SANTA FE

Downtown

Post Office ⊠

Becker's Delicatessen ❶
Cafe Pasqual's ❷
Carlos' Gosp'l Cafe ❸
The Compound ❹
Coyote Cafe ❺
Delhi Palace Cuisine
   of India ❻
Guadalupe Cafe ❼
Inn of the Anasazi
   Restaurant ⓫
Josie's Casa de Comida ❽
La Casa Sena ❾

La Tertulia ❿
Ore House on the Plaza ⑫
The Palace ⑬
Paul's ⑯
Patis CorBae ⑭
The Pink Adobe ⑮
Pranzo Italia Grill ⑰
San Francisco Street
   Bar & Grill ⑱
Santacafe ⑲
The Shed ⑳
Tomasita's Santa
   Fe Station ㉑

$ Prices: Lunch $6–$9.25; dinner appetizers $4.75–$9, main courses $17–$28 Sun–Thurs, prix fixe Fri–Sat $27–$35. MC, V.

Open: Lunch Sat–Sun 11:30am–2pm; dinner daily 6–10pm (9pm in winter).

Closed: Tues in Jan and Feb.

This is still the number-one "trendy" place to dine in Santa Fe. Owner Mark Miller has talked extensively about his restaurant and cuisine on national television, with the result that he is universally identified with "Santa Fe cuisine." Tourists throng here: In summer, in fact, reservations are recommended two to three days in advance. The café overlooks Water Street from tall windows on the second floor of a downtown building. Beneath the skylight, set in a cathedral ceiling, is a veritable zoo of animal sculptures in modern folk-art forms. Nonsmokers can breathe freely: The atmosphere is completely smoke free.

The cuisine, prepared on a pecan-wood grill in an open kitchen, is southwestern with a modern twist. The menu changes daily, but diners might start with wild boar bacon and fresh corn tamale with glazed granny apples and corn-cumin coulis or griddled buttermilk and wild rice-corn cakes with chipotle shrimp and salsa fresca. Main courses might include pecan-grilled pork tenderloin or grilled tolenas farm sonoma quail with spicy bourbon apple stuffing and la caretta cider glaze. You can get drinks from the full bar or wines by the glass.

The Coyote Café has two adjunct establishments, the Rooftop Cantina (open May through October) serves light Mexican fare and cocktails. It's open from 11:30am to 9:30pm daily, entrée prices range from $5 to $9, and there is entertainment nightly. Recently opened on the ground floor is the Coyote Café General Store, a retail gourmet southwestern food market, featuring a deli for carry-out sandwiches (open daily 10am to 8pm).

INN OF THE ANASAZI RESTAURANT, 113 Washington Ave. Tel. 988-3236.

Cuisine: NORTHERN NEW MEXICAN/NATIVE AMERICAN. **Reservations:** Highly recommended.

$ Prices: Breakfast $2.75–$10.50; lunch appetizers $4–$6.50, main courses $6.50–$12; dinner appetizers $5.75–$9, main courses $14–$24.

Open: Breakfast Mon–Fri 7–10am, Sat–Sun 7–11am; lunch daily 11:30am–2:30pm; dinner Mon–Fri 5:30–10pm, Sat–Sun 5:30–11pm.

In keeping with the theory behind the Inn of the Anasazi, everything offered in this restaurant is all natural. The meats are chemical free, and fruits and vegetables are organic whenever possible. They even serve water only on request "in the interest of conservation." The setting is comfortable, with an exposed beam ceiling, exposed adobe walls, and traditional Southwest decor—it's not at all kitsch, it's very elegant.

For breakfast you can have anything from fruit to a breakfast burrito with ranchero sauce and chile potatoes or a whole wheat quesadilla with lamb sausage, poached eggs, and black-bean hollandaise. At lunch, you could get roasted acorn squash soup with ancho cream and a warm spinach salad with cider vinaigrette and house dried apples; or, perhaps you'd like to try the Anasazi bean felafel in a pita with Quinoa tabbouleh and yogurt. For dinner, try the Navajo flat bread with fire roasted peppers to start, then perhaps pecan grilled range chicken with garlic and sage and corn pudding. Maybe you'd rather have "cota" tea smoked duckling with wild rice cakes and tart apple.

There are daily specials, as well as a nice list of wines by the glass and special wines of the day.

LA CASA SENA, 125 E. Palace Ave. Tel. 988-9232.

Cuisine: CREATIVE SOUTHWESTERN. **Reservations:** Recommended.

$ Prices: Lunch appetizers $1.75–$8.75, main courses $7–$10; dinner appetizers $3.50–$7, main courses $15.95–$21.50. Cantina tapas $3.25–$11, main courses $10–$18.50. AE, CB, DC, DISC, MC, V.

Open: Lunch Mon–Sat 11:30am–3pm, dinner daily 5:30–10pm; Sun brunch in main dining room only, 11am–3pm.

★ Opposite St. Francis Cathedral, two restaurants look into a spacious garden patio. The elegant main dining room occupies the Territorial-style adobe house built in 1867 by Civil War hero Maj. Jose Sena for his wife and 23 children. Today, it's a veritable art gallery with museum-quality landscapes on the walls and Taos-style handcrafted furniture. In the adjacent La Cantina, waiters and waitresses sing arias and tunes from Broadway shows, like *Phantom of the Opera, Les Misérables,* and *Little Shop of Horrors,* as they carry platters from kitchen to table.

The cuisine in the main dining room might be described as northern New Mexican with a continental flair. Lunches include chicken enchiladas on blue-corn tortillas and baby coho salmon with a cilantro lime pesto. In the evenings, diners might start with caldo de frijole negro (purée of black beans with amontillado sherry), then move to piñon free range chicken breast with mulato chile-lignonberry sauce or wild boar scaloppine.

The more moderately priced Cantina menu offers the likes of fire roasted chicken salad and carne adovada burrito (prime pork roasted with red chile, served with Hatch green chiles and cheeses). Both restaurants have exquisite desserts and fine wines by the glass.

THE PINK ADOBE, 406 Old Santa Fe Trail. Tel. 983-7712.
Cuisine: CONTINENTAL. **Reservations:** Recommended.
$ Prices: Appetizers $5.75–$7.50; lunch $6.50–$8.50; dinner $10.25–$21. AE, CB, DC, MC, V.
Open: Lunch Mon–Fri 11:30am–2:30pm, dinner daily 5:30–10pm.

★ San Pasqual, patron saint of the kitchen, keeps a close eye on this popular restaurant, in the center of the 17th-century Barrio de Analco, across the street from the San Miguel mission. A Santa Fe institution since 1946, it occupies an adobe home believed to be at least 350 years old. Guests enter through a narrow side door to a series of quaint, informal dining rooms with tile or hardwood floors. Stuccoed walls display original modern art or Priscilla Hoback pottery on built-in shelves.

At the dinner hour the Pink Adobe is at its continental best, with the likes of escargots and shrimp remoûlade as appetizers. Main courses include shrimp creole, poulet Marengo, tournedos bordelaise, lamb curry, and porc Napoleone. Lunch has more New Mexican and Cajun dishes, including a house enchilada topped with an egg, turkey-seafood gumbo, and gypsy stew (chicken, green chile, tomatoes, and onions in sherry broth).

Smoking is allowed only in the Dragon Room, the lounge across the alleyway from the restaurant. Under the same ownership, the Dragon Room has a separate menu from its parent establishment with traditional Mexican foods in the $5.25 to $9.50 range. The full bar is open from 11:30am to 2am daily, until midnight Sunday.

SANTACAFE, 231 Washington Ave. Tel. 984-1788.
Cuisine: CONTEMPORARY AMERICAN. **Reservations:** Recommended.
$ Prices: Appetizers $4–$8; lunch $8–$12.50; dinner $16.50–$20. MC, V.
Open: Lunch Mon–Fri 11:30am–2pm, dinner daily 6–10pm.

★ A casually formal restaurant in the 18th-century Padre Gallegos House, 2½ blocks north of the Plaza, its service and presentation are impeccable. Low lighting, soft jazz, and simple white decor dominate all four dining rooms. Each of the rooms has a fireplace for winter heat, and there's an outside courtyard for ⑤ summer diners.

The menu varies seasonally. A year-round lunchtime favorite is the "sampler" of four specials daily—for example, cilantro ravioli filled with chicken, mushrooms, yellow bell peppers, and Sonoma Jack cheese with sun-dried tomato butter; and pizza with roasted vegetables, bresaola, fresh mozzarella and marjoram on grilled roasted corn and green chile crust. Appetizers include Chinese dumplings filled with shrimp and spinach served with tahini sauce, and smoked pheasant spring rolls with chile dipping sauce. Dinner grills include grilled Asian glazed pork chop with red pepper hoisin barbecue sauce, herbed Chinese noodles and warm pepper salad. Grilled filet mignon with tomatilla ketchup and green chile mashed potatoes will keep the "meat and potatoes" eater happy. All breads and desserts are homemade, and the full bar offers wines by the glass.

MODERATE

CAFE PASQUAL'S, 121 Don Gaspar Ave. Tel. 983-9340.

Cuisine: NEW MEXICAN. **Reservations:** Recommended for dinner.

$ Prices: Breakfast $4.75–$7.75, lunch $6.25–$8.95; dinner appetizers $4.75–$8.75, main courses $10.50–$19.75. MC, V.

Open: Breakfast Mon–Sat 7am–3pm, brunch Sun 8am–2pm, lunch Mon–Sat 11am–3pm, dinner Thurs–Tues 6–10pm.

This classic New Mexican style establishment one block southwest of the plaza is a big favorite of locals and travelers alike. Not only does it have a common table where solo journeyers can meet locals and get acquainted; it has an innovative menu, and one that especially appeals to budget watchers at breakfast and lunch. Omelets, pancakes, cereals, and huevos motulenos—like rancheros but with fried bananas—are among the breakfast options. Soups, salads, sandwiches, and Mexican dishes are popular at lunch, and there's a delectable grilled trout in cornmeal with green chile and toasted piñon. There are also daily specials.

The frequently changing dinner menu offers grilled meats and seafoods, plus vegetarian specials. Oaxacan mango, whole roasted garlic, and corn cakes with squash are typical appetizers. Main courses might include chile-marinated New York steak, rack of lamb with tomato-mint salsa, chipotle shrimp on blue-corn tortillas, or an enchilada with spinach and Jack cheese. Pasqual's also boasts house-made desserts, imported beers, and wine by the bottle or glass.

LA TERTULIA, 416 Agua Fria St. Tel. 988-2769.

Cuisine: NEW MEXICAN. **Reservations:** Recommended.

$ Prices: Lunch $4.95–$6.75, dinner $7.50–$16.95. AE, MC, V.

Open: Lunch Tues–Sun 11:30am–2pm; dinner Tues–Sun 5–9pm.

Housed in a former 18th-century convent, La Tertulia's thick adobe walls separate six dining rooms, among them the old chapel and a restored *sala* (living room) containing a valuable Spanish colonial art collection. There's also an outside garden patio for summer dining. Dim lighting and *viga*-beamed ceilings, shuttered windows and wrought-iron chandeliers, lace tablecloths and hand-carved *santos* in wall niches lend a feeling of historic authenticity. La Tertulia means "The Gathering Place."

A highlight of the menu is Spanish paella (for two or more), an olio of seafood, chicken, chorizo sausage, vegetables, and rice, served with black bean/jalapeño soup and sopaipillas. Gourmet regional dishes include filet y rellenos, carne adovada, pollo adovo, and camarónes con pimientas y tomates (shrimp with peppers and tomatoes). If you feel like dessert, try capirotada (bread pudding) or natillas (custard). Many diners request the bar to bring them a pitcher of the homemade sangría.

ORE HOUSE ON THE PLAZA, 50 Lincoln Ave. Tel. 983-8687.

Cuisine: STEAKS & SEAFOOD. **Reservations:** Recommended.

$ Prices: Appetizers $3.50–$9; lunch $6.25–$8.50; dinner $12.95–$20. AE, MC, V.

Open: Lunch daily 10:30am–2:30pm, dinner daily 5:30–10pm.

The Ore House's second-story balcony, at the southwest corner of the Plaza, is an ideal spot from which to watch the passing parade while enjoying lunch or cocktails. When the weather gets chilly, radiant heaters keep the balcony warm, and there's a big fireplace indoors. The decor is southwestern, with plants and lanterns hanging amid white walls and booths.

The menu is heavy on fresh seafood and steaks. Daily fresh fish specials include salmon and swordfish (poached, blackened, teriyaki, or lemon), rainbow trout, lobster, and shellfish. Steak Ore House, wrapped in bacon and topped with crabmeat and béarnaise sauce, and chicken Ore House, a grilled breast stuffed with ham, Swiss cheese, green chile, and béarnaise, are local favorites. The Ore House also caters to vegetarians with vegetable platters. Luncheon diners often opt for the spinach salad or the prime rib sandwich.

The bar, with solo music Wednesday through Saturday nights, is proud of its 66 "custom margaritas." It has a selection of domestic and imported beers, and an excellent wine list. An appetizer menu is served from 2:30 to 5pm daily, and the bar stays open until midnight or later (only until midnight on Sunday).

THE PALACE, 142 W. Palace Ave. Tel. 982-9891.
   Cuisine: NORTHERN ITALIAN & CONTINENTAL. **Reservations:** Recommended.
   $ Prices: Lunch $5.25–$10.50; dinner appetizers $5.95–$8.50, main courses $9.50–$18.95. AE, MC, V.
   Open: Lunch Mon–Sat 11:30am–5pm, dinner Mon–Sat 5:45–10pm.
When construction crews in 1959 were excavating the Burro Alley site of Dona Tules's notorious 19th-century gambling hall, they came across an unusual artifact: a brass door knocker, half in the shape of a horseshoe, the other half resembling a saloon girl's leg, complete with stocking and high-heel boot. That knocker today is the logo of the Palace, which maintains the Victorian flavor but none of the ill repute of its predecessor. Red velvet wallpaper, dimly lit chandeliers, marble-topped tables, and high-backed chairs provide a classy yet casual decor for the restaurant.

Brothers Lino, Piedro, and Bruno Pertusini have carried on a long family tradition in the restaurant business: Their father was chef at the famous Villa d'Este on Lake Como, Italy. The Pertusinis' menu is predominantly northern Italian but contains a few French and continental dishes as well. Lunches include Caesar salad and coquille of fresh seafood. Full dinners include steak, veal scaloppine with shiitake mushrooms, sautéed sea scallops on artichoke hearts. There are a variety of fresh pastas daily; the wine list is long and well considered.

You can see the famous door knocker above the bar of the spiffy saloon, open Monday through Saturday from 11:30am to 2am. There's a nightly piano bar.

PRANZO ITALIA GRILL, 540 Montezuma St., Sanbusco Center. Tel. 984-2645.
   Cuisine: NORTHERN ITALIAN. **Reservations:** Recommended.
   $ Prices: Appetizers $4.25–$6.95; lunch $4.50–$7.95; dinner $6.95–$17.95. AE, MC, V.
   Open: Lunch Mon–Sat 11:30am–3pm; dinner Sun–Thurs 5–10pm, Fri–Sat 5–11pm.
Housed in a renovated warehouse, this sister to Albuquerque's redoubtable Scalo restaurant caters to local Santa Feans with a contemporary atmosphere of modern abstract art. An open grill is the centerpiece: The menu has few fried foods.

Homemade soups, salads, creative pizzas, and fresh pastas mark the low end of the menu. Bianchi e nere al capesante (black-and-white linguine with bay scallops in a light seafood sauce) and the pizza Mediterranea (with shrimp, zucchini, and roasted garlic) are consistent favorites. Steaks, chicken, veal, and fresh seafood grills, heavy on the garlic, dominate the dinner menu.

The bar boasts the Southwest's largest collection of grappa, as well as a wide choice of wines and champagnes by the glass. The restaurant's deli, Portare Via, offers Santa Fe's largest selection of Italian deli meats and cheeses.

INEXPENSIVE

DELHI PALACE CUISINE OF INDIA, 142 Lincoln Ave. Tel. 982-6680.
   Cuisine: EAST INDIAN. **Reservations:** Recommended.
   $ Prices: Appetizers 95¢–$3.95; main courses $5.95–$12.95. AE, MC, V.
   Open: Lunch daily 11:30am–2:30pm; dinner daily 5–10pm.
If you get a craving for Indian food, I'd recommend a visit to Delhi Palace—one of the very few restaurants like it in all of Santa Fe. The restaurant is extremely comfortable, and there's a mural on the wall directly in front of you as you walk in that, along with

the Indian music playing quietly in the background, might make you feel like you're out in the desert somewhere.

For lunch or dinner, you can get the traditional vegetable samosas or mulligatawny soup to start, and then tandoori chicken or shrimp or beef, lamb, or shrimp curry. Chef's specialties include lamb fraizee, cooked in gravy with onions, tomatoes, and bell pepper and tossed in an Indian iron skillet (karahai). There's an "all you can eat" lunch buffet served from 11:30am to 2:30pm daily for $5.95 a person, and complete dinners are served from 5 to 10pm. There are some desserts, including mango kulfi (ice cream served with fresh mangoes), and rasmalai (fresh homemade chunks of cottage cheese in evaporated milk, almonds, and pistachios). The food is good, and it's a real bargain.

GUADALUPE CAFE, 313 Guadalupe St. Tel. 982-9762.
Cuisine: NEW MEXICAN.
$ Prices: Breakfast $3.50–$6.75; lunch $3.95–$8.95; dinner appetizers $1.95–$5.25, main courses $5.95–$11.95. MC, V.
Open: Breakfast and lunch Tues–Fri 8am–2pm, brunch Sat–Sun 8am–2pm, dinner Tues–Sat 5:30–10pm.

Santa Feans line up at all hours to dine in this casually elegant café with tall potted plants and cushioned seats. Breakfasts include sausage and potato burritos and huevos rancheros; on the lunch menu are Mexican chicken salad and blue-corn enchiladas. Dinner includes everything from breast of chicken relleno to chile-cheese chimichangas. Daily specials feature fresh fish, crêpes, and pastas; don't miss the famous chocolate-amaretto adobe pie for dessert. Beer and wine are served.

PAUL'S, 72 W. Marcy St. Tel. 982-8738.
Cuisine: CREATIVE SOUTHWESTERN. **Reservations:** Recommended for dinner.
$ Prices: Breakfast $2–$4.25; lunch $5.50–$6.95; dinner appetizers $3.95–$6.50, main courses $10.25–$14.25. MC, V.
Open: Mon–Fri 7am–9pm, Sat lunch and dinner 11am–9pm.

Once just a home-style deli, then a little gourmet restaurant called Santa Fe Gourmet, Paul's is taking another step forward. With a new chef, new menu, and new decor, Paul's is a great place for any meal. Breakfast includes a breakfast burrito, a bagel with cream cheese, pancakes, or crêpes (with apple, pecans, and cheddar). The lunch menu has a few entrées, like sausage and lentils or fettucine, hot or cold sandwiches, and a short vegetarian menu. At dinner, the lights are lowered, and the bright Santa Fe interior (with folk art on the walls and colorfully painted screens that divide the restaurant into smaller, more intimate areas) becomes a great place for a romantic dinner. The menu includes a black-bean crêpe filled with curried vegetables to start and as a main course, stuffed pumpkin bread with pine nuts, corn, green chile, red chile sauce, queso blanco and caramelized apples. A wine list is available, and the restaurant is entirely nonsmoking.

SAN FRANCISCO STREET BAR AND GRILL, 114 W. San Francisco St. Tel. 982-2044.
Cuisine: AMERICAN.
$ Prices: Lunch $3.95–$6.50; dinner $4.75–$9.95. MC, V.
Open: Daily 11am–11pm.

This easygoing eatery offers casual dining amid simple decor in three seating areas: the main restaurant, an indoor courtyard beneath the three-story Plaza Mercado atrium, and an outdoor patio with its own summer grill.

It's perhaps best known for its hamburger, yet it offers a variety of daily specials. The lunch menu consists mainly of soups, sandwiches, and salads; dinners include fresh Boston bluefish, grilled pork tenderloin medallions, and New York strip steak. There are also nightly pasta specials. There's full bar service with draft beers and daily wine specials.

TOMASITA'S SANTA FE STATION, 500 S. Guadalupe St. Tel. 983-5721.

Cuisine: NEW MEXICAN.

$ Prices: Appetizers $1.95–$4.25; lunch $3.95–$9.25; dinner $4.50–$9.70. MC, V.

Open: Mon–Sat 11am–10pm.

(S) This may be the restaurant most consistently recommended by local Santa Feans. Why? Some point to the atmosphere; others cite the food and prices. Hanging plants and wood decor accent this spacious brick building, adjacent to the old Santa Fe railroad station. Traditional New Mexican main courses, including vegetarian dishes and daily specials, are served, and there's full bar service.

BUDGET

BECKER'S DELICATESSEN, 403 Guadalupe St. Tel. 988-2423.

Cuisine: DELI.

$ Prices: Breakfast $3.75–$5.95; lunch $5.25–$7.65. MC, V.

Open: Mon–Fri 7:30am–5:30pm, Sat 8am–5:30pm Sun 9am–2:30pm.

This is perhaps the most charming deli in town. Fresh flowers and clean paper doilies are placed on the wood tables daily, and wrought-iron windows lend an Old World touch to the nonsmoking atmosphere. Sandwiches combine a fine selection of imported and domestic cheeses, smoked fish and meats, and/or homemade sausage. Pasta, salads, breads, desserts, and espresso are also available.

CARLOS' GOSP'L CAFE, 125 Lincoln Ave. Tel. 983-1841.

Cuisine: DELI.

$ Prices: $2.25–$6.60. No credit cards.

Open: Mon–Sat 11am–4pm.

(S) You may sing the praises of the "Say Amen" desserts at this café in the inner courtyard of the First Interstate Bank Building. First, though, try the tortilla or hangover (potato-corn) soups or the deli sandwiches. Carlos' has outdoor tables, but many diners prefer to sit indoors, reading newspapers or sharing conversation at the large common table. Gospel and soul music play continually; oil paintings of churches and of many performers cover the walls.

JOSIE'S CASA DE COMIDA, 225 E. Marcy St. Tel. 983-5311.

Cuisine: NEW MEXICAN.

$ Prices: Full meals $6 and under. No credit cards.

Open: Mon–Fri 11am–4pm.

(★)(S) This unpretentious little white house, with casual Mexican decor, is open for lunch only. Everything is home cooked and made to order, which means there's a 20-minute minimum wait for diners. But it's worth it for a complete Mexican dinner, with a taco, rolled enchilada, chile relleno, tortilla, lettuce, and beans. Josie's caters to vegetarians by offering a variety of appropriate selections.

PATIS CORBAE, 422 Old Santa Fe Trail. Tel. 983-2422.

Cuisine: DELI.

$ Prices: Breakfast $4–$8.50; lunch $3.75–$9.25. No credit cards.

Open: Mon–Fri 7am–3:30pm, Sat–Sun 7am–1pm.

Croissant lovers appreciate this bakery and café behind the State Capitol. There are 14 varieties of the French sandwich rolls, from chocolate almond to egg, ham, and Swiss cheese. Quiche, soup, and weekday luncheon specials round out the midday menu. Early risers can enjoy fruit granola for breakfast with a cup of espresso or cappuccino. The café has indoor and outdoor seating.

THE SHED, 113½ E. Palace Ave. Tel. 982-9030.

Cuisine: NEW MEXICAN.

$ Prices: Main dishes $4.20–$6.25. No credit cards.

Open: Mon–Sat 11am–2:30pm.

Queues often form outside the Shed, a half block east of the Palace of the Governors. A luncheon institution since 1954, it occupies several rooms and the patio of a rambling hacienda built in 1692. Festive folk art adorns the doorways and walls. The food is basic but delicious, a compliment to traditional Hispanic Pueblo cooking. Enchiladas, tacos, and burritos, all served on blue-corn tortilla with pinto beans and posoles, are standard courses. There are dessert specials, and beer and wine are available.

SOUTHSIDE/CERRILLOS ROAD

MODERATE

OLD MEXICO GRILL, 2434 Cerrillos Rd., College Plaza South. Tel. 473-0338.

Cuisine: REGIONAL MEXICAN. **Reservations:** Requested for large parties.

$ **Prices:** Lunch $4.55–$7.50; dinner $6.25–$15.50. AE, DISC, MC, V.

Open: Lunch Mon–Sat 11:30am–3pm; dinner Sun–Thurs 5–9pm, Fri–Sat 5–9:30pm. Extended hours in summer.

Here's something unique in Santa Fe: a restaurant that specializes not in northern New Mexico food, but in authentic regional Mexican cuisine. Waitpersons offer attentive service; the centerpiece is an exhibition cooking area with an open mesquite grill and French rotisserie, behind bright-blue tiles and beneath a raft of hanging copperware.

A tempting array of fajitas, tacos al carbón, and other specialties are prepared on the grill. Popular dishes include turkey mole poblano, chiles en nogada (in a walnut cream sauce), shrimp in orange-lime tequila sauce, and paella Mexicana. There's a good choice of soups and salads at lunch, and a choice of homemade desserts, including hazelnut-apricot torte. A full bar serves Mexican beers and margaritas.

STEAKSMITH AT EL GANCHO, Old Las Vegas Hwy. Tel. 988-3333.

Cuisine: STEAKS & SEAFOOD. **Reservations:** Recommended.

$ **Prices:** Appetizers $3.95–$5.95, main courses $9.95–$24.95. AE, MC, V.

Open: Daily 5:30–10pm.

Santa Fe's most highly regarded steak house is a 15-minute drive up the Old Pecos Trail toward Las Vegas. Guests enjoy attentive service in a pioneer atmosphere of adobe walls and *viga* ceilings.

New York sirloin, filet mignon, and other complete steak dinners are served, along with barbecued ribs and such nightly fresh seafood specials as oysters, trout, and salmon. A creative appetizer menu ranges from ceviche Acapulco to grilled pasilla peppers and beef chupadero. There are also outstanding salads, homemade desserts and bread, and a full bar and lounge that even caters to cappuccino lovers.

SZECHWAN CHINESE CUISINE, 1965 Cerrillos Rd. Tel. 983-1558.

Cuisine: NORTHERN CHINESE. **Reservations:** Recommended.

$ **Prices:** Lunch $4.50–$5.25; dinner $5.25–$20. AE, MC, V.

Open: Daily 11am–9:30pm.

Spicy northern Chinese cuisine pleases the southwestern palate. There's plenty of it here. Some diners love the Peking duck, made to order with 24-hours notice, served with traditional pancakes and plum sauce. Also excellent is the seafood platter of shrimp, scallops, crab, fish, and vegetables stir-fried in a wine sauce. Other specialties include Lake Tung Ting shrimp, sesame beef, and General Chung's chicken. Wine is served, along with Tsingtao beer from China.

INEXPENSIVE

MARIA'S NEW MEXICAN KITCHEN, 555 W. Cordova Rd. near St. Francis Drive. Tel. 983-7929.

Cuisine: NEW MEXICAN. **Reservations:** Accepted

$ Prices: Lunch $4.50–$7.95; dinner $6.50–$15.25. MC, V.

Open: Mon–Fri 11am–10pm, Sat–Sun noon–10pm.

Built in 1949 by Maria Lopez and her politician husband, restaurant is a prime example of what charm can come from sca bricks came from the old New Mexico State Penitentiary, and mo furniture was once used in La Fonda Hotel. The five wall frescoes in the cantina painted by master muralist Alfred Morang (1901–58) in exchange for food.

Maria's boasts an open tortilla grill, where cooks can be seen making flour and corn tortillas by hand. Generous portions are on every plate, from the award-winning beef, chicken, shrimp, and vegetarian fajitas to blue-corn enchiladas, chile rellenos, green chile and posole stews, and huge steaks. Children's plates are available. From September through April, Tuesday is "Twos-day," when diners pay only $2 for a second meal. Strolling mariachi troubadours perform nightly.

THE NATURAL CAFE, 1494 Cerrillos Rd. Tel. 983-1411.

Cuisine: VEGETARIAN. **Reservations:** Recommended.

$ Prices: Lunch $4.95–$7.50; dinner $8.50–$11.50.

Open: Lunch Tues–Fri 11:30am–2:30pm, dinner Tues–Sun 5–9:30pm.

An international menu of tasty and healthy dishes is served in an artsy garden atmosphere by a competent cosmopolitan staff.

No fewer than four national cuisines—Mexico (black-bean enchiladas), China (Szechuan vegetables), Indonesia (tempeh burger), Lebanon (hummus with pita bread), and the United States—are represented on the everyday menu. There are a small number of seafood and chicken dishes. Daily specials include the likes of walnut fettuccine and mushroom Stroganoff. A children's menu is available. Homemade desserts are sweetened with maple syrup or honey. There are a couple of dozen wines and several beers (including Kaliber nonalcoholic beer), plus herbal teas, grain coffee, and other beverages.

BUDGET

SOUPER SALADS, 2428 Cerrillos Rd., College Plaza South. Tel. 473-1211.

Cuisine: SOUP & SALAD.

$ Prices: $2.95–$4.95. No credit cards.

Open: Mon–Sat 11am–9pm, Sun noon–9pm.

The all-you-can-eat salad bar is Santa Fe's largest, with more than 60 items. There's also a soup stove with four homemade soups daily, a baked-potato bar with eight different toppings, and a deli sandwich counter. Gingerbread and honey-buttered corn bread are served with all meals. Beer and wine are available.

TECOLOTE CAFE, 1203 Cerrillos Rd. Tel. 988-1362.

Cuisine: NEW MEXICAN.

$ Prices: Main dishes $3.75–$8.50. No credit cards.

Open: Tues–Sun 7am–2pm.

This is a breakfast lovers' favorite. The decor is simple, but the food is elaborate: eggs any style, omelets, huevos rancheros, served with fresh-baked muffins or biscuits and maple syrup. Luncheon specials include carne adovada burritos and green-chile stew, served with beer or wine.

5. ATTRACTIONS

SUGGESTED ITINERARIES

IF YOU HAVE 1 DAY Start at the Palace of the Governors to get a visual grasp of New Mexico's four centuries of Hispanic and American history. As you leave, visit

crafts and jewelry beneath the portal facing the
ed walking tour of old Santa Fe, starting from the
thedral.

te your second day to the arts. Spend the morning
in the Museum of Fine Arts, and the afternoon
Canyon Road.

isit the cluster of museums on Camino Lejo—the
Art, the Museum of Indian Arts and Culture, and the
American Indian. Then wander through the historic
yourself the rest of the afternoon to shop.

R MORE You'll definitely want to leave the city and
explore   ountryside. One day could be devoted to the pueblos,
including San ju   o, headquarters of the Eight Northern Indian Pueblos
Council, and Santa Clara Pueblo, with its amazing Puye Cliff Dwellings. Another
could take you along the High Road to Taos, with a stop at the spiritually profound El
Santuario de Chimayo, returning down the valley of the Rio Grande. Yet another day
trip might include Los Alamos, birthplace of the atomic bomb and home of the
Bradbury Science Museum and Bandelier National Monument, where an Anasazi
culture thrived more than 500 years ago.

THE TOP ATTRACTIONS

PALACE OF THE GOVERNORS, North Plaza. Tel. 827-6483.

Built in 1610 as the original capitol of New Mexico, the Palace has been in
continuous public use longer than any other structure in the United States. It
was designated the Museum of New Mexico in 1909, two years before New
Mexico became a state, and has become (appropriately) the state history museum,
with an adjoining library and photo archives. A model shows how the adobe palace
itself has evolved through the centuries, alternately shrinking and expanding. Some
cutaways of doors and windows show off early architecture.

A series of exhibits chronicle four centuries of New Mexico's Hispanic and
American history, from the 16th-century Spanish explorations through the frontier
era to modern times. Among Hispanic artifacts, there are early Jesuit maps and rare
Franciscan hide paintings—historic chronicles on elk and buffalo hides—from the
early 1700s. There's even an entire mid-19th-century chapel, with a simple,
bright-colored altarpiece made in 1830 for a Taos church by a folk artist named Jose
Rafael Aragon.

Governor's offices of the Mexican and 19th-century U.S. eras have been restored
and preserved. Displays out of early New Mexico life include a stagecoach, an early
working printing press, and a collection of *mestizajes*, portraits of early Spanish
colonists detailing typical costumes of the time. A great door from a jail in the Santa
Ana pueblo was apparently used at one time as a testing board for a blacksmith who
made branding irons: It has the scores of dozens of ranches all over it.

From the 20th century, kitsch items show how Indian designs and symbols have
been wrenched into commercial forms: a liquor bottle in the form of an eagle dancer,
a neon motel sign with the Zia sun symbol, a quilted toaster cover made to resemble a
pueblo apartment complex. Also on display are pieces from the silver service used
aboard the battleship USS *New Mexico* from 1918 to 1939, and a tiny New Mexico
state flag, 3″ by 4″, that was smuggled to the moon.

Reminders of the native heritage are scant in this museum, most having been
moved to the Museum of Indian Arts and Culture. Among those remaining are some
ancient pottery from the Puye Plateau culture, and a series of artifacts and
photographs depicting a museum-sponsored study of Mayan sites in Mexico's
Yucatán.

There are two shops here that visitors should not miss. One is the bookstore, with
one of the finest selections of art, history, and anthropology books in the Southwest.

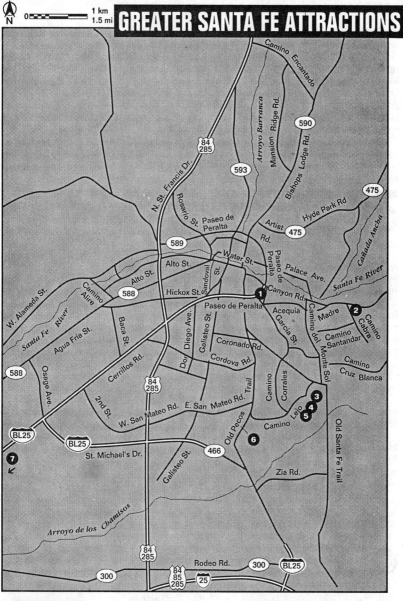

GREATER SANTA FE ATTRACTIONS

1 km
1.5 mi

N. St. Francis Dr.
Camino Encantado
Arroyo Barranca
Mansion Ridge Rd.
Bishops Lodge Rd.
590
84 285
593
Rosario St.
Paseo de Peralta
Hyde Park Rd.
475
Artist Rd.
475
Cañada Ancha
589
Water St.
Alto St.
Alto St.
Palace Ave.
Santa Fe River
Sandoval St.
Paseo de Peralta
W. Alameda St.
Camino Alire
588
Hickox St.
Canyon Rd.
Paseo de Peralta
Acequia
Camino del Monte Sol
Camino Madre
2
Santa Fe River
Agua Fria St.
Baca St.
Diego Ave.
Galisteo St.
Garcia St.
Camino Santandar
Camino Cabra
Don
Coronado Rd.
588
Osage Ave.
Cerrillos Rd.
Cordova Rd.
Camino Cruz Blanca
2nd St.
84 285
W. San Mateo Rd.
E. San Mateo Rd.
Old Pecos Trail
Camino Corrales
Camino Lejo
3
4
5
Old Santa Fe Trail
BL25
BL25
St. Michael's Dr.
Galisteo St.
466
Camino
6
7
Zia Rd.
Arroyo de los Chamisos
84 285
Rodeo Rd.
300
BL25
300
84 85 285
25

Greater Santa Fe Area

NEW MEXICO

Cristo Rey Church 2

El Rancho de
Las Golondrinas 7

Indian Art
Research Center 1

Museum of Indian
Arts & Culture 3

Museum of International
Folk Art 4

Santa Fe Children's
Museum 6

Wheelwright Museum
of the American Indian 5

The other is the print shop and bindery, in which limited-edition works are produced on hand-operated presses.

One of the most lasting impressions Santa Fe visitors bring home is not of the museum itself, but of the Indian artisans squatting shoulder-to-shoulder beneath the long covered portal facing the Plaza. Here on the shaded sidewalk, several dozen colorfully dressed members of local Pueblo tribes, plus an occasional Navajo, Apache, or Hopi, spread their handcrafts: mainly jewelry and pottery, but also woven carpets, beadwork, and paintings. The museum's Portal Program restricts selling space to Indians only.

Admission: Adults $3.50; free for children under 16. Two-day passes good at all four branches of the Museum of New Mexico cost $6 for those 16 and older.

Open: Mar–Dec daily 10am–5pm. **Closed:** Mon in Jan and Feb; Thanksgiving Day, Christmas, and New Year's Day.

MUSEUM OF FINE ARTS, Palace and Lincoln Aves. Tel. 827-4455.

Located cater-corner from the Plaza and immediately opposite the Palace of the Governors, this was the first Pueblo Revival–style building constructed in Santa Fe, in 1917. As such, it was a major stimulus in Santa Fe's development as an art colony earlier this century.

The museum's permanent collection of more than 8,000 works emphasizes regional art, including numerous Georgia O'Keeffe paintings, landscapes and portraits by all the Taos masters, and more recent works by such contemporary greats as Luis Jimenez and Fritz Scholder.

Typical of the early 20th-century works are aquatints by Doel Reed, an Indiana-born painter who lived in New Mexico for a quarter century. His feelings for nudes, jagged lines of rocky horizons, and the contrasting dark-and-light facades of southwestern buildings, mark him an original; especially in his nudes, there is a pleasingly familiar hint of Picasso, or even of early impressionists. On another level, a vast mural that for size at least could vie with the famous ones in Mexico shows an early scene out of some imagined Spanish colonial history, a priest giving bread to a hungry Indian child; this bit of sweetness takes up a whole wall in the auditorium.

The museum also has a collection of Ansel Adams photography. Modern artists, many of them far from the mainstream of traditional southwestern art, are featured in temporary exhibits throughout the year.

Beautiful St. Francis Auditorium, patterned after the interiors of traditional Hispanic mission churches, adjoins the Museum of Fine Arts. (See "Evening Entertainment," below.) A museum shop sells books on southwestern art, plus prints and postcards of the collection.

Admission: Adults $3.50; free for children under 16.

Open: Mar–Dec, daily 10am–5pm. **Closed:** Mon Jan–Feb; Thanksgiving Day, Christmas, and New Year's Day.

ST. FRANCIS CATHEDRAL, Cathedral Place at San Francisco St. (P.O. Box 2127). Tel. 982-5619.

Santa Fe's grandest religious structure is just a block east of the Plaza. An architectural anomaly in Santa Fe, it was built between 1869 and 1886 by Archbishop Jean-Baptiste Lamy to resemble the great cathedrals of Europe. French architects designed the Romanesque building—named after Santa Fe's patron saint—and Italian masons assisted with its construction.

The small adobe Our Lady of the Rosary chapel on the northeast side of the cathedral reflects a Spanish look. Built in 1807, it is the only parcel remaining from Our Lady of the Assumption Church, founded with Santa Fe in 1610. The new cathedral was built over and around the old church.

A wooden icon set in a niche in the wall of the north chapel, *La Conquistadora,* "Our Lady of Conquering Love," is the oldest representation of the Madonna in the United States. Rescued from the old church during the 1680 Pueblo rebellion, it was carried back by Don Diego de Vargas on his peaceful reconquest 12 years later, thus the name. Today *La Conquistadora* plays an important part in the annual Feast of Corpus Christi in June and July.

In 1986 a $600,000 renovation project relocated an early 18th-century wooden statue of St. Francis of Assisi to the center of the altar screen. Around the cathedral's exterior are front doors featuring 16 bronze door panels of historic note, and a plaque memorializing the 38 Franciscan friars who were martyred in New Mexico's early years. There's also a large bronze statue of Bishop Lamy himself; his grave is under the main altar of the cathedral.

Admission: Donations appreciated.

Open: Daily. Visitors may attend mass Mon–Sat at 6, 7, and 7:45am and 5:15pm and Sun at 6, 8, and 10am, noon, and 7pm.

MORE ATTRACTIONS

MUSEUMS

MUSEUM OF INTERNATIONAL FOLK ART, 706 Camino Lejo. Tel. 827-8350.

This property of the Museum of New Mexico may not seem quite as typically southwestern as other Santa Fe museums, but it's the largest of its kind in the world. With a collection of well over 200,000 objects from more than 100 countries, it is my personal favorite of the city museums.

It was founded in 1953 by Chicago collector Florence Dibell Bartlett, who said: "If peoples of different countries could have the opportunity to study each others' cultures, it would be one avenue for a closer understanding between men." That's the basis on which the museum operates today.

The special collections include Spanish Colonial silver, traditional and contemporary New Mexican religious art, Mexican Indian costumes, Mexican majolica ceramics, Brazilian folk art, European glass, African sculptures, East Indian textiles, and the marvelous Morris Miniature Circus. Particularly delightful are numerous dioramas of people around the world at work and play in typical town, village, and home settings. Recent acquisitions include American weather vanes and quilts, Palestinian costume jewelry and amulets, and Bhutanese and Indonesian textiles. Children love to look at the hundreds of toys on display. About half the pieces comprise the 1982 contribution of Alexander and Susan Girard. A new wing was built to hold the vast assemblage of dolls, animals, and entire towns.

In 1989, the museum opened a new Hispanic Heritage Wing. Folk art demonstrations, performances, and workshops are often presented here. The 80,000-square-foot museum also has a lecture room, a research library, and a gift shop where a variety of folk art is available for purchase.

The museum is located two miles south of the Plaza, in the Sangre de Cristo foothills off Old Santa Fe Trail.

Admission: Adults $3.50; free for children under 16.

Open: Mar–Dec daily 10am–5pm. Jan–Feb Tues–Sun 10am–5pm. **Closed:** Thanksgiving Day, Christmas, and New Year's Day.

MUSEUM OF INDIAN ARTS AND CULTURE, 710 Camino Lejo. Tel. 827-8941.

Next door to the folk-art museum, this new museum opened in 1987 as the showcase for the adjoining Laboratory of Anthropology. Interpretive displays detail tribal history and contemporary life-styles of New Mexico's Pueblo, Navajo, and Apache cultures. More than 50,000 pieces of basketry, pottery, clothing, carpets, and jewelry—much of it quite ancient—is on continual rotating display.

There are daily demonstrations of traditional skills by Indian artisans, and regular programs in a 70-seat multimedia theater. Native educators run a year-round workshop that encourages visitors to try such activities as weaving and corn grinding. As well, there are regular performances of Indian music and dancing by native groups. Concession booths purvey Native American foods.

The laboratory is a point of interest in itself, an exquisite example of Pueblo revival architecture by well-known Santa Fe architect John Gaw Meem. Since the museum opened, the lab has expanded its research and library facilities into its former display wing. It was founded in 1931 by John D. Rockefeller, Jr.

Admission: $3.50 adults, free for children under 16.

Open: Mar–Dec daily 10am–5pm. Jan–Feb Tues–Sun 10am–5pm. **Closed:** Thanksgiving Day, Christmas, and New Year's Day.

WHEELWRIGHT MUSEUM OF THE AMERICAN INDIAN, 704 Camino Lejo. Tel. 982-4636.

Though not a member of the state museum system, the Wheelwright is often visited on the same trip as the folk-art and Indian arts museums by virtue of its proximity: next door. Once known as the Museum of Navajo Ceremonial Art, it was founded in 1937 by Boston scholar Mary Cabot Wheelwright in collaboration with a Navajo medicine man, Hastiin Klah, to preserve and document Navajo ritual beliefs and practices. Klah took the designs of sand paintings used in healing ceremonies and adapted them into the textiles that are a major part of the museum's treasure.

In 1977 the museum's focus was changed to include the living arts of all American Indian cultures. Built in the shape of a Navajo hogan, with its doorway facing east (toward the rising sun) and its ceiling made in the interlocking "whirling log" style, it offers rotating single-subject shows of silverwork, jewelry, tapestry, pottery, basketry, and paintings. There's a permanent collection, of course, plus an outdoor sculpture garden with works by Allan Houser and other noted artisans.

In the basement is the Case Trading Post, an arts-and-crafts shop built in the image of a turn-of-the-century trading post such as was found on Navajo reservations. A storyteller gathers listeners outside a teepee at 7pm on Saturday and Sunday in July and August.

Admission: Suggested donation, adults $2, children $1.

Open: Mon–Sat 10am–5pm, Sun 1–5pm. **Closed:** Thanksgiving Day, Christmas, and New Year's Day.

EL RANCHO DE LAS GOLONDRINAS, Rte. 14, Box 214, La Cienega. Tel. 471-2261.

 Otherwise known as Old Cienega Village Museum, this 400-acre ranch, 15 miles south of the Santa Fe Plaza via I-25, was once the last stopping place on the 1,000-mile El Camino Real from Mexico City to Santa Fe. Today, it is a living 17th- and 18th-century Spanish village, comprising a hacienda, village store, schoolhouse, and several chapels and kitchens. There's also a working molasses mill, wheelwright and blacksmith shops, shearing and weaving rooms, a threshing ground, a winery and vineyards, and four water mills, as well as dozens of farm animals. A walk around the entire property is 1¾ miles in length.

Highlights of the year for Las Golondrinas (The Swallows) are the Spring Festival (the first weekend of June) and the Harvest Festival (the first weekend of October). Authentically costumed volunteers demonstrate shearing, spinning, weaving, embroidery, wood carving, grain milling, blacksmithing, tinsmithing, soap making, and other activities. There's an exciting atmosphere of Spanish folk dancing, music, and theater, and traditional oven-cooked food. Each festival Sunday the museum opens with a procession and mass dedicated to San Ysidro, patron saint of farmers.

Admission: Adults $3, youths 13–18 $2, children 5–12 $1. Festival weekends, adults $5, youths 13–18 $3, children 5–12 $2.

Open: June–Aug Wed–Sun 10am–4pm. Guided tours Apr–Oct Sat–Sun, by advance arrangement.

CHURCHES

LORETTO CHAPEL, The Inn at Loretto, 211 Old Santa Fe Trail at Water St. Tel. 984-7971.

Though no longer consecrated for worship, the Loretto chapel is an important site in Santa Fe. Patterned after the famous Sainte-Chapelle church in Paris, it was constructed in 1873—by the same French architects and Italian masons

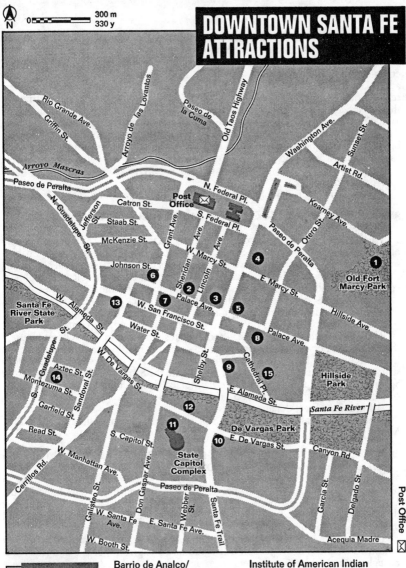

DOWNTOWN SANTA FE ATTRACTIONS

0 — 300 m / 330 y
N

Rio Grande Ave.
Griffin St.
Paseo de la Cuma
Arroyo de las Lovantos
Old Taos Highway
Washington Ave.
Sunset St.
Artist Rd.
Arroyo Mascras
Paseo de Peralta
N. Federal Pl.
Post Office ✉
Catron St.
Staab St.
McKenzie St.
Johnson St.
S. Federal Pl.
Kearney Ave.
Otero St.
N. Guadalupe St.
Jefferson St.
Grant Ave.
Sheridan St.
Lincoln Ave.
W. Marcy St.
E. Marcy St.
Palace Ave.
Paseo de Peralta
Old Fort Marcy Park **1**
Hillside Ave.
6
2
7
3
5
Palace Ave.
W. Alameda St.
Santa Fe River State Park
13
W. San Francisco St.
Water St.
W. De Vargas St.
Shelby St.
Cathedral Pl.
8
9
15
Hillside Park
E. Alameda St.
Santa Fe River
Guadalupe
Aztec St.
Montezuma St.
Sandoval St.
Garfield St.
Read St.
14
S. Capitol St.
12
11
De Vargas Park
E. De Vargas St.
10
Canyon Rd.
State Capitol Complex
W. Manhattan Ave.
Cerrillos Rd.
Galisteo St.
Don Gaspar Ave.
Webber St.
Santa Fe Trail
Paseo de Peralta
Garcia St.
Delgado St.
W. Santa Fe Ave.
E. Santa Fe Ave.
W. Booth St.
Acequia Madre
Post Office ✉

SANTA FE
Downtown

Barrio de Analco/
    East De Vargas Street
    area historic houses: **12**
    Adolph Bandelier House
    Boyle House
    Gregoria Crespin House
    José Alarid House
    Oldest House
    Tudesqui House
Bergere House **6**
Casa de Ortiz **13**
Delgado House **7**
Footsteps Across
    New Mexico **9**

Institute of American Indian
    Arts Museum **15**
Loretto Chapel **9**
Mission of San Miguel **10**
Museum of Fine Arts **2**
Old Fort Marcy Park **1**
Padre de Gallegos House **4**
Palace of the Governors **3**
Prince Plaza **5**
St. Francis Cathedral **8**
Santa Fe Adventures **14**
State Capitol **11**

who were building Archbishop Lamy's cathedral—as a chapel for the Sisters of Loretto, who had established a school for young ladies in Santa Fe in 1852.

The chapel is especially notable for its remarkable spiral staircase: It makes two complete 360-degree turns with no central or other visible support! (A railing was added later.) Legend has it that the building was nearly finished in 1878 when workers realized the stairs to the choir loft wouldn't fit. Hoping for a solution more attractive than a ladder, the sisters made a novena to St. Joseph—and were rewarded when a mysterious carpenter appeared astride a donkey and offered to build a staircase. Armed with only a saw, a hammer, and a T square, the master constructed this work of genius by soaking slats of wood in tubs of water to curve them, and holding them together with wooden pegs. Then he disappeared without waiting to collect his fee.

Today, the chapel is maintained by the Inn at Loretto Hotel.

Admission: $1.

Open: Daily 9am–4:30pm. Entry is through the Inn at Loretto.

MISSION OF SAN MIGUEL, Old Santa Fe Trail at E. De Vargas St. Tel. 983-3974.

This is one of the oldest churches in America, having been erected within a couple of years of the 1610 founding of Santa Fe. Tlaxcala Indians, servants of early Spanish soldiers and missionaries, may have used fragments of a 12th-century pueblo on this site in its construction. Severely damaged in the 1680 Pueblo revolt, it was almost completely rebuilt in 1710, and has been altered numerous times since.

Because of its design, with high windows and thick walls, the structure was occasionally used as a temporary fortress during times of raiding Indians. One painting in the sanctuary has holes that, according to legend, were made by arrows.

The mission and a nearby house—today a gift shop billed as "The Oldest House," though there's no way of knowing for sure—were bought by the Christian Brothers from Archbishop Lamy for $3,000 in 1881, and the order still operates both structures. Among the treasures in the mission are the San Jose Bell, reputedly cast in Spain in 1356 and brought to Santa Fe via Mexico several centuries later; and a series of buffalo hides and deerskins decorated with Bible stories.

Admission: Free; donations welcomed.

Open: Mon–Sat 11:30am–4pm, Sun 1–4:30pm. Summer hours start earlier. Mass 5pm daily.

SANTUARIO DE NUESTRA SEÑORA DE GUADALUPE, 100 Guadalupe St. at Agua Fria St. Tel. 988-2027.

Built between 1795 and 1800 at the end of El Camino Real by Franciscan missionaries, this is believed to be the oldest shrine in the United States honoring the Virgin of Guadalupe, patroness of Mexico. The sanctuary's adobe walls are almost three feet thick, and the deep-red plaster wall behind the altar was dyed with oxblood in traditional fashion when the church was restored earlier this century.

On one wall is a famous oil painting, *Our Lady of Guadalupe,* created in 1783 by renowned Mexican artist Jose de Alzibar. Painted expressly for the church, it was brought from Mexico City by mule caravan.

Today administered as a museum by the nonprofit Guadalupe Historic Foundation, the sanctuary is frequently used for chamber music concerts, flamenco dance programs, dramas, lectures, and religious art shows.

Admission: Donations accepted.

Open: Mon–Fri 9am–4pm, Sat 10am–3pm. **Closed:** Weekends Nov–Apr.

OTHER ATTRACTIONS

STATE CAPITOL, Paseo de Peralta and Old Santa Fe Trail. Tel. 984-9589.

Some are surprised to learn that this is the only round capitol building in America. It's also the newest. Built in 1966 in the shape of a Pueblo Indian *zia* emblem, it symbolizes the Circle of Life: four winds, four seasons, four directions, and four sacred obligations. Surrounding the capitol is a lush 6½-acre garden boasting more than 100 varieties of plants—roses, plums, almonds, nectarines, Russian olive trees, and sequoias among them. Benches are placed around the grounds for the enjoyment of visitors.

FOOTSTEPS ACROSS NEW MEXICO, The Inn at Loretto, 211 Old Santa Fe Trail. Tel. 982-9297.

This multimedia presentation is an impressive introduction to the state. From Pre-Hispanic Pueblo culture to the landing of the space shuttle at White Sands, slides, music, and a sculptured, three-dimensional map combine to tell the New Mexico story. There's a fine bookstore here for browsing before or after the show.

Admission: Adults $3.50, $2.50 children 6–16.
Open: Shows every half hour, Mon–Sat 9:30am–5pm, Sun 9:30am–4pm.

COOL FOR KIDS

Don't miss taking the kids to the Museum of International Folk Art, where they'll love the international dioramas and the toys, and to El Rancho de las Golondrinas, a living Spanish colonial village. Other children's attractions include:

SANTA FE CHILDREN'S MUSEUM, 1050 Old Pecos Trail. Tel. 989-8359.

Designed for whole families to share, this museum offers interactive exhibits and hands-on displays in the arts, humanities, science, and technology. Special art and science activities and family performances are regularly scheduled.

Admission: Adults $2, children $1.
Open: Thurs–Sat 10am–5pm, Sun noon–5pm.

SANTA FE ADVENTURES, Sanbusco Center, 500 Montezuma St. Tel. 983-0111.

This creative summer day-care program appeals to children age four and older with a wide variety of activities. The youngest can practice clay sculpture with a native artisan, learn how to spot animal tracks in the mountains or desert, and take field trips to El Rancho de las Golondrinas. Kids seven and older can raft on the Rio Grande and design sand paintings and *kachina* dolls. Middle-school students and older can do any of these activities, plus look into the future through a video-imaging program or take a dinner "ghost walk" to haunted places around downtown Santa Fe. Call for information or write for a brochure: P.O. Box 15086, Santa Fe, NM 87506.

Admission: Varies by activity; averages $10–$17 an hour, minimum $20.
Open: June–Aug, daily; limited dates in May, Sept, and Oct.

ORGANIZED TOURS

CITY TOURS

Chamisa Touring Service, 2076 Calle Ensenada (Tel. 438-9656). Chamisa's Nicholas and Sandra Cobb offer customized tours in your private car or rental vehicle. They will plan specific tours based on your interests and at the pace you desire.

Gray Line Tours, 220 N. Guadalupe St. (tel. 983-9491). The trolleylike Roadrunner departs several times daily in summer (less often in winter) from the Plaza, beginning at 9am, for 2½ hour city tours. Buy tickets (adults $15, children under 12 $7.50) as you board.

Rojo Tours, 228 Old Santa Fe Trail, Suite A (tel. 983-8333). Customized private tours.

Santa Fe Detours, La Fonda Hotel, 100 E. San Francisco St. (tel. 983-6565 or toll free 800/DETOURS). Perhaps the city's most extensive booking service.

Studio Entrada Tours, P.O. Box 4934, Santa Fe, NM 87502 (tel. 505/983-8786). Personalized tours to galleries of leading painters, sculptors, craftspersons, and furniture makers.

WALKING TOURS

Afoot in Santa Fe, The Inn at Loretto, 211 Old Santa Fe Trail (tel. 983-3701). Twice-daily, 2½-hour personalized tours.

    Ghost Tours of Santa Fe, Santa Fe Adventures, Sanbusco Center, 500 Montezuma St. (tel. 983-0111). Visits 14 haunted places around the city. Nightly June through August, weekends April and May and September and October.

    Historical Walking Tours of Santa Fe, 418 Cerrillos Rd. (tel. 984-8235). Three basic tours are offered several times daily, from morning to early evening.

    Pathways Customized Tours, 663 Washington (tel. 982-5382). Don Dietz offers several planned tours, including a downtown Santa Fe walking tour and a full city tour.

    Santa Fe Walks, La Fonda Hotel, 100 E. San Francisco St. (tel. 983-6565 or toll free 800/DETOURS). Tours of 2½ hours leave twice daily in summer.

6. SPORTS & RECREATION

SPECTATOR SPORTS

HORSE RACING The ponies run at the **Downs at Santa Fe,** 11 miles south of Santa Fe off U.S. 85, near La Cienega, from Memorial Day through September. Post time for 10-race cards is 3:30pm Wed and Fri; for 12-race cards, 1:30pm Saturday and Sunday, plus Memorial Day, the Fourth of July, and Labor Day. Admission starts at $1 and climbs depending upon seating. A closed-circuit TV system shows instant replays of each race's final stretch run and transmits out-of-state races for legal betting.

RECREATION

BALLOONING Champagne brunches in hot-air balloons are made romantic by **Balloons Over Santa Fe** (tel. 471-2937 or 982-8178).

BICYCLING **First Powder** on Hyde State Park Road (tel. 982-0495) rents bikes. Several U.S. Cycling Federation–sanctioned events are scheduled throughout the year, including the Santa Fe Century and the Tour de Los Alamos road race. Contact the **Sangre de Cristo Cycling Club** (tel. 471-4473) for details.

FISHING Rainbow trout are the favorite fish for most high-lakes anglers: The season runs April through December. Check with the **New Mexico Game and Fish Department** (tel. 827-7882) for specific laws and licenses. **High Desert Angler,** 435 S. Guadalupe St. (tel. 988-7688), specializes in fly-fishing gear.

GOLF There are two public courses in the Santa Fe area. The 18-hole **Santa Fe Country Club,** Airport Road (tel. 471-0601); and the oft-praised 18-hole **Cochiti Lake Golf Course,** 5200 Cochiti Hwy., Cochiti Lake, 29 miles southwest of Santa Fe via I-25 and N.M. 16 and 22.

HIKING & BACKPACKING It's hard to decide which of the 900 miles of nearby national forest trails to challenge. Three wilderness areas are especially attractive: **Pecos Wilderness,** with 223,000 acres east of Santa Fe; **Dome Wilderness,** 5,200 acres of rugged canyon land adjacent to Bandelier National Monument; and **San Pedro Parks Wilderness,** 41,000 acres west of Los Alamos. Information on these and other wilderness areas is available from the **Santa Fe National Forest,** 1220 St. Francis Dr. (P.O. Box 1689), Santa Fe, NM 87504 (tel. 988-6940). If you're looking for company on your trek, contact the Santa Fe group of the **Sierra Club** (tel. 983-2703).

HORSEBACK RIDING Trips ranging in length from a few hours to a few days can be arranged by **Camel Rock Ranch,** Tesuque (tel. 986-0408). Rides are also major activities at two local guest ranches, the **Bishop's Lodge** (see "Accommodations," above) and **Rancho Encantado.**

HUNTING   Mule deer and elk are taken by hunters in the Pecos Wilderness and Jemez Mountains, as well as occasional black bear and bighorn sheep. Wild turkey and grouse are frequently bagged in the uplands, geese and ducks at lower elevations. Check with the **New Mexico Game and Fish Department** (tel. 827-7882) for specific laws and licenses.

RIVER RAFTING   Although Taos is the real rafting center of New Mexico, several companies serve Santa Fe during the April-October white-water season. They include the **Southwest Wilderness Center,** P.O. Box 2840, Santa Fe, NM 87501 (tel. 983-7262); **New Wave Rafting,** 107 Washington Ave. (tel. 984-1444); **Rio Bravo River Tours,** 1412 Cerrillos Rd. (tel. 988-1153 or toll free 800/451-0708); and the **Santa Fe Rafting Co.,** 80 E. San Francisco St. (tel. 988-4914).

RUNNING   Despite its elevation, Santa Fe is popular with runners, and hosts numerous competitions, including the annual Old Santa Fe Trail Run on Labor Day. Fun runs begin from the Plaza at 6pm Wednesday year-round (5:30pm in winter).

SKIING   There's something for all skiing ability levels at the   **❂ Santa Fe Ski Area,** 16 miles northeast of Santa Fe via Hyde Park (Ski Basin) Road. Built on the upper reaches of 12,000-foot Tesuque Peak, the area has an average annual snowfall of 250 inches and a vertical drop of 1,650 feet. Six lifts, including a 5,000-foot triple chair and a quad chair, serve 39 runs and 700 acres of terrain; the lifts have a capacity of 7,300 skiers an hour. Base facilities, at 10,350 feet, center around La Casa Mall, with a cafeteria, lounge, ski shop, and boutique. Another restaurant, the Sierra Lodge, has a midmountain patio. The ski area is open daily from 9am to 4pm, often from Thanksgiving to Easter, depending on snow conditions. Rates for all lifts are $28 for adults, $17 for children and seniors, free for kids under 3 feet, 10 inches (in their ski boots). For more information, write the Santa Fe Ski Area, 1210 Luisa St., Suite 10, Santa Fe, NM 87501 (tel. 982-4429). For 24-hour taped reports on snow conditions, call 983-9155. The New Mexico Snophone (tel. 984-0606) gives statewide reports.

Cross-country skiers find seemingly endless miles of snow to track in the **Santa Fe National Forest** (tel. 988-6940). A favorite place to start is at the Black Canyon campground, 9 miles from downtown en route to the Santa Fe Ski Area. In the same area are the Borrega Trail and the Aspen Vista Trail. Basic nordic lessons, telemarking instruction, backcountry tours, and overnight packages are all offered by Bill Neuwirth's **Tracks,** P.O. Box 173, Santa Fe, NM 87504 (tel. 982-2586).

SPAS   A common stop for skiers coming down the mountain road from the Santa Fe Ski Area is   **❂ Ten Thousand Waves,** a Japanese-style health spa 3 miles northeast of Santa Fe on Hyde Park Road (tel. 988-1047 or 982-9304). This serene retreat, nestled in a grove of piñon, offers hot tubs, saunas, and cold plunges, plus a variety of massage and other bodywork techniques. Bathing suits are optional in the 10-foot communal hot tub, where you can stay as long as you want for $8.50. Eight private hot tubs cost $14 to $19 an hour, with discounts for seniors and children. You can also get therapeutic massage, facials, herbal wraps, and salt glows. The spa is open June 1 to Sept 30, Sunday, Monday, Wednesday, and Thursday from 10am to 10pm, Tuesday from 4:30 to 10pm, and Saturday and Sunday from 10am to 11:30pm. Reservations are recommended, especially on weekends.

SWIMMING   The city operates four indoor pools and one outdoor pool. Nearest downtown is the **Fort Marcy Complex** (tel. 984-6725) on Camino Santiago off Bishop's Lodge Road. Admission is $1.25 for adults, $1 for students, and 50¢ for children 8 to 13. Call the city Swimming Pools Division (tel. 984-6671) for details.

TENNIS   Santa Fe has 27 public tennis courts and four major private facilities. The City Recreation Department (tel. 984-6864) can locate all indoor, outdoor, and lighted public courts.

7. SAVVY SHOPPING

From traditional native crafts to Hispanic folk art to abstract contemporary works, Santa Fe is the place to shop. Galleries speckle the downtown area, and Canyon Road is well known as an artists' thoroughfare. Of course, the greatest concentration of Indian crafts is displayed beneath the portal of the Palace of the Governors.

Business hours vary quite a bit between establishments, but nearly everyone is open weekdays *at least* from 10am to 5pm, with mall stores open until 9pm. Most shops are open similar hours Saturday; and many are also open Sunday afternoons during the summer. Winter hours are often more limited.

BEST BUYS

Few visitors to Santa Fe leave the city without having bought at least one item—and often several—from the native artisans at the Palace of the Governors. In considering purchases, keep the following pointers in mind:

Silver jewelry should have a harmony of design, clean lines, and neatness in soldering. Navajo jewelry typically features large stones, with designs shaped around the stone. Zuni jewelry usually has patterns of small or inlaid stones. Hopi jewelry rarely uses stones, instead displaying a darkened motif incised into the top layer of silver.

Turquoise of a deeper color is usually higher quality, so long as it hasn't been color treated. *Heishi* bead necklaces usually use stabilized turquoise.

Pottery is traditionally hand coiled and of natural clay, not thrown on a potter's wheel using commercial clay. It is hand polished with a stone, hand painted, and fired in an outdoor oven rather than an electric kiln. Look for an even shape; clean, accurate painting; a high polish (if it is a polished piece); and an artist's signature.

Navajo rugs are appraised according to tightness and evenness of weave, symmetry of design, and whether natural (preferred) or commercial dyes have been used.

Kachina dolls are more highly valued according to the detail of their carving: fingers, toes, muscles, rib cages, feathers, for example. Elaborate costumes are also desirable. Oil staining is preferred to the use of bright acrylic paints.

Sand paintings should display clean narrow lines, even colors, balance, an intricacy of design, and smooth craftsmanship.

Local museums, particularly the Wheelwright Museum and the Institute of American Indian Art, can give a good orientation to contemporary craftsmanship.

Contemporary artists are mainly painters, sculptors, ceramicists, and fiber artists, including weavers. Peruse one of the outstanding catalogs that introduce local galleries—*The Collector's Guide to Santa Fe & Taos* by Wingspread Communications (P.O. Box 13566, Albuquerque, NM 87192), *Santa Fe & Taos Arts* by the Book of Santa Fe (535 Cordova Rd., Suite 241, Santa Fe, NM 87501), or the *Santa Fe Catalogue* by Modell Associates (P.O. Box 1007, Aspen, CO 81612). They're widely distributed at shops or can be ordered directly from the publishers.

An outstanding introduction to Santa Fe art and artists is the personalized studio tours offered by **Studio Entrada,** P.O. Box 4934, Santa Fe, NM 87502 (tel. 983-8786). For $50 per person (minimum two), director Linda Morton takes small groups into private studios to meet the artists and learn about their work. Each itinerary lasts about 2½ hours, and includes two or three studio/gallery visits.

SHOPPING A TO Z

ANTIQUES

CLAIBORNE GALLERY, 558 Canyon Rd. Tel. 982-8019.
Original Spanish colonial furniture.

ROBERT F. NICHOLS AMERICANA, 419 Canyon Rd. Tel. 982-2145.
Prehistoric pottery and country antiques.

ART

ELAINE HORWITCH GALLERIES, 129 W. Palace Ave. Tel. 988-8997.
Oils, acrylics, etchings, sculptures, and ceramics, mainly of southwestern themes, including works by Havard, Fincher, Palmore, Mason, and Wade.

EL TALLER GALLERY, 235 Don Gaspar Ave. Tel. 988-9298.
Southwestern art of many media, with work by the renowned Amado Pena, Jr.

FENN GALLERIES, 1075 Paseo de Peralta. Tel. 982-4631.
Early Taos and Santa Fe painters; classic American impressionism, historical western, modernism, as well as contemporary southwestern landscapes and monumental sculpture.

GERALD PETERS GALLERY, 439 Camino del Monte Sol. Tel. 988-8961.
Taos school and other classical artists; modern oils, watercolors, and ceramics.

LEWALLEN GALLERY, 225 Galisteo St. Tel. 988-5387.
Paintings, sculptures, and mixed-media work by 25 artists.

LINDA DURHAM GALLERY, 400 Canyon Rd. Tel. 988-1313.
Contemporary painting, sculpture, and photography.

LINDA MCADOO GALLERY, 503 Canyon Rd. Tel. 983-7182.
Impressionist painters and sculptors.

MEYER GALLERY, 225 Canyon Rd. Tel. 983-1434.
Bronze sculpture, paintings, jewelry, and handcrafts.

NEDRA MATTEUCCI FINE ART, 300 Garcia St. at Canyon Road. Tel. 983-2731.
Classics by the Taos school and early Santa Fe artists, plus contemporary sculpture and painting.

NIGHT SKY GALLERY, 826 Canyon Rd. Tel. 982-1468.
Works of important emerging artists; etchings, lithographs, monoprints, and watercolors.

OWINGS-DEWEY FINE ART, 74 E. San Francisco St. Tel. 982-6244.
Specializes in 19th and 20th century American art, including works by Georgia O'Keeffe, Charles Russell, Robert Henri, and Andrew Dasburg.

PRESDEN GALLERY, 125 E. Water St. Tel. 983-1014.
Paintings, ceramics, sculpture, neon, and wood carvings.

RIO GRANDE GALLERY, 80 E. San Francisco St. Tel. 983-2458.
Exclusively features R. C. Gorman paintings and bronzes.

SANTA FE EAST, 200 Old Santa Fe Trail, Santa Fe, NM 87501. Tel. 988-3103.
Across from the Loretto Chapel, this gallery has some great museum quality artwork, including sculpture, pottery, paintings, and one-of-a-kind pieces of jewelry.

SENA GALLERIES WEST, Plaza Mercado, 112 W. San Francisco St. Tel. 982-8808.
Contemporary painters and sculptors.

SHIDONI FOUNDRY AND GALLERY, Bishop's Lodge Rd., Tesuque. Tel. 988-8008.
Sculpture garden, with bronze casting; foundry tour available, call for details.

WOODROW WILSON FINE ARTS, 319 Read St. Tel. 983-2444.

High-profile Taos and Santa Fe artists, plus modern impressionism and realism.

BOOKS

In addition to independent bookstores in Santa Fe, the nationwide chains B. Dalton and Waldenbooks are represented. Specialty bookstores include **Cornerstone Books Etc.,** 1722 St. Michael's Dr. (tel. 473-0306), for Christian literature and music; **Horizons,** 328 Guadalupe St. (tel. 983-1554), for books on travel, nature, and science; **Margolis & Moss,** 129 W. San Francisco St. (tel. 982-1028), for rare books and prints; **Parker Books of the West,** 142 W. Palace Ave. (tel. 988-1076), for new and old books about western history and fiction; **Nicholas Potter** (tel. 983-5434), 203 E. Palace Ave., for used and rare hardbacks; and **Santa Fe Bookseller,** 203 W. San Francisco St. (tel. 983-5278), for new and out-of-print art books. Among the most interesting stores are:

CAXTON BOOKS & MUSIC, 216 W. San Francisco St. Tel. 982-8911.

Probably downtown Santa Fe's best bookstore. Its collection includes a wide choice of regional works, art books, and music.

FOOTSTEPS ACROSS NEW MEXICO, Inn at Loretto, 211 Old Santa Fe Trail. Tel. 982-9297.

The bookstore here specializes only in works about New Mexico and the Southwest.

LOS LLANOS BOOK STORE, 500 Montezuma Ave. Tel. 982-9542.

Located about 10 blocks from the Plaza in the delightful shopping area known as the Sanbusco Center, Los Llanos is the most complete bookstore in Santa Fe, with major sections on southwestern Americana, children's books, literature, and fine arts.

CRAFTS

BELLAS ARTES, 653 Canyon Rd. Tel. 983-2745.

Contemporary sculpture, paintings, drawings, and clay and fiber. Also, Pre-Columbian and African.

DAVIS MATHER FOLK ART GALLERY, 141 Lincoln Ave. Tel. 983-1660 or 988-1218.

★ New Mexican animal wood carvings. Folk, Hispanic, and unpredictable arts.

ECONOMOS WORKS OF ART, 225 Canyon Rd. Tel. 982-6347.

Classic American Indian art, Pre-Columbian, and antique Mexican pieces.

GALLERY 10, 225 Canyon Rd. Tel. 983-9707.

★ Museum-quality pottery, weavings, and basketry; contemporary paintings and mixed media.

INDIAN TRADER WEST, 204 W. San Francisco St. Tel. 988-5776.

Navajo baskets, jewelry, rugs, Pueblo pottery, Hopi *kachinas* and baskets, and other handcrafts.

JOSHUA BAER & COMPANY, 116 E. Palace Ave. Tel. 988-8944.

★ Nineteenth-century Navajo blankets, pottery, jewelry, and tribal art.

KANIA-FERRIN GALLERY, 662 Canyon Rd. Tel. 982-8767.

Fine American Indian baskets, pottery, jewelry, textiles, and beadwork. Antique *santos* and *retablos.*

MORNING STAR GALLERY, 513 Canyon Rd. Tel. 982-8187.

North American Indian artifacts.

NAMBE MILLS, INC., 924 Paseo de Peralta at Canyon Rd. Tel. 988-5528.

An exquisite alloy is sand-cast and handcrafted to create cooking, serving, and decorating pieces. Also at Plaza Mercado, 112 W. San Francisco St. (tel. 988-3574), and 216 Paseo del Pueblo Norte (Yucca Plaza), Taos (tel. 758-8221).

THE RAINBOW MAN, 107 E. Palace Ave. Tel. 982-8706.
Photography, trade blankets, pawn jewelry, kachinas, folk arts, railroad china, and western memorabilia.

RUNNING RIDGE GALLERY, 640 Canyon Rd. Tel. 988-2515.
Ceramics, fiber and paper art, and glass work.

SALON & GALLERY OF THE FRIGHTENED OWL, 1117 Canyon Rd. Tel. 983-7607.
Spanish Colonial art and furniture.

STREETS OF TAOS, 200 Canyon Rd. Tel. 983-8268 or 983-4509.
Navajo rugs, Pueblo jewelry, pottery, and baskets.

FASHIONS

ORIGINS, 135 W. San Francisco St. Tel. 988-2323.
Wearable folk art, including handwoven southwestern apparel and jewelry.

SANTA FE FIESTA FASHIONS, 651 Cerrillos Rd. Tel. 983-1632.
Designer and manufacturer of southwestern apparel, created by Just Lindee.

THREE SISTERS, Inn at Loretto Hotel 211 Old Santa Fe Trail. Tel. 988-5045.
Traditional and contemporary Southwest attire and accessories, including ribbon shirts and fiesta wear.

WOOL PALACE, 53 Old Santa Fe Trail. Tel. 983-5855.
Indian trade blankets; men's and women's apparel.

FOOD

SANTA FE SCHOOL OF COOKING, Plaza Mercado (upper level), 116 W. San Francisco St. Tel. 983-4511.
A 2-hour demonstration class discusses the flavors and history of traditional New Mexican and contemporary Southwest cuisines; $25 includes a meal and recipes. Specialized classes are well attended; call for schedules and rates. An adjoining market offers a variety of traditional foods and cookbooks, with gift baskets available.

FURNITURE

DELL WOODWORKS, 1326 Rufina Circle. Tel. 471-3005.
Handcrafted Santa Fe–style furniture.

DOOLINGS OF SANTA FE, 525 Airport Rd. Tel. 471-5956.
Southwestern country furniture.

SOUTHWEST SPANISH CRAFTSMEN, Plaza Mercado, 116 W. San Francisco St. Tel. 982-1767 or toll free 800/777-1767.
Spanish Colonial and Spanish provincial furniture, doors, and home accessories.

GIFTS/SOUVENIRS

EL NICHO, 227 Don Gaspar Ave. Tel. 984-2830.
Handcrafted folk art, including *kachinas,* jewelry, tiles, and drums.

TIN-NEE-ANN TRADING CO., 923 Cerrillos Rd. Tel. 988-1630.
Indian arts, moccasins, T-shirts, and other low-cost souvenirs.

JEWELRY

JAMES REID LTD., 114 E. Palace Ave. Tel. 988-1147.
⭐ Silversmithing, gold jewelry, antique Native American art, contemporary paintings, sculpture, furniture, and folk art.

MILLENNIUM TURQUOISE MINES, 221 E. De Vargas St. Tel. 983-1589.
⭐ Jewelry straight from the mountains. Tours can be arranged of the mines, 15 miles south on N.M. 586.

THINGS FINER, La Fonda, 100 E. San Francisco St. Tel. 983-5552.
Estate and antique jewelry and gift items as well as Russian objets d'art and silverwork.

MARKETS

SANTA FE TRADERS MARKET, 1241 Siler Rd. Tel. 438-0011.
This huge indoor flea market, offering new and antique goods, is open Friday through Sunday from 10:30am to 5:30pm.

WINES

THE WINERY, Sanbusco Center, 510 Montezuma St. Tel. 982-WINE.
⭐ Perhaps the most extensive wine shop in New Mexico, it carries gourmet foods and beers, gift baskets, and publishes a monthly newsletter.

8. EVENING ENTERTAINMENT

Full information on all major cultural events can be obtained from the Santa Fe Convention and Visitors Bureau (tel. 984-6760 or toll free 800/777-CITY) or from the City of Santa Fe Arts Commission (tel. 984-6707). Current listings can be found in Friday's "Pasatiempo" edition of the *New Mexican,* Santa Fe's daily newspaper, and in the *Santa Fe Reporter,* published weekly on Wednesdays.

The **Galisteo News & Ticket Center,** 201 Galisteo St. (tel. 984-1316), is the primary outlet for tickets to the opera and other major entertainment events. **Nicholas Potter, Bookseller,** 203 E. Palace Ave. (tel. 983-5434), also has tickets to select events. You can order by phone from **TicketMaster** (tel. 842-5387 for information, 884-0999 to order). Discount tickets may be available on the nights of performances; the opera, for example, makes standing-room tickets available at a greatly reduced rate just one hour ahead of time.

A variety of free concerts, lectures, and other events are presented in the summer, cosponsored by the City of Santa Fe and the chamber of commerce under the name **Santa Fe Summerscene.** From mid-June through August, Tuesday and Thursday at 7pm, they are held either on the Plaza, in Fort Marcy Park, or Amelia White Park (Old Santa Fe Trail at Camino Corrales), and run the gamut from classical to rock. There's also a wide-ranging Noon Concert Series on Tuesday and Thursday on the Plaza. Call 983-7317 for more information.

The **Santa Fe Summer Concert Series,** at Paolo Soleri Outdoor Amphitheatre on the Santa Fe Indian School campus on Cerrillos Road, has brought such name performers as Frank Zappa, Kenny Loggins, and B. B. King to the city. More than two dozen concerts and special events are scheduled each summer.

Note: Many companies listed here perform at locations other than their headquarters, so check the site of the performance you plan to attend.

THE PERFORMING ARTS

MAJOR PERFORMING ARTS COMPANIES

Opera & Classical Music

SANTA FE OPERA, P.O. Box 2408, Santa Fe, NM 87504. Tel. 982-3851 or 982-3855 for tickets.

Even if your visit isn't timed to coincide with the opera season, you shouldn't miss seeing its open-air amphitheater. Located on a wooded hilltop seven miles north of the city off U.S. 84/285, the sweeping curves of this serene structure seem perfectly attuned to the contour of the surrounding terrain. At night, the lights of Los Alamos can be seen in the distance under clear skies.

Many rank the Santa Fe Opera behind only the Metropolitan Opera of New York as the finest company in the United States today. Established in 1957 by John Crosby, still the opera's artistic director, it consistently attracts famed conductors, directors, and singers, the list of whom has included Igor Stravinsky.

The opera is noted for its performances of great classics, little-known works by classical European composers, and American premieres of 20th-century works.

The 9-week, 37-performance opera season runs from late June to late August. All performances begin at 9pm.

Tours: July 6–Aug 29, Mon–Sat 2pm; $5 for adults, free for children 7 to 15.

Prices: Fri–Sat $83, $63, $54, $45, $30, $15; Mon–Thurs $5 less for all seats. Wheelchair seating $12; standing room (sold 1 hour before the show) $6.

SANTA FE CHAMBER MUSIC FESTIVAL, 640 Paseo de Peralta (P.O. Box 853), Santa Fe, NM 87504. Tel. 983-2075 or 982-1890 (box office), toll free 800/962-7286.

The festival, whose 7-week season of some 50 concerts runs from the second week of July through the third week of August, has been held in beautiful St. Francis Auditorium since its founding in 1973. Performances, which are later broadcast in a 13-week series over the Chicago-based WFMT Fine Arts Network, include selections by great classical and contemporary composers and a week of baroque music on original instruments. Also part of the festival is a "Music of the Americas" series, emphasizing the traditions of different Western Hemisphere cultures. A noted string quartet and composer are "in residence" each season.

Performances are nightly at 8pm, except Sunday at 6pm. At 1pm Sunday, there's a "musical conversation" session, combining performance with dialogue between artists and the audience. Other days during the season, open rehearsals are free to the public from 10am to 5pm.

Prices: Evening performances $15–$25; Sun matinee $5.

THE SANTA FE SYMPHONY ORCHESTRA AND CHORUS, P.O. Box 9692, Santa Fe, NM 87504. Tel. 983-3530.

This 60-piece professional symphony orchestra has grown rapidly in stature since its founding in 1984. Weekend performances of classical and popular works are presented in a subscription series at Sweeney Center from September to May. Each performance is preceded by a lecture, "Reflections on Music," given by music director Stewart Robertson. There is a mid-February children's program ($4.50 children, $6.50 adults). A free concert is offered at the Cristo Rey Church in early December.

Prices: Single tickets $10–$30 (six seating categories).

THE ORCHESTRA OF SANTA FE, 111 N. Guadalupe St. (P.O. Box 2091), Santa Fe, NM 87504. Tel. 988-4640.

A chamber orchestra founded in 1974, this group is best known for its holiday production of Handel's *Messiah* and its January/February Bach or Mozart festivals. In all, it offers 15 classical concerts a year, between mid-September and early May. Noon lectures are given five times a season at St. Francis Auditorium and in Los Alamos.

All regular concert performances are at the Lensic Theatre, 211 W. San Francisco St. (tel. 988-4640). This early 20th-century Spanish Colonial–style theater, otherwise a United Artists cinema, has a state-of-the-art acoustical sound shell installed in 1989. It seats about 850.

Prices: Single tickets $6–$27 (five seating categories). Students are half-price. Ask about the Sunday family-saver package.

THE ENSEMBLE OF SANTA FE, P.O. Box 8427, Santa Fe, NM 87504. Tel. 984-2501.

The Ensemble is a professional chamber music group composed of leading musicians from the western United States and guests of national and international acclaim. The Ensemble performs monthly public concerts (21 in all) from September through May in the historic Loretto Chapel and the Santuario de Guadalupe. Christmas and Holy Week concerts sell out in advance.

Prices: $12–$20.

SANTA FE CONCERT ASSOCIATION, P.O. Box 4626, Santa Fe, NM 87504. Tel. 984-8759.

Founded in 1938, the oldest musical organization in northern New Mexico has an October-to-May season that includes more than 20 annual events. Among them are a distinguished artist series featuring renowned instrumental and vocal soloists and ensembles; a free youth concert series; a Sunday-afternoon recital series by local performers; a master class for vocalists; a Christmas Eve special; and occasional master classes. All performances are at St. Francis Auditorium; tickets are sold by Nicholas Potter, Bookseller (tel. 983-5434).

Prices: $12.50–$20.

Theater Companies

NEW MEXICO REPERTORY THEATRE, 1050 Old Pecos Trail (P.O. Box 9279), Santa Fe, NM 87504. Tel. 983-2382 or 984-2226 (box office).

The state's sole resident professional company, founded in 1983, splits its production schedule equally between Santa Fe and Albuquerque (see "Albuquerque Evening Entertainment"). It has its own 340-seat theater, the former Armory for the Arts, where it stages six plays in a mid-October to early May season.

The company performs a variety of innovative classical plays and contemporary American and European works.

The 1991–92 season featured Lanford Wilson's seething drama *Burn This,* the outrageous *The Mystery of Irma Vep,* Athol Fugard's South African drama *The Blood Knot,* Luis Santiero's warm family comedy *Our Lady of the Tortilla,* and the Tennessee Williams classic, *The Glass Menagerie.* Performances during 2-week runs are Tuesday through Saturday at 8pm, with 2pm matinees Saturday and Sunday.

Prices: $18.50–$24, depending upon performance and seatings; $13.50 for seniors and students, weekdays and matinees only.

SANTA FE COMMUNITY THEATRE, 142 E. De Vargas St. (P.O. Box 2084), Santa Fe, NM 87504. Tel. 988-4262.

Founded in the 1920s, this is the oldest existing theater group in New Mexico. Still performing in a historic adobe theater in the Barrio de Analco, it attracts thousands for its dramas (October, March, and May) and comedies. Its January/February Fiesta Melodrama series, and a Labor Day show, are especially popular: One-act melodramas call upon the public to boo the sneering villain and swoon for the damsel in distress.

At press time, the theater had plans to move to the Center for Contemporary Arts, so be sure to check the address before heading out.

Dance Companies

MARIA BENITEZ SPANISH DANCE COMPANY, Picacho Plaza Hotel, 750 N. St. Francis Dr. Tel. 982-1237.
The Benitez Company's "Estampa Flamenca" summer series is performed from mid-June to mid-September at the Picacho Plaza. True flamenco is one of the most thrilling of all dance forms, displaying the inner spirit and verve of the gypsies of Spanish Andalusia.
Prices: $14–$18 (subject to change).

MAJOR CONCERT HALLS & ALL-PURPOSE AUDITORIUMS

CENTER FOR CONTEMPORARY ARTS, 291 E. Barcelona Rd. (P.O. Box 148) Santa Fe, NM 87504. Tel. 982-1338.
The Center for Contemporary Arts presents the work of international, national, and regionally known artists through gallery exhibitions, contemporary dance and new music concerts, poetry readings, performance art events, theater, video and film screenings. Events are offered nightly. The Cinematheque screens international cinema; there is an Ethnographic Films Series; and the Santa Fe Film Expo, which showcases the newest of international independent cinema. CCA is the site of a permanent outdoor James Turrell SKYSPACE.
The gallery is open from 10am to 4pm Tuesday through Friday; Saturday noon to 4pm; office hours are 9am to 5pm Monday through Friday.
Tickets: Prices vary with performance.

PAOLO SOLERI AMPHITHEATRE, 1501 Cerrillos Rd., Santa Fe Indian School. Tel. 989-6310.
This outdoor arena is the locale of many warm-weather events. More than two dozen concerts are presented here each summer, including the Santa Fe Summer Concert Series. In recent years, the series has attracted such big-name acts as Joan Armatrading, the Grateful Dead, B. B. King, Kenny Loggins, Anne Murray, Suzanne Vega, Frank Zappa, and the Reggae Sunsplash. Most are booked by Big River Productions, P.O. Box 8036, Albuquerque, NM 87198 (tel. 505/256-1777).
Tickets: Vary according to performer.

ST. FRANCIS AUDITORIUM, Museum of Fine Arts. Tel. 827-4455.
⭐ This beautiful music hall, patterned after the interiors of traditional Hispanic mission churches, is noted for its acoustics. It hosts a wide variety of musical events, including the Santa Fe Chamber Music Festival in July and August. The Santa Fe Symphony Festival Series, the Santa Fe Concert Association, the Santa Fe Women's Ensemble, and various other programs are also held here.
Tickets: $5–$25, depending upon event; see listings for specific performing arts companies.

SWEENEY CONVENTION CENTER, Marcy and Grant Sts. Tel. 984-6760.
Santa Fe's largest indoor arena hosts a wide variety of trade expositions and other events during the year. It's also the home of the Santa Fe Symphony Orchestra.
Tickets: $10–$30, depending upon seating and performances.

THE CLUB & MUSIC SCENE
COUNTRY MUSIC

RODEO NITES, 2911 Cerrillos Rd. Tel. 473-4138.
There's live country dance music nightly at this popular club at the Vagabond Inn. Free dance lessons are offered Monday from 7 to 9pm.
Admission: Fri–Sat $3, Sun $2; free weekdays.

ROCK

THE BULL RING, 414 Old Santa Fe Trail. Tel. 983-3328.
This restaurant near the State Capitol is also a lively bar with dance music after

9pm Wednesday through Saturday. Bands, normally booked for a week at a time, may be rhythm-and-blues, reggae, rock, or tunes from the sixties and seventies.
Admission: Thurs–Sat $3.

CHELSEA STREET PUB, Villa Linda Mall, Rodeo and Cerrillos Rds. Tel. 473-5105.
Burgers and beer are served here during the lunch and dinner hours, but when the shopping mall closes at 9pm, the pub really starts hopping. Top bands from throughout the Southwest play dance music until 2am Monday through Saturday and until 7pm Sunday.
Admission: Free.

CHEZ WHAT, 213 W. Alameda St. Tel. 982-0099.
There's original live music here nightly from 11am to 2am. Performers could be local, regional, national, or even international, and the music runs the gamut from rock to reggae and pop to jazz and blues.
Admission: $2–$3 Mon–Thurs, $5–$6 Fri–Sun; $10 or more for major acts.

JAZZ, BLUES & FOLK

EL FAROL, 808 Canyon Rd. Tel. 983-9912.
The original neighborhood bar of the Canyon Road artists' quarter (its name means the Lantern) is the place to head for local ambience. Its low ceilings and muraled walls are the home of Santa Fe's largest and most unusual selection of *tapas* (bar snacks and appetizers), from stuffed calamari to grilled cactus with ramesco sauce. Jazz, folk, and ethnic musicians, some of national note, perform most nights.
Admission: $2–$6.

FIESTA LOUNGE, La Fonda Hotel, 100 E. San Francisco St. Tel. 982-5511.
This lively lobby bar offers live entertainment nightly, including a variety of country, jazz, Latin, and big-band show tunes.
Admission: Free.

THE BAR SCENE

CARGO CLUB IN THE BACK, 519 Cerrillos Rd. at Sandoval St. Tel. 989-8790.
Publicized as an "alternative dance club," the Cargo Club hosts a mixed bag of funk, rock, rap, and soul groups, as well as a mixed clientele of gays and straights. Male strip revues sometimes are booked here on weeknights.
Admission: Fri–Sat $3; other nights free except for special events.

VANESSIE OF SANTA FE, 434 W. San Francisco St. Tel. 982-9966.
This is unquestionably Santa Fe's most popular piano bar. The talented Charles Tichenor and Taylor Kundolf have a loyal local following. Their repertoire ranges from Bach to Billy Joel, Gershwin to Barry Manilow. They play Monday through Saturday from 4:30pm to 2am and Sunday from 4:30pm to midnight.
Admission: Free.

MORE ENTERTAINMENT

Ever since *The Santa Fe Trail*, a splashy western starring Errol Flynn, Olivia de Havilland, Ronald Reagan, and Raymond Massey, premiered in Santa Fe in 1940, northern New Mexico has been a prime site for major studio movie productions. Films like *Butch Cassidy and the Sundance Kid* (1968), *Easy Rider* (1968), *Billy Jack* (1970), *Silverado* (1984), *Young Guns* (1988), and *The Milagro Beanfield War* (1988) have become big national hits. In fact, an estimated 500 movies have been shot in this region since 1900.
In addition to films shown at the Center for Contemporary Arts, several theaters

present first-run movies. They include **Cinema 6,** 4250 Cerrillos Rd. (tel. 471-0666), the **Coronado Twin Theatres,** 508 Cordova Rd. (tel. 983-3179), **The Movies,** De Vargas Center (tel. 988-2775), and the **Yucca Drive-In,** Cerrillos Road (tel. 471-1000). The **Jean Cocteau Cinema,** 418 Montezuma St. (tel. 988-2711), and the **Grand Illusion,** St. Michael's Drive and Llano Street (tel. 471-8935), show selected comercial, foreign, and art films.

9. EASY EXCURSIONS

PUEBLOS

Within easy driving distance of Santa Fe are the "Eight Northern Pueblos." Nambe, Pojoaque, San Ildefonso, San Juan, Santa Clara, and Tesuque are all within about 30 miles. Picuris (San Lorenzo) is on the "High Road to Taos," and Taos Pueblo, of course, is just outside of the northern New Mexico town of Taos.

The southern six pueblos of this group can easily be seen in a day's round-trip from Santa Fe. Plan to focus most of your attention on San Juan and Santa Clara, including the former's arts cooperative and the latter's Puye Cliff Dwellings.

Certain rules of etiquette apply in visits to pueblos. These are personal dwellings, and must be respected as such. Don't climb on the buildings or peek into doors or windows. Don't enter sacred grounds, such as cemeteries and *kivas*. If you attend a dance or ceremony, remain silent during it, and refrain from applause when it's over. Many pueblos prohibit photography or sketches; others require you to pay a fee for a permit.

TESUQUE PUEBLO, Rte. 11, Box 1, Santa Fe, NM 87501. Tel. 983-2667.

Located eight miles north of Santa Fe northbound on U.S. 84/285, Tesuque's (*teh-SOO-keh*) most visible signs are the unusual Camel Rock and a large roadside Bingo operation (nightly 6:30–11pm; tel. 984-8414). Despite this concession to the late 20th century, the 400 pueblo dwellers are faithful to traditional religion, ritual, and ceremony. Excavations confirm that there was a pueblo here in A.D. 1250; a mission church and adobe houses surround the plaza.

Some Tesuque women are skilled potters; Ignacia Duran's black-and-white and red micaceous pottery is particularly noted.

Admission: Free. Still cameras $10, movie cameras $50, sketching $100.
Open: Daily 9am–5pm.

POJOAQUE PUEBLO, Rte. 11, Box 71, Santa Fe, NM 87501. Tel. 455-2278.

Seven miles farther north on U.S. 84/285, at the junction of N.M. 503, is Pojoaque (*po-HWA-keh*). Though small (pop. 125) and without a definable village, Pojoaque is important as a center for traveler services. Indigenous pottery, embroidery, silverwork, and beadwork are available for sale at the Pojoaque Pueblo Tourist Center. Camera and sketching permits must be obtained in advance through the governor's office.

Admission: Free. No photography on feast days.
Open: Daylight hours.

NAMBE PUEBLO, Rte. 1, Box 117, Santa Fe, NM 87501. Tel. 455-2036.

Drive east three miles from Pojoaque on N.M. 503, then turn right at the Bureau of Reclamation sign for Nambe Falls. Two miles farther is Nambe, a 700-year-old Tewa-speaking pueblo (pop. 450) with a solar-powered tribal headquarters, at the foot of the Sangre de Cristo range. A few of the original pueblo buildings still exist, including a large round *kiva*, used today in ceremonies. Pueblo artisans make woven belts, beadwork, and brown micaceous pottery.

Nambe Falls make a stunning three-tier drop through a cleft in a rock face four miles beyond the pueblo, tumbling into Nambe Reservoir. A recreational site at the reservoir offers fishing, boating, hiking, camping, and picnicking.

Admission: Pueblo free; still cameras $3, movie cameras $5, sketching $10. Recreational site, fishing $5/day adults, $3/day children, camping $7 first night, $4 additional nights.

Open: Pueblo daily 8am–5pm; recreational site Apr–May and Sept–Oct 7am–7pm, June–Aug 6am–9pm.

SAN ILDEFONSO PUEBLO, Rte. 5, Box 315A, Santa Fe, NM 87501. Tel. 455-3549 or 455-2273.

If you turn left on N.M. 502 at Pojoaque, it's about six miles to the turnoff to this pueblo, nationally famous for the matte-finish black-on-black pottery developed by tribeswoman Maria Martinez in the 1920s. The pottery-making process is explained at the **San Ildefonso Pueblo Museum,** where exhibits of pueblo history, arts, and crafts are presented on weekdays. Tours of the pueblo (pop. 650) are offered from the visitor center.

San Ildefonso Feast Day, January 22–23, is a good time to observe the social and religious traditions of the pueblo, when buffalo, deer, and Comanche dances are presented. There are also dances for Easter, St. Anthony's Day on June 13, Santiago's Day on July 25, and the Harvest Festival in early September, as well as Christmas.

The pueblo has a 4½-acre fishing lake open April through October. Picnicking is encouraged; camping is not.

Admission: $1 noncommercial vehicle, $10 commercial vehicle, plus 50¢ per passenger. Still cameras $5, movie cameras and sketching $15. Fishing $5 adults, $3 children 6–12.

Open: Summer Mon–Fri 8am–5pm, Sat–Sun 9am–6pm; winter Mon–Fri 8am–4:30pm. **Closed:** Major holidays and San Ildefonso Feast Day.

SAN JUAN PUEBLO, P.O. Box 1099, San Juan Pueblo, NM 87566. Tel. 852-4400.

The largest (pop. 1,950) and northernmost of the Tewa- (not Tiwa-) speaking pueblos and the headquarters of the Eight Northern Indian Pueblos Council, San Juan is located on the east side of the Rio Grande—opposite the 1598 site of San Gabriel, the first Spanish settlement west of the Mississippi River and the first capital of New Spain. The pueblo is reached via N.M. 74, a mile off N.M. 68, four miles north of Espanola.

Past and present cohabit here. San Juan Indians, though Roman Catholics, still practice traditional religious rituals; thus two rectangular *kivas* flank the church in the main plaza, and *caciques* (pueblo priests) share influence with civil authorities.

The **Eight Northern Indian Pueblos Council** (tel. 852-4265) is a sort of chamber of commerce and social-service agency.

Aguino's Indian Arts and Crafts features paintings, wood carvings, rasps, and corn dolls. It is open Saturday from 8am to 5pm and Sunday from 9am to 5pm and by appointment. Call Juan B. Aguino at 667-8175. Another crafts store, **O'ke Oweenge Arts and Crafts Cooperative** (tel. 852-2372), focuses on local wares: This is a fine place to seek out San Juan's distinctive red pottery, a lustrous ceramic incised with traditional geometric symbols. Also exhibited and sold are seed, turquoise, and silver jewelry, wood and stone carvings, indigenous clothing and weavings, embroidery, and paintings. Artisans often work in the center for visitors to watch. The co-op is open Monday through Saturday from 9am to 5pm; closed San Juan Feast Day.

Right on the main road through the pueblo is the **Tewa Indian Restaurant,** serving traditional pueblo chile stews, breads, blue-corn dishes, posole, teas, and desserts. It's open weekdays from 9am to 2:30pm, except holidays and feast days.

Fishing and picnicking are encouraged at the **San Juan Tribal Lakes,** open year-round.

Admission: Free. Photography or sketching may be allowed with prior permission from the governor's office. The fee for each is $5. Fishing $7 adults, $4 children and seniors.

Open: Daylight hours.

SANTA CLARA PUEBLO, P.O. Box 580, Espanola, NM 87532. Tel. 753-7326.

Just across the Rio Grande from Espanola on N.M. 5, Santa Clara has a population of about 1,600, making it one of the larger pueblos. Driving and walking tours are offered weekdays, with a week's notice, and include visits to the pueblo's historic church and artists' studios. Visitors are welcome to enter studios so marked, and watch the artists making baskets and a highly polished red-and-black pottery.

The Puye Cliff Dwellings (see below) are on the Santa Clara reservation.

Admission: Free. Still cameras $5, movie cameras $10, sketching $15.

Open: Daylight hours. Visitor's center open daily 9am–4:30pm.

PUYE CLIFF DWELLINGS, Santa Clara Pueblo. Tel. 753-7326.

The Santa Clara people migrated to their home on the Rio Grande in the 13th century from a former home high on the Pajarito Plateau to the west. The ruins of that past life have been preserved in this site, an 11-mile climb west of the pueblo. Thought to have been occupied from about 1250–1577, this site at the mouth of the Santa Clara Canyon is a national landmark.

High on a nearly featureless plateau, the volcanic tuff rises in a soft tan facade 200 feet high. Here the Anasazi found niches to build their houses. Visitors can descend via staircases and ladders from the 7,000-foot mesa top into the 740-room pueblo ruin, which includes a ceremonial chamber and community house. Petroglyphs are evident in many of the rocky cliff walls.

Six miles farther west is the **Santa Clara Canyon Recreational Area,** a sylvan summer setting for camping, open year-round for picnicking, hiking, and fishing in ponds and Santa Clara Creek.

Admission: $4 adults, $3 children and seniors. Guided tours additional $1 charge. Tues–Thurs package tour including pueblo feast and dance, $15–$20. Use of recreational area, $8/day per vehicle; camping $10; fishing $8 adults, $4 children.

Open: Daily 9am–6pm.

LOS ALAMOS

The atomic bomb was born in Los Alamos, a city of 12,000 spread on the craggy, fingerlike mesas of the Pajarito Plateau, between the Jemez Mountains and Rio Grande valley, 33 miles northwest of Santa Fe. Pueblo Indians lived in this rugged area for well over 1,000 years, and an exclusive boys' school operated atop the 7,300-foot plateau from 1928 to 1943. Then Los Alamos National Laboratory was founded in secrecy as Project Y of the Manhattan Engineer District, the hush-hush wartime program to split the atom and develop the world's first nuclear weapons.

Project director J. Robert Oppenheimer, later succeeded by Norris E. Bradbury, worked with a team of 30 to 100 scientists in research, development, and production of the weapons. Today 3,000 scientists and another 4,800 support staff work at **Los Alamos National Laboratory,** making it the largest employer in northern New Mexico. Still operated by the University of California for the federal Department of Energy (which provides more than 80% of its $600-million annual budget), its 32 technical areas occupy 43 square miles of mesa-top land.

The laboratory is known today as one of the world's foremost scientific institutions. It's still geared heavily to the defense industry—the Trident and Minuteman strategic warheads were created here, for example—but it has many other research programs, including studies in nuclear fusion and fission, energy conservation, nuclear safety, the environment, and nuclear wastes. Its international resources include a genetic sequence data bank, with wide implications for medicine and agriculture, and an Institute for Geophysics and Planetary Physics among others.

WHAT TO SEE & DO

BRADBURY SCIENCE MUSEUM, Los Alamos National Laboratory, Diamond Dr. Tel. 667-4444.

This outstanding museum is the laboratory's public showcase. It offers a glimpse into World War II's historic Manhattan Project as well as today's advanced science and technology.

Visitors may explore the museum, experiment with lasers, use computers, and view laboratory research in energy, defense, environment, and health. The laboratory's weapon research program is displayed with historical and current exhibits. Self-guided exhibits have interesting hands-on features and video monitors to enhance the visitor's understanding. Educational and historical films are shown continuously.

Note: As this book was going to press, the museum was scheduled to move, so call ahead to find out its current location.

Admission: Free.

Open: Tues–Fri 9am–5pm, Sat–Mon 1–5pm. **Closed:** Major holidays.

LOS ALAMOS HISTORICAL MUSEUM, 2132 Central Ave. Tel. 662-4493.

The massive log building that once housed the dining and recreation hall for the Los Alamos Ranch School for boys is now a National Historic Landmark known as the Fuller Lodge. Its current occupants include this museum, the Fuller Lodge Art Center (see below), and the **Los Alamos County Chamber of Commerce,** P.O. Box 460, Los Alamos, NM 87544 (tel. 662-8105), which doubles as a visitor information center. The museum recounts area history, from prehistoric cliff dwellers to the present, with a variety of exhibits ranging from Indian artifacts to school memorabilia and wartime displays. The museum sponsors guest speakers and operates a bookstore.

Admission: Free.

Open: Mon–Sat 10am–4pm, Sun 1–4pm.

FULLER LODGE ART CENTER, 2132 Central Ave. Tel. 662-9331.

Works of northern New Mexico artists, and traveling exhibitions of regional and national importance, are displayed here.

Admission: Free.

Open: Mon–Sat 10am–4pm, Sun 1–4pm.

WHERE TO STAY

HILLTOP HOUSE HOTEL, Trinity at Central, Los Alamos, NM 87544. Tel. 505/662-2441 or toll free 800/462-0936. Fax 505/662-5913. 87 rms, 5 suites. A/C FRIDGE TV TEL

$ Rates: $60 single. $68 double, $95–$150 suite. AE, CB, DC, MC, V.

Recently renovated, this hotel's tastefully furnished rooms include 33 efficiency units with kitchenettes. Each room has standard furnishings, satellite TV, and other modern conveniences. There are rooms for nonsmokers and women travelers.

The third-floor Trinity Sights Restaurant, which affords a stunning view across the Rio Grande to Santa Fe, offers a lengthy dinner menu that includes the likes of Cajun-style prime rib, chicken saltimbocca, and scallops Portofino. Dinner main courses range from about $14 to $17. A full breakfast is included in weekday rates. The restaurant is open from 6:30am to 10pm daily. There's a lounge on the mezzanine level above. The hotel also offers room service, valet laundry, secretarial service, and complimentary coffee 24 hours. Pets are accepted with a $25 deposit. Facilities include an indoor swimming pool, coin-op laundry, Avis car-rental agency, travel agent, realty office, beauty salon, 24-hour convenience store, adjacent gas station and liquor store, and meeting and conference facilities.

LOS ALAMOS INN, 2201 Trinity Dr., Los Alamos, NM 87544. Tel. 505/662-7211 or toll free 800/279-9279. Fax 505/662-7211 (ask for fax). 116 rms, suites. A/C MINIBAR TV TEL

$ Rates: $60 single, $65 double. AE, CB, DC, MC, V.

Located just a few minutes from Los Alamos National Laboratory, the inn's comfortable, spacious rooms, including some for nonsmokers and the disabled, have queen-size or double beds, large writing tables, remote-control in-room movies, and minibars. Ashley's restaurant is open from 7am to 2pm and 5 to 9pm, with a big salad bar and dinner Mexicana and teriyaki shrimp and scallops in the $10 to serves happy-hour hors d'oeuvres and late-night snacks. service, outdoor swimming pool, hot tub, and meeting facility

BANDELIER NATIONAL MON

Fewer than 15 miles south of Los Alamos along N major prehistoric site to Santa Fe. It combines the ex cliff-dwelling Anasazi pueblo culture with 46 square miles of canyon-and-mesa wilderness.

Most visitors, after an orientation stop in the visitor center and museum to learn about the culture that persisted here between A.D. 1100 and 1550, follow a cottonwood-shaded 1½-mile trail along Frijoles Creek to the principal ruins. The pueblo site, including a great underground *kiva*, has been partially reconstructed. The biggest thrill for most folks, though, is climbing hardy piñon ladders to explore the interiors of cliff dwellings carved into ancient volcanic rock 140 feet above the canyon floor. Tours are self-guided or led by a National Park Service ranger.

At night around a campfire, the rangers or local Indians talk to groups of visitors about the history, culture, and geology of the ruins, or about Indian legends. On a moonlit evening, the guided night walks reveal a different, spooky aspect of the ruins and cave houses, outlined in the two-dimensional chiaroscuro of the thin cold light from the starry sky. Daytime, there are nature programs for adults and children. A small museum at the visitor center shows artifacts found in the area.

Elsewhere in the monument, 60 miles of maintained trails lead to more Indian ruins and ceremonial sites, waterfalls, and wildlife habitats. The separate **Tsankawi** section of the monument, reached by an ancient 2-mile trail close to White Rock, contains a large unexcavated ruin on a high mesa overlooking the Rio Grande valley.

Areas are set aside for picnicking and camping. Admission is $5 per vehicle. The national monument—named after Swiss American archaeologist Adolph Bandelier, who explored here in the 1880s—is open year-round during daylight hours, except Christmas.

Most people are surprised to learn that the largest volcanic caldera in the world is here in northern New Mexico. **Valle Grande,** a vast meadow 16 miles in diameter and 76 square miles in area, is all that remains of a massive volcano that erupted nearly a million years ago. When the mountain spewed ashes and dust as far as Kansas and Nebraska, its underground magma chambers collapsed, forming this great valley. Lava domes which pushed up after the collapse obstruct a full view across the expanse. N.M. 4 skirts the caldera beginning about 15 miles west of Los Alamos.

HIGH ROAD TO TAOS

Unless you're in a hurry to get from Santa Fe to Taos, the "high road"—also called the Mountain Road or the King's Road—is by far the most fascinating route. It transits tiny ridge-top villages where Hispanic life-styles and traditions persist as they did a century ago.

The historic weaving center of **Chimayo** is 16 miles north of Pojoaque junction, at the junction of N.M. 520 and 76 via N.M. 503. Families like the Ortegas maintain a tradition of handwoven textiles begun by their ancestors seven generations ago, in the early 1800s, in this small village. **Ortega's Weaving Shop** and **Galeria Ortega** are fine places to take a close look at this ancient craft.

Today, however, many more people come to Chimayo to visit ✪ **El Santuario de Nuestro Señor de Esquipulas** (the Shrine of Our Lord of Esquipulas), better known simply as El Santuario de Chimayo. Attributed with miraculous powers of healing, this church has been the destination of countless thousands of pilgrims since its construction in 1814–16. Some 30,000 people may participate in the annual Good Friday pilgrimage, many of them walking from as far away as Albuquerque.

nly the earth in the anteroom beside the altar has healing powers , the entire shrine has a special serene feeling that's hard to ignore. It's ng to peruse the testimonies of rapid recoveries from illness or injury on the the anteroom, and equally poignant to read the as yet unanswered entreaties on behalf of loved ones.

Designated a National Historic Landmark in 1970, the church contains five beautiful *reredos,* or panes of sacred paintings, one behind the main altar and two on each side of the nave. Each year during the fourth weekend in July, the 9th-century military exploits of the Spanish saint Santiago are celebrated in a weekend fiesta, supported by the National Endowment for the Arts, including the historic play *Los Moros y Cristianos* (Moors and Christians).

Many travelers schedule their drives to have lunch at the ✪ **Restaurante Rancho de Chimayo** (tel. 351-4444) on N.M. 76 east of the junction. The adobe home, built by Hermenegildo Jaramillo in the 1880s, has been in the food business for nearly three decades. Native New Mexican cuisine, prepared from generations-old Jaramillo family recipes, is served on terraced patios and in cozy dining rooms beneath hand-stripped *vigas.* Dinners run $10 to $17. The restaurant is open daily from noon to 10pm from June through August and Tuesday through Sunday from noon to 9pm the rest of the year.

The Jaramillo family also owns a bed-and-breakfast inn, **Hacienda Rancho de Chimayo,** P.O. Box 11, Chimayo, NM 87522 (tel. 505/351-2222). Once the residence of Epifanio Jaramillo, Hermenegildo's brother, its seven guest rooms all open onto an enclosed courtyard. Each room, furnished with turn-of-the-century antiques, has a private bath and sitting area. Rates are $55 to $95. The office is open daily from 9am to 9pm.

Lovely **Santa Cruz Lake** has a dual purpose: the artificial lake provides water for Chimayo valley farms, but also offers a recreation site for trout fishing and camping at the edge of the Pecos Wilderness. To reach it, turn south 4 miles on N.M. 503, 2 miles east of Chimayo.

Just as Chimayo is famous for its weaving, the village of **Cordova,** 7 miles east on N.M. 76, is noted for its wood carvers. Small shops and studios along the highway display *santos* (carved saints) and various decorative items.

Anyone who saw Robert Redford's 1988 movie production, *The Milagro Beanfield War,* has seen **Truchas.** A former Spanish colonial outpost built at 8,000 feet atop a mesa 4 miles east of Cordova, it was chosen as the site for filming in part because traditional Hispanic culture remains pervasive. Subsistence *acequia* farming has a high profile here. The scenery is spectacular: 13,101-foot Truchas Peak dominates one side of the mesa, and the broad Rio Grande valley the other. **Rancho Arriba,** P.O. Box 338, Truchas, NM 87578 (tel. 505/689-2374), is a small working farm/bed-and-breakfast for those who seek a little solitude. Four rooms are priced at $40 to $55.

Las Trampas, 6 miles east of Truchas on N.M. 76, is most notable for its **San Jose Church,** to some the most beautiful church built during the Spanish colonial period. It was placed on the National Register of Historic Places in 1966 through the efforts of preservationists who felt it was threatened by a highway project.

Near the regional education center of **Penasco,** 24 miles from Chimayo near the junction of N.M. 75 and 76, is the **Picuris (San Lorenzo) Pueblo** (tel. 587-2519). The 270 citizens of this 15,000-acre mountain pueblo, native Tiwa speakers, consider themselves a sovereign nation: Their forebears never made a treaty with any foreign country, the United States included. Thus they observe a traditional form of tribal council government. Their annual feast day at San Lorenzo Church is August 10.

Still, the people are modern enough to have fully computerized their public showcase, Picuris Tribal Enterprises. Besides the Hotel Santa Fe in the state capital, components include the **Picuris Pueblo Museum,** where weaving, beadwork, and the distinctive reddish-brown clay cooking pottery are exhibited weekdays from 8am to 4:30pm. Guided tours through the old village ruins begin from the museum; camera fees start at $5. **Hidden Valley Restaurant** serves a native Picuris menu, along with an American menu. There's also an information center, crafts shop,

grocery, and other shops. Permits ($3 for adults, $2 for chilc
camp at Pu-Na and Tu-Tah lakes, regularly stocked with t

One mile east of Penasco on N.M. 75 is **Vadito,** which
center for the conservative Catholic brotherhood, the Penit

Taos is 24 miles north of Penasco via N.M. 518. But da
can loop back to the capital by taking N.M. 75 west from Pi
miles west of Picuris, and its twin village of **Embudo,** a mil
the Rio Grande, are the homes of many artists and craftspe
works during an annual autumn show sponsored by the Dixor
can follow signs to **La Chiripada Winery** (tel. 579-44:
surprisingly good. The winery is open Monday through Saturc   ___ ⌐pm.
There is a tasting room in Taos at the Plaza Real Building th.. .ɔ open Monday to
Saturday from 10am to 5pm and noon to 5pm on Sunday.

Near Dixon is the **Harding Mine,** a University of New Mexico property where
visitors can gather mineral specimens without going underground. If you haven't
signed a liability release at the Albuquerque campus, ask at Labeo's Store in Dixon.
They'll direct you to the home of a local resident who can get you started fossicking
almost immediately.

Two more small villages lie in the Rio Grande valley at 6-mile intervals south of
Embudo on N.M. 68. **Velarde** is a fruit-growing center; in season, the road here is
lined with stands selling fresh fruit or crimson chile *ristras* and wreaths of native
plants. **Alcalde** is the location of Los Luceros, an early 17th-century home planned
for refurbishment as an arts and history center. The unique Dance of the Matachines,
a Moorish-influenced production brought from Spain by the conquistadors, is
performed here on holidays and feast days.

The commercial center of **Espanola** (pop. 7,000) no longer has the railroad that
was responsible for its establishment in the 1880s, but it does have perhaps New
Mexico's greatest concentration of "low riders." Their owners give much loving
attention to these late-model customized cars, so called because their suspension
leaves them sitting exceedingly close to the ground. You can't miss seeing them cruise
the main streets of town, especially on weekend nights.

Significant sights in Espanola include the **Bond House Museum,** a Victorian-era
adobe home displaying exhibits of local history and art; and the **Santa Cruz
Church,** built in 1733 and renovated in 1979, which houses many fine examples of
Spanish Colonial religious art. Major events include the July **Fiesta de Oñate,**
commemorating the valley's founding in 1596; the **Tri-Cultural Art Festival** in
October on the Northern New Mexico Community College campus; and the
weeklong **Summer Solstice** celebration, staged in June by the nearby, 200-strong
Ram Das Puri ashram of the Sikhs (tel. 753-9438).

Santa Feans sometimes take the half-hour drive to Espanola simply to dine at
Matilda's Café, Corlett Road (tel. 753-3200). Open Tuesday through Sunday from
9am to 9pm, it's noted for its New Mexican food, including vegetarian plates. There's
also **El Paragua,** 603 Santa Cruz Rd. (tel. 753-3211).

Full information on Espanola and vicinity can be obtained from the **Espanola
Valley Chamber of Commerce,** 417 Big Rock Center, Espanola, NM 87532 (tel.
505/753-2831).

PECOS NATIONAL MONUMENT

About 15 miles east of Santa Fe, I-25 meanders through **Glorieta Pass,** site of an
important Civil War skirmish. In March 1862 volunteers from Colorado and New
Mexico, along with Fort Union regulars, defeated a Confederate force marching on
Santa Fe, thereby turning the tide of Southern encroachment in the West.

Take N.M. 50 east to **Pecos,** a distance of about 7 miles. This quaint town, well
off the beaten track since the interstate was constructed, is the site of a noted
Benedictine monastery. North of here 26 miles on N.M. 63 is the village of **Cowles,**
gateway to the natural wonderland of the Pecos Wilderness. There are many camping,
picnicking, and fishing locales en route.

...onal Monument (tel. 757-6414), 2 miles south of the town of Pecos ..., contains the ruins of a 14th-century pueblo and 17th-century mission. ...o was well known to Coronado in 1540: "It is feared through the land," he ...With a population of about 2,000, the Indians farmed in irrigated fields and ...ted wild game. Their pueblo had 660 rooms and many *kivas*. By 1620 Franciscan monks had established a church and convent. Military and natural disasters took their toll, however, and in 1838 the 20 surviving Pecos Indians abandoned their ancestral home and took up residence with relatives at the Jemez Pueblo.

The E. E. Fogelson Visitor Center tells the history of the Pecos people in a well-done, chronologically organized exhibit, complete with dioramas or Pre-Hispanic life-styles. A 1¼-mile loop trail departs from the center and leads through Pecos Pueblo and the Mission de Nuestra Senora de Los Angeles de Porciuncula, as the church was formally known. This excavated structure—170 feet long and 90 feet wide at the transept—was once the most magnificent church north of Mexico City.

Visitors to the national monument are asked to pay $1 admission, which goes to further preservation. Hours are 8am to 6pm from Memorial Day to Labor Day; 8am to 5pm the rest of the year.

TAOS

Taos is one of those gemlike little towns where the local regard for traditional architecture, combined with surrounding natural beauty, has drawn the eye of artists. For nearly a century painters, graphic artists, and sculptors have made Taos an art center, many of them settling here to form a sort of informal colony. It is one of the very oldest American towns: The Tiwa Indians living in the traditional apartment complexes in Taos Pueblo nearby have been in residence for at least 1,000 years, perhaps 5,000; prehistoric ruins exist throughout the Taos Valley. The village itself was settled by the Spanish in 1617.

Taos is just 40 miles south of the Colorado border, 70 miles north of Santa Fe, and 130 miles from Albuquerque. Life here moves in and out of, and around, the Plaza, just as did life in old villages in Spain and Mexico. Although the population is only about 5,000, the summertime scene is one of crowded sidewalks, shops, and restaurants, with a never-ending traffic jam on the main road through town, for Taos has become a major tourist attraction in the Southwest. With several fine museums and a wide choice of accommodations and restaurants for visitors, it is well worth a visit of two to three days.

Its 6,900-foot elevation and dry climate give Taos sharp clear air that is mild in summer and invigorating in winter—especially for skiers who since the 1950s have flocked to the Taos area in increasing numbers to take to the slopes at five resorts. The winter season in Taos has become even busier than the summer.

Taos began as the northernmost outpost of Spain's Mexican empire. It was a hotbed of revolutionary activity throughout the late 17th century; the suppression of three rebellions helped spark the Pueblo Revolt of 1680. Through the 18th and 19th centuries Taos was an important trade center: New Mexico's annual caravan to Chihuahua, Mexico, couldn't leave until after the annual midsummer Taos Fair. French trappers began attending the fair in 1739. Plains Indians, even though they often attacked the Pueblos at other times, also attended the market festivals under a temporary annual truce. By the early 1800s Taos had become a headquarters for American "mountain men," the most famous of whom, Kit Carson, made his home in Taos from 1826 to 1868.

Taos was firmly Hispanic, and stayed loyal to Mexico during the Mexican War of 1846. The city rebelled against its new U.S. landlord in 1847, killing newly appointed Gov. Charles Bent in his Taos home. Nevertheless it became a part of the territory of New Mexico in 1850. It fell into Confederate hands for just six weeks during the Civil War, at the end of which time Carson and two other statesmen raised the Union flag over Taos Plaza and guarded it day and night. Since then Taos has had the honor of flying the flag 24 hours a day.

The town's international renown as an art center had its start in 1898 when two young eastern artists on a sketching tour through the Rockies had a wheel break on their horse-drawn buggy north of Taos. The pair, Ernest Blumenschein and Bert Phillips, took the wheel in for repairs, and were captivated by the dramatic light changes and their visual effect upon buildings and landscapes. They soon settled in Taos, and by 1912 the Taos Society of Artists had placed the town on the international cultural map. Today, by some estimates, more than 10% of the townspeople are painters, sculptors, writers, musicians, or otherwise earn income from an artistic pursuit.

1. ORIENTATION

ARRIVING IN TAOS By Plane Taos Airport (tel. 758-4995) is about eight miles northwest of town on U.S. 64, en route to the Rio Grande Gorge Bridge. **Horizon Air Services** (tel. 758-9501) provides local Cessna 310 services to communities and national parks of the region.

Pride of Taos (tel. 758-8340) meets incoming flights and provides shuttle-bus service to Taos and the Taos Ski Valley.

By Bus The **Taos Bus Center,** Paseo del Pueblo Sur across from the Chevron Station (tel. 758-1144), is not far from the Plaza. **Greyhound** and **TNM&O Coaches** arrive and depart from this depot several times a day.

Two local bus services provide transportation throughout the region. **Pride of Taos** (tel. 758-8340) offers twice-daily shuttle-bus service to and from Albuquerque airport and downtown Santa Fe. **Faust's Transportation** (tel. 758-3410 or 758-7359) runs a similar service once a day, as well as shuttling to and from Red River, Angel Fire, and other area resort towns. Both services charge similar rates of $25 one-way, $45 round-trip, to Albuquerque.

By Car Most visitors arrive in Taos either via N.M. 68 or U.S. 64. Northbound travelers exit I-25 at Santa Fe, follow U.S. 285 as far as San Juan Pueblo, and continue on the divided highway when it becomes N.M. 68. Taos is 79 miles from the I-25 junction. Travelers southbound from Denver on I-25 exit 6 miles south of Raton at U.S. 64, and follow it 95 miles to Taos. Another major route is U.S. 64 from the west (214 miles from Farmington).

TOURIST INFORMATION The **Taos County Chamber of Commerce,** P.O. Drawer I, Taos, NM 87571 (tel. 505/758-3873 or toll free 800/732-TAOS) is located on Paseo del Pueblo Sur; however, it was in the process of moving at press time, so be sure to call ahead for its present location. It's open from 8am to 5pm daily, year-round except major holidays. **Carson National Forest** has an information center connected to the chamber.

CITY LAYOUT The Plaza is a short block west of Taos's major intersection— where **U.S. 64 (Kit Carson Road)** from the east joins N.M. 68, **Paseo del Pueblo Sur** (also known as South Pueblo Road or South Santa Fe Road). U.S. 64 proceeds north from the intersection as **Paseo del Pueblo Norte** (North Pueblo Road). **Camino de la Placita** (Placitas Road) circles the west side of downtown, passing within a block of the other side of the Plaza. Many of the streets that join these thoroughfares are winding lanes lined by traditional adobe homes, many of them a century or more old.

MAPS To find your way around town, pick up a copy of the Town of Taos map from the chamber of commerce.

2. GETTING AROUND

BY BUS OR TAXI Two private companies serve Taos. **Pride of Taos** (tel. 758-8340) operates a summer trolley that runs daily from 9am to 4:30pm from Taos

Plaza and the chamber of Commerce. The tour is a 50-minute narrated sightseeing trolley tour of historic Taos for $5 ($3 for children). In winter, Pride of Taos's shuttle-bus service links town hotels and Taos Ski Valley four times a day for $5 round-trip. A night bus ($10) brings skiers staying at the ski valley into town for dinner and returns them to their lodgings.

Faust's Transportation (tel. 758-3410) offers town taxi service from 7am to 11pm daily, with fares of $5 anywhere in the city limits for up to two people ($2 per additional person), $12 to the airport, $25 to Taos Ski Valley.

BY CAR With offices at the airport plus in-town pick up and delivery, **Rich Ford Rental Cars** (tel. 758-9501) is reliable and efficient. **Hertz** (tel. 758-1668) is at the Sagebrush Inn, Paseo del Pueblo Sur.

Parking can be difficult during the summer rush, when the stream of tourists' cars moving north and south through town never ceases. Not everyone knows about all the free parking lots, however, especially about the municipal lot behind Taos Community Auditorium, just off Paseo del Pueblo Norte a block north of the Plaza traffic signal. Another lot just to the north of the Plaza has parking meters. Two commercial lots, one behind the Plaza and another off Kit Carson Road, charge a small fee for all-day parking.

A *note for outdoor enthusiasts:* Reliable paved roads lead to takeoff points for side trips up poorer forest roads to many recreation sites. Once you get off the main roads, you won't find gas stations or cafés. Four-wheel-drive vehicles are recommended on snow and much of the otherwise-unpaved terrain of the region. If you're doing some off-road adventuring, it's wise to go with a full gas tank, extra food and water, and warm clothing—just in case. At the more-than-10,000-foot elevations of northern New Mexico, sudden summer snowstorms are not unknown.

BY BICYCLE Rentals are available from the **Taos Mountain Outfitters** at 114 S. Plaza (tel. 758-9292), or **Native Sons Adventures** at 813 A Paseo del Pueblo Sur (tel. 758-9342).

FAST   TAOS

Business Hours Most businesses are open Monday to Friday 9am to 5pm. Some may open an hour earlier and close an hour later. Many also open on Saturday mornings, and some art galleries are open all day Saturday and Sunday, especially during peak tourist seasons. Call for specific hours.

Drugstores The **Taos Pharmacy,** in Piñon Plaza on Paseo del Pueblo Sur (tel. 758-3342 or 758-3507), next door to Holy Cross Hospital, is open 9am to 6pm Monday to Friday and 9am to 5pm Saturday.

Emergencies Dial 911 for police, fire, and ambulance.

Hairdressers & Barbers **Spirits of Beauty,** 223 Paseo del Pueblo Sur (tel. 758-1178), next door to the chamber of commerce, and **Kachina Beauty Salon,** 413 Paseo del Pueblo Norte (tel. 758-8727), welcome drop-ins of either sex. There are numerous other shops in town.

Hospital The **Holy Cross Hospital,** on Paseo del Pueblo Sur (tel. 758-8883), is a 29-bed unit with 24-hour emergency service.

Hot lines **Rape Crisis Center,** 758-2910, **Battered Women,** 785-9888. **Environmental Improvement Division,** 1-827-9329. **Poison Control Center,** toll free 800/432-6866.

Laundry & Dry Cleaning The **Peralta Laundromat,** 1018 Paseo del Pueblo Sur (tel. 758-0239), a couple of miles south of downtown, is open daily.

Library The **Harwood Public Library and Museum,** on Ledoux Street near the Plaza (tel. 758-3063), has a general collection for Taos residents; a children's library; and special collections featuring the Taos Society of Artists as its permanent collection, and changing exhibitions of contemporary artists.

Mail   The main **Taos Post Office** is on Paseo del Pueblo Norte (tel. 758-2081), a few blocks north of the Plaza traffic light. There are smaller offices in Ranchos de Taos (tel. 758-3944) and at El Prado (tel. 758-4810). The ZIP code for Taos is 87571.

Newspapers   The *Taos News* (tel. 758-2241) and the *Sangre de Cristo Chronicle* (tel. 377-2358) appear on Thursday. The *Albuquerque Journal* and *Tribune,* the *New Mexican* from Santa Fe, and the *Denver Post* are easily obtained at the Fernandez de Taos Bookstore on the Plaza.

Photographic Needs   Check **Plaza Photo,** 106B Juan Largo Lane, just off North Plaza (tel. 758-3420).

Police   In case of emergency, dial 911. All other inquiries should be directed to **Taos Police,** Civic Plaza Drive (tel. 758-2216). The **Taos County Sheriff,** with jurisdiction outside the city limits, is located in the county courthouse on Paseo del Pueblo Sur (tel. 758-3361).

Radio   Local stations are KKIT-AM (1340) for news, sports, and weather (tel. 758-2231); and KTAO-FM (101.7), which broadcasts an entertainment calendar at 6pm daily (tel. 758-1017).

Religious Services   The biggest church in town is **Our Lady of Guadalupe Church,** west of the Plaza on Camino de la Placita (tel. 758-9208). Visitors often enjoy attending a service at the famous **San Francisco de Asis Church,** four miles south of the Plaza in Ranchos de Taos (tel. 758-2754). Masses are mainly in English, but each church has a Sunday-morning Spanish-language mass.

Other denominations active in Taos include Assemblies of God, Baptist, Brethren, Church of Christ, Episcopal, Foursquare Gospel, Friends, Jehovah's Witnesses, Methodist, Presbyterian, Mormon, and Jewish.

Taxes   There is a local bed tax of 3.5% in Taos Town and 3% on hotel rooms in Taos County.

Useful Telephone Numbers   For information on **road conditions** in the Taos area, call the state police (tel. 758-8878) or dial 800/432-4269 (within New Mexico) for the State Highway Department. **Taos County offices** are at 758-8834. The KKIT 24-hour weather line is 758-4267.

3. ACCOMMODATIONS

During peak seasons, visitors without reservations may find a vacant room hard to come by. **Taos Central Reservations,** P.O. Box 1713, Taos, NM 87571 (tel. 505/758-9767 or toll free 800/821-2437) might be able to help.

There are another 300-or-so rooms in 15 condos and lodges at or near the Taos Ski Valley. If they're full, the **Taos Valley Resort Association,** P.O. Box 85, Taos Ski Valley, NM 87525 (tel. 505/776-2233 or toll free 800/776-1111) frequently knows of unadvertised condominium or lodge vacancies.

Unlike Santa Fe, there are two high seasons in Taos, with winter (Christmas-to-Easter ski season) usually busier and sometimes more expensive than summer. Spring and fall are shoulder seasons, often with lower rates. The period between Easter and Memorial Day is notoriously slow in the tourist industry here, and many restaurants and other businesses take their annual vacations at this time. Book well ahead during ski holiday periods (especially Christmas) and during the annual arts festivals (late May to mid-June and late September to early October).

In these listings, the following categories describe peak-season price ranges: **expensive,** over $100 per night double; **moderate,** $75 to $100; **inexpensive,**

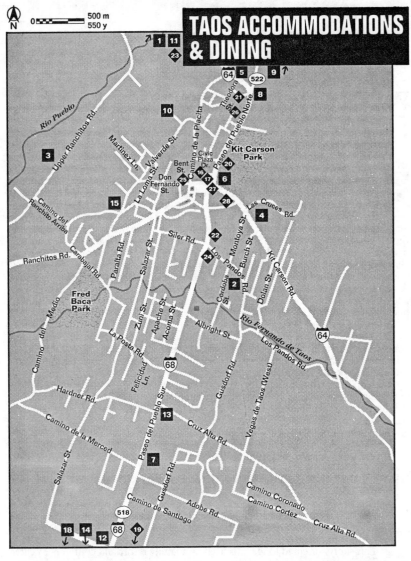

TAOS ACCOMMODATIONS & DINING

0 — 500 m / 550 y

N

ACCOMMODATIONS:
Abominable Snowmansion Skiers' Hostel **1**
Adobe & Pines Inn **14**
Casa de las Chimeneas **2**
Casa Europa **3**
El Monte Lodge **4**
El Pueblo Lodge **5**
The Historic Taos Inn **6**
Holiday Inn Don Fernando de Taos **7**
Kachina Lodge de Taos **8**

Laughing Horse Inn **9**
Orinda **10**
Quail Ridge Inn **11**
Sagebrush Inn **12**
Sun God Lodge **13**
Taos Hacienda Inn **15**

DINING:
The Apple Tree ◆**16**
Bent Street Deli & Café ◆**17**
Casa de Valdez ◆**19**
Doc Martin's, Taos Inn ◆**20**

Dori's Bakery & Café ◆**21**
La Cigale de Paris ◆**22**
Lambert's of Taos ◆**24**
Mainstreet Bakery ◆**25**
Michael's Kitchen ◆**26**
Ogelvie's Bar & Grill ◆**27**
Roberto's Restaurant ◆**28**
Stakeout at Outlaw Hill ◆**18**
Villa Fontana ◆**23**

$50 to $75; **budget,** less than $40 per night double. Tax of 9% to 11% is added to every hotel bill.

EXPENSIVE

THE HISTORIC TAOS INN, 125 Paseo del Pueblo Norte (P.O. Drawer N), Taos, NM 87571. Tel. 505/758-2233 or toll free 800/TAOS-INN. Fax 505/758-5776. 39 rms. A/C TV TEL

$ Rates: $80–$125, according to type of room and season. Rates are often lower during spring and fall. AE, CB, DC, MC, V.

The last century of Taos history is alive and well within the walls of this atmospheric inn. The inn is made up of several separate adobe houses dating from the mid-1800's, which surrounded a small plaza complete with communal town well. Dr. T. Paul Martin purchased the complex in 1895: He was Taos County's first physician, and for many years, the only one. In 1936, a year after the doctor's death, his widow, Helen, enclosed the plaza, now the inn's magnificent two-story lobby, installed indoor plumbing (the first in Taos!), and opened the Hotel Martin. In 1981–82, the inn was restored; it is now listed on the state and national registers of historic places. Today, hotel visitors find an inn of hospitality and charm, combining 20th-century elegance with 19th-century ambience. The lobby is graced with interior balconies overlooking the town well, reborn as a tiered fountain. Above it rises a stained-glass cupola. Large *vigas* adorn the ceiling, handwoven rugs and outstanding artwork cover the walls, and Taos-style *bancos* face a sunken pueblo-style fireplace in one corner of the room.

No two guest rooms are alike. While all are furnished in regional style, they differ in size, shape, and craft items—and thus each has a distinct personality. All rooms contain Taos-style furniture built by local artisans; and original Native American, Hispanic, and New Mexican arts decorate the interiors. All have custom hand-loomed bedspreads and 31 rooms have fireplaces.

Dining/Entertainment: Doc Martin's, with outstanding contemporary American cuisine, is one of Taos's leading dining establishments. (See "Dining," below). The Adobe Bar, popular among Taos artists and other locals, has live entertainment weekends and a late-night food menu.

Services: Room service, valet laundry.

Facilities: Rooms for nonsmokers and the disabled, seasonal outdoor swimming pool, year-round Jacuzzi in greenhouse.

QUAIL RIDGE INN, Ski Valley Rd. (P.O. Box 707), Taos, NM 87571. Tel. 505/776-2211 or toll free 800/624-4448. Fax 505/776-2949. 110 rms (60 suites). TV TEL

$ Rates (range covers seasonal variations): $75–$125 single or double; $125–$300 suite. A 2% gratuity is added to all rates. Extra person $10. Children under 18 stay free with parent. AE, CB, DC, MC, V.

This sports-oriented lodge bills itself as a family resort and conference center. Tennis and skiing are the recreations of note at this contemporary pueblo-style hotel, which spreads across several acres of open sagebrush about 4 miles north of Taos and three-quarters of a mile east of U.S. 64, en route to the Ski Valley 14 miles distant.

Four room options are available at the Quail Ridge Inn, which won a *Western Home* magazine award for architect Antoine Predock when it opened in 1978. Smallest are "hotel rooms," which can sleep four on a queen-size bed and queen-size sleeper sofa. Next are studios, actually semisuites with full kitchens and patios or balconies. One-bedroom suites, the most popular accommodations, consist of a studio with a connecting hotel room. A half-dozen separate *casitas* contain spacious two-bedroom suites of about 1,600 square feet each.

Every room, no matter its size, has a big fireplace, huge closets and full shower/baths with private hot-water heaters. Kitchenettes are fully stocked and include a stove, refrigerator, microwave oven, and dishwasher. Decor is breezy southwestern pastel, with light woods, dried-flower arrangements in handcrafted pottery, and various pieces of local art and artifacts.

Dining/Entertainment: Carl's French Quarter (tel. 776-8319), specializing in Cajun/creole cuisine, is one of the most popular restaurants in the Taos area. Breakfasts are served to hotel guests only, and lunches are strictly group affairs; but dinners and Sunday brunches are when Carl's bounces like Basin Street. Appetizers like seafood filet gumbo or shrimp and artichoke bisque, run $3.50 to $7.95; main courses, including shrimp creole, blackened chicken, and Cajun prime rib, are $12.95 to $22.95. Dessert favorites are chocolate marquise cake and key lime pie. There's a kids' menu. The lounge serves authentic New Orleans cocktails, like hurricanes and mint juleps.

Services: Valet laundry.

Facilities: Rooms for nonsmokers, year-round heated swimming pool, hot tubs and saunas. Six outdoor and two indoor tennis courts, four racquetball/squash courts, summer volleyball pit. Fitness center with weights and exercise room.

MODERATE

HOLIDAY INN DON FERNANDO DE TAOS, Paseo del Pueblo Sur (P.O. Drawer V), Taos, NM 87571. Tel. 505/758-4444 or toll free 800/759-2736. Fax 505/758-0055. 124 rms, 26 suites. A/C TV TEL

$ Rates: $69–$125 single, $79–$125 double, $95–$135 suites, depending upon season. Christmas season rates $20 higher. Children 19 and under stay free with parent. AE, CB, DC, DISC, JCB, MC, V.

Taos's newest major hotel, opened in 1989, is like a modern Pueblo village spread across landscaped grounds on the south side of town. A half-dozen adobe-style building clusters, each named for a noted New Mexico artist, surround private courtyards. The two-story structures are linked with one another, and with the main lobby and restaurant, by a web of walkways.

Standard rooms, appointed in a soft Southwest-motif decor with Pueblo paintings on the walls, feature hand-carved New Mexican wood furnishings, two queen-size beds or a king-size bed and sleeper sofa, and a special doorside niche for skis and boots. King suites offer a sitting room, fireplace, and wet bar; deluxe suites have full living rooms with fireplaces, a sleeper-sofa and a queen-size Murphy bed to accommodate six people. Rooms for nonsmokers and the disabled are available.

Don Fernando's Restaurant, open daily from 6:30am to 2pm and 5 to 10pm, serves a variety of regional breakfasts and lunches. An all-you-can-eat soup-and-salad lunch buffet ($4.95) is served weekdays from 11:30am to 2pm. Dinner main courses ($6.95–$17.95) include steaks, chicken Gusdorf (stuffed with green chiles and Jack cheese), and broiled shrimp Veracruz. The Fernando's Hideaway Lounge, built around a large adobe fireplace, has a daily happy hour (5–7pm). The hotel provides room service, valet laundry, courtesy van, and a 24-hour desk, as well as an outdoor swimming pool, hot tub, and tennis court.

KACHINA LODGE DE TAOS, Paseo del Pueblo Norte (P.O. Box NN), Taos, NM 87571. Tel. 505/758-2275 or toll free 800/522-4462. Fax 505/758-9207. 118 rms, 4 suites. A/C TV TEL

$ Rates: $60–$100 single or double. Additional person $8. Children under 12 free with parent. AE, CB, DC, DISC, MC, V.

A pueblo-style motel with bright blue trim, this long-established lodge is an art lover's dream. The art gallery, which connects the lobby to the lodge's restaurants, has a changing exhibit of paintings and other works from the Taos Gallery. The Navajo Living Room, a comfortable space for indoor games or fireside reading, is full of valuable antique Navajo rugs.

Rooms—of which there are a wide variety, including nonsmoking—are appointed with custom-made Taoseno furniture, including armoire, headboards, table, and chairs. Many have a couch or love seat; all have huge bathrooms and a second sink at the vanity in an outer dressing area.

The Hopi Dining Room (open daily from 5:30 to 10pm for dinner) is an elegant restaurant with a gourmet family-style menu (steaks, chicken, seafood) priced at $10 to $14. The Kiva Coffee House, open daily (6am–5:30pm), serves filling breakfasts and Mexican-style lunches for prices under $8. The Zuni Lounge is open nightly, and the Kachina Cabaret (see "Evening Entertainment," below) draws big-name acts. A Taos Pueblo dance troupe performs nightly in summer. The hotel has concierge service, valet laundry, 24-hour desk, an outdoor swimming pool, hot tub, and coin-op laundry. A ski shop is adjacent. No pets are permitted.

SAGEBRUSH INN, Paseo del Pueblo Sur (P.O. Box 557), Taos, NM 87571. Tel. 505/758-2254 or toll free 800/428-3626. 81 rms, 19 suites. A/C TV TEL

$ Rates (including breakfast): $55 single, $77 double, $92–$127 suite. Extra person $7. AE, CB, DC, MC, V.

Georgia O'Keeffe, probably the most famous artist to have worked extensively in the Southwest, lived and painted for six months in the 1930s in a third-story room at this venerable hotel. The artistic legacy persists in the rare antiques, pottery, Navajo rugs, and painted masterpieces that adorn many walls. Originally called the Chamisa Inn, the hotel was built in Pueblo Mission style in 1929, three miles south of the Plaza near Ranchos de Taos.

Most of the rooms face either an open grass courtyard, the outdoor swimming pool, or the stables. Traditional *viga* ceilings are complemented by earth-patterned decor and standard furnishings. Suites in "Sagebrush Village" have *kiva* fireplaces and beautiful hand-carved furniture. There's a king-size bed in the bedroom, a Murphy bed in the main living area, two full baths, and charcoal drawings of local Indians on the walls. There are rooms for nonsmokers and the disabled.

The Los Vaqueros Room is open for dinner from 5:30 to 10pm daily. Most American and New Mexican meals run $9.95 to $15, although beef-and-seafood specials cost as much as $24.50. A children's menu is priced at $4.95. A complimentary full breakfast is served daily (6:30 to 11am) in the Sagebrush Dining Room. The lobby bar is one of Taos's most active nightspots for live music and dancing (see "Evening Entertainment," below). Services and facilities include valet laundry, courtesy van, swimming pool, two Jacuzzis, and tennis courts.

INEXPENSIVE

EL MONTE LODGE, 317 Kit Carson Rd. (P.O. Box 22), Taos, NM 87571. Tel. 505/758-3171. 13 rms. TV TEL

$ Rates: $65 single, $75 double. Higher rate for kitchenette units. AE, CB, DC, DISC, MC, V.

Century-old cottonwood trees stand in a parklike picnic area, complete with barbecue grills and children's playground, outside this friendly 1930s motel. Four blocks east of the Plaza, it's old-fashioned but homey, built in traditional adobe style with protruding *vigas*, painted yellow and framed by flower gardens. The rooms, many of them with fireplaces, occupy eight small buildings. The eclectic decor features considerable Pueblo Indian art. Many rooms have fully stocked kitchenettes; there's a free guest laundry.

EL PUEBLO LODGE, P.O. Box 92, Taos, NM 87571. Tel. 505/758-8700 or toll free 800/433-9612. 42 rms, 4 suites. FRIDGE TV TEL

$ Rates (including continental breakfast): $40–$45 single, $50–$100 double. Additional person $5–$7. AE, MC, V.

The setting here is special: nicely landscaped 2½-acre grounds, complete with fir trees, rose gardens, a barbecue pit, lawn furniture, and a slide for children. Throw in a year-round outdoor swimming pool and hot tub and it's no surprise this motel is popular with families. All of the brightly colored rooms have hand-carved furniture and *viga* ceilings; many rooms have furnished minikitchens with a microwave oven and hot pot; 12 have *kiva* fireplaces or Franklin stoves. Laundry facilities are free to guests.

LAUGHING HORSE INN, 729 Paseo del Pueblo Norte (P.O. Box 4889),

Taos, NM 87571. Tel. 505/758-8350 or toll free 800/776-0161. 11 rms, 3 guest houses. TV.
$ Rates: $42–$52 single, $48–$65 double; $98–$150 penthouse and guest houses.

Occupying the print shop of the 1920s "Laughing Horse Press," the inn is an unmistakable adobe structure with lilac-purple trim. Guests can choose between sunny dorm-type loft rooms, cozy private rooms, a deluxe solar-heated penthouse, spacious private guest houses across the street, or a house on the mesa complete with views of Taos Mountain. All accommodations have cassette decks, TVs, and VCRs. Some have fireplaces. Bathrooms are shared in the lower portion of the inn. The penthouse has a private bedroom, enclosed sleeping loft, and a bunk set with double beds. A private bath, wood stove, big-screen TV, video and audio decks, and a small refrigerator complete the room. The inn has a common room around a *kiva* fireplace where a wide variety of audio- and videotapes are shelved. Breakfasts (which might be continental or full), may be eaten in the kitchen or the dining room. The refrigerator is stocked on the honor system. There's an outdoor hot tub, and mountain bikes are free for guest use. Psychic readings are available from the innkeepers, and a massage therapist is available by appointment.

BUDGET

ABOMINABLE SNOWMANSION SKIERS' HOSTEL, Taos Ski Valley Rd. (P.O. Box 3271), Taos, NM 87571. Tel. 505/776-8298. 95 beds.
$ Rates (including full breakfast in winter) $13–$50, depending on size of accommodation and season. No credit cards.

Located in the small community of Arroyo Seco, about 8 miles north of Taos and 10 miles from the Taos Ski Valley, this lodging attracts many young people. It's clean and comfortable for those happy with dormitory-style accommodation. Toilets, shower rooms, and dressing rooms are segregated by sex. A two-story lodge room focuses around a circular fireplace, and features a piano and games area. Tent camping is permitted outside. Guests can cook their own meals or indulge in home-cooked fare.

SUN GOD LODGE, 919 Paseo del Pueblo Sur (P.O. Box 1713), Taos, NM 87571. Tel. 505/758-3162. TV TEL
$ Rates: Summer and winter $67.65 single, $74.30–$85.40 double, $100.90 suite, $105.35–$138.60 casita.

An adobe structure, this motel offers 1½ acres of landscaped grounds. After a recent renovation, the rooms are of Southwest decor, all have ceiling fans, double-, queen-, or king-sized beds (with Navajo patterned spreads), prints and lithographs by Taos artists on the walls, and complimentary bedside coffee service. There are some new accommodations with kitchenette areas (fully supplied with dishes and utensils), coffee makers, a minirefrigerator; living rooms with *kiva* fireplaces (wood and fire starter are supplied), remote controlled TVs, and niches with howling coyotes or kachinas in them. There are outdoor grills and a hot-tub room.

BED & BREAKFASTS

Some three dozen bed-and-breakfasts are listed with the Taos Chamber of Commerce. The **Taos Bed & Breakfast Association** (tel. 505/758-4747 or toll free 800/876-7857), with strict guidelines for membership, will provide information and make reservations for member homes. The following are some of my favorites.

ADOBE & PINES INN, P.O. Box 837, Ranchos de Taos, NM 87557. Tel. 505/751-0947 or toll free 800/723-8267. Fax 505/758-8423. 3 rms (all with bath). TV **Directions:** The inn is located directly off Hwy. 68, about 1½ miles from the recreation area at Hwy. 570 (driving north from Santa Fe), or 0.3 miles from St. Francis Plaza (driving south from Taos town). Driving from Santa Fe, the Adobe & Pines Inn will be on your right. You can't really see the inn from the street, but you will see the multicolored posts that mark the driveway.
$ Rates: $85–$110 single or double. AE, MC, V.

After some traveling in Europe, the owners, Chuck and Charil, decided that they wanted to open a bed-and-breakfast inn. The only problem is that they didn't quite know where—until they ended up in Taos and fell in love with what, after six months of renovation, is now the Adobe & Pines Inn.

As you drive down to the house you'll see the horses out front, and you'll undoubtedly be awed by the length of the Grand Portal (it's 80 feet long). The inn is a 150-year old adobe home that has been turned into one of the most beautiful and peaceful guesthouses in which I have stayed. The inn rests amid four acres of pine and fruit trees, and each room has a private entrance, which affords you all the privacy you could ever need. All three rooms have fireplaces (one even has a fireplace in the bathroom), and they are each decorated uniquely. Puerta Azul is a wonderful, little, cozy space with an antique writing desk and royal blue accents. Puerta Verde, done in deep greens, has a wonderful old *retablo* (ask Chuck and Charil about it), a sitting area, and a queen-sized canopy bed. Puerta Turquese, my favorite, is a guest cottage that is separate from the rest of the house, it has a full kitchen and is done in bright pastels. A wonderful "broken tile mosaic" floor, that was done about a hundred years ago by a man who did only a select few in the whole town of Taos, runs throughout the whole guesthouse. The colors (turquoise, yellow, maroon, black, and peach) in the tile floor have been picked up in the rest of the decor. You can get cozy in bed under a down comforter while the bedroom fireplace warms the room, or you can relax in a jet whirlpool bath in front of a blaze in the bathroom fireplace.

In the evening, Chuck, Charil, and Rascal (the dog) serve hors d'oeuvres in front of a roaring fire in the living room, which is decorated with local art (on sale), including paintings, sculptures, and greeting cards. Charil does some of her own work—in fact, the paper sculpture hanging above the reception desk is hers. In the morning you're in for a treat with a delicious full breakfast in front of the fire in the glassed-in breakfast room. Chuck and Charil are very gracious hosts and they will help you plan any activities of interest, and they'll also give you suggestions as to how you might want to spend your time in Taos. You really can't go wrong here!

CASA DE LAS CHIMENEAS, 405 Cordoba Lane at Los Pandos Road (P.O. Box 5303), Taos, NM 87571. Tel. 505/758-4777. 3 rms, 1 suite. TV

$ Rates: $93 single, $103 double, $130 suite (for two). MC, V.

 The "House of Chimneys" qualifies as one of Taos's luxury B&Bs. Its three rooms, each of them a work of art and each with a private entrance, look out on a beautifully landscaped private garden. The two-room suite incorporates an old library and two fireplaces; it is furnished with marble-topped antiques, a comfortable reading couch, a bentwood rocker, and a game table complete with chess and backgammon. Beautiful bed linens over a sheepskin mattress pad guarantee a great night's sleep. The Blue Room and Willow Room have similar charm and amenities. Attention to detail is a top priority here, with plush towels, down pillows, extra firewood, books and magazines for reading, and owners eager to share tips on best restaurants, ski runs, or scenic drives. Complimentary juices and sodas are always available and a full gourmet breakfast is served daily. Guests gather in the main house for complimentary afternoon hors d'oeuvres. A courtesy telephone is in the main dining room and a large hot tub is located adjacent to a well maintained herb, vegetable, and rose garden. Smoking is not permitted. As we go to press, several improvements have been made to this B&B, and the rates may be restructured, so call ahead.

CASA EUROPA, Upper Ranchitos Rd. (Los Cordovas Rte., Box 157), Taos, NM 87571. Tel. 505/758-9798. 6 rms.

$ Rates: $70–$95. MC, V.

This cream-colored, Mediterranean-style pueblo, 1.7 miles west of the Plaza, was built of adobe and *vigas* two centuries ago. The elegant rooms, each with full private bath, vary in furnishings: One, for example, has a marble whirlpool and enamel wood stove; another has a full-size Jacuzzi and fireplace, with glass doors opening onto a courtyard. In fact, there are eight fireplaces and 14 skylights in Casa Europa. Regional artwork in the rooms can be purchased. There's a sitting room for reading and/or conversation; coffee and pastries are offered here each day between 3 and 4pm. A full or continental breakfast is served each morning. Smoking is not permitted.

ORINDA, 1 Orinda Lane off Val Verde St. (P.O. Box 4451), Taos, NM 87571. Tel. 505/758-8581. 2 rms, 1 suite.
$ Rates: $75 double, $20 per additional guest. MC, V.
This B&B has the delightful advantage of being in town but also in the country. Though only a 10-minute walk from the Plaza, it's tucked beneath huge cottonwood trees with a view across pasture land to Taos Mountain. Thick adobe walls keep it warm in winter and cool in summer. Innkeepers Dave and Karol Dondero share their living room, including a TV, sound system, and wood-burning stove, with guests. Dave's black-and-white photo collection adorns the wall of the dining room, where a hearty continental breakfast is served daily. Two rooms comprise the Vigil Suite, where a sitting room with a fireplace and refrigerator separates two bedrooms. The Truchas Room, with traditional southwestern decor, has a private entrance. Bathrooms have showers but no baths; a hot tub is planned. Children are welcome, but pets and smoking are not.

TAOS HACIENDA INN, 102 LaLoma Plaza (Box 4159), Taos, NM 87571. Tel. 505/758-1717 or toll free 800/530-3040. 7 rms (all with bath). TV TEL
$ Rates: $95–$125 standard double; $145–$165 artist's studio; $135–$300 suite. Discounts available. MC, V.
As you drive into the parking area, you'll see the Taos Hacienda Inn perched atop a small hill. As you enter the reception area, you are immediately relaxed by the abundance of green plants and a slow, gurgling fountain. Local art is displayed, for sale, in all public spaces of this comfortable, spacious, adobe home (some of which was built in the 1800s).

Each room is differently decorated, though all have the same amenities, such as bathrobes, fireplaces, fresh flowers, televisions, telephones, and queen- or king-sized beds. Some rooms have patios, and there are a couple of suites and artists' studios with kitchenettes. Cary's Studio, named for Cary Moore who was a longtime resident of the home, has a full kitchenette and sleeps up to six. The Happy Trails Room, which is distinctly different from the rest of the rooms in the house, has wonderful pine paneling, a brass bed, and chaps and spurs hanging decoratively. A couple of the rooms have incredible views of Taos Mountain. All the furniture in the rooms is handcrafted.

In the morning, a breakfast of fresh fruit, different kinds of juice, fresh breads, muffins, croissants, and a daily special hot item, perhaps a breakfast burrito with Jerry's special green chile, is served. In the early evening, you'll find southwestern hors d'oeuvres or homemade cookies and coffee waiting for you to snack on while you're planning your evening.

4. DINING

In the listings below, an **expensive** restaurant is one with most main courses for $15 or higher; **moderate** has main courses for $10 to $15; **inexpensive,** $6 to $10; and **budget,** most main courses cost less than $6.

EXPENSIVE

DOC MARTIN'S, Taos Inn, 125 Paseo del Pueblo Norte. Tel. 758-1977.
Cuisine: CONTEMPORARY AMERICAN. **Reservations:** Recommended.
$ Prices: Breakfast $3.50–$7; lunch $4.95–$9; dinner, appetizers $4–$9, main courses $13–$20. AE, CB, DC, MC, V.
Open: Daily 7:30am–2:30pm and 5:30–10pm.

This portion of the Taos Inn comprises Dr. Paul Martin's former home, office, and delivery room. In 1912, painters Bert Phillips (Doc's brother-in-law) and Ernest Blumenschein hatched the concept of the Taos Society of Artists in the Martin dining room. Art still predominates here, from paintings to cuisine. The food here is widely acclaimed, and the wine list has received numerous "Awards of Excellence" from the *Wine Spectator* magazine.

Breakfast may include homemade sopaipillas stuffed with scrambled eggs, onions, cheese, and green chile, or blue corn and blueberry hotcakes. Luncheon favorites include New Mexican onion rings spiced with chile and cilantro, chile stew with jalapeño Jack cheese, shrimp burritos, and cobb salad. Dinner might start with a crab quesadilla, Caesar salad or beef carpaccio, followed by seared salmon with grilled red onions and cucumber *raita;* roasted pheasant breast with a Michigan cherry vodka sauce; or grilled New Zealand venison with a lignonberry-zinfandel sauce. Doc's nightly features fresh seafood and game specialties.

LAMBERT'S OF TAOS, 309 Paseo del Pueblo Sur. Tel. 758-1009.
  Cuisine: CONTEMPORARY AMERICAN. **Reservations:** Recommended.
$ Prices: Appetizers $4–$8, main courses $13–$17.50. AE, MC, V.
  Open: Daily 6–9pm.

Zeke Lambert, a former San Francisco restaurateur who was head chef at Doc Martin's for four years, opened this fine dining establishment in late 1989 in the historic Randall Home near Los Pandos Road. Now, in simple but elegant surroundings, he presents a new and different menu every night.

Diners can start with the likes of homemade duck pâté with roasted garlic, a spinach-and-basil salad with sautéed mushrooms, or grilled swordfish niçoise. Main courses always include grilled fresh seafood, such as tuna with yams and garlic butter, or mahimahi with red pepper sauce and couscous. Other more-or-less typical main dishes could be veal chop with chard Dijon, chicken stewed in green chile and served with black beans, or cassoulet with duck confit and lamb sausage. Desserts are outstanding, like chocolate oblivion truffle torte and sour-cream cognac cake. Espresso coffees, beers, and wines are poured.

STAKEOUT AT OUTLAW HILL, Stakeout Dr. (just off N.M. 68). Tel. 505/758-2042.
  Cuisine: INTERNATIONAL. **Reservations:** Highly recommended.
$ Prices: Appetizers $2.95–$8.95; main courses $8.95–$24.95. MC, V.
  Open: 6pm until the last diners leave.

I love this restaurant. Maybe it's because of the fact that you have to drive about a mile up a dirt road towards the base of the Sangre de Cristo Mountains and once you get there (you'll think I'm insane for sending you up Stakeout Drive in the black of night, and you'll think you're never going to get there) you've got one of the greatest views of Taos. Or, maybe it's because after you're inside, you're enveloped in the warmth of its rustic decor (which is a great contrast to the close-to-white exterior), the paneled walls and creaking hardwood floors, and the crackling fireplace in the winter. Or, maybe it's the food. You can start with baked Brie with sliced almonds and apples or escargots with walnuts and garlic. Then move on to a wonderful filet mignon which is wrapped in bacon and cooked to your liking, or my favorite (and the chef's), the honey almond duck, which is never fatty and always leaves you feeling a little sticky but *very* satisfied. Finish it off with some fresh pastry and a cappucino. You'll really be missing something if you don't get to Stakeout while you're in Taos.

VILLA FONTANA, Highway 522, 5 miles north of Taos. Tel. 758-5800.
  Cuisine: ITALIAN. **Reservations:** Recommended.
$ Prices: Appetizers $4–$11.50; main courses $15.25–$24. AE, DC, MC, V.
  Open: Mon–Sat 5:30pm–closing.

Carlo and Siobhan Gislimberti like to talk about "peccato di gola"—lust of the palate. The couple brought it with them to Taos when they left their home in the Italian Dolomites, near the Austrian border. They have their own herb garden, and Carlo, a master chef, is a member of the New Mexico Mycological Society . . . so wild mushrooms are a major element in many of his kitchen preparations.

Meals are truly gourmet. Diners can start with scampi alla veneziana (shrimp in a brandy Aurora sauce) or pâté ricco de fegatini alla moda (homemade chicken liver pâté). Main courses include socliola di Dover alle erbe aromatiche (whole Dover sole with fresh herbs) and filetto di bue al cognac papato alla Verdi (beef tenderloin sautéed with brandy, green peppercorns, cream, and demiglaze). Dinners are served with salad, fresh vegetables, and potatoes or rice.

MODERATE

THE APPLE TREE, 123 Bent St. Tel. 758-1900.

Cuisine: INTERNATIONAL. **Reservations:** Recommended.

$ **Prices:** Appetizers $2.50–$6.95; lunch $2.95–$7.95; dinner $8.95–$17.95; children's menu $3.95–$5.95; Sunday brunch $3.95–$7.95. AE, MC, V.

Open: Lunch Mon–Fri 11:30am–3pm, brunch Sun 10am–3pm, dinner daily 5:30–9pm.

Classical and baroque music pervades the four elegant adobe rooms of this fine restaurant, a block north of the Plaza. Original paintings by Taos masters overlook the candlelit, white-linen service indoors; outside, diners sit at wooden tables on a graveled courtyard beneath spreading apple trees.

Daily specials supplement a standing menu with international flavor: drunken shrimp boiled in Harp's Irish beer, tandoori chicken (East Indian), fried tofu and noodles with Indonesian peanut sauce, Chinese stir-fry, even mango-crab enchiladas. Of course, there's filet mignon and fresh fish specials, too. There's a limited children's menu. Homemade desserts, cappuccinos, and fine wines and beer are offered. Classical guitar, harp, and/or flute music is presented live nightly in the summer.

CASA DE VALDEZ, Paseo del Pueblo Sur. Tel. 505/758-8777.

Cuisine: NEW MEXICAN. **Reservations:** Suggested. **Directions:** Drive south of the plaza for about 2½ miles.

$ **Prices:** Appetizers, dinner, $5.95–$6.50; main courses $7.95–$18.95. AE, DISC, MC, V.

Open: Mon, Tues, Thurs–Sat 11:30am–9:30pm, Sun 4–9:30pm.

You can't really miss Casa de Valdez—it's the only A-frame building in the area. The interior looks more like a mountain home than a New Mexican restaurant because of the wood paneling, which makes it a cozy environment for a quiet dinner for two. The staff is extremely friendly, and they know many of their customers by name. The menu is predictable as far as New Mexican cuisine goes, with blue-corn enchiladas, bean burritos, and tamales. You can also get spare ribs and barbecued chicken. Personally, I think the sopaipillas served at Casa de Valdez are the best around—they practically melt in your mouth.

LA CIGALE CAFE DE PARIS, Pueblo Alege Mall, off Paseo de Pueblo Sur. Tel. 751-0500.

Cuisine: FRENCH BISTRO. **Reservations:** Not necessary.

$ **Prices:** Appetizers, dinner, $4–$5.50; main courses, dinner, $11.25–$15.95. AE, MC, V.

Open: Mon–Sat lunch 11:30am–2:30pm, dinner daily 6–10pm.

If, by the time you reach Taos, you've had your fill of spicy New Mexican food, you're in for a treat at La Cigale—for any meal. The decor is typical bistro style with its bare wood tables and green and white tile floor. It's bright and refreshing with little posters and turn-of-the-century photographs on the walls. Of course you can get croissants in the morning (absolutely fresh and buttery enough to melt in your mouth), and for lunch there's a variety of sandwiches, including a hamburger with melted Brie, onion, and Dijon mustard. The dinner menu includes terrine de foie de volaille, the chef's special fowl pâté, as an appetizer; les poissons, like rouget grondin à la nicoise (red snapper with garlic tomato sauce), entrecôte frites (ribeye steak with french fries), and magret de canard (duck breast sautéed and garnished with berry sauce). If none of the above items strike your fancy, there's always fondue! The prices are incredibly low as far as French cuisine goes; however, they are fairly high by Taos standards.

OGELVIE'S BAR & GRILL, 1031 E. Plaza. Tel. 758-8866.
Cuisine: STEAKS & SEAFOOD. **Reservations:** Recommended.
$ Prices: Appetizers $3.95–$6.95; lunch $4.50–$10.25; dinner $8.95–$17.95. AE, MC, V.
Open: Daily 10am–4pm and 5–10pm; from 11am in winter.

Like Ogelvie's in Albuquerque and Santa Fe, this is a casual restaurant with rich wood decor. Homemade soups, burgers and other sandwiches, and huevos (eggs) de casa Ogelvie's are hits on the lunch menu. Dinners place emphasis on regional preparations of poultry, steak, and seafood. Fajitas—strips of beef or chicken sautéed with onions and bell peppers—are a specialty. Other dishes include fresh trout piñon, blue-corn enchiladas, pollo verde (sautéed with pinons, shredded zucchini, and green chile), and steak ranchero. A lively bar with an outdoor deck overlooks the Plaza.

INEXPENSIVE

BENT STREET DELI & CAFE, 120 Bent St. Tel. 758-5787.
Cuisine: DELI.
$ Prices: Breakfast $2–$6.50; lunch $2–$7; dinner $9.50–$12.50. MC, V.
Open: Mon–Sat 8am–8pm.

This popular café is a short block north of the Plaza. Outside, a flower box surrounds sidewalk café-style seating beneath large blue-and-white umbrellas. Inside, baskets and bottles of homemade jam lend a homey, country feel. The menu features breakfast burritos and homemade granola for the morning hours; 17 deli sandwiches, plus a "create-your-own" column, for lunch; and various quiche, pasta, chicken, and fish dishes for dinner.

MICHAEL'S KITCHEN, 305 Paseo del Pueblo Norte. Tel. 758-4178.
Cuisine: NEW MEXICAN & AMERICAN.
$ Prices: Breakfast $2.85–$8.45; lunch $2.65–$8.25; dinner $5.25–$10.75. MC, V.
Open: Daily 7am–8:30pm.

A couple of blocks north of the Plaza is this eatery, a throwback to earlier days. Between its hardwood floor and *viga* ceiling are various knickknacks on posts, walls, and windows: a deer head here, a Tiffany lamp there, several scattered antique wood stoves. Seating is at booths and tables. Meals, too, are old-fashioned, as far as quality and quantity for price. Breakfasts, including a great variety of pancakes and egg dishes, are served all day, as are luncheon sandwiches. Dinners range from veal Cordon Bleu to knackwurst-and-sauerkraut, plantation fried chicken to enchiladas rancheros, fish-and-chips to New York steak. There's also a children's menu.

ROBERTO'S RESTAURANT, 122 Kit Carson Rd. Tel. 758-2434.
Cuisine: NEW MEXICAN. **Reservations:** Recommended.
$ Prices: Dinner, appetizers $2.85–$5, main courses $6.50–$9.95. MC, V.
Open: Summer Wed–Mon noon–2:30pm and 6–9pm; most weekends in winter.
Closed: Tues year-round.

Hidden within a warren of art galleries opposite the Kit Carson Museum is this local gem, which for 25 years has focused on authentic native dishes. Within this 160-year-old adobe are three small, high-ceilinged dining rooms, each with hardwood floors, a maximum of five tables, and a corner fireplace in one of them. Everyday dishes include tacos, enchiladas, tamales, and chile rellenos. All meals start with sopaipillas and are accompanied by homemade refried beans with chicos (dried kernels of corn). Beer and wine only are served.

BUDGET

DORI'S BAKERY & CAFE, Paseo del Pueblo Norte. Tel. 758-9222.
  Cuisine: NEW MEXICAN/AMERICAN.
$ Prices: Breakfast $3.45–$5.25; lunch $2.25–$4.25. No credit cards.
  Open: Mon–Fri 7:30am–2:30pm, Sat 7:30am–noon, Sun 9am–1pm.

This delightful find, next door to the Taos Post Office, serves breakfasts like "hash brown heaven," eggs, pancakes, bagels, and granola all day. Deli sandwiches are popular lunch fare, as well as burgers, pizza, and homemade soups and salads. French pastries are homemade daily and espresso coffees are served. There is outside seating in the summer.

MAINSTREET BAKERY, Guadalupe Plaza, 112 Dona Luz. Tel. 758-9610.
  Cuisine: VEGETARIAN/NATURAL FOOD.
$ Prices: $4–$5.50. No credit cards.
  Open: Mon–Fri 7:30am–11:30am, Sat–Sun 8am–2pm; bakery open until 3pm.
About a block and a half west of the Plaza, this has become possibly Taos's biggest counterculture hangout. The image is fostered by the health-conscious cuisine and the wide selection of newspapers, magazines, and other reading material advocating alternative life-styles. Coffee and pastries are served all day; vegetarian breakfasts and (on weekends) lunches are very popular.

5. ATTRACTIONS

SUGGESTED ITINERARIES

IF YOU HAVE 1 DAY   Spend at least two hours at the Taos Pueblo. You'll also have time to see the Millicent Rogers Museum, and to browse in some of the town's fine art galleries. Try, too, to make it to Ranchos de Taos to see the San Francisco de Asis Church.

IF YOU HAVE 2 DAYS   Explore the Kit Carson Historic Museums—the Martinez Hacienda, the Kit Carson Home, and the Ernest L. Blumenschein Home. And get out of town for the view from the Rio Grande Gorge Bridge.

IF YOU HAVE 3 DAYS OR MORE   Drive the "Enchanted Circle" through Red River, Eagle Nest, and Angel Fire. You may want to leave a full day for shopping, or perhaps drive up to the Taos Ski Valley for a look-see. Of course, if you're here in the winter with skis, that's your first priority.

THE TOP ATTRACTIONS

TAOS PUEBLO, P.O. Box 1846, Taos Pueblo, NM 87571. Tel. 758-9593.
No other site in Taos is as important or as famous. The community of 1,500, 2½ miles north of the Plaza, forms a world of its own. The northernmost of New Mexico's 19 pueblos, it has been the home of Tiwa Indians for more than 900 years.

Two massive, multistoried adobe apartment buildings appear much the same today as when a regiment from Coronado's expedition first saw them in 1540. Houses are built one upon another to form porches, balconies, and roofs reached by ancient ladders. The distinctive, flowing lines of shaped mud, with a straw-and-mud exterior plaster, are typical of pueblo architecture throughout the Southwest. The buildings blend in with the land around them, as the houses are made of the earth itself. Bright blue painted doors repeat the clear blue of the sky that frames the brown buildings. Between the complexes trickles a fast-flowing creek, the Rio Pueblo de Taos. A footbridge joins the two shores. To the northeast looms Taos Mountain, its long fir-covered slopes forming a timeless backdrop to the old pueblo.

Though the Tiwa were essentially a peaceful agrarian people, they are better remembered as having spearheaded the only successful revolt by Native Americans in U.S. history. Launched by Pope (*po-PAY*) in 1680, the uprising drove the Spanish from Santa Fe until 1692, and from Taos until 1698.

Native culture and religion have persisted since. Taos is one of the most conservative of all North American Indian communities, still eschewing such modern conveniences as electricity and plumbing. (The town well predates Columbus's arrival in America.) Arts and crafts and other tourism-related businesses support the economy, along with government services, and ranching and farming.

As you explore the pueblo and absorb insights into its people's life-style, you can visit those studios, munch on homemade oven bread, look into the new **San Geronimo Chapel,** and wander past the fascinating ruins of the old church and cemetery. You're expected to ask permission from individuals before taking their photos; some ask a small payment, but that's for you to negotiate. *Kivas* and other ceremonial underground areas are taboo.

San Geronimo is the patron saint of the Taos Pueblo, and his feast day on September 30 combines Catholic and Pre-Hispanic traditions. The **San Geronimo Day Trade Fair** is a joyous occasion, with footraces, pole climbs, and crafts booths. Dances are performed the evening of September 29. Other annual events include a turtle dance on New Year's Day, deer or buffalo dances on Three Kings Day (January 6), and corn dances for Santa Cruz Day (May 3), San Antonio Day (June 13), San Juan Day (June 24), Santiago Day (July 23), and Santa Ana Day (July 24). The **Taos Pueblo Pow Wow,** a dance competition and parade drawing tribes from throughout North America, is held the weekend after July 4 on reservation land off N.M. 522. Christmas Eve bonfires mark the start of the children's corn dance, the Christmas Day deer dance, or the three-day-long Matachines dance.

Admission: $5 per vehicle or $1 per person. Still camera $5, video camera $10, sketching or painting $25. No photography permitted on feast days.

Open: Daily summer 8am–5pm; winter 9am–4:30pm.

MILLICENT ROGERS MUSEUM, off N.M. 522, 4 miles north of Taos. Tel. 758-2462.

Taos's most interesting collection is this museum, founded in 1953 by family members after the death of Millicent Rogers. Rogers was a wealthy Taos émigré who compiled a magnificent array of aesthetically beautiful Native American arts and crafts beginning in 1947. Included are Navajo and Pueblo jewelry, Navajo textiles, Pueblo pottery, Hopi and Zuni *kachina* dolls, paintings from the Rio Grande Pueblo people, and basketry from a wide variety of southwestern tribes. The collection continues to grow through gifts and museum acquisitions.

Since the 1970s the scope of the museum's permanent collection has been expanded to include Hispanic religious and secular arts and crafts, from Spanish and Mexican colonial to contemporary times. Included are *santos* (religious images), furniture, weavings, *colcha* embroideries, and decorative tinwork. Agricultural implements, domestic utensils, and craftspeoples' tools dating from the 17th and 18th centuries are also displayed.

The museum gift shop has some superior regional art. Temporary exhibits, classes and workshops, lectures, and field trips are scheduled throughout the year.

Admission: Adults $3, children (6–16) and seniors $1, families $6.

Open: Daily 9am–5pm. **Closed:** Easter Day, San Geronimo Day (Sept 30), Thanksgiving Day, Christmas, New Year's Day.

KIT CARSON HISTORIC MUSEUMS, Drawer CCC, Taos, NM 87571. Tel. 758-0505.

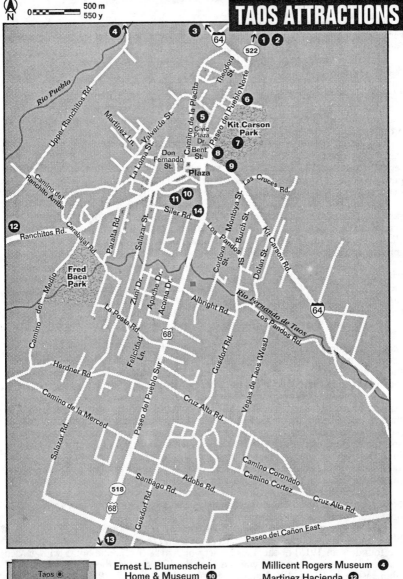

TAOS ATTRACTIONS

N

0 — 500 m
    550 y

Rio Pueblo

Upper Ranchitos Rd.

Martinez Ln.

Camino del Ranchito Arriba

Valverde St.

La Loma St.

Camino de la Placita

Theodora St.

Paseo del Pueblo Norte

Kit Carson Park

Civic Plaza Dr.

Don Fernando St.

Bent St.

Plaza

Las Cruces Rd.

Siler Rd.

Carabajal Rd.

Ranchitos Rd.

Peralta Rd.

Salazar St.

Montoya St.

Burch St.

Kit Carson Rd.

Fred Baca Park

Camino del Medio

Zuni Dr.

Apache Dr.

Acoma Dr.

Albright Rd.

Cordova St.

Los Pandos St.

Dolan St.

Rio Fernando de Taos

Los Pandos Rd.

La Posta Rd.

Felicidad Ln.

68

Gusdorf Rd.

Vegas de Taos (West)

Herdner Rd.

Camino de la Merced

Cruz Alta Rd.

Salazar Rd.

Santiago Rd.

Adobe Rd.

Camino Coronado

Camino Cortez

Cruz Alta Rd.

518

68

Gusdorf Rd.

Paseo del Pueblo Sur

Paseo del Cañon East

64

522

64

Taos

Santa Fe

NEW MEXICO

Ernest L. Blumenschein Home & Museum ⑩

The Fechin Institute ⑥

Governor Bent House Museum ⑧

Harwood Foundation Museum of the University of New Mexico ⑪

Kit Carson Home and Museum of the West ⑨

Kit Carson Park and Cemetery ⑦

Millicent Rogers Museum ④

Martinez Hacienda ⑫

Rio Grande Gorge Bridge ③

San Francisco de Asis Church ⑬

San Geronimo Chapel, Taos Pueblo ②

Taos Institute of Arts ⑭

Taos Fire Department ⑤

Taos Pueblo ①

This foundation operates three historical homes as museums, affording glimpses of early Taos life-styles. The Martinez Hacienda, Kit Carson Home, and the Ernest Blumenschein Home each has its individual appeal.

Martinez Hacineda, Lower Ranchitos Road, Highway 240 (tel. 758-1000), is one of the only Spanish Colonial haciendas in the United States that is open to the public year round. This was the home of merchant and trader Don Antonio Severino Martinez, who bought it in 1804 and lived there until his death in 1827. Located on the west bank of the Rio Pueblo de Taos about two miles southwest of the Plaza, the hacienda was built like a fortress, with thick adobe walls and no exterior windows to protect against raids by Plains tribes.

Twenty-one rooms were built around two placitas, or interior courtyards. Most of the rooms open today contain period furnishings: They include the bedrooms, servant's quarters, stables, a kitchen, and even a large fiesta room. Exhibits in one newly renovated room tell the story of the Martinez family and life in Spanish Taos between 1598 and 1821, when Mexico assumed control.

Don Antonio Martinez, who for a time was alcalde (mayor) of Taos, owned several caravans that he used in trade on the Chihuahua Trail to Mexico. This business was carried on by his youngest son, Don Juan Pascual, who later owned the hacienda. His eldest son was Padre Antonio Jose Martinez, northern New Mexico's controversial spiritual leader from 1826 to 1867.

Kit Carson Historic Museums has developed the hacienda into a living museum with weavers, blacksmiths, and wood carvers. Demonstrations are scheduled daily; including during the Old Taos Trade Fair the last weekend in September when they run virtually nonstop. The Trade Fair recalls days when Indians, Spanish settlers, and mountain men met here to trade with each other. Hours are daily from 9am to 5pm.

Kit Carson Home and Museum of the West, East Kit Carson Road (tel. 758-4741), located a short block east on the Plaza intersection, is the town's only general museum of Taos history. The 12-room adobe home with walls 2½ feet thick, was built in 1825 and purchased in 1843 by Carson, the famous mountain man, Indian agent, and scout, as a wedding gift for his young bride, Josefa Jaramillo. It remained their home for 25 years, until both died (a month to the day apart) in 1868.

A living room, bedroom, and kitchen are furnished as they might have been when occupied by the Carsons. The Indian Room contains artifacts crafted and utilized by the original inhabitants of Taos Valley; the Early American Room has an array of pioneer items, including a large number of antique firearms and trappers' implements; and the Carson Interpretive Room presents memorabilia from Carson's unusual life. In the kitchen is a Spanish plaque that reads: *Nadie sabe lo que tiene la olla mas que la cuchara que la menea* (Nobody better knows what the pot holds than the spoon that stirs it).

The museum bookshop, with perhaps the town's most comprehensive inventory of New Mexico historical books, is adjacent to the entry. Hours are daily from 8am to 6pm in summer, 9am to 5pm in winter.

Ernest Blumenschein Home & Museum, 222 Ledoux St. (tel. 758-0330), a block and a half southwest of the Plaza, recalls and re-creates the life-style of one of the founders (in 1915) of the Taos Society of Artists. An adobe home with garden walls and a courtyard, parts of which date to the 1790s, it was the home and studio of Blumenshchein (1874–1960) and his family beginning in 1919. Period furnishings include European antiques and handmade Taos furniture in Spanish colonial style. Blumenschein was born and raised in Pittsburgh. His arrival in Taos in 1898 came somewhat by accident. After training in New York and Paris, he and fellow painter Bert Phillips were on assignment for *McClure's* magazine of New York when a wheel of their wagon broke during a mountain traverse 30 miles north of Taos. Blumenschein drew the short straw and carried the wheel by horseback to Taos for repair. He later recounted his initial reaction to the valley he entered: "No artist had ever recorded the New Mexico I was now seeing. No writer had ever written down the smell of this air or the feel of that morning sky. I was receiving . . . the first great unforgettable inspiration of my life. My destiny was being decided."

That spark later led to the foundation of Taos as an art colony. An extensive collection of work by early 20th-century Taos masters is on display in several rooms of the home. Among the modern works are paintings by Blumenschein's daughter, Helen. Hours are daily from 9am to 5pm.

Admission: Three museums, $7 adults, $6 seniors, $4 children (6–16), family rate $13. Two museums, $5 adults, $4 seniors, $3 children, family rate $11. One museum, $3 adults, $2.50 seniors, $2 children, family rate $6.

Open: Daily except Thanksgiving Day, Christmas, and New Year's Day.

MORE ATTRACTIONS

SAN FRANCISCO DE ASIS CHURCH, Ranchos de Taos. Tel. 758-2754.

From the side of N.M. 68, four miles south of Taos, this famous church appears as a modernesque adobe sculpture with no doors or windows. It's often photographed (as by Ansel Adams) and painted (by the likes of Georgia O'Keeffe) from this angle. Visitors must walk through the garden on the west side of this remarkable two-story church to enter and get a full perspective on its massive walls, authentic adobe plaster, and beauty.

Displayed on the wall of an adjacent building is an unusual painting, *The Shadow of the Cross* by Henri Ault (1896). In ordinary light it portrays a barefoot Christ at the Sea of Galilee; in darkness, however, the portrait becomes luminescent and the shadow of a cross forms over the left shoulder of Jesus' silhouette. The artist reportedly was as shocked as everyone else. The reason for the illusion remains a mystery.

The church office and gift shop are just across the driveway to the north of the church. A slide show is also presented here. Several crafts shops surround the square.

Admission: Donations appreciated.

Open: Daily. Visitors may attend mass at 5:30pm Sat and 7am (Spanish), 9am, and 11:30am Sun.

HARWOOD FOUNDATION MUSEUM OF THE UNIVERSITY OF NEW MEXICO, 238 Ledoux St. Tel. 758-3063.

Some of the finest works of art ever produced in or about Taos hang on the walls of this pueblo-style library-and-museum complex, a cultural and community center since 1923.

The museum shows paintings, drawings, prints, sculpture, and photographs by the artists of the Taos area from 1800 to the present. Featured are paintings from the early days of the art colony by members of the Taos Society of Artists, including Oscar Berninghaus, Ernest Blumenschein, Herbert Dunton, Victor Higgins, Bert Phillips, and Walter Ufer. In addition, there are works by Emil Bisttram, Andrew Dasburg, Leon Gaspard, Louis Ribak, and Thomas Benrimo.

Also on display are 19th-century *retablos,* religious paintings of saints which have traditionally been used for decoration and inspiration in the homes and churches of New Mexico. The permanent collection of art shows sculptures by Patrocinio Barela, one of the leading Hispanic artists of 20th-century New Mexico.

The museum also has five or six changing exhibitions each year, many of which feature the best artists currently working in Taos.

Admission: Free.

Open: Mon–Fri noon–5pm, Sat 10am–4pm.

GOVERNOR BENT HOUSE MUSEUM, 117 Bent St. Tel. 758-2376.

A short block north of the Plaza, this was the residence of Charles Bent, the New Mexico Territory's first American governor. Bent, a former trader who established Fort Bent, Colorado, was murdered in the 1847 Indian and Hispanic rebellion, as his wife and children escaped by digging through an adobe wall into the house next door. The hole is still visible. Period art and artifacts are displayed.

Admission: Adults $1, children 50¢.

Open: Daily, summer 9:30am–5pm, winter 10am–4pm.

THE FECHIN INSTITUTE, 227 Paseo del Pueblo Norte (P.O. Box 832), Taos, NM 87571. Tel. 758-1710.

★ The home of Russian artist Nicolai Fechin (*feh-SHEEN*) from 1927 to 1933, this historic house memorializes the career of a 20th-century Renaissance man. Born in Russia in 1881, Fechin came to the United States in 1923, already acclaimed as a master of painting, drawing, sculpture, architecture, and woodwork. In Taos, he built a huge adobe home and embellished it with hand-carved doors, windows, gates, posts, fireplaces, and other features of a Russian country home. The house and adjacent studio are now used for Fechin Institute educational activities, as well as concerts, lectures, and other programs. Fechin's daughter, Eya, in her late 70s, directs the institute.

Admission: Suggested donation $3.

Open: May 30–third week of Sept, Wed–Sun 1–5:30pm; Taos Arts Festival (late Sept–early Oct), daily 1–5:30pm; other times by appointment.

KIT CARSON PARK AND CEMETERY, Paseo del Pueblo Norte.

Major community events are held in the park in summer. The cemetery, established in 1847, contains the graves of Carson and his wife, Gov. Charles Bent, the Don Antonio Martinez family, Mabel Dodge Luhan, and many other noted historical figures and artists. Plaques describe their contributions.

RIO GRANDE GORGE BRIDGE, U.S. Hwy. 64, 10 miles west of Taos.

★ This impressive bridge spans the Southwest's greatest river, west of the Taos Airport. At 650 feet above the canyon floor, it's one of America's highest bridges. If you can withstand the vertigo, it's interesting to come more than once, at different times of day, to observe how the changing light plays tricks with the colors of the cliff walls.

D. H. LAWRENCE RANCH, San Cristobal. Tel. 776-2245.

The shrine of the controversial early 20th-century author is a pilgrimage site for literary devotees. A short uphill walk from the ranch home, it is littered with various mementos—photos, coins, messages from fortune cookies—placed by visitors. The guestbook is worth a long read.

Lawrence lived in Taos off and on between 1922 and 1925. The ranch was a gift to his wife, Frieda, from art patron Mabel Dodge Luhan. Lawrence repaid Luhan the favor by giving her the manuscript of *Sons and Lovers*. Lawrence died in southern France in 1930 of tuberculosis; his ashes were returned here for burial. The grave of Frieda, who died in 1956, is outside the shrine.

The shrine is the only public building at the ranch, operated today by the University of New Mexico as an educational and recreational retreat. To reach the site, head north from Taos 15 miles on N.M. 522, then another 6 miles east into the forested Sangre de Cristo range via a well-marked dirt road.

TAOS INSTITUTE OF ARTS, P.O. Box 1389, Taos, NM 87571. Tel. 505/758-2793.

Perhaps you're visiting Taos because it is so well-known as an art community, but galleries and studio visits just aren't enough to satisfy your urge to create. Well, if you're interested in pursuing an artistic adventure of your own while visiting Taos, you should definitely investigate the week-long classes in sculpture, painting, jewelry making, photography, clay working, textiles, and quite a few other media. Class sizes are limited, so if you're thinking about giving these workshops a try, you should call ahead for information and prices well in advance. The fees vary from class to class and usually don't include the price of materials; they remain, however, quite reasonable.

ORGANIZED TOURS

Pride of Taos Tours, P.O. Box 1192, Taos, NM 87571 (tel. 758-8340). Damaso and Helen Martinez's young company offers several packages, including a historical tour that lasts one hour and takes tourists to the Plaza, Martinez Hacienda, and Ranchos de Taos Church for $5 adults, $2 children 12 and under.

6. RECREATION

SKIING

There are numerous popular cross-country skiing trails in Carson National Forest, including some so marked en route to Taos Ski Valley. One of the more popular is **Amole Canyon**, off N.M. 518 near Sipapu Ski Area, where the Taos Nordic Ski Club maintains set tracks and signs along a 3-mile loop. It's closed to snowmobiles, a comfort to lovers of serenity.

Just east of Red River, with 18 miles of groomed trails in 600 acres of forest land atop Bobcat Pass, is the ✪ **Enchanted Forest Cross Country Ski Area** (tel. 505/754-2374). Full-day trail passes, good from 9am to 4:30pm, are $8 for adults, much less for children. Equipment rentals and lessons can be arranged at **Millers Crossing** ski shop on Main Street in Red River (tel. 754-2374). Qualified nordic skiers can get further instruction in skating, mountaineering, and telemarking.

The **Southwest Nordic Center**, P.O. Box 3212, Taos, NM 87571 (tel. 505/758-4761), offers lessons and tours in various locations around northern New Mexico. The center also owns two private Mongolian yurts north of Chama for overnight skiing or (in summer) mountain-biking excursions.

Taos Mountain Outfitters, South Plaza (tel. 758-9292), offers cross-country sales, rentals, and guide service.

Five alpine resorts are located within an hour's drive of Taos. All offer complete facilities, including equipment rentals. Although opening and closing dates may vary according to snow conditions, it's safe to say that skiing usually begins Thanksgiving weekend and continues into early April.

Ski vacationers who can't decide which area to patronize should look into the **Enchanted Circle Explorer,** a discount ticket book containing vouchers for all-day adult lifts at any three of the four Enchanted Circle ski areas—Taos Ski Valley, Angel Fire, Red River, and Ski Rio—at a discount of about 15% over current rates. They're not good over the Christmas holidays, President's Day weekend, or during school vacation week in mid-March. The book is available for purchase at all ski ticket offices.

SKI RESORTS

TAOS SKI VALLEY, Taos Ski Valley, NM 87525. Tel. 505/776-2291.

✪ The preeminent ski resort in the southern Rocky Mountains was founded in 1955 by a Swiss-German immigrant, Ernie Blake. According to local legend, Blake searched for two years in a small plane for the perfect location for a ski resort equal to his native Alps. He found it at the abandoned mining site of Twining, high above Taos. Ernie died in 1989, aged 76; but the area is still in the family, under the command of two younger generations of Blakes. The resort has become internationally renowned for its light, dry powder (323 inches annually), its superb ski school, and its personal, friendly manner. Even the esteemed London *Times* called the valley "without any argument the best ski resort in the world. Small, intimate and endlessly challenging, Taos simply has no equal."

Of the 73 trails and bowls, more than half are designated for expert or advanced skiers. But between the 11,800-foot summit and the 9,200-foot base, there are also ample opportunities for novice and intermediate skiers. The area has an uphill capacity of 10,600 skiers per hour on its six double chairs, one triple, two quad, and two surface tows.

Taos Ski Valley has 14 lodges and condominiums with nearly 300 beds. All offer ski-week packages; six of them have restaurants. There are two more restaurants on the mountain in addition to the expansive facilities of Village Center at the base. For reservations, call the **Taos Valley Resort Association** (tel. 505/776-2233 or toll free 800/776-1111).

Tickets: All lifts, adults $35 full day, $23 half day; children (12 or younger) $20

full day, $15 half day; seniors 65–69, $10 full day; seniors over 70, free. Novice lifts, adults $20, children $15. Full rental packages, $15 adults, $7 children.
Open: Daily, Thanksgiving Day–first week of April 9am–4pm.

RED RIVER SKI AREA, P.O. Box 900, Red River, NM 87558. Tel. 505/754-2382 or toll free 800/348-6444 for reservations.

Lodgers in Red River can walk out their doors and be on the slopes. Two other factors make this 32-year-old, family-oriented area special: first, its 27 trails are geared to the intermediate skier, though beginners and experts have their share; and second, good snow is guaranteed early and late in the year by snowmaking equipment that can work on 75% of the runs, more than any other in New Mexico. There's a 1,500-foot vertical drop here to a base elevation of 8,750 feet. Lifts include three double chairs, two triple chairs, and one surface tow, with a skier capacity of 6,720 per hour.
   Tickets: All lifts, adults $28 full day, $20 half day; children (12 and under) and seniors (60 and over) $17 full day, $11 half day. Full rental packages, from $12 adults, $9 children.
   Open: Daily, Thanksgiving Day–Apr 1 9am–4pm.

ANGEL FIRE SKI AREA, P.O. Drawer B, Angel Fire, NM 87710. Tel. 505/377-6401 or toll free 800/633-7463.

The 30 miles of ski runs here are heavily oriented to beginning and intermediate skiers. Still, with a vertical drop of 2,180 feet to a base elevation of 8,500 feet, advanced skiers are certain to find something they like. The area's lifts—four double and two triple chairs—have an hourly capacity of 1,900 skiers.
   Tickets: All day, adults $25, children $17.
   Open: Daily, in season 8:30am–4:30pm.

SIPAPU SKI AREA, P.O. Box 29, Vadito, NM 87579. Tel. 505/587-2240.

The oldest ski area in the Taos region, Sipapu is 25 miles southeast on N.M. 518 in Tres Rios canyon. It prides itself on being a small local area, especially popular with schoolchildren. There are just one triple chair and two tows, with a vertical drop of only 865 feet to the 8,200-foot base elevation. There are 18 trails, half classified as intermediate. A bunkhouse provides some overnight lodging.
   Tickets: Adults $20, children under 9 $1.
   Open: Daily, in season 9am–4pm.

MORE RECREATION

BALLOONING   The Taos Mountain Balloon Rally, P.O. Box 3096, Taos, NM 87571 (tel. 758-8321), is held each year the third weekend of October. A hot-air balloon workshop is held in Taos the weekend before the rally. Recreational trips are offered by **Taos Mountain Magic** (tel. 776-8746).

BICYCLING   Taos Mountain Outfitters, South Plaza (tel. 758-9292), offer mountain bikes for rent or sale. Carson National Forest rangers recommend several biking trails in the greater Taos area, including Garcia Park and Rio Chiquito for beginner to intermediate mountain bikers, Gallegos and Picuris peaks for experts. Inquire at the U.S. Forest Service office next to the Chamber of Commerce for an excellent handout. Annual touring events include Red River's **Enchanted Circle Century Bike Tour** (tel. 754-2366) in mid-September.

FISHING   Fishing season in the high lakes and streams opens April 1 and continues through December, though spring and fall are known as the best times for success. Rainbow, cutthroat, and brown trout, and kokanee, a freshwater salmon, are commonly stocked and caught. The Rio Grande also has pike and catfish. Many experienced anglers prefer fly fishing, but those who don't recommend using jigs, spinners, or woolly worms as lures, or worms, corn, or salmon eggs as bait. A license is required; they are sold, along with tackle, at several Taos sporting-goods shops. For backcountry guides, try **Deep Creek Wilderness** (tel. 776-8423) in Red River, the **Fish Eagle** (tel. 377-3359) in Eagle Nest, **Los Rios Anglers** (tel. 758-2798) in Taos.

GOLF   The par-72 18-hole course in **Angel Fire** has been endorsed by the Professional Golfers Association. Surrounded by stands of ponderosa pine, spruce, and aspen, it's one of the highest regulation golf courses in the world at 8,600 feet. It also has a driving range and putting green. Carts and clubs can be rented at the course, and the club pro provides instruction. **The Taos Country Club** (tel. 758-7300) has opened a driving range and a new golf course. As of July 1992, 9 holes were open for play.

HIKING & BACKPACKING   There are many hundreds of miles of hiking trails in Taos County's mountain and high-mesa country. They're especially popular in summer and fall, although nights turn chilly and mountain weather fickle by September.

Maps (at $2 each) and free handouts and advice on all **Carson National Forest** trails and recreation areas can be obtained from the Forest Service Building, 208 Cruz Alta Rd. (tel. 758-6200) and from the office adjacent to the chamber of commerce on Paseo del Pueblo Sur. Both are open Monday through Saturday from 8am to 4:30pm. Detailed USGS topographical maps of backcountry areas can be purchased from **Taos Mountain Outfitters** on the Plaza (tel. 758-9292). This is also the place to rent camping gear, if you came without your own. Tent rentals are $9 a day or $21 a weekend; sleeping bags, $9 a day or $21 a weekend.

Two nearby wilderness areas offer outstanding hiking possibilities. The 19,663-acre **Wheeler Peak Wilderness** is a wonderland of alpine tundra encompassing New Mexico's highest (13,161 feet) peak. The 20,000-acre **Latir Peak Wilderness,** north of Red River, is noted for its high lake country. Both are under the jurisdiction of the Questa Ranger District, P.O. Box 110, Questa, NM 87556 (tel. 505/586-0520).

HORSE & PACK TRIPS   The **Taos Indian Horse Ranch,** on pueblo land off Ski Valley Road just before Arroyo Seco (tel. 758-3212 or toll free 800/659-3210), offers a variety of guided rides. Open daily from 10am to 4pm and by appointment, the ranch provides horses for all types of riders (English, western, bareback) and ability levels. Call ahead to reserve. Rates are $55 to $95 for a 2-hour trail ride. Horse-drawn trolley rides are also offered in summer. From late November to March, the ranch offers evening sleigh rides to a bonfire and marshmallow roast at $37.50 a head.

Horseback riding is also offered by the **Shadow Mountain Guest Ranch,** 6 miles east of Taos on U.S. 64 (tel. 758-7732). Rates are $17 to $20 per hour for trail rides. Shadow Mountain also takes llamas into the backcountry for "luncheons with llamas."

HUNTING   Hunters in Carson National Forest bag deer, turkey, grouse, band-tailed pigeons, and elk by special permit. On private land, where hunters must be accompanied by qualified guides, there is also black bear and mountain lion. Hunting seasons vary year to year, so it's important to inquire ahead with the **New Mexico Game and Fish Department** in Santa Fe (tel. 505/827-7882).

Several Taos sporting-goods shops sell hunting licenses. Backcountry guides include **Agua Fria Guide Service** (tel. 377-3512) in Angel Fire, **United States Outfitters** (tel. 758-9774) in Taos, and **Rio Costilla Park** (tel. 586-0542) in Costilla.

RIVER RAFTING   Half- or full-day white-water rafting trips down the Rio Grande and Rio Chama originate in Taos and Red River. The wild **Taos Box,** south of the **Wild Rivers Recreation Area,** is especially popular. Early May, when the water is rising, is a good time to go. Experience is not required, but you should wear a life jacket (provided) and be willing to get wet.

One convenient rafting service is **Rio Grande Rapid Transit,** P.O. Box A, Pilar, NM 87571 (tel. 505/758-9700 or toll free 800/222-RAFT). Its headquarters is at the entrance to the BLM-administered **Orilla Verde Recreation Area,** 16 miles south of Taos, where most excursions through the Taos Box exit the river. Several other serene but thrilling floats through the Pilar Racecourse start at this point. Other rafting outfitters in the Taos area include **Far Flung Adventures** (tel. 758-2628), **Los Rios River Runners** (tel. 758-1550 or toll free 800/338-6877), and **Rio Grande River Tours** (tel. 758-0762 or toll free 800/525-4966).

Note: Taos is not the place in which to experiment if you are not an experienced rafter. Do yourself a favor and check with the **Bureau of Land Management** (tel. 758-8851) to make sure that you are fully equipped to go white-water rafting without a guide. Have them check your gear to make sure it's sturdy enough—this is serious rafting!

SPAS After a day outside, **Taos Water Gardens,** in Pueblo Alegre Mall on Paseo del Pueblo Sur (tel. 758-1669), can treat the sore muscles of skiers, rafters, and others with private and public hot tubs and massage.

Ojo Caliente Mineral Springs, Ojo Caliente, NM 87549 (tel. 505/583-2233), is on U.S. 285, 50 miles (a 1-hour drive) southwest of Taos. This National Historic Site was considered sacred by prehistoric Indians. When Spanish explorer Cabeza de Vaca discovered and named the springs in the 16th century, he called them "the greatest treasure that I found these strange people to possess." No other hot spring in the world has Ojo Caliente's combination of iron, soda, lithium, sodium, and arsenic. The resort offers herbal wraps and massages, lodging and meals. Summer hours are from 10am to 8pm daily; in winter the springs don't open until 1pm on weekdays.

SWIMMING **Don Fernando Pool** on Civic Plaza Drive at Camino de la Placita, opposite the new convention center, admits swimmers over age six without adult supervision.

TENNIS There are free public courts in Taos at **Kit Carson Park** on Paseo del Pueblo Norte and **Fred Baca Memorial Park** on Camino del Medio south of Ranchitos Road, and indoor courts at the **Quail Ridge Inn** (see "Accommodations," above).

7. SAVVY SHOPPING

Visitors come to Taos to buy fine art. Some 50-odd galleries are located within easy walking distance of the Plaza, and a couple of dozen more are a short drive from downtown. Most artists display in one or more of the galleries, which are generally open seven days a week, especially in high season. Some artists show their work by appointment only.

The best-known Taos artist is R. C. Gorman, a Navajo Indian from Arizona who has made his home in Taos for over two decades. Now in his 50s, Gorman is internationally acclaimed for his bright, somewhat surrealistic depictions of Navajo women. His ✪ **Navajo Gallery,** next door to the Blumenschein House at 5 Ledoux St. (tel. 758-3250), is a showcase for his widely varied work: acrylics, lithographs, silk screens, bronzes, tapestries, hand-cast ceramic vases, etched glass, and more.

A good place to start an exploration of galleries is the **Stables Art Center,** operated by the Taos Art Association at 133 Paseo del Pueblo Norte (tel. 758-2036). A changing series of fine and performing arts exhibits introduce many of Taos's emerging artists on a rotating basis. All types of work are exhibited, including painting (from expressionism to nonrepresentationalism), sculpture, printmaking, photography, and ceramics. Admission is free; it's open Monday through Saturday from 10am to 5pm and Sunday from noon to 5pm, year-round.

SHOPPING A TO Z
ANTIQUES
DWELLINGS REVISITED, 10 Bent St. Tel. 758-3377.
Mexican and New Mexican primitive furniture.

STEWART'S FINE ART, 102B S. Taos Plaza. Tel. 758-0049.
Historical paintings for collectors.

ART

BURKE ARMSTRONG FINE ART, 121 N. Plaza. Tel. 758-9016.
Historic oils, watercolors, and sculptures, including works by Taos Pueblo sculptor John Suazo.

DESURMONT-ELLIS GALLERY, 121 N. Plaza. Tel. 758-3299.
Abstract and impressionist oils and watercolors, sculpture, ceramics, and jewelry, including Angie Coleman woodcuts.

EL TALLER GALLERY, 119A Kit Carson Rd. Tel. 758-4887.
The Amado Pena gallery, with paintings, graphics, sculpture, jewelry, and weavings of southwestern theme.

MAGIC MOUNTAIN GALLERY, 107A N. Plaza. Tel. 758-9604.
Contemporary paintings, sculpture, ceramics, jewelry, and turned wood bowls.

NEW DIRECTIONS GALLERY, 107B N. Plaza. Tel. 758-2771.
Features Larry Bell's latest glass sculptures and mirage works, as well as work by acclaimed Taos sculptor Ted Egri.

PHILIP BAREISS CONTEMPORARY EXHIBITIONS, 15 Ski Valley Rd. Tel. 776-2284.
The works of some 30 leading Taos artists, including sculptor Gray Mercer and watercolorist Patricia Sanford.

QUAST GALLERIES, 229 Kit Carson Rd. Tel. 758-7160.
Representational landscapes and figurative paintings of the West, distinguished sculpture, occasional international exhibits.

SHRIVER GALLERY, 401 Paseo del Pueblo Norte. Tel. 758-4994.
Traditional paintings, drawings, etchings, and bronze sculpture, featuring Star Liana York.

TALLY RICHARDS GALLERY, Ledoux St. Tel. 758-2731.
Contemporary art, especially surrealism.

THE TAOS GALLERY, 403 Paseo del Pueblo Sur. Tel. 758-2475.
Contemporary paintings, sculptures, lithographs, serigraphs, and etchings. Also operates the Taos Gallery 2 at 124 Bent St.

TAOS TRADITIONS GALLERY, 221 Paseo del Pueblo Norte. Tel. 758-0016.
Contemporary to traditional landscapes, still lifes, and figuratives in oil, pastel, watercolor, and bronze. Also featured are works by exceptional emerging artists.

WESTERN HERITAGE GALLERY, 110 S. Plaza. Tel. 758-4489.
Paintings, sculpture, and jewelry of western and southwestern Indian themes.

BOOKS

Among the most interesting bookstores in Taos are the following. The **Taos Book Shop,** 122D Kit Carson Rd. (tel. 758-3733), founded in 1947, is the oldest general bookstore in New Mexico. **Moby Dickens Bookshop,** 124A Bent St., #6 Dunn House (tel. 758-3050), has a children's as well as an adult collection. The **Kit Carson House** (see "Attractions," above) is well stocked with regional history books. The **Fernandez de Taos Bookstore** is located right on the Plaza (tel. 758-4391). It carries local and regional newspapers as well as a large array of magazines and a substantial offering of books on various southwestern subjects.

CRAFTS

BROOKS INDIAN SHOP, 108G Cabot Plaza Mall, 108 Kit Carson Rd. Tel. 758-9073.
Jewelry, pottery, artifacts, and accessories.

CLAY & FIBER GALLERY, 126 West Plaza Dr. Tel. 758-8093.
Contemporary crafts, ceramics, jewelry, textiles, and sculpture.

OPEN SPACE GALLERY, 103B E. Taos Plaza. Tel. 758-1217.
A cooperative gallery of contemporary arts and crafts.

TAOS ARTISANS GALLERY, Bent St. Tel. 758-1558.
Local handmade jewelry and wearables, clay-work glass, leather, silk, and *retablos*.

WEAVING SOUTHWEST, 216B Paseo del Pueblo Norte. Tel. 758-0433.
Contemporary tapestries by New Mexico artists, and one-of-a-kind rugs, blankets, and pillows.

FASHIONS

MARTHA OF TAOS, 121 Paseo del Pueblo Norte. Tel. 758-3102.
Southwestern-theme original designs.

TWINING WEAVERS AND CONTEMPORARY CRAFTS, 135 Paseo del Pueblo Norte. Tel. 758-9000.
Handwoven rugs, blankets, and other fabrics by designer and weaver Sally Bachman.

FURNITURE

TAOS BLUE, 101A Bent St. Tel. 758-3561.
An unusual collection of fine contemporary and Native American crafts and furniture.

GIFTS & SOUVENIRS

BROKEN ARROW LTD., N. Plaza. Tel. 758-4304.
Ceramics, weaving, jewelry, baskets, paintings, and sculpture.

ORIGINAL TRADING POST OF TAOS, El Rincon, 114 Kit Carson Rd. Tel. 758-9188.
Hispanic and Indian artifacts and jewelry.

RAINY MOUNTAIN TRADING POST, S. Plaza. Tel. 758-4489.
Jewelry, pottery, artifacts.

JEWELRY

ARTWARES, N. Plaza. Tel. 758-8850.
Innovative contemporary works, featuring Phil Poirier's one-of-a-kind and limited-edition silverwork.

TAOS GEMS AND MINERALS, Paseo del Pueblo Sur. Tel. 758-3910.
Gems, jewelry, and crystals.

---

8. EVENING ENTERTAINMENT

Many occasional events are scheduled by the **Taos Art Association,** P.O. Box 198, Taos, NM 87571 (tel. 758-2036), with headquarters at the Stables Art Center on Paseo del Pueblo Norte. The TAA imports local, regional, and national performers in theater, dance, and concerts—Dave Brubeck, Dizzy Gillespie, the American String Quartet, and the American Festival Ballet have performed here—and offers two weekly film series, including one for children. The TAA is also the best place to purchase tickets for most events.

You can get details on current events in the weekly *Taos News,* published on Thursday. The Taos County Chamber of Commerce (tel. 505/758-3873 or toll free 800/732-TAOS) publishes semiannual listings of "Taos County Events."

THE PERFORMING ARTS

MAJOR ANNUAL PROGRAMS

TAOS SCHOOL OF MUSIC, P.O. Box 198, Taos, NM 87571. Tel. 505/ 758-2052.

⭐ One of the oldest chamber music programs of its kind in the United States offers an intensive eight week (mid-June to mid-August) chamber music study and performance program to advanced students of violin, viola, cello, and piano. There is daily coaching by the American String Quartet and pianist Robert McDonald. The school is located at the Hotel St. Bernard in Taos Ski Valley in northern New Mexico.

The eight week Chamber Music Festival is an important adjunct to the school, offering 16 concerts and seminars to the public by the American String Quartet, pianist Robert McDonald, and guest violist Michael Tree of the Guarneri Quartet, as well as concerts by the international young artists in attendance. Concerts are given at the Taos Community Auditorium and the Hotel St. Bernard.

Hosted by the Taos Art Association, the school was founded in 1963.

FORT BURGWIN RESEARCH CENTER, State Hwy. 518 (south of Taos). Tel. 758-8322.
This historic site (of the 1,000 year-old Pot Creek Pueblo), located about 10 miles south of Taos, is a summer campus of Southern Methodist University. From mid-May through mid-August, the SMU-IN-TAOS curriculum (among other studio arts, humanities, and sciences) includes courses in music and theater. There are regularly scheduled orchestral concerts, guitar and harpsichord recitals, and theater performances that are available to the community, without charge, throughout the summer.

MUSIC FROM ANGEL FIRE, P.O. Box 502, Angel Fire, NM 87710. Tel. 377-6932 or 989-4772.

⭐ This acclaimed program of chamber, folk, and jazz music begins in mid-August with weekend concerts and continues up to Labor Day. Based in the small resort community of Angel Fire, about 21 miles east of U.S. 64, it also presents numerous concerts in Taos and Raton.

MAJOR CONCERT HALLS & ALL-PURPOSE AUDITORIUMS

TAOS CIVIC PLAZA AND CONVENTION CENTER, 121 Civic Plaza Dr. Tel. 758-4160.
Taos's pride and joy is this new center, located just three short blocks north of the Plaza. Opened in 1990, it accommodates groups of 610 in Rio Grande Hall and

another 500 in adjacent Bataan Auditorium. Major concerts and other entertainment events will be scheduled here.

TAOS COMMUNITY AUDITORIUM, Kit Carson Memorial State Park. Tel. 758-2052.

The town's primary arts facility before the construction of the Civic Plaza, this auditorium—located behind the Stables Art Center—seats 235 for theater. A film series is offered at 8pm every Wednesday (admission $4).

THE CLUB & MUSIC SCENE

ADOBE BAR, The Historic Taos Inn, 125 Paseo del Pueblo Norte. Tel. 758-2233.

A favorite gathering place for locals as well as visitors, the Adobe Bar is known for its live music series (Wednesday and Sunday from 6 to 9pm) devoted to the eclectic talents of Taos musicians. The schedule offers a little of everything—classical, jazz, folk, Hispanic, and acoustic. The Adobe Bar features a wide selection of international beers, wines-by-the-glass, light New Mexican dining, desserts, and an espresso menu.

Admission: Free.

CARL'S FRENCH QUARTER, Quail Ridge Inn, Ski Valley Rd. Tel. 776-8319.

This popular Cajun-style restaurant features Thursday night dinner shows by classical or jazz artists. Seating is at 7pm; the show, at 8pm. Musical revues are often presented at other times of year.

Admission: $20 dinner show.

KACHINA CABARET, Kachina Lodge, 413 Paseo del Pueblo Norte. Tel. 758-2275.

Top-name country and Hispanic acts, including the Desert Rose Band, the Nitty Gritty Dirt Band, and Eddie Rabbit, perform in the cabaret. Saturday night is the big night, starting at 9pm. The adjacent Zuni Lounge has rock bands nightly.

Admission: Varies according to performer. Usually $5 Fri–Sat.

SAGEBRUSH INN, Paseo del Pueblo Sur. Tel. 758-2254.

Taos's highest-energy dancing spot has country or rock performers nightly, year-round, from 9pm. During ski season, country singer/guitarist Michael Martin Murphey ("Wildfire") presents a cocktail show every other Saturday night, sometimes more frequently.

Admission: Dance bands, free. Murphey show, $16.

THUNDERBIRD LODGE, Taos Ski Valley. Tel. 776-2280.

The first two weeks of January, the Thunderbird Jazz Festival brings leading contemporary jazz musicians to perform week-long gigs at the foot of the ski slopes. Shows start at 8:30pm; dinner-and-show packages are available. The rest of the ski season, the Twining Tavern has country, soft rock, jazz music, and Warren Miller ski movies.

Admission: Jazz festival $8–$18 depending on seats.

9. EASY EXCURSIONS

THE ENCHANTED CIRCLE

This 90-mile loop, a National Forest Scenic Byway, runs through the towns of Questa, Red River, Eagle Nest, and Angel Fire, incorporating portions of N.M. 522, N.M. 38,

and U.S. 64. It can be driven in two hours round-trip from Taos—k
a full day, and many several days, to accomplish it.

Traveling north from Taos via N.M. 522, it's a 24-mile drive t
whose residents are employed at a molybdenum mine 5 miles ea
north, the highway passes near **San Cristobal,** where a side
D. H. Lawrence Shrine, and **Lama,** site of an isolated spiritu:

If you turn west off N.M. 522 onto N.M. 378 about 3 miles nortn
descend 11 miles on a gravel road into the gorge of the Rio Grande at the bu..
Land Management–administered ✪ **Wild Rivers Recreation Area** (tel. 758-
8851). Here, where the Red River enters the gorge, is the most accessible starting point
for river-rafting trips through the infamous Taos Box. Some 48 miles of the Rio
Grande, south from the Colorado border, are protected under the national Wild and
Scenic River Act of 1968. Information on geology and wildlife, as well as hikers' trail
maps, can be obtained at the Visitors Center here. Ask for directions to the impressive
petroglyphs in the gorge. River-rafting trips can be booked in Taos, Santa Fe, Red
River, and other communities.

The village of **Costilla,** near the Colorado border, is 20 miles north of Questa.
This is the turnoff point for four-wheel-drive jaunts into Valle Vidal, a huge U.S.
Forest Service–administered reserve with 42 miles of roads.

✪ **RED RIVER**   Turn east at Questa onto N.M. 38 for a 12-mile climb to **Red
River,** a rough-and-ready 1890s gold-mining town which has parlayed its Wild West
ambience into a pleasant resort village. Especially popular with families from Texas
and Oklahoma, this community at 8,750 feet is a center for skiing and snowmobiling,
fishing and hiking, off-road driving and horseback riding, river rafting, and other
outdoor pursuits. Frontier-style celebrations, honky-tonk entertainment, and even
staged shoot-outs on Main Street are held throughout the year.

The **Red River Chamber of Commerce,** P.O. Box 868, Red River, NM
87558 (tel. 505/754-2366 or toll free 800/348-6444), lists more than 40 accommodations, including lodges and condominiums. Some are open winters or summers only.

EAGLE NEST   About 16 miles east of Red River, on the other side of 9,850-foot
Bobcat Pass, is the village of **Eagle Nest,** resting on the shore of Eagle Nest Lake in
the Moreno Valley. There was gold mining in this area as early as 1866, starting in
what is now the ghost town of Elizabethtown 5 miles north; but Eagle Nest itself
(pop. 200) wasn't incorporated until 1976. The 4-square-mile lake is considered one
of the top trout producers in the United States, and attracts ice fishermen in winter as
well as summer anglers. Sailboaters and windsurfers also use the lake, although
swimming, waterskiing, and camping are not permitted. The **Laguna Vista Lodge,**
P.O. Box 65, Eagle Nest, NM 87718 (tel. 505/377-6522 or toll free 800/821-2093) is
the village's best hotel/restaurant.

If you're heading to Cimarron (see Chapter 7, "Northeastern New Mexico") or
Denver, proceed east on U.S. 64 from Eagle Nest. But if you're circling back to Taos,
continue southwest on U.S. 38 and 64 to Agua Fria and Angel Fire.

Shortly before the Agua Fria junction, you'll see the ✪ **DAV Vietnam
Veterans Memorial.** It's a stunning structure, its curved white walls soaring high
against the backdrop of the Sangre de Cristo range. Consisting of a chapel and
underground visitor center, it was built by Dr. Victor Westphall in memory of his son,
David, a marine lieutenant killed in Vietnam in 1968. The chapel has a changing
gallery of photographs of Vietnam veterans who gave their lives in the Southeast Asian
war, and a poignant inscription by young Westphall.

✪ **ANGEL FIRE**   The full-service resort community of **Angel Fire,** 12 miles south
of Eagle Nest, 21 miles east of Taos, and 2 miles south of the Agua Fria junction on
N.M. 38, dates only from the late 1960s, but already has some 30 lodges and
condominiums. Winter skiing and summer golf are the most popular activities, but
there's also ample opportunity for sailing and fishing on Angel Fire Lake, tennis,
racquetball, and horseback riding. The unofficial community center is the **Legends**

& Conference Center, P.O. Drawer B, Angel Fire, NM 87710 (tel. 377-6401 or toll free 800/633-7463), a 157-room inn and restaurant with rates ting at $55.

For more information and full accommodations listings on the Moreno Valley, contact the **Angel Fire/Eagle Nest Chamber of Commerce,** P.O. Box 547, Angel Fire, NM 87710 (tel. 505/377-6353 or toll free 800/446-8117).

It's 21 miles back to Taos, over 9,100-foot Palo Flechado Pass, down the valley of the Rio Fernando de Taos, and through the small community of Shady Brook.

CHAPTER 7

NORTHEASTERN NEW MEXICO

1. LAS VEGAS
2. RATON
3. THE I-40 CORRIDOR

The region north from I-40, and east of the Sangre de Cristo Mountains, is a vast prairie that, over many thousands of years, has been trodden by dinosaurs and buffalo, by early humans and Plains Indians, by pioneers and settlers. Dinosaurs left footprints at Clayton Lake State Park, and Folsom Man roamed this region 12,000 years ago. Coronado passed through during his 16th-century search for Cíbola; some 300 years later, covered wagons followed the Santa Fe Trail west.

Cattle baron Lucien Maxwell controlled most of these prairies as his private empire in the latter half of the 19th century. During his era, this was truly the Wild West. The notorious town of Cimarron attracted nearly every gunslinger ever made famous by a Hollywood film, from Butch Cassidy to Clay Allison, Black Jack Ketchum to Jesse James; bullets still decorate the ceiling of the St. James Hotel.

Las Vegas, established long before its Nevada namesake, was the largest city in New Mexico at the turn of the 20th century, with a cosmopolitan population from all over the world. Doc Holliday, Bat Masterson, and Wyatt Earp walked its wild streets in the 1880s. A decade later, it was the headquarters of Teddy Roosevelt's Rough Riders, and early in the 20th century, it was a silent film capital (Tom Mix made movies here) and the site of a world heavyweight boxing match. Today, with a population of 16,000, it is the region's largest city, and the proud home of 900 historic properties.

Raton (pop. 9,000), on I-25 in the Sangre de Cristo foothills, is the gateway to New Mexico from the north. Clayton (pop. 3,000), Tucumcari (pop. 8,000), and Santa Rosa (pop. 3,000) are all transportation hubs and ranching centers.

Two national monuments are particular points of interest. Fort Union, 24 miles north of Las Vegas, was the largest military installation in the Southwest in the 1860s and 1870s. Capulin Volcano, 33 miles east of Raton, last erupted 10,000 years ago; visitors can walk inside the crater. Kiowa National Grasslands preserve 136,000 acres of pure prairie.

Drained by the Pecos and Canadian rivers, northeastern New Mexico is otherwise notable for the number of small lakes that afford opportunities for fishing, hunting, boating, camping, and other recreational pursuits. There are 11 state parks and six designated wildlife areas within the region. Philmont Scout Ranch, south of Cimarron, is known by Boy Scouts throughout the world.

Use Las Vegas, just over an hour's drive east of Santa Fe, as your base for exploring this region. After seeing the sights of this historic city, head north a short distance via I-25 and N.M. Highway 161 to Fort Union National Monument. Then follow state roads up the Mora River valley, turning north at Mora on N.M. 434 to Angel Fire and Eagle Nest. Where U.S. 64 turns east off the Enchanted Circle, follow it to Cimarron. You'll need a day to absorb this frontier village.

U.S. 64 traces the Santa Fe Trail northeast to Raton. Explore the town's historic district, then take U.S. 64/87 east to Capulin Volcano National Monument. Continue east to the ranching center of Clayton, then south on N.M. 402 and southwest on U.S. 54 to Tucumcari. This city and Santa Rosa, an hour west on I-40, are oases in the arid east. Return to Las Vegas via N.M. 3 through Villanueva.

1. LAS VEGAS

64 miles E of Santa Fe; 106 miles W of Tucumcari;
324 miles S of Denver, Colorado

GETTING THERE   By Plane   Las Vegas Municipal Airport handles private flights and charters. There is no regularly scheduled commercial service.

By Train   Amtrak (tel. toll free 800/USA-RAIL) has a depot on Railroad Avenue, but there are no ticket sales: You must book ahead. The *Southwest Chief,* which runs between Los Angeles and Chicago, stops in Las Vegas once daily eastbound and once westbound.

By Bus   Greyhound/Trailways, 508 Seventh St. (tel. 425-8689), stops in Las Vegas three times daily northbound, and three times southbound, on its Denver-Albuquerque runs. The station may change location, so call ahead.

By Car   From Santa Fe, take I-25 north (1¼ hours); from Raton, take I-25 south (1¾ hours); from Taos, follow N.M. 518 southeast 78 miles through Mora (2 hours); from Tucumcari, follow N.M. 104 west (2 hours).

ESSENTIALS   Orientation   Las Vegas is on the eastern slope of the Sangre de Cristo range, on a Pecos River tributary known as the Gallinas River. Grand Avenue (U.S. 85) parallels I-25, which runs northeast-southwest through the city. Old Town Plaza is at the intersection of four main streets: Hot Springs Boulevard (to the north), Pacific Street (south), Bridge Street (east), and National Avenue (west). Bridge and Pacific intersect Grand.

Information   The **Las Vegas/San Miguel Chamber of Commerce** is at 727 Grand Ave. (P.O. Box 148), Las Vegas, NM 87701 (tel. 505/425-8631 or toll free 800/832-5947). It's at the north end of town, between University Avenue and Bridge Street.

Fast Facts   The **area code** is 505. **Northeastern Regional Hospital** is at 1235 Eighth St. (tel. 425-6751). The main **post office** is located at 1001 Douglas Ave. (tel. 425-9387). In case of **emergencies,** dial 911.

Once known as the "gateway to New Mexico," this pleasant town was founded by a land grant in 1835. The Santa Fe Trail came through beginning in the 1850s, and with the advent of the Atchison, Topeka & Santa Fe Railway in 1879, Las Vegas boomed. As prosperity came from shipping cattle raised on millions of acres of surrounding ranch land, Las Vegas put up scores of fancy Queen Anne and Victorian-style houses and hotels that remain today as a visual entry to that lavish era.

WHAT TO SEE & DO

A WALKING TOUR OF HISTORIC LAS VEGAS   Start next door to the chamber of commerce on Grand Avenue, at the ✪ **Rough Riders Memorial and City Museum** (tel. 425-8726). About 40% of Teddy Roosevelt's Spanish-American War campaigners in 1898 came from this frontier town, and the museum chronicles their contribution to U.S. history. It's open Monday to Saturday to 9am to 4pm except holidays.

Most of the notable structures can be found district. The 1879 **Stern and Nahm Building** and folded sheet-metal ornaments above. Deco **Winternitz Block.** The Italianate commercia arched windows of the **Anicito Baca Buildi** The **E. Romero Hose and Fire Company,** piers capped by pressed-metal capitals with d tecture.

The 1888 **Hedgcock Building** has arche building, and has served both as police static store. Presently, it is the home of the Citizens

The **Plaza Hotel** gave the town the finest ho in 1881. Its three-story facade topped with a fan the town's pride and joy, and it has been happi below.) The **Charles Ilfeld Building** began as a one grew to two stories in 1882, and finally reached three stories with an in 1890. The **Louis Ilfeld Building**, nearby, shows the classic architecture con into favor at the turn of the century in a storefront now serving as a bookstore.

The town's earlier history, going back to the first Spanish visits in the 16th century, is also seen in adobe architecture still standing alongside the ornate structures of the late 1800s. In addition, there are few places in the West with a better preserved collection of Territorial-style buildings.

OTHER ATTRACTIONS   Las Vegas has two colleges. **New Mexico Highlands University,** a 4-year liberal arts school of 2,000 students, was established in 1893. In 1971, it hired the nation's first Hispanic college president. Located at Seventh Street and University Avenue, just west of U.S. 85, it is especially strong in its minority education curriculum, and fields outstanding small-college athletic teams.

✪ **Armand Hammer United World College,** the U.S. branch of an international system of secondary and postsecondary schools, is 5 miles west on N.M. 65 at **Montezuma Hot Springs.** The college occupies the former Montezuma Hotel, a luxury resort built by the Santa Fe Railroad in 1888. The multistoried, turreted, balconied, 343-room "Montezuma Castle" is on every historic landmark list. Three U.S. presidents, Kaiser Wilhelm II, and Japan's Meiji Emperor Mutsuhito all stayed here. In 1981, the Armand Hammer Foundation purchased the run-down building and renovated it for the college.

The springs have been known for their curative powers for over 1,000 years; there are legends that Aztecs journeyed here from Mexico before the arrival of the Spanish. They are open to visitors; for information, call the City of Las Vegas Arts and Recreation Program (tel. 454-1401). A short drive north of the springs, a pond on the Gallinas River provides a fine place for summer fishing and midwinter ice-skating. The ice is free; skate rentals are available weekends.

Nearby parklands include **Las Vegas National Wildlife Refuge** (tel. 425-3581), 6 miles southeast via N.M. 104 and N.M. 281, open daily from 8am to 4:30pm, boasting 220 species of birds and animals on 8,750 acres of wetland; and **Storrie Lake State Park,** 4 miles north via N.M. 518, with fishing, swimming, waterskiing, camping, and a visitor center with historic exhibits.

Villanueva State Park, 36 miles southwest via I-25 and N.M. 3, offers hiking, camping, and picnicking between red sandstone bluffs in the Pecos River Valley. Nearby are the Spanish colonial villages of **Villanueva** and **San Miguel del Vado,** the latter a national historic district built around its impressive 1805 church.

NEARBY ATTRACTIONS

Mora, a village of about 450 people, 31 miles north via N.M. 518, is the main center between Las Vegas and Taos, and the seat of sparsely populated Mora County. The 15-mile long Mora Valley is one of New Mexico's prettiest but most economically depressed regions, where large ranches have more or less pushed out small farmers.

Beautiful and isolated **Morphy Lake State Park** is reached via N.M. 518 to

road south. The pretty lake is set in a basin of pine forest; it
ng and trout fishing. Eighteen miles north via N.M. 434 is
ay beauty, **Coyote Creek State Park,** with campsites beside
with beaver ponds. The fishing is good and several well-marked
d into the Sangre de Cristo from here.

les south of Mora and 27 miles northwest of Las Vegas, on N.M. 105
is the **Pendaries Lodge and Country Club,** P.O. Box 820, Rociada,
2 (tel. 505/425-6076). This lovely foothills lodge boasts the region's finest
golf course, tennis courts, stables for horseback riding, and a swimming pool.
has overnight accommodations and a restaurant/lounge.

EVELAND ROLLER MILL, P.O. Box 287, Cleveland, NM 87715, N.M. 518, about 2 miles west of Mora. Tel. 387-2645.

One vestige of a more prosperous past is this two-story adobe mill, which ground
out 50 barrels of wheat flour a day, virtually every day from 1901 to 1947. It was the
last flour mill to be built in New Mexico, the last to stop running, and is the only
roller mill in the state to have its original milling works intact. Today, it's been
converted into a museum with exhibits on regional history and culture.

Admission: $2 adults, $1 children 6–17, under 6, free.
Open: Memorial Day to Oct 31 10am–5pm and by appointment.

FORT UNION NATIONAL MONUMENT, P.O. Box 127, Watrous, NM 87753. Tel. 425-8025.

Established in 1851 to defend the Santa Fe Trail against attacks from Plains
Indians, Fort Union was expanded in 1861 in anticipation of a Confederate
invasion, subsequently thwarted at Glorieta Pass. Its location on the Santa Fe
Trail made it a welcome way station for travelers, but when the railroad replaced the
trail in 1879, the fort was on its way out. It was abandoned in 1891. Today Fort Union,
the largest military installation in the 19th-century Southwest, is in ruins. There's little
to see but adobe walls and chimneys, but the very scope of the fort is impressive. Santa
Fe Trail wagon ruts can still be seen nearby. The national monument visitor center has
interpreted the fort's history through exhibits, booklets, and a walking trail.

To reach the site from Las Vegas, drive 18 miles north on I-25 to the Watrous exit,
then another 8 miles northwest on N.M. 161.

Admission: $3 per car, $1 per person.
Open: Memorial Day–Labor Day, daily 8am–6pm; rest of year, daily 8am–5pm.
Closed: Christmas and New Year's Day.

WHERE TO STAY

Most motels are on U.S. Highway 85 (Grand Avenue), the main north-south highway
through downtown Las Vegas. (An exception is the Plaza Hotel, below.) Local
lodging tax is 4%; including state tax (6%), a total tax of 10% is assessed to each
hotel/motel bill.

INN ON THE SANTA FE TRAIL, 1133 Grand Ave., Las Vegas, NM 87701. Tel. 505/425-6791. 33 rms (all with bath). A/C TV TEL

$ Rates: $34–$44 single, $39–$44 double, $49 suite. Extra person $4. MC, V.
Parking: Free.

Built in the 1920's, the Inn on the Santa Fe Trail has been remodeled in a hacienda
style with all rooms looking out onto the central courtyard and sculptured gardens,
creating a quiet, intimate retreat just off the busy Grand Avenue. The rooms are small
but comfortable and have all the amenities of a major hotel. Done in pink and teal
with Southwest furnishings, designed and handcrafted by local artisans, they offer full
baths, direct dial telephones, and cable TV. Every morning a complimentary "sunrise
coffee buffet" is served in the fireplace room.

PLAZA HOTEL, 230 Old Town Plaza, Las Vegas, NM 87701. Tel. 505/425-3591 or toll free 800/626-4886. 36 rms, 2 suites. A/C TV TEL

$ Rates: $53–$63 single, $58–$68 double, $70–$95 suite. AE, CB, DC, MC, V.

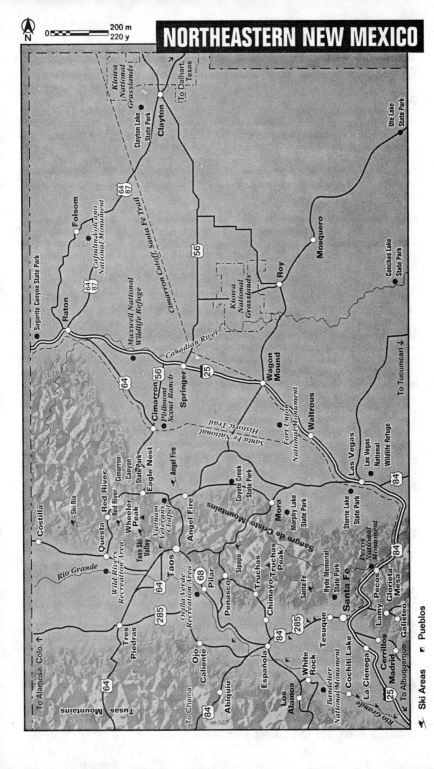

NORTHEASTERN NEW MEXICO

0 ⊨▬▬▬▬ 200 m
           220 y

To Dalhart, Texas
Kiowa National Grasslands
Clayton Lake State Park
Clayton
Ute Lake State Park
Folsom
64 87
Capulin Volcano National Monument
Cimarron Cutoff Santa Fe Trail
56
Mosquero
Sugarite Canyon State Park
64 87
Maxwell National Wildlife Refuge
Roy
Kiowa National Grasslands
Conchas Lake State Park
Raton
Canadian River
64
Cimarron 56
Springer
25
Wagon Mound
To Tucumcari →
Philmont Scout Ranch
Santa Fe National Historic Trail
Fort Union National Monument
Waltrous
Red River
Cimarron Canyon State Park
Angel Fire
Eagle Nest
Las Vegas
Las Vegas National Wildlife Refuge
84
Costilla
Ski Rio
Red River
Wheeler Peak
Vietnam Veterans' Chapel
Angel Fire
Coyote Creek State Park
Mora
Morphy Lake State Park
Storrie Lake State Park
Questa
Taos Ski Valley
Sangre de Cristo Mountains
Wild Rivers Recreation Area
Rio Grande
Taos
Sipapu
Truchas
Truchas Peak
Pecos National Monument
64
68
Pilar
Penasco
Chimayo
Santa Fe
Hyde Memorial State Park
Pecos
Glorieta Mesa
84
Orilla Verde Recreation Area
Tres Piedras
285
Lamy
285
To Alamosa, Colo. ↑
Rio Grande
Ojo Caliente
White Rock
Tesuque
Cerrillos
Galisteo
84
Española
Bandelier National Monument
Cochiti Lake
Madrid
25
To Albuquerque
Abiquiu
Los Alamos
La Cienega
To Chama
84
64
Tusas Mountains

✈ Ski Areas   ▣ Pueblos

The windows of this stately old inn look out on the center of Las Vegas life, the Plaza, where in 1846 a ceremony led by Gen. Stephen Kearny marked the takeover of New Mexico by the United States. It was built in Italianate bracketed style in 1882, in the days when western towns, newly connected with the East by train, vied with one another in constructing fancy "railroad hotels," as they were known. Considered the finest hotel in the New Mexico Territory when it was built, it was renovated with a $2 million investment exactly 100 years later. Stately walnut staircases frame the lobby and conservatory (with its piano), and throughout the hotel, the architecture is true to the era.

All rooms have antique furnishings, of course, and a queen-size or two double beds. Numerous second- and third-floor units adjoin, and a pair of hexagonal rooms overlook the conservatory. The rooms all open onto spacious hallways with casual seating areas.

Services and facilities include room service, valet laundry, courtesy car to/from rail and bus stations, handicapped rooms, saunas, a hair salon, and meeting space.

The Plaza Dining Room is considered the fanciest restaurant in town. Notice the walls: The original 19th-century stenciling has been restored. The restaurant is open nightly, from 5 to 9pm (9:30 on Friday and Saturday), as well as for breakfast and lunch from 7am to 2pm. Prices range from $6.95 to $9.95 for New Mexican dishes, $10.95 to $16.95 for continental cuisine. There's often live music in the evenings at Byron T's 19th-century saloon.

REGAL MOTEL, 1809 Grand Ave., Las Vegas, NM 87701. Tel. 505/454-1456. 50 rms, 1 suite. A/C TV TEL
$ Rates: $27–$30 single, $32–$39 double. AE, DC, DISC, MC, V.
A pleasant one-story motel stretched around a large parking area, the Regal has spacious rooms appointed in Southwest motif and standard furnishings. It's adjacent to the municipal golf course and nearby restaurants. There's limited courtesy-car service. No pets.

TOWN HOUSE MOTEL, 1215 Grand Ave., Las Vegas, NM 87701. Tel. 505/425-6717. 42 rms. A/C TV TEL
$ Rates: June 15–Aug $28–$37 single, $37–$45 double. May–June 14 and Sept–Oct 15 $25–$29 single, $29–$37 double. Oct 16–Apr $25 single, $29–$35 double. AE, CB, DC, MC, V.
One for the budget watchers, the Town House is an adequate place to lay your head—clean, comfortable, and AAA rated. It has all standard furnishings, and there's a restaurant opposite.

WHERE TO DINE

EL ALTO SUPPER CLUB, Sapello St. off New Mexico Ave. Tel. 454-0808.
Cuisine: STEAKS & NEW MEXICAN. **Reservations:** Recommended.
$ Prices: $5.95–$13.95. AE, MC, V.
Open: Daily 6–9pm.

Situated atop a hill overlooking the city, El Alto is a local legend: 50 years under one owner. It's known for its steaks—New York, T-bone, sirloin, filet mignon, all guaranteed an inch-and-a-half thick. It also has limited seafood offerings, including lobster, shrimp, trout, and frogs' legs; plus combination New Mexican meals, like enchiladas and tacos. Dinner comes with salad and tortilla chips. The adjoining lounge has music most nights.

EL RIALTO RESTAURANT, 141 Bridge St. Tel. 425-0037.
Cuisine: NEW MEXICAN. **Reservations:** Suggested weekends.
$ Prices: Dinner $6.95–$19.95. AE, MC, V.
Open: Daily 10:30am–9pm.
This colorful family restaurant adjacent to the Plaza offers an extensive Mexican-style menu as well as steaks and seafood. Desserts are all homemade, and there's a special children's menu. The Rye Lounge has full bar service.

HILLCREST RESTAURANT, 1106 Grand Ave. Tel. 425-72
   Cuisine: AMERICAN.
$ Prices: Dinner $6.95–$12.95. MC, V.
   Open: Daily 6am–8:45pm.
Known throughout the city as a "home-style" dining establishment, the Hillcres
everything from chicken-fried steaks to country-fried chicken to corn-fried catfish,
also has a good selection of Mexican food. The dining room is open evenings only;
the coffee shop is busy all day. The adjoining Flamingo Lounge offers full bar service.

SEMILLA NATURAL FOODS, 510 University Ave. Tel. 425-8139.
   Cuisine: DELI.
$ Prices: $2.25–$6. No credit cards.
   Open: Mon–Fri 11am–2pm.
Near New Mexico Highlands University is this natural-food store with a deli counter
and indoor/outdoor seating. It's a great place for a midweek lunch stop. There are
daily soup-and-quiche specials, a variety of salads, tostadas, and sandwiches like
chicken avocado and tuna salad. No red meat is served.

2. RATON

95 miles NE of Taos; 165 miles NE of Santa Fe;
220 miles S of Denver, Colo.

GETTING THERE   By Plane   Private planes can land at **Raton Municipal
Airport,** 10 miles south of Raton (tel. 445-3076).

By Train   The *Southwest Chief* stops in Raton twice a day—once eastbound
toward Chicago, once westbound toward Albuquerque and Los Angeles. Make
reservations with **Amtrak** (tel. toll free 800/USA-RAIL). The 1903 Santa Fe Depot,
First Street and Cook Avenue, still serves passengers.

By Bus   Greyhound/Trailways (tel. 445-9071) and **TNM&O Coaches** both
serve Raton, making their stops at McDonald's Restaurant, 419 Clayton Hwy.
Albuquerque–Denver buses stop in Raton four times daily northbound, and four
times southbound. Dallas–Denver buses pass through once each day each direction.

By Car   From Santa Fe, take I-25 north (3 hours); from Taos, take U.S. 64 east (2
hours); from Denver, take I-25 south (4 hours).

ESSENTIALS   Orientation   Raton is located at the foot of 7,834-foot Raton
Pass, the main route into Colorado from the south. Second Street, which runs to the
west of north-south I-25, is the main thoroughfare through downtown.

Information   The tourist information center is in the **Raton Chamber and
Economic Development Council,** 100 Clayton Hwy. at Second Street (P.O. Box
1211), Raton, NM 87740 (tel. 505/445-3689 or toll free 800/638-6161).

Fast Facts   The **area code** is 505. Raton's hospital, **Miners Colfax Medical
Center,** 1064 Hospital Dr. (tel. 445-3661), is on the south side of town. The main
post office is at 245 Park Ave. (tel. 445-2681). In case of **emergencies,** phone
445-2704 for police or ambulance, 445-2701 for fire.

Raton was founded in 1879 at the site of Willow Springs, a watering stop on the
Santa Fe Trail. Mountain man "Uncle Dick" Wootton, a closet entrepreneur, had
blasted a pass through the Rocky Mountains just north of the spring, and began
charging toll. When the railroad bought Wootton's toll road, Raton developed as the
railroad, mining, and ranching center for this part of the New Mexico Territory.
Today it has a well-preserved historic district, a horse-racing track, and the finest
shooting facility in the United States; and it's the gateway to a wide-ranging
mountain-and-prairie district.

WHAT TO SEE & DO

OF HISTORIC RATON Explore the city's historic
...ks of Raton's original townsite are listed on the National
...s, with some 70 significant buildings.

...useum, 216 S. First St. (tel. 445-8979), where you can pick
...he museum, open Tuesday through Saturday from 10am to
...iety of mining, railroad, and ranching items from the early
...sed in the Coors Building (1906), previously a Coors Brewing
...ext door is the **Haven Hotel** (1913), built of ivory brick with
...dorned with a pair of pineapples and three lion heads. At the
corner of ...st ... ok is the **Palace Hotel** (1896).

The **Santa Fe Depot,** First and Cook, was built in 1903 in Spanish mission
revival style. It is still used by Amtrak passengers today. Next door, built in 1910, is
the **Wells Fargo Express Company.**

Opposite the station, heading north on First, is the **Roth Building** (1893), whose
ornate metal facade boasts Corinthian pilasters and a bracketed cornice; the
Abourezk Building (1906), with two female figureheads on the upper storefront;
the **Marchiondo Building** (1882), a former dry-goods store painted bright yellow
with green trim; and the **Joseph Building** (1890s), which still retains the cupids
painted on its walls when it was the Gem Saloon.

Across Park Avenue, on First, the **VFW/Bennett's Transportation Building**
(1882) is the oldest structure in the historic district. Built with stone sidewalls and a
brick front, it had wooden lap siding added around the turn of the century.

Walk west 1 block to Second Street, and proceed south. At 131 N. Second St. is
the **Shuler Theatre.** Built in 1915, it housed the opera company, fire station, and
city offices. The interior of the theater, designed in European rococo style, has superb
acoustics. The lobby is decorated with murals recalling local history. It's still in active
use, especially in summer.

At the intersection of Second and Cook are the **Raton Realty Building** (1928),
characterized by a red tile roof and terra-cotta trimmed windows; and the **De Lisio
Building** (1918), a former bank with three Doric columns at its entrance and stained
glass topping the lower windows. At Third and Cook, the neoclassical U.S. Post Office
(1917) is now the **Arthur Johnson Memorial Library,** with a fine collection on
southwestern art. The south side of Cook between Second and Third is dominated by
the **Swastika Hotel** (1929), now the International State Bank, a seven-story brick
building decorated at the roofline with the swastika, an Indian symbol of good luck.
The hotel's name was changed to the Yucca Hotel when the German Nazis adopted
the swastika as their symbol.

OTHER ATTRACTIONS The **NRA Whittington Center,** off U.S. Highway 64
about 10 miles south of Raton, is considered the most complete nonmilitary shooting
and training facility in the world. Operated by the National Rifle Association, it spans
50 square miles of rolling hills. It has 14 instructional and competitive ranges, a
handful of condominium units, and hookups for campers. Classes in pistol, rifle, and
shotgun shooting, firearm safety, and conservation are offered. National championship events are held annually. The center is open daily to the public for tours.

Eight miles northeast of Raton, **Sugarite Canyon State Park** (tel. 445-5607)
offers camping, boating, and fishing at three trout-stocked lakes.

NEARBY ATTRACTIONS

THE CLAYTON HIGHWAY There are a number of attractions on the Clayton
Highway, U.S. 64/87 running 83 miles east-southeast from Raton to Clayton.

Thirty-three miles east of Raton in **Capulin,** visitors have the rare opportunity to
walk inside a volcanic crater at ✪ **Capulin Volcano National Monument** (tel.
278-2201). A 2-mile road spirals up over 1,000 feet to the top of the 8,182-foot peak,
where two self-guiding trails leave from the parking area: the 1-mile Crater Rim Trail,
and the 1,000-foot descent to the ancient volcanic vent. The mountain was last active

about 10,000 years ago, when it exploded and sent out the last of three lava flows. At the Visitor Center, an audiovisual program discusses volcanism, and park personnel will answer questions. A short nature trail behind the center introduces plant and animal life of the area. Admission is $3 per car, $1 per person. The visitor center is open Memorial Day through Labor Day daily from 7am to 7pm, the rest of the year daily from 8am to 4:30pm.

Just north of Capulin Mountain, on N.M. 325 off the Clayton Highway, is the town of **Folsom,** near which 12,000-year-old "Folsom Man" was discovered in 1928. The find, excavated by the Denver Museum of Natural History, represented the first association of the artifacts of prehistoric people (spear points) with the fossil bones of extinct animals (a species of bison). Today the site, on private property, is closed to the public. But artifacts (prehistoric as well as from the 19th century) are displayed at the **Folsom Museum,** Main Street, Folsom (tel. 278-2155).

Clayton (pop. 3,000) is a ranching center just 9 miles west of the Texas and Oklahoma panhandle borders. Rich prairie grasses, typical of nearby **Kiowa National Grasslands** (tel. 374-9652), led to its founding in 1887. In New Mexico history, it's known as the town where Thomas "Black Jack" Ketchum, a notorious train robber, was executed and buried in 1901 after a decade of legendary heists.

North of town, near the distinctive Rabbit Ears mountains, dinosaur tracks can be clearly seen at **Clayton Lake State Park** (tel. 374-8808). The park has a visitor center, and offers fishing and camping.

Information on other area attractions, as well as lodging and dining, can be obtained from the **Clayton-Union County Chamber of Commerce,** 1103 S. First St. (P.O. Box 476) Clayton, NM 88415 (tel. 505/374-9253).

SOUTH OF RATON   Heading down I-25, **Maxwell National Wildlife Refuge** (tel. 375-2331) on the Canadian River, 24 miles from Raton, has a rich resident and migratory bird population, and numerous native mammals. In the little town of **Springer** (pop. 2,000), 39 miles south of Raton via I-25, the **Santa Fe Trail Museum** (tel. 438-2394) is housed in the 1881 Colfax County Courthouse. It contains pioneer artifacts and memorabilia from trail travelers, as well as a livery stable. The Colfax County Fair is held in Springer annually in mid-August. At the same time there is also a car show.

About 30 miles east of Springer via U.S. 56 is the **Dorsey Mansion,** a two-story log-and-stone home built in the 1880s by cattleman Stephen Dorsey. With 36 rooms, hardwood floors, Italian marble fireplaces, hand-carved cherry staircase, and dining-room table that sat 60, it was quite a masterpiece! Public tours are offered by appointment (tel. 375-2222) Monday to Saturday 10am to 4pm, Sunday 1 to 5pm, for an admission charge of $2 adults, $1 for children under 12.

South of U.S. 56 via N.M. 39 is the western of the two parcels that comprise **Kiowa National Grasslands.** Travel this route to reach **Chicosa Lake State Park,** on N.M. 120; 55 miles southeast of Springer, this Goodnight-Loving Trail stop has a visitor center, camping, and trout fishing.

۞ CIMARRON   Few towns in the American West have as much lore or legend attached to them as Cimarron, 41 miles southwest of Raton via U.S. 64. Nestled against the eastern slope of the Sangre de Cristo range, the town (its name is Spanish for "wild" or "unbroken") achieved its greatest fame as an outpost on the Santa Fe Trail between the 1850s and 1880s. Frontier personalities like Kit Carson and Wyatt Earp, Buffalo Bill Cody and Annie Oakley, Bat Masterson and Doc Holliday, Butch Cassidy and Jesse James, painter Frederic Remington and novelist Zane Grey, all passed through and stayed—most of them at the St. James Hotel (see "Where to Stay," below)—at one time or another.

Land baron Lucien Maxwell founded the town in 1848 as base of operations for his 1.7-million-acre empire. In 1857, he built the **Maxwell Ranch,** which he furnished opulently with heavy draperies, gold-framed paintings, and two grand pianos. In the gaming room the tables saw high stakes, as guests bet silver Mexican pesos or pokes of yellow gold dust. Gold was struck in 1867 on Maxwell's land, near

Baldy Mountain, and the rush of prospectors that followed caused him to sell out three years later.

The ranch isn't open for inspection today, but Maxwell's 1864 stone grist mill, built to supply flour to Fort Union, is. The **Old Mill Museum** houses an interesting collection of early photos and memorabilia. It's open May to October Monday to Wednesday and Friday and Saturday from 9am to 5pm and Sunday from 1 to 5pm. Admission is $2 adults, $1 seniors and children.

Cimarron has numerous other buildings of historic note: the **Dahl Brothers Trading Post** (1854), **Swink's Gambling Hall** (1854), the **National Hotel** (1854), the **Old Jail** (1872), the **Cimarron News and Press Building** (1872), and the **Colfax County Courthouse** (1872).

Cimarron is the gateway to the ✪ **Philmont Scout Ranch,** a 137,000-acre property donated to the Boy Scouts of America by Texas oilman Waite Phillips in 1938. Scouts from all over the world use it for backcountry camping and leadership training from June through August and for conferences the remainder of the year.

There are three museums on the ranch, all open to the public. **Villa Philmonte,** Phillips's Mediterranean-style summer home, was built in 1927 and remains furnished with the family's European antiques from that era. Three miles south of Cimarron, it's open daily in summer for guided tours, other times by appointment. The **Philmont Museum and Seton Memorial Library** (tel. 376-2281) commemorates the art and taxidermy of the naturalist and author who founded the Boy Scouts of America, and has exhibits on the varied history of the Cimarron area. It's open year-round, daily from June to August; closed Sunday the rest of the year. The **Kit Carson Museum,** 7 miles south of Philmont headquarters in Rayado, is a period hacienda furnished in 1850s style. Staff in historic costumes lead tours daily June through August. Admission is free to all ranch museums.

The **Cimarron Chamber of Commerce,** P.O. Box 604, Cimarron, NM 87714 (tel. 505/376-2417), has complete information on the region.

U.S. 64 from Cimarron leads west 24 miles to Eagle Nest, passing en route **Cimarron Canyon State Park,** a designated state wildlife area at the foot of crenellated granite formations known as the Palisades. Just east of Cimarron, County Road 204 offers access to the Carson National Forest's **Valle Vidal** wilderness recreation area, discussed in Chapter 6.

WHERE TO STAY

Most motels are found along U.S. 64/87, the Clayton Highway, between Second Street and the I-25 interchange. Local lodging tax is 5.5%, highest in the state; including the 6% state levy, each motel bill has 11.5% added tax.

BEST WESTERN SANDS MANOR MOTEL, 300 Clayton Hwy., Raton, NM 87740. Tel. 505/445-2737 or toll free 800/528-1234. 50 rms. A/C TV TEL
$ Rates: $42–$65 single, $48–$65 double. Extra person $2. AE, CB, DC, DISC, MC, V.
A rambling, one-story motel, the Sands Manor has spacious rooms with a king-size or two queen-size beds and all standard furnishings. Nonsmoking and handicapped rooms are available. There's an outdoor swimming pool, a playground for children, and a gift shop. The coffee shop is open daily, serving three family-style meals from 6am to 10pm.

HARMONY MANOR MOTEL, 351 Clayton Rd., Raton, NM 87740. Tel. 505/445-2763 or toll free 800/922-0347. 18 rms (all with bath). A/C TV TEL
$ Rates: Memorial Day–Labor Day $40–$58 single or double; rest of the year $36–$50 single or double. AE, MC, V. **Parking:** Free.
The Harmony Manor Motel, located just off I-25, is a great buy. The rooms are spotlessly kept by Loyd and Doris Wilkins (the owners) and contain all the amenities you need for a comfortable stay. Each is enormous and has king- or queen-size beds, cable TV, and direct dial phones. The decor is bright and airy, accented by floral

bedspreads—a welcome change from the dark paneling and outdated colors of other motels in the area. You won't be disappointed with the accommodations at the Harmony Manor.

HOLIDAY CLASSIC MOTEL, Clayton Hwy. at I-25 (P.O. Box 640), Raton, NM 87740. Tel. 505/445-5555 or toll free 800/255-8879. 87 rms, 7 suites. A/C TV TEL.
$ Rates: $54–$66 single, $58–$70 double. Children 17 and under free with parent. AE, CB, DC, DISC, MC, V.
Raton's most "high profile" accommodation, the Holiday Classic's rooms surround an enclosed courtyard with a heated indoor swimming pool. Rooms are spacious, nicely appointed, and recently remodeled. The hotel has a guest Laundromat, a games room, and a separate billiard room. The Holiday Inn restaurant, open from 6am to 10pm, offers meals in the $5 to $15 range; a plush lounge adjoins.

MELODY LANE MOTEL, 136 Canyon Dr., Raton, NM 87740. Tel. 505/ 445-3655. 26 rms, 2 suites. A/C TV TEL
$ Rates: Mid-May–Labor Day $32–$49 single, $36–$55 double. Labor Day–mid-May $29–$38 single, $33–$45 double. AE, CB, DC, DISC, MC, V.
This nice property on the I-25 business loop has a wide variety of room options. Eight rooms have steam baths; many of them have king-size beds. Most have HBO cable reception. All have thermostat-controlled hot-water heating. Pets are permitted here. The fully licensed restaurant serves daily from 6:30am to 1:30pm and 4:30 to 9pm, with dinners in the $7 to $15 price range.

IN NEARBY CIMARRON

ST. JAMES HOTEL, Rte. 1, Box 2, Cimarron, NM 87714. Tel. 505/376-2664. 26 rms, 2 suites.
$ Rates: Hotel $65 single or double, $75 suite; motel $35 single, $37 double. MC, V.
This landmark hotel looks much the same today as it did in 1873, when it was built by Henri Lambert, previously a chef for Napoleon, Abraham Lincoln, and Gen. Ulysses S. Grant. In its early years, as a rare luxury on the Santa Fe Trail, it had a dining room, a saloon, gambling rooms, and lavish guest rooms fitted out with Victorian furniture. Today, the lace and cherry wood have returned to the bedrooms, but without televisions or phones—the better to evoke the days when famous guests such as Zane Grey, who wrote *Fighting Caravans* at the hotel, were residents. Annie Oakley's bed is here, and a glass case holds a register with the signatures of Buffalo Bill Cody and the notorious Jesse James.
Unfortunately, the St. James also was a place of some lawlessness: 26 men were said to have been killed within the two-foot-thick adobe walls, and owner Ed Sitzberger (a Cimarron native son) can point out bullet holes in the pressed-tin ceiling of the dining room. The ghosts of some are believed to inhabit the hotel still.
The hotel itself has 15 rooms. There are 11 more in a modern annex; these lack the historic atmosphere of the hotel, but they do provide TV and telephone for those who prefer the late 20th century.
The St. James Dining Room serves the finest meals in this part of New Mexico. The menu is ambitious: main courses like shrimp Diablo, tournedos of beef, and veal marsala, most of them priced from $11 to $16. A separate coffee shop serves three meals daily; the bar offers live solo entertainment weekends. The hotel also offers room service, a seasonal outdoor swimming pool, gift shop, package store, and meeting room for 30.

WHERE TO DINE

THE CAPRI, 304 Canyon Dr. Tel. 445-9755.
   Cuisine: ITALIAN.
$ Prices: Main courses $5.45–$9.95. MC, V, AE.
   Open: Daily 7am–9pm.

This casual café draws rave reviews from locals for its homemade pastas, including stuffed manicotti, and its chicken cacciatore. It also offers a Mexican menu, steaks, and limited seafood, including a popular combination of tenderloin and brook trout.

EL MATADOR, 445 S. 2nd St. Tel. 445-9575.
  Cuisine: NEW MEXICAN.
  $ Prices: Lunch and dinner $3.25–$10.25.
  Open: Tues–Sun 7am–8:30pm.
Festive Mexican decor makes this café a lively spot. Tacos, enchiladas, burritos, tostadas, and other menu favorites are prepared à la carte or as part of combination plates. Steaks and other American dishes are also on the menu.

SWEET SHOP RESTAURANT, 1201 S. 2nd St. Tel. 445-9811.
  Cuisine: AMERICAN & TEX-MEX. **Reservations:** Suggested at dinner in summer.
  $ Prices: Lunch $3.95–$7.95; dinner $5.95–$24.95. AE, DC, DISC, MC, V.
  Open: Daily 9am–2pm and 5–9pm. **Closed:** Sun in winter.
This isn't a bakery, as the name might suggest: It's a fine restaurant, known for its quality beef. Prime rib, filet mignon, and steak-and-seafood combinations are popular, along with broiled breast of chicken and deep-fried shrimp. Across-the-border dishes include a Tex-Mex steak, fajitas, and enchiladas. A full-service lounge adjoins the restaurant.

---

3. THE I-40 CORRIDOR

Tucumcari: 172 miles E of Albuquerque; 101 miles W of Amarillo, Texas;
Santa Rosa: 113 miles E of Albuquerque; 170 miles W of Amarillo, Texas

GETTING THERE By Plane There's no regularly scheduled commercial service into either Tucumcari or Santa Rosa. Private planes can land at **Tucumcari Municipal Airport** (tel. 461-3229).

By Bus Greyhound Lines, Inc. buses pass through both towns several times daily. Coaches stop in Tucumcari at 118 E. Center St. (tel. 461-1350) and in Santa Rosa at the West Side Shell Station, 432 W. Coronado Dr. (tel. 472-5263).

By Car I-40 extends from southern California to North Carolina. Travel time from Albuquerque to Tucumcari is 2 hours, 40 minutes; to Santa Rosa, 1 hour, 45 minutes.

ESSENTIALS Orientation Tucumcari (pop. 8,000), 44 miles from the Texas border, is reached from three freeway exits. Tucumcari Boulevard (east-west U.S. 66) and First Street (north-south N.M. 209, to Clovis) are the principle arteries. **Santa Rosa** (pop. 3,000), situated where I-40 crosses the Pecos River, also is served by three freeway exits. Parker Avenue downtown is the same road as Will Rogers Drive (East Business Loop 40) and Coronado Drive (West Business Loop 40).

Information Contact the **Tucumcari-Quay County Chamber of Commerce**, 404 W. Tucumcari Blvd. (P.O. Drawer E), Tucumcari, NM 88401 (tel. 505/461-1694) or the **Santa Rosa Chamber of Commerce**, 486 Parker Ave., Santa Rosa, NM 88435 (tel. 505/472-3763).

Fast Facts The **area code** is 505. Hospitals are **Dr. Dan C. Trigg Memorial Hospital**, 301 E. Liel De Luna Ave. (tel. 461-0141), in Tucumcari; and **Guadalupe County Hospital**, 535 Lake Dr. (tel. 472-3417), in Santa Rosa. City **post offices** can be found at First and Aber streets (tel. 461-0370) in Tucumcari, and at 120 Fifth St. (tel. 472-3743) in Santa Rosa. In case of **emergency**, dial 911 in Santa Rosa. In Tucumcari, call for police/ambulance (tel. 461-2160), fire (tel. 461-3473), or Quay County sheriff (tel. 461-2720).

The 216 freeway miles from Albuquerque to the Texas border cross straight, featureless prairie and very few towns. But the valleys of the Pecos River (site of Santa Rosa) and Canadian River (location of Tucumcari) have several attractions, including natural lakes. There's not a lot to explore here, unless you're a bird hunter or a fisherman, but both towns can make a day's stopover worthwhile.

WHAT TO SEE & DO

The **Tucumcari Historical Museum,** 416 S. Adams, one block east of First Street, is open from 9am to 6pm Monday through Saturday, 1 to 6pm Sunday in summer; Tuesday through Saturday 9am to 5pm, 1 to 5pm Sunday in winter. An early sheriff's office, an authentic western schoolroom, a hospital room of the early West, a real chuck wagon, a historic windmill, and a barbed-wire collection are among the treasures.

The moonlike **Mesa Redondo,** rising 11 miles south of town via N.M. 209, gives visitors a sense of entering a strange unknown world. To the northwest, 27 miles distant over N.M. 104, is **Conchas Lake State Park,** with a reservoir 25 miles in length. Two modern marinas provide facilities for boating, fishing, and waterskiing. Camping and picnic areas attract visitors to the south side of the lake—there are full hookups available as well as a nine-hole golf course. The northern site offers rental cabins, a trailer park with hookups, a marina, a store, and a restaurant. **Ute Dam** is 22 miles northeast on U.S. 54, near the town of Logan. It has docking facilities on a lake, campsites, and rental boats. Quay County around Tucumcari is noted for its blue-quail hunting, said to be the best anywhere in the United States.

Caprock Amphitheatre (tel. 505/576-2779), 30 miles southeast of Tucumcari, is a natural amphitheater. Here the New Mexico Outdoor Drama Association presents an outdoor musical drama for eight weeks each summer, Friday and Saturday nights from July 3 to August 22. *Billy the Kid,* in its sixth season in 1992, is a romantic dramatization of New Mexico's Wild West days. The 1¾-hour show starts at 8pm, following a 6:30pm barbecue on-site. Show tickets are $8 for adults, $7 for seniors, $2.50 for children 5 to 12. Dinner costs $6 for adults, $4.50 for children. The amphitheater is on N.M. 469, south of San Jon off I-40 (Exit 356). For advance information, write the NMODA, P.O. Box 337, San Jon, NM 88434 (tel. 505/576-2455).

Santa Rosa calls itself "the city of natural lakes." Those bodies of water include **Blue Hole,** a crystal-clear, 90-foot-deep artesian spring just east of downtown. Fed by a subterranean river that flows 3,000 gallons per minute, it's a favorite of scuba divers. More than 100 per week come here to be certified. There's a bathhouse on site. **Park Lake,** in the middle of town, offers swimming, picnicking, and extensive recreational facilities. **Santa Rosa Lake State Park,** P.O. Box 384, Santa Rosa (tel. 472-3110), on a dammed portion of the Pecos River, has camping, hiking, excellent fishing, and a visitor information center. Ten miles south of town via N.M. 91, the village of **Puerto de Luna** is a 19th-century county seat with a 111-year-old church, Nuestra Senora del Refugio. Coronado bridged the Pecos near this point in 1541.

WHERE TO STAY

In both Tucumcari and Santa Rosa, major hotels are at I-40 interchanges. Smaller "ma and pa" hostelries can be found along the main streets—Tucumcari Boulevard in Tucumcari, Will Rogers Drive in Santa Rosa. All told, there are about 2,000 rooms in Tucumcari and Santa Rosa. City lodging taxes, charged in addition to the state levy of 6%, are 3% in Tucumcari, 2.75% in Santa Rosa.

TUCUMCARI

BEST WESTERN DISCOVERY MOTOR INN, 200 E. Estrella Ave. at Exit 332, Tucumcari, NM 88401. Tel. 505/461-4884 or toll free 800/528-1234. 107 rms. A/C TV TEL

$ Rates: June 1–Sept 1 $44–$48 single, $52–$56 double; Sept 2–May 31 $40–$44 single, $46–$50 double. AE, CB, DC, DISC, MC, V.

This spacious new motor hotel has the advantage of being off the "strip"—it's still central, but it's more quiet than many others. Many rooms, all of which have king-size or two queen-size beds, look down upon the outdoor swimming pool. The hotel also has an indoor spa, guest Laundromat, game room, and gift shop. Complimentary morning coffee is an added touch. Nonsmoking and handicapped rooms are available, and small pets are permitted with payment of a damage deposit.

The Headquarters House Restaurant, open from 6am to 10pm, with dinners in the $7 to $13 range, is considered one of Tucumcari's better eating places.

BEST WESTERN POW WOW INN, 801 W. Tucumcari Blvd. (P.O. Box 1306), Tucumcari, NM 88401. Tel. 505/461-0500 or toll free 800/528-1234. Fax 505/461-0135. 90 rms, 16 suites. A/C TV TEL

$ Rates: May–Oct $40–$50 single, $44–$54 double, $62–$87 suite. Nov–Apr $36–$46 single, $42–$52 double, $62–$87 suite. AE, CB, DC, DISC, MC, V.

A full-service downtown motor inn, the Pow Wow focuses around its beautiful outdoor swimming pool, with an artificial-turf deck. One-third of the units, including 15 ground-level suites, have kitchens (utensils not provided). Other facilities include a children's playground, a coin-op Laundromat, and a gift shop. Guests get complimentary greens fees at the local golf club. Pets are accepted, but must not be left unattended.

The Pow Wow Restaurant, open from 6am to 10pm, has a daily luncheon buffet; dinners priced from $5 to $12; and a cool, low-lit lounge with live entertainment evenings.

SANTA ROSA

BEST WESTERN ADOBE INN, E. Business Loop 40 at I-40 (P.O. Box 410), Santa Rosa, NM 88435. Tel. 505/472-3446 or toll free 800/528-1234. 58 rms. A/C TV TEL

$ Rates: May–Oct $44–$54 single, $50–$60 double; Nov–Apr $36–$46 single, $42–$52 double. AE, DC, CB, DISC, MC, V.

This pleasant motel has clean, comfortable rooms with all standard furnishings, including queen-size beds in every room. There's a swimming pool and gift shop, a courtesy car, and an attached coffee shop. Small pets are allowed.

MOTEL 6, 3400 Will Rogers Dr., Santa Rosa, NM 88435. Tel. 505/472-3045. 90 rms. A/C TV TEL

$ Rates: $27.95 single, $33.95 double. Under 18 free with parent. AE, CB, DC, DISC, MC, V.

Rooms are basic but clean; and with double beds, table and chairs, three-quarter bath, TV and phones, they meet the needs of many travelers. The motel has an outdoor swimming pool, open seasonally. It's on the north side of I-40, opposite the town.

SUPER 8 MOTEL, 1201 Will Rogers Dr., Santa Rosa NM 88435. Tel. 505/472-5388. Fax 505/472-5388. 88 rms (all with bath). A/C TV TEL

$ Rates: $31.90 single, $38.90 double. AE, CB, DC, MC, V. **Parking:** Free.

Located near the historic Club Café, this Super 8 is like other Super 8s in that it's clean and has large rooms with double beds and standard furnishings. The decor is simple—green carpeting and floral bedspreads. There's cable TV with pay movies, a guest laundry, and rooms for nonsmokers. Pets are not welcome.

WHERE TO DINE
TUCUMCARI

DEL'S, 1202 E. Tucumcari Blvd. Tel. 461-1740.
    Cuisine: AMERICAN & NEW MEXICAN.
$ Prices: $3.95–$14.95. MC, V.

Open: Mon–Sat 11am–8pm.
The big cow atop Del's neon sign is not only a Route 66 landmark; it points to the fine steaks inside, priced from just $6.95. T-bones, sirloins, rib eyes, and other cuts highlight the menu. Del's also offers burgers, Mexican plates, and seafood, including an 8-ounce catfish filet. A trip through the large salad bar is a satisfying meal for many. Del's is not licensed for alcoholic beverages.

LA CITA, 812 S. 1st St. Tel. 461-3930.
   Cuisine: NEW MEXICAN.
$ Prices: $2.95–$9.95. MC, V.
   Open: Mon–Sun 11am–9pm.
A modern café in downtown Tucumcari, La Cita is best known for its tasty fajitas, green chile enchiladas, spicy salsa, and flat enchiladas—served with an egg on top. There's a gift shop attached.

CHAPTER 8

NORTHWESTERN NEW MEXICO

1. GRANTS
2. GALLUP
3. FARMINGTON
4. CHAMA

This is Indian country, past and present. Pueblo, Navajo, and Apache share this colorful country of sandstone bluffs, treading the same ground their Anasazi ancestors did many centuries ago.

The Zuni, Acoma, and Laguna pueblos make their homes within shouting distance of I-40. Acoma's "Sky City" has been continually occupied for more than nine centuries. A huge chunk of the northwest is taken up by a part of the Navajo Reservation, largest in America; and the Jicarilla Apache Reservation stretches 65 miles south from the Colorado border. All share their arts and crafts, and their distinctive cultures, with visitors.

The past lives here, too, side by side with the present. Chaco Culture National Historical Park, with 12 major ruins and hundreds of smaller ones, represents the highest development of Anasazi civilization in the 11th century. Aztec Ruins National Monument and the nearby Salmon Ruins are similarly spectacular pueblo preservations.

Two other national monuments in northwestern New Mexico are El Morro and El Malpais—the former a sandstone monolith that bears centuries of inscriptions by passing travelers, the latter a volcanic badlands.

The metropolitan centers of the region are Farmington, center of the fertile San Juan valley and gateway to the Four Corners region, with about 37,000 people; Gallup, "Indian capital of the world" and a mecca for silver-jewelry shoppers, about 20,000; and Grants, a former uranium-mining boomtown, near 9,000.

Well east of Farmington, about equidistant from Santa Fe, is a fourth regional center of sorts: Chama (pop. 1,250). It's best known as the New Mexico depot for the Cumbres & Toltec Railroad and as a center for hunting and fishing expeditions into New Mexico's high country.

Albuquerque is your base for exploring northwestern New Mexico. Head west on I-40 via Laguna to Acoma Pueblo to tour the amazing "Sky City." Then proceed west on I-40 to Grants, after another turnoff on N.M. 117 to see El Malpais National Monument. Don't miss the New Mexico Museum of Mining in Grants.

From Grants, head south and west on N.M. 53 to Bandera Volcano and Ice Caves, El Morro National Monument, and the Zuni Pueblo. Then proceed north on N.M. 602 to Gallup, self-proclaimed "Indian Capital of the World," where you'll want to browse in trading posts for native jewelry and crafts.

Leaving Gallup, take I-40 east to Thoreau, N.M. 371 north to Crownpoint, and N.M. 57 east and north again to Chaco Canyon National Historical Park, the crown jewel of ancient Anasazi culture in North America. Spend the day here, leaving in time to travel north to Farmington for the night, via N.M. 44 and U.S. 64.

Essential sights in the Farmington area are Aztec Ruins National Monument and the Salmon Ruins, near Bloomfield. Afterward, take U.S. 64 east. Detour briefly to Navajo Lake State Park, then continue to Dulce, in the Jicarilla Apache Indian Reservation. Stay either here or a half hour down the highway in Chama.

Chama is the home of the Cumbres & Toltec Scenic Railroad, one of New Mexico's premier attractions. When you've waved the train good-bye, follow U.S. 84 south to Santa Fe, leaving time for a midway stop at the Ghost Ranch Living Museum north of Abiquiu. Return to Albuquerque via I-25. This itinerary will take you five to seven days.

1. GRANTS

78 miles W of Albuquerque; 60 miles E of Gallup

GETTING THERE   By Plane   Private planes are served by **Grants-Milan Municipal Airport,** U.S. 66 west (tel. 287-4700). There is no commercial service.

By Bus   The buses of **Greyhound Lines, Inc.,** 1801 W. Santa Fe Ave. (tel. 285-6268), stop several times a day.

By Car   From Albuquerque, take I-40 west (¼ hour). From Gallup, take I-40 east (1 hour).

ESSENTIALS   Orientation   Route 66 (Santa Fe Avenue) parallels I-40 as the main street through Grants, on the north side of the east-west freeway. It is bisected by N.M. 547 (First Avenue), which extends north to Roosevelt Avenue and Grants' "second" downtown, where many civic buildings and a large shopping mall are located.

Information   The Grants/Cíbola County Chamber of Commerce is at 100 N. Iron Ave. (P.O. Box 297), Grants, NM 87020 (tel. 505/287-4802 or toll free 800/748-2142). It's located in the same building as the Mining Museum.

Fast Facts   The **area code** is 505. **Cíbola General Hospital** is at 1212 Bonita St. in Grants (tel. 287-4446). The main **post office** is located at 120 N. Third St. (tel. 287-3143). In case of **emergencies,** dial 911.

Grants was established in the late 19th century as a railroad town and ranching center. It didn't really come of age until 1950, when Paddy Martinez, a Navajo sheep rancher, discovered uranium near Haystack Mountain, northwest of town. Grants has boomed and declined twice since then. Mines remain active today, though in some decline. The city is the seat of expansive Cíbola County, which stretches from the Arizona border nearly to Albuquerque.

WHAT TO SEE & DO

THE NEW MEXICO MUSEUM OF MINING, 100 N. Iron St. at Santa Fe Ave. Tel. 287-4802.

The world's only uranium-mining museum is structured over a re-creation of an actual underground mine, complete with original machinery and equipment.
Begin your tour on the first level of the museum, following a time line of dinosaur bones and ancient Pueblo pottery from the prehistory of the Grants area to the industry of the late 20th century. Then an elevator, representing the "cage" of deep-rock mining, carries you into the mine shaft.
Once underground, you can touch and feel the mining tools, equipment, and cement walls. You'll start at the station, a dimly lit cavern where workers, materials, and yellow uranium ore entered and left the mine. You'll see huge ore cars and actual

blasting caps. Deep in the mine, you'll duck into an open "stope," stripped of all ore and off-limits in an actual mine. Retired miners often lead tours, and their memories are worth 10 times the price of admission.

Admission: $2 includes guided tour or self-guiding "sound stick." Free for children 8 and under.

Open: Summer Mon–Sat 9am–7pm, Sun 1–7pm; winter Mon–Sat 10am–4pm, Sun 1–4pm.

ACOMA PUEBLO, P.O. Box 309, Acomita, NM 87034. Tel. 252-1139 or toll free 800/747-0181.

⭐ The spectacular "Sky City," a walled adobe village perched high atop a sheer rock mesa 367 feet above the 6,600-foot valley floor, is said to have been lived in at least since the 11th century—the longest continuously occupied community in the United States. Native legend says it has been inhabited since before the time of Christ. Both the pueblo and its mission church of San Estevan del Rey are National Historic Landmarks. When Coronado visited in 1540, he suggested that Acoma was "the greatest stronghold in the world"; those who attempt to follow the cliffside footpath to the top, rather than take the modern road, might agree.

The Keresan-speaking Acoma (pronounced *Ack*-uh-mah) Pueblo boasts about 4,400 inhabitants, but only about 50 reside year round on the 70-acre mesa top. Many others maintain ancestral homes and occupy them during ceremonial periods. The terraced three-story buildings face south for maximum exposure to the winter sun. Most of Sky City's permanent residents make livings from tourists who throng here to see the magnificent church, built in 1639 and containing numerous masterpieces of Spanish colonial art, and to purchase the thin-walled white pottery, with brown-and-black designs, for which the pueblo is famous.

Start your tour of Acoma at the visitor center at the base of the mesa. While waiting for your tour to begin, peruse the excellent little museum of Acoma history and crafts, or dine on native food in an adjoining café. Then board your 13-seat tour bus, which climbs through a rock garden of 50-foot sandstone monoliths and past precipitously dangling outhouses to the mesa's summit. There's no running water or electricity in this medieval-looking village; a small reservoir collects rainwater for most uses, and drinking water is transported up from below. Wood-hole ladders and mica windows are prevalent among the 300-odd adobe structures.

The annual San Estevan del Rey feast day is September 2, when the pueblo's patron saint is honored with a midmorning mass, a procession, an afternoon corn dance, and an arts-and-crafts fair. Traditional "rooster pulls" take place June 24 and 29 and July 25; a Governor's Feast is held annually in February; and four days of Christmas festivals run from December 25 to 28. Cameras are not allowed on the mesa during feast days.

Other celebrations are held in low-lying pueblo villages at Easter (in Acomita), early May (Santa Maria feast at McCartys), and August 10 (San Lorenzo Day in Acomita). Many Acomas work in Grants, 15 miles west of the pueblo, or in Albuquerque; others are cattle ranchers or operate a tribal bingo parlor.

To reach Acoma from Grants, drive east 15 miles on I-40 to McCartys, then south 13 miles on paved tribal roads to the visitor center. From Albuquerque, drive west 52 miles to the Acoma-Sky City exit, then 12 miles southwest.

Admission: Adults $6, seniors $5, children $4. Still photography $5, sketching or painting $40.

Open: Nov–Mar 8am–4:30pm; Apr–Oct 8am–7pm. One-hour tours every 20 minutes. **Closed:** Easter weekend, long weekend after July 4, and first weekend of Oct.

LAGUNA PUEBLO, P.O. Box 194, Laguna Pueblo, NM 87026. Tel. 552-6654.

The major Keresan-speaking pueblo consists of a central settlement and five smaller villages some 32 miles east of Grants (46 miles west of Albuquerque) along I-40 and U.S. 66. Laguna is the youngest of New Mexico's pueblos, and with 6,800 residents, the largest after Zuni. Founded after the 1680 Pueblo Revolt by refugees

N

0 ——— 15 mi
25.5 km

UTAH

Cortez

Durango

160

Mesa Verde
National Park

550

Ute Mountain
Reservation

Antimas River

Four Corners
Monument

574

160

ARIZONA

San Juan River

Aztec Ruins
National Monument

Aztec

511

Navajo
Lake

Carson
National
Forest

Shiprock

170

544

173

539

Navajo Lake
State Park

550

Ship Rock

Fruitland

64

Farmington

Bloomfield

64

Navajo   Indian   Reservation

Salmon
Ruins

To Chama
and Taos

371

Angel Peak
Recreational Area

44

Blanco
Trading Post

Jicarilla
Apache
Reservation

666

Bisti
Badlands

57

Nageezi

44

Sheep Springs

To Cuba and
Albuquerque

134

Chaco Cultural
National Historic Park

371

57

Tohatchi

White
Horse

197

Continental Divide

Crownpoint

Window
Rock

Gallup

Red Rock
State Park

40

57

509

666

Thoreau

To Holbrook and
Flagstaff, Ariz.

602

Bluewater Lake
State Park

Cibola
National
Forest

605

Cebolleta

Cibola   National   Forest

Mt. Taylor

Zuni
Pueblo

Ramah

Grants

53

40

Laguna

53

El Moro
National Monument

Zuni Reservation

36

Bandera Volcano
& Ice Caves

El Malpais
National Monument

Laguna
Reservation

Hawikuh
Ruins

Ramah
Navajo
Reservation

117

Acoma
Pueblo

Acoma Reservation

Laguna
Reservation

Pueblo

from the Rio Grande valley, it features the Mission of San Jose de los Lagunas, famous for its interior artwork.

Many Laguna Indians are engaged in uranium mining as employees of Laguna Enterprises, which has a contract with the U.S. Defense Department. Others are in agriculture or private business, including a tribal-operated residential center for Indian elderly. Permits for fishing in Paguate Reservoir can be obtained in the village of Paguate.

Pueblo and Navajo people from throughout the region attend the Fiesta de San Jose (September 19) at the Laguna mission. The fair kicks off with a mass and procession, followed by a harvest dance, sports events, and carnival. New Year's Day (January 1) and Three Kings Day (January 6) are also celebrated at the pueblo with processions and dances. Each smaller village has its own feast day between August 28 and October 17; call the pueblo office for details.

Seboyeta, the oldest Hispanic community in western New Mexico, is 3½ miles north of Paguate, outside Laguna Pueblo. It still shows ruins of adobe fortress walls built in the 1830s to protect the village from Navajo attack. The Mission of Our Lady of Sorrows was built in the 1830s, as was the nearby Shrine of Los Portales, built in a cave north of town.

Admission: Free. No photo fee, but some restrictions apply from village to village.

Open: Daylight hours year-round.

EL MALPAIS NATIONAL MONUMENT, 620 E. Santa Fe Ave., Grants, NM 87020. Tel. 285-5406.

America's newest national monument, designated only in 1987, is considered one of the outstanding examples of volcanic landscapes in the United States. El Malpais (the badlands) contains 115,000 acres of cinder cones, vast lava flows, hundreds of lava-tube and ice caves, sandstone cliffs, natural bridges and arches, Anasazi ruins, ancient Indian trails, and Spanish and Anglo homesteads.

There are two approaches to El Malpais, via N.M. 117 and N.M. 53. Route 117 exits I-40 7 miles east of Grants, then enters the national monument 10 miles south. From **Sandstone Bluffs Overlook,** many craters are visible in the lava flow, which extends for many miles along the eastern flank of the Continental Divide. The most recent flows date back only 1,000 years: Indian legends tell of rivers of "fire rock." Seventeen miles south of I-40, **La Ventana** is the largest natural arch in New Mexico.

From N.M. 53, which exits I-40 just west of Grants, visitors have access to the **Zuni-Acoma Trail,** an ancient Pueblo Indian trade route that crosses four major lava flows in a 7½-mile (one-way) hike. A printed trail guide is available. **El Calderon,** 20 miles south of I-40, is a trailhead for exploration of a cinder cone, lava tubes, and a bat cave (with restricted access).

The largest of all Malpais cinder cones, **Bandera Crater,** is on private property 25 miles south of I-40. The National Park Service has laid plans to absorb this commercial operation, known as **Ice Caves Resort** (tel. 783-4303). For now, however, visitors must pay $6 to hike up the crater or walk to the edge of an ice cave.

Perhaps the most fascinating phenomenon of El Malpais are the lava tubes, formed when the outer surface of a lava flow cooled and solidified. When the lava river drained, tunnellike caves were left. Ice caves within some of the tubes have delicate ice-crystal ceilings, ice stalagmites, and floors like ice rinks.

The national monument is surrounded by El Malpais National Conservation Area, 262,000 acres administered by the Bureau of Land Management. Hunting and trapping are permitted in the conservation area, and cattle grazing will continue after ranchers' leases on national monument land expire in 1997. The conservation area includes 30 cinder cones in the Chain of Craters.

Admission: Free.

Open: Daily year-round. Visitor center in Grants open daily 8am–4:30pm.

EL MORRO NATIONAL MONUMENT, Rte. 2, Box 43, Ramah, NM 87321. Tel. 783-4226.

Travelers who like to look history straight in the eye are fascinated by "Inscription Rock," 43 miles west of Grants along N.M. 53. Looming up out of the sand and sagebrush is a bluff 200 feet high, holding some of the most captivating messages in North America. Its sandstone face displays a written record of nearly every explorer, conquistador, missionary, Army officer, surveyor, and pioneer emigrant who passed this way between 1605—when Gov. Don Juan de Onate carved the first inscription—and 1906, when it was preserved by the National Park Service. Onate's inscription, dated April 16, 1605, was perhaps the first graffiti left by any white in America, but El Morro also boasts earlier petroglyph carvings by Indians.

A paved walkway makes it easy to walk to the writings, and there is a stone stairway leading up to other treasures. One reads: "Year of 1716 on the 28th of August passed by here Don Feliz Martinez, Governor and Captain General of this realm to the reduction and conquest of the Macaw." Confident of success as he was, Martinez actually got nowhere with any "conquest of the Macaw," or Hopi, Indians. After a 2-month battle they chased him back to Santa Fe. Another special group was the U.S. Camel Corps, trekking past on their way from Texas to California in 1857. The camels worked out fine in mountains and deserts, outlasting horses and mules 10 to 1, but the Civil War ended the experiment. When Peachy Breckinridge, fresh out of the Virginia Military Academy, came by with 25 camels, he noted the fact on the stone here.

El Morro was at one time as famous as the Blarney Stone of Ireland: Everybody had to stop by and make a mark. But when the Santa Fe Railroad was laid 25 miles to the north, El Morro was no longer on the main route to California—and from the 1870s, the tradition began to die out.

Atop Inscription Rock via a short, steep trail are ruins of an Anasazi pueblo occupying an area 200 by 300 feet. Its name, Atsinna, suggests that carving one's name here is a very old custom indeed: The word, in Zuni, means "writing on rock."

Self-guided trail booklets are available at the visitor center.

Two private enterprises near El Morro are worthy of special note. **El Morro Lodge,** Route 2, Box 44, Ramah, NM 87321 (tel. 783-4612), has cabins ($24.95 double), RV and tent camping, and an old-fashioned barbecue at 7pm every Friday and Saturday from Memorial Day to Labor Day. Adults pay $9, children $5. It's held in and around a 1920s schoolhouse and includes an Old West shoot-out and music by the Sarsaparilla Kids.

East of El Morro, the **Blue Corn Restaurant,** Mile 57, N.M. 53 (tel. 783-4671), serves some of the most innovative contemporary American cuisine imaginable in an isolated location like this. Daily specials, in the $10-to-$12 range, include apricot-stuffed chicken breast and red snapper with cilantro cream sauce. It's open from 11am to 8:30pm, Thursday to Sunday in summer.

Admission: Free.

Open: Visitor center, summer 8am–8pm, winter 8am–5pm. Campground open year-round.

CÍBOLA NATIONAL FOREST, 1800 Lobo Canyon Rd. Tel. 505/287-8833.

Two major parcels of the forest flank I-40 on either side of Grants. To the northeast, N.M. 547 leads some 20 miles into the San Mateo Mountains. The range's high point, 11,301-foot Mount Taylor, is home of the annual Mount Taylor Winter Quadrathlon in February. The route passes two campgrounds, Lobo Canyon and Coal Mine Canyon. Hiking and elk hunting are popular in summer, cross-country skiing in winter.

To the west run the Zuni Mountains, a heavily forested range topped by 9,253-foot Mount Sedgewick. Ask at the convention and visitor bureau or the Forest Service office for the "Zuni Mountain Historic Auto Tour" brochure. This describes a 91-mile loop, including over 45 miles of unpaved road with no gas or water en route, that gives unusual insight into the region's early 20th-century logging and mining activities.

On the northern slope of the Zuni Mountains, but outside of the national forest, is **Bluewater Lake State Park** (tel. 876-2318). At 7,400 feet, this forested recreational site offers fishing for rainbow trout, boating (rentals available), hiking, picnicking, and camping. There is a café and store on the east shore, 7 miles south of I-40 Exit 63 (18 miles west of Grants). Ice fishing is popular in winter.

SPORTS & RECREATION

Grants offers **golf** on a nine-hole city course (tel. 287-9239), open Tuesday through Sunday, with $6 weekday greens fees and $10 on weekends; **swimming** at the Grants Swimming Pool (tel. 287-7927), with free swimming from 1:30 to 5:30pm daily, for $1.50 admission; and **tennis** on 11 city courts (tel. 287-7927).

WHERE TO STAY

Grants hotels are all on or near Route 66, with major properties near I-40 interchanges, and smaller or older motels nearer downtown.

THE INN AT GRANTS, E. Grants Spur Hwy. at I-40 (P.O. Drawer T), Grants, NM 87020. Tel. 505/287-7901 or toll free 800/528-1234 or 800/548-6758. 125 rms 19 suites. A/C FRIDGE TV TEL
$ Rates: $52–$62 single, $62–$72 double, $67–$77 suite. AE, CB, DC, DISC, MC, V.
Owned by Maloof Hotels, which operates six others in New Mexico, and affiliated with Best Western, the inn offers a touch of the tropics to this semiarid land. Skylights nourish a junglelike central courtyard of lush trees and tall plants, which surround an indoor swimming pool and café.
Rooms are pleasant and modern. Standard units have king-size or two queen-size beds with southwestern, pastel-colored bedspreads, light purple carpeting, table and chairs, and two sinks: one at the vanity. All rooms have a small refrigerator and bedtime reading lamps. "King suites" are set up for executive travel with a phone at a working desk, an oversize dresser, and a sleeper sofa in a sitting area. Some rooms are designated for nonsmokers and the disabled.
The inn's café offers an outdoor experience indoors beneath the skylight. Umbrellas shade the tables, while silk fuchsias and draping vines lend atmosphere. It serves American fare daily for breakfast and dinner. Services and facilities include room service during restaurant hours, valet laundry, 24-hour desk, an indoor swimming pool, men's and women's saunas, hot tub, weight and exercise room, guest Laundromat, video games area, gift shop, and meeting rooms. Pets are welcome.

SANDS MOTEL, 112 McArthur St. (P.O. Box 1437), Grants, NM 87020. Tel. 505/287-2996 or toll free 800/424-7679. 24 rms. A/C FRIDGE TV TEL
$ Rates: $38 single, $42 double. AE, CB, DC, DISC, MC, V.
A family-style motel set back a block from Highway 66, the Sands has two dozen nicely appointed rooms. Some have king- and queen-size beds; all are partially wood paneled, with a dressing area between the bedroom and bathroom. Nonsmoking rooms are available.

WHERE TO DINE

EL JARDIN, 912 Lobo Canyon Rd. Tel. 285-5231.
Cuisine: NEW MEXICAN.
$ Prices: $2.50–$6.95. MC, V.
Open: Mon–Fri 11am–3pm, Mon–Sat 5–9pm.
This friendly restaurant, owned and operated by the Palacio family, is located on N.M. 247 behind the Lobo Canyon Shopping Mall, 2½ miles north of Route 66. Plants hang in the windows of El Jardin (the garden), original oils adorn the walls, and the brick-tile floor gives it a homey feeling.
The food is of high quality. Beef is shredded and sautéed for tacos, not ground and fried; vegetable oil is used in making shrimp and chicken fajitas;

and only chicken breasts are used in enchiladas and other dishes. If you have room, try the florencita, a dessert special with fruit filling. Beer and wine are served.

GRANTS STATION, 200 W. Santa Fe Ave. Tel. 287-2334.

Cuisine: AMERICAN/NEW MEXICAN.
$ Prices: Breakfast $2.29–$4.70; lunch $2.40–44.95; dinner $4.50–$7.25. AE, MC, V.
Open: Daily 6am–11pm.

You can't miss this place: an old red Santa Fe Railroad caboose stands outside on a length of track. And the train theme extends inside with old railroad signs and other paraphernalia, donated by numerous aficionados—many of them "just passing through."

Good, inexpensive American food is served here—chicken-fried steak, top sirloin, barbecued spare ribs, filet of perch. A few Mexican dishes, like tacos, burritos, and fajitas are also on the menu, and there's an all-you-can-eat soup-and-salad bar (just $3.60). Grants Station is not licensed for alcoholic beverages.

LA VENTANA, 110½ Geis St., Hillcrest Center. Tel. 287-9393.

Cuisine: STEAKS. **Reservations:** Recommended.
$ Prices: Appetizers $1.75–$4.95; lunch $1.75–$6.95; dinner $3.75–$13.50. AE, CB, DC, DISC, MC, V.
Open: Mon–Sat 11am–11pm.

Beneath a rustic exterior of weathered wood planks, behind the long-closed Iron Blossom Saloon, hides this sophisticated surprise. Though the exterior doesn't give it away, there's elegant white-linen service within. Original oils hang on the walls and a Roman bust peers from a niche.

Prime rib and steaks are the top sellers here and fresh seafood is served weekends. Chicken and beef fajitas are also popular. La Ventana is fully licensed.

MONTE CARLO RESTAURANT, 721 W. Santa Fe Ave. Tel. 287-9250.

Cuisine: NEW MEXICAN & STEAKS.
$ Prices: Appetizers $2.25–$3.50; main courses, breakfast $1.30–$6.60, lunch $2.50–$5.50, dinner $5.75–$12.95. AE, DISC, MC, V.
Open: Daily 7am–10pm.

Open since the 1940s, this adobe restaurant is one of the few buildings in Grants that predates the uranium boom. The menu hasn't changed a lot over the years: It includes steak Marie (topped with green chile and melted cheese), chile rellenos del mar (with shrimp and crabmeat), even Navajo tacos (frybread with borracho beans, chile, and vegetables) and Mexican pizza. There's live music as well as a full bar in the Cíbola Room. Children's menu available.

---

2. GALLUP

138 miles W of Albuquerque; 122 miles SSW of Farmington; 190 miles E of Flagstaff, Ariz.

GETTING THERE   By Plane   Gallup Municipal Airport, West Highway 66 (tel. 722-4896), is served several times daily by **Mesa Airlines** (tel. 722-5404 or toll free 800/MESA-AIR). There are regular connections to and from Albuquerque, Farmington, and Phoenix, Arizona.

By Train   Amtrak stops at the Santa Fe Railroad depot, 201 E. Hwy. 66 at Strong Street (tel. toll free 800/USA-RAIL). No tickets are sold here; passage must be booked ahead. The *Southwest Chief,* which runs between Los Angeles and Chicago, stops once daily eastbound and once westbound.

By Bus   Greyhound Lines, Inc., 105 S. Dean St. at Aztec Avenue (tel.

863-6761), stops several times daily on runs to Albuquerque, Farmington, and Flagstaff, Arizona.

By Car   From Albuquerque, take I-40 west (2½ hours). From Farmington, take U.S. 64 west to Shiprock, then U.S. 666 south (2½ hours). From Flagstaff, Arizona, take I-40 east (3 hours).

ESSENTIALS   Orientation   Gallup stretches for about 11 miles east and west along the I-40 corridor. U.S. Highway 66, which parallels the freeway on the south side of the Rio Puerco of the West, is the principal avenue. Through downtown Gallup, it's known as 66 Avenue. Second and Third streets cross 66 as the main north-south arteries of downtown Gallup. A loop bypass is formed by N.M. 564 (east of downtown) and N.M. 602 (west of downtown, extending south to Zuni).

Information   The **Gallup Convention and Visitors Bureau,** 701 Montoya Blvd. (P.O. Box 600), Gallup, NM 87305 (tel. 505/863-3841 or toll free 800/242-4282), is conveniently located in Miyamura Park, just north of the main I-40 interchange for downtown Gallup. Or contact the **Gallup–McKinley County Chamber of Commerce,** P.O. Box 1395, Gallup, NM 87305 (tel. 505/722-2228).

Fast Facts   The **area code** is 505. **Rehoboth McKinley Christian Hospital** is located at 1901 Red Rock Dr. (tel. 863-7000). The main **post office** is at 500 S. Second St. (tel. 863-3491). In case of **emergencies,** dial 911.

There's more to Gallup than the city's seemingly endless Route 66 neon strip might at first indicate. Founded on the rail line in 1881 as a coal supply town, Gallup has a frontier atmosphere that lingers among the late 19th- and early 20th-century buildings. A proliferation of Indian trading posts and pawnbrokers offers opportunities for shopping and bargaining. The city is the market center for the Navajo Reservation to the north and the Zuni Pueblo to the south.

WHAT TO SEE & DO

A WALKING TOUR OF GALLUP

Gallup has 20 buildings that are either listed on, or have been nominated to, the National Register of Historic Places. Start at the **Santa Fe Railroad depot,** East 66 Avenue and Strong Street. Built in 1923 in modified mission style with heavy Spanish Pueblo revival style massing, it is earmarked to be renovated into a community transportation and cultural center. Across the highway, the **Drake Hotel** (now the Turquoise Club), built of blond brick in 1919, had the Prohibition-era reputation of being controlled by bootleggers, with wine running in the faucets in place of water. Two blocks west, the 1928 **White Café,** 100 W. 66 Ave., is an elaborate decorative brick structure that catered to the early auto tourist traffic. **Kitchen's Opera House** (now Zimmermans and the Eagle Café), 218 W. 66 Ave., dates from 1895; it had a second-floor stage for all kinds of functions and performances, and a first-floor saloon and café. A block farther, the **Rex Hotel,** 300 W. 66 Ave., was constructed of locally quarried sandstone; it's now a police substation.

A block north of the police station, at 101 N. Third St., is the **C. N. Cotton Warehouse** (now Associated Grocers). Built about 1897 in the New Mexico vernacular style, with a sandstone foundation and adobe-block walls, it has a statue in front that is a city landmark: **Manuelita,** the last Navajo chief to surrender to U.S. soldiers. Mr. Cotton, a trader who admired the Indian's bravery, commissioned the statue.

Reverse course, and head back south two blocks on Third. Turn east on Coal Avenue. The **Grand Hotel** (now Ricca Mercantile), 306 W. Coal Ave., was built in 1925 as the depot for transcontinental buses on Route 66, as well as a travelers' hotel. The **Chief Theater** (now City Electric Shoe Shop), 228 W. Coal Ave., was built in

1920; but in 1936 it was completely redesigned in Pueblo deco style, with zigzag relief and geometric form, by R. E. "Griff" Griffith. Almost across the street, the 1928 **El Morro Theater** is of Spanish colonial revival style with an ornate symmetry from the parapet to the corbels. Next door, the **Ruiz Optical Building** has been decorated with Indian *kachinas* between the second-floor windows.

South two blocks at 201 W. Hill Ave., the **McKinley County Court House** was built in 1938 in picturesque Spanish Pueblo revival style. The bell tower and upper stories display stylized projecting *vigas,* while wood beams and corbels define the entry. Indian-motif reliefs, tiles, and paintings are found throughout. Back at the corner of First and Coal, the **Old Post Office** (now United Cable Television) is an eclectic mix of Mediterranean, decorative brick commercial, and Spanish Pueblo revival styles. Large carved eagles are used as corbels, and the beams have brightly painted rope molding lines.

OTHER ATTRACTIONS

RED ROCK STATE PARK, N.M. 566 (P.O. Box 328), Church Rock, NM 87311. Tel. 722-6196.

Six miles east of downtown Gallup, this park—with its natural amphitheater—is set against red sandstone buttes. It includes an auditorium/convention center, historical museum, post office, trading post, stables, and modern campgrounds.

Native dancers perform nightly from Memorial Day to Labor Day at the 8,000-seat Marland Aitson Amphitheater. This arena is also the site of numerous annual events, including the Inter-Tribal Indian Ceremonial in mid-August. Red Rock Convention Center accommodates 600 for trade shows or concert performances.

The Red Rock Museum has displays on prehistoric Anasazi and modern Zuni, Hopi, and Navajo cultures, and changing art gallery exhibits. From June through September, corns, beans, and squash are grown outside in a traditional Pueblo "waffle garden."

Admission: Dance performances $4; free for children under 5. Museum, adults $1, children 50¢.

Open: Dances, summer 7:30pm; museum, Mon–Fri 8:30am–4:30pm, with extended hours in summer.

NAVAJO INDIAN RESERVATION, P.O. Box 663, Window Rock, AZ 86515. Tel. 602/871-6659 or 871-6436.

Navajos are the largest tribe in the United States, with about 150,000 members. Their reservation, known to them as Navajoland, spreads across 24,000 square miles of Arizona, Utah, and New Mexico. The New Mexico portion, extending in a band 45 miles wide from just north of Gallup to the Colorado border, comprises only about 15% of the total area.

Until the 1920s, the Navajo nation governed itself with a complex clan system. When oil was discovered on reservation land, the Navajos established a tribal government to handle the complexities of the 20th century. Today, the Navajo Tribal Council has 88 council delegates representing 109 regional chapters, some two dozen of which are in New Mexico. They meet at least four times a year as a full body in **Window Rock,** Arizona, capital of the Navajo nation, on the New Mexico border 24 miles northwest of Gallup.

Natural resources and tourism are the mainstays of the Navajo economy. Coal, oil, gas, and uranium earn some $45 million a year, with coal alone providing about two-thirds of that sum. Tourism provides nearly the same amount, especially on the Arizona side of the border, which contains or abuts Grand Canyon and Petrified Forest national parks, Canyon de Chelly, Wupatki, and Navajo national monuments, and Monument Valley Navajo Tribal Park; and in Utah, Glen Canyon National Recreation Area, and Rainbow Bridge and Hovenweep national monuments.

The Navajos, like their linguistic cousins, the Apaches, belong to the large family of Athapaskan Indians found across Alaska and northwestern Canada and in parts of the northern California coast. They are believed to have migrated to the Southwest about the 14th century. In 1864, after nearly two decades of conflict with the U.S. Army, the entire tribe was rounded up and forced into internment at an agricultural colony near Fort Sumner, New Mexico—an event still recalled as "The Long March." Four years of near-starvation later, the experiment was declared a failure, and the now-contrite Navajos returned to their homeland.

Three to four generations later, 320 Navajo young men served in the U.S. Marine Corps as communications specialists in the Pacific during the Second World War. The code they created, 437 terms based on the extremely complex Navajo language, was never broken by the Japanese. Among those heroes still alive is artist Carl Gorman, coordinator of the Navajo Medicine Men Organization and father of internationally famed painter R. C. Gorman.

While Navajos express themselves artistically in all media, they are best known for their work in silversmithing, sand painting, basketry, and weaving. Distinctive styles of handwoven rugs from Two Grey Hills, Ganado, and Crystal are known worldwide.

The place to stay on the reservation is the **Navajo Nation Inn,** Highway 264 (P.O. Box 1687), Window Rock, AZ 86515 (tel. 602/871-4108). Modern rooms are comfortable and inexpensive, and the Sheepherder Restaurant offers Navajo specialties. The inn has an attractive weekend package that for $140 includes two nights' lodging and a Saturday bus trip that takes in **Hubbell Trading Post National Historic Site** at Ganado, 30 miles west of Window Rock; **Canyon de Chelly National Monument,** 39 miles north of Ganado; **Navajo Community College** and its Hatathli Gallery at Tsaile, 28 miles northeast of Chinle; and the 56-mile return to Window Rock.

Attractions in Window Rock itself include the **Navajo Nation Council Chambers,** the **Navajo Nation Arts and Crafts Enterprise,** the **Navajo Museum and Tribal Zoo, St. Michael's Mission Museum,** and **Window Rock Tribal Park,** containing the natural red-rock arch after which the community is named.

In early September, the annual 5-day **Navajo Nation Fair** attracts more than 100,000 people to Window Rock for a huge rodeo, parade, carnival, Miss Navajo Nation contest, arts-and-crafts shows, intertribal powwow, concerts, country dancing, and agricultural exhibits. Among smaller annual tribal fairs are the traditional October **Shiprock Navajo Fair,** 90 miles north of Gallup, and the **Eastern Navajo Fair** in Crownpoint, 55 miles northeast of Gallup.

The Crownpoint Rug Weavers Association has 12 public auctions a year, normally on Friday evenings, about five weeks apart.

ZUNI PUEBLO, N.M. 53 (P.O. Box 339), Zuni, NM 87327. Tel. 782-4481.

The largest and westernmost of New Mexico's 19 pueblos is located 38 miles south of Gallup. In many regards it's the most unique of all pueblos: The language spoken by the 8,084 Zuni is different from any other dialect, and their traditional religion has persisted despite missionary influence.

Zuni was built upon the ruins of the ancient site of Halona, an early pueblo destroyed by the conquistadors. Zuni Mission was built in the early 1600s, razed during the 1680 Pueblo revolt; rebuilt and destroyed again in 1849. Finally, after 119 years, it was reconstructed in 1968 as **Our Lady of Guadalupe Church.** The builders, Auro and John Cattaneo of Zuni, were recognized by Pope Paul VI for their fine workmanship and authenticity in restoration. Roman Catholic mass is said each Sunday beneath life-size *kachinas* painted on the walls by Zuni artist Alex Seowtewa, "the Michelangelo of New Mexico." Franciscan fathers conduct guided tours.

Thirteen miles southwest of Zuni are the ruins of **Hawikuh,** in all probability the "city of gold" spied in 1539 by the friar who incited the Hispanic rush for the fabled Seven Cities of Cíbola. It was certainly the largest Zuni pueblo of its day, until forcefully conquered by the Spanish.

Today the largest number of Zuni live at the pueblo, 9 miles west of the intersection of N.M. 602 and 53. Others live in nearby **Black Rock, Ojo Caliente, Lower Nutria** and outlying settlements. Many Zuni work in Gallup, but others are employed in diverse local occupations, including the Zuni School District and tribal governmental programs and services.

Though traditionally farmers, the Zuni are best known for their turquoise-and-silver inlay jewelry and other handcrafts, including stone animal fetishes and the new hand-painted and hand-carved furniture. Zuni needlepoint is an elaborate art form in its own right—finely cut turquoise set in intricate patterns of silver.

Camping, fishing, and hunting permits can be obtained from the tribal Game and Fish Department. Guide service can also be arranged. Several trading posts offer jewelry, arts, and crafts for sale at reservation prices.

The **Zuni Fair and Rodeo** attracts large crowds each year during Labor Day weekend. Better known is the **Zuni Shalako Ceremony** in late November or early December, a highly spiritual all-day, all-night celebration marked by dances, chants, processions, prayers, fasting and feasting. In 1990, however, it was closed to non-Indians in response to a lack of sensitivity and respect shown by tourists to Zuni traditions. Some, for example, insisted on photographing the ceremony without permission—a major transgression.

Admission: Free. Photo permits $2 still, $4 video.
Open: Pueblo office Mon–Fri 8am–4:30pm.

TOURS

Indian Land Adventure Tours, 1400 Second St., Gallup, NM 87301 (tel. 505/722-2264 or toll free 800/748-1611), operates tours to scenic areas in New Mexico and Arizona, and shopping tours to trading posts and pawnshops in Gallup.

SPORTS & RECREATION

Fishing and hunting are popular in adjacent national forests and mesa land, and in small lakes and streams in the Chuska and Zuni mountains. Tribal permits may be required.

The 18-hole **Gallup Municipal Golf Course,** 111 Susan St. (tel. 863-9224), is set on rolling hills and canyonland in the southeastern part of town. It's open Friday through Sunday and Tuesday and Wednesday from 6am to dusk and Monday and Thursday from noon to dusk.

The Fitness Center, 700 Old Zuni Rd. (tel. 722-7271), offers health-clubgoers a place for aerobics or racquetball. It also has free weights and Nautilus equipment, a gym, an indoor track, tennis courts, sauna, whirlpool, steam room, massage, and tanning. There's a nursery on the premises.

SHOPPING

Nowhere are the jewelry and crafts of Navajo, Zuni, and Hopi tribes less expensive than in Gallup. The most intriguing places to shop are the trading posts and pawnshops, which provide a surprising range of services for their largely native clientele and have little in common with the pawnshops of large American cities.

Navajoland ✪ **pawnbrokers** in essence are bankers, at least from the Navajo and Zuni viewpoint. They're like savings-and-loan institutions, but a lot less likely to fold. In fact, they're an integral part of the economic structure of the Gallup area, providing native Americans with such services as the safekeeping of valuable personal goods and the payment of small collateral loans.

Security systems in Navajo hogans and Zuni pueblos are nonexistent. So Indians go to the trading post with their turquoise and silver jewelry, ceremonial baskets, hand-tanned hides, saddles, and guns, and "pawn" them for safekeeping. They may accept a payment far less than the value of the goods, because the smaller the amount of the loan, the easier it is to redeem the items when they are needed.

Pawnbrokers are also collateral lenders. Traditionally, Navajos visited trading posts to exchange handmade goods for cash or other products. Today, banks won't take jewelry or guns as loan collateral—but the trading post will. What's more, the trader will hold onto the items for months or even years before deeming it "dead" and putting it up for sale. Less than 5% ever go unredeemed.

Some larger trading posts even have pens for livestock, storage warehouses for wool and mohair, and refrigeration units for fresh lamb and mutton. Lynn Tanner, who runs the Ellis Tanner Trading Post founded by his grandfather, said the company philosophy is to "try to have for sale whatever they need to buy, and try to buy whatever they have for sale."

If you're shopping for jewelry, look for silver concho belts, worn with jeans and southwestern skirts; cuff bracelets; and necklaces, from traditional squash blossoms to silver beads and *heishi,* very fine beads worn in several strands. Earrings may be only in silver, or they may be decorated with varying stones. The bigger and bolder are the more fashionable.

For men, bolo ties and belt buckles of silver and/or turquoise are hot with jeans. Silver concho hatbands go great on Stetson hats. A silver or gold handcrafted earring, sometimes decorated with turquoise, is a big seller.

Handwoven Indian rugs may be draped on couches, hung on walls, or used on floors. Also look for pottery, *kachinas,* and sculpture.

Most shops are open Monday through Saturday from 9am to 5pm.

ART & CRAFTS   Art-related activities complement exhibits at some of these emporiums: **Gallup Gallery,** 108 W. Coal Ave. (tel. 863-4563); **Kiva Gallery,** 202 E. 66 Ave. (tel. 722-5577); **Red Mesa Art Center,** 105 W. Hill Ave. (tel. 722-4209); and **Windy Mesa Gallery,** 230 W. 66 Ave. (tel. 863-5077).

Three interesting crafts shops are **Denny Pino's Indian Supply,** 116 W. 66 Ave. (tel. 722-6455); and **Pat Yellowhorse's Reservation Crafts,** 1302 S. Second St. (tel. 863-6809).

CLOTHING   For western attire for the whole family, try **Sherman's Boots & Jeans,** 920 E. 66 Ave. (tel. 722-5477) and 1304 W. Lincoln St. (tel. 722-6166); and **Trice's Western Wear,** 210 W. Coal Ave. (tel. 863-4631).

GIFTS/SOUVENIRS   A wide range of items can be found at **Gifts of Love,** 120 W. Coal Ave. (tel. 722-6443); and **OB's Indian America,** 3310-30 E. Hwy. 66 (tel. 722-5846 or toll free 800/545-3819).

JEWELRY   Prominent local dealers include **Cousins Indian Jewelry,** 2000 E. Hwy. 66 (tel. 722-4471); **Felix Indian Jewelry,** 1001 W. Hwy. 66 (tel. 722-5369); **Martinez Indian Jewelry,** 1624 S. Second St., Cedar Hills Plaza (tel. 722-5217); **Ortega's Indian Jewelry,** 3306 E. Hwy. 66 (tel. 722-6666); **Silver House,** 210 W. 66 Ave. (tel. 722-2335); and **Trailblazer,** 210 W. Hill Ave. (tel. 722-5051).

MARKETS   The ✪ **Gallup Indian Market,** between Aztec and Coal avenues and Second and Third Streets is open from 10am to 4pm Saturday, mid-June to mid-August.

PAWNBROKERS   These distinctive area merchants include **Jean's All Indian Pawn Shop,** 2000 E. Hwy. 66 (tel. 722-4471); **T & R Pawn,** 1300 W. I-40 Frontage Rd., Rio West Mall (tel. 722-3473); and **Trader Billy K's,** 118 W. 66 Ave. (tel. 722-5151).

TRADING POSTS   For a look at everything from livestock to unusual souvenirs, visit ✪ **Ellis Tanner Trading Company,** Munoz Boulevard and Highway 602 Bypass (tel. 722-7776); **First American Traders of Gallup,** 2201 W. Hwy. 66 (tel. 722-6601); **Galanis Trading Co.,** 306 E. 66 Ave. (tel. 722-5464); **Richardson Trading Co. and Cash Pawn, Inc.,** 222 W. 66 Ave. (tel. 722-4762); **Shi'ma Traders,** 216 W. Coal Ave. (tel. 722-5500); **Silver Dust Trading Co.,** 120 W. 66

Ave. (tel. 722-4848); ✪ **Tobe Turpen's Indian Trading Company,** 1710 S. Second St. (tel. 722-3806); and **Turney's Inc.,** 207 S. Third St. (tel. 863-6504).

WHERE TO STAY

Virtually every accommodation in Gallup is somewhere along Route 66, either near the I-40 interchanges or on the highway through downtown. Local lodging tax is 5%; added to the 6% state tax, a total of 11% is levied on hotel bills.

MODERATE

THE INN AT GALLUP, 3009 W. Hwy. 66, Gallup, NM 87301. Tel. 505/722-2221 or toll free 800/528-1234. Fax 505/722-7442. 124 rms, 21 suites. A/C FRIDGE TV TEL
$ Rates: $52–$67 single, $57–$77 double, $70–$97 suite. AE, CB, DC, DISC, MC, V.
The trademark of this Best Western/Maloof Hotels property, an otherwise nondescript white brick building, is its huge central Atrium Courtyard that contains the hotel café at one end, the swimming pool at the other, and skylit trees and plants in between. Three 8-foot paintings of native dancers dominate the lobby.
The rooms are large and well kept, with one king-size or two queen-size beds and a big desk-dresser combination. The vanity has its own sink in addition to that within the bathroom. There are rooms for nonsmokers and the disabled. The Café, under the roof of the Atrium Courtyard, serves breakfast daily from 6 to 10am and dinner daily from 5 to 9pm. O'Henry's Lounge serves drinks Monday to Saturday from 2pm. The hotel has room service, valet laundry service, 24-hour desk, an indoor swimming pool, hot tub, men's and women's saunas, weight/exercise room, video games, guest laundry, and gift shop. Meeting facilities accommodate 600. Pets are allowed.

HOLIDAY INN, 2915 W. Hwy. 66, Gallup, NM 87301. Tel. 505/722-2201 or toll free 800/432-2211. Fax 505/722-9616. 212 rms. A/C TV TEL
$ Rates: $49–$65 single, $56–$72 double. AE, CB, DC, DISC, JCB, MC, V.
The spacious lobby of this hotel makes indoors feel like outdoors. A small fountain and various plants stand beneath a high ceiling, while Indian motifs and small murals are painted on some of the walls.
Rooms, many decorated with Southwest decor in tones of purple and rust, contain a king-size or two double beds, hideabed sofa or leisure chairs, desk, and clock radio. Some rooms accommodate nonsmokers or the disabled.
Nicole's offers fine continental cuisine from 5:30 to 10pm Tuesday through Saturday. The specialty in this intimate setting is table-side preparation of dishes like scampi provençale, steak Diane, and veal scaloppine Nicole. The Cactus Rose serves three meals daily, from 6am to 10pm, in a more casual setting. The City Lights lounge, open from 11:30am to 1:30am Monday to Saturday, has live country-and-western music for dancing nightly. The hotel has room service, valet laundry service, 24-hour desk, courtesy van, an indoor swimming pool, hot tub, sauna, weight equipment, guest laundry, gift shop, and meeting facilities for 800. Pets are allowed.

INEXPENSIVE

DAYS INN—WEST, 3201 W. Hwy. 66, Gallup, NM 87301. Tel. 505/863-6889 or toll free 800/325-2525. 74 rms, 2 suites. A/C TV TEL
$ Rates: $35–$55 single, $40–$60 double. $80–$120 suite. AE, CB, DC, DISC, MC, V.
New in September 1990, this handsome two-story pink adobe building is built in Spanish style with a tile roof. Rooms are of average size, but they're nicely done in desert rose color schemes, with prints of regional native crafts on the walls.

Complimentary coffee and rolls are served in the lobby in the morning. The hotel offers a 24-hour desk, nonsmoking and handicapped rooms, an indoor swimming pool, hot tub, and guest laundry. No pets.

EL RANCHO HOTEL & MOTEL, 1000 E. 66 Ave., Gallup, NM 87301. Tel. 505/863-9311 or toll free 800/543-6351. Fax 505/722-5917. 98 rms, 2 suites. A/C TV TEL

$ Rates: $36–$51 single, $44–$63 double, $75 suite. AE, CB, DC, DISC, MC, V.

⭐ This historic hotel owes as much to Hollywood as to Gallup. Built in 1937 by R. E. "Griff" Griffith, brother of movie mogul D. W. Griffith, it became *the* place for film companies to set up headquarters in the Southwest. Between the 1940s and 1960s, a who's who of Hollywood stayed here. Their autographed photos line the walls of the hotel's mezzanine. Spencer Tracy and Katharine Hepburn stayed here during production of *The Sea of Grass;* Burt Lancaster and Lee Remick were guests when they made *The Hallelujah Trail.* Gene Autry, Lucille Ball, Jack Benny, Humphrey Bogart, James Cagney, Rhonda Flemming, Errol Flynn, Henry Fonda, John Forsythe, Paulette Goddard, Susan Hayward, William Holden, the Marx Brothers, Fred MacMurray, Robert Mitchum, Gregory Peck, Tyrone Power, Ronald Reagan, Rosalind Russell, James Stewart, Robert Taylor, Gene Tierney, John Wayne, and Mae West have all been here. . . . The list goes on and on.

In 1986, Gallup businessman Armand Ortega, a longtime jewelry merchant, bought a run-down El Rancho and restored it to its earlier elegance. The lobby staircase rises to the mezzanine on either side of an enormous stone fireplace, while heavy ceiling beams and railings made of tree limbs give the room a hunting-lodge ambience. The hotel is on the National Register of Historic Places.

Rooms in El Rancho differ one to the next. Many are named after the stars who stayed in them. My cozy room had a double bed with a wagon-wheel headboard, a leisure armchair, and Southwest art prints on the walls. The corridors bear small wall paintings of native life-style. Many rooms have balconies.

El Rancho's full-service restaurant, open from 6:30am to 10pm daily, has pleasant hacienda decor. Egg and pancake breakfasts run from $1.75 to $6.45; lunches (salads, burgers, and other sandwiches), from $2.50 to $6.95. Dinner main dishes—standard American meals like steaks, pork chops, and fried chicken—range from $3.75 to $12.95. The '49er Lounge stays lively later. Services and facilities include a 24-hour desk, courtesy car (by request), a seasonal outdoor pool, guest Laundromat, Ortega's Indian Store, and meeting space for 125.

BUDGET

BLUE SPRUCE LODGE, 1119 E. 66 Ave., Gallup, NM 87301. Tel. 505/863-5211. 20 rms. A/C TV TEL

$ Rates: $20 single, $26 double. AE, CB, DC, DISC, MC, V.

Ⓢ This little motel is nothing fancy, but it's clean, hospitable, and a step ahead of others in friendliness: Rooms have standard furnishings; some have shower-bath combinations, others showers only. Small pets are allowed.

EL CAPITAN MOTEL, 1300 E. 66 Ave., Gallup, NM 87301. Tel. 505/863-6828. 42 rms, 5 suites. A/C TV TEL

$ Rates: $26 single, $28–$40 double, $40–$50 suite. AE, CB, DC, DISC, MC, V.

A one-story adobe-style motel, El Capitan has recently been remodeled. Rooms are very spacious, simply but comfortably furnished with full-size beds, desk-dresser, table and chairs, and vanity/dressing area. Family suites that sleep five are a bit more eclectic in appearance than the standard guest rooms. Pets are accepted.

WHERE TO DINE

Keep in mind that Gallup is dry on Sunday.

PANZ ALEGRA, 1201 E. 66 Ave., Gallup. Tel. 722-7229.
   Cuisine: MEXICAN, STEAK & SEAFOOD. **Reservations:** Recommended.

$ Prices: Appetizers $2.95–$3.95; lunch $3–$7.95; Mexican dinner $4.95–$8.95; American dinner $8–$22. AE, CB, DC, MC, V.
Open: Mon–Sat 11am–10pm.

⭐ This brown stone and yellow adobe building harbors what may be Gallup's finest restaurant. Behind brick arches and planter boxes of silk flowers, diners enjoy steak-and-seafood platters, or opt for the fine New Mexican food. House specialties include carne adovada, arroz con pollo, and the Alegra steak with green chile and cheese. The restaurant is licensed for beer and wine.

THE RANCH KITCHEN, 3001 W. Hwy. 66, Gallup. Tel. 722-2537.
Cuisine: AMERICAN & MEXICAN. **Reservations:** For large parties.
$ Prices: Appetizers $2.95–$3.75; breakfast $1.95–$5.25; lunch $3.50–$7.95; dinner $5.95–$12.95. AE, CB, DC, MC, V.
Open: Daily, summer 6am–10pm, winter 6am–9pm.

Ⓢ An institution since 1954, the Ranch Kitchen has the perfect location to attract tourists—wedged between Gallup's two largest accommodations at the west end of the city. It takes full advantage of that advantage, with two gift shops flanking the entrance, and a variety of colorful pinatas, *kachinas,* and other folk art hanging everywhere. The food, though, is up to the boast. It's hard to pass up on the chicken and ribs, barbecued outside when weather permits. There's great chili, excellent Navajo tacos and rancho grande burritos, fine steaks, and a big soup-and-salad buffet. Children and seniors can order smaller portions from their own menus. The restaurant serves wine and beer.

---

3. FARMINGTON

182 miles NW of Albuquerque; 122 miles NNE of Gallup;
214 miles W of Taos; 49 miles S of Durango, Colo.

GETTING THERE By Plane All commercial flights arrive at busy **Four Corners Regional Airport** on Navajo Drive (tel. 327-7701, ext. 1396). The principal carrier is **Mesa Airlines** (tel. 326-3338 or toll free 800/MESA-AIR), with 15 arrivals daily from Albuquerque, five from Phoenix, Arizona, via Gallup, and three from Denver, Colorado. **United Express** (tel. 326-6400 or toll free 800/241-6522) links Farmington with Denver's Stapleton Field several times daily.
　　Car-rental agencies at Four Corners airport include **Avis** (tel. 327-9864), **Budget** (tel. 327-0700), **Hertz** (tel. 327-6093), and **National** (tel. 327-0215).

By Bus Farmington is served by **Texas, New Mexico & Oklahoma (TNM&O) Coaches,** 101 E. Animas St. (tel. 325-1009). Buses depart twice a day for Albuquerque (10:50am and 5:45pm) and Durango, Colorado (6:05 and 11:30am), once daily for Salt Lake City, Utah (6:30am), and Dallas and Houston, Texas (10:50am).

By Car From Albuquerque, take N.M. 44 (through Cuba) from the I-25 Bernalillo exit, then turn left (west) on U.S. 64 at Bloomfield (¾ hour). From Gallup, take U.S. 666 north to Shiprock, then turn right (east) on U.S. 64. (2¼ hours). From Taos, follow U.S. 64 all the way (4½ hours). From Durango, take U.S. 500 south (1 hour).

ESSENTIALS Orientation Farmington lies at the confluence of the Animas and San Juan rivers, and at the junction of U.S. 64 (from Taos) and U.S. 550 (from Durango). As Highway 64 crosses the Animas and enters downtown Farmington, it becomes Broadway; it is paralleled one block north by Highway 550, here known as Main Street. They join at the west end of downtown. Other main thoroughfares are 20th Street, a quarter mile north of Main, which intersects Highway 550 at its east end; Butler Avenue, a north-south thoroughfare which links Broadway and Main with

20th; and Scott Avenue, a quarter mile east of Butler, where most major accommodations are located.

Information The **Farmington Convention and Visitors Bureau,** 203 W. Main St. (tel. 505/326-7602 or toll free 800/448-1240), is the clearing house for tourist information. It shares an address with the **Farmington Chamber of Commerce** (tel. 505/325-0279).

Fast Facts The **area code** is 505. **San Juan Regional Medical Center,** 801 W. Maple St. (tel. 325-5011), is the principal hospital. The main **post office** is at 2301 E. 20th St. (tel. 325-5047). Cab service is provided by **Roadrunner Taxi** (tel. 327-1909). In case of **emergencies,** dial 911, or 325-3501 for an ambulance.

A river city of 37,000 residents, Farmington is the gateway to the Four Corners area. Its pride and joy is a system of five parks it's developed along the San Juan River and its tributaries, the Animas and La Plata rivers. In this desert country, it follows that Farmington is an agricultural oasis. It's also an industrial center (for coal, oil, natural gas, and hydroelectricity), and a takeoff point for explorations of the Navajo Reservation, Chaco Culture National Historical Park, and Mesa Verde National Park in Colorado.

WHAT TO SEE & DO

THE RUINS

CHACO CULTURE NATIONAL HISTORICAL PARK, Star Rte. 4 (P.O. Box 6500), Bloomfield, NM 87413. Tel. 505/988-6727.

⭐ Chaco represents the high point of Pre-Columbian pueblo civilization. A must-see attraction for any visitor even vaguely interested in ancient Indians, it includes more than a dozen large Anasazi ruins occupied from the early 900s to about A.D. 1200, and hundreds of smaller sites in the wide streambed of the normally dry Chaco Wash.

A series of pueblo ruins stand within 5 or 6 miles of each other on the broad, flat, treeless canyon floor. Pueblo Bonito is the largest. Other ruins accessible directly from an auto road running up and down the canyon are Chetro Ketl, Pueblo del Arroyo, Kin Kletso, Casa Chiquita, Casa Rinconada, Hungo Pavi, and Una Vida. Some ruins demand half-day backcountry hikes to reach; they include Penasco Blanco, Pueblo Alto, Tsin Kletsin, and Wijiji.

Most ruins are on the north side of the canyon. **Pueblo Bonito,** constructed over three acres of land in the 11th century A.D., may have been the largest apartment house built anywhere in the world prior to 1887. It had four stories, 600 rooms and 40 *kivas,* and may have housed as many as 1,200 people. **Chetro Ketl** had some 500 rooms, 16 *kivas,* and an impressive enclosed plaza. **Pueblo del Arroyo** was a four-story, D-shaped structure, with about 280 rooms and 20 *kivas;* **Kin Kletso** had three stories, 100 rooms, and five *kivas.* **Una Vida,** a short walk from the visitor center, was one of the first pueblos built and has been left only partially excavated; it had 150 rooms and five *kivas.* **Casa Rinconada,** which stands alone on the south side of the canyon, is the largest "great *kiva*" in the park, and is astronomically aligned to the cardinal directions and the summer solstice. It may have been a center for the community at large, used for major spiritual observances.

The Chacoans were skilled masons, building their cities of sandstone blocks mortared with mud, with no metal tools or formal mathematical knowledge. The use of different masonry styles has helped to date the buildings.

The sweeping magnificence of this lost and ruined city, as seen from 100 feet above on the rim of the canyon, impresses visitors most—the outline of Pueblo Bonito, its many *kivas* forming circles within the great half circle of the community, all of it in the glowing sandstone browns and tans of the land and stone around it. Eventually there were 75 such compact towns all connected with one another in this region of New Mexico.

Aerial photos show 300 miles of roads connecting these towns with the Chaco pueblos, one of the longest running 42 miles straight north to Salmon Ruin and the Aztec Ruins (see below). Settlements were spaced along the road at travel intervals of one day. They were not simple trails worn into the stone by foot travel, but engineered roadways 30 feet wide with a berm of rock to contain the fill. Where the road went over flat rock, walls were built along the sides of it. It is this road network that leads some scholars to believe Chaco was the center of a unified Anasazi society.

The Chacoans' trade network, as suggested by artifacts found here, stretched from California to Texas and south into Mexico. Seashell necklaces, copper bells, and the remains of macaws or parrots were found among Chaco artifacts. Some of these items are displayed in the museum at the visitor center. Self-guiding trail brochures are obtained here, as well as permits for the overnight campground (with a water supply, tables, and fireplaces: Bring your own wood or charcoal).

The only snag to visiting Chaco is its isolation. Farmington is the nearest population center, and it's still a 75-mile, 2-hour drive to these ruins. N.M. 44 takes you as far as the Nageezi Trading Post, but the final 26 miles are graded dirt—fine in dry weather but dangerous when it rains, and often flooded where arroyos cross it. Inquire before leaving the paved highway. (A turnoff at Blanco Trading Post, 8 miles before Nageezi, cuts 5 miles off the trip, but the road is more subject to hazardous conditions. The park can also be reached from the south via Crownpoint, with the final 19 miles graded dirt.) There's no food, gas, or lodging nearer than Nageezi.

Admission: $3 per car or $1 per person; seniors 62 and older free.

Open: Memorial Day–Labor Day daily 8am–6pm; rest of year daily 8am–5pm. Campground open 24 hours.

AZTEC RUINS NATIONAL MONUMENT, U.S. Hwy. 550, P.O. Box 640 Aztec. Tel. 334-6174.

The ruins of a fabulous 500-room Indian pueblo, abandoned by the Anasazi seven centuries ago, make up this site, 14 miles northeast of Farmington in the town of Aztec on the Animas River. The ruins were named after ancient Mexican Indians because of a misunderstanding by the pioneers who discovered them, but the name stuck when the town was founded.

The influence of the Chaco culture is strong at Aztec, as evidenced in the preplanned architecture, the open plaza, and the fine stone masonry in the old walls. But Aztec is best known for its Great Kiva, the only completely reconstructed Anasazi *kiva* in existence. About 50 feet in diameter, with a main floor sunken eight feet below the surface of the surrounding ground, this circular ceremonial room rivets the imagination. It's hard not to feel spiritually overwhelmed, and perhaps to feel the presence of people who walked here nearly 1,000 years ago.

The visitor center displays some outstanding examples of Anasazi ceramics and basketry found in the ruins.

Admission: $1 per person, children and seniors free.

Open: Daily in summer 8am–6:30pm in winter 8am–5pm. **Closed:** Christmas and New Year's Day.

SALMON RUIN AND SAN JUAN COUNTY ARCHAEOLOGICAL RESEARCH CENTER, 975 U.S. Hwy. 64 (P.O. Box 125), Bloomfield. Tel. 632-2013.

This massive C-shaped pueblo, overlooking the San Juan River, was built in the 11th century as a Chacoan colony. A planned community of some 250 rooms, it offers not only a great *kiva* in its plaza, but a remarkable, elevated ceremonial chamber or "tower *kiva*." Just 11 miles east of Farmington, it is one of the most recently excavated ruins in the West.

The site was actually occupied twice—first, for two generations in the 11th century, by the Chacoans; then, in the 13th century, by emigrants from the great Mesa Verde complex to the north. But they, too, soon abandoned the site.

The site today is only 30% excavated, by design. It's being saved for future generations of archaeologists, who, it's assumed, will be able to apply advanced research techniques. For now, the archaeological research center studies regional sites earmarked for natural-resource exploitation.

In 1990, Heritage Park was established on an adjoining plot of land. It comprises a series of reconstructed ancient and historic dwellings representing the area's cultures, from a paleoarchaic sand-dune site to an Anasazi pit house, Apache wickiups and tepees to Navajo hogans, and an original pioneer homestead. Visitors are encouraged to enter the re-creations; several have arts-and-crafts exhibits or living-history demonstrations.

In the visitor center are a small museum displaying artifacts found at the site, a gift shop, and a scholarly research library.

Admission: Adults $1, children 6–15 50¢.
Open: Daily 9am–5pm.

OTHER ATTRACTIONS

FARMINGTON MUSEUM, 302 N. Orchard St. Tel. 599-1174 or 599-1179.
Area pioneer history is the forte here. Exhibits include a replica of an early frontier business street (depicting the era 1876 to 1912), and a "Pathfinder" series highlighting the lives of different Farmington homesteaders. Fine traveling and temporary exhibits share space. There's also a children's hands-on exploration area, including giant puzzles, a shadow room, and a walk-in giant kaleidoscope; and a gift shop.
Admission: Free.
Open: Tues–Fri noon–5pm, Sat 10am–5pm.

INDUSTRIAL TOURS

BHP-Utah International Inc. operates three large surface coal mines in the Farmington area. Mine tours of one to two hours are offered weekly at each of them. Appointments are requested for groups of eight or more. Tours of the **Navajo Mine** (tel. 598-5861), the largest open-pit coal mine in the western United States, are 10am Monday. It's 27 miles southwest of Farmington on reservation Road 4048. Tours of the **San Juan Mine** (tel. 598-5871), just north of U.S. 64 about 15 miles west of Farmington, are 10am Wednesday. Tours of **La Plata Mine** (tel. 599-4100), 22 miles north of Farmington via N.M. 170, are 10am Friday. Picnic and barbecue facilities are available in a park near the La Plata Mine.

Tour groups (ages 12 and older) are requested to give two weeks' notice to visit the **Four Corners Power Plant,** 18 miles west of Farmington at the community of Fruitland (tel. 598-8204). Tours describe the plant's use of coal to generate 2 million kilowatts of power. **Morgan Lake,** which provides cooling water for the plant's condenser, has picnic grounds; it's also extremely popular with local windsurfers. Swimming is not allowed, even though the water is 80 degrees year-round.

SPORTS & RECREATION

Baseball The **Connie Mack World Series** is held annually in mid-August at Ricketts Park. Top amateur baseball teams from all over the United States and Puerto Rico compete in a 7-day, 17-game series. Players are in their late teens, so they attract a great many professional scouts and college coaches. Many current major-league baseball players have competed in this tournament.

Fishing & Hunting See Navajo Lake State Park, below.

Golf **Piñon Hills Municipal Golf Course,** 2101 Sunrise Pkwy. (tel. 326-6066), is an 18-hole course open daily except Tuesday. **Civitan Municipal Golf Course,** 2200 N. Dustin St. (tel. 599-1194), is a nine-hole course open daily except Monday.

Horse Racing **San Juan Downs,** 593 U.S. 64 between Farmington and

Bloomfield (tel. 326-4551), has live racing from late April to Labor Day. Post time is 1:30pm Saturday, Sunday, and Monday holidays. Races from Santa Fe Downs are simulcast Monday and Tuesday and from Ruidoso Downs on Friday.

Rodeo   The **Farmington Pro-Rodeo Roundup** is held the first weekend of April at McGee Park, between Farmington and Bloomfield on U.S. 64. The event draws professionals from throughout the country. The **San Juan County Sheriff Posse Rodeo,** held the second weekend of June, is northern New Mexico's largest open rodeo, attracting amateurs as well as pros. It's at the San Juan County Rodeo Grounds, U.S. 550 northeast of Farmington.

SHOPPING

Downtown Farmington shops are open 9am to 6pm Monday to Friday. Shops in the **Animas Valley Mall,** in the northeast part of the city on U.S. 550 north of 30th Street, are open from 10am to 9pm Monday through Friday, 10am to 6pm Saturday, and noon to 6pm Sunday. The mall contains five department stores, Beall's, Best, Dillard's, J.C. Penney, and Sears, and 65 smaller stores. It's worth a visit even if you're not shopping, to see the two dozen wall-size Indian murals that decorate the mall.
　　Native arts and crafts are best purchased at trading posts, either downtown on Main or Broadway streets, or west of Farmington on U.S. 64/550 toward Shiprock. Some recommended stores include: **Aztec Ruins Trading Post,** Ruins Road, Aztec (tel. 334-2943); **Beasley Manning's Trading Co.,** 113 E. Main St. (tel. 327-6741); **Blanco Trading Post,** N.M. 44, 25 miles south of Bloomfield (tel. 632-1597); **Foutz Indian Room,** 301 W. Main St. (tel. 325-9413); **Hogback Trading Co.,** U.S. 64/550, Waterflow, 17 miles west of Farmington (tel. 598-5154); and **Navajo Curio Shop,** 126 E. Main St. (tel. 325-1685).

EVENING ENTERTAINMENT

The annual **Anasazi Pageant** is a summer musical about the region's multicultural heritage. Presented in the outdoor Lions Wilderness Park Amphitheater (off College Boulevard) against a sandstone backdrop, *Anasazi, the Ancient Ones* weaves a story around the early history of San Juan area settlers through original music and dance. A southwestern-style dinner is served with the performance. For information and tickets contact the Anasazi Reservation Desk at 505/327-9336 or the Farmington Convention and Visitors Bureau at toll free 800/448-1240.
　　Admission: Dinner and pageant, adults $16, seniors $14, children under 11 $10. Pageant only, adults $10, seniors $8, children $5. Tickets sold at Farmington Convention and Visitors Bureau and at the gate.
　　Open: Wed–Sat, mid-June to Labor Day, dinner 6:30pm, performance 8pm.

NEARBY ATTRACTIONS

SHIP ROCK, Navajo Indian Reservation southwest of Shiprock, 29 miles west of Farmington via U.S. 64.

This distinctive landmark is known to the Navajo as *Tes be dahi,* "Rock with wings." Composed of igneous rock flanked by long upright walls of solidified lava, it rises 1,700 feet off the desert floor to an elevation of 7,178 feet. There are viewpoints off U.S. 666, 6 to 7 miles south of the town of Shiprock. You can get closer by taking the tribal road to the community of Red Rock; but to get any nearer this sacred Navajo rock, you must have permission. Climbing is not permitted.
　　The town named after the rock is a gateway to the Navajo reservation and the Four Corners region. There's a tribal visitor center here.
　　From Shiprock, it's a 32-mile drive west on N.M. 504 to Teec Nos Pos, Arizona, then north on U.S. 160, to the **Four Corners Monument.** A marker here sits

astride the only point in the United States where four states meet—New Mexico, Colorado, Utah, and Arizona. There are no facilities.

NAVAJO LAKE STATE PARK, N.M. 511, 40 miles east of Farmington.
Three recreation sites (San Juan River, Pine River, and Sims Mesa) with camping, fishing, and boating make this the most popular water sports destination for residents of northwestern New Mexico. Trout, kokanee, largemouth bass, and catfish are caught in lake and river waters, and the surrounding hills attract hunters seeking deer and elk. A visitor center at Pine River Recreation Area has interpretive displays on natural history and on the construction and purposes of the dam.

Navajo Lake, with an area of 15,610 acres, extends from the confluence of the San Juan and Los Pinos rivers 25 miles north into Colorado. Navajo Dam, an earthen embankment, is three-quarters of a mile long and 400 feet high. It provides Farmington-area cities, industries, and farms with their principal water supply. It's also the main storage reservoir for the Navajo Indian Irrigation Project, designed to irrigate 110,000 acres.

ANGEL PEAK RECREATION AREA, N.M. 44, 35 miles south of Farmington. Tel. 327-5344.
The distinctive pinnacle of 6,880-foot Angel Peak can often be spotted from Farmington. This area at its foot offers a variety of unusual, colorful geological formations and canyons to explore on foot. The Bureau of Land Management has developed two campgrounds and a third picnic area, all with rest rooms. The last 6 miles of access, after turning off from Highway 44, are over a rough graded dirt road.

BISTI BADLANDS, Old N.M. 371, 32 miles south of Farmington. Tel. 327-5344.
A federally protected area of weird rock formations, petrified logs, and prehistoric fossils, this wilderness is like an undiscovered planet. Walk among its huge turrets, buttes, spires, and pinnacles. Seventy million years ago, this was a swampland that attracted many dinosaurs and primitive mammals; many fossils remain, but may not be removed from the site. There are no facilities here. The site is administered by the BLM.

WHERE TO STAY

There are about 1,500 rooms in 22 accommodations in the Farmington area. Lodging tax is 10.75% (including 4.69% local).

MODERATE

HOLIDAY INN, 600 E. Broadway at Scott Ave., Farmington, NM 87401. Tel. 505/327-9811 or toll free 800/HOLIDAY. Fax 505/325-2288. 150 rms, (5 suites). A/C TV TEL
$ Rates: $50–$60 single, $56–$62 double. $75–$120 suite. AE, CB, DC, DISC, JCB, MC, V.
Primarily a businessperson's hotel, the Holiday Inn focuses its attention on guest rooms rather than lobby appointments. Southwestern decor predominates throughout the hotel. Standard units have two double beds and normal furnishings. King rooms (with king-size beds, of course) feature a sofa sleeper, leisure chair, and executive desk. There are rooms for nonsmokers and the disabled.

The Brass Apple Restaurant, open daily from 6am to 2pm for breakfast and lunch and 5 to 10pm for dinner, specializes in American and continental cuisine. A modern dining room with big windows and garden decor, the Brass Apple offers luncheon buffets ($4.95) and full dinner priced from $7.95–$15.95. Save room for the special desserts that are baked fresh daily. The Sportz Club Lounge, open from 3pm to midnight daily, has four TV monitors, two of them big screens. The hotel provides room service during restaurant hours, valet laundry, 24-hour desk, an outdoor swimming pool, sauna, hot tub, fitness center, and meeting space for 200. Pets are accepted; a kennel is also available.

THE INN AT FARMINGTON, 700 Scott Ave., Farmington, NM 87401.
   Tel. 505/327-5221 or toll free 800/528-1234 or 800/548-6758. 194 rms, (28 suites). A/C FRIDGE TV TEL
$ Rates: $52–$67 single, $67–$77 double, $77–$87 suite. AE, CB, DC, DISC, MC, V.

Owned by Albuquerque-based Maloof Hotels and affiliated with Best Western, the inn (like its related properties in Gallup, Grants, and Roswell) is focused around a skylit central courtyard, with luxuriant trees and plants shading a café at one end and a swimming pool at the other.

Pleasant, modern rooms have king- or two queen-size beds with rose or lilac decor, serigraph art on the walls, bedside remote controls for TV and lights, and minirefrigerators. All rooms have standard furnishings and two sinks, one outside the toilet at the vanity. King suites have a phone at a working desk, an oversize dresser, and a sleeper sofa in a sitting area. Some rooms accommodate nonsmokers or the disabled.

An American menu is served daily from 6 to 10am for breakfast and 5 to 9pm for dinner in the sidewalk-café atmosphere of the Coffee Shop. The lounge has live entertainment most nights, and the Sports Room offers big-screen viewing of games and events. The hotel has room service during restaurant hours, valet laundry, 24-hour desk, an indoor swimming pool, sauna, Jacuzzi, weight and exercise room, guest Laundromat, video games area, and gift shop. Pets are welcome.

LA QUINTA, 675 Scott Ave., Farmington, NM 87401. Tel. 505/327-4706 or toll free 800/531-5900. Fax 505/325-6583. 106 rms. A/C TV TEL
$ Rates: $47–$62 single, $55–$70 double. AE, CB, DC, DISC, ER, JCB, MC, V.
A homey, family-style motel, La Quinta is a purveyor of affordable luxury. Good-sized rooms with southwestern decor have a king-size or two double beds, hardwood furnishings, dressing area (with vanity) behind an accordion door, remote-control television, free local phone calls, clock radios, and reading lamps. The Kettle, a 24-hour restaurant, is next door. Complimentary coffee and tea is always available at the front desk. The hotel also offers valet laundry service, 24-hour desk, nonsmoking and handicapped rooms, and an outdoor swimming pool. Small pets are permitted.

INEXPENSIVE

ANASAZI INN, 903 W. Main St., Farmington, NM 87401. Tel. 505/325-4564. 66 rms, (8 suites). A/C TV TEL
$ Rates: $37.95 single, $43.95 double, $45.95–$51.95 suite. AE, CB, DC, DISC, MC, V.

This newly renovated property, built in Pueblo style, is a real bargain. The spacious lobby displays Navajo crafts and gift items. Pastel colors and Navajo motifs brighten the guest rooms, which are decorated with native paintings and metal sculptures. The rooms each have one king- or two queen-size beds, maple furnishings, a dressing table backed by a large mirror, and a ceiling fan. There's a courtesy car and gift shop. Nonsmoking rooms are available; small pets are permitted.

The ranch-style Coyote Restaurant, with its howling coyote motif, is open for three meals daily, from 7am to 10pm. Steaks, seafood, and Mexican food run from $3.30 to $9 for lunch, $6.30 to $15 for dinner. The adjoining lounge, done in a sort of nouveau-rustique style, sometimes features live solo entertainment.

SUPER 8 MOTEL, 1601 Bloomfield Hwy. at Carlton Ave., Farmington, NM 87401. Tel. 505/325-1813 or toll free 800/800-8000. 60 rms. A/C TV TEL

$ Rates: $27.90 single, $36.90–$40.90 double. Children under 12 free with parent. AE, CB, DC, DISC, MC, V.

A handsome new property on U.S. Highway 64, just across the Animas River from central Farmington, the Super 8 has comfortable, amply sized rooms with standard furnishings, including queen-size or two double beds. Some rooms have water beds. A game room keeps the kids from getting bored. The motel has nonsmoking rooms and a 24-hour desk and accepts pets (with prior arrangement).

BUDGET

MOTEL 6, 1600 Bloomfield Hwy. at Cedar St., Farmington, NM 87401. Tel. 505/326-4501. 134 rms. A/C TV TEL
$ Rates: $20.95 single, $26.95 double. AE, DC, DISC, MC, V.

This rambling motel on U.S. Highway 64, just east of downtown Farmington, stacks its cubicles in two stories. Rooms are clean but cozy, with all the essentials (double bed, table and chairs, dresser, and wardrobe rack) but none of the luxuries of a more expensive room. An outdoor swimming pool is open seasonally.

WHERE TO DINE

MODERATE

K.B. DILLON'S, 101 W. Broadway at Orchard Avenue. Tel. 325-0222.
Cuisine: STEAKS & SEAFOOD. **Reservations:** Recommended.
$ Prices: Appetizers $3–$7.75; lunch $4–$14.25; dinner $9.95–$21.25. AE, MC, V.
Open: Lunch Mon–Fri 11am–2pm, dinner Mon–Sat 5:30–10:30pm.

Rough wooden walls, brick arches, historical photos, and early 20th-century decor, including signs used in advertising and at railroad crossings, make this downtown restaurant seem like a page out of grandfather's scrapbook.

The menu, by contrast, is quite modern. Selections include Fracosta (an 8-ounce top sirloin broiled and topped with sautéed sweet peppers, mushrooms, green onions, and white wine); chicken à la Dillon (a sautéed breast topped with fresh tomato, avocado, and melted provolone cheese); and fresh mountain trout amandine, Cajun or Oscar. The restaurant has a full bar that stays open between lunch and dinner.

SEÑOR PEPPER'S RESTAURANTE Y CANTINA, Four Corners Regional Airport, Navajo St. Tel. 327-0436.
Cuisine: NEW MEXICAN.
$ Prices: Appetizers $3.25–$6.50; breakfast $2.95–$7.50, lunch $1.75–$8.50; dinner $4.95–$15.95. AE, DC, DISC, MC, V.
Open: Sun–Thurs 5:30am–10pm, Fri–Sat 5:30am–10:30pm. **Closed:** Christmas.

For an airport restaurant and lounge, Señor Pepper's is very "with it." Waitresses in colorful fiesta dress serve diners at booths and tables, beneath hanging lamps and perched tropical birds (not real). Meals are also served in the lounge, where classic rock is piped nonstop and neon lights surround a dance floor that hosts a DJ from 9pm nightly. Painted above the bar is Senor Pepper himself—a reclining red pepper wearing sunglasses.

Meals are very generous, from breakfast burritos to enchiladas de Guaymas (crab) or de Cancún (shrimp). The steak Mazatlán has drawn raves from *Bon Appetit* readers, and the carne São Paulo (with green chile sauce and cheese) deserves to. Stacked enchiladas, burritos, tacos, tostadas, chiles rellenos, tamales, sopaipillas, and every other Mexican standby is also on the menu.

THE TROUGH, U.S. 550, Flora Vista. Tel. 334-6176.

Cuisine: STEAK & SEAFOOD. **Reservations:** Not accepted.
$ Prices: Dinners only $10.50–$29. AE, DISC, MC, V.
Open: Mon–Thurs 5:30–10:30pm, Fri–Sat 5:30–11pm.

Eight miles northeast of central Farmington is this find, tucked behind the often-rowdy Country Palace nightclub. With a rustic, candlelit decor brightened by planter boxes, it feels like a home on the range. Obviously, the staff feels at home here—most of them have been with the restaurant five years or longer.

The oversize menu is your first clue as to the size of the meals. (Everything is for sale here, including the business itself . . . for a price!) Opt for prime rib, steaks, pork chops, ribs, chicken, half duckling, shrimp, lobster, or Alaskan king crab legs. Or choose any of 5 to 10 nightly fresh fish specials, from salmon to tuna to shark. (It's flown in three times a week.) If you still have room, ask to see the dessert tray. There's an extensive California and European wine list and a full bar.

INEXPENSIVE

CLANCEY'S PUB, 2703 E. 20th St. at Hutton Rd. Tel. 325-8176.
Cuisine: AMERICAN & MEXICAN.
$ Prices: Appetizers $2.50–$4.95; main courses $4–$7.75. AE, MC, V.
Open: Mon–Sat 11am–2am, Sun noon–midnight.

The owners of this old adobe building call it "an Irish cantina." Family photographs and regional art line the walls of this dim-lit establishment, and rock music (sometimes live) plays almost continually.

The menu is heavy on sandwiches and finger food, including the Olde English burger (with cheddar cheese and bacon) and the Rueben O'Rourke (with Thousand Island dressing). There's fish-and-chips, of course; and Mac McMulligan stew; and "build-your-own" baked potatoes. Enchiladas, burritos, and tacos are also served.

SOMETHING SPECIAL, 116 N. Auburn Ave. near Main St. Tel. 325-8183.
Cuisine: GOURMET HOME COOKING.
$ Prices: Breakfast $3–$6; lunch $6; desserts $2.50. AE, MC, V.
Open: Tues–Fri 7am–5pm, Sat 7am–noon.

If the aroma didn't tip you off, you might walk right past this unimposing white house, with its yellow shutters and yellow door, and not think it to be a bakery and restaurant. It's just like home, or like home ought to be. Dine indoors amid the fresh bakery smells, or outdoors beneath a vine-draped arbor.

A set lunch menu, announced a month ahead, is served daily. It varies from beef Stroganoff to spinach and feta cheese croissants, manicotti to orange-pecan chicken with avocados. Breakfasts also vary, with one criterion: Nothing is ever fried. There's always a difficult choice of nine desserts each day—from butterscotch-pecan pie to ambrosia cake to chocolate-banana torte.

4. CHAMA

106 miles N of Santa Fe; 101 miles NW of Taos; 113 miles E of Farmington

GETTING THERE   By Plane   There's a private airstrip at El Vado State Park (tel. 588-7470).

By Car   From Santa Fe, take U.S. 84 north (2 hours). From Taos, take U.S. 64 west (2½ hours). From Farmington, take U.S. 64 east (2¼ hours).

ESSENTIALS   Orientation   Historic downtown Chama spreads along the west side of N.M. 17 opposite the Cumbres & Toltec railroad depot, 1.4 miles north of the U.S. 64/84 junction (known as the "Y"). N.M. 17 is Terrace Avenue through downtown, Main Street south of there. Various accommodations and restaurants are strung down the highway south for several miles.

Information   The **New Mexico Welcome Center** (tel. 756-2235) is at the south end of town, at the "Y" junction of U.S. 64/84 and N.M. 17. It's open from 8am to 5pm daily. For complete local information, contact the **Chama Valley Chamber of Commerce**, 532 S. Terrace Ave. (P.O. Box 306), Chama, NM 87520 (tel. 505/756-2306 or toll free 800/477-0149).

Fast Facts   The **area code** is 505. **Dr. J. I. Dunham Memorial Clinic,** Pine Street east of First Street (tel. 756-2143). The **post office** is at Fifth and Maple streets (tel. 756-2240). In case of **emergencies,** phone police (tel. 756-2319), ambulance (tel. 756-2929), fire (tel. 756-2213), state highway patrol (tel. 756-2343), or the Rio Arriba County sheriff (tel. 588-7271 in Tierra Amarilla).

A village of just 1,250 people, Chama's importance exceeds its small size. It's the largest New Mexico community for two hours in any direction, the head of the fertile Rio Chama valley, and the southern terminal of the world-famous Cumbres & Toltec Scenic Railroad. Lumber and ranching, along with tourism and outdoor recreation, support the economy today. It's a hunting and fishing center in summer, a cross-country skiing and snowmobiling haven in winter. Tierra Amarilla, the Rio Arriba County seat, is 14 miles south; Dulce, governmental seat of the Jicarilla Apache Indian Reservation, is 27 miles west.

WHAT TO SEE & DO

CUMBRES & TOLTEC SCENIC RAILROAD, P.O. Box 789, Chama, NM 87520. Tel. 505/756-2151.

America's longest and highest narrow-gauge steam railroad, the historic C&T operates on a 64-mile track between Chama and Antonito, Colorado. Built in 1880 as an extension of the Denver & Rio Grande line to serve the mining camps of the San Juan Mountains, it is perhaps the finest surviving example of what once was a vast network of remote Rocky Mountain railways.

The C&T passes through forests of pine and aspen, past striking rock formations, and through the magnificent Toltec Gorge of the Rio de los Pinos. It crests at the 10,015-foot Cumbres Pass, the highest in the United States used by scheduled passenger trains.

Halfway through the route, at Osier, Colorado, the *New Mexico Express* from Chama meets the *Colorado Limited* from Antonito. They stop to exchange greetings, engines, and through passengers. Round-trip day passengers return to their starting point after enjoying a picnic or catered lunch beside the old water tank and stock pens in Osier.

A walking tour brochure, describing 23 points of interest in the Chama railroad yards, can be picked up at the 1899 depot in Chama. A registered National Historic Site, the C&T is owned by the states of Colorado and New Mexico, and operated by a concessionaire, Kyle Railways, Inc.

Fares: Round-trip to Osier and return, adults $29, children 11 and under $11. Through trip to Antonito, return by van (or to Antonito by van, return by train), adults $45.50, children $23. Reservations highly recommended. MC, V.

Open: Memorial Day weekend to mid-Oct trains leave Chama daily at 10:30am; vans depart for Antonito at 8pm.

JICARILLA APACHE INDIAN RESERVATION, P.O. Box 507, Dulce, NM 87528. Tel. 759-3242.

About 3,200 Apaches live on this reservation along U.S. Highway 64 and N.M. 537. Its 768,000 acres stretch from the Colorado border south 65 miles to N.M. 44 near Cuba. The word *jicarilla* (pronounced hick-ah-*ree*-ah) means "little basket," so it's no surprise that tribal craftspeople are noted for their basket weaving and beadwork. See their work, both contemporary and museum quality, at the **Jicarilla Apache Arts and Crafts Shop and Museum,** a lime green building along U.S. 64 west of downtown (tel. 759-3362). Two isolated pueblo ruins are found on the reservation—the **Cordova Canyon** ruins on tribal Road 13 and the **Honolulu** ruin on Road 63.

This area of New Mexico offers some of the finest hunting in North America. Tribe members guide fishermen and trophy hunters, most of whom seek elk, mule deer, or bear, into the reservation's rugged wilderness backcountry. Just south of Chama on Jicarilla's northeastern flank is the **Horse Lake Mesa Game Park,** P.O. Box 313, Dulce, NM 87528 (tel. 505/759-3442), a 20,000-acre reserve surrounded by a predator-proof fence. At an altitude of around 8,500 feet, this is the home of the Rocky Mountain elk, mule deer, and countless numbers of bobcat, bear, and coyote.

Fishing permits for seven reservation lakes and the Navajo River run $5 per day for adults, $2 for seniors and children under 12. Rainbow, cutthroat, and brown trout are regularly stocked.

Highlights of the Jicarilla calendar are the Little Beaver Roundup (the second or third weekend in July) and the Stone Lake Fiesta (September 14–15 annually).

Admission: Free.
Open: Year-round.

NEARBY ATTRACTIONS

U.S. HIGHWAY 84 SOUTH   Distinctive yellow earth provided a name for the town of **Tierra Amarilla,** 14 miles south of Chama at the junction of U.S. 84 and 64. Throughout New Mexico, this name is synonymous with a continuing controversy over the land-grant rights of the descendants of the original Hispanic settlers. But the economy of this community of 1,000 is dyed in the wool, literally.

The organization Ganados del Valle (Livestock Growers of the Valley) is at work to save the long-haired Spanish churro sheep from extinction through breeding; to introduce other unusual wool breeds to the valley; and to perpetuate a 200-year-old tradition of shepherding, spinning, weaving, and dyeing. Many of the craftspeople work in conjunction with ✪ **Tierra Wools,** P.O. Box 118, Los Ojos, NM 87551 (tel. 588-7231), which has a showroom and workshop in a century-old mercantile building just north of Tierra Amarilla. One-of-a-kind blankets and men's and women's apparel are among the products displayed and sold.

Two state parks are a short drive west from Tierra Amarilla. **El Vado Lake,** 14 miles on N.M. 112, offers boating and waterskiing, fishing, and camping in summer; cross-country skiing and ice fishing in winter. **Heron Lake,** 8 miles west on N.M. 95, has a 3-m.p.h. speed limit for motor vessels, adding to its appeal for fishing, sailing, and windsurfing. There's an interpretive center, and camping and picnic sites. The scenic 5½-mile Rio Chama trail connects the two lakes.

East of Tierra Amarilla, the Rio Brazos cuts a canyon through the Tusas Mountains and around 11,403-foot Brazos Peak. From just north of Los Ojos, N.M. 512 heads east 7½ miles up the **Brazos Box Canyon.** High cliffs that rise straight from the valley floor give it a Yosemite-like appearance—one that is made more apparent from an overlook on U.S. 64, 18 miles east of Tierra Amarilla en route to Taos. **El Chorro,** an impressive waterfall at the mouth of the canyon, usually flows only from early May to mid-June, but this is a tremendous hiking area any time of year. There are a couple of resort lodges in the area.

About 27 miles south of Tierra Amarilla on U.S. 84, and 3 miles north of Ghost Ranch, is **Echo Canyon Amphitheater,** with a campground and picnic area. A natural "theater," hollowed out of sandstone by thousands of years of erosion, it is a 10-minute walk from the parking area. Some 13 miles west of here, via a dirt road into the Chama River Canyon Wilderness, is the isolated **Christ-in-the-Desert Monastery,** built in 1964 by Benedictine monks. The brothers produce crafts, sold at a small gift shop, and operate a guest house.

The ✪ **Ghost Ranch Living Museum** (tel. 685-4312) is a U.S. Forest Service–operated exhibit of regional plant and animal life, geology, paleontology, and ecology. Short trails lead past re-created marsh, grassland, canyon, and forest land, inhabited by 27 species of native New Mexican animals and birds, most of them brought here injured or orphaned. A miniature national forest, complete with a fire lookout tower, illustrates conservation techniques; a trail through a severely eroded arroyo affords an opportunity to study soil ecology. Temporary exhibits from the New Mexico Museum of Natural History are presented in an indoor display hall. It's open May through September (daily 8am to 6pm) and October through April (Tuesday to Sunday 8am to 4:30pm). There's no admission, though donations are welcomed.

There's no museum to mark her former residence, but the celebrated artist Georgia O'Keeffe spent most of her adult life in **Abiquiu,** a tiny town in a bend of the Rio Chama 14 miles south of the Ghost Ranch, and 22 miles north of Espanola, on U.S. 84. The inspiration for O'Keeffe's startling landscapes is clear in the surrounding terrain. Many dinosaur skeletons have been found in rocks along the base of cliffs near **Abiquiu Reservoir,** a popular fishing spot formed by the Abiquiu Dam.

In successive miles south, keep your eyes open for **Dar al-Islam,** a spiritual community with a circular adobe replica of a Middle Eastern mosque; **Medanales,** a small village famous for its weaving (seek out Cordelia Coronado's shop); and **Hernandez,** a village 6 miles north of Espanola that was immortalized in Ansel Adams's famous photograph of a full moon rising.

WHERE TO STAY

Virtually all accommodations are found on N.M. 17 or south of the "Y" on U.S. 64/84. Lodging tax is 9% (including 3% local tax).

BEST WESTERN JICARILLA INN, U.S. Highway 64 (P.O. Box 23), Dulce, NM 87528. Tel. 505/759-3663 or toll free 800/528-1234. Fax 505/759-3170. 42 rms, 6 suites. A/C TV TEL

$ Rates: $50–$70 single; $60–$80 double; $70–$90 suite. AE, CB, DC, DISC, JCB, MC, V.

The best motel in the Chama area is actually 27 miles west in Dulce, in the northeastern corner of the Jicarilla Apache Indian Reservation. Modern and well maintained—Best Western has honored the inn with its prestigious Gold Key award—it features a skylit indoor garden down the middle of the corridor between rooms.

Guest units all have queen-size beds and nice wood furnishings. Upstairs rooms are particularly spacious, with cathedral ceilings. Six suites have kitchenettes; kitchenware is provided on request. Some rooms accommodate nonsmokers or the disabled.

The inn offers a popular "Trains & Indians" package, which combines lodging and meals with a ride on the C&T Railroad for rates starting at $130 double for one night, $195 for two nights.

The Hill Crest Restaurant serves New Mexican and American cuisine in traditional wickiup decor, with historical black-and-white photographs on the walls. It's open from 6:30am to 9pm daily (and from 4:30am during the October-to-December hunting season). Breakfast and lunch run $2.50 to $6.95, dinner $5.50 to $15.95, including Jicarillo beef-and-potato stew. The cozy Timber Lake Lounge, open at 4pm daily, stages bingo games Friday and Saturday. The hotel also has a tourist information center, 24-hour desk, Apache Mesa Gallery and Gift Shop, video shop, and meeting space for 150.

BRANDING IRON MOTEL, West Main St. (P.O. Box 557), Chama, NM 87520. Tel. 505/756-2162 or toll free 800/446-2650. 41 rms (1 suite). A/C TV TEL

$ Rates: $45 single, $52 double. DISC, MC, V.

This modern two-story motel, set back off the highway, has spacious, colorfully appointed motel units with all standard furnishings. Wildlife photos on the walls are reminders of the popularity of hunting in this area. The restaurant/lounge offers coffee-shop fare, three meals a day.

CHAMA TRAILS INN, West Main St. at the "Y," Chama (P.O. Box 816),

NM 87520. Tel. 505/756-2156 or toll free 800/289-1421. 16 rms. FRIDGE TV TEL

$ Rates: $35 single, $41 double, $75 suite. AE, DISC, MC, V.

An art gallery as well as a motel, this white stucco building with dangling chile *ristras* incorporates the work of a different artist into the decor of each room. All rooms have queen-size beds and Santa Fe–style furnishings, custom-made of pine. Some units have ceiling fans, gas fireplaces, and/or Mexican-tiled bathroom floors. Several rooms have been designated for nonsmokers and a redwood sauna is available for guest use. The small but impressive art gallery here began as a hobby; now it's a major outlet for local artists' work.

ELK HORN LODGE, on Hwy. 84, Chama, NM 87520. Tel. 505/756-2105. 33 units. TV TEL

$ Rates: Rooms $32.50 single, $39–$44 double; cabins $48–$75 single or double. Extra person $5. AE, MC, V. **Parking:** Free.

Situated just outside the center of the sleepy little town of Chama, the Elk Horn Lodge is a bargain for those who enjoy outdoor sports—fishing gear is even sold in the lodge's office. The rooms and cabins are clean and spacious and are done in dark wood paneling with beige carpeting and orange bedspreads. The furnishings include two double beds, a desk, and a table accompanied by a Naugahyde chair. Outside the door of each room, on the motel-style porch, a folding chair is provided. There are barbecue pits available for guest use, and there is a small café that is also run by the owners of the Elk Horn Lodge.

THE JONES HOUSE, 311 Terrace Ave. at 3rd St., Chama, NM 87520. Tel. 505/756-2908. 4 rms.

$ Rates (including full breakfast): Private bath $45 single, $65 double; shared bath $35 single, $55 double. AE, MC, V.

Phil and Sara Cole's bed-and-breakfast, at the north end of the historic downtown district across from railroad yard, occupies a 1928 adobe home of Tudor design. It's notable for its pressed-tin ceilings and homey decor. Two guest rooms have private baths; the other two share. Phone and TV are available on request. The living room has a wood stove, games table, and small library, and there's a big yard for bird watching. No smoking or pets are allowed.

WHERE TO DINE

THE CHUCK BOX EATERY & DINING HALL, Cumbres Mall, Terrace Ave. Tel. 756-2975.

Cuisine: AMERICAN & NEW MEXICAN.

$ Prices: Breakfast $1.25–$3.50; lunch $1.25–$4.50; dinner $3.95–$10.50; dinner and Fri–Sat show $6.95–$13.95. MC, V.

Open: Eatery daily 8am–2pm; Dining Hall Tues–Thurs and Sun 6–9pm, Fri–Sat 6–11pm.

At the back of a small shopping mall is this little cook house, which boasts a "down home" atmosphere with farming antiques on the walls. You can get cackleberries and pig patties (two eggs with sausage) or saddle anchors (pancakes) for breakfast, an oink-and-gobble (club sandwich) or a Navajo taco (on a sopaipilla) for lunch. Dinners in the Dining Hall focus on steak and chicken. There's live music here nightly, and a special weekend dinner show in the "stage barn." Box lunches, including sandwich, chips or salad, and dessert, are prepared for train passengers or outdoor excursionists.

HIGH COUNTRY RESTAURANT, Main St. (0.1 mile north of "Y"). Tel. 756-2384.

Cuisine: STEAKS & SEAFOOD.

$ Prices: Lunch $2.95–$8.95; dinner $4.95–$12.95. AE, MC, V.

Open: Mon–Sat 11am–10:30pm, Sun 11am–9:30pm.

This rustic wood-plank restaurant/saloon is like a country lodge with a big stone fireplace. The dinner menu features fried chicken, barbecued pork ribs, a variety of steaks, prime rib, and such seafood as trout, beer-battered shrimp, and Alaskan snow crab. There's also enchiladas, hamburgers, baked potatoes, and a soup-and-salad bar. A children's menu starts at $1.95.

VIVA VERA'S, Main St. (0.2 mile north of "Y"). Tel. 756-2557.
   Cuisine: NEW MEXICAN & AMERICAN.
$ Prices: Lunch $3.25–$6; dinner $5.50–$9.95. AE, MC, V.
   Open: Daily 7am–10pm.

A small white Territorial-style roadside café, Vera's may be Chama's most popular hangout. Portions are generous. Try the chile stew and posole. Beer and wine are served with meals.

CHAPTER 9

SOUTHWESTERN NEW MEXICO

1. SOCORRO

2. TRUTH OR CONSEQUENCES

3. LAS CRUCES

4. DEMING & LORDSBURG

5. SILVER CITY

This region belongs to the Old West. Billy the Kid lived here; so did Geronimo.

The Rio Grande is southwestern New Mexico's lifeline, throughout history nourishing the Indian, Hispanic, and Anglo settlers who have built their homes beside its shores. It sketches a distinct boundary between the rugged mountains of the southwest and the desert reaching toward the southeast. The river land was especially fertile around modern Las Cruces; the settlement of La Mesilla was southern New Mexico's major center for three centuries.

West of the river, the Black Range and Mogollon Mountains rise in the area now cloaked by Gila National Forest. This was the homeland of the Mogollon Indians 1,000 years ago; Gila Cliff Dwellings National Monument preserves one of their great legacies. It was also the homeland of the fiercely independent Chiricahua Apaches in the 19th century—considered the last North American Indians to succumb to the whites, they numbered Cochise and Geronimo among their chieftains. Mining and outdoor recreation, centered in historic Silver City (pop. 11,000), now are the economic stanchions. But dozens of mining towns have boomed and busted in the past 140 years; a smattering of ghost towns throughout the region are grim reminders.

Las Cruces, at the foot of the Organ Mountains, is New Mexico's second largest city with 60,000 people. It's a busy agricultural and education center. North up the valley are Truth or Consequences (pop. 11,500), a spa town named for a 1950s radio and TV game show, and Socorro (pop. 9,200), a historic city with Spanish roots. West, on the I-10 corridor to Arizona, are the ranching centers of Deming (pop. 12,000) and Lordsburg (pop. 3,000).

If you're coming by car from Albuquerque, follow I-25 south to Socorro. Turn west on U.S. Highway 60 through Magdalena to see the Very Large Array radio telescope. At Datil Well Recreation Area, turn off U.S. 60 onto N.M. 12, which will take you to the Catron County seat of Reserve. Join U.S. 180 just south of Reserve, with stops in Mogollon and the Catwalk near Glenwood. Then proceed to Silver City, a full day's drive from Socorro on this route.

Use Silver City as a base to visit the downtown historic district and Gila Cliff Dwellings National Monument. U.S. 180 continues past City of Rocks State Park to Deming; there, pick up I-10 into Las Cruces, where you'll want to spend time at Old Mesilla Plaza.

Return to Albuquerque from Las Cruces. Head north up I-25, giving yourself a long stop in Truth or Consequences, and returning via Socorro. Ideally, this is a week's journey, with a night in Socorro, two nights each in Silver City and Las Cruces, and a night in T or C.

1. SOCORRO

77 miles S of Albuquerque; 149 miles N of Las Cruces

GETTING THERE **By Plane** There is no direct commercial air service to Socorro. A shuttle service, the **Socorro Roadrunner** (tel. 835-1010), runs four times daily—at 9am, 2pm, 7pm, and midnight—from Albuquerque International Airport.

By Bus   Socorro is served by **TNM&O/Greyhound** (tel. 835-3361) on its Albuquerque–El Paso run. The depot address changes frequently; at this writing, it is at 915 California St. Buses depart twice daily southbound (at 3:10am and 4:40pm) and twice daily northbound (at 3:45am and 12:55pm).

By Car   From Albuquerque, take I-25 south (1¼ hours). From Las Cruces, take I-25 north (2¾ hours).

ESSENTIALS Orientation   Socorro is nestled in the valley of the Rio Grande. Highway 85 (California Street) is the main street of Socorro, with access from I-25 at both ends of town.

Information   The **Socorro County Chamber of Commerce,** which is also the visitor information headquarters, is just off North California Street (Highway 85) at 103 Francisco de Avondo (P.O. Box 743), Socorro, NM 87801 (tel. 505/835-0424).

Fast Facts   The **area code** is 505. **Socorro General Hospital** is located on West Highway 60 (tel. 835-1140). The **post office** is 124 Plaza NW (tel. 835-0542). In case of **emergencies,** dial 911.

This quiet, pleasant town of 9,200 is an unusual mix of the 19th and 20th centuries. Established as a mining settlement and ranching center, its downtown area is dominated by numerous mid-1800s buildings and the 17th-century San Miguel Mission. The New Mexico Institute of Mining and Technology (New Mexico Tech) is a major research center. Socorro is also the gateway to a vast and varied two-county region that includes the Bosque del Apache National Wildlife Refuge, the Very Large Array national radio astronomy observatory, and three national forests.

WHAT TO SEE & DO

A WALKING TOUR OF HISTORIC SOCORRO

The best introduction to Socorro is a walking tour of the historic district. Start from the parklike **Plaza,** one block west of California Street on Manzanares Street. A brochure published by the chamber points out several Territorial-style buildings from the mid 1800s, including the **J. N. Garcia Opera House,** the **Juan Nepomoceno Garcia House,** and the **Juan José Baca House.** Several impressive late 19th-century Victorian homes stand in the blocks south of the Plaza. A historical museum in the old **Hammel Brewery** on Sixth Street is temporarily closed.

OTHER ATTRACTIONS

OLD SAN MIGUEL MISSION, 403 El Camino Real, NW, 2 blocks north of the Plaza.

Built in 1615–26 but abandoned during the Pueblo Revolt of 1680, this church was subsequently restored, and a new wing built in 1853. It boasts thick adobe walls, large carved *vigas,* and supporting corbel arches. English-language masses are Saturday at 6:30pm and Sunday at 10am and noon.
   Admission: Free.
   Open: Daily 6am–6pm.

NEW MEXICO INSTITUTE OF MINING AND TECHNOLOGY, College St. at Leroy St.

Founded in 1889, New Mexico Tech is a highly regarded institution of 1,200 enrollment whose course work focuses on science and mineral engineering. Its research facilities—including centers for petroleum recovery, explosives technology,

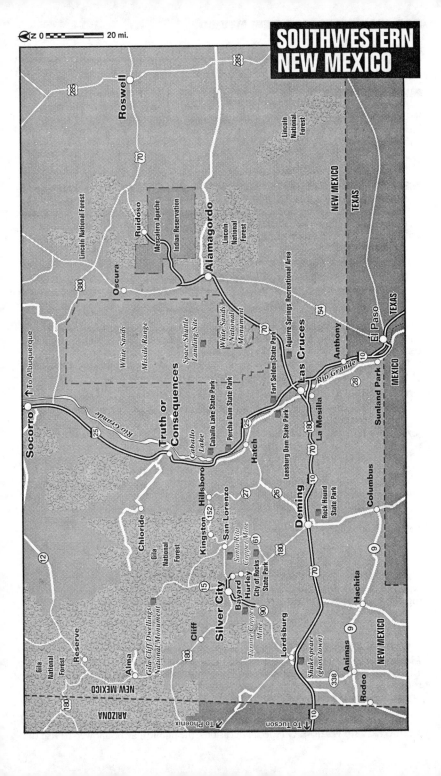

SOUTHWESTERN
NEW MEXICO

and terminal effects and analysis—are internationally acclaimed. Golfers also visit to play the 18-hole university course, considered one of the best in the state. **Macey Center** has a 600-seat auditorium for performing arts and a gallery of rotating art.

MINERAL MUSEUM, Campus Rd., New Mexico Tech campus.

Run by the New Mexico Bureau of Mines and Mineral Resources, this museum has the largest geological collection in the state. Its more than 10,000 specimens include mineral samples from all over the world, fossils, mining artifacts, and photographs.

Admission: Free.
Open: Mon–Fri 8am–5pm.

NEW MEXICO FIREFIGHTERS TRAINING ACADEMY, 2 miles northwest via Highway 60. Tel. 835-7500.

Socorro's newest educational institution opened in 1985 at a cost of $6 million. Its facilities, spread across 121 acres, include a three-story control tower and four-story drill tower for rescue practices.

Admission: Free.
Open: Tours Mon–Fri 9am–noon and 1–4pm, by appointment only.

NEARBY ATTRACTIONS

SOUTH OF SOCORRO

The village of **San Antonio,** the boyhood home of Conrad Hilton, is 10 miles from Socorro via I-25. During the panic of 1907, his merchant father, Augustus Hilton, converted part of his store into a rooming house. This gave Conrad his first exposure to the hospitality industry, and he went on to worldwide fame as a hotelier. Only ruins of the store/boardinghouse remain.

BOSQUE DEL APACHE NATIONAL WILDLIFE REFUGE, 8 miles south of San Antonio via State Hwy. 1 (P.O. Box 1246, Socorro, NM 87801). Tel. 835-1828.

An estimated 300 permanent and migratory birds and over 100 amphibians, reptiles, and mammals make their homes in the 57,000-acre reserve. It's an especially busy place in winter, when the population includes more than 40,000 snow geese, 30,000 ducks, 15,000 sandhill cranes, and about a dozen endangered whooping cranes. Photographers and nature watchers can start their 15-mile driving tour or 1¾-mile Bosque Trail walk at the Visitor Center.

Admission: $2 per vehicle.
Open: 1 hour before sunrise to 1 hour after sunset, year-round. Visitor center open daily in winter, Mon–Fri in summer.

NORTH OF SOCORRO

It's about 15 miles to **Sevilleta National Wildlife Refuge,** location of one of the National Science Foundation's 17 long-term ecological research sites. Coordinated by the University of New Mexico, it is open to the public by permission only.

WEST OF SOCORRO

U.S. Highway 60, running west to Arizona, is the avenue to several points of interest. **Magdalena,** 27 miles from Socorro, is a mining and ranching town that preserves an 1880s Old West spirit. Its **Woman on the Mountain Inn** (tel. 505/854-2757) has rooms ($20–$35) with a country inn atmosphere. It's popular with families and rock hounds. Three miles south, the ghost town of **Kelly** produced over $40 million worth of lead, zinc, copper, silver, and gold in the late 19th and early 20th centuries.

Thirty-two miles north of Magdalena on a dead-end road is the home of the **Alamo Navajo Nation.** On special occasions, the public may be allowed to visit the band of 1,400 Navajo who live on this reservation: Inquire with the Alamo Chapter Office (tel. 854-2686).

Southeast of Magdalena, atop 10,783-foot South Baldy Mountain, the **Langmuir Research Laboratory** studies thunderstorms and atmospheric electricity from June through August. Nearby is the **Joint Observatory for Cometary Research,** where comets are observed and studied under the direction of the NASA/Goddard Space Flight Center. The research centers can be reached by four-wheel-drive vehicles only; would-be visitors should call 835-5423 in advance.

VERY LARGE ARRAY NATIONAL RADIO ASTRONOMY OBSERVATORY, 54 miles west of Socorro on U.S. 60. Tel. 835-7000.

Twenty-seven dish-shaped antennae, each 82 feet in diameter, extend across an ancient lake bed in three 13-mile-long arms. The antennae are interconnected to form a single enormous radio telescope, the world's premier instrument for researching the physics of radio sources beyond the Milky Way. Fully operational since 1981, it cost $78.6 million. The VLA is controlled by computers in Socorro; data is shipped to the Array Operations Center. A Visitor Center has displays on radio astronomy and the operation of the VLA, and offers a self-guided walking tour around the central part of the observatory.

Admission: Free.
Open: Daily 8:30am–sunset.

WHERE TO STAY

All accommodations are along California Street, the main highway through town, or the adjacent I-25 frontage road. A 9.5% tax is imposed on all lodging bills (6% state tax and 3.5% city lodging tax).

THE EATON HOUSE, 403 Eaton Ave., (P.O. Box 536) Socorro, NM 87801. Tel. 505/835-1067. 3 rms (all with bath). A/C
$ Rates (including full breakfast): $75–$85 single or double. No credit cards.
Parking: Free.
This charming bed-and-breakfast, originally constructed in 1881 by Col. E. W. Eaton for himself and his descendants, is on the register of New Mexico State Historic Buildings. Tom Harper and Anna Appleby, the current owners, have created an oasis in the Eaton House. Each room is uniquely decorated. For instance, the Daughters' Room is done in an early 19th-century style with twin beds and claw-foot tub and shower, while the Vigilante Room has a full bed and is done in a traditional Southwest style with handmade Southwest furnishings and a Mexican tiled bathroom. The Colonel Eaton Room, on the other hand, is Victorian in style and has a queen-size four poster bed. All beds are covered with crisp linens and cozy goose-down comforters. If privacy is what you want, each room has a separate entrance, but if you'd like to socialize, you can either sit out on the portal and enjoy the hummingbirds that hover around the bird feeders hanging there, or you can go into the main house and sit in the sunny wicker-furnished sitting room.

Breakfast is served in the main house at the large dining table and might consist of fruit, coffee cake or homemade bread, huevos rancheros or egg soufflé, turkey chile sausage, or blue-corn pancakes with piñon nuts. All ingredients are organic, and the eggs come only from free-range chickens. Believe me, the breakfast is nothing short of full, and nothing short of delicious. Children 14 and over are welcome. No pets.

MOTEL 6, 807 S. California St., Socorro, NM 87801. Tel. 505/835-4300. 123 rms. A/C TV TEL
$ Rates: $22.95 single, $29.95 double. Under 18 free with parent. AE, CB, DC, DISC, MC, V.
Rooms are small and Spartan—no bathtubs (showers only), no pictures on the walls—but they're clean and sufficient. Decorated in earth tones, all have double

beds, and three-quarter baths. Some have a table and chairs. The motel has an outdoor swimming pool.

SUPER 8 MOTEL, 1211 Frontage Rd. NW, Socorro, NM 87801. Tel. 505/835-4626 or toll free 800/848-8888. Fax 505/835-3988. 63 rms, 8 suites. A/C TV TEL

$ **Rates:** $38.90 single, $42.90–$48.90 double, $46.90–$65.90 suite. AE, CB, DC, DISC, MC, V.

Regular patrons of Super 8 motels return in part because their accommodations are so predictable. Each room here is clean and cozy, with particleboard furnishings and paper flowers on the desk. A big blue stuffed armchair brings out the mauve colors of the rest of the room. Coffee is always on at the 24-hour desk. Facilities include a swimming pool, hot tub, and guest laundry.

WHERE TO DINE

DON JUAN'S, 118 Manzanares Rd. Tel. 835-9967.
   Cuisine: NEW MEXICAN. **Reservations:** Not necessary.
$ **Prices:** Appetizers 95¢–$2.50; à la carte $1.50–$4.25, Mexican plates $3.90–$15.75. AE, MC, V.
   Open: Mon–Fri 10am–9pm.

The decor at Don Juan's is nothing to speak of in the main dining room, but the festive outdoor patio has some extraordinary murals painted on its surrounding walls. If you're not particularly interested in the decor, you'll be very interested in the food—it's excellent and inexpensive. Breakfast is served all day and might consist of the standard huevos rancheros or a breakfast burrito. Appetizers at lunch and dinner include taquitos, chile cheese fries, and sopaipillas. You can order your main course à la carte (tacos, burritos, enchiladas, and tostadas), or you might prefer to get a full Mexican plate with refried beans and rice. Beer and wine are available, but you'd be better off to have one of their incredible margaritas.

EL SOMBRERO, 210 Mesquite St., Socorro. Tel. 835-3945.
   Cuisine: NEW MEXICAN & AMERICAN.
$ **Prices:** Main courses $1.70–$6.95. CB, DC, MC, V.
   Open: Daily 11am–9pm.

Located just out of town on an I-25 frontage road on the east side of the freeway, this popular establishment has a playful atmosphere, with flower baskets hanging from the ceilings and various Mexican knickknacks on the walls. It has a wide variety of Mexican cuisine, including chalupas, as well as steaks and burgers. Beer and wine are served. Luncheon buffets are frequently offered.

OWL BAR & CAFE, State Hwy. 1 and U.S. Hwy. 380, San Antonio. Tel. 835-9946.
   Cuisine: AMERICAN.
$ **Prices:** Lunch $1.80–$9.95; dinner $6–$9.95. MC, V.
   Open: Daily 11am–1pm. Steak house open 5–9:30pm Fri–Sat only.

   A low-lit tavern in a one-story adobe building, 7 miles south of Socorro, the Owl has earned a regionwide reputation for "the world's greatest hamburgers." It's especially proud of its chili cheeseburger. The steak house serves T-bones and filet mignons for under $10.

LA PASADITA, 326 N. 6th St., Socorro. Tel. 835-4373.
   Cuisine: NEW MEXICAN.
$ **Prices:** $1.50–$3.50. No credit cards.
   Open: Mon–Fri 8am–8pm, Sat 8am–4pm.

   A tiny café a block east of the highway, La Pasadita shares La Belle Square's long building with a print shop. Though this unlicensed restaurant is easily missed, its food attracts a big local following–especially for the enchiladas.

VAL VERDE STEAK HOUSE, 203 Manzanares Ave., Socorro. Tel. 835-3380.

Cuisine: AMERICAN. **Reservations:** Recommended.

$ **Prices:** Appetizers $2.25–$5.75; lunch $4.50–$6.75; dinner $6.75–$31.50. AE, CB, DC, DISC, MC, V.

Open: Mon–Thurs 11am–2pm and 5–9:30pm; Fri 11am–2pm and 5–10pm, Sat 5–9:30pm, Sun noon–9pm.

The horseshoe-shaped Val Verde Hotel is a national historic landmark, built in 1919 in California mission style. The hotel has been converted to apartments, but the public can enjoy the old dining room. The lunch menu is simple but tasty: homemade soups, salads, sandwiches, plus steaks and seafood. Dinner is more elaborate. House specials include beef Stroganoff and pepper steak Capri (in madeira sauce). Gourmet southwestern dishes are also served. The restaurant is about two blocks off California Street (Highway 85), directly east of the Plaza. Beer and wine are served.

2. TRUTH OR CONSEQUENCES

151 miles S of Albuquerque; 75 miles N of Las Cruces

GETTING THERE **By Plane** Private flights and charters arrive at **Truth or Consequences Municipal Airport,** North Highway 85 (tel. 894-6199).

By Bus Truth or Consequences is served by **TNM&O/Greyhound,** which at this writing stops at the Black Range Restaurant (tel. 894-3649), on its Albuquerque–El Paso run. Buses depart twice daily southbound (at 4:55am and 6:15pm) and twice daily northbound (at 2:40am and 11:15pm).

By Car From Albuquerque take I-25 south (2½ hours). From Las Cruces take I-25 north (1¼ hours).

ESSENTIALS **Orientation** Best known as "T or C," this year-round resort town and retirement community of 7,500 is spread along the Rio Grande between Elephant Butte and Caballo reservoirs, two of the three largest bodies of water in the state. Business Loop 25 branches off from I-25 to wind through the city, splitting into Main Street (one-way west) and South Broadway (one-way east) in the downtown area. Third Avenue connects T or C with the Elephant Butte resort community, 5 miles east.

Information The visitor information center is located at the corner of Main Street (Business Loop 25) and Foch Street in downtown T or C. It is administered by the **Truth or Consequences/Sierra County Chamber of Commerce,** P.O. Drawer 31, Truth or Consequences, NM 87901 (tel. 505/894-3536 or toll free 800/831-9487).

Fast Facts The **area code** is 505. **Sierra Vista Hospital** is located at 800 E. Ninth Ave. (tel. 894-2111). The **post office** is downtown, at the corner of Main and Jones streets (tel. 894-3137). For police dial 894-7111, fire 894-2345, ambulance 894-6617.

Originally known as Hot Springs, after the therapeutic mineral springs bubbling up near the river, the town took the name Truth or Consequences in 1950. That was the year that Ralph Edwards, producer of the popular radio and television program "Truth or Consequences," began his weekly broadcast with these words: "I wish that some town in the United States liked and respected our show so much that it would like to change its name to Truth or Consequences." The reward to any city willing to make this change was to become the site of the 10th anniversary broadcast of the program—which would put it on the national map in a big way. The locals voted for the name change, which has survived three protest elections over the years.

Although the "Truth or Consequences" television program was canceled decades ago, Ralph Edwards, now in his 70s, continues to return for the annual T or C Fiesta, the first weekend of May. Another popular annual festival is Geronimo Days, the first weekend of October.

WHAT TO SEE & DO

THE HOT SPRINGS

T or C's "original" attraction is its hot springs. The entire downtown area is located over a table of odorless hot mineral water, 98 to 115 degrees, that bubbles to the surface through wells or pools. The first bathhouse was built in the 1880s; most of the eight historic spas extant today date from the 1930s. Generally open from morning to early evening, these spas welcome visitors for soaks and massages. Baths of 20 minutes or longer start at $1.50 per person.

The chamber of commerce has information on all eight local spas; I suggest visiting **Indian Springs Apartments and Pools,** 200 Pershing St. (tel. 894-3823), which has longer hours (7am to 11pm daily) than other spas, naturally flowing pools, and payment on the honor system.

GERONIMO SPRINGS MUSEUM, 211 Main St. Tel. 894-6600.

Outside is Geronimo's Spring, where the great Chiricahua Apache war chief is said to have taken his warriors to bathe their battle wounds. Turtleback Mountain, looming over the Rio Grande east of the city, is believed to have been sacred to the Indians.

Exhibits of prehistoric Mimbres pottery (A.D. 950–1250); Spanish colonial artifacts; artists' work, including historical murals and sculptured bronzes. Exhibits in the other rooms feature army forts and mining towns; the construction of Elephant Butte Dam; local history, featuring photos and artifacts; Indian artifacts, both prehistoric and of more recent culture; the story of ranching and farming in the county; the rise and fall of mining camps and cattle towns. Ralph Edwards Wing contains the history and highlights of the annual fiestas, and celebrates the city's name change. Geothermally heated museum. Gift counter.

Admission: Adults $1.50, students 75¢.
Open: Mon–Sat 9am–5pm.

ELEPHANT BUTTE LAKE STATE PARK. Tel. 744-5421.

Five miles from T or C is the largest lake in New Mexico, covering 38,000 acres. A state park has 5,000 acres of shoreside land. Fishing for black and white bass, catfish, walleye and Northern pike, and crappie goes on all year long. Trout are stocked in the Rio Grande below Elephant Butte Dam. The park has sandy beaches for tanning and swimming, boating, sailing, waterskiing, and camping. There are frequent regattas. The lake was named for a huge rock formation that makes an island; before the inundation that created the lake, it clearly looked like an elephant! Today, it's partially submerged.

ALAMOSA CELLARS, Hwy. 195 (P.O. Box 690), Elephant Butte. Tel. 744-5319.

German-style wines from vineyards east of Elephant Butte Lake. Varieties produced include Pinot noir, chenin blanc, ruby cabernet, Riesling, chardonnay, sauvignon blanc, and muscat Canelli.
Open: Daily 11am–6pm. MC, V.

NEARBY ATTRACTIONS

NORTH OF T OR C A couple of so-called ghost towns—abandoned mining centers that nevertheless do have a few live residents—are Winston and Chloride. **Winston,** 37 miles northwest of T or C on N.M. 52, was abandoned in the early 1900s when silver prices dropped and local mining became unprofitable. Some of the original structures are still standing from that era. A similar fate befell **Chloride,** 5 miles west of Winston on a side road off N.M. 52, where famed silver mines had such names as Nana, Wall Street, and Unknown. Chloride also figured in many battles in the turn-of-the-century war between cattle-ranching and sheep-ranching interests.

SOUTH OF T OR C   Twenty miles via I-25 is another recreation area, **Caballo Lake State Park,** which like Elephant Butte has year-round water sports, fishing, and campsites. The lake has the lofty ridge of the Caballo Mountains just to the east to make a handsome backdrop. There is a marina with full-service and a shop for boaters, as well as full hookups for recreational vehicles. Reached from the same exit off I-25 is still another area, **Percha Dam State Park,** a lovely shaded spot under great cottonwood trees, part of the ancient *bosque,* or woods, the Spanish found bordering the Rio Grande when they first arrived in this area in the 1530s. The dam here diverts river water for irrigation. There are campsites, rest rooms and showers, hiking trails, and access to fishing here.

Thirty-two miles from T or C, via I-25 south to N.M. 152, then west, is ❂ **Hillsboro,** another ghost town fast losing its ghosts to a small invasion of artists and craftspeople, antique shops, and galleries. This town boomed after an 1877 gold strike nearby, and during its heyday produced $6 million in silver and gold. It was the county seat from 1884 to 1938. Its Labor Day weekend Apple Festival is famous throughout the state; the Black Range historical museum is also located here.

The Enchanted Villa bed-and-breakfast, P.O. Box 456, Hillsboro, NM 88042 (tel. 505/895-5686), charges $35 single, $50 double. **General Store and Country Café** serves inexpensive meals amid early 20th-century curios; this local hangout is closed Tuesday.

Nine miles west of Hillsboro on N.M. 152 is **Kingston,** which was born with the rich silver strike at the Solitaire Mine a century ago, and is locally reputed to have been the wildest mining town of the region, with 7,000 people, 22 saloons, a notorious red-light district, and a famous opera house. It was once the residence of the infamous Albert Fall, one of the perpetrators of the Teapot Dome Scandal. Today, by contrast, life in Kingston is pretty quiet.

For overnight stays, the **Black Range Lodge,** Star Route 2, Box 119, Kingston, NM 88042 (tel. 505/895-5652), has rooms for $30 to $40 single, $50 to $60 double. **Sarah's Closet,** Main Street off Virtue (tel. 895-5607), is open from 11am Friday through Sunday for sandwiches, desserts, and homemade coffee. It also has a gift shop and boutique.

WHERE TO STAY

There's a wide choice of accommodations in and near T or C. Tax of 9% (3% city, 6% state) is added onto all lodging bills of less than 30 days' stay.

BEST WESTERN HOT SPRINGS INN, 2270 N. Date St. at I-25, Truth or Consequences, NM 87901. Tel. 505/894-6665 or toll free 800/528-1234. 40 rms. A/C TV TEL

$ Rates: $41.50–$43.50 single, $46.50–$48.50 double; less Nov–Feb. AE, CB, DC, DISC, MC, V.

This freeway-exit motel lives up to the Best Western standard with spacious, comfortable units in a pleasant setting. Rooms are appointed in desert rose and cornflower blue, with large beds, two sinks (one at the full-mirrored vanity), remote-control television, and clock radio. There's an outdoor pool, open seasonally; K-Bob's steak house is adjacent.

ELEPHANT BUTTE INN, Hwy. 195 (P.O. Box E), Elephant Butte, NM 87935. Tel. 505/744-5431. 49 rms, 1 suite. A/C TV TEL

$ Rates: $45–$55 single, $50–$60 double. $125–$135 suite. AE, CB, DC, MC, V.

★ Situated above the shores of Elephant Butte Reservoir, this homey inn caters to boaters, fishermen, and other relaxation lovers. Rooms are standard motel-style units, with king- or queen-size beds; there's a great 3½-room penthouse suite. The restaurant serves American and New Mexican meals (dinners $6 to $14) from 6am to 9pm daily, an hour later on Friday and Saturday. Chuck-wagon dinners may be served outside. The White Cap Lounge offers live entertainment. The inn has a swimming pool, hot tub, tennis courts, and room service.

RIO GRANDE MOTEL, 720 S. Broadway, Williamsburg, NM 87942. Tel. 505/894-9769. 50 rms. A/C TV TEL

$ Rates: $24–$34 single, $29–$39 double. MC, V.

Located in the suburb of Williamsburg near the south access to T or C from I-25, the Rio Grande offers clean, comfortable rooms for a budget price. Some rooms have kitchenettes. There's an outdoor swimming pool, a guest Laundromat, and a restaurant next door.

RIVER BEND HOT SPRINGS HOSTEL, 100 Austin St., Truth or Consequences, NM 87901. Tel. 505/894-6183. 16 dormitory beds and 2 apartments.

$ Rates: Dorm beds $10 for International Youth Hostel Association members, $13 for nonmembers; apartments $25.

This pleasant hostel, situated beside the Rio Grande, has the added attraction of hot mineral baths on the premises! The apartments are kitchenette units.

STOUT'S GREASEWOOD BED & BREAKFAST, 400 W. 2nd St. (P.O. Box 2280), Truth or Consequences, NM 87901. Tel. 505/894-3157. 1 rm, 1 casita. A/C **Directions:** I-25 to Exit 79, follow Date St. into town. Look for water tank with mural atop a hill. Go right at the stop light; go left at the first stop sign (Foch St.); go left at 2nd St.; drive to the top of the hill.

$ Rates: $40–$50 single or double. MC, V. **Parking:** Free.

You really can't miss the water tank with the mural, "Journey to the Sacred Springs" by Tony Pennock (water tank mural painter of Las Cruces)—it stands high above everything else in T or C. Greasewood (in case you're wondering about the name, it's named for a desert plant that grows in the area) is the only other thing atop the same hill and, as a result, has the greatest view in town. Laverne Stout has carved quite a place out of her hill. Her double-wide mobile home has been rooted to the ground, stuccoed, and surrounded by beautiful landscaped gardens. There is one room in the main house, and it holds a queen-size bed and has light paneling and a full bath. The casita (for those who prefer complete autonomy and privacy) has a full kitchen, full bath, dining area, stereo with CDs and cassettes, and queen-size four poster bed (covered by a down comforter, of course). At night you are treated to fine gourmet chocolates by the bed, and perhaps a small bottle of champagne. Whether you're there for a romantic retreat or not, you can take advantage of the spa (set under a portal) at sunset and enjoy the original R. C. Gorman bronze as well as other fine original pieces of art (including paintings by Delmas Howe and bronzes by Bill Girard). Ask Laverne about her collection of Native American pottery and basketry. Over breakfast, which can be large or small according to your taste and appetite, you can ask Laverne to help you plan your day of sightseeing—she's a veritable font of information about Truth or Consequences and the surrounding area.

WHERE TO DINE

DAM SITE RESTAURANT, Hwy. 177, Elephant Butte. Tel. 894-2073.
   Cuisine: MEXICAN/STEAKS.
$ Prices: Dinners $8–$20. AE, DISC, MC, V.
   Open: Wed–Mon 11am–9pm. **Closed:** Oct–Apr.

It was inevitable that this lakeside restaurant and lounge would give itself the sobriquet "a dam site better." Part of the Dam Site Recreation Area, it overlooks picturesque Elephant Butte Island and bustling marina. Steaks and spicy Mexican dishes are the fare.

K-BOB'S, 2260 N. Date St. Tel. 894-2127.
   Cuisine: STEAKS.
$ Prices: Lunch $3.95–$9.95; dinner $4.95–$13.20. AE, MC, V.
   Open: Sun–Thurs 7am–10pm, Fri–Sat 7am–11pm.

K-Bob's, a New Mexico–wide family steak-house chain, succeeds because it caters to everyone. For example, all meals come with a choice of any of 15 "homestyle veggies." There's a large salad bar; a children's menu; and a selection of beers and wines. Soups, sandwiches, and burgers are always available.

LA COCINA, 228 N. Date St. Tel. 894-6499.
  Cuisine: NEW MEXICAN.
$ **Prices:** Main courses $1.35–$14.50. No credit cards.
  Open: Mon–Sat 11am–11pm, Sun 11am–10pm.

This nicely appointed traditional restaurant serves New Mexican and American meals, including excellent compuestas and chile rellenos. You'll smile at the faces whimsically painted on the restaurant's hanging lamps, draped with sombreros, and you'll be astonished by the size of their sopaipillas.

LA PINATA, 1990 South Broadway. Tel. 894-9047.
  Cuisine: MEXICAN/AMERICAN. **Reservations:** Not necessary.
$ **Prices:** $1.75–$5.50 main courses. No credit cards.
  Open: Mon–Sat 7am–8pm.

For authentic Mexican food at low prices, La Pinata is your best bet. You'll find all the old standbys, including tostadas, chile rellenos, tamales, burritos, and stacked or rolled enchiladas, as well as hamburgers and sandwiches on the menu. The decor is a little more "flashy" than other restaurants in town and the service is fast and friendly. You can order à la carte, or you can get a full meal complete with rice and beans. Portions are large.

LOS ARCOS, 1400 N. Date St. (Hwy. 85). Tel. 894-6200.
  Cuisine: AMERICAN. **Reservations:** Recommended.
$ **Prices:** Appetizers $1.95–$8.95; main courses $9–$23.95. AE, CB, DC, DISC, MC, V.
  Open: Mon–Thurs 5–10:30pm, Fri–Sat 5–11pm, Sun 11am–2pm and 5–10:30pm. **Closed:** Thanksgiving Day, Christmas, 5 days in midwinter, and 1 day in summer.

A spacious hacienda-style restaurant fronted by a lovely desert garden, Los Arcos offers diners an intimate atmosphere and friendly service, as if you're at an old friend's home. Its steaks are regionally famous, and its fish dishes include fresh local catches like walleye pike and catfish. The restaurant also has a fine dessert list and cordial selection.

---

3. LAS CRUCES

225 miles S of Albuquerque; 45 miles N of El Paso, Texas; 272 miles E of Tucson, Ariz.

GETTING THERE   By Plane   Las Cruces International Airport, 8 miles west, has 12 arrivals and departures a day to Albuquerque. Contact **Mesa Airlines** (tel. 526-9743 or toll free 800/MESA-AIR). El Paso International Airport, 47 miles south, is connected 20 times a day to Phoenix, 21 to Dallas, and 32 to Houston. The **Las Cruces Shuttle Service,** 201 E. University Ave. (tel. 525-1784 or toll free 800/288-1784), provides continuing service between the El Paso airport and Las Cruces. It leaves Las Cruces nine times daily between 5am and 11:30pm, with a charge of $21 ($35 round-trip). There's a $5 pick-up or drop-off charge for service elsewhere than its regular stops at the Las Cruces Hilton and Holiday Inn.

By Bus   Greyhound and **TNM&O** both service Las Cruces from a bus depot at 415 S. Valley Dr. near Amador and Lohman (tel. 524-8518 or toll free 800/528-0447). The city is a stop on the Denver–Albuquerque–El Paso, Salt Lake–Albuquerque–El Paso, and Los Angeles–El Paso routes, with 10 departures daily.

By Car   From Albuquerque, take I-25 south (4 hours). From El Paso, take I-10 north (¾ hour). From Tucson, take I-25 east (5 hours).

ESSENTIALS   Orientation   New Mexico's second-largest city is beautifully set in the Mesilla Valley with the spectacular Organ Mountains as a backdrop to the east. I-25 from Albuquerque and I-10 from San Diego intersect here.

Information   The **Las Cruces Convention & Visitors Bureau** is at 311 N. Downtown Mall, Las Cruces, NM 88001 (tel. 505/524-8521 or toll free 800/FIESTAS). The **Las Cruces Chamber of Commerce** is at 760 W. Picacho Ave., Las Cruces, NM 88005 (tel. 524-1968).

Fast Facts   The **area code** is 505. Public transportation is provided by the **RoadRunner** city bus system (tel. 525-2500), with eight routes throughout the city. One-ride fares start at 50¢ for adults, 25¢ for children 6 to 18 and seniors 60 and over. For a taxi, call **Yellow Cab** (tel. 524-1711). **Memorial Medical Center** is located at University Avenue and Telshor Boulevard (tel. 522-8641). The main **post office** is on Las Cruces Avenue at Church Street (tel. 524-2841).

Established in 1849 on the Camino Real, the "royal highway" between Santa Fe and Mexico City, Las Cruces (the crosses) was named for the graves of travelers who had been ambushed here a generation earlier by Apaches. It became a supply center for miners prospecting the Organ Mountains and soldiers stationed at nearby Fort Selden. Today, it is New Mexico's second-largest urban area, with 60,000 people in the city and 100,000 in Dona Ana County. It is noted as an agricultural center, especially for its cotton, pecans, and chiles; as a regional transportation hub; and as the gateway to the White Sands Missile Range and other defense installations.

WHAT TO SEE & DO

Las Cruces's early history is the domain of adjacent ✪ **La Mesilla.** This picturesque village on Las Cruces's southwestern flank was established in the late 1500s by Mexican colonists. It became the crossroads of El Camino Real and the Butterfield Overland Stagecoach route. The Gadsden Purchase, which annexed La Mesilla to the United States and fixed the current international boundaries of New Mexico and Arizona, was signed in this village in 1854.

La Mesilla's most notorious resident, William Bonney (Billy the Kid), was sentenced to death at the county courthouse, but escaped before the sentence was carried out. Legendary hero Pat Garrett eventually tracked down and killed the Kid at Fort Sumner; later, Garrett was mysteriously murdered in an arroyo just outside Las Cruces. He is buried in the local Masonic cemetery.

Thick-walled adobe buildings, which once protected residents against Apache attacks, now house art galleries, restaurants, museums, and gift shops. Throughout Mesilla, colorful red-chile *ristras* decorate homes and businesses.

A WALKING TOUR OF HISTORIC LAS CRUCES

Downtown Las Cruces has numerous historical buildings which make a walking tour well worthwhile. **Bicentennial Log Cabin,** 671 N. Main St., Downtown Mall (tel. 524-1422), is a circa 1879 structure with authentic furnishings and artifacts that was moved here from the Black Range; it's open from June through mid-August from 9:30am to noon, or by appointment. The **Branigan Cultural Center,** 106 W. Hadley Ave., Downtown Mall (tel. 524-1422), has displays of works by local artists and craftspersons, and artifacts from Fort Selden. It includes a gallery, a museum, and an auditorium for lectures, concerts, and performing arts. The **Fountain Theater** was built in 1905 by the Fountain family as a vaudeville house; it is said to be haunted by the ghost of a frustrated actress.

The **Old Armijo House,** Lohman Avenue at Main Street, is an 1860s home that was at one time restored with original furnishings and second-floor display rooms. Now Pioneer Savings and Loan, it is open weekdays from 9am to 4pm but the display rooms are no longer open to the public. **Our Lady at the Foot of the Cross Shrine,** near Main Street and Lohman Avenue, is a reproduction of Michelangelo's

Pietà, dedicated to the Sisters of Loretto. **El Molino,** a grinding wheel from an 1853 flour mill at Water Street and Lohman Avenue, commemorates the work and hardships of early pioneers. The **Amador Hotel,** Amador Avenue and Water Street, built in 1850, once hosted Benito Juarez, Pat Garrett, and Billy the Kid; restored, it now houses county offices, and is not open to the public.

OTHER ATTRACTIONS

SAN ALBINO CHURCH, north side of Old Mesilla Plaza.

This is one of the oldest churches in the Mesilla valley. Constructed in 1851, the present structure was built some 55 years later (1906) on its original foundation. It was named for St. Albin, medieval English bishop of North Africa, on whose day an important irrigation ditch from the Rio Grande was completed. The church bells date to the early 1870s; the pews were made in Taos of Philippine mahogany.

Admission: Free; donations appreciated.

Open: Tours Tues–Sun 1–3pm; English-language masses Sat 6:30pm and Sun 11am.

GADSDEN MUSEUM, Hwy. 28 and Barker Rd. Tel. 526-6293.

A famous painting of the signing of the Gadsden Purchase is a highlight of this collection, donated by the Albert Jennings Fountain family. The museum, three blocks east of the Old Mesilla Plaza, also houses Indian and Civil War relics and Old West artifacts. Visitors must go on the museum's guided tour.

Admission: Adults $2, children 6–12 $1.

Open: Mon–Sat 9–11am, daily 1–5pm.

NEW MEXICO STATE UNIVERSITY, University Ave. and Locust St. Tel. 646-0111.

Established in 1888, this institution of 14,300 students is especially noted for its schools of business, engineering, and agriculture. Its facilities include the Solar Energy Institute, the Water Resources Institute of New Mexico, and the New Mexico Environmental Institute.

University Museum in Kent Hall (tel. 646-3739) has exhibits of historic and prehistoric Indian culture and art exhibits; it's open Tuesday through Saturday from 10am to 4pm and Sunday from 1 to 4pm, with free admission. The **Williams Hall Art Gallery** (tel. 646-2545) features monthly exhibits of contemporary and historical art, and a permanent collection of prints, photographs, and folk art. **Corbett Center Gallery,** in the student center (tel. 646-3200), has various exhibits throughout the year; a 12-foot copper-alloy triangle outside has a notch that symbolizes the shift from youth to adulthood. **Clyde Tombaugh Observatory,** named for the discoverer of the planet Pluto (who is a current resident of Las Cruces), has a high-powered telescope open for public viewing one evening a month. The **Southwest Residential Experiment Station** has eight working solar-photovoltaic prototypes on view; guided tours are available by reservation from the visitor center (tel. 646-1049).

COOL FOR KIDS

LAS CRUCES MUSEUM OF NATURAL HISTORY, Mesilla Valley Mall, Telshor Boulevard. Tel. 522-3120.

This small city-funded museum offers a variety of exhibits, changing quarterly, that emphasize zoology, microbiology, meteorology, cartography, and local history. Permanent exhibits present baby spadefoot toads, leopard frogs, a gopher snake, an aquarium of native fish, and box turtles.

Admission: Free.

Open: Tues–Thurs and Sun noon–5pm, Fri noon–9pm, Sat 10am–6pm.

SPORTS & RECREATION

New Mexico State University football, basketball, baseball, and other teams play intercollegiate schedules in the Big West Conference, against schools from California,

Nevada, and Utah. The "Aggies" play their home games on the NMSU campus, south of University Avenue on Locust Street. Football is played in the Chili Bowl, basketball in Pan Am Center arena.

Fishing   The **Rio Grande** is considered one of the nation's great fishing streams and **Burn Lake,** Amador Avenue at I-10, is also stocked with panfish.

Golf   Two year-round public courses are the **Las Cruces Country Club,** Highway 70 North at Solano Drive (tel. 526-8731), open from 8am to dusk Tuesday through Sunday; and the **NMSU Golf Course,** Telshore Boulevard and University Avenue (tel. 646-3219), open dawn to dusk daily except Thanksgiving and Christmas.

Hiking   The most popular spot for day hikes near Las Cruces is **Aguirre Springs Recreation Area** (tel. 525-8228), 20 miles east of the city off U.S. Highway 70, on the eastern flanks of the Organ Mountains.

Horse Racing   New Mexico's only winter racing takes place 40 miles south of Las Cruces at **Sunland Park.** The ponies run Friday, Saturday, and Sunday, October to May.

Swimming   There are public pools at **Apodaca Park,** 801 E. Madrid St. (tel. 524-7008); **Frenger Park,** Parkview and West Park drives (tel. 523-0362); and **LAABS,** 750 W. Picacho Ave. (tel. 524-3168). All are open mid-May to Labor Day. There's also swimming at little **Burn Lake,** Amador Avenue at I-10.

Tennis   Public courts can be found at **Apodaca Park,** 801 E. Madrid St.; **Frenger Park,** 800 Parkview Dr.; and **Young Park,** 1905 E. Nevada Ave.

SHOPPING

Before you get started with cash and credit, be aware that in Las Cruces, Monday is a notoriously quiet day. Most downtown stores, and many in La Mesilla, close their doors for the day, preferring to serve customers on Saturday instead. Business hours, therefore, are commonly Tuesday to Saturday from 10am to 5pm.

For **art,** visit **Linda Lundeen Galleries,** 618 Alameda Blvd. (tel. 526-3327), open from 9am to 6pm daily; **Rising Sky Artworks,** 415 E. Foster (tel. 525-8454), from 9am to 5pm Monday to Saturday; **Universal & Community Center of the Arts,** 207 Avenida de Mesilla (tel. 523-0014), from 10am to 5pm Tuesday to Friday, 1 to 5pm Saturday and Sunday; and the **William Bonney Gallery,** 3 Calle Parian, in the old courthouse at the southeast corner of Old Mesilla Plaza (tel. 526-8275), open Monday to Saturday from 10am to 6pm, Sunday noon to 5pm.

For **books,** try **Mesilla Book Center,** in an 1856 mercantile building on the west side of Old Mesilla Plaza (tel. 526-6220), open from 11am to 5:30pm Tuesday to Saturday and 1 to 5pm on Sunday.

For native **crafts and jewelry,** check out **Silver Assets,** Calle de Santiago (tel. 523-8747), 1½ blocks east of San Albino Church in La Mesilla.

Got a sweet tooth? **J. Eric Chocolatier,** on the east side of Old Mesilla Plaza (tel. 526-2744), is open Tuesday to Saturday from 11am to 5pm and noon to 5pm on Sunday.

Mesilla Valley Mall is a full-service shopping center on Telshor Boulevard, just off the I-25 interchange with Lohman Avenue.

Farmers Market operates Wednesday and Saturday mornings (from 8am to noon) on the Downtown Mall (tel. 526-1737). Local produce, baked goods, arts, and crafts are commonly available.

EVENING ENTERTAINMENT

National recording artists frequently perform at NMSU's **Pan Am Center** (tel. 646-4413). The NMSU Music Department (tel. 646-2421) offers free jazz, classical and pop concerts, and the **Las Cruces Symphony** often performs here as well.

Hershel Zohn Theater (tel. 646-4515), at NMSU, presents plays of the **American Southwest Theatre Company**—dramas, comedies, musicals, and original works. ASTC is headed by Mark Medoff, who won a Tony Award for his play, *Children of a Lesser God.*

The **Las Cruces Community Theatre** (tel. 523-1200) mounts six productions a year at its own facility on the Downtown Mall. Other important local companies are the **Las Cruces Chamber Ballet** and the **Right Combination Dance Company.**

A popular country-music and dancing club is **Cowboys,** 2205 S. Main St. (tel. 525-9050), with no cover Wednesday, $1 Monday, $2 Tuesday, $2.50 Thursday through Saturday. Closed Sunday. For rock music, try the **Sports Connection,** 855 S. Valley Dr. (tel. 525-9534), $2 Wednesday, $2 men only Thursday, $3 Friday and Saturday.

NEARBY ATTRACTIONS
NORTH OF LAS CRUCES

The town of **Hatch,** 39 miles via I-25 or 34 miles via N.M. 185, calls itself the "chile capital of the world." It is the center of a 22,000-acre agricultural belt which grows and processes more chile than anywhere else in the world. The annual Hatch Chile Festival over the Labor Day weekend celebrates the harvest. For information, call the Hatch Chamber of Commerce (tel. 267-3021).

FORT SELDEN STATE MONUMENT, 15 miles north of Las Cruces between I-25 and N.M. 185. Tel. 526-8911.

Founded in 1865, it housed the famous Black Cavalry, the "Buffalo Soldiers" who protected settlers from marauding Indians. It was subsequently the boyhood home of Gen. Douglas MacArthur, whose father, Arthur, was in charge of troops patrolling the U.S.-Mexican border in the 1880s. There are only eroding ruins remaining today. Displays in the visitor center tell Fort Selden's story, including photos of young Douglas and his family. The fort closed permanently 100 years ago, in 1891. Adjacent to the state monument, **Leasburg Dam State Park** (tel. 524-4068) offers picnicking, camping, boating, and swimming.

Admission: Adults $2; free for children 15 and under.
Open: Daily 9am–6pm.

SOUTH OF LAS CRUCES

Stahmann Farms, 10 miles south of La Mesilla on N.M. 28 (tel. 526-2453), is one of the world's largest single producers of pecans. Several million pounds are harvested annually from orchards in the bed of an ancient lake. Tours are given by appointment. **Stahmann's Country Store** sells pecans and pecan candy; it's open weekdays from 9am to 5:30pm, weekends from noon to 4pm.

Local wineries are glad to give tours and tastings. They include **Binns Vineyards & Winery** (tel. 526-6738), **Estrada Winery** (tel. 526-4017), and **La Vina Winery** (tel. 882-2092).

EAST OF LAS CRUCES

The **Organ Mountains,** so-called because they resemble the pipes of a church organ, draw inevitable comparisons to Wyoming's Grand Tetons. Organ Peak, at 9,119 feet, is the highest point in Dona Ana County.

The **Aguirre Springs Recreation Area** (tel. 525-8228), off U.S. Highway 70 on the western slope of the Organ Mountains, is operated by the Bureau of Land Management. Activities include hiking, camping, and picnicking, and there are horse trails here, too.

White Sands Testing Facility and Missile Range, NASA's "Man to the Moon" Apollo Site, 19 miles east of Las Cruces and 4 miles south of U.S. 70, is in the bone-dry Tularosa Valley at the eastern foot of the Organ Mountains. The guidance rocket control systems for the space shuttle were tested here, and a "low-level satellite communications system" is being installed. The missile range covers 4,000 square miles primarily north and east from here; it is the largest land-based missile testing facility in the United States.

WHERE TO STAY

Las Cruces has the wide variety of accommodations expected in a town of its size and importance. Local lodging tax of 5% is added to the state tax for a whopping 11.25% addition to every hotel bill.

MODERATE

BEST WESTERN MESILLA VALLEY INN, 901 Avenida de Mesilla at I-25, Las Cruces, NM 88005. Tel. 505/524-8603 or toll free 800/528-1234. Fax: 505/526-8437. 167 rms, 4 suites. A/C FRIDGE TV TEL

$ Rates: $40–$51 single, $48–$58 double. Suites to $120. AE, CB, DC, DISC, MC, V.

A large motel set on spacious grounds near the north-south freeway, the Mesilla Valley Inn offers rooms that are standard in almost every way but their paneled Oriental-motif artwork. Each has a king-size or two double beds, particleboard furnishings, a vanity, and a wardrobe rack instead of a closet. The newer Executive Building has a security entrance; its upgraded rooms are more spacious, with all king-size beds, maple furnishings, and historical photos on the walls. Children are not allowed in this wing. A refrigerator is available free on request in any room. Some rooms have kitchenette facilities.

Eddie's Bar and Grill serves three American or continental-style meals daily (6am to 2pm and 5 to 10pm) in a sidewalk-café atmosphere. Lunches (including buffalo burgers) run $3.95 to $7.50, dinners $9.50 to $16.95. There's an enormous salad bar here. The adjacent lounge has a piano bar and sometimes books light jazz combos. The inn has room service, valet laundry, handicapped and nonsmoking rooms, an outdoor swimming pool, Jacuzzi, guest laundry, and meeting space for 350. There is a nominal membership fee to use a nearby health and racquet club.

HOLIDAY INN DE LAS CRUCES, 201 E. University Ave. at I-10 (P.O. Drawer HI), Las Cruces, NM 88004. Tel. 505/526-4411 or toll free 800/HOLIDAY. Fax: 505/524-0530. AC, TV, TEL.

$ Rates: $61–$64 single, $69–$72 double. AE, CB, DC, DISC, JCB, MC, V.

⭐ This is like a traditional Mexican village indoors! Steep tiled roofs and wrought-iron balconies hang above the blue-tiled registration desk. To your left at the entry, the Pancho Villa Café and Cantina occupy a mock adobe courtyard with trees and street lamps. Several 19th-century stagecoaches are nearby; shops and offices face them. On your right, the swimming pool area is surrounded by greenery.

Standard rooms, all of which face in toward the courtyard or out toward garden landscaping, have king-size or two double beds, big wood headboards, solid wood furnishings, southwest-style bedspreads, and full mirrors on the vanity. There are rooms for nonsmokers and the disabled.

The Pancho Villa Café, open from 6am to 10pm daily, serves Mexican food and sandwiches in the $4.95-to-$7.95 range. The adjoining cantina has photos of Pancho Villa and his gang on the back wall. The Billy the Kid ("BK's") Restaurant and Saloon offers fine dining in a Wild West atmosphere, complete with photos, guns, and "Reward" posters. Steak, chicken, seafood, and barbecue dinners run $8.95 to $22.95, the top price for a 28-ounce T-bone steak. BK's has good desserts, a full bar, and live entertainment Tuesday through Sunday nights for dancing after dinner. Services and facilities include room service, valet laundry, a large indoor swimming pool and wading pool, guest laundry, video game room, two gift shops, newsstand, jogging path, and convention facilities for 1,000. Pets are welcome.

LUNDEEN'S INN OF THE ARTS, 618 S. Alameda Blvd., Las Cruces, NM 88005. Tel. 505/526-3327 or toll free 800/553-4ART. Fax: 505/526-3355. 15 rms, 2 suites. A/C

$ Rates (including breakfast): $55 single, $60 double, $75–$90 suite. AE, MC, V. Operated by Gerald Lundeen, an architect and circuit preacher, and his wife Linda, who operates an art gallery in the front of the inn, this bed-and-breakfast establishment is worth a trip in itself. A late 1890s adobe built in Territorial style, it displays the works of about 30 Southwest painters, sculptors, and potters in its 14,000 square feet of floor space. Outside, guests can help Gerry make adobe bricks for building a large *horno* (outdoor oven) and courtyard with mission archways.

Rooms are named for noted regional artists, like Georgia O'Keeffe, Amado Pena, R. C. Gorman, Frederic Remington, Nicolai Fechin, and Gordon Snidow, and each features the flavor of that artist. Every room is different, but all have wooden floors, tubs or bidets, and regional touches. Two suites have kitchenettes, a private TV and telephone. Others share the TV and telephone in a downstairs common area. Some rooms have fireplaces. Breakfast is a full gourmet occasion, including fresh fruit and eggs, pancakes, strudels, and so forth.

The inn is a popular spot for weddings and artists' workshops. The ElderHostel program also stays here. Guests get reduced rates at local health club, and Gerry Lundeen will take them on architectural walking tours of La Mesilla. Lundeen's Inn of the Arts is only five minutes from La Mesilla.

LAS CRUCES HILTON, 705 S. Telshor Blvd., Las Cruces, NM 88001. Tel. 505/522-4300 or toll free 800/284-0616. Fax 505/521-4707. 202 rms, 7 suites. A/C TV TEL
$ Rates: $56–$63 single, $58–$68 double, $90–$145 suite. Weekend packages from $55 for a family, including breakfast. AE, CB, DC, DISC, MC, V.

Las Cruces's finest hotel was built in 1987 on a hill on the east side of the city, across the street from the Mesilla Valley Mall. Its pleasant tiled lobby has southwestern-style furnishings in pastel shades. That motif carries to the decor of the spacious rooms, each of which has a king- or two queen-size beds, and all standard furnishings, including a working desk. Some rooms accommodate nonsmokers or the disabled.

The Ventana Terrace serves breakfast and lunches daily from 6am to 2pm, then does a make-over to fine gourmet dining from 5 to 10pm nightly, with southwestern and continental specialties in the $10.95-to-$15.95 range for main courses. The Opus piano lounge has live music Thursday through Saturday nights. Illusions, the only Top-40 dance club in Las Cruces, offers a mixed bag of Tuesday comedy, Wednesday-and-Thursday live jazz, and Friday-and-Saturday disco dancing.

The hotel offers room service (6am to 10pm), 24-hour desk, courtesy van, valet laundry, secretarial service, an outdoor swimming pool, Jacuzzi, gift shop, car rental, and discount guest passes to a local athletic club. There is meeting space for 700.

MESÓN DE MESILLA, 1803 Avenida de Mesilla (P.O. Box 1212), La Mesilla, NM 88046. Tel. 505/525-9212. Fax: 505/525-2380. 13 rms, 2 suites. A/C TV TEL
$ Rates (including breakfast): $52–$82 single or double. AE, CB, DC, DISC, MC, V.

This large adobe home is a landmark on Highway 28 into Mesilla, and host Chuck Walker likes to say it has the "ambience of a Wine Country inn." Surrounded by beautiful gardens and adjacent to cotton fields, it certainly has the setting.

A portico surrounds the second floor, where the homey guest rooms are located. Appointed in southwestern motifs with clock radios, brass headboards, antiques, and ceiling fans, each room has a private bath, shower, and tub. Phones can be used for outgoing calls only; incoming messages are taken at the switchboard. A full breakfast is served in the garden atrium of the gourmet restaurant (see "Where to Dine," below).

Facilities include an outdoor swimming pool, horseshoes, bicycles (including a tandem) free for guests' use.

INEXPENSIVE

BEST WESTERN MISSION INN, 1765 S. Main St., Las Cruces, NM 88005. Tel. 505/524-8591 or toll free 800/528-1234. 70 rms, 2 suites. A/C TV TEL

$ Rates: $40 single, $55 double, $65 suite. AE, CB, DC, DISC, MC, V.

The grounds of this two-story motel have several trees, including a big weeping willow shading a picnic table. Rooms are spacious, with a king- or two queen-size beds. Colorful flowers are stenciled on the walls, big mirrors are surrounded by Mexican tiles, and there's a tile shelf behind the beds, giving it the mission look of its name. There are rooms for nonsmokers and the disabled.

Senor Toucan's Coffee Shop is open daily from 6am–2pm. The Hidden Forrest restaurant serves steaks and seafood nightly (see "Where to Dine," below). The Sports Connection is a big-screen lounge with a deejay dance floor. The inn provides room service, 24-hour desk, valet laundry, an outdoor swimming pool, and a small playground with shuffleboard; VCRs and movies are available at the front desk.

HIGH COUNTRY INN, 2160 W. Picacho Ave., Las Cruces, NM 88004. Tel. 505/524-8627. 120 rms, 5 suites. A/C TV TEL

$ Rates (including morning doughnuts and coffee): $19–$26 single, $26–$32 double, $38 suite. AE, CB, DC, DISC, MC, V.

An older property built around a central swimming pool, the High Country is in need of a renovation. Its sparse lobby offers few amenities other than video games and a billiards table. Rooms are made to look larger than they are by a full mirrored wall behind the bed/s. The soft goods are gray, with dark-wood furnishings, vinyl-upholstered chairs, and a dressing table outside the bathroom. Next door to the motel is the Dynasty Restaurant. There are nonsmoking and handicapped rooms, an outdoor swimming pool, guest Laundromat, and meeting space for 200.

HILLTOP HACIENDA, 2520 Westmoreland Rd., Las Cruces, NM 88001. Tel. 505/382-3556. 3 rms. A/C

$ Rates (including continental breakfast): $45 single, $55 double. MC, V.

The bed-and-breakfast home of Bob and Teddi Peters is situated on 10 acres of land, 10 minutes' drive north of the city. A two-story, arched-adobe brick dwelling of Spanish Moorish architectural style, it offers spectacular views of the city, Rio Grande valley, and Organ Mountains. Breakfast is served outdoors on a wide patio or indoors beside a large fireplace. No smoking or pets are permitted.

WHERE TO DINE

EXPENSIVE

THE DOUBLE EAGLE, east side of Old Mesilla Plaza. Tel. 523-6700.
Cuisine: CONTINENTAL. **Reservations:** Recommended.

$ Prices: Appetizers $3.50–$6.25; lunch $4.95–$8.25; dinner $11.95–$20.95. AE, CB, DC, DISC, MC, V.

Open: Mon–Sat 11am–10pm, Sun noon–9pm.

The recent restoration of this 150-year-old hacienda has put the imposing Territorial-style premises on the National Historic Sites register. Its 30-foot-long bar has Corinthian columns in gold leaf, and there are Gay Nineties oil paintings of nudes, and 18-armed brass chandeliers hung with Baccarat crystals. A woman's ghost is said to frequent one of the several exquisite small dining rooms. The lush red of carpet and chair upholstery contrasts richly with the dark tones of polished wood in tables, sideboards, and paneling. Specialties of the house include quail, breast of chicken Mesilla, 16-ounce pink mountain trout, and an 18-ounce filet mignon. All portions are generous. There is a lavish salad bar, international-style desserts and coffees, and a good wine and beer list. Sandwiches and light meals are served at lunch.

MESÓN DE MESILLA, 1803 Avenida de Mesilla, La Mesilla. Tel. 525-9212.
 Cuisine: CONTINENTAL. **Reservations:** Required.
$ **Prices:** Appetizers $4.95; lunch $4.75–$7.60; Sun brunch $12.95, dinner $14.25–$20.50. AE, CB, DC, DISC, MC, V.
 Open: Lunch Wed–Fri 11am–2pm, dinner Tues–Sat 5:30–8:45pm, champagne brunch Sun 11am–2pm.

Located in an elegant bed-and-breakfast at the northeast gateway to La Mesilla, this gourmet restaurant has a Spanish colonial ambience with carved wooden pillars, stained-glass windows, wrought-iron chairs, and a rich burgundy color scheme. Chef Bob Herrera's blackboard menu changes weekly, but always presents several varieties of fresh fish, chicken, beef, and Eastern veal. All meals include soup, salad, main course, vegetables, and dessert. Main courses might be sautéed quail à la meson, black sea bass, shrimp Cardinale, or chateaubriand. Lunches feature salads, sandwiches, quiches, and a buffet. There's a new lounge in Cueva de Vina (the Wine Cavern), and an extensive wine and beer list.

MODERATE

CATTLE BARON, 709 S. Telshore Blvd. Tel. 522-7533.
 Cuisine: STEAKS & SEAFOOD. **Reservations:** Not taken for parties under 6.
$ **Prices:** Appetizers $2.50–$5.75; lunch $3.95–$6.50, dinner main courses $6.75–$19.95. AE, DISC, MC, V.
 Open: Sun–Thurs 11am–9:30pm, Fri–Sat 11am–10pm.
An elegant restaurant with burgundy decor, green marble tabletops, and suspended brass lamps, the Cattle Baron is within walking distance of the Hilton. Its lounge displays unique works of original southwestern art on the walls.
 The menu, ranging from filet Oscar to broiled mahimahi, features a wide choice of steaks, chicken, and seafood, including fresh catches of the day. There are homemade soups, a huge salad bar, a children's menu, and desserts such as mud pie. The most expensive thing on the menu is *not* the prime rib/crab legs combination ($18.95); it's a peanut butter sandwich with jelly ($19.95).

HIDDEN FORREST, at Best Western Mission Inn, 1765 S. Main St. Tel. 524-8591.
 Cuisine: STEAKS & SEAFOOD. **Reservations:** Recommended.
$ **Prices:** Appetizers $3.50–$5.95, main courses $8.25–$18.95. AE, CB, DC, DISC, MC, V.
 Open: Daily 5–10pm.
Here's the place to come for intimate candlelight dining in a forest green decor. In summer, you can opt to dine in the outside courtyard. Meals include the likes of steak Delmonico, veal piccata, and Lost Padre Island brochette (shrimp and artichoke hearts wrapped in bacon and skewered). An extensive wine list accompanies dinner.

PEPPERS, east side of Old Mesilla Plaza. Tel. 523-4999.
 Cuisine: NEW MEXICAN. **Reservations:** For large parties only.
$ **Prices:** Tapas (appetizers) $1.35–$4.95, lunch $4.95–$7.50, dinner $7.50–$14.95. AE, CB, DC, DISC, MC, V.
 Open: Mon–Sat 10am–10pm, Sun 11am–9pm.

This restaurant shares a building and the same ownership with the Double Eagle, but the resemblance ends there. The Eagle has age and grace; Peppers has youthful exuberance. Hispanic folk art, including traditional masks and *santiagos,* greets guests in the entryway. Music from the sixties and seventies plays continuously. There are cacti on the tables. A regional artist is featured in the gallery.
 The cuisine is Santa Fe–style New Mexican, heavy on seafood, such as the seafood

chimichanga and blue-corn catfish. Other dishes include the La Fonda strip (sirloin with black beans and a guacamole-and-chipotle sauce). Tapas include green-chile wontons and tortilla-wrapped shrimp with pineapple-chile salsa.

TATSU, 930 El Paseo Dr. Tel. 526-7144.
  Cuisine: JAPANESE.
  $ Prices: Appetizers $3–$6.25; main courses $7.95–$13.95. AE, DC, MC, V.
  Open: Mon–Thurs 11am–9pm, Fri 11am–10pm, Sat noon–10pm, Sun 11am–2pm and 5–9pm.

Tatsu may not be classic Japanese by New York or L.A. standards, but it does well for southern New Mexico. There are no tatami rooms here, but hanging paper lanterns and other designer touches lend a feeling of authenticity. Big windows face the street in the front room. There's somewhat more traditional decor in a rear chamber which houses a Japanese garden.

Sushi, sukiyaki, and soba plates are integral to the menu. The tempura is excellent—seafood, vegetables, and a spicy relleno pepper. "East Meets West" specials include pecan chicken katsu, ginger beef, and soft-shell crab. Imported Japanese beers, saké, and wines are served with meals. There's a children's menu as well.

INEXPENSIVE

EL PATIO RESTAURANTE Y CANTINA, south side of Old Mesilla Plaza. Tel. 524-0982.
  Cuisine: NEW MEXICAN & AMERICAN.
  $ Prices: Lunch $3.75–$4.50, dinner $4.50–$10.95. AE, MC, V.
  Open: Lunch Mon–Fri 11am–2pm, dinner Mon–Thurs 5:30–9:30pm, Fri–Sat 5:30–9:30pm.

This early 19th-century adobe home has been a Customs house, Wells Fargo office, and newspaper office. Today it's a popular restaurant giving new twists to old Mexican recipes, such as enchiladas, rellenos, tacos, and burritos. Steaks and burgers are also served. The adjoining cantina is a classic New Mexican bar!

FAJITAS, 600 E. Amador Ave. at Tornillo St. Tel. 523-6407.
  Cuisine: NEW MEXICAN.
  $ Prices: Main dishes $3.45–$9.95. AE, DISC, MC, V.
  Open: Daily 11am–2pm and 5–9pm.

A turn-of-the-century adobe that still has its original *vigas* and hardwood floors, Fajitas also has rebuilt fireplaces and an indoor brick patio. Its mesquite-broiled beef, chicken, pork or shrimp fajitas are served with grilled, marinated onions and green chile on a sizzling platter, with frijoles, guacamole, pico de gallo, and flour or corn tortillas. Enchiladas, tacos, and nachos are also on the menu, and there's a full bar.

HENRY J'S GOURMET HAMBURGERS, 523 E. Idaho St. Tel. 525-2211.
  Cuisine: AMERICAN.
  $ Prices: Sandwiches and hamburgers $2.95–$4.75; full meals $5.95–$12.95. AE, DISC, MC, V.
  Open: Sun–Thurs 10:30am–9pm, Fri–Sat 10:30am–10pm.

Much more than a huge fifties soda fountain—which it incorporates—Henry J's has seating on three levels amidst big bay windows, brass railings, framed period advertisements, and a Wurlitzer jukebox. Besides great hamburgers, the restaurant has a large salad bar and a "bottomless" soup bowl priced at just $2.

LA POSTA, southeast corner of Old Mesilla Plaza. Tel. 524-3524.
  Cuisine: NEW MEXICAN & STEAKS. **Reservations:** Recommended.
  $ Prices: Main courses $2.80–$11.95. AE, CB, DC, DISC, MC, V.
  Open: Sun–Thurs 11am–9pm, Fri–Sat 11am–9:30pm.

The only surviving stagecoach station of the Butterfield, Overland Mail Route from Tipton, Missouri, to San Francisco, in the late 19th century, La Posta occupies an adobe building over 175 years old. Kit Carson, Pancho Villa, and Billy the Kid all ate here. The entrance leads through a jungle of tall plants beneath a Plexiglas roof, past a tank of piranhas and a noisy aviary of macaws, cockatiels, and Amazon parrots, to nine dining rooms with bright, festive decor.

The menu features steaks and such Mexican dinners as "Specialty of La Posta"—chile con queso and corn tortillas, guacamole and salad; rolled red enchiladas, tamale, frijoles, chili con carne, rolled taco, hot corn tortillas; ice cream and coffee. That's a lot of food! Beer and wine are served with meals.

MY BROTHER'S PLACE, 334 Main St. at Amador Ave. Tel. 523-7681.
   Cuisine: NEW MEXICAN.
$ **Prices:** Lunch specials from $4.10; dinner $4.65–$14.25. AE, MC, V.
   Open: Mon–Thurs 11am–9pm, Fri–Sat 11am–10pm.
Located between the Downtown Mall and the historic Amador Hotel, the Gutierrez brothers' modern adobe hacienda boasts a central fountain, tiled planters, *vigas,* and arches. Mexican menu favorites include fajitas and a hot-hot green enchilada; barbecues and burgers are also popular.

Three lounges adjoin the restaurant. The Main Street Lounge has an indoor patio overlooking the street from the second story. PM's Billiards Club and the Cantina Game Room have 15 pool tables between them. Margaritas are served by the glass and the pitcher.

SANTA FE RESTAURANT, 1410 S. Solano Dr. at Foster Rd. Tel. 522-0466.
   Cuisine: SOUTHWESTERN. **Reservations:** Recommended on weekends.
$ **Prices:** Appetizers $2.50–$5.95; lunch $3.25–$12.50; dinner $4.25–$13.95. AE, DISC, MC, V.
   Open: Sun–Thurs 11:30am–2pm and 5–10pm, Fri–Sat 11:30am–10pm.
There's not much atmosphere here—merely a nonsmoking area with fishbowl windows on a busy intersection, and a more cloistered smoking section. But then, this is a young restaurant—owner Scott Bannister is 28, and its eldest chef is 30—and they're still excited about being on stage. "It's us against the world," says Bannister. "It's a storybook, man. We're all real tight here."

The menu is Old World Mexican . . . with Italian touches and French presentation. Examples: Free-range chicken with smoked chile butter, panfried and served atop fried Tabasco onions; filet mignon Jerez, sautéed in marsala sauce with mushrooms, onions, peppers, and Dijon mustard; shrimp three continents, stuffed with scallops, sole, crab, atop a cream chile reduction. Beer and wine are served.

4. DEMING & LORDSBURG

Deming is 59 miles W of Las Cruces, 213 miles E of Tucson, Ariz.
Lordsburg is 119 miles W of Las Cruces, 153 miles E of Tucson

GETTING THERE By Plane Deming's **Grant County Airport** serves private planes only. A van line, **DART** (tel. 546-6511), shuttles to and from El Paso airport on a request basis.

By Train **Amtrak** trains pass through three times weekly, each direction, on their Los Angeles–El Paso run. The depot in Deming is at 301 E. Railroad Ave.; in Lordsburg on Motel Drive at Main Street. (Neither has a phone.) Tickets must be booked in advance with a travel agent or Amtrak (tel. toll free 800/USA-RAIL).

By Bus Coaches on **Greyhound**'s Las Cruces–Tucson line stop daily, each direction, in Deming and Lordsburg. The bus station in Deming is at 300 E. Spruce St. (tel. 546-3881); in Lordsburg, buses stop at McDonald's restaurant, South Main and Pine streets.

By Car   From Las Cruces, take I-10 west (1 hour to Deming, 2 hours to Lordsburg). From Tucson, take I-10 east (3 hours to Lordsburg, 4 hours to Deming).

ESSENTIALS   Orientation   Both towns are on the northern edge of the Chihuahuan Desert. Deming's downtown area lies just south of I-10, Lordsburg's just north. In each case, the main street parallels the east-west freeway.

Information   The **Deming–Luna County Chamber of Commerce,** 800 E. Pine St., Deming, NM 88030 (tel. 505/546-2674); and the **New Mexico Welcome Center,** Exit 20, I-10, Deming, NM 88045 (tel. 505/542-8149), are the most reliable sources. The **Lordsburg Hidalgo County Chamber of Commerce** maintains a part-time office at 1000 S. Main St., Lordsburg, NM 88045.

Fast Facts   The **area code** is 505. **Mimbres Memorial Hospital** in Deming is located at 900 W. Ash St. (tel. 546-2761). The Deming **post office** is at Spruce and Copper streets (tel. 546-9461); in Lordsburg, it's at Third and Shakespeare streets. In case of **emergency,** dial 911 or 0 for an operator.

New Mexico's least populated corner is this one, which includes the "boot heel" of the Gadsden Purchase that pokes 40 miles down into Mexico. These two railroad towns, an hour apart on I-10, see a lot of traffic; but whereas Deming (pop. 12,000) is thriving as a ranching center, Lordsburg (pop. 3,000) is watching its population dwindle. This is a popular area for rock hounds, aficionados of ghost towns, and history buffs: Columbus, 32 miles south of Deming, was the site of the last foreign incursion on continental American soil, by the Mexican bandit-revolutionary Pancho Villa in 1916.

WHAT TO SEE & DO

DEMING

DEMING LUNA MIMBRES MUSEUM, 301 S. Silver St., Deming. Tel. 546-2382.

Deming was the meeting place of the second east-west railroad to connect the Pacific and Atlantic coasts, and that heritage is recalled in this museum, run by the Luna County Historical Society. In the basement of the old Deming Armory, it's one of those charming everybody's-attic museums, with the left-hand oven built into a stove for an early left-handed cook, and an old wooden sign: "Warning: Fine of $2 to $10 for Leaving Your Team Untied." It shows some pioneer-era quilts and laces, a military room containing mementos of 19th century forts and raids, a doll room with over 800 dolls, and pottery from the Mimbres people who lived here around A.D. 1000. There's a gem and mineral room, a display of ladies' fashions from the Gay Nineties to the Roaring Twenties, a variety of pioneer silver, china, and crystal, and a new Transportation Annex with a chuck wagon—a "traveling kitchen." The museum also houses a collection of 2,200 bells from all over the world, as well as about 1800 liquor decanters.

Admission: By donation.

Open: Mon–Sat 9am–4pm, Sun 1:30–4pm. **Closed:** Thanksgiving Day and Christmas.

ROCKHOUND STATE PARK, 14 miles southeast of Deming via N.M. 11 South.

Here at the base of the wild Florida Mountains is an arid, cactus-covered land with trails leading down into dry gullies and canyons. Visitors are encouraged to pick and take home with them as much as 15 pounds of minerals—jasper, agate, quartz crystal, flow-banded rhyolite, and other rocks. (You may have to walk a bit, as the more accessible minerals have been largely picked out.)

The campground here, which has shelters, rest rooms, showers, and a playground, gives a distant view of the untroubled mountain ranges all the way south to the Mexican border. The mountains offer hunting for bear, cougar, Barbary sheep, bighorn sheep, oryx, ibex, elk, antelope, deer, javelina, and turkey.

Admission: Free.
Open: Year round.

PANCHO VILLA STATE PARK, N.M. Highway 11, Columbus. Tel. 505/ 531-2708.

Some 32 miles south of Deming is the tiny border town of Columbus, looking across at Mexico. The state park here marks the last time there was a foreign invasion of American soil. A temporary fort, where a tiny garrison was housed in tents, was attacked in 1916 by 600 Mexican revolutionaries, who cut through the boundary fence at Columbus. Eighteen Americans were killed, 12 wounded; an estimated 200 Mexican died. The Mexicans immediately retreated across their border. An American punitive expedition, headed by Gen. John J. Pershing, was launched into Mexico, but got nowhere. Villa restricted his banditry to Mexico after that, until his assassination in 1923.

Some ruins of the border fort, called Camp Furlong, are to be seen at the state park, which has a strikingly beautiful desert botanical garden worth the trip alone. It also has campsites with shelters, rest rooms, showers, a dump station, and a playground. For information, write the **Columbus Historical Society,** P.O. Box 562, Columbus, NM 88029.

Three miles south is Las Palomas, Chihuahua (pop. 1,500), the only U.S.-Mexico border crossing from New Mexico. The port of entry is open 24 hours. Numerous restaurants and tourist-oriented businesses are located in Las Palomas.

LORDSBURG

Visitors to Lordsburg can go ✪ **rockhounding** in an area rich in minerals of many kinds. Desert roses can be found near Summit, and agate is known to exist in many abandoned mines locally. Mine dumps, southwest of Hachita, contain lead, zinc, and gold. There is manganese in the Animas mountains. Volcanic glass can be picked up in Coronado National Forest, and there is panning for gold in Gold Gulch.

Rodeo, 30 miles southwest via I-10 and U.S. 80, is the home of the **Chiricahua Gallery** (tel. 557-2225), open Tuesday through Saturday from 10am to 4pm, Arizona time. Regional artists have joined in a nonprofit, cooperative venture to exhibit works and offer classes in a variety of media. Many choose to live on the high-desert slopes of the Chiricahua Range. The gallery is on Highway 80 en route to Douglas, Arizona.

SHAKESPEARE GHOST TOWN, P.O. Box 253, Lordsburg. Tel. 542- 9034.

✪ A national historic site, Shakespeare was once the home of 3,000 miners, promoters, and dealers of various kinds. Under the name "Ralston" it enjoyed a silver boom in 1870. This was followed by a notorious diamond fraud in 1872 in which a mine was salted with diamonds in order to raise prices on mining stock with many notables being sucked in, particularly William Ralston, founder of the Bank of California. It enjoyed a mining revival in 1879 under its new name, Shakespeare. It was a town with no church, no newspaper, and no local law, giving it a reputation for lawlessness. Some serious fights resulted in hangings from the roof timbers in the Stage Station.

Since 1935, it's been privately owned by the Hill family, who have kept it uncommercialized with no souvenir hype or gift shop. They offer 2-hour guided tours on a limited basis, and reenactments and special events four times a year. Six original buildings and two reconstructed buildings survive in various stages of repair or disrepair.

To reach Shakespeare, drive 1.3 miles south from I-10 on Main Street. Before the town cemetery, turn right, to .6 mile and turn right on a dirt road for .4 mile.

Admission: $3 adults, $2 children 6–12; for shoot-outs and special events $4 adults, $3 children.

Open: 10am and 2pm second and fourth weekends of every month, except the fourth weekend of December, when it is closed. Special tours by appointment.

STEINS RAILROAD GHOST TOWN, Exit 3, I-10 (P.O. Box 185, Roadforks), Steins. Tel. 542-9791.

This settlement 19 miles west of Lordsburg started as a Butterfield Stage stop, then was a railroad town of about 1,000 residents from 1905 to 1945. It was so isolated that water, hauled from Doubtful Canyon, brought $1 a barrel!

Today there remain 10 buildings, with 16 rooms filled with artifacts and furnishings from the 19th and early 20th century. There is also a petting zoo for kids and the Steins Mercantile shop. The owners have plans to build a hotel, RV facilities, and an ice-cream shop.

Admission: $1.50 over 12 years; under 12, free.
Open: Daily 9am–5pm.

WHERE TO STAY

Lodging tax is 8.75% in Deming (6% state, 2.75% local) and 11% in Lordsburg (6% state, 5% local).

DEMING

BEST WESTERN CHILTON INN, 1709 E. Spruce St. (P.O. Box 790), Deming, NM 88031. Tel. 505/546-8813 or toll free 800/528-1234. Fax: 505/546-7095. 57 rms. A/C TV TEL

$ Rates: $41–$43 single, $47–$49 double. AE, CB, DC, DISC, MC, V.

Tall pillars, a brick facade, and white-shuttered windows lend an elegant appearance to this main-drag motel, which is more than adequate in many respects. Rooms are clean and comfortable, appointed in shades of brown, with plush chairs, working desks, and vanities. The Branding Iron restaurant (open 5:30am to 10pm daily) has American-style dinners in the $6.75 to $12.50 range. The property has a swimming pool and courtesy car service (8am to 4pm).

GRAND MOTOR INN, Hwy. 70/180 east of downtown (P.O. Box 309), Deming, NM 88031. Tel. 505/546-2631. 60 rms. A/C TV TEL

$ Rates: $38 single, $45–$48 double. AE, CB, DC, DISC, MC, V.

Looking like a redbrick Colonial Williamsburg manor, the Grand is built around a lovely central lawn and shrubbery garden with an outdoor swimming pool and hot tub. The pleasant rooms have floral decor and standard furnishings, including a large bathroom and an anteroom with a dressing table and wardrobe rack. A coffeehouse is open from 6am to 9pm daily (full dinners $4.95 to $11.95); a lounge is adjacent. There's courtesy car service to and from the train station. Nonsmoking rooms are available.

HOLIDAY INN, off I-10 (P.O. Box 1138), Deming NM 88031. Tel. 505/546-2661. Fax 505/546-6308. 80 rms. A/C TV TEL

$ Rates: $30–$48 single; $42–$52 double. AE, DC, MC, V. **Parking:** Free.

Though the building has been in existence for quite some time, it has only recently become Deming's newest Holiday Inn. The new owners practically gutted the place and have done a wonderful job of redecorating and refurbishing the large comfortable rooms. Many of the guest rooms look out onto the heated outdoor pool, which is open April through October, and all are decorated in soft pastels and have cable TV, direct dial phones, and vanity areas separate from the bathroom. The staff is friendly and extraordinarily efficient—which is due in part to the fact that the owners live in an apartment on the premises (a rarity for hotel chains). There is a coin-operated laundry as well as valet laundry.

Fat Eddie's, the hotel's restaurant, is open for breakfast, lunch, and dinner and serves New Mexican and American cuisine. Prices are very reasonable, and there's a children's menu. Room service is available during restaurant hours. The Lazy Lizard Lounge is open for cocktails Monday through Saturday from 2pm to midnight and until 11pm on Sundays. There are rooms for nonsmokers and the disabled. Pets are welcome. You won't find anything to complain about at this Holiday Inn.

MOTEL 6, I-10 and Motel Dr. (P.O. Box 970), Deming, NM 88031. Tel. 505/546-2623. Fax 505/892-8667. 102 rms. A/C TV TEL
$ Rates: $22.95 single, $28.95 double. AE, DC, DISC, MC, V.
Typically Spartan but comfortable, the Motel 6 has double beds, a table and chairs, and other essential furnishings. Bathrooms have showers only. This is a place to rest your head, and little more. It does have an outdoor swimming pool, and immediate freeway access.

LORDSBURG

BEST WESTERN AMERICAN MOTOR INN, 944 E. Motel Dr. (Alt. I-10), Lordsburg, NM 88045. Tel. 505/542-3591 or toll free 800/528-1234. 92 rms. A/C TV TEL
$ Rates: $39–$59 single; $44–$59 double. AE, CB, DC, DISC, MC, V.
Located well off I-10 on the old highway through town, the American caters to families with an outdoor swimming pool and Jacuzzi, a small playground with swings, and a handful of family units. Rooms have sturdy maple furnishings and scenic Southwest prints on the walls. Some king-size beds are available, along with non-smoking rooms. A friendly adjacent restaurant, under separate management, serves three American and New Mexican meals daily, with dinner priced from $4.25 to $12.95. They also have kids' menus.

BEST WESTERN WESTERN SKIES INN, 1803 S. Main St. at I-10, Lordsburg, NM 88045. Tel. 505/542-8807 or toll free 800/528-1234. 40 rms. A/C TV TEL
$ Rates: $41.50 single, $45–$47 double. AE, CB, DC, DISC, MC, V.
A newer property at the I-10 interchange, this motel has appointed its spacious rooms in earth tones with southwestern motifs. Each has solid maple furnishings, a large bathroom area, and dressing table/vanity. There's an outdoor pool and free coffee in the lobby beginning at 5:30am. Kranberry's family-style restaurant is next door.

WHERE TO DINE
DEMING

CACTUS CAFE, 218 W. Cedar St. off I-10. Tel. 546-2458.
   Cuisine: AMERICAN & NEW MEXICAN.
$ Prices: Lunch or dinner $4.25–$7.25. DISC, MC, V.
   Open: Daily 7am–9pm.
The Perrault family restaurant has a friendly atmosphere that carries into the colorful regional decor. There's a wide choice of menu selections, including the popular Tampiquena steak with green chiles and onions.

K-BOB'S, 316 E. Cedar St. off I-10. Tel. 546-8883.
   Cuisine: STEAKS.
$ Prices: Lunch $3.95–$9.95, dinner $4.95–$13.20. AE, MC, V.
   Open: 7am–9pm Sun–Thurs, 7am–10pm Fri–Sat.
This family-style steak house offers a wide selection of steaks, chicken, and deep-fried seafood. It has a large salad bar; a children's menu; and a selection of beers and wines. Soups, sandwiches, and burgers are always available.

LA FONDA RESTAURANT, 601 E. Pine St. Tel. 546-8731.
   Cuisine: NEW MEXICAN.
$ Prices: Main courses, New Mexican $2.50–$7.25, American $5.45–$12.25. AE, DISC, MC, V.

Open: Daily 6am–9:30pm.

Another family-style spot, La Fonda is thoroughly Mexican, with serapes adorning the walls and mariachi music playing. House specials include delicious burritos and fajitas.

LORDSBURG

EL CHARRO CAFE, 209 Southern Pacific Blvd. Tel. 542-3400.
Cuisine: NEW MEXICAN & AMERICAN.
$ Prices: Breakfast $2.40–$7.05; lunch/dinner, New Mexican $2–$5.95, American $4.50–$11.95. AE, CB, DC, DISC, MC, V.
Open: 24 hours daily.

On the north side of the railroad tracks, El Charro has two sections: an informal, unlicensed café, with Formica-topped tables and counter service, and the Maverick Room lounge, with licensed dining. The menu is the same in both rooms—enchiladas, tacos, burritos, chiles rellenos, and the like, plus American dishes.

5. SILVER CITY

240 miles SW of Albuquerque; 112 miles NW of Las Cruces;
197 miles E of Tucson, Ariz.

GETTING THERE   By Plane   Mesa Airlines (tel. 388-4115 or toll free 800/MESA-AIR) flies twice daily from Albuquerque to Silver City–Grant County Airport, 15 miles south of Silver City near Hurley. Pick up a car there from **Grimes Aviation and Car Rental** (tel. 538-2142). **Silver Stage Lines** (tel. 388-2586) offers daily shuttle service to the El Paso airport, leaving Silver City at 7am and returning at 5pm.

By Bus   There's no regular commercial service into Silver City. A shuttle provides connection with **Greyhound** (tel. 388-3475) at Deming.

By Car   From Albuquerque take I-25 south, 15 miles past Truth or Consequences; then west on N.M. 152 and U.S. 180 (5 hours). From Las Cruces take I-10 west to Deming, then north on U.S. 180 (2 hours).

ESSENTIALS   Orientation   Silver City rests in the foothills of the Pinos Altos Range of the Gila Wilderness, at 6,000 feet elevation. U.S. Highway 180 is the main east-west artery through town; N.M. 90 (Hudson Street) comes north from Lordsburg and intersects 180 north of downtown. Bullard Street (north-south) and Broadway (east-west) are the main routes in downtown. N.M. 15, the highway to Gila Cliff Dwellings National Monument, turns off U.S. 180 at the east end of Silver City.

Information   The **Silver City–Grant County Chamber of Commerce,** at 1103 N. Hudson St., Silver City, NM 88061 (tel. 505/538-3785 or toll free 800/548-9378), maintains a visitor information headquarters on N.M. 90, a few blocks south of U.S. 180. The chamber produces extremely useful tourist publications.

Fast Facts   The **area code** is 505. Medical emergencies are treated at the **Gila Regional Medical Center,** 1313 E. 32nd St. (tel. 388-1591). The **post office** is located at 500 N. Hudson St. (tel. 538-2831). In case of **emergencies,** dial 911 or 0 for an operator.

Silver City (pop. 11,000) is an old mining town, located in the foothills of the Pinos Altos Range of the Mogollon Mountains, and gateway to the Gila Wilderness. Early Indians mined turquoise from these hills, and by 1804 the Spanish were digging for copper. In 1870, a group of prospectors discovered silver, and the rush was on. In

10 short months, the newly christened Silver City grew from a single cabin to over 80 buildings. Early visitors included Billy the Kid, Judge Roy Bean, and William Randolph Hearst.

This comparatively isolated community kept pace with every modern convenience: telephones in 1883, electric lights in 1884, only two years after New York City installed its lighting, and a water system in 1887. Typically, the town should have busted with the crash of silver prices in 1893. But unlike many western towns, Silver City did not become a picturesque memory. Silver City capitalized on its high dry climate to become today's county seat and trade center. Copper mining and processing are still the major industry. But Silver City also can boast that it produces astronauts: Harrison (Jack) Schmitt, the first civilian geologist to visit the moon and later a U.S. senator, was born and raised in nearby Santa Rita.

WHAT TO SEE & DO

Silver City's downtown ✪ **historic district,** the first such district to receive National Register recognition, is a must for visitors. The downtown core is marked by the extensive use of brick in construction: Brick clay was discovered in the area soon after the town's founding in 1870, and an 1880 ordinance prohibited frame construction within the town limits. Mansard-roofed Victorian houses, Queen Anne and Italianate residences, and commercial buildings show off the cast-iron architecture of the period. Some are still undergoing restoration.

An 1895 flood washed out Main Street and turned it into a gaping chasm, which was eventually bridged over; finally, the **Big Ditch,** as it's called, was made into a green park in the center of town. Facing downtown, in the 500 block of North Hudson Street, was a famous red-light district from the turn of the century that wasn't shut down until the late 1960s.

Billy the Kid lived in Silver City as a youth. You can see his cabin site a block north of the Broadway bridge, on the east side of the Big Ditch. The Kid (William Bonney) waited tables at the Star Hotel, Hudson Street and Broadway. He was jailed (at 304 N. Hudson St.) in 1875 at the age of 15, after being convicted of stealing from a Chinese laundry, but he escaped—a first for the Kid. The grave of Bonney's mother, Catherine McCarty, is in Silver City Cemetery, east of town on Memory Lane, off U.S. 180. She died of tuberculosis about a year after the family moved here in 1873.

SILVER CITY MUSEUM, 312 W. Broadway. Tel. 538-5921.

✪ This very well-presented museum of city and regional history contains collections of early ranching and mining displays, Indian pottery and early photographs. Exhibits of pioneer life include one room about Silver City women, among them silent film actress Lillian Knight. There are also displays of Casas Grandes pottery.

The main gallery features changing exhibits. For most of 1993 there will be an exhibit of Victorian costumes.

The museum is lodged in the 1881 H. B. Ailman House, a former city hall and fire station remarkable for its cupola and Victorian mansard roof. Ailman came to Silver City penniless in 1871, made a fortune in mining, and went on to start the Meredith and Ailman Bank.

Admission: Free.
Open: Tues–Fri 9am–4:30pm, Sat–Sun 10am–4pm.

WESTERN NEW MEXICO UNIVERSITY MUSEUM, 1000 W. College Fleming Hall, WNMU. Tel. 538-6386.

Spread across 80 acres on the west side of Silver City, WNMU will celebrate its centennial in 1993. The university boasts a 2,000-student enrollment and 24 major buildings. Among them is Fleming Hall, which houses this interesting museum.

The WNMU museum has the largest permanent exhibit of prehistoric Mimbres pottery in the United States. Also displayed are Casas Grandes Indian pottery, stone tools, ancient jewelry, historical photographs, mining and military artifacts. Displays are changed regularly, so there is always something new to see in the museum—such

as Pancho Villa memorabilia, riparian fossils, Nigerian folk art, or a collection of 18th- to 20th-century timepieces. There is a gift shop here.
Admission: By donation.
Open: Mon–Fri 8am–4:30pm, Sun 1–4pm.

SPORTS & RECREATION

Scott Park Golf Course, Silver Acres (tel. 538-5041), is open 7am to 7pm daily.
Silver City Municipal Swimming Pool, 2700 N. Silver St. (tel. 388-4165), has open hours daily.

NEARBY ATTRACTIONS
NORTH OF SILVER CITY

The virtual ghost town of ✪ **Pinos Altos,** straddling the Continental Divide, is six miles north of Silver City on N.M. 15. Dubbed "Tall Pines" when it was founded in the gold- and silver-rush era, it has retired from Apache attacks and mine failures to doze amid apple orchards planted in the 1860s.

Visitors can see restored buildings, homes, and churches dating from the time when a miner was worth $1.20 per day from the neck down. The adobe **Methodist-Episcopal Church** was built with William Randolph Hearst's money in 1898 and now houses the Grant County Art Guild. The **Pinos Altos Museum** displays Sheriff Pat Garrett's funeral hearse and other horse-drawn vehicles, as well as a three-quarter-scale reproduction of the Santa Rita del Cobre Fort & Trading Post, built at Santa Rita copper mine in 1804 to protect the area from Apaches. (It was renamed Fort Webster in 1851.) It's still possible to pan for gold in Pinos Altos. The town also has a gift shop and the Buckhorn Saloon restaurant (see "Where to Dine," below).

GILA CLIFF DWELLINGS NATIONAL MONUMENT, Rte. 11, Box 100, Silver City, NM 88061. Tel. 536-9461.

✪ It takes at least 1½ hours to reach the Gila Cliff Dwellings from Silver City, 44 miles up narrow, winding N.M. 15 into the Mogollon Mountains. It's definitely worth the trip. First-time visitors are inevitably awed by the climactic sight. At this stone-within-stone-on-stone relic of a disappeared civilization, reality is somehow exaggerated in the dazzling sunlight and contrasting shadow, making the dwellings look, from a distance, as two-dimensional as a stage set. The solid masonry walls are well preserved, even though they've been abandoned for seven centuries.

The cliff dwellings were discovered by Anglo settlers in the early 1870s, near where the three forks of the Gila River rise. Seven natural caves occur in the southeast-facing cliff of a side canyon; six of them contain the ruins of dwellings, which had about 42 rooms. Probably not more than 8 or 10 Mogollon families (40 to 50 people) lived in these dwellings at any one time. Tree-ring dating indicates their residence didn't last longer than 30 to 40 years at the end of the 13th century.

Today, the dwellings allow a rare glimpse inside the homes and lives of prehistoric Indians. About 75% of what is seen is original, although the walls have been capped and the foundations strengthened to prevent further deterioration. It took a great deal of effort to build these homes: The stones were held in place by mortar, and all of the clay and water for the mortar had to be carried up from the stream, as the Mogollon did not have any pack animals. The *vigas* for the roof were cut and shaped with stone axes or fire.

The people who lived here were farmers, as shown by the remains of beans, squash, and corn in their homes. The fields were along the valley of the west fork of the Gila River and on the mesa across the canyon. No signs of irrigation have been found.

A 1-mile loop trail, rising 175 feet from the canyon floor, provides access to the dwellings.

Near the visitor center, about a mile away, the remains of an earlier (A.D. 100–400) pit house, built below ground level, and later pit houses (up to A.D. 1000), aboveground structures of adobe or wattle, have been found.

Camping and picnicking are encouraged in the national monument. There are no accommodations here; most visitors stay in Silver City, and the nearby town of Gila Hot Springs has overnight lodging and a grocery store, as well as horse rentals and guided pack trips.

Admission: Free.

Open: Visitor center, Memorial Day–Labor Day daily 8am–5pm; rest of year 8am–4:30pm. Cliff dwellings, summer daily 8am–6pm; rest of year 9am–4pm.

SOUTH OF SILVER CITY

South 12 miles on N.M. 90 is the ✪ **Phelps Dodge Open Pit Copper Mine** (tel. 538-5331). Some 80 million tons of rock are taken out every year. An observation point is open Monday through Friday from 7am to sunset; free guided tours are offered on weekdays with a day's advance reservation.

Phelps Dodge consolidated its Tyrone holdings in 1909 and hired famous architect Bertram Goodhue to design a "Mediterranean-style" company town. **Tyrone,** later referred to as the Million Dollar Ghost Town, was constructed in 1914–18. A large bank and shop building, administration office, mercantile store, and passenger depot were grouped around a central plaza. Eighty-three single and multiple-unit dwellings, accommodating 235 families, were built on the nearby hillsides; and a school, chapel, garage, restaurant, justice court, hospital, morgue, and recreation building were added. A drop in copper prices caused it to be abandoned virtually overnight.

After a pre–World War II incarnation as a luxurious dude ranch, Tyrone lay dormant for years until the late 1960s, when the town made way for the present-day open pit mine and mill. A new townsite was created 7 miles north. Most of the original homes and major buildings were removed between 1967 and 1969; today, the only remaining structures are Union Chapel, the justice court, and the pump house. The copper mine supplies copper concentrates to the modern Hidalgo Smelter near Playas, southeast of Lordsburg.

EAST OF SILVER CITY

The oldest active mine in the Southwest, and the fourth largest in America, is the **Chino Mines Co. Open Pit Copper Mine** at Santa Rita, 15 miles east of Silver City via U.S. 180 and N.M. 152. The multicolored open pit is a mile wide and 1,000 feet deep, and can be viewed from a spectacular observation point with a small museum. Apache Indians once scratched the surface for metallic copper. By 1800, the Spanish, under Col. Jose Manuel Carrasco, were working "Santa Rita del Cobre." Convict labor from New Spain mined the shafts, with mule trains of ore sent down the Janos Trail to Chihuahua, Mexico. An impressive adobe fort was built near the mine, along with smelters and numerous buildings, but Apache raids finally forced the mine's abandonment. In the late 19th century, the mine was reopened, and the town of Santa Rita was reborn. The huge open pit, started around 1910, soon consumed Santa Rita. Giant-sized machines scoop the ore from the earth and huge 175-ton ore trucks transport it to the reduction mill to the southwest of the pit.

✪ **City of Rocks State Park** (tel. 536-2800), 30 miles from Silver City via U.S. 180 and N.M. 61, is an area of fantastically shaped volcanic rock formations, formed in ancient times from thick blankets of ash that hardened into tuff. This soft stone, eroded by wind and rain, was shaped into monolithic blocks reminiscent of Stonehenge. For some, the park resembles a medieval village; for others, it is a collection of misshapen, albeit benign giants. Complete with a desert garden, the park offers excellent camping and picnic sites. Hot water is solar heated, while windmills pump it and make electricity; the park is thus self-sufficient.

WEST OF SILVER CITY

U.S. 180, heading northwest from Silver City, is the gateway to Catron County and most of the Gila National Forest, including the villages of Glenwood, Reserve, and Quemado.

✪ **Gila National Forest,** 2610 N. Silver St., Silver City, NM 88061 (tel. 388-8201), comprises 3.3 million acres in four counties. Nearly one-fourth of that acreage (790,000) comprises the **Gila, Aldo Leopold,** and **Blue Range wildernesses.** Within the forest are 1,490 miles of trails for hiking and horseback riding, and in winter, cross-country skiing and snowmobiling; outside of the wildernesses, trail bikes and off-road vehicles are also permitted. The 41-mile Middle Fork Trail, with its east end near Gila Cliff Dwellings, is among the most popular. More than 50 trailheads provide roadside parking.

There are 18 campgrounds in the national forest, 11 of them undeveloped (no drinking water). Gila National Forest also contains numerous lakes, 360 miles of mountain streams, and the largest virgin ponderosa-pine forest in the United States. Its highest peak is Whitewater Baldy, 10,892 feet. Big-game animals found here include mule deer, elk, antelope, black bear, mountain lion, and bighorn sheep.

The ✪ **Catwalk,** 68 miles north of Silver City on U.S. 180, then 5 miles east of Glenwood, is reached by foot from a parking area. It follows the route of a pipeline built in 1897 to carry water to the now-defunct town of Graham and its electric generator. About a quarter of a mile above the parking area is the beginning of a striking 250-foot metal causeway clinging to the sides of the boulder-choked Whitewater Canyon, which in spots is 20 feet wide and 250 feet deep. Spectacular vistas are found farther up the canyon, where a suspension bridge spans the chasm. Picnic facilities are located near the parking area.

The scenic ghost town of ✪ **Mogollon** is 3½ miles north of Glenwood on U.S. 180, then 9 miles east on N.M. 159, a narrow mountain road. The village bears witness to silver and gold mining booms beginning in the late 19th century, and to the disastrous effects of floods and fire in later years. Remains of its last operating mine, the Little Fanny (which ceased operation in the 1950s), are still visible, along with dozens of other old buildings, miner's shacks, and mining paraphernalia. An art gallery and museum are found along Mogollon's main street. The movie *My Name Is Nobody,* starring Henry Fonda, was shot here.

Reserve (pop. 550), Catron County seat, is noted as the place where, in 1884, Deputy Sheriff Elfego Baca made an epic stand in a shoot-out with 80 cowboys. Cochise, Geronimo, and other Apache war chiefs held forth in these mountains in the late 19th century.

WHERE TO STAY

Standard motels are strung along U.S. 180 east of N.M. 90. Some of the more interesting accommodations, however, are not! An 11.125% tax is imposed on all lodging bills (6% state tax and 5.125% city lodging tax).

BEAR MOUNTAIN GUEST RANCH, Bear Mountain Rd., Silver City, NM 88061. Tel. 505/538-2538. 13 rms, 2 cottages.

$ Rates (including 3 meals daily): $65 single, $114 double; cottage with kitchenette (meals not included), $55–$80 for 1 to 4 persons. No credit cards.

Spread across 160 acres just 3½ miles northwest of downtown Silver City, Myra McCormick's ranch has been a New Mexico institution since 1959. This is a nature lover's delight—McCormick hosts birding, wild plant, and archaeological workshops throughout the year, a "Lodge and Learn" series (for adults of all ages) is a feature every month. The ranch doesn't have horses, but visitors are urged to "bring your own." All rooms have private baths, and home-cooked meals are served in a family-style setting.

To reach the ranch, turn north off Highway 180 on Alabama Street, a half mile west of Route 90 intersection. Proceed 2.8 miles (Alabama becomes Cottage San Road, then Bear Mountain Road) to turnoff; the ranch is another 0.6 miles.

THE CARTER HOUSE, 101 N. Cooper St., Silver City, NM 88061. Tel. 505/388-5485. 5 rms and 24 youth-hostel bunks.

$ Rates: $50–$65 per room, bed-and-breakfast; $14 per bed ($11 for hostel association members) in youth hostel. MC, V.

⭐ The top floor of this renovated 1906 mansion, situated next door to the Grant County Courthouse, is a classic bed-and-breakfast establishment. The lower floor is an official American Youth Hostel. It's a unique combination, but seems to work. B&B patrons feel at home with a living and dining room, library and TV room, all decorated with 19th-century prints—family heirlooms of owners Jim and Lucy Nolan. They also can share the laundry and kitchen facilities with the youth hostelers in the basement.

COPPER MANOR MOTEL, 710 Silver Heights Blvd. (Hwy. 180), Silver City, NM 88061. Tel. 505/538-5392. 68 rms. A/C TV TEL
$ Rates: $34–$39 single, $40–$45 double. AE, CB, DC, MC, V.
A standard roadside motel, the Copper Manor has the advantage of being part of a one-ownership complex that includes the Red Barn Steak House next door and the Drifter Motel and Restaurant across the street. Room decor is bold; the bathrooms quite small. Facilities include an indoor pool and Jacuzzi; guests can also use the Drifter's outdoor pool.

HOLIDAY MOTOR HOTEL, Hwy. 180 E., Silver City, NM 88061. Tel. 505/538-3711, toll free 800/828-8291. 79 rms. A/C TV TEL
$ Rates: $40–$45 single, $46–$58 double. AE, CB, DC, MC, V.
Located about three miles east of downtown near the junction of U.S. 180 and State 15, this motel is a step above the ordinary with its landscaped grounds, attractive outdoor swimming pool, and guest Laundromat. Rooms are clean and comfortable, with custom-made furnishings. The restaurant serves three meals daily from 6am to 9:30pm, with a menu superior to the typical hotel coffee shop: For example, you can have a dinner of broiled swordfish or maple-cured ham.

THE PALACE HOTEL, 106 W. Broadway (P.O. Box 5093), Silver City, NM 88061. Tel. 505/388-1811. 22 rms, 7 suites. TV
$ Rates (including continental breakfast): $28–$38 single or double; $45–$55 suite. AE, DC, MC, V.

⭐ Old-fashioned elegance and Victorian decor are earmarks of this hotel, first established 1882 and reopened in July 1990 as a historic small European-style hotel. Each of the rooms on the second floor is shaped and decorated differently. All have standard furnishings and steam heat, but bed sizes vary from king to single; some have refrigerators; three share baths; all of the others have bathtubs and showers. That's a sight better than in 1882! The owners provide fresh fruit bread for breakfast. The hotel has a guest laundry and a games room in the basement.

WHERE TO DINE

BUCKHORN SALOON AND OPERA HOUSE, N.M. 15, Pinos Altos. Tel. 538-9911.
  Cuisine: CONTINENTAL & STEAKS. **Reservations:** Strongly recommended.
$ Prices: Main courses $7.95–$18.95. MC, V.
  Open: Dinner served Mon–Sat at 6:10pm.

⭐ Seven miles north of Silver City in Pinos Altos, the surprising Buckhorn offers tuxedo-clad service in 1860's decor. It's noted for its western-style steaks, seafood, homemade desserts, and excellent wine list. There's live entertainment nightly; the saloon opens at 3pm during the week.

THE RED BARN STEAK HOUSE, 708 Silver Heights Blvd. (Hwy. 180). Tel. 538-5666.
  Cuisine: AMERICAN.
$ Prices: Appetizers $3.25–$7.25; lunch $3.25–$7.95; dinner $7.95–$19.95. AE, CB, DC, MC, V.

Open: Daily 11am–10pm. **Closed:** Thanksgiving Day, Christmas, and New Year's Day.

This big red barn, with its white silo, is unmistakable on the south side of U.S. 180 as it enters Silver City from the east. The interior is spacious and comfortable, with atmospheric wagon-wheel chandeliers. Steaks are the specialty, from beef teriyaki to steak Oscar. A 20-ounce T-bone is just $18.95. There's an enormous salad bar. At the rear of the restaurant is the Watering Hole Lounge.

CHAPTER 10

SOUTHEASTERN NEW MEXICO

1. ALAMAGORDO
2. RUIDOSO
3. ROSWELL
4. CARLSBAD

Southeastern New Mexico—that part of the state east of the Rio Grande (the I-25 corridor) and south of I-40—is a vast and surprising region which in many ways is typical of the "real" West.

Here are the spectacular Carlsbad Caverns and the awesome White Sands National Monument. This is the home of the fierce Mescalero Apaches and of the world's richest horse race. Billy the Kid lived and died in southeastern New Mexico in the 19th century, and the world's first atomic bomb was exploded here in the 20th. From west to east, barren desert gives way to high, forested peaks, snow-covered in winter; to the fertile valley of the Pecos River; and to high plains beloved by ranchers along the Texas border.

The main city in this section of the state is Roswell, a city of about 50,000. Carlsbad (pop. 30,000), 76 miles south of Roswell; and Alamogordo (pop. 32,000), 117 miles west of Roswell, are of more immediate interest to tourists. Other sizable towns are Clovis (pop. 32,000) and Hobbs (pop. 30,000), both on the Texas border; and Artesia (pop. 13,000), between Roswell and Carlsbad. Ruidoso (pop. 5,000), in the mountains between Alamogordo and Roswell, is a booming resort town.

A good way to approach the region, if you're coming by car from Albuquerque, is to head south on I-25 to San Antonio, just beyond Socorro, then turn east of U.S. Highway 380 through Carrizozo. This will bring you first to the Ruidoso area, whose major attractions can be defined by a triangle formed by Highway 380, U.S. Highway 70, and N.M. Highway 48.

Drive south on U.S. 70 to explore Alamogordo and White Sands. Then follow U.S. Highway 82 east through the charming mountain village of Cloudcroft and down the valley of the Rio Penasco with its fruit orchards. At Artesia, turn south on U.S. Highway 285 to Carlsbad and its famous caverns.

From Carlsbad, you can either reverse course back up Highway 285 to Roswell and (via N.M. Highway 20) Fort Sumner, site of Fort Sumner State Monument and Billy the Kid's grave, or meander through the Llano Estacado along the Texas border, taking U.S. Highway 62/180 to Hobbs, then turning north on N.M. 206 to Clovis. From the latter city, Fort Sumner is an hour's drive west on U.S. Highway 60/84. Return to your starting point by heading north from Fort Sumner on U.S. 84 to I-40 at Santa Rosa; it's a 2-hour drive west to Albuquerque.

1. ALAMOGORDO

191 miles S of Albuquerque; 68 miles NE of Las Cruces;
87 miles N of El Paso, Texas

GETTING THERE By Plane Mesa Airlines (tel. toll free 800/MESA-AIR) has connections three times daily with Albuquerque. **Avis** (tel. 437-3140), **Hertz** (tel. 437-7760), and **National** (tel. 437-4126) rent cars at the Municipal Airport.

By Bus **TNM&O/Greyhound** (tel. 437-3050) serves Alamogordo from Albuquerque, Las Cruces, Roswell, Carlsbad, and El Paso, with 12 arrivals and departures each day from the **Union Bus Station** (tel. 437-3050).

By Car From Albuquerque take I-25 south 87 miles to San Antonio; turn east on U.S. 380, 66 miles to Carrizozo; then south on U.S. 54 (4 hours). From Las Cruces, take U.S. 70 northeast (1½ hours). (This road may be closed for up to 2 hours during times of missile testing on White Sands Missile Range.) From El Paso, take U.S. 54 north (1½ hours).

ESSENTIALS Orientation Alamogordo is on the eastern edge of the Tularosa Valley, at the foot of the Sacramento Mountains. U.S. 54 (White Sands Boulevard) is the main street, extending several miles north and south. The downtown district is actually three blocks east of White Sands Boulevard, off 10th Street.

Information The **Alamogordo Chamber of Commerce** and visitor center is at 1301 N. White Sands Blvd. Write P.O. Box 518, Alamogordo, NM 88311 (tel. 505/437-6120 or toll free 800/545-4021 outside New Mexico, 800/826-0294 within New Mexico).

Fast Facts The **area code** is 505. **Gerald Champion Memorial Hospital,** 1209 Ninth St. (tel. 439-2100), has its emergency entrance at 10th and Cuba streets. The **post office,** 900 Alaska Ave. (tel. 437-9390), is one block south of 10th Street, three blocks east of White Sands Boulevard. For **emergencies,** dial 911.

Famous for its leading role in America's space research and military technology industries, Alamogordo (population 32,000) first achieved worldwide fame on July 16, 1945, when the first atomic bomb was exploded at the nearby Trinity Site. Today, it is home of the Space Center and International Space Hall of Fame, White Sands National Monument, and Holloman Air Force Base. Twenty miles east and twice as high, the resort village of Cloudcroft (elevation 9,000 feet) attracts vacationers to the forested heights of the Sacramento Mountains.

WHAT TO SEE & DO

In addition to the attractions in Alamogordo itself, worth visiting is the small, historic village of **La Luz,** just 3 miles north of Alamogordo. It has attracted a number of resident artists and craftspeople who live and work here, and display some of their products for sale. Worth seeing are the old adobe corral and the small Our Lady of Light Church.

TULAROSA BASIN HISTORICAL SOCIETY MUSEUM, 1301 N. White Sands Blvd. Tel. 437-6120.
Located beside the chamber of commerce, this museum displays artifacts and photographs recalling regional history.
Admission: Free.
Open: Mon–Sat 10am–4pm and Sun 1–4pm.

ALAMEDA PARK ZOO, 1321 N. White Sands Boulevard. Tel. 437-8430.
Next to the historical society museum is this 7-acre zoo, the oldest zoo in the Southwest. Established in 1898, its collection includes hundreds of mammals and birds from around the world, including a variety of American and African mammals.
Admission: $1 children 11–16, 50¢ children 3–11 and seniors 62 and older.
Open: Daily 9am–5pm.

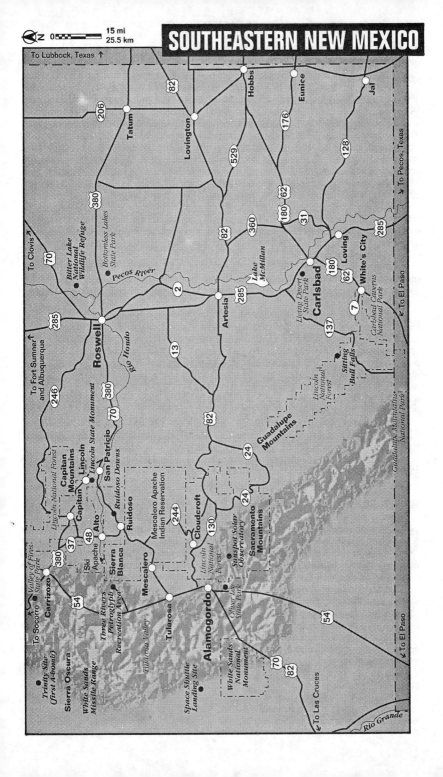

ALAMOGORDO SPACE CENTER, Scenic Dr. and Indian Wells Rd. Tel. 437-2840, 800/545-4021 out-of-state.

★ The Space Center comes in two parts—the **International Space Hall of Fame** and the **Clyde W. Tombaugh Space Theater.** Both are located on the lower slopes of the Sacramento Mountains, 2 miles east of U.S. Highway 54, and just above New Mexico State University's Alamogordo branch campus.

The Space Hall of Fame occupies the "Golden Cube," a five-story building with walls of golden glass. Visitors are encouraged to start on the top floor and work their way down. En route, they recall the accomplishments of the first astronauts and cosmonauts, including America's Mercury, Gemini, and Apollo programs, and the early Soviet orbital flights. Spacecraft and a lunar exploration module are exhibited. There's a space-station plan, a hands-on cutaway of crew module "Space Station 2001," and explanations of life in space aboard Skylab and Salyut. Other displays tell the history and purposes of rocketry, missiles, and satellites; provide an orientation to astronomy and exploration of other planets; and tell about New Mexico's role in space exploration history, from ancient Indians to rocketry pioneer Robert Goddard to astronauts. Exhibits on the first floor focus on current issues in space, such as the Hubble space telescope.

On adjacent grounds is the "Sonic Wind" sled, which tested human endurance to speeds exceeding 600 m.p.h. in preparation for future space flights; the "Little Joe II" rocket, which tested Apollo launch escape systems; and other historic artifacts of space travel.

Each year, on the first Saturday of October, new members of the Space Hall of Fame are inducted in a special ceremony here. As of 1990, there were 43 members.

At the Tombaugh Theater, OMNIMAX and Spitz 512 Planetarium Systems create earthly and cosmic experiences on a 2,700-square-foot screen. Twenty special-effects projectors can show 2,354 stars, the Milky Way, all the visible planets, the sun and the moon, and can duplicate the night sky anywhere on earth, anytime of the year. Special programs allow visitors to white-water raft down the Colorado River, share the splendor of a space sunset with a shuttle crew, or take part in a laser-concert symphony of sight and sound.

Admission: Space Hall, adults $2.25, youth (6–12) and seniors (62 and older) $1.75; free for children under 5. Theater, adults $3.75, youths and seniors $2.50. Combined visit, adults $5.25, youths and seniors $3.50.

Open: Daily 9am–6pm summer, 9am–5pm winter. Theater show times Mon–Fri 10am, noon, 2pm, 4pm; Sat–Sun 10am, 11am, noon, 2pm, 3pm, 4pm. **Closed:** Christmas.

WHITE SANDS NATIONAL MONUMENT, 15 miles southwest of Alamogordo via U.S. Hwy. 70/82. Tel. 505/479-6124.

★ Arguably the most memorable natural area in this part of the Southwest, White Sands National Monument preserves the best part of the world's largest gypsum dune field. An area of 275 square miles of pure white gypsum sand reaches out over the floor of the Tularosa Basin in wavelike dunes. Plants and animals have evolved in special ways to adapt to the bright white environment.

The surrounding mountains, the Sacramentos to the east, with their forested slopes, and the sere San Andres to the west, are composed of sandstone, limestone, sedimentary rocks, and pockets of gypsum. These have been slowly eroded over the past millions of years by rains and melting snows; the silt from the mountains has been washed down into Lake Lucero. Here the hot sun and dry winds evaporate the water, leaving the pure white gypsum in crystals, in the dry lake bed. Then the persistent winds blow these crystals, in the form of minuscule bits of sand, in a northeastern direction, adding them to growing dunes. As each dune grows and moves farther from the lake, new ones form, rank after rank, in what seems an endless procession.

Some creatures that have evolved here have a bleached coloration to match the whiteness all around them. Some plants have also evolved means for surviving against the smothering pressures of the blowing sands. The plants and animals together make up a special community of living things adapted to a strange world. The plants and animals, dependent on each other, can thus survive this desert environment.

A 16-mile Dunes Drive loops through the "heart of sands" from the visitor center. Information available at the center will tell you what to look for on your drive. Sometimes the winds blow the dunes over the road, which must then be rerouted around a dune. The dunes are in fact all moving slowly to the northeast, pushed by prevailing southwest winds, some at the rate of as much as 20 feet a year.

In the center of the monument, the road itself is made of hard-packed gypsum. (This part of the road can be especially slick after an afternoon thunderstorm, so drive cautiously!) Visitors are invited to get out of their cars at established parking areas and explore a bit; climb a dune for a better view of the endless sea of sand.

A couple of safety tips are emphasized by the Park Service: one, that tunneling in this sand can be dangerous, for it collapses easily and could suffocate a person; and two, that sand-surfing down the dune slopes, although permitted, can also be hazardous, so it should be undertaken with care, and never near an auto road. Hikers are warned about the possibility of getting lost in a sudden sandstorm should they stray from marked trails or areas.

In summer there are nature walks and evening programs at the visitor center. Ranger-guided activities include orientation talks and nature walks. When driving near or in the monument, tune a radio to 1610 AM for information on what's doing.

Admission: $3 per vehicle.

Open: Memorial Day–Labor Day, visitor center 8am–7pm, Dunes Drive 7am–10pm; rest of year, visitor center 8am–4:30pm, Dunes Drive 7am–sunset. Due to missile testing on the adjacent White Sands Missile Range, the drive is sometimes closed for up to 2 hours at a time.

OLIVER LEE MEMORIAL STATE PARK, 15 miles southeast of Alamogordo via U.S. Hwy. 54 and Dog Canyon Rd. Tel. 437-8284.

Nestled at the mouth of Dog Canyon, a stunning break in the steep escarpment of the Sacramento Mountains, the site has drawn human visitors for thousands of years. Springs and seeps support a variety of rare and endangered plant species, as well as a rich wildlife. Hiking trails into the foothills are well marked; the park also offers picnic and camping grounds, with showers, electricity, and a dump station.

Dog Canyon was one of the last strongholds of the Mescalero Apache, and was the site of battles between the Indians and the U.S. Cavalry in the 19th century. Around the turn of the 20th century, rancher Oliver Lee built a home near here and raised cattle; guided tours from the visitor center to his restored house give a taste of early ranch life in southern New Mexico.

Admission: $3 per car.

Open: Daily 7am–sunset; visitor center 9am–4pm. Guided tours Sat–Sun at 3pm, weather permitting.

TRINITY SITE, west slope of Sierra Oscura, 60 air miles northwest of Alamogordo.

The world's first atomic bomb was exploded in this desert never-never land on July 16, 1945. It is strictly off-limit to civilians—except twice a year, in early April and early October, when free 1-day tours are organized by the Alamogordo Chamber of Commerce. A small lava monument commemorates the explosion, which left a crater a quarter-mile across, 25 feet deep at its center, and transformed the desert sand into a jade green glaze called "Tritinite" that remains today. The McDonald House, where the bomb's plutonium core was assembled 2 miles from Ground Zero, has been restored to its 1945 condition. Call 505/437-6120 for reservations.

NEARBY ATTRACTIONS

✪ **Cloudcroft** is a quaint mountain village of 600 people high in the Sacramento Mountains, surrounded by Lincoln National Forest. Though only about 20 miles east of Alamogordo via U.S. Highway 82, it is twice as high, overlooking the Tularosa Valley from a dizzying elevation of about 9,000 feet. It was founded in 1898 when railroad surveyors reached the mountain summit and built a lodge for Southern Pacific Railroad workers. Today, the Lodge is Cloudcroft's biggest attraction and biggest employer (see "Where to Dine," below). There are 17 other accommodations in town, and lots of recreational opportunities and community festivals. For information, contact the **Cloudcroft Chamber of Commerce,** P.O. Box 125, Cloudcroft, NM 88317 (tel. 505/682-2733).

The **Sacramento Mountains Historical Museum,** U.S. Highway 82 east of downtown, recalls the town's settlement days. The **Sunspot Solar Observatory,** about 17 miles south via Forest Service Road 64, offers self-guided daily tours at one of the world's largest solar observatories, atop Sacramento Peak; guided tours are available on Saturdays, May to October. An unusual footpath fitted out with storyboards in braille make **La Pasada Encantada**—the Enchanted Walk—a destination for the blind within the quiet stretches of national forest. The loop departs from the Sleep Grass Campground, off N.M. Highway 24 south of town. Signs invite strollers to touch the various barks, leaves, and plants along the way.

Ski Cloudcroft, 2 miles east of the village on U.S. Highway 82 (tel. 682-2333 or toll free 800/333-7542), has 20 runs and a 650-foot vertical, served by two T-bars and two rope tows. It appeals primarily to beginning and intermediate skiers, but has a few advanced pitches. When there's snow (usually December through March), it's open from 9am to 4pm daily. Snowboarding is permitted. Lift rates are $25 for adults, $15 for children.

WHERE TO STAY

All accommodations are along White Sands Boulevard, the north-south highway through town. A 9% tax is imposed on all lodging bills (6% state tax and 3% city lodging tax).

DESERT AIRE MOTOR INN, 1021 S. White Sands Blvd., Alamogordo, NM 88310. Tel. 505/437-2110 or toll free 800/528-1234. Fax 505/437-1898. 102 rms, 5 suites. A/C FRIDGE TV TEL
$ Rates (including continental breakfast): $47 single, $54 double, $65 suite. AE, CB, DC, DISC, MC, V.
This hotel of yellow-and-white concrete-block construction, surrounds a huge central parking area. Rooms are cozy, with a king-size or two double beds, photo art posters on the walls, and standard furnishings. There are minirefrigerators in all rooms and three-foot-deep Jacuzzis that dominate a dozen "spa rooms." The hotel offers a guest Laundromat, gift shop, and outdoor swimming pool, a hot tub and a sauna.

HOLIDAY INN, 1401 S. White Sands Blvd., Alamogordo, NM 88310. Tel. 505/437-7100 or toll free 800/HOLIDAY. Fax 505/437-7100, ext. 299. 107 rms, 1 suite. A/C TV TEL
$ Rates: $47–$52 single, $55–$60 double. AE, CB, DC, DISC, JCB, MC, V.
A lovely desert garden fronts this single-story hotel, and a stream cascades through black lava rocks on the left side of the lobby, blessed by a carving of St. Francis. Rooms have all standard furnishings, with a king-size bed or two doubles, and a full mirror behind the vanity. Room service and valet laundry service are offered; there's also an outdoor swimming pool, an adjacent children's pool, and a guest Laundromat. Yesterdays, a low-lit restaurant with wooden booths and ceiling fans, serves three meals daily in a moderate price range; cuisine is American with Mexican specials. The lounge has daily hors d'oeuvres and a big-screen TV.

SUPER 8 MOTEL, 3204 N. White Sands Blvd., Alamogordo, NM 88310. Tel. 505/434-4205 or toll free 800/800-8000. 60 rms. A/C TV TEL

$ **Rates** (including continental breakfast): $27.90 single, $33.90 double. AE, CB, DC, DISC, MC, V.

Like other Super 8s, this no-frills accommodation at the north end of town offers basic facilities for low cost. Rooms are clean and comfortable, if somewhat Spartan. Facilities include a guest Laundromat and vending machines. The desk is open 24 hours a day.

WHERE TO DINE

FURGI'S PUB, 817 Scenic Dr. Tel. 437-9564.

Cuisine: AMERICAN.
$ **Prices:** Appetizers $2.95–$4.95; main courses $3.95–$11.95. MC, V.
Open: Daily 11am–10pm.

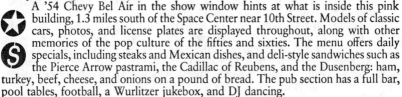

A '54 Chevy Bel Air in the show window hints at what is inside this pink building, 1.3 miles south of the Space Center near 10th Street. Models of classic cars, photos, and license plates are displayed throughout, along with other memories of the pop culture of the fifties and sixties. The menu offers daily specials, including steaks and Mexican dishes, and deli-style sandwiches such as the Pierce Arrow pastrami, the Cadillac of Reubens, and the Dusenberg: ham, turkey, beef, cheese, and onions on a pound of bread. The pub section has a full bar, pool tables, football, a Wurlitzer jukebox, and DJ dancing.

K-BOB'S, 504 1st St. Tel. 437-5592.

Cuisine: STEAKS.
$ **Prices:** Appetizers $3.95–$4.95, main courses $5.95–$11.95. AE, MC, V.
Open: Mon–Sat 11am–9pm.

A friendly family restaurant, K-Bob's occupies a re-created Territorial-style adobe lodge. Steaks of all sizes and kinds are the specialty here; smaller meals are available for kids and seniors. A large salad bar satisfies vegetable lovers. Beer and wine are served.

RAMONA'S, 2913 N. White Sands Blvd. Tel. 437-7616.

Cuisine: NEW MEXICAN & AMERICAN.
$ **Prices:** Appetizers $2.95–$4.75; breakfast $2.10–$6.95; lunch $2.25–$8.95; dinner $4.50–$8.95. AE, MC, V.
Open: Daily 6am–10pm.

Huge arched windows face the highway from the indoor patio of this tile-roofed adobe, and a huge wallpapered mural of a Mexican city covers one wall. A favorite meal is Ramona's special: a chicken enchilada, chile relleno, and chicken burrito, with guacamole, sour cream, refried beans, rice, and salad. American dishes include chicken-fried steak and fresh mountain trout. Beer and wine are served.

YEE'S ORIENTAL EXPRESS, 1115 S. White Sands Blvd. Tel. 437-RICE.

Cuisine: CHINESE FAST FOOD.
$ **Prices:** All dishes $2.50–$4.25/pint, $3.95–$6.95/quart. No credit cards.
Open: Mon–Thurs 11am–9pm, Fri–Sat 11am–10pm.

Yee's "drive-through buffet" is a novel concept, especially popular among the men and women stationed at nearby Holloman Air Force Base. The menu includes daily specials like Szechuan beef or cashew chicken, and everyday favorites like sweet-and-sour pork, fried wontons, and butterfly shrimp. Yee's makes deliveries, or you can eat inside the bright red building, located between the Holiday Inn and the Desert Aire Motor Inn.

NEARBY PLACES TO STAY & DINE

CHIPPEWAY PARK, N.M. Highway 130, 6 miles east of Cloudcroft. Tel. 682-2407 or 682-2943.

Cuisine: CHUCK WAGON.

$ Prices: Dinner $12 adults, $7 children. No credit cards.

Open: Dinner served at 7pm, Saturdays in June, Fridays and Saturdays July–Aug and the first weekend in October, and Memorial and Labor Day weekends.

The Fuller Family serves up chuck-wagon dinners from an open-pit barbecue, followed by a show of homespun country music, during the summer season. You'll feast on a meal of beef, beans, baked potatoes, coleslaw, garlic toast, lemonade, and coffee. Afterward, four generations of the family sing and play together on banjo, fiddle, guitar, bass, piano, and drums.

THE LODGE AT CLOUDCROFT, 1 Corona Place (P.O. Box 497), Cloudcroft, NM 88317. Tel. 505/682-2566 or toll free 800/395-6343 in New Mexico. Fax 505/682-2715. 58 rms, 9 suites. TV TEL

$ Rates: $55–$79 single or double, $95–$150 suite. Tax in Cloudcroft is 8.75% (including 6% state tax). AE, DC, DISC, ER, MC, V.

The only hotel in New Mexico listed in the "Top 100 Hotels in the U.S.," the Lodge is an antique jewel, a well-preserved survivor of another era. From the big fireplace in the lobby to the homey Victorian decor in the guest rooms, this mansion exudes gentility and class. Its nine-hole golf course, one of the nation's highest, challenges duffers across rolling hills between 8,600 and 9,200 feet elevation, and is the site of numerous regional tournaments.

Rooms in the Lodge are filled with antiques, from sideboards and lamps to mirrors and steam radiators. They're decorated in deep burgundy or peach colors; each has a king-size or two double beds. New guests are greeted by a stuffed bear sitting on their bed with a sampler of homemade fudge from the Lodge Mercantile! In 1991 more rooms were added in the form of the Pavilion and the Retreat, which were built adjacent to the Lodge. The Retreat is an entire house with four bedrooms, kitchen, living room, and dining room. The Pavilion is an 11-room bed-and-breakfast inn with pine paneled walls, down comforters, and fireplaces. Of course, the guests of the recent additions also have the privilege of enjoying the amenities and facilities of the Lodge.

Rebecca's (tel. 682-3131) is named for the Lodge's resident ghost, believed to have been a chambermaid in the '30s who was killed by her lumberjack lover. Breakfast and lunch are served from 7am to 2pm Monday to Saturday; brunch from 11:30am to 2pm on Sunday; and fine continental cuisine in a moderate-to-expensive price range is offered for dinner Sunday through Thursday from 5 to 9pm and Friday and Saturday from 5 to 10pm. The Red Dog Saloon, in the basement, has live country entertainment weekend nights. The hotel has room service, valet laundry, concierge (May 15–Sept 15), a golf course, heated outdoor swimming pool, hot tub, sauna, massage, art gallery, gift shop, and goldsmith.

---

2. RUIDOSO

191 miles S of Albuquerque; 48 miles NE of Alamogordo; 71 miles W of Roswell

GETTING THERE   By Plane   Ruidoso is served by **Sierra Blanca Regional Airport** (tel. 336-8111), 17 miles north near Fort Stanton. **Mesa Airlines** (tel. toll free 800/MESA-AIR) has two flights daily to and from Albuquerque and to and from El Paso on weekdays, one flight daily weekends.

By Bus   The Ruidoso **bus station** is on Sudderth Drive just west of Reese Drive (tel. 257-2660). The town is served by **TNM&O,** with three stops daily each direction on its Amarillo–El Paso run, and **Greyhound Lines, Inc.,** which stops once daily each way on its Alamogordo–Roswell run.

By Car   From Albuquerque, take I-25 south 87 miles to San Antonio; turn east on U.S. 380, 74 miles; then south on N.M. 37 and 48 (4 hours). From Alamogordo, take U.S. 70 northeast via Tularosa (1 hour). From Roswell, take U.S. 70 west (1½ hours).

ESSENTIALS Orientation   Ruidoso (most New Mexicans pronounce it Ree-uh-do-so) is situated at 6,900 feet in the timbered Sacramento Mountains, the southernmost finger of the Rockies. U.S. Highway 48 is the main artery through the sprawling town; it's called Sudderth Drive west of its junction with U.S. 70, and Mechem Drive when it turns suddenly north a few miles later.

Information   The **Ruidoso Valley Chamber of Commerce** and visitor center is at 720 Sudderth Dr. Write P.O. Box 698, Ruidoso, NM 88345 (tel. 505/257-7395).

Fast Facts   The **area code** is 505. **Lincoln County Medical Center** is on Sudderth Drive near the U.S. 70 junction, at Nob Hill (tel. 257-7381). The **post office** is on Sudderth Drive just west of its junction with Mechem Drive. In case of **emergencies,** call 257-9111 in Ruidoso; 378-4001 in Ruidoso Downs; 258-5608 in Alto; or 671-4419 in Mescalero.

Ruidoso is a mountain resort town named for its site on a noisy stream. It is most famous for its racetrack, where the world's richest race is run for a $2.5-million purse. Outdoors lovers, hikers, horseback riders, fishermen, and hunters are drawn to the surrounding Lincoln National Forest. Southern New Mexico's most important ski resort, Ski Apache, is just out of town. The nearby Mescalero Apache Indian Reservation includes the magnificent Inn of the Mountain Gods resort hotel. Not far away, the restored village of Lincoln recalls the Wild West days of Billy the Kid.

WHAT TO SEE & DO

Ruidoso itself, while a lovely town for wandering, shopping, and enjoying outdoor pursuits, doesn't have any sightseeing attractions *per se*—no museums, no Indian ruins, no astounding sights. Its surrounding area, however, has plenty.

NEARBY ATTRACTIONS

Ruidoso Downs

In nearby Ruidoso Downs, 2 miles east on U.S. 70, is the famous **Ruidoso Downs racetrack** (see "Sports and Recreation," below) with its new **Museum of the Horse** (tel. 378-4142) with a collection of over 10,000 horse related items, including saddles from all over the world, a Russian sleigh, a horse-drawn "fire engine," and an 1860 stagecoach. Several great American artists including Frederic Remington, Charles M. Russell, Frank Tenney Johnson, and Henry Alkins are represented here as well. The Anne C. Stradling Collection, also housed here, is composed of family memorabilia that spans six generations. There is a gift shop with some interesting books and curios. Admission is $4 for adults, $3 for seniors, and $2.50 for children 5 to 18 (under 5, free).

Mescalero

MESCALERO APACHE INDIAN RESERVATION, P.O. Box 176, Mescalero, NM 88340. Tel. 505/671-4495.

★ Immediately south and west of Ruidoso, the reservation covers over 460,000 acres (719 square miles) and is home to about 2,800 members of the Mescalero, Chiricahua, and Lipan bands of Apaches. Established by order of Pres. Ulysses S. Grant in 1873, it sustains a profitable cattle-ranching industry and the Apache-run logging firm of Mescalero Forest Products.

Even if you're not staying or dining there, don't fail to visit the **Inn of the Mountain Gods,** a luxury four-seasons resort owned and operated by the tribe (see "Nearby Places to Stay," below). It's the crowning achievement of Wendell Chino, president of the Mescalero Apache tribe for all but four years since 1952.

Also on the reservation, on U.S. Highway 70 about 17 miles southwest of Ruidoso, is the ✪ **Mescalero Cultural Center,** open from 8am to 4:30pm Monday through Friday. Photos, artifacts, clothing, craftwork, and other exhibits demonstrate the history and culture of the tribe. Throughout the year, the center hosts powwows of colorful dancing and traditional drumming, open to the public and unrestricted as far as photography.

Restrictions do apply, however, to the annual **Coming of Age Ceremony,** held over four days in early July. A traditional rite reenacted in the tribal community of Mescalero, it includes an Apache maidens' puberty rites ceremony at dawn and a mountain spirits dance at night. Check ahead to learn what you can and can't see, and what you can and can't photograph.

St. Joseph's Mission, just off Highway 70 on a hill overlooking the reservation, is a Gothic-style structure with walls eight feet thick, built by the Apaches between the two world wars. The interior has the symbols of Apache mountain gods along with Roman Catholic saints in paintings and carvings.

Lincoln

LINCOLN STATE MONUMENT, P.O. Box 36, Lincoln, NM 88338. Tel. 505/653-4372.

★ One of the last historic yet uncommercialized 19th-century towns remaining in the American West, this tiny community lies 37 miles northeast of Ruidoso on U.S. Highway 380, in the valley of the Rio Bonito. Only 70 people live here today, but it was once the seat of the largest country in the United States, and the focal point of the notorious Lincoln County War of 1878–79. The entire town is now a New Mexico State Monument and a National Historic Landmark.

The bloody Lincoln County War was fought between various ranching and merchant factions over the issue of beef contracts for nearby Fort Stanton. A sharpshooting teenager named William Bonney—soon to be known as "Billy the Kids"—took sides in this issue with "the good guys," escaping from the burning McSween House after his employer and colleague were shot and killed. Three years later, after shooting down a sheriff, he was captured in Lincoln and sentenced to be hanged. But he shot his way out of his cell in the **Old Courthouse,** now a state museum which still has a hole made by a bullet from the Kid's gun.

Many of the original structures from that era have been preserved and restored by State Monuments, under the aegis of the Museum of New Mexico; the Lincoln County Historical Society; or the Lincoln County Heritage Trust (tel. 653-4025).

At the trust's ✪ **Historical Center,** exhibits explain the role in Lincoln's history of Apaches, Hispanics, Anglo cowboys, and the black Buffalo Soldiers, and detail the Lincoln County War. A brief slide show on Lincoln history is presented in an old-fashioned theater. Start your visit here and either join a tour or pick up a brochure describing the trust's self-guided walking tour (50¢). Across the courtyard is the **Luna Museum Store.**

The trust also owns the **Wortley Hotel** (see "Nearby Places to Stay," below). The Old Courthouse and the **Tunstall Store** are operated as museums by the State Monument, while the historical society runs **Dr. Woods' House** and conducts historical research. Many other 19th-century adobes are still private homes.

An annual folk pageant, *The Last Escape of Billy the Kid,* has been presented outdoors since 1949 as a highly romanticized version of the Lincoln County War. It's staged Friday and Saturday nights and Sunday afternoon during the first full weekend in August as part of the **Old Lincoln Days** celebration. The festival also includes living-history demonstrations of traditional crafts, musical programs, and food booths throughout the village. From mid-June to mid-August, other weekend activities, including Apache dancing, historical dramas, and lectures, are scheduled.

Admission: Adults $2, children under 16 free.

Open: Daily May 1–Sept 15 9:30am–5:30pm, rest of year 8:30am–4:30pm.

The Lincoln Loop

It's wise to include Lincoln on a 1-day "loop tour" from Ruidoso, to see many other significant sights within a short drive from the resort center.

Heading east from Ruidoso on U.S. 70, about 18 miles past Ruidoso Downs, is the hamlet of **San Patricio.** This picturesque community on the Rio Hondo is known as the home of painters Peter Hurd, Henriette Wyeth, and their son Michael Hurd. Their work is displayed in the **Hurd-La Rinconada Gallery** on the late Peter Hurd's Sentinel Ranch.

At Hondo, 4 miles farther at the confluence of the Rio Bonito and Rio Hondo, turn west on U.S. Highway 380. Lincoln's a 10-mile drive from here. The high plains rising gently to the 10,000-foot Capitan Mountains in the north, look like a scene from a classic western movie. Eight miles farther, a turnoff to the south leads 3 miles to **Fort Stanton,** a frontier outpost from 1855 to 1896. Today it is a state school and hospital for retarded children. Many of the original fort buildings remain. The Fort Stanton Road continues to Sierra Blanca Airport and Alto, just north of Ruidoso.

But return to Highway 380 and continue another 4 miles to **Capitan.** Smokey the Bear, national symbol of forest fire prevention, was born near here, found as an orphaned cub by firefighters in the early 1950s. He lived a long life in the National Zoo in Washington, D.C., and after his death was returned to his home turf for burial. You can visit his grave and walk nature paths in ✪ **Smokey Bear Historic State Park,** learn his story, and find out more about fire prevention at its Smokey Bear Museum. It's open 8:30am to 5pm daily; admission is 25¢.

West from Capitan 20 miles is **Carrizozo,** seat of Lincoln County since 1912 and the crossroads of U.S. 380, U.S. 54, and a Southern Pacific rail line. Carrizozo is on the eastern edge of the Malpais lava flow; **Valley of Fires Recreation Area,** a BLM-administered site just west of the town on U.S. 380, preserves this 44-mile-long volcanic finger, a geologic "baby" just 1,500 years old. Picnicking and hiking on well-trodden trails is encouraged.

Twelve miles northeast of Carrizozo on N.M. 349 is the ghost town of ✪ **White Oaks,** an 1879 gold-mining town that once had a population of 4,000. When the railroad bypassed the town in favor of Carrizozo, it fell into a decline. Few live here today, except a handful of artists. A museum, saloon, and lovely Victorian homes surround the townsite. Twenty miles farther north, in **Ancho,** the eclectic **My House of Old Things** displays thousands of items, from kitchenware to railroad and industrial memorabilia, in a turn-of-the-century railroad depot. It's open May through October 15 from 9am to 5pm daily; admission is $2 for adults, 50¢ for children.

If you turn south at Oscura and travel 28 miles via U.S. 54, then another 8 miles east on a well-marked side road, you'll reach ✪ **Three Rivers Petroglyphs National Recreation Site** (tel. 525-8228). A three-quarter-mile trail through a vast plain, on the west side of the White Mountain Wilderness, reveals more than 5,000 petroglyphs, or rock inscriptions, carved by the Mogollon people who lived there between A.D. 900 and 1400. Ruins of an ancient village may also be seen just south of the inscription trail. The area, run by the BLM, has camping and picnicking facilities. There's no fee.

From the Three Rivers turnoff, it's another 17 miles south on U.S. 54 to Tularosa. Turn east here on U.S. 70 to return to Ruidoso via the Mescalero Apache Reservation.

SPORTS & RECREATION

CAMPING   Lincoln National Forest has 13 campgrounds in the region; four of them are within the immediate area. Maps (at $2) and details can be obtained from all campground offices, including the **Smokey Bear Ranger Station,** 902 Mechem Dr., Ruidoso (tel. 257-4995), open from Memorial Day to Labor Day, Saturday 7:30am to 4:30pm.

FISHING   Bonito Lake, Alto Lake, and Rio Ruidoso are popular destinations in the national forest. A New Mexico fishing license is required (see "Sports and Recreation," in Chapter 1), **Conley's Trout Lake,** 4 miles east of Ruidoso Downs on U.S. 70, is privately owned; a family permit costs $1, including poles and bait. You pay for what you catch at 30¢ an inch. The lake is open 8am to 4pm daily.

FITNESS CLUB   **Ruidoso Athletic Club** (tel. 257-4900), has Nautilus equipment and free weights, Lifecycles, racquetball, aerobics, hot tub, sauna, and massage. Day visits are $5 for nonmembers. It's open daily except major holidays.

GOLF   There are plenty of opportunities here. **Cree Meadows Country Club,** Country Club Road off Sudderth Drive (tel. 257-5815), is an 18-hole public course. Also public are the 18-hole course at the **Inn of the Mountain Gods,** Carrizo Canyon Road (tel. 257-5141); and the nine-hole **Carrizozo Golf Course** in Carrizozo. **Alto Lakes Golf and Country Club,** High Mesa Drive, Alto Village, is an 18-hole private course. **Mark's Driving Range,** across from Cree Meadows, is open from 8am to 8pm daily. Miniature golf can be played at two courses: **Pan-O-Rama Mini Golf,** Eagle Drive at Rio Ruidoso (tel. 257-7164), and **Executive Golf Course,** Rainbow Lake Fun Park (tel. 257-9039).

HIKING   More than 300 miles of trails weave a web through Lincoln National Forest. From Ruidoso, a favorite destination of hikers is the **White Mountain Wilderness,** with nine major trailheads, and the **Capitan Mountain Wilderness,** with 11 major trails. Smokey Bear Ranger Station, 901 Mechem Dr., Ruidoso, has an excellent map for $4. **Monjeau Lookout** is a popular destination off Ski Run Road.

HORSE RACING   The world's richest quarter-horse race, the $2.5 million All-American Futurity, is run each year on Labor Day at ✪ **Ruidoso Downs** racetrack (tel. 378-4431). Seventy-seven other days of quarter-horse and thoroughbred racing lead up to the big one, beginning the second week of May. Post time in May and June is 1pm Thursday through Sunday, and July through Labor Day Thursday through Monday. Grandstand admission is free.

HORSEBACK RIDING   Numerous private stables in the area offer trail rides between 8am and 6pm, at rates from $7.50 to $8.50 per hour. Stables include **Buddies** (tel. 258-4027), the **Grindstone Stables** (tel. 257-2241), and the **Inn of the Mountain Gods** (tel. 257-5141).

SKIING   Southern New Mexico's premier ski resort is **Ski Apache** (snow report tel. 257-9001, information tel. 336-4356), only 20 miles northwest of Ruidoso in the Mescalero Apache Reservation. Situated on an 11,500-foot ridge of 12,003-foot Sierra Blanca, the resort boasts a gondola, five triple chairs, two double chairs, a day lodge, sport shop, rental shop, ski school, first-aid center, four snack bars, and a lounge. Ski Apache has 37 trails and slopes (25% beginner, 35% intermediate, and

40% advanced), with a vertical drop of 1,900 feet and a total skier capacity of 15,300 an hour. In 1992, all-day, all-lift rates were $30 adult, $18 child (12 and under). The mountain is open Thanksgiving to Easter daily from 8:45am to 4pm. Lift-and-lodging packages can be booked through the Inn of the Mountain Gods.

SWIMMING   Ruidoso Municipal Swimming Pool, 515 Sudderth Dr. (tel. 257-2795), is open in summer, 11:30am to 4:45pm daily; admission is $2.75. Private indoor heated pool is open daily year-round at **Cree Meadows Country Club** (tel. 257-5815).

MISCELLANEOUS   Rainbow Lake Fun Park, Carrizo Canyon Road (tel. 257-9039), appeals to kids of all ages with miniature golf, including roughs and water hazards; bumper boats; batting cages; a trout lake; a video arcade; and a restaurant. It's open Sunday through Thursday from 10am to 10pm, 10am to midnight Friday and Saturday.

SHOPPING

Many noted artists—among them Peter Hurd, Henriette Wyeth, and Gordon Snidow—have made their homes in Ruidoso and the surrounding Lincoln County. Dozens of other art-world hopefuls have followed them here, with the result that there is a proliferation of galleries in town. Among them are: **California Colors,** 201 Country Club Rd., open Tuesday to Sunday from 11am to 5pm; the **Camel House,** 714 Mechem Dr., open Monday to Saturday from 10am to 5pm; **Crucis Art Bronze Foundry & Gallery,** 524 Sudderth Dr., open from 10am to early evening daily; **Fenton's Gallery,** 2629 Sudderth Dr., open daily from 10am to 6pm; **Grace's Art & Frame Chalet,** 1108 Sudderth Dr., open Monday to Saturday from 10am to 5pm; **Gray Fox Gallery,** 2312 Sudderth Dr., open Monday to Saturday from 10am to 5pm and from 11am to 4pm on Sunday; **Knapp Gallery,** Glencoe, open by appointment (tel. 378-4126); ✪ **La Rinconada (Michael Hurd Gallery),** San Patricio, open Monday to Saturday from 10am to 5pm; **Lindavida,** 1085 Mechem Dr., open Saturday from 10am to 5pm; **McGary Studios,** Loma Grande Estates, off Nogal Highway, open by appointment (tel. 354-2402); **Meigs Gallery,** San Patricio, open 9am to 5pm daily; **Mountain Arts,** 2530 Sudderth Dr., open Monday to Saturday from 10am to 6pm and from 10am to 4pm on Sunday; **Rio Mercado,** 2200 Sudderth Dr., open daily from 9:30am to 7pm; **Savage Arts,** 2609 Sudderth Dr., open from 9am to 6pm daily; **Spirit Winds,** 103 Mechem Dr., open from 10am to 5pm Monday through Thursday and from 10am to 6pm Friday and Saturday; and **Travis Gallery,** 2342 Sudderth Dr., open from 10am to 6pm Monday to Saturday.

WHERE TO STAY

A 9.75% tax is imposed on all lodging bills (6% state tax and 3.75% city lodging tax). The only exception is the Inn of the Mountain Gods, governed by Mescalero Apache Reservation laws (7.5% tax).

Moderate

BEST WESTERN SWISS CHALET INN, 1451 Mechem Dr. (P.O. Box 759), Ruidoso, NM 88345. Tel. 505/258-5325 or toll free 800/47-SWISS or 800/528-1234. 82 rms, 2 suites. A/C TV TEL
$ Rates: $54–$74 double. AE, CB, DC, DISC, MC, V.
This blue-and-white chalet-style motel, with Swiss flags hanging outside its entry, looks right at home in a mountain resort. The spacious rooms feature burgundy color schemes and gray Taoseno-style furnishings.

In Ahna-Michelle's Restaurant restaurant, Swiss and American food is served in an alpine atmosphere of Swiss bells and other souvenirs. The menu includes the likes of wienerschnitzel, wursts, Luzern Cordon Bleu, and Davos Platz (peppered beef tips). Prices range from $4.95 to $13.95 for dinner main courses. The restaurant is open for breakfast daily from 7:30am to 11am, and for dinner daily, except Tuesday from 6pm to 9pm. The Inn has room service, valet laundry, nonsmoking rooms, an indoor swimming pool, Jacuzzi, and guest Laundromat. VCRs and videos are available at the front desk.

CARRIZO LODGE, Carrizo Canyon Rd. (P.O. Box 1371-M513), Ruidoso, NM 88345. Tel. 505/257-9131. 90 rms and suites. A/C TV TEL

$ Rates: $40–$79 single or double, $90–$135 3-bedroom apartment. MC, V.
Nestled among the pines beside a stream flowing east toward Ruidoso from Lake Mescalero, this lodge, on 32 acres, is the home of the Carrizo Art School, one of America's oldest. Built in 1879 on a natural river-rock foundation, Carrizo has been designated a New Mexico cultural property and is on the National Register of Historic Places. The lodge, a rose-colored building with stucco walls, and its renovated bungalows retain their original *viga* ceilings, hardwood floors, and brass fixtures. Modern luxury condominium suites all have fireplaces.

The lodge has a restaurant and cocktail lounge. Facilities include a swimming pool, sauna, hot tub, video arcade, and convenience store.

DAN DEE CABINS RESORT, 310 Main Rd., Upper Canyon (P.O. Box 844), Ruidoso, NM 88345. Tel. 505/257-2165 or toll free 800/345-4848. 12 cabins. FRIDGE TV

$ Rates: June 15–Labor Day $72 1 bedroom, $92 2 bedrooms, $108 3 bedrooms; Dec 15–Easter $72 1 bedroom, $89 2 bedroom, $105 3 bedroom; rest of year $56 1 bedroom, $72 2 bedroom, $84 3 bedrooms. DISC, MC, V.
Rustic, woodsy, back-to-nature—these adjectives apply to the Dan Dee Cabins, some of which date back to 1940. Built beside a stream in five acres of forest, the cabins have sitting porches, fireplaces, kitchens with gas stoves, and their own hot-water heaters. They're popular with honeymooners who don't want to be disturbed: The only phone is in the office. For families, there's a barbecue area and children's playground.

THE INN AT PINE SPRINGS CANYON, off U.S. Hwy. 70 (P.O. Box 2100), Ruidoso Downs, NM 88346. Tel. 505/378-8100 or toll free 800/237-3607. Fax 505/378-8215. 100 rms, 4 suites. A/C TV TEL

$ Rates (including continental breakfast): May–Sept $67–$73 single, $74–$88 double, $140–$169 suite; Oct–Apr $40–$55 single, $55–$68 double, $115 suite. Children 12 and under free with parent. AE, CB, DC, DISC, MC, V.
High on a hill overlooking the racetrack, this motel is set on beautifully manicured grounds sprinkled with flowers and pine, spruce, and juniper trees. The rooms are almost too spacious; they're nicely appointed with standard furnishings and limited-edition prints on the walls. A big Jacuzzi on an open-air deck is a favorite of guests.

SHADOW MOUNTAIN LODGE, 107 Main Rd., Upper Canyon (P.O. Box 1427), Ruidoso, NM 88345. Tel. 505/257-4886 or toll free 800/441-4331. 19 rms. A/C FRIDGE TV TEL

$ Rates: July–Aug and weekends Memorial Day–Labor Day $77 single or double; Oct 1–May 30, weekdays, $49.50 single or double; high-season weekends and low-season weekends $63 single or double. Ski and golf packages. AE, CB, DC, DISC, MC, V.

Advertising "luxury lodging for couples," this property doesn't accept children, let alone pets. It's a place of rustic elegance, an outstanding spot for a romantic getaway. Each unit has a king-size bed, a fireplace (wood is provided), and a coffee maker (with complimentary coffee and tea). Ten rooms have full kitchens; the other nine have a wet bar and microwave. There's a barbecue area outside. Guests get a discount off greens fees at a local country club, where they can play golf, swim, or jump in a Jacuzzi.

Inexpensive

RUIDOSO INN, U.S. Hwy. 70 (0.3 miles S. of N.M. 48 junction), Ruidoso, NM 88345. Tel. 505/378-4051 or toll free 800/332-4051. Fax 505/378-4051; request fax. 52 rooms and 20 condominium units. A/C TV TEL
$ Rates: $35–$50 single, $40–$55 double, $85–$175 condo. MC, V.
Operated by Vacation Resorts International, this highway motel is rather ordinary. Rooms are clean but dimly lit and ordinary in size and furnishings. They have a pastel decor with southwestern motifs. The Fifth Season Restaurant and Lounge (open 7am–2pm and 5–9pm daily), serves American and New Mexican dinners. The inn offers room service and a guest laundry. Facilities include an indoor swimming pool, Jacuzzi, and outdoor barbecue deck.

NEARBY PLACES TO STAY

CASA DE PATRON, on U.S. 380 (P.O. Box 27) Lincoln, NM 88338. Tel. 505/653-4676. 3 rms, 2 casitas.
$ Rates (including breakfast): $59 single, $69 double, $79–$89 casita. DISC, MC, V. **Parking:** Off-street parking is available.
If you really want to get away from it all and experience the solitude of a small New Mexico village nestled amidst the hills of the Rio Bonito valley and a bit of the history of Billy the Kid, Casa de Patron is your best bet. The main building of Casa de Patron, an adobe, was built around 1860 and is said to have housed Juan Patron's old store. It is also thought that Billy the Kid used part of the house as a hideout at some point during his time in the Lincoln area.

Jeremy and Cleis Jordan, the gracious hosts of this charming bed-and-breakfast, have created some lovely rooms in the main house and two wonderful casitas. You enter the main house from the side and turn right to the guest sitting room where you'll find a fireplace, comfortable couches, a wood rocking chair, and a grand piano (Cleis is a musician—you'll also see the practice organ in the breakfast room). The Turnstall Room is the only one with twin beds and it is ideal for single travelers. The McSween Room and Juan's Old Store both have queen size beds, and the latter has a patio and a private entrance. People traveling with children are encouraged to take advantage of the casitas. Casita de Paz has two bedrooms, a full bath, and a sitting area. The casita also holds a small refrigerator and coffee maker. Casita Bonita (my personal favorite) was built with adobe bricks by Cleis and Jeremy and can best be described as a small house with everything you might need contained within its walls—a full kitchen (completely stocked with dishes, pots, and pans, and the like), a loft bedroom with a queen-size bed (and a carved antique headboard), bathroom, and living room (with a futon that sleeps two). The cathedral ceiling in Casita Bonita gives it a spacious feeling even though it is quite small. If you choose to stay in a casita, you will get a continental breakfast delivered to your door in the morning, but if you stay in the main house, Cleis and Jeremy will prepare a full breakfast with a hot dish, sausage, juice, fresh fruit, and coffee or tea.

INN OF THE MOUNTAIN GODS, Carrizo Canyon Rd. (P.O. Box 269), Mescalero, NM 88340. Tel. 505/257-5141 or toll free 800/545-9011. Fax 505/257-6173. 250 rms, 10 suites. A/C TV TEL
$ Rates (including breakfast): June 1–Labor Day $115 single or double, $125 suite; Apr–May and Sept–Oct $95 single or double, $105 suite; Nov–Mar $80 single or double, $90 suite. Golf, tennis, and ski packages. AE, CB, DC, DISC, MC, V.
Southern New Mexico's most luxurious resort is this impressive property on the Mescalero Apache Indian Reservation, 3½ miles southwest of Ruidoso. It is the successful dream of the tribal president, Wendell Chino, who wanted to help his people get into the recreation and tourism business. They picked a spectacularly beautiful location, overlooking pristine Lake Mescalero and, behind it, 12,003-foot-high Sierra Blanca.

Nine interconnected brown-shake buildings comprise the hotel and an associated convention center. Guests cross a covered wooden bridge over a cascading stream to reach the three-story lobby, dominated by a huge conelike, copper fireplace. Modern tribal art and trophies of wild animals bagged on the reservation are on display. The property includes an 18-hole golf course designed by Ted Robinson, whose work includes the famed course at the Princess in Acapulco; eight tennis courts; horseback riding stables; boating and fishing; and many other recreations. In winter, buses shuttle skiers to the Ski Apache resort, also owned by the tribe.

The guest rooms are spacious and sophisticated, with high ceilings and tasteful furnishings. All are appointed in shades of desert rose or mesquite green. Lithographs on the walls depict typical 19th-century tribal scenes. Each room has a big closet, two sinks, and a dressing table with mirrors. There are rooms for nonsmokers and the disabled.

The Dan Li Ka Room (open 7am to 2:30pm and 6 to 10pm daily) is a huge dining room with a view of lake and mountain beyond. The menu features steak, poultry, seafood, and pasta, plus reservation specialties like Southwest sauté (venison, chicken breast, and beef medallions with marsala-cilantro sauce) and broiled fresh mountain trout. Appetizers run $4.95 to $7.95, dinner main courses $12.95 to $17.95. The Top o' the Inn, on the mezzanine above the lobby, has casual dining from 2:30 to 9pm. Ina Da Lounge has ample seating and a big floor for dancing and drinks. There's a piano bar off the lobby.

The hotel offers room service (7am to 10pm), valet laundry, a gift shop, and a gaming room for poker, Lotto, and bingo. Facilities include a golf course, stables, outdoor tennis courts, swimming pool, whirlpool, saunas, fishing lake stocked with rainbow trout, trap and skeet shooting, archery, boating (rowboats, pedal boats, and canoes rented), and a base for hunting trips. A convention center is attached. No pets.

SIERRA MESA LODGE, Fort Stanton Road (P.O. Box 463), Alto, NM 88312. Tel. 505/336-4515. 5 rms.
$ Rates (including full breakfast): $75 single, $85 double. DISC, MC, V.

★ Southern California transplants Larry and Lila Goodman operate what may be Ruidoso's friendliest and most elegant B&B for nonsmokers. Each room is faithful to its particular theme. The Country Western Room, for instance, has a huge step-up bed and steamer trunk; the Victorian Room boasts an eagle-claw bathtub/shower. There's also the Oriental Room, the Queen Anne Room, and the French Country Room. All have private baths, period furnishings, comforters and goose-down pillows on the brass and/or four-poster beds, rocking chairs and chaise longues. The lodge has a large private spa and each afternoon offers silver tea service. The rates include high tea as well as evening wine and cheese.

WORTLEY HOTEL, P.O. Box 96 (Hwy. 380) Lincoln, NM 88338. Tel. 505/653-4500. 8 rms.
$ Rates: $53 single or double. MC, V.
Built in 1878 as the Lincoln County wars began to flare, this one-story, Territorial-style inn, surrounded by a board veranda and a white picket fence, retains the flavor of the last century. Each room has a brass bed, ceiling fan, and marble-topped table. Antiques and fireplaces are found throughout the hotel. The hotel's Victorian dining room serves a full menu with an emphasis on western meals. It closes during January and February. If you're here for lunch, try the homemade green chile and tortillas; and don't miss the "cobbler of the day."

WHERE TO DINE

Expensive

**LA LORRAINE, 2523 Sudderth Dr., Ruidoso. Tel. 257-2954.
Cuisine:** FRENCH. **Reservations:** Recommended.

$ Prices: Appetizers $4.95–$6.25; lunch $5.95–$12.95; dinner $9.95–$19.95. AE, MC, V.
Open: Lunch Mon–Sat 11am–2pm, dinner Mon–Sat 6–9:30pm.

This piece of Paris is a bit hard to imagine in a New Mexico mountain town, but here it is, in an adobe building on the main street. International flags drape over an awning above wild roses in a window planter. Inside, there's French provincial decor, with lace curtains and candlelight; diners can also opt for outdoor courtyard service beside a mural of a Parisian sidewalk café.

Le menu? Pâtés, bisques, salades . . . and wonderful dishes like canard (duck) à l'orange, côtes d'agneau (lamb) with apricot-mint chutney, veal au calvados, and steak au poivre.

Moderate

THE BULL RING, 1200 Mechem Dr., Ruidoso. Tel. 258-3555.
   Cuisine: AMERICAN. **Reservations:** Recommended for dinner.
$ Prices: Appetizers $1.95–$5.95; main courses $4.95–$15.95. AE, MC, V.
   Open: Daily 5–10pm.
Better known as a popular night spot, with live rock music weekend nights, the Bull Ring—located at the north end of town, en route to the ski area—also serves steaks and other meals in a comfortable, unpretentious dining room. New York strip, T-bone, rib-eye, sirloin, filet mignon, and more are offered up, along with shrimp, trout, chicken, and Mexican dishes. It's a rustic, comfortable spot.

CATTLE BARON STEAK HOUSE, 657 Sudderth Dr., Ruidoso. Tel. 257-9355.
   Cuisine: STEAK & SEAFOOD. **Reservations:** Recommended.
$ Prices: Appetizers $2.75–$5.95; lunch $3.95–$6.50; dinner $5.75–$20.95. AE, DISC, MC, V.
   Open: Sun–Thurs 11am–9:30pm, Fri–Sat 11am–10:30pm.
A casually elegant restaurant with several levels of seating in a white adobe-style interior, the Cattle Baron serves up a variety of fine steaks and chicken dishes. It also boasts an extensive seafood menu, including fresh catches from the Atlantic, Pacific, and Gulf of Mexico. Filet Oscar (tenderloin wrapped with bacon, crowned with béarnaise sauce, topped with crabmeat and asparagus spears) is always a big seller. There's a large salad bar and a great lounge.

Inexpensive

CASA BLANCA, 501 Mechem Dr., Ruidoso. Tel. 257-2495.
   Cuisine: NEW MEXICAN.
$ Prices: Appetizers $1.95–$5.95; main courses $4.95–$8.25. AE, MC, V.
   Open: Daily 11am–10pm.
This large white-stucco building, a half mile north of the Sudderth/Mechem junction toward Alto, commands a lovely valley view from its hilltop garden location. Contemporary regional art hangs on the walls inside, and a large beer garden/patio, shaded by ponderosa pines, is the location of afternoon "jams" from 2 to 6pm every summer Sunday. There's a small cantina downstairs. The menu features a wide variety of southwestern favorites, include chimichangas and green-chile enchiladas.

DON VICTOR'S, 2911 Sudderth Dr., Uptown, Ruidoso. Tel. 257-9900.
   Cuisine: NEW MEXICAN. **Reservations:** Recommended in evening.
$ Prices: Appetizers $2.50–$4.95, main courses $4.75–$7.95. MC, V.
   Open: Daily 7am–9pm.
Hanging baskets of silk flowers, wrought-iron designs, and prominent *vigas* give this Uptown restaurant a pleasant atmosphere. An especially popular dish is the Mexican steak—a breaded, top-round steak smothered with salsa, garnished with cheese, and

served with rice and beans. The menu also includes stuffed sopaipillas, enchiladas, chimichangas, fajitas, and other regional favorites.

Budget

BLUE GOOSE, 2963 Sudderth Dr., Ruidoso. Tel. 257-5271.
  Cuisine: DELI.
$ **Prices:** Lunch $5.45–$5.95. No credit cards.
  Open: Tues–Sat 11:30am–2:30pm.

A delightful little lunchroom with lace curtains and blue everywhere, the Blue Goose also caters evening functions. It's lodged in the historic Wingfield House. The everyday menu caters to vegetarians with meatless tacos, sandwiches, and fruit-and-veggie plates, but roast-beef sandwiches and daily specials like chicken cacciatore and apple-glazed pork chops light up carnivores' eyes. The sour-cream lemon pie is hard to say no to.

HUMMINGBIRD TEAROOM, 2306 Sudderth Dr., Village Plaza, Ruidoso. Tel. 257-5100.
  Cuisine: DELI.
$ **Prices:** $2.95–$4.95. No credit cards.
  Open: Tues–Sat 11am–4pm.
A little ice-cream and dessert shop, the Hummingbird also offers sandwiches, salads, and delicious homemade soups on an outdoor patio. It also draws throngs to afternoon tea!

NEARBY PLACES TO DINE

CHANGO'S, 1st and Lincoln Sts. (Hwys. 48 and 380), Capitan. Tel. 354-4213.
  Cuisine: INTERNATIONAL. **Reservations:** Highly recommended.
$ **Prices:** Dinner $10.95–$12.95. No credit cards.
  Open: Thurs–Sun 5pm till closing.

Jerrold Donti Flores, the owner of Chango's (it's named after his cat), left San Francisco a few years ago and returned to the village of his birth. An avant-garde sculptor and acrylic/airbrush artist, Flores is also extremely adept in the kitchen. So he opened this small (24-seat) restaurant in a circa-1900 adobe building, and decorated it with his own works and a collection of primitive art.

A selection of four gourmet home-style main dishes changes every few nights. The main course—such as Spanish paella, beef manicotti, or whitefish in an asparagus-pistachio sauce—is cooked in terra-cotta, accompanied by fresh vegetables and fruit, and followed by dessert. The restaurant serves no alcohol.

FLYING J RANCH, Hwy. 48, 1 mile north of Alto. Tel. 336-4330.
  Cuisine: CHUCK WAGON. **Reservations:** Highly recommended.
$ **Prices:** $10.50 adults; reduced children's rates. MC, V.
  Open: May–Labor Day, Mon–Sat 7:30pm.

A treat for the whole family, this ranch is like a western village, complete with staged gunfights . . . and pony rides for the kids. Gates open at 6pm; a chuck-wagon dinner of beef, baked potato, beans, biscuit, applesauce cake, and coffee or lemonade is served promptly at 7:30. Then, at 8:15pm, the Flying J Wranglers present a fast-paced stage show with western music and a cheer-the-hero, boo-the-villain melodrama.

INNCREDIBLE RESTAURANT & SALOON, Hwy. 48 North at Ski Run Rd., Alto Village. Tel. 336-4312.
  Cuisine: STEAKS & CONTINENTAL. **Reservations:** Recommended.

$ Prices: Appetizers $3.25–$5.50; dinner $7.95–$18.25. AE, MC, V.
  Open: Daily 11:30am–3pm and 5–10pm.
Old West–style art hangs on the walls of this modern rustic establishment. Fine etched-glass and stained-glass work is accented by large skylights. The restaurant (open only for dinner) serves a variety of steaks, including the teriyaki Inncredible; prime rib, Alaskan king crab, shrimp de Jonghe (in a sour cream and herb sauce), veal and chicken dishes, and pastas. There are special children's meals. You can get a light lunch (soups, sandwiches, and salads) in the bar.

TINNIE'S SILVER DOLLAR, Hwy. 70 E., Tinnie. Tel. 653-4425.
  Cuisine: STEAKS & SEAFOOD. **Reservations:** Recommended.
$ Prices: Appetizers $3.95–$8.95; main courses $9.95–$23.50. MC, V.
  Open: Wed–Sun 11:30am–10pm.

Housed in a Territorial-style building dating from the 1880s, this Victorian eatery is truly a relic from another era. An ornate 19th-century European music box still plays tunes on ancient metal disks. Four stained-glass windows from an old El Paso church cover the entire wall of one room; above the fireplace in another, Neptune is attended by mermaids in an 1880s stained-glass window from a San Francisco seafood restaurant. The restaurant has a massive oak bar, milkglass gaslights, a bell tower, and a veranda offers a fine view of the Rio Honda valley.

For an appetizer, you can't miss with the layered Brie, with pesto and piñon nuts. Selections include everything from rib-eye steak, grilled lamb chops, and lobster tail, to Silver Dollar prawns (basted in drawn butter), pasta Scandiffio, and enchiladas suizas. Tinnie's serves espresso coffees.

---

3. ROSWELL

199 miles SE of Albuquerque; 185 miles NE of Las Cruces;
76 N of Carlsbad.

GETTING THERE By Plane Roswell Airport, at Roswell Industrial Air Center on South Main Street (tel. 347-5703), is served commercially by **Mesa Airlines** (tel. 347-5501 or toll free 800/MESA-AIR). Mesa flies to Albuquerque almost hourly throughout the day and direct to Dallas, Texas, twice daily.

By Bus Texas, New Mexico & Oklahoma (TNM&O) Coaches serve Roswell with connections three times daily each way on the Amarillo–El Paso run, four times daily to and from Alamogordo and Ruidoso, twice to and from Albuquerque and Las Cruces, once daily to and from Carlsbad. The **bus station** is at 515 N. Main St. (tel. 622-2510).

By Car From Albuquerque take I-40 east 59 miles to Clines Corners; turn south on U.S. 285, 140 miles to Roswell (4 hours). From Las Cruces, take U.S. 70 east (4 hours). From Carlsbad, take U.S. 285 north (1½ hours).

ESSENTIALS Orientation Roswell is at the intersection of east-west U.S. Highway 380, which runs through the city as Second Street, and north-south U.S. Highway 285, known here as Main Street. City streets east and west of Main, and north and south of First (just south of Second), are so designated. On the south side of the city, Main Street branches, with South Main heading due south to the airport and Southeast Main continuing as U.S. 285 to Carlsbad.

Information The **Roswell Chamber of Commerce** is at 131 W. Second St. (P.O. Drawer 70), Roswell, NM 88201 (tel. 505/623-5698).

Fast Facts The **area code** is 505. The main **hospital,** Eastern New Mexico

Medical Center, has a north campus at 405 W. Country Club Rd. (tel. 622-8170) and a south campus on South Main at Chisum Street (tel. 622-1110). The **post office** is located at 415 N. Pennsylvania St., at West Fifth Street (tel. 622-3741). **Eastern New Mexico University-Roswell** is located at Roswell Industrial Air Center on South Main Street (tel. 624-7000). In the event of an **emergency,** dial 911.

oswell (pop. 50,000) dominates a vast, scantily populated prairie of ranch land. From its founding in 1871, it has been a center for cattle and sheep raising. It has also become a major industrial center: The city is home to the largest bus-manufacturing business in the Northern Hemisphere. Its elevation of 3,650 feet gives it a hot climate in summer, mild in winter. The city has a very active cultural life, and a visit to its museums and nearby natural areas make it worth spending some time.

WHAT TO SEE & DO

ROSWELL MUSEUM AND ART CENTER, 100 W. 11th St., Roswell. Tel. 624-6744.

This highly acclaimed small museum is deservedly Roswell's number one attraction. Established in the 1930s through the efforts of city government, local archaeological and historical societies, and the WPA, the museum proclaims this city's role as a center for the arts and a cradle of America's space industry.

The art center contains the world's finest collection of works by Hurd and his wife, Henriette Wyeth, as well as representative works by Georgia O'Keeffe, Ernest Blumenschein, Joseph Sharp, and others famed from the early 20th-century Taos and Santa Fe art colonies. There are also permanent and temporary exhibits of late 20th-century works, as well as Native American and Hispanic art. The museum has an early historical section, but its pride and joy is the Robert Goddard Collection, which presents actual engines, rocket assemblies, and specialized parts developed by Goddard in the 1930s, when he lived and worked in Roswell. Goddard's workshop has been re-created for the exhibit. A special display commemorates the Apollo XVII, which undertook the last manned lunar landing in 1972; it includes the spacesuit worn on the moon by New Mexican Harrison Schmitt. The Goddard Planetarium is used as a science classroom for local students and for special programs. Ask about "the Roswell Incident," an alleged UFO crash near here in 1947 that was reported by the local newspaper but quickly hushed up by the U.S. Army.

Admission: Free.

Open: Mon–Sat 9am–5pm, Sun and holidays 1–5pm. **Closed:** Christmas and New Year's Day.

HISTORICAL CENTER FOR SOUTHEAST NEW MEXICO, 200 N. Lea Ave. at W. 2nd St., Roswell. Tel. 622-8333.

The handsome mansion that houses this historical collection is as much a part of the museum as the collection itself. A three-story yellow-brick structure built in 1910–12 by rancher J. P. White, its gently sweeping rooflines and large porches reflect the prairie style of architecture made popular by Frank Lloyd Wright. The White family lived here until 1972; today this home, on the National Register of Historic Places, is a monument to turn-of-the-century life-styles.

First- and second-floor rooms, including the parlor, bedrooms, dining room, and kitchen, have been restored and furnished with early 20th-century antiques. The kitchen includes such vintage appliances as a wood-burning cookstove, an icebox, and a pie safe. The second floor has a gallery of changing historic exhibits, from fashions to children's toys to business machines. The third floor, once White's private library, now houses the Pecos Valley Collection and the archives of the Historical Center for Southeast New Mexico.

Admission: Donations welcomed.

Open: Fri–Sun 1–4pm.

**NEW MEXICO MILITARY INSTITUTE, N. Main St. and College Blvd.,
Roswell. Tel. 622-6250** or 624-8100.

"West Point of the West" celebrated its centennial in 1991. Established 100 years earlier, it is one of the most distinguished military schools in the United States, and the alma mater of luminaries as disparate as football star Roger Staubach and network newsman Sam Donaldson. The state-supported, coeducational institute includes a 4-year college preparatory high school and a 2-year junior college, and is the only J.C. in the country that offers graduates an Army ROTC commission in just two years.

On campus is the **General Douglas L. McBride Military Museum,** with a fine collection of artillery and artifacts that document New Mexico's role in America's wars. Among the memorabilia are items from the Bataan Death March. **Godfrey Athletic Center** is open to Roswell visitors with payment of a small fee; in fact, the whole campus is open. Tours are offered by appointment.

Admission: Free.

Open: Daily (museum hours) 8am–4pm.

**SPRING RIVER PARK AND ZOO, 1400 E. College Blvd. at Atkinson
Ave., Roswell. Tel. 624-6760.**

This lovely park, covering 48 acres on either side of a stream a mile east of NMMI, incorporates a miniature train, an antique carousel, a large prairie-dog town, a children's fishing pond, a picnic ground, and playgrounds. Capitan Trail takes zoo visitors on a simulated walk from the river bottom to the plains, foothills, and mountains, with regional animals grouped into their appropriate habitats. There's also a children's petting zoo, a Texas longhorn ranch, and (in the planning stages) a World Safari enclosure for exotic species.

Admission: Free.

Open: Zoo, year-round, daily 10am–sunset, weather permitting. Rides and concessions, June–Labor Day daily 1–6pm; Apr–May and Sept–Oct, Sat–Sun 1–6pm.

NEARBY ATTRACTIONS

**BITTER LAKE NATIONAL WILDLIFE REFUGE, Pecos River, off U.S.
Hwy. 70, 15 miles NE of Roswell. Tel. 622-6755.**

A great variety of waterfowl—including cormorants, herons, pelicans, sandhill cranes, and snow geese—find a winter home on these 24,000 acres of river bottomland, marsh, stands of salt cedar, and open range. Seven gypsum sinkhole lakes, covering an area of 700 acres, are of a peculiar beauty. If you're here between December and February, don't miss this place: The sky actually darkens with birds. Once threatened with extinction, the sandhill crane now appears in numbers of 10,000 to 50,000 every winter. Snow geese were unknown here 20 years back, but now turn up to the tune of some 60,000 every winter. All told, over 300 species of birds have been sighted. You can get information at the headquarters building at the entrance.

Admission: Free.

Open: Dawn to dusk year-round.

**BOTTOMLESS LAKES STATE PARK (HC 12 Box 1200), N.M. Highway
409 off U.S. Hwy. 380, 16 miles east of Roswell.**

This chain of seven lakes, surrounded by rock bluffs, got its name from early cowboys, who tried to fathom the lakes' depth by plumbing them with lariats. No matter how many ropes they tied together and lowered into the limpid water, they never touched bottom. In fact, no lake is deeper than 100 feet. The largest, Lea Lake, is so clear that skin divers frequent it. Another is so shaded by surrounding bluffs that the sun rarely reaches it, so its name is Devil's Inkwell. Mirror, Cottonwood, Pasture, and Figure 8 lakes got their monikers with similar logic; No Name Lake, which apparently didn't have anything to distinguish it has been renamed, Lazy Lagoon.

This park is a popular recreation site for Roswell residents. There's fishing for rainbow trout, swimming and windsurfing, campsites for trailers or tents, and shelters, showers, a dump station, and a snack bar (open 9am to 6pm Memorial Day to Labor Day).

Admission: $3 per vehicle.
Open: Daily 6am–9pm year-round.

FORT SUMNER, 84 miles north of Roswell via U.S. Hwy. 285 and N.M. Hwy. 20.

⭐ This little town of 1,500 people is important in New Mexico history for two big reasons: It's the site of Fort Sumner State Monument and the burial place of Billy the Kid.

Fort Sumner State Monument recalls a tragic U.S. Army experiment (1864–68) to create a self-sustaining agricultural colony for captive Navajos. That native tribe still recalls it as the "Long March," the saddest chapter in their noble history. Today, a visitor center (open daily 9am to 5pm) tells the story of the fort, and the **Old Fort Sumner Museum** displays artifacts, pictures, and documents. It's located 7 miles southeast of the modern town, via U.S. 60/84 and N.M. 272.

Behind the museum is the **Grave of Billy the Kid,** a 6-foot tombstone engraved to "William H. Bonney, alias 'Billy the Kid,' died July 16, 1881," and to two previously slain comrades with whom he was buried. Those curious about the notorious young outlaw, just 21 when Sheriff Pat Garrett shot him in Fort Sumner, can learn more at the **Billy the Kid Museum,** 2 miles east of downtown Fort Sumner on U.S. Highway 60/84. It contains more than 60,000 relics of the Old West, including some recalling the life of young Bonney himself.

The **Old Fort Days** celebration, the second week of June, is Fort Sumner's big annual event. It includes the World's Richest Tombstone Race (inspired by the actual theft of Billy's tombstone, since recovered), the Pat Garrett Swim for Law and Order, the Billy the Kid Outlaw Run, a country music show, barbecue, and parade.

Lake Sumner State Park (tel. 355-2541), 16 miles northwest of Fort Sumner via U.S. Highway 84 and N.M. Highway 203, is a 1,000-acre property with a campground and cabin sites. Boating, fishing, swimming, and waterskiing are popular recreations.

For more information on the town, write or phone the **De Baca County Chamber of Commerce,** P.O. Box 28, Fort Sumner, NM 88119 (tel. 505/355-7705). To learn more about Billy the Kid and Pat Garrett, write **Billy the Kid Outlaw Gang Inc.,** P.O. Box 1881, Taiban, NM 88134 (tel. 505/355-2555).

CLOVIS/PORTALES, 110 miles northeast of Roswell via U.S. Hwy. 70.

Clovis is a major market center on the Texas border. Founded in 1906 as a railway town, it is now the focus of an active ranching and farming region, with about 32,000 population. **Cannon Air Force Base,** a part of the Tactical Air Command, is just northwest of the city. The **Lyceum Theatre,** 411 Main St. (tel. 763-6085), is a magnificent restoration of a former vaudeville theater; it's now the city's center for performing arts. The **H. A. "Pappy" Thornton Homestead and Museum** in Ned Houk Park (no phone) displays antique farming equipment in a prairie farmhouse. A major rodeo on the national circuit is held the first weekend in June. "Clovis Man," who hunted mammoths in this region about 10,000 B.C., was first discovered at a site near the city.

South of Clovis 19 miles is **Portales,** a town of 16,000 people that is the home of the main campus of **Eastern New Mexico University.** On campus are the **Roosevelt County Historical Museum** (tel. 562-2592) of regional ranching history and the **Natural History Museum** (tel. 562-2723), with wildlife exhibits, including a bee colony. There are anthropology and paleontology exhibits at the **Blackwater Draw Museum** (tel. 562-2254), 7 miles northeast of Portales on U.S. Highway 70 toward Clovis.

For lodging in the Clovis/Portales area, try the **Best Western LaVista Inn,** 1516 Mabry Dr. (U.S. Highway 60/70/84), Clovis, NM 88101 (tel. 505/762-3808 or toll free 800/528-1234), or the **Holiday Inn,** 2700 E. Mabry Dr., Clovis, NM 88101 (tel. 505/762-4491). Clovis is the flagship of the **K-Bob's Steakhouse** chain, when you're hungry. The restaurant is at 1600 Mabry Dr. (tel. 763-4443).

SPORTS & RECREATION

Roswell has 24 parks and playgrounds, 30 tennis courts, three golf courses, and numerous other recreational facilities. For full information, check with the **City of Roswell Recreation & Park Departments,** 1101 W. Fourth St. in Cahoon Park (tel. 624-6724).

Racquetball courts, weights, and full health-club facilities are available at the **Roswell Racquet Club & Spa,** 200 E. Mescalero St. (tel. 622-0962).

Most spectator events take place at the **Roswell Sports Complex,** including the Wool Bowl football stadium, east of NMMI on College Boulevard at Garden Avenue.

SHOPPING

Nearly every need can be met at the **Roswell Mall,** 4501 N. Main St. (tel. 623-8553), a modern 300,000-square-foot complex with a wide choice of stores spaced among fountains and indoor garden areas.

EVENING ENTERTAINMENT

The **Roswell Symphony Orchestra,** 3201 N. Main St. (tel. 623-5882), a 65-member professional orchestra founded in 1959, gives an annual October-to-April series of five concerts at NMMI's Pearson Auditorium. Tickets are $7 to $15 for adults, $2.50 to $5 for students, depending upon seating. Orchestra members also present a three-part chamber series at the Roswell Museum; tickets are $10 adults, $5 students. Six free youth concerts are scattered through the year.

The **Roswell Community Little Theatre** (tel. 622-1982), which enters its 35th season in 1993–94, presents five light dramas and comedies a year, including the likes of Agatha Christie and Neil Simon. The season runs from September to June. All performances are in the troupe's own 142-seat theater at 1101 N. Virginia St., a block east of Main at 12th. Tickets are $5 adults, $2.50 students; productions run five nights over two weekends, with curtain time 8:15pm.

WHERE TO STAY

An 11% tax is imposed on all lodging bills (6% state tax and 5% city lodging tax).

MODERATE

ROSWELL INN, 1815 N. Main St. (P.O. Box 2065), Roswell, NM 88202. Tel. 505/623-4920 or toll free 800/426-3052 in New Mexico, 800/323-0913 out-of-state. Fax 505/623-4920, ext. 165. 121 rms, 4 suites. A/C TV TEL
$ Rates: $55 single, $59 double, $95 suite. Weekend packages available. AE, CB, DC, DISC, MC, V.

This hotel's classic four-column portico is a landmark beside U.S. Highway 285 north, opposite the New Mexico Military Institute. It's indicative of the sophistication and elegance of the property. Off the lobby, there's a fine art gallery, and throughout the hotel are hung original paintings, prints, and signed lithographs. A large central lawn and garden is shaded by big cottonwood trees.

Guest rooms, which perpetuate the arty feeling, have a king- or two queen-size beds and light-wood furnishings, including a big working table; there are rooms for nonsmokers and the disabled. Fifteen king deluxe units have minifridges, hair dryers, and executive desks. Rooms are entered off the 1½-acre parking lot, but look inward toward the landscaped grounds.

Impressionist paintings and a garden setting give the Roswell Inn coffee shop a French café atmosphere. A landscape by Peter Rogers, Peter Hurd's son-in-law, dominates the back wall of the inn's dining room. Both dining spots are open from 6am, to 10pm daily, with steaks, chicken, fish, and other American-style dinners priced from $6.95 to $13.95. The dining room has weekday luncheon buffets, low-calorie and children's menus, and nightly specials such as lemon-pepper cod. The

Pecos Pub has solo entertainment most nights. The inn offers room service, concierge, valet laundry, courtesy limousine to Roswell Airport, a year-round outdoor swimming pool, hot tub, adjacent running track, and meeting space for 150. The NMMI athletic center, open to guests for a small fee, has a weight room, racquetball courts, and a golf course.

SALLY PORT INN, 2000 N. Main St., Roswell, NM 88201. Tel. 505/622-6430 or toll free 800/528-1234 or 800/548-6758. Fax 505/623-7631. 124 rms. A/C TV TEL

$ Rates: $49–$64 single, $59–$74 double. Summer weekend specials. AE, CB, DC, DISC, MC, V.

A Best Western property and one of the Maloof Hotels group that includes the Inns at Grants, Gallup, and Farmington, this two-story white-brick building adjacent to NMMI boasts a huge atrium courtyard. A café and swimming pool are at opposite ends of this skylit area, which gives a feeling of being outside while actually being inside.

Guest rooms, all of which have interior access, have double and queen-size beds and blue or green pastel decor. Each has two sinks (one at the vanity), brass fixtures, and a working table. Executive king units have a refrigerator as well as a king-size bed. Some rooms are designated for nonsmokers and the disabled.

The atrium café serves American cuisine 6am to 1:30pm and 5 to 10pm daily, with dinners in the $4.25-to-$12.95 range. O'Henry's Lounge (open 11am to 1am Monday to Saturday is a lively local dance spot, with country-and-western bands performing from 9pm. The Sports Bar, more quiet except during Monday night football, is open from 11am to 10pm Monday to Saturday. The inn has room service, courtesy van, valet laundry, a swimming pool, whirlpool, men's and women's saunas, weight room, coin-op laundry, hair salon, and gift shop.

INEXPENSIVE

COMFORT INN, 2803 W. Second St., Roswell, NM 88201. Tel. 505/623-9440 or toll free 800/221-2222. 60 rms. A/C FRIDGE TV TEL

$ Rates (including continental breakfast): May–Oct $39–$42 single, $42–$45 double; Nov–Apr $36–$39 single, $39–$42 double. AE, CB, DC, DISC, ER, JCB, MC, V.

Located on the western edge of Roswell on the road to Ruidoso, this hotel—pale yellow with brown trim—focuses around a central lawn and outdoor swimming pool. Rooms are clean and comfortable, with a brown-and-white southwestern decor and standard furnishings.

DAYS INN, 1310 N. Main St., Roswell, NM 88201. Tel. 505/623-4021. 62 rms. A/C TV TEL

$ Rates (including continental breakfast): $33–$38 single, $42–$52 double. AE, CB, DC, MC, V.

A colonial-style inn with a redbrick and white-wood facade, Days Inn is located on the north side of town, not far past the Roswell Museum and Art Center. Guest rooms, appointed in Southwest colors and shades of brown, have a king-size or two double beds, a plush easy chair with an ottoman, a TV in a handsome armoire, a working desk, and a small vanity. Outdoors are a large swimming pool and hot tub.

To reach The Claim Restaurant and Saloon, you must descend a flight of stairs as into a mine shaft. Steak-and-seafood dinners start at $6.25 and go all the way up to $24.95 for African lobster tail. It's open for lunch from 11am to 2pm Monday to Friday, dinner 5 to 9pm Monday to Thursday, 5 to 10pm Friday and Saturday.

WHERE TO DINE

EL TORO BRAVO, 102 S. Main St. at 1st St. Tel. 622-9280.
Cuisine: NEW MEXICAN.
$ Prices: Lunch $3.25–$6.95; dinner $5.75–$10.95. AE, MC, V.
Open: Lunch Mon–Fri 11am–2:30pm, dinner Mon–Sat 5–9pm.

Mexican souvenirs adorn the walls of this low-lit restaurant, which occupies two large rooms. Plants hang from the high ceiling. The menu has a wide selection of regional dishes, including stuffed sopaipillas, chalupas, chile Colorado, and carne asada.

KEUKEN DUTCH RESTAURANT, 12th and N. Main Sts. Tel. 624-2040.
Cuisine: DUTCH & AMERICAN.
$ Prices: Appetizers $1.50–$4.30; breakfast $2–$4.80; lunch $2.70–$5; dinner $4.80–$10. AE, CB, DC, MC, V.
Open: Daily 5am–11pm.

This is just like New Holland. Blue-and-white delft pottery and Dutch dolls brighten the decor of this family restaurant, while waitresses in traditional outfits, wearing bonnets and aprons, provide attentive service. Standard American dishes share the menu with Dutch specialties like eggs hollandaise and fruit koeken (pancakes) for breakfast, a Dutch burger with Gouda cheese for lunch, and Metworst sausage with aardappel salad (potato-and-red cabbage salad) for dinner. There's free coffee for early risers (5 to 6am).

MARIO'S, 200 E. 2nd St. Tel. 623-1740.
Cuisine: AMERICAN.
$ Prices: Appetizers $2.25–$5.50; lunch $3.25–$5.95; dinner $5.95–$13.95. AE, MC, V.
Open: Mon–Thurs 11am–9pm, Fri–Sat 11am–10pm.

The works of regional artists like Peter Hurd and R. C. Gorman hang on the walls, while stained-glass lamps/ceiling fans are suspended above the booths and tables. Dinners include prime rib and New York strip steak, country chicken, and blackened or southern (cornmeal-fried) catfish. "Heart Smart" (low fat, low cholesterol) items are indicated on the menu. All dinners include the expansive salad bar and a miniloaf of bread. An adjoining lounge has complimentary hors d'oeuvres and a big-screen TV.

PEPPER'S GRILL, Sunbank Building, 500 N. Main St. (off 6th St.). Tel. 623-1700.
Cuisine: NEW MEXICAN & AMERICAN.
$ Prices: Appetizers $1.45–$4.85; main courses $3.90–$8.95. AE, MC, V.
Open: Mon–Thurs 11am–9pm, Fri–Sat 11am–10pm.

It's hard to take too seriously a restaurant with cartoon mariachi chile characters painted on its walls, including one cute little jalapeño pulling a burro. But the frivolous decor is merely a reminder to have fun. And eating here is certainly fun! The menu offers a variety of salads, soups, burgers and other sandwiches, including a charbroiled tuna-steak sandwich. It also features standard Mexican main courses plus regional specialties: marinated mesquite catfish, steak or chicken fajitas, southwestern chicken or shrimp, country-fried steak, barbecued baby back ribs. Beer and wine are served.

---

4. CARLSBAD

275 miles SE of Albuquerque; 164 miles E of El Paso, Texas; 180 miles W of Lubbock, Texas

GETTING THERE **By Plane** **Cavern City Air Terminal** (tel. 885-5236) is 4 miles south of the city via National Parks Highway (U.S. 62/180). **Mesa Airlines** (tel. 885-0245 or toll free 800/MESA-AIR) provides commercial service with four flights to and from Albuquerque and two flights to and from Dallas, Texas. You can rent a car at the airport from **Hertz** (tel. 887-1500).

By Bus From Carlsbad's **Union Bus Depot,** 1000 S. Canyon St. near Pompa Street (tel. 887-1108), there's daily service aboard **Texas, New Mexico & Oklahoma Coaches.** Three buses pass through daily each way on TNM&O's Oklahoma

City–El Paso route and one daily each way on the Albuquerque–Roswell–Fort Stockton, Texas, run. From White's City, south of Carlsbad, van service to Carlsbad Caverns National Park is provided by **Sun Country Tours** (tel. 785-2291).

By Car From Albuquerque take I-40 east 59 miles to Clines Corners; turn south on U.S. 285, 216 miles to Carlsbad via Roswell (6 hours). From El Paso, take U.S. 62/180 east (3 hours).

ESSENTIALS Orientation Carlsbad straddles the Pecos River, a beautiful stream which gives it its particular character. Downtown spreads along the west side of the river, with the primary artery, Canal Street (U.S. 285), about three blocks from the Pecos. Carlsbad is located at the crossroads of Highway 285, a north-south route linking Albuquerque with southern Texas, and Highway 62/180, an east-west highway connecting El Paso and Dallas.

Information The **Carlsbad Chamber of Commerce,** Canal Street (Highway 285) at Green Street (Highway 62/180), Carlsbad, NM 88220 (tel. 505/887-6516 or toll free 800/221-1224), is open from 8am to 5pm Monday to Friday.

Fast Facts The **area code** is 505. **Guadalupe Medical Center** provides full hospital services at 2430 W. Pierce St., U.S. Highway 285 north (tel. 887-4100). The **post office** is located at 301 N. Canyon St. (tel. 885-5717). In case of **emergency,** dial 911.

Carlsbad is a city of 29,000 on the Pecos River. Founded in the late 1800s, its area was controlled by Apaches and Comanches until just a little over a century ago. Besides a good tourist business from Carlsbad Caverns, the town thrives on farming, with irrigated crops of cotton, hay, and pecans. Pecans grow so well in Carlsbad that it is said the nuts from just two trees in your yard will pay your property taxes. The area also has potash mines producing 85% of the U.S. total of this fertilizer. The town was named for the Czech spa of the same name.

The caverns are the big attraction, having drawn more than 28 million visitors since opening in 1923. A satellite community, White's City, has sprung up 20 miles south of Carlsbad at the park entrance junction. The family of Jack White, Jr. owns all of its motels, restaurants, gift shops, and other attractions.

WHAT TO SEE & DO

Carlsbad's pride and joy is its riverfront. The city has 27 miles of beaches along the **Pecos River.** Its centerpiece is **Presidents Park,** a small amusement park featuring a 2-mile narrow-gauge steam locomotive ride, a carousel, Ferris wheel, and other diversions. The little 1858 **George Washington Paddlewheel Boat** offers diesel-powered tours along the river's course (adults $2.50, children $1.50). Carlsbad boasts 30 parks, including more than 100 baseball and softball fields!

The **Carlsbad Museum and Art Center,** Fox Street, one block west of Canal Street (tel. 887-0276), is well displayed and described. Everything from dinosaur bones to Apache relics, pioneer artifacts to paintings from the early 20th-century Taos school, is exhibited. Admission is by donation; it's open from 10am to 6pm Monday to Saturday.

Though it may sound frightening, the **Waste Isolation Pilot Plant (WIPP),** has pumped new life into the Carlsbad economy. Located 26 miles east of Carlsbad, this Department of Energy facility is designed for "safe disposal of defense-generated radioactive waste." Visitor tours can be arranged on request. Downtown at 101 W. Greene St. (tel. 885-8883), WIPP has an exhibit area where skeptical and sometimes hostile visitors are told the why and how of disposing of nuclear waste in salt beds. There are hands-on demonstrations; a diorama re-creates the salt tunnels. It's open Monday to Friday from 8am to 4pm.

Recreational facilities in Carlsbad and vicinity include 23 parks, three golf courses, five indoor swimming pools, 14 tennis courts, and an elaborate shooting and archery range. Contact the **City of Carlsbad Recreation Department** (tel. 887-1191) for full information.

LIVING DESERT STATE PARK, Skyline Dr. (P.O. Box 100), Carlsbad, NM 88220. Tel. 887-5516.

Officially called Zoological & Botanical State Park of the Southwest, this is a 45-acre piece of authentic Chihuahuan Desert preserved with all its flora and fauna. There are more than 50 species of mammals, birds, and reptiles in this open-air park, and hundreds of varieties of plants. A trail leads past extravagant cacti and other desert plants, and a greenhouse shelters more delicate flora, including exotic succulents. Animals arrive in the park through a rehabilitation program to care for sick or injured creatures.

Golden eagles and great horned owls are among birds of prey reigning over the aviary. An exhibit of nocturnal animals shows badgers, spotted skunks, kit foxes, and ringtail cats in underground burrows. A prairie-dog town is a favorite with the kids. Larger mammals such as deer, antelope, elk, javelina, buffalo, and bobcat all share the little wilderness. Regional plants may be purchased at the gift shop.

The view from the park, high atop the Ocotillo Hills on the northwest side of Carlsbad, is superb. To reach it, take Skyline Drive off U.S. 285 west of town and proceed just over a mile.

Admission: $3 for adults and children 7 and older.

Open: Mid-May to Labor Day 8am–7pm; rest of year 9am–4pm.

CARLSBAD CAVERNS NATIONAL PARK, 3225 National Parks Hwy., Carlsbad, NM 88220. Tel. 785-2232 or 785-2107 (recorded information).

One of the largest and most spectacular cave systems in the world, Carlsbad Caverns comprise some 75 caves that snake through the porous limestone reef of the Guadalupe Mountains. Fantastic and grotesque formations fascinate visitors, who find every shape imaginable (and unimaginable) naturally sculpted in the underground—from frozen waterfalls to strands of pearls, soda straws to miniature castles, draperies to ice-cream cones.

Although Indians had known of the caverns for centuries, they were not discovered by whites until about a century ago, when settlers were attracted by sunset flights of bats from the cave. Jim White, a guano miner, began to explore the main cave in the early 1900s, and to share its wonders with tourists. By 1923 it had become a national monument, upgraded to national park in 1930.

Two caves, Carlsbad Cavern and New Cave, are open to the public. The National Park Service has provided facilities to make it easy for everyone to visit the cavern, with elevators, a kennel for pets, and a nursery. Visitors in wheelchairs are common.

Visitors to the cavern can either walk down through its natural entrance or go by elevator to a point 750 feet below the surface and begin walking there. The paved walkway through the natural entrance winds into the depths of the cavern and leads through a series of underground rooms. This walk is 1¾ miles in length and takes about an hour and 45 minutes. Parts of it are steep. At its lowest point, the trail reaches 830 feet below the surface, ending finally at an underground lunchroom whose existence seems to amaze many visitors.

Here, those who have taken the elevator join the tour of the spectacular 14-story-high Big Room, with a ceiling looming 255 feet over the trail. The floor of this room covers 14 acres; a tour, over a relatively level path, is 1¼ miles in length and takes about an hour. Visitors may either join one of the frequent guided tours or simply wander through the cavern by themselves.

Everyone is advised to wear flat shoes with rubber soles and heels because of the slippery paths. A light sweater or jacket feels good in the constant temperature of 56°, especially when it's 100° outside in the sun. The cavern is well lit. Rangers are stationed in the cave to answer questions.

At sunset, a crowd gathers at the cave entrance to watch a quarter-million bats take off for the night, mid-May through October. (The bats, and some of the people, winter in Mexico.) All day long the Mexican free-tail bats sleep in the cavern, then strike out on an insect hunt at night. A ranger program is offered about 7pm. On the second Thursday in August, a "bat flight breakfast" from 5 to 7am encourages visitors to watch the bats return to the cavern.

New Cave was discovered in 1937 and was mined for bat guano commercially until the 1950s. It consists of a corridor 1,140 feet long with many side passageways. The lowest point is 250 feet below the surface, and the passage traversed by tours is 1¾ miles long, but more strenuous than hiking through the main cavern; there is also a 500-foot rise in the trail from the parking lot to the cave mouth. The tour lasts about 2½ hours. No more than 25 people may take part in a tour, and then by reservation only. Everyone needs a flashlight, hiking boots or shoes, and a container of drinking water. New Cave is reached via U.S. 180, south 5 miles from White's City, to a marked turnoff that leads 11 miles into a parking lot.

Spelunkers who seek access to the park's undeveloped caves require special permission from the park superintendent.

Aside from the caves, the national park offers the Walnut Canyon Loop Drive, a 9½-mile nature study of the Chihuahuan Desert, which starts a half mile from the visitor center; and the Rattlesnake Springs Picnic Area, on County Road 418 near New Cave, a water source for hundreds of years for the Indians. Backcountry hikers must register at the visitor center before going out on any of the trails in the 46,755 acres of the park.

Admission: $5 adults, $3 children 6–15, under 6, free.
Open: Daily 8:30am–2:30pm. **Closed:** Christmas Day.

NEARBY ATTRACTIONS

GUADALUPE MOUNTAINS NATIONAL PARK, HC 60, Box 400, Salt Flat, TX 78947. Tel. 915/828-3251.

Some 250 million years ago, the Guadalupe Mountains were an immense reef poking up through a tropical ocean. Marine organisms fossilized this 400-mile-long Capitan Reef as limestone; later, as the sea evaporated, a blanket of sediments and mineral salts buried the reef. Then just 10 to 12 million years ago, a mountain-building uplift exposed a part of the fossil reef. This has given modern scientists a unique opportunity to explore earth's geologic history and outdoor lovers a playground for wilderness experience.

The steep southern end of the range makes up the park, while the northern part lies within Lincoln National Forest and Carlsbad Caverns National Park. Deer, elk, mountain lion, and bear are found in the forests, which contrast strikingly with the desert around them. In these isolated basins and protected valleys is a proliferation of vegetation rare elsewhere in the Southwest.

The Frijole Visitors Center, 55 miles southwest of Carlsbad via U.S. Highway 180, offers a variety of exhibits and slide programs telling the story of the Guadalupe Mountains, as well as ranger-guided walks and lectures. Information, maps, and backcountry permits are also obtained at McKittrick Canyon Visitor Center (10 miles northeast via U.S. 180 and a side road) and Dog Canyon Ranger Station (reached through Carlsbad via N.M. 137 and County Road 414, about 70 miles).

McKittrick Canyon is one of the few spots accessible by paved road. Protected by its high sheer walls, with a green swatch of trees growing along the banks of its spring-fed stream, it is a beautiful location. It is a great spot for bird-watching and viewing other wildlife, and an especially lovely sight during fall foliage time, late October to mid-November. Most of the national park's 76,293 acres are reached only by 80 miles of foot or horse trail through desert, canyon, and high forest. Backcountry hikers require water and permits; camping must be in designated areas. There are developed camping areas at Pine Springs and Dog Canyon.

Admission: Free; Pine Springs Campground $5 per night.
Open: Visitor center, June–Aug 7am–6pm; Sept–May 8am–4:30pm.

Artesia

In this quiet town of 13,000 people, 36 miles north of Carlsbad on U.S. 285, the principal attraction is the **Artesia Historical Museum & Art Center,** housed in a

Victorian home at 505 W. Richardson Ave., Artesia (tel. 748-2390). Open Tuesday to Saturday from 10am to noon and from 1 to 5pm, it exhibits Indian and pioneer artifacts and the work of local artists.

Visitors looking for a stopover in Artesia might consider the **Best Western Pecos Inn,** 2209 W. Main St. (Highway 82), Artesia, NM 88210 (tel. 505/748-3324). A good restaurant is **Señor Peppers,** 816 S. First St. (tel. 746-4881). Further information can be obtained from the **Artesia Chamber of Commerce,** P.O. Box 99, Artesia, NM 88210 (tel. 505/746-2744).

Hobbs

Located 69 miles east of Carlsbad on U.S. 62/180, on the edge of the Llano Estacado tableland, Hobbs (pop. 35,000) is at the center of New Mexico's richest oilfield. Many oil companies have their headquarters here.

Points of interest include the **Lea County Cowboy Hall of Fame and Western Heritage Center** at New Mexico Junior College, on the Lovington Highway (tel. 392-4510, ext. 317). It honors the area's ranchers and rodeo performers and is open from 8am to 5pm Monday through Thursday, 8am to 3pm on Friday, 9am to 5pm Saturday and from 1 to 5pm on Sunday. The **Confederate Air Force Museum** (tel. 392-5342) at Lea County/Hobbs Airport displays World War II aircraft; the **Soaring Society of America** (tel. 392-1177) has its national headquarters at the adjacent Hobbs Industrial Air Park. West of the airport on U.S. Highway 180, Indian artifacts and pioneer mementos are displayed by appointment at the **Linam Ranch Museum** (tel. 393-4784).

Twenty-two miles northwest of Hobbs via N.M. 18, at the junction of U.S. Highway 82, is the town of **Lovington** (pop. 10,000), another ranching and oil center. The **Lea County Historical Museum,** 103 S. Love St. (tel. 396-5311), presents memorabilia of the region's unique history in a First World War–era hotel.

If you plan to stay in Hobbs, try **Hobbs Motor Inn,** 501 N. Marland St. (tel. 397-3251), or the **Zia Motel,** 619 N. Marland St. (tel. 397-3591). You can get a good square meal at the **Cattle Baron Steak House,** 1930 N. Grimes St. (tel. 393-2800), or **La Fiesta,** 604 E. Broadway (tel. 397-1235). **Harry McAdams State Park,** 4 miles north of Hobbs on N.M. 18 (tel. 392-5845), has campsites and a visitor center. For more information, contact the **Hobbs Chamber of Commerce,** 400 N. Marland St. (tel. 397-3202).

WHERE TO STAY

Most properties are along the highway south toward Carlsbad Caverns. An 11% tax is imposed on all lodging bills (6% state tax and 5% city lodging tax).

BEST WESTERN CAVERN INN, 17 Carlsbad Cavern Hwy. at N.M. Hwy. 7 (P.O. Box 128), White's City, NM 88268. Tel. 505/785-2291 or toll free 800/CAVERNS out-of-state, 800/THE-CAVE in New Mexico. Fax 505/785-2283. 63 rms. A/C TV TEL
$ Rates: May 15–Sept 15 $65–$80 single or double; Sept 16–May 14 $51–$65 single or double. AE, CB, DC, DISC, MC, V.

This motel and the overflow properties flanking it—the 44-room Guadalupe Inn and the 25-unit adobe Walnut Canyon Inn—suffice as places to rest one's head before or after a visit to Carlsbad Caverns. Guest registration is in the arcade with the western facade on the south side of the highway; the motel is on the north side.

Rooms are very spacious if a bit austere. The white-painted fabric walls are without pictures. The carpeting is brown, the bedspreads and drapes of a brown Southwest motif. The vanity is quite large, the adjacent bathroom quite small.

Most folks dine and drink across the highway at the Velvet Garter Saloon and Restaurant (see "Where to Dine," below). The White's City arcade contains a post office, grocery store, gift shop, Million Dollar Museum of various antiques and paraphernalia, and Granny's Opera House, a theater for weekend melodramas.

Between the Cavern Inn and its neighbor properties, there are two swimming pools, two hot tubs, and a court for tennis, volleyball, and basketball. Pets are not allowed.

BEST WESTERN MOTEL STEVENS, 1829 S. Canal St., Carlsbad, NM 88220. Tel. 505/887-2851 or toll free 800/528-1234. Fax 505/887-6338. 202 rms, 15 suites. A/C TV TEL

$ Rates: $45 single, $55 double, $55-$60 suite. AE, CB, DC, DISC, MC, V.

Well-landscaped gardens surround this handsome property, composed of several buildings spread across the spacious grounds. The homey lobby and restaurants are located in a central brick building with a tile roof.

Rooms are good-sized, with gray/burgundy decor and southwestern motifs; some are designated for nonsmokers or the disabled. All have remodeled bathrooms with large mirrors. Some units, with peaked ceilings to make them feel even larger, have back-door patios. Suites have kitchenettes.

Fifty new suite units with kitchenettes (including a stove, refrigerator, and microwave oven, but no pots and pans or dishes) were added in 1991.

The Flume (see "Where to Dine," below), open daily from noon to 10pm, is a beautiful fine-dining establishment specializing in American cuisine. Breakfast and lunch buffets are served in the Green Tree, from 6am to 2pm. The Silver Spur Lounge has live country music for dancing, Monday through Saturday nights. The motel has room service, courtesy car, guest laundry, 24-hour desk, swimming and wading pool, playground for kids, and volleyball net.

LA CASA MUNECA, 213 N. Alameda St. at W. Shaw St., Carlsbad, NM 88220. Tel. 505/887-1891 or 887-5738. 5 rms, 1 suite. A/C

$ Rates (including continental breakfast): $45 single, $55-$65 double, $72-$85 suite. MC, V.

Carlsbad's only B&B is a big beige stucco house two blocks west of Canal Street. The name means "The Doll House," and throughout, owner M. J. Lawrence has placed her handmade Raggedy Ann–style dolls. In the living room, there's even a real doll house under construction; guests can help with the building. Historical photos line the staircase, and local art on the walls is for sale.

Rooms are quaint and nicely furnished. Guests have access to the television and VCR in the living room and to the downstairs telephone (hookups are available in rooms). A continental breakfast of cereal, fruit, muffins, coffee, and juice is served each morning. This is a nonsmoking property. Children five and older are welcome.

PARK INN INTERNATIONAL, 3706 National Parks Hwy. (U.S. 62/180), Carlsbad, NM 88220. Tel. 505/887-2861 or toll free 800/437-PARK. Fax 505/887-2861, ext. 310. 123 rms, 1 suite. A/C TV TEL

$ Rates: May–Sept $45–$58 single, $58–$68 double, $85 suite; Oct–Apr $29–$38 single, $44–$48 double, $85 suite. AE, CB, DC, DISC, JCB, MC, V.

Spacious rooms and nicely landscaped grounds give this former Holiday Inn a character of tranquility. Guest rooms—including nonsmoking and handicapped accommodations—are decorated in earth tones with southwestern-motif bedspread and drapes and contain all standard furnishings.

Three meals are served daily in the Café in the Park, which has an open grill and windows that open onto the grounds. Lunch and dinner are served in the Chaparral Grill Room, which features steaks and seafood in the $7.95-to-$12.95 range. The hotel lounge has a duo playing easy-listening country music for dancing, Tuesday through Saturday nights. Services and facilities include room service, courtesy van, valet laundry, guest Laundromat, swimming pool, hot tub, video games, gift shop, and meeting space for 300.

STAGECOACH INN, 1819 S. Canal St., Carlsbad, NM 88220. Tel. 505/887-1148. 55 rms. A/C TV TEL

$ Rates: $28 single, $32-$36 double. AE, CB, DC, DISC, MC, V.

A large playground area set back from the highway is the earmark of this motel, which also features an adult pool and children's wading pool separated for safety's sake by a fence. The one-story inn is gaily decorated with red doors and white-brick walls. Rooms have ample space, queen-size beds, ceiling fans, and nice furnishings, including dressing tables. Facilities include a coin-op guest laundry.

The adjacent restaurant specializes in Texas-style barbecue, with meals from $3.50 to $7.95; it's open from 5am to 9pm Monday to Saturday, from 5am to 2pm Sunday.

WHERE TO DINE

THE FLUME, at Best Western Motel Stevens, 1829 S. Canal St. Tel. 887-2851.
  Cuisine: AMERICAN. **Reservations:** Recommended for dinner.
$ **Prices:** Appetizers $3.95–$7.75; lunch $3.25–$7.95; dinner $7.75–$15.95. AE, CB, DC, DISC, MC, V.
  Open: Daily noon–10pm.

Carlsbad's most elegant restaurant is entered through the motel off a skylit atrium, flanked by trees and cacti, facing a decorator mirror depicting an Apache spirit dancer. Once inside, there's a rich wood decor with dark green upholstery, a large chandelier, and candlelight.

The menu focuses on wholesome foods: lots of steaks, a New Orleans shrimp plate, a special teriyaki chicken breast, even Rocky Mountain oysters! Lighter dinners, called "Young and Young-at-Heart" meals, are available at reduced prices.

FLYING X RANCH, 7505 Old Cavern Hwy. Tel. 885-6789.
  Cuisine: AMERICAN. **Reservations:** Required.
$ **Prices:** Adults $10, children 5–10 $6; children under 4 free when sharing plate with adult.
  Open: Memorial Day–Labor Day Mon–Sat 7:30pm.

Five miles south of town, a chuck-wagon (ranch-style) supper is served during the summer months in a big cow shed. It's followed by an Old West stage show. The meal includes barbecued beef, potatoes, beans, biscuits, applesauce, cake, coffee, and lemonade.

LUCY'S, 701 Canal St. Tel. 887-7714.
  Cuisine: MEXICAN. **Reservations:** Recommended on weekends.
$ **Prices:** Main courses $3.45–$8.95. AE, MC, V.
  Open: Mon–Sat 11am–10pm.

Since 1973, Lucy and Justo Yanez's friendly, casual downtown restaurant has made diners—visitors and locals alike—feel right at home. It's dedicated to the words of a Mexican proverb printed on the menu: *El hambre es un fuego, y la comida es fresca* (Hunger is a burning, and eating is a coolness). The food is superb, with Lucy's personal adaptations of old favorites—steak ranchero, caldillo de Miguel (beef stew), Tucson chimichanga, and shrimp fajitas. Finish with a dessert of buenelos, sprinkled with cinnamon sugar. Children's plates are available; all diners indicate the strength they like their red or green chiles.

SIRLOIN STOCKADE, 710 S. Canal St. Tel. 887-7211.
  Cuisine: STEAKS.
$ **Prices:** Main courses $2.80–$11. MC, V.
  Open: Daily 11am–10pm.

A Sizzler-style establishment, the Stockade offers seating within a beige stuccoed building or in a smoked-glass garden atrium area. Orders are placed at the counter; the food is then delivered to your table. There are a variety of steaks, as well as hamburgers, chicken, and fried fish. The restaurant offers a children's menu and a good-sized salad bar.

VELVET GARTER SALOON AND RESTAURANT, 26 Carlsbad Cavern Hwy., White's City. Tel. 785-2291.
  Cuisine: AMERICAN. **Reservations:** Recommended in summer.
$ **Prices:** Appetizers $2.95–$3.25; main courses $6.95–$12.95. AE, CB, DC, MC, V.
  Open: Daily 4–9pm.

This comfortable coffee shop–style establishment near the Carlsbad Caverns Highway junction boasts two beautiful stained-glass windows portraying the caverns and the Guadalupe Mountains. The food is somewhat more ordinary—steaks, chicken, and limited seafood (catfish and rainbow trout). Nearby Fat Jack's caters to fast-food diets with three meals daily; the saloon is unmistakable with the longhorns mounted over the door.

INDEX

GENERAL INFORMATION

DESTINATIONS

KEY TO ABBREVIATIONS: *B* = Budget; *B&B* = Bed & Breakfast; *CG* = Campground; *E* = Expensive; *I* = Inexpensive; *M* = Moderately priced; *VE* = Very Expensive; * = Author's Favorites; *$* = Super-Special Value

Now Save Money on All Your Travels by Joining
FROMMER'S ™ TRAVEL BOOK CLUB
The World's Best Travel Guides at Membership Prices

FROMMER'S TRAVEL BOOK CLUB is your ticket to successful travel! Open up a world of travel information and simplify your travel planning when you join ranks with thousands of value-conscious travelers who are members of the FROMMER'S TRAVEL BOOK CLUB. Join today and you'll be entitled to all the privileges that come from belonging to the club that offers you travel guides for less to more than 100 destinations worldwide. Annual membership is only $25 (U.S.) or $35 (Canada and all foreign).

The Advantages of Membership

1. Your choice of three free FROMMER'S TRAVEL GUIDES. You can pick two from our FROMMER'S COUNTRY and REGIONAL GUIDES (listed under Comprehensive, $-A-Day, and Family) and one from our FROMMER'S CITY GUIDES (listed under City and City $-A-Day).
2. Your own subscription to **TRIPS & TRAVEL** quarterly newsletter.
3. You're entitled to a **30% discount** on your order of any additional books offered by FROMMER'S TRAVEL BOOK CLUB.
4. You're offered (at a small additional fee) our **Domestic Trip Routing Kits.**

Our quarterly newsletter **TRIPS & TRAVEL** offers practical information on the best buys in travel, the "hottest" vacation spots, the latest travel trends, world-class events and much, much more.

Our **Domestic Trip Routing Kits** are available for any North American destination. We'll send you a detailed map highlighting the best route to take to your destination—you can request direct or scenic routes.

Here's all you have to do to join:
Send in your membership fee of $25 ($35 Canada and foreign) with your name and address on the form below along with your selections as part of your membership package to **FROMMER'S TRAVEL BOOK CLUB, P.O. Box 473, Mt. Morris, IL 61054-0473**. Remember to check off 2 FROMMER'S COUNTRY and REGIONAL GUIDES and 1 FROMMER'S CITY GUIDE on the pages following.

If you would like to order additional books, please select the books you would like and send a check for the total amount (please add sales tax in the states noted below), plus $2 per book for shipping and handling ($3 per book for all foreign orders) to:

FROMMER'S TRAVEL BOOK CLUB
P.O. Box 473
Mt. Morris, IL 61054-0473
1-815-734-1104

[ ] **YES**. I want to take advantage of this opportunity to join FROMMER'S TRAVEL BOOK CLUB.

[ ] **My check is enclosed**. Dollar amount enclosed_____*
(all payments in U.S. funds only)

Name_____

Address_____

City_____ State_____ Zip_____

To ensure that all orders are processed efficiently, please apply sales tax in the following areas: CA, CT, FL, IL, NJ, NY, TN, WA, and CANADA.

*With membership, shipping and handling will be paid by FROMMER'S TRAVEL BOOK CLUB for the three free books you select as part of your membership. Please add $2 per book for shipping and handling for any additional books purchased ($3 per book for all foreign orders).

Allow 4-6 weeks for delivery. Prices of books, membership fee, and publication dates are subject to change without notice.

Please Send Me the Books Checked Below

FROMMER'S COMPREHENSIVE GUIDES

(Guides listing facilities from budget to deluxe, with emphasis on the medium-priced)

	Retail Price	Code		Retail Price	Code
☐ Acapulco/Ixtapa/Taxco 1993–94	$15.00	C120	☐ Jamaica/Barbados 1993–94	$15.00	C105
☐ Alaska 1990–91	$15.00	C001	☐ Japan 1992–93	$19.00	C020
☐ Arizona 1993–94	$18.00	C101	☐ Morocco 1992–93	$18.00	C021
☐ Australia 1992–93	$18.00	C002	☐ Nepal 1992–93	$18.00	C038
☐ Austria 1993–94	$19.00	C119	☐ New England 1993	$17.00	C114
☐ Austria/Hungary 1991–92	$15.00	C003	☐ New Mexico 1993–94	$15.00	C117
☐ Belgium/Holland/ Luxembourg 1993–94	$18.00	C106	☐ New York State 1992–93	$19.00	C025
			☐ Northwest 1991–92	$17.00	C026
☐ Bermuda/Bahamas 1992–93	$17.00	C005	☐ Portugal 1992–93	$16.00	C027
			☐ Puerto Rico 1993–94	$15.00	C103
☐ Brazil, 3rd Edition	$20.00	C111	☐ Puerto Vallarta/Manzanillo/ Guadalajara 1992–93	$14.00	C028
☐ California 1993	$18.00	C112			
☐ Canada 1992–93	$18.00	C009	☐ Scandinavia 1993–94	$19.00	C118
☐ Caribbean 1993	$18.00	C102	☐ Scotland 1992–93	$16.00	C040
☐ Carolinas/Georgia 1992–93	$17.00	C034	☐ Skiing Europe 1989–90	$15.00	C030
☐ Colorado 1993–94	$16.00	C100	☐ South Pacific 1992–93	$20.00	C031
☐ Cruises 1993–94	$19.00	C107	☐ Spain 1993–94	$19.00	C115
☐ DE/MD/PA & NJ Shore 1992–93	$19.00	C012	☐ Switzerland/Liechtenstein 1992–93	$19.00	C032
☐ Egypt 1990–91	$15.00	C013	☐ Thailand 1992–93	$20.00	C033
☐ England 1993	$18.00	C109	☐ U.S.A. 1993–94	$19.00	C116
☐ Florida 1993	$18.00	C104	☐ Virgin Islands 1992–93	$13.00	C036
☐ France 1992–93	$20.00	C017	☐ Virginia 1992–93	$14.00	C037
☐ Germany 1993	$19.00	C108	☐ Yucatán 1993–94	$18.00	C110
☐ Italy 1993	$19.00	C113			

FROMMER'S $-A-DAY GUIDES

(Guides to low-cost tourist accommodations and facilities)

	Retail Price	Code		Retail Price	Code
☐ Australia on $45 1993–94	$18.00	D102	☐ Mexico on $50 1993	$19.00	D105
☐ Costa Rica/Guatemala/ Belize on $35 1993–94	$17.00	D108	☐ New York on $70 1992–93	$16.00	D016
			☐ New Zealand on $45 1993–94	$18.00	D103
☐ Eastern Europe on $25 1991–92	$17.00	D005	☐ Scotland/Wales on $50 1992–93	$18.00	D019
☐ England on $60 1993	$18.00	D107			
☐ Europe on $45 1993	$19.00	D106	☐ South America on $40 1993–94	$19.00	D109
☐ Greece on $45 1993–94	$19.00	D100			
☐ Hawaii on $75 1993	$19.00	D104	☐ Turkey on $40 1992–93	$22.00	D023
☐ India on $40 1992–93	$20.00	D010	☐ Washington, D.C. on $40 1992–93	$17.00	D024
☐ Ireland on $40 1992–93	$17.00	D011			
☐ Israel on $45 1993–94	$18.00	D101			

FROMMER'S CITY $-A-DAY GUIDES

(Pocket-size guides with an emphasis on low-cost tourist accommodations and facilities)

	Retail Price	Code		Retail Price	Code
☐ Berlin on $40 1992–93	$12.00	D002	☐ Madrid on $50 1992–93	$13.00	D014
☐ Copenhagen on $50 1992–93	$12.00	D003	☐ Paris on $45 1992–93	$12.00	D018
			☐ Stockholm on $50 1992–93	$13.00	D022
☐ London on $45 1992–93	$12.00	D013			

FROMMER'S TOURING GUIDES
(Color-illustrated guides that include walking tours,
cultural and historic sights, and practical information)

	Retail Price	Code		Retail Price	Code
☐ Amsterdam	$11.00	T001	☐ New York	$11.00	T008
☐ Barcelona	$14.00	T015	☐ Rome	$11.00	T010
☐ Brazil	$11.00	T003	☐ Scotland	$10.00	T011
☐ Florence	$ 9.00	T005	☐ Sicily	$15.00	T017
☐ Hong Kong/Singapore/ Macau	$11.00	T006	☐ Thailand	$13.00	T012
			☐ Tokyo	$15.00	T016
☐ Kenya	$14.00	T018	☐ Venice	$ 9.00	T014
☐ London	$13.00	T007			

FROMMER'S FAMILY GUIDES

	Retail Price	Code		Retail Price	Code
☐ California with Kids	$17.00	F001	☐ San Francisco with Kids	$17.00	F004
☐ Los Angeles with Kids	$17.00	F002	☐ Washington, D.C. with Kids	$17.00	F005
☐ New York City with Kids	$18.00	F003			

FROMMER'S CITY GUIDES
(Pocket-size guides to sightseeing and tourist accommodations
and facilities in all price ranges)

	Retail Price	Code		Retail Price	Code
☐ Amsterdam 1993–94	$13.00	S110	☐ Miami 1993–94	$13.00	S118
☐ Athens, 9th Edition	$13.00	S114	☐ Minneapolis/St. Paul, 3rd Edition	$13.00	S119
☐ Atlanta 1993–94	$13.00	S112			
☐ Atlantic City/Cape May 1991–92	$ 9.00	S004	☐ Montréal/Québec City 1993–94	$13.00	S125
☐ Bangkok 1992–93	$13.00	S005	☐ New Orleans 1993–94	$13.00	S103
☐ Barcelona/Majorca/ Minorca/Ibiza 1993–94	$13.00	S115	☐ New York 1993	$13.00	S120
			☐ Orlando 1993	$13.00	S101
☐ Berlin 1993–94	$13.00	S116	☐ Paris 1993–94	$13.00	S109
☐ Boston 1993–94	$13.00	S117	☐ Philadelphia 1993–94	$13.00	S113
☐ Cancún/Cozumel/Yucatán 1991–92	$ 9.00	S010	☐ Rio 1991–92	$ 9.00	S029
			☐ Rome 1993–94	$13.00	S111
☐ Chicago 1993–94	$13.00	S122	☐ Salt Lake City 1991–92	$ 9.00	S031
☐ Denver/Boulder/Colorado Springs 1990–91	$ 8.00	S012	☐ San Diego 1993–94	$13.00	S107
			☐ San Francisco 1993	$13.00	S104
☐ Dublin 1993–94	$13.00	S128	☐ Santa Fe/Taos/Albuquerque 1993–94	$13.00	S108
☐ Hawaii 1992	$12.00	S014			
☐ Hong Kong 1992–93	$12.00	S015	☐ Seattle/Portland 1992–93	$12.00	S035
☐ Honolulu/Oahu 1993	$13.00	S106	☐ St. Louis/Kansas City 1993–94	$13.00	S127
☐ Las Vegas 1993–94	$13.00	S121			
☐ Lisbon/Madrid/Costa del Sol 1991–92	$ 9.00	S017	☐ Sydney 1993–94	$13.00	S129
			☐ Tampa/St. Petersburg 1993–94	$13.00	S105
☐ London 1993	$13.00	S100			
☐ Los Angeles 1993–94	$13.00	S123	☐ Tokyo 1992–93	$13.00	S039
☐ Madrid/Costa del Sol 1993–94	$13.00	S124	☐ Toronto 1993–94	$13.00	S126
			☐ Vancouver/Victoria 1990–91	$ 8.00	S041
☐ Mexico City/Acapulco 1991–92	$ 9.00	S020	☐ Washington, D.C. 1993	$13.00	S102

Other Titles Available at Membership Prices

SPECIAL EDITIONS

	Retail Price	Code		Retail Price	Code
☐ Bed & Breakfast North America	$15.00	P002	☐ Where to Stay U.S.A.	$14.00	P015
☐ Caribbean Hideaways	$16.00	P005			
☐ Marilyn Wood's Wonderful Weekends (within a 250-mile radius of NYC)	$12.00	P017			

GAULT MILLAU'S "BEST OF" GUIDES
(The only guides that distinguish the truly superlative
from the merely overrated)

	Retail Price	Code		Retail Price	Code
☐ Chicago	$16.00	G002	☐ New England	$16.00	G010
☐ Florida	$17.00	G003	☐ New Orleans	$17.00	G011
☐ France	$17.00	G004	☐ New York	$17.00	G012
☐ Germany	$18.00	G018	☐ Paris	$17.00	G013
☐ Hawaii	$17.00	G006	☐ San Francisco	$17.00	G014
☐ Hong Kong	$17.00	G007	☐ Thailand	$18.00	G019
☐ London	$17.00	G009	☐ Toronto	$17.00	G020
☐ Los Angeles	$17.00	G005	☐ Washington, D.C.	$17.00	G017

THE REAL GUIDES
(Opinionated, politically aware guides for youthful budget-minded travelers)

	Retail Price	Code		Retail Price	Code
☐ Able to Travel	$20.00	R112	☐ Kenya	$12.95	R015
☐ Amsterdam	$13.00	R100	☐ Mexico	$11.95	R016
☐ Barcelona	$13.00	R101	☐ Morocco	$14.00	R017
☐ Belgium/Holland/Luxembourg	$16.00	R031	☐ Nepal	$14.00	R018
			☐ New York	$13.00	R019
☐ Berlin	$11.95	R002	☐ Paris	$13.00	R020
☐ Brazil	$13.95	R003	☐ Peru	$12.95	R021
☐ California & the West Coast	$17.00	R121	☐ Poland	$13.95	R022
☐ Canada	$15.00	R103	☐ Portugal	$15.00	R023
☐ Czechoslovakia	$14.00	R005	☐ Prague	$15.00	R113
☐ Egypt	$19.00	R105	☐ San Francisco & the Bay Area	$11.95	R024
☐ Europe	$18.00	R122			
☐ Florida	$14.00	R006	☐ Scandinavia	$14.95	R025
☐ France	$18.00	R106	☐ Spain	$16.00	R026
☐ Germany	$18.00	R107	☐ Thailand	$17.00	R119
☐ Greece	$18.00	R108	☐ Tunisia	$17.00	R115
☐ Guatemala/Belize	$14.00	R010	☐ Turkey	$13.95	R027
☐ Hong Kong/Macau	$11.95	R011	☐ U.S.A.	$18.00	R117
☐ Hungary	$14.00	R118	☐ Venice	$11.95	R028
☐ Ireland	$17.00	R120	☐ Women Travel	$12.95	R029
☐ Italy	$13.95	R014	☐ Yugoslavia	$12.95	R030